NORTHLANDERS

BOOK 2 THE ICELANDIC SAGA

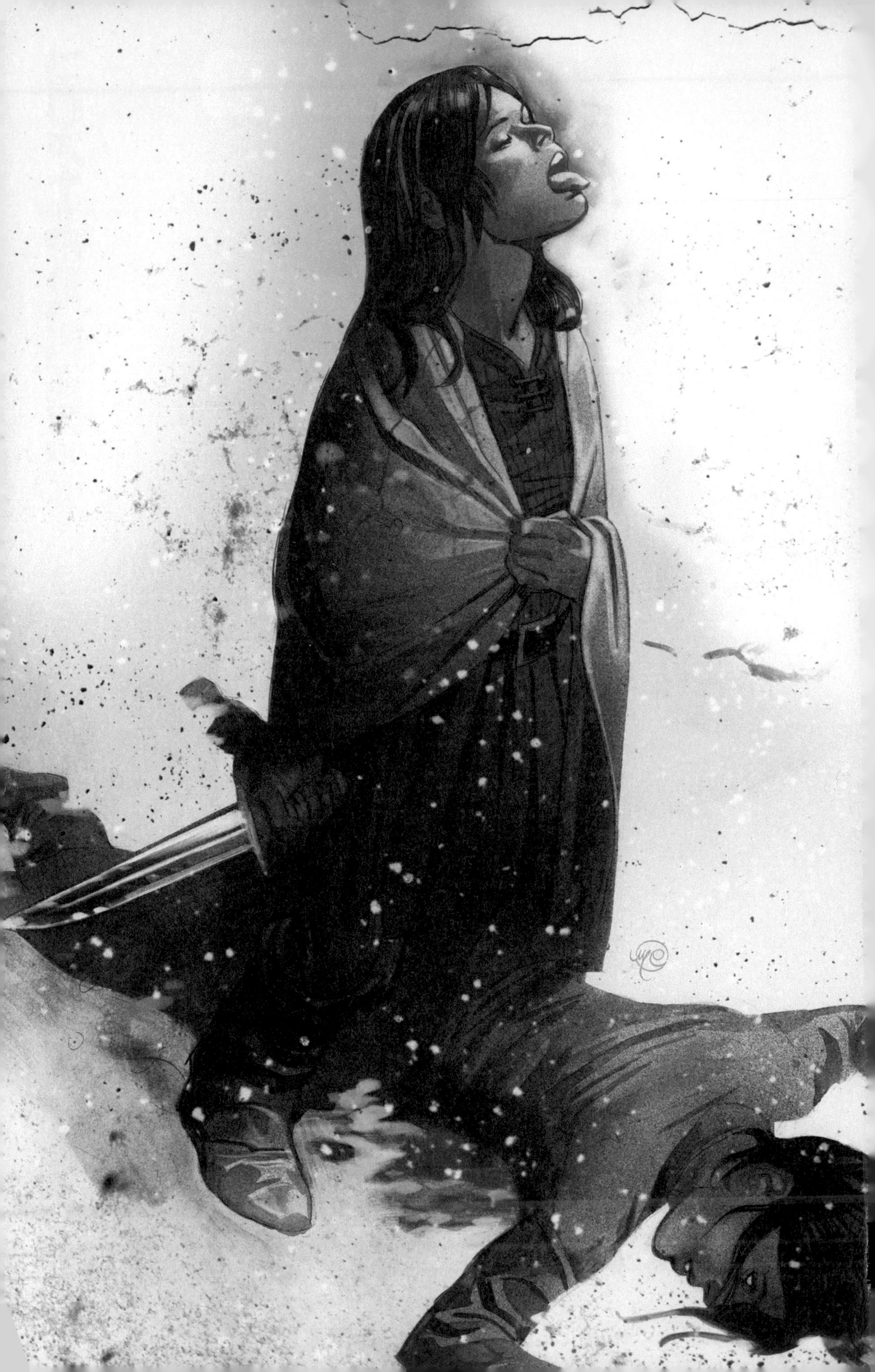

NORTHLANDERS

BOOK 2 THE ICELANDIC SAGA

BRIAN WOOD writer

FIONA STAPLES DAVIDE GIANFELICE BECKY CLOONAN

PAUL AZACETA DECLAN SHALVEY DANIJEL ŽEŽELJ artists

DAVE McCAIG colorist TRAVIS LANHAM letterer

MASSIMO CARNEVALE series and collection cover artist

NORTHLANDERS created by BRIAN WOOD

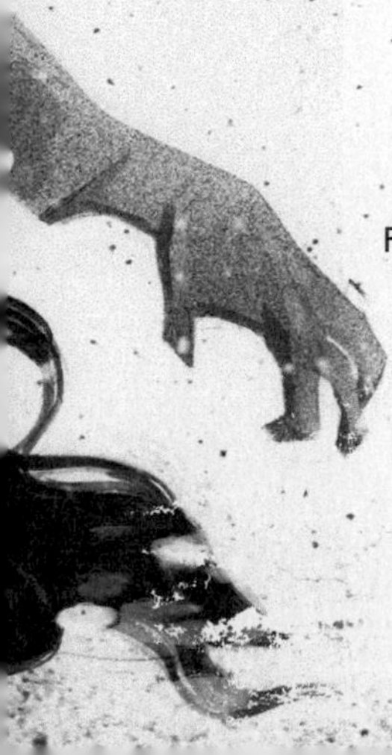

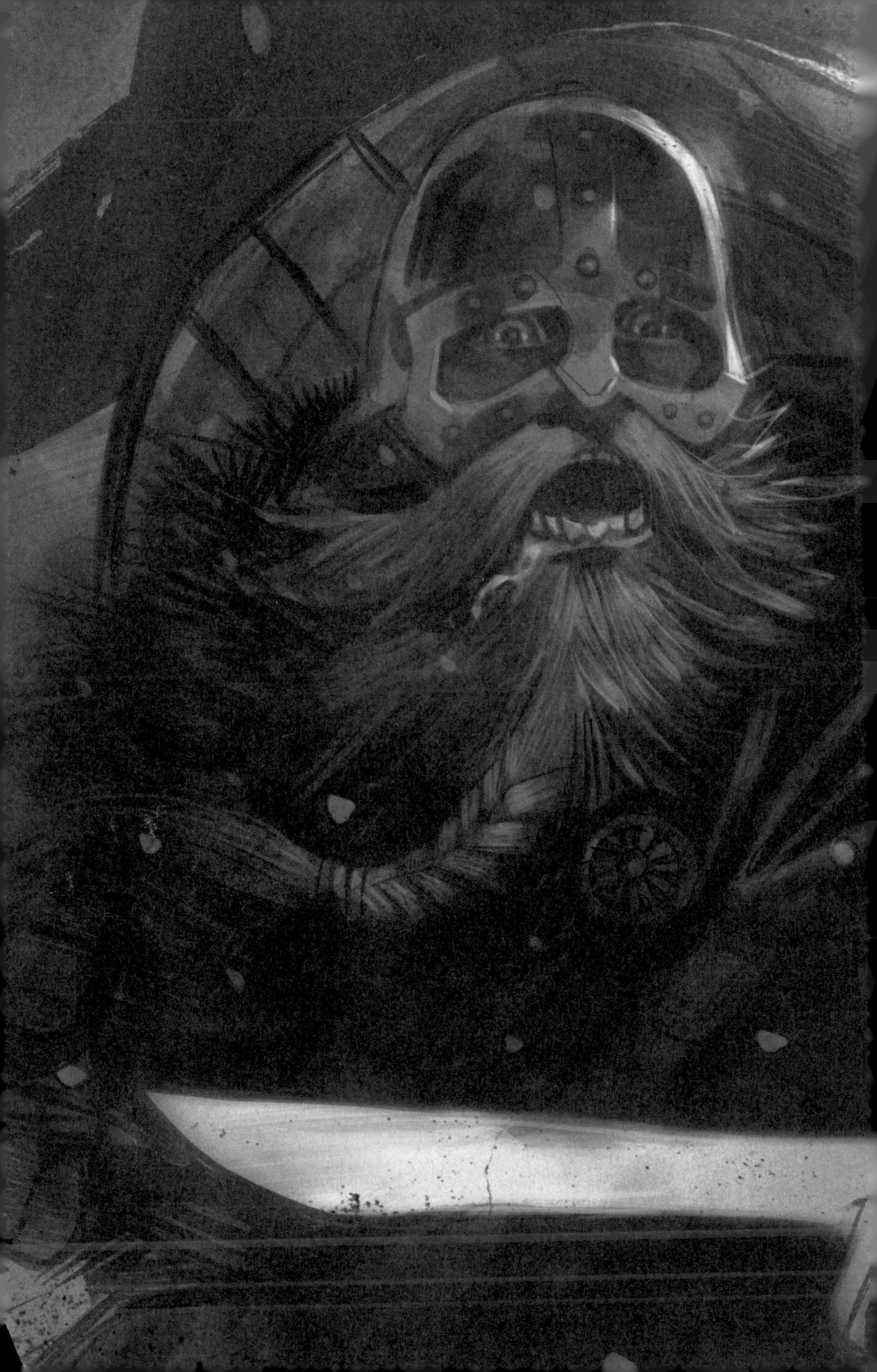

MARK DOYLE Editor – Original Series
JAMIE RICH Group Editor – Vertigo Comics
JEB WOODARD Group Editor – Collected Editions
STEVE COOK Design Director – Books
LOUIS PRANDI Publication Design

DIANE NELSON President
DAN DiDIO Publisher
JIM LEE Publisher
GEOFF JOHNS President & Chief Creative Officer
AMIT DESAI Executive VP – Business & Marketing Strategy, Direct to Consumer
& Global Franchise Management
SAM ADES Senior VP – Direct to Consumer
BOBBIE CHASE VP – Talent Development
MARK CHIARELLO Senior VP – Art, Design & Collected Editions
JOHN CUNNINGHAM Senior VP – Sales & Trade Marketing
ANNE DePIES Senior VP – Business Strategy, Finance & Administration
DON FALLETTI VP – Manufacturing Operations
LAWRENCE GANEM VP – Editorial Administration & Talent Relations
ALISON GILL Senior VP – Manufacturing & Operations
HANK KANALZ Senior VP – Editorial Strategy & Administration
JAY KOGAN VP – Legal Affairs
THOMAS LOFTUS VP – Business Affairs
JACK MAHAN VP – Business Affairs
NICK J. NAPOLITANO VP – Manufacturing Administration
EDDIE SCANNELL VP – Consumer Marketing
COURTNEY SIMMONS Senior VP – Publicity & Communications
JIM (SKI) SOKOLOWSKI VP – Comic Book Specialty Sales & Trade Marketing
NANCY SPEARS VP – Mass, Book, Digital Sales & Trade Marketing

NORTHLANDERS BOOK 2:
THE ICELANDIC SAGA

Published by DC Comics. Compilation and all new material Copyright © 2016 Brian Wood
and DC Comics. All Rights Reserved. Originally published in single magazine form in
NORTHLANDERS 20, 29, 35-36, 42-50. Copyright © 2009, 2010, 2011, 2012 Brian Wood and
DC Comics. All Rights Reserved. All characters, their distinctive likenesses and related ele-
ments featured in this publication are trademarks of DC Comics. VERTIGO is a trademark
of DC Comics. The stories, characters and incidents featured in this publication are entirely
fictional. DC Comics does not read or accept unsolicited submissions of ideas, stories or
artwork.

DC Comics, 2900 West Alameda Ave., Burbank, CA 91505
Printed in the USA. First Printing.
ISBN: 978-1-4012-6508-3

Library of Congress Cataloging-in-Publication Data is available.

FSC
www.fsc.org
MIX
Paper from
responsible sources
FSC® C101537

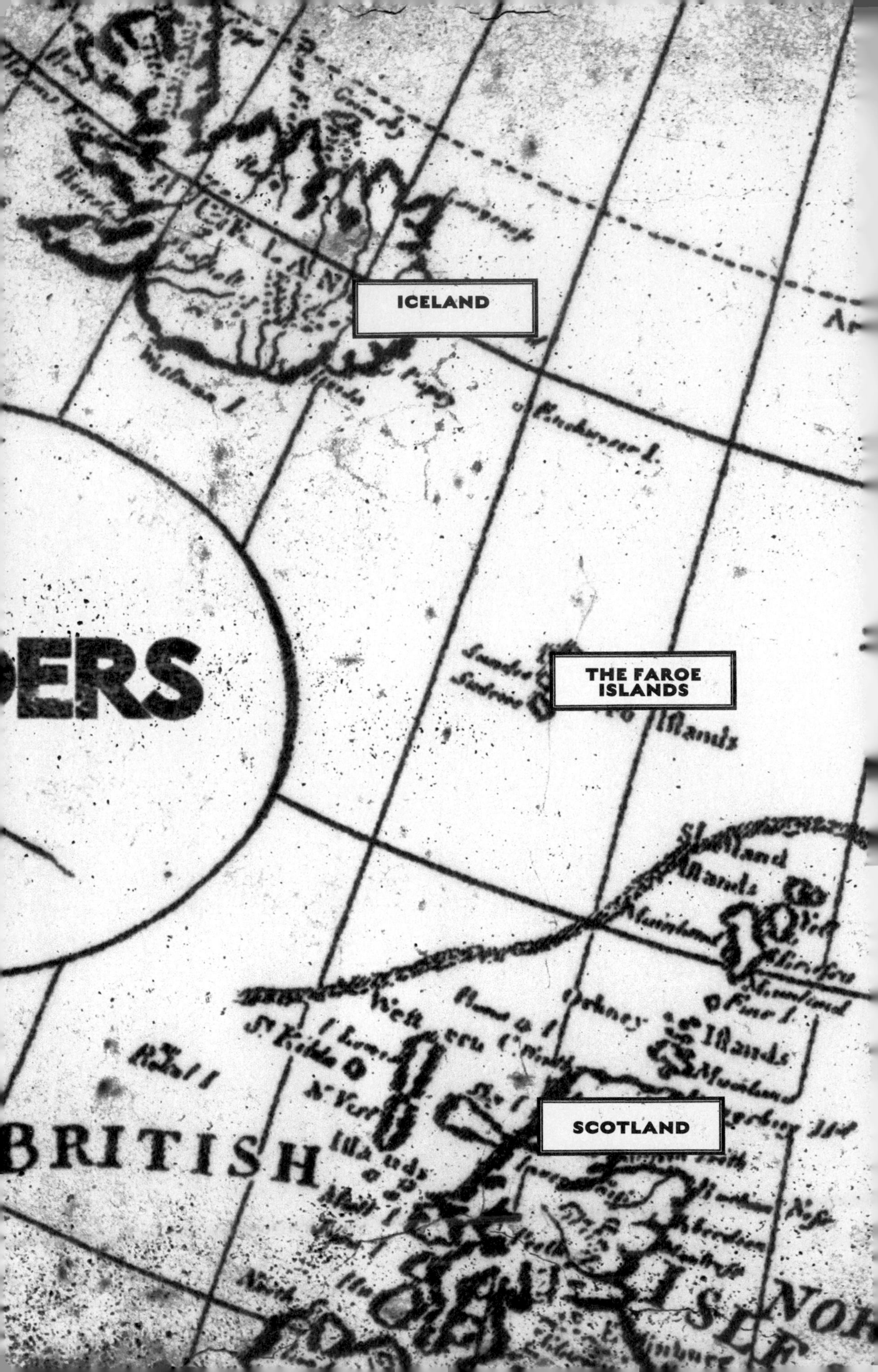

ICELAND
THE FAROE ISLANDS
SCOTLAND
ERS
BRITISH

60
55
50
45
40
35
London
Circle

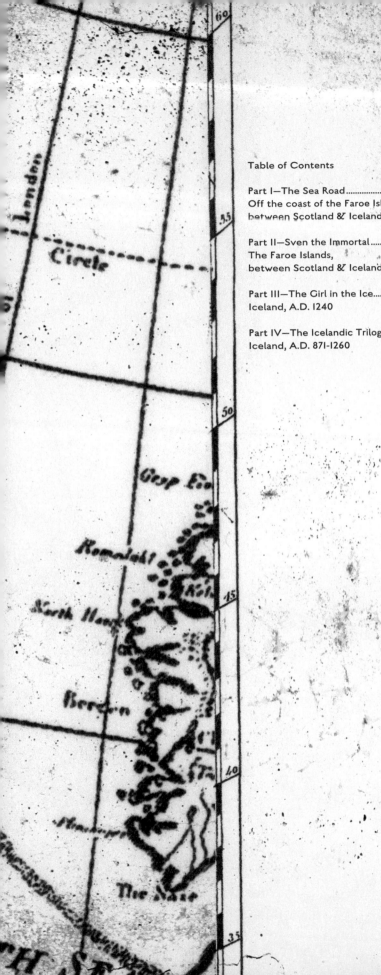

Table of Contents

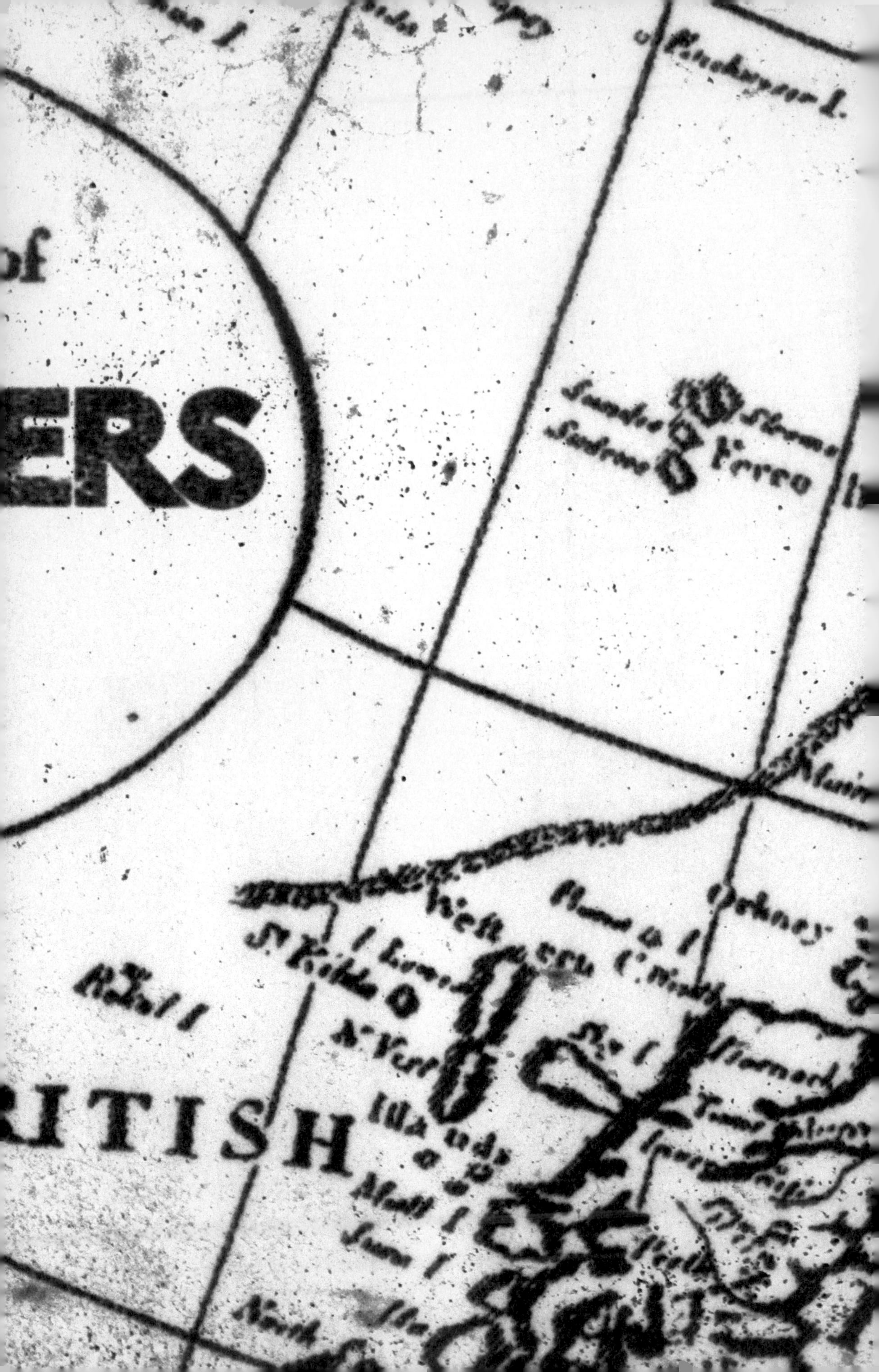
of
ERS
RITISH
Ferro
Orkney
St Kilda
Rokol I

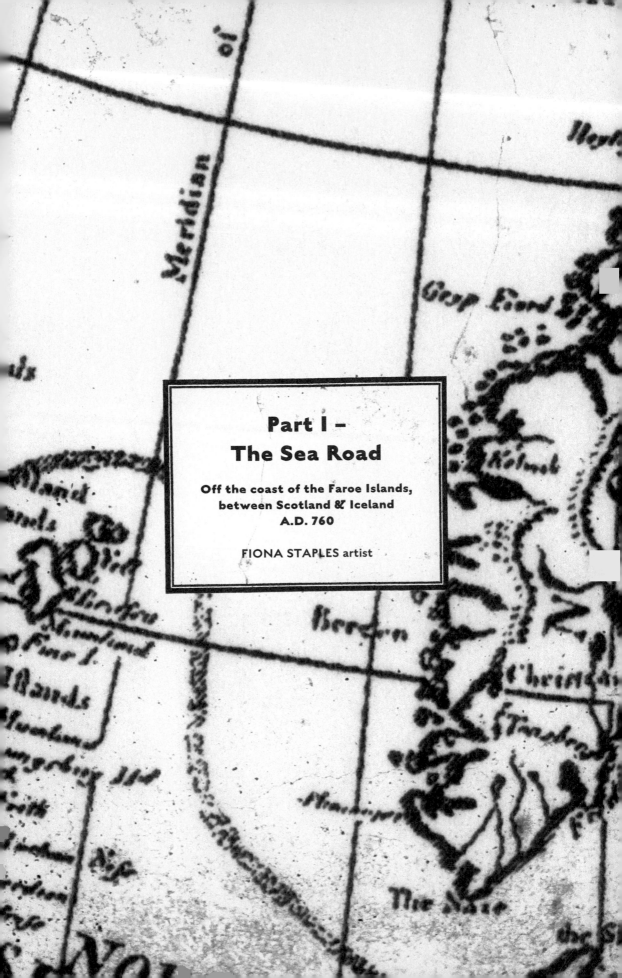

Part I –
The Sea Road

Off the coast of the Faroe Islands,
between Scotland & Iceland
A.D. 760

FIONA STAPLES artist

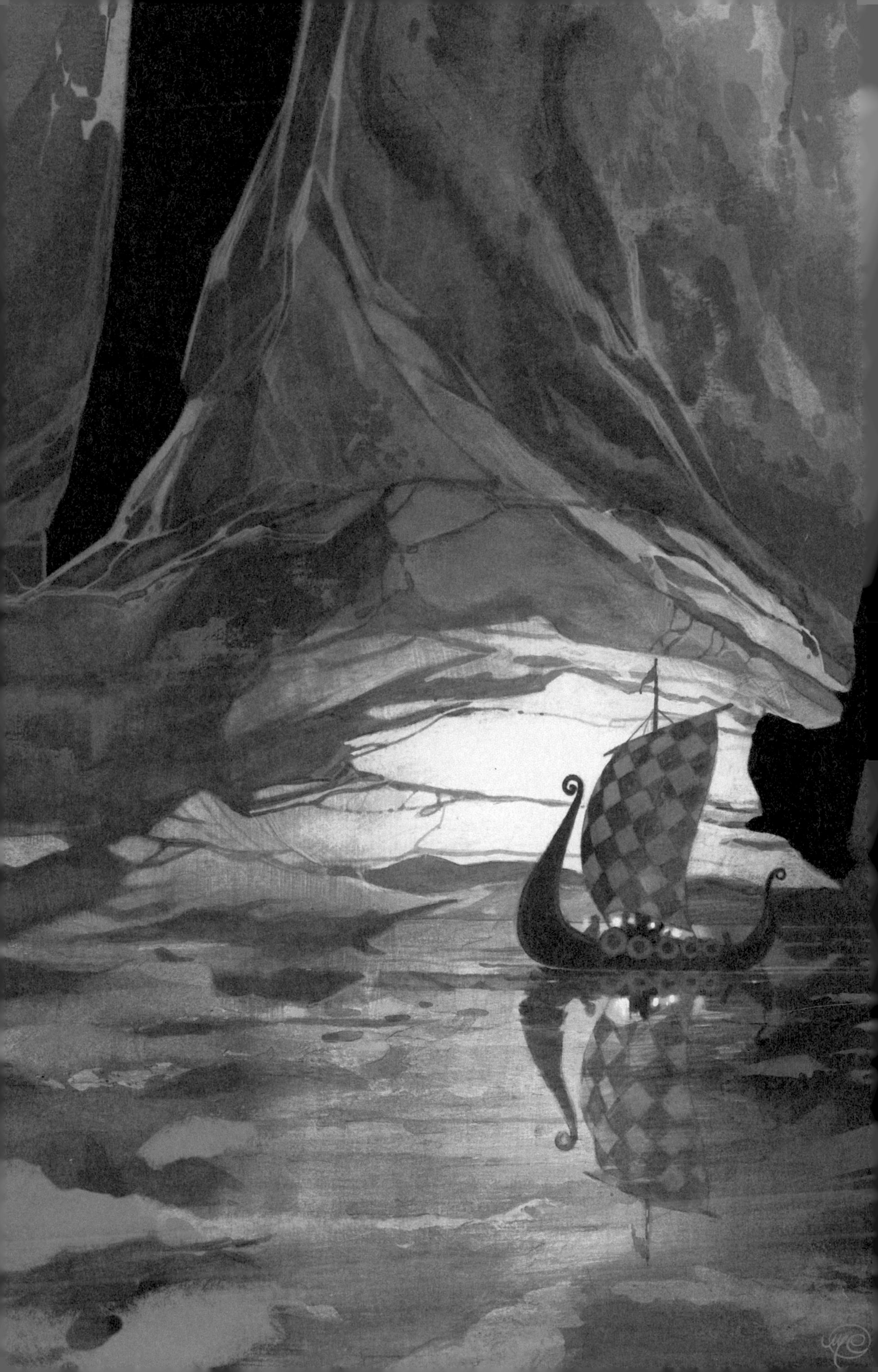

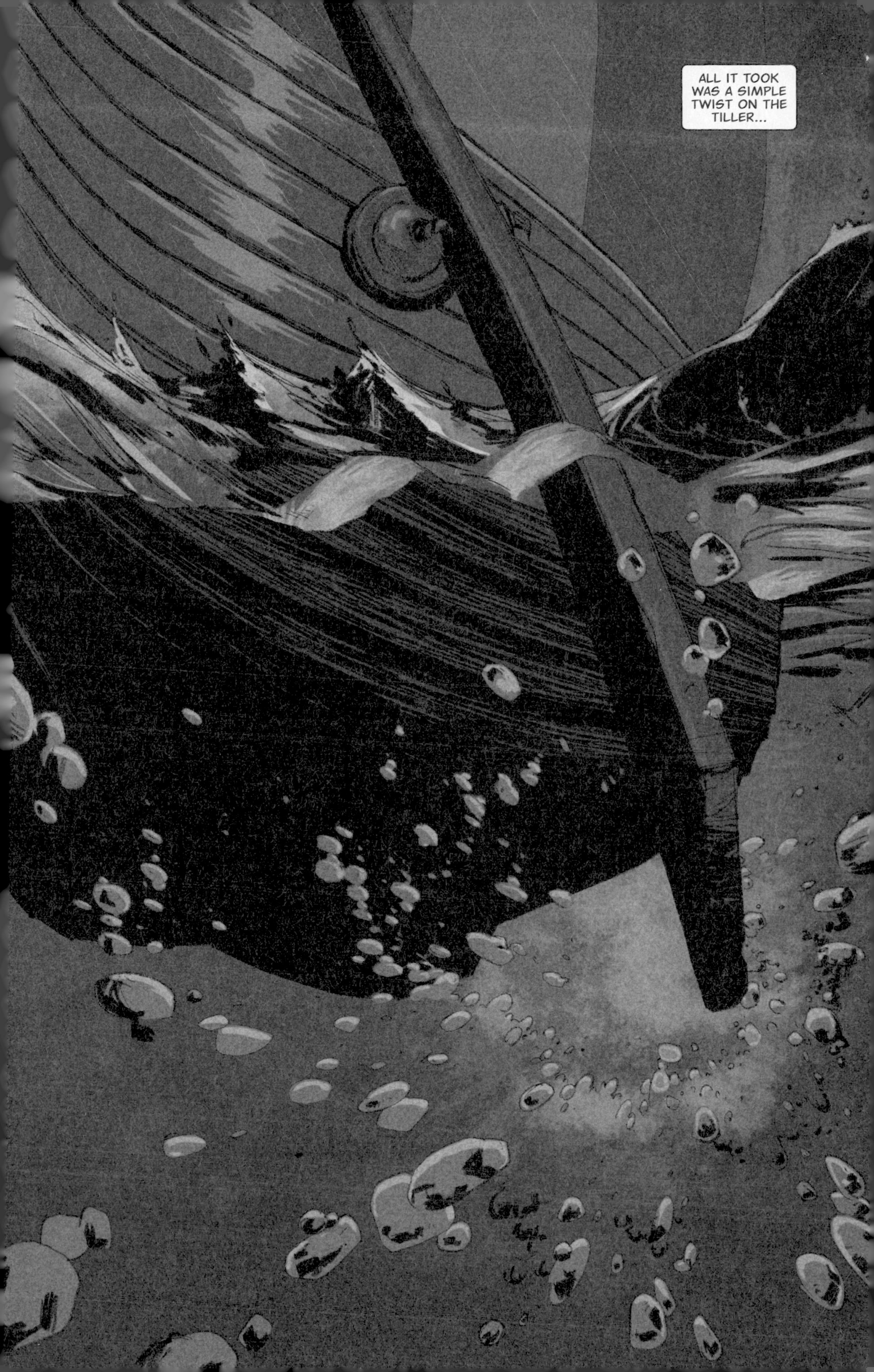
ALL IT TOOK WAS A SIMPLE TWIST ON THE TILLER...

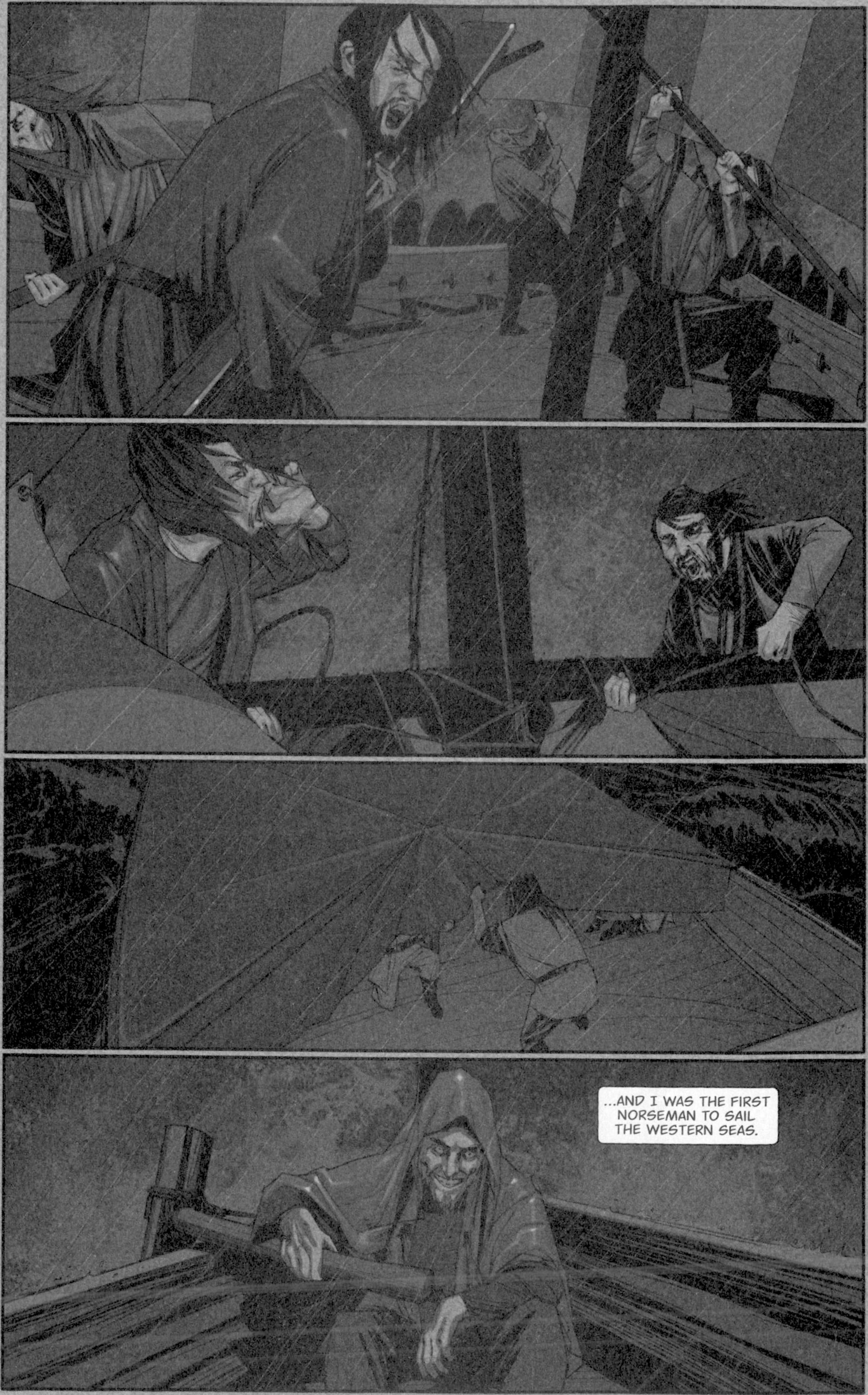
...AND I WAS THE FIRST NORSEMAN TO SAIL THE WESTERN SEAS.

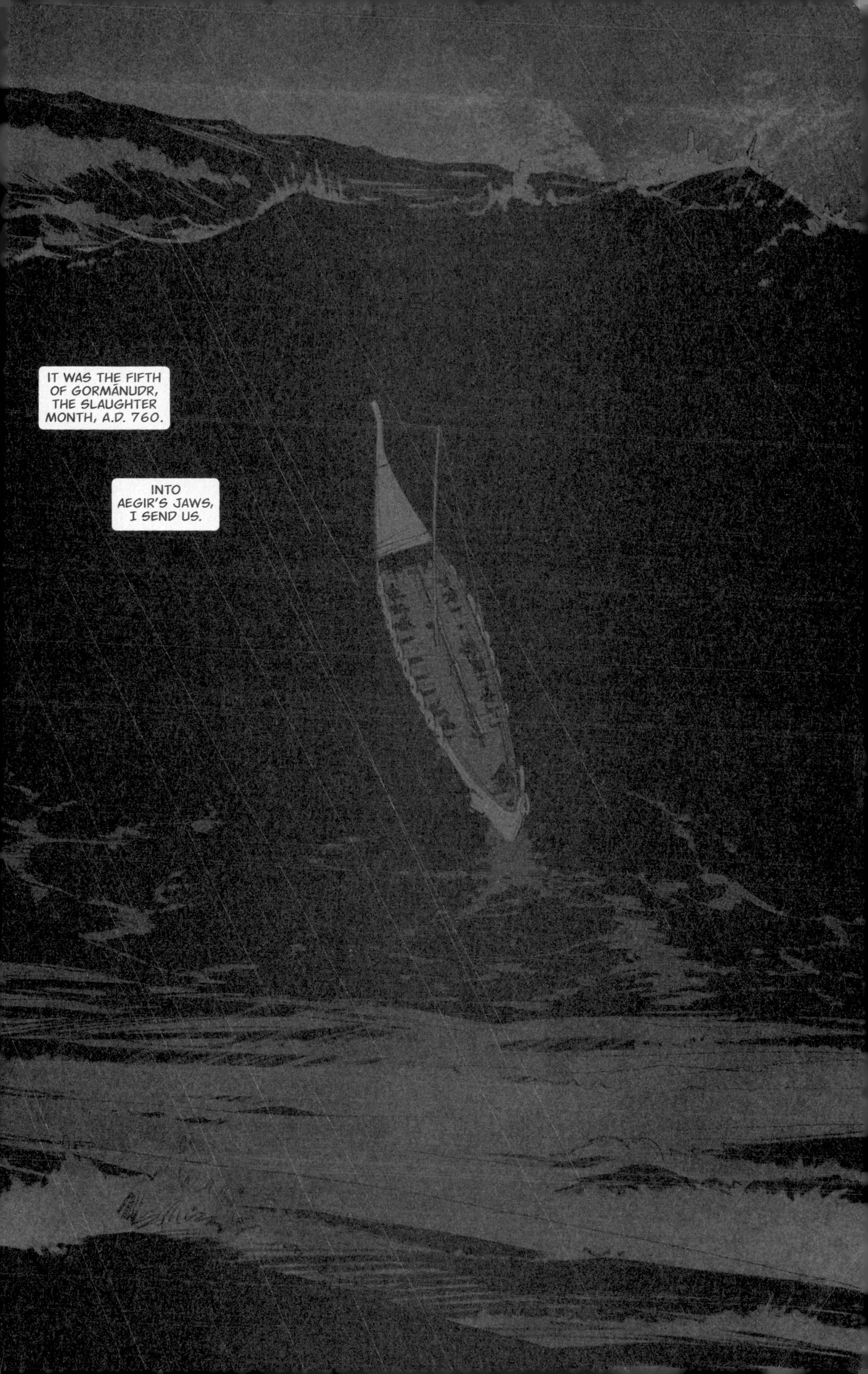
IT WAS THE FIFTH OF GORMÁNUDR, THE SLAUGHTER MONTH, A.D. 760.
INTO AEGIR'S JAWS, I SEND US.

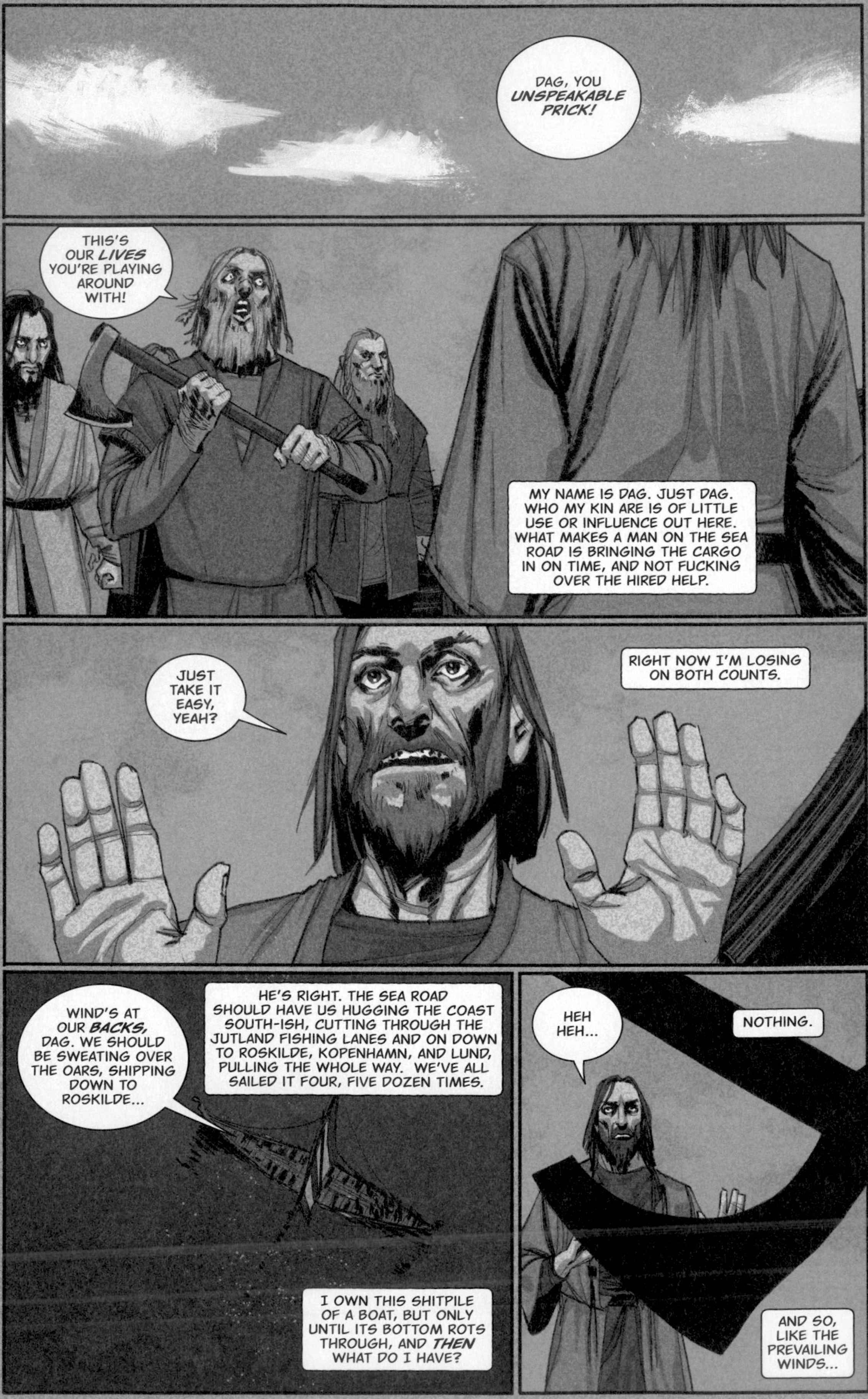
DAG, YOU *UNSPEAKABLE* PRICK!
THIS'S OUR *LIVES* YOU'RE PLAYING AROUND WITH!
MY NAME IS DAG. JUST DAG. WHO MY KIN ARE IS OF LITTLE USE OR INFLUENCE OUT HERE. WHAT MAKES A MAN ON THE SEA ROAD IS BRINGING THE CARGO IN ON TIME, AND NOT FUCKING OVER THE HIRED HELP.
JUST TAKE IT EASY, YEAH?
RIGHT NOW I'M LOSING ON BOTH COUNTS.
WIND'S AT OUR *BACKS,* DAG. WE SHOULD BE SWEATING OVER THE OARS, SHIPPING DOWN TO ROSKILDE...
HE'S RIGHT. THE SEA ROAD SHOULD HAVE US HUGGING THE COAST SOUTH-ISH, CUTTING THROUGH THE JUTLAND FISHING LANES AND ON DOWN TO ROSKILDE, KOPENHAMN, AND LUND, PULLING THE WHOLE WAY. WE'VE ALL SAILED IT FOUR, FIVE DOZEN TIMES.
I OWN THIS SHITPILE OF A BOAT, BUT ONLY UNTIL ITS BOTTOM ROTS THROUGH, AND *THEN* WHAT DO I HAVE?
HEH HEH...
NOTHING.
AND SO, LIKE THE PREVAILING WINDS...

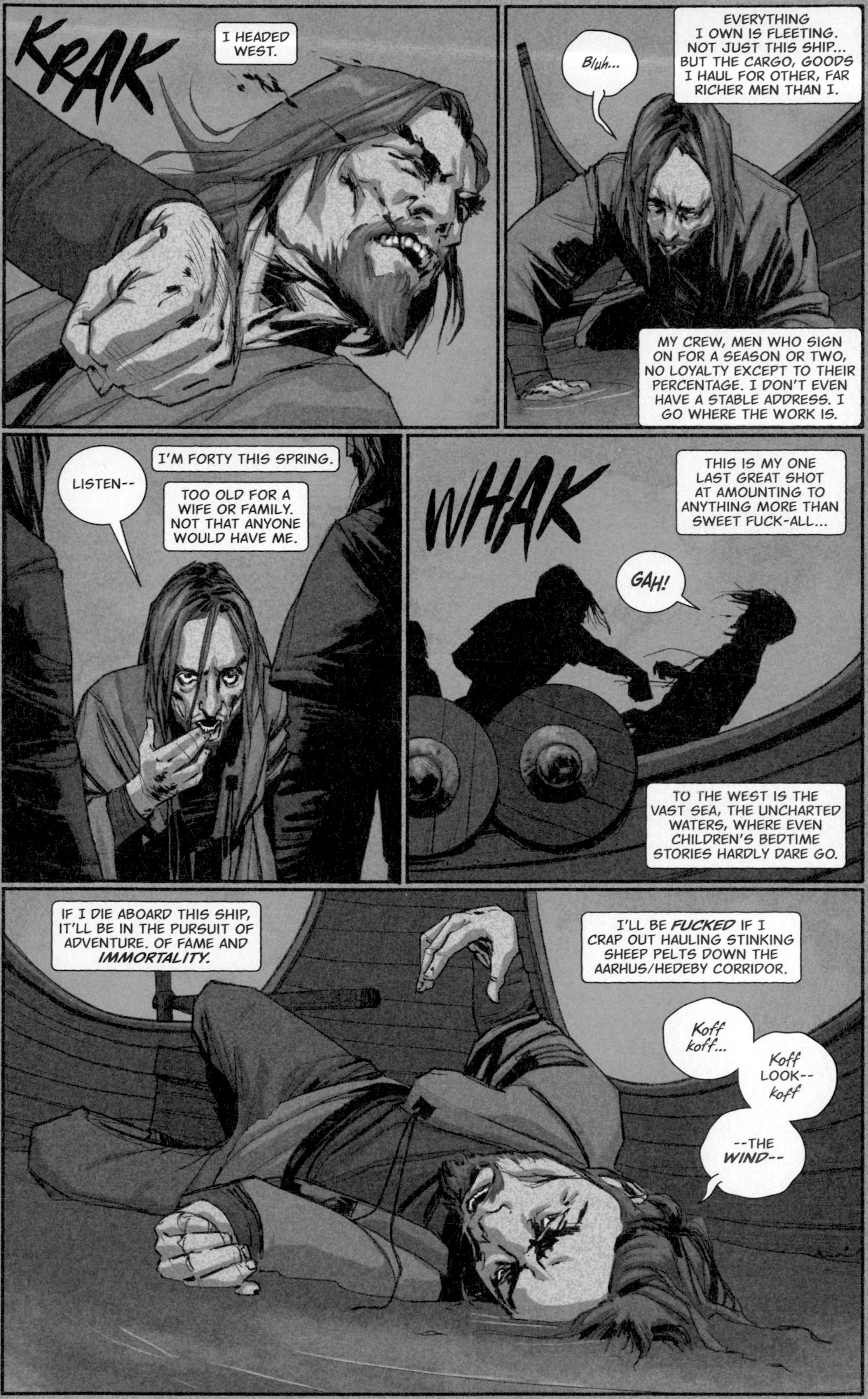
KRAK
I HEADED WEST.
Bluh...
EVERYTHING I OWN IS FLEETING. NOT JUST THIS SHIP... BUT THE CARGO, GOODS I HAUL FOR OTHER, FAR RICHER MEN THAN I.
MY CREW, MEN WHO SIGN ON FOR A SEASON OR TWO, NO LOYALTY EXCEPT TO THEIR PERCENTAGE. I DON'T EVEN HAVE A STABLE ADDRESS. I GO WHERE THE WORK IS.
LISTEN--
I'M FORTY THIS SPRING.
TOO OLD FOR A WIFE OR FAMILY. NOT THAT ANYONE WOULD HAVE ME.
WHAK
THIS IS MY ONE LAST GREAT SHOT AT AMOUNTING TO ANYTHING MORE THAN SWEET FUCK-ALL...
GAH!
TO THE WEST IS THE VAST SEA, THE UNCHARTED WATERS, WHERE EVEN CHILDREN'S BEDTIME STORIES HARDLY DARE GO.
IF I DIE ABOARD THIS SHIP, IT'LL BE IN THE PURSUIT OF ADVENTURE. OF FAME AND IMMORTALITY.
I'LL BE FUCKED IF I CRAP OUT HAULING STINKING SHEEP PELTS DOWN THE AARHUS/HEDEBY CORRIDOR.
Koff koff...
Koff LOOK-- koff
--THE WIND--

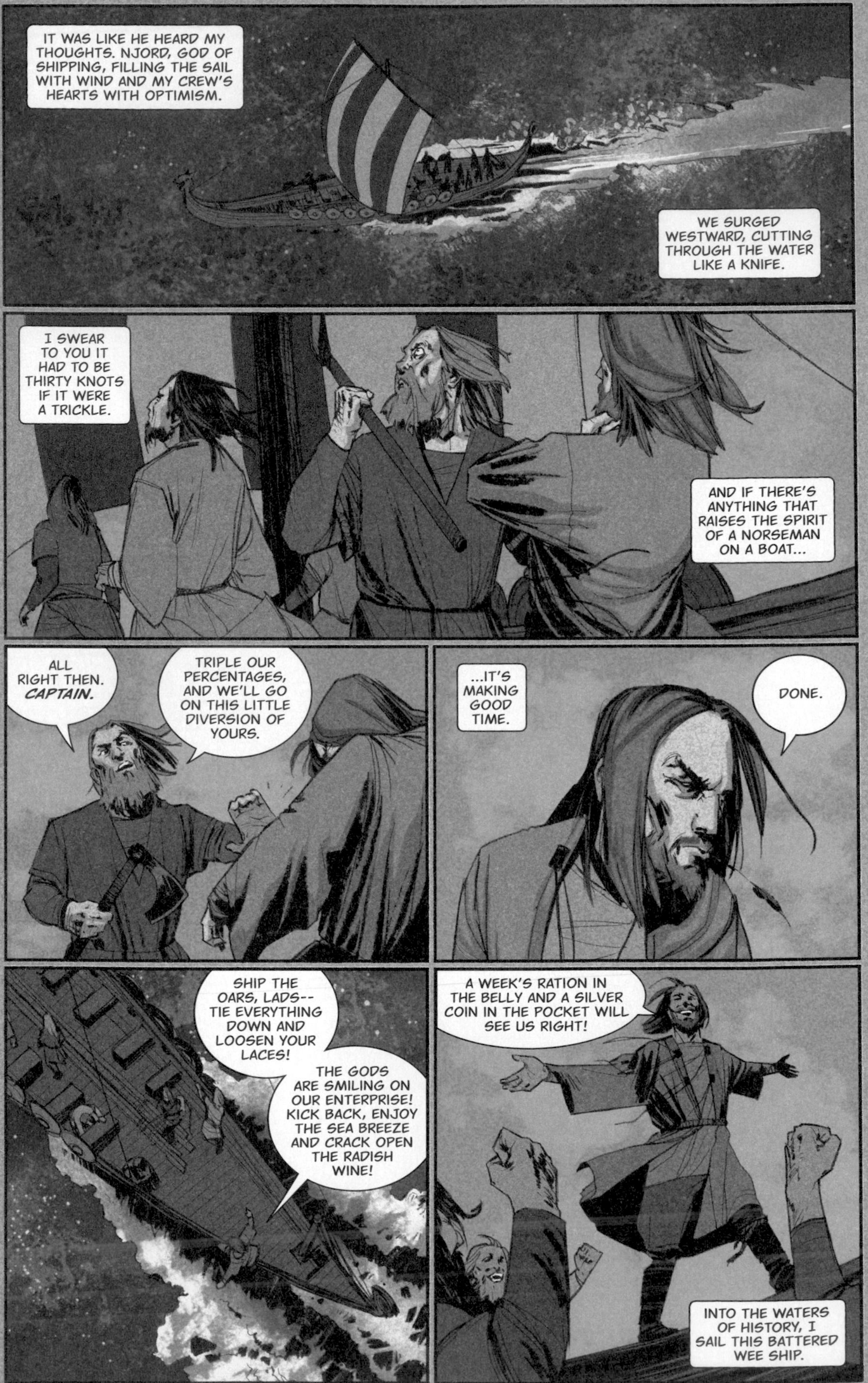
IT WAS LIKE HE HEARD MY THOUGHTS. NJORD, GOD OF SHIPPING, FILLING THE SAIL WITH WIND AND MY CREW'S HEARTS WITH OPTIMISM.
WE SURGED WESTWARD, CUTTING THROUGH THE WATER LIKE A KNIFE.
I SWEAR TO YOU IT HAD TO BE THIRTY KNOTS IF IT WERE A TRICKLE.
AND IF THERE'S ANYTHING THAT RAISES THE SPIRIT OF A NORSEMAN ON A BOAT...
ALL RIGHT THEN. *CAPTAIN.*
TRIPLE OUR PERCENTAGES, AND WE'LL GO ON THIS LITTLE DIVERSION OF YOURS.
...IT'S MAKING GOOD TIME.
DONE.
SHIP THE OARS, LADS-- TIE EVERYTHING DOWN AND LOOSEN YOUR LACES!
THE GODS ARE SMILING ON OUR ENTERPRISE! KICK BACK, ENJOY THE SEA BREEZE AND CRACK OPEN THE RADISH WINE!
A WEEK'S RATION IN THE BELLY AND A SILVER COIN IN THE POCKET WILL SEE US RIGHT!
INTO THE WATERS OF HISTORY, I SAIL THIS BATTERED WEE SHIP.

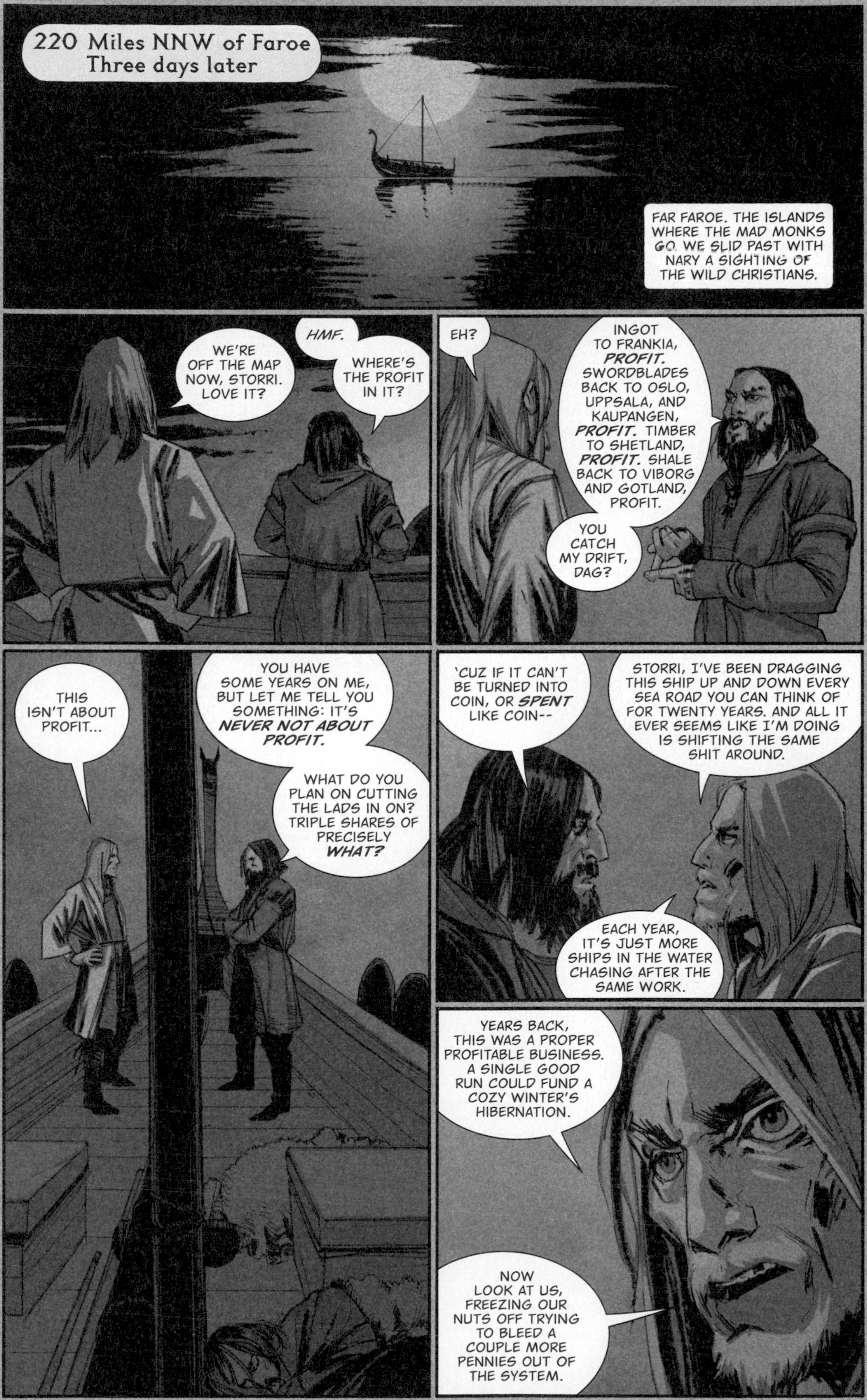
220 Miles NNW of Faroe
Three days later
FAR FAROE. THE ISLANDS WHERE THE MAD MONKS GO. WE SLID PAST WITH NARY A SIGHTING OF THE WILD CHRISTIANS.
WE'RE OFF THE MAP NOW, STORRI. LOVE IT?
HMF.
WHERE'S THE PROFIT IN IT?
EH?
INGOT TO FRANKIA, PROFIT. SWORDBLADES BACK TO OSLO, UPPSALA, AND KAUPANGEN, PROFIT. TIMBER TO SHETLAND, PROFIT. SHALE BACK TO VIBORG AND GOTLAND, PROFIT.
YOU CATCH MY DRIFT, DAG?
THIS ISN'T ABOUT PROFIT...
YOU HAVE SOME YEARS ON ME, BUT LET ME TELL YOU SOMETHING: IT'S NEVER NOT ABOUT PROFIT.
WHAT DO YOU PLAN ON CUTTING THE LADS IN ON? TRIPLE SHARES OF PRECISELY WHAT?
'CUZ IF IT CAN'T BE TURNED INTO COIN, OR SPENT LIKE COIN--
STORRI, I'VE BEEN DRAGGING THIS SHIP UP AND DOWN EVERY SEA ROAD YOU CAN THINK OF FOR TWENTY YEARS. AND ALL IT EVER SEEMS LIKE I'M DOING IS SHIFTING THE SAME SHIT AROUND.
EACH YEAR, IT'S JUST MORE SHIPS IN THE WATER CHASING AFTER THE SAME WORK.
YEARS BACK, THIS WAS A PROPER PROFITABLE BUSINESS. A SINGLE GOOD RUN COULD FUND A COZY WINTER'S HIBERNATION.
NOW LOOK AT US, FREEZING OUR NUTS OFF TRYING TO BLEED A COUPLE MORE PENNIES OUT OF THE SYSTEM.

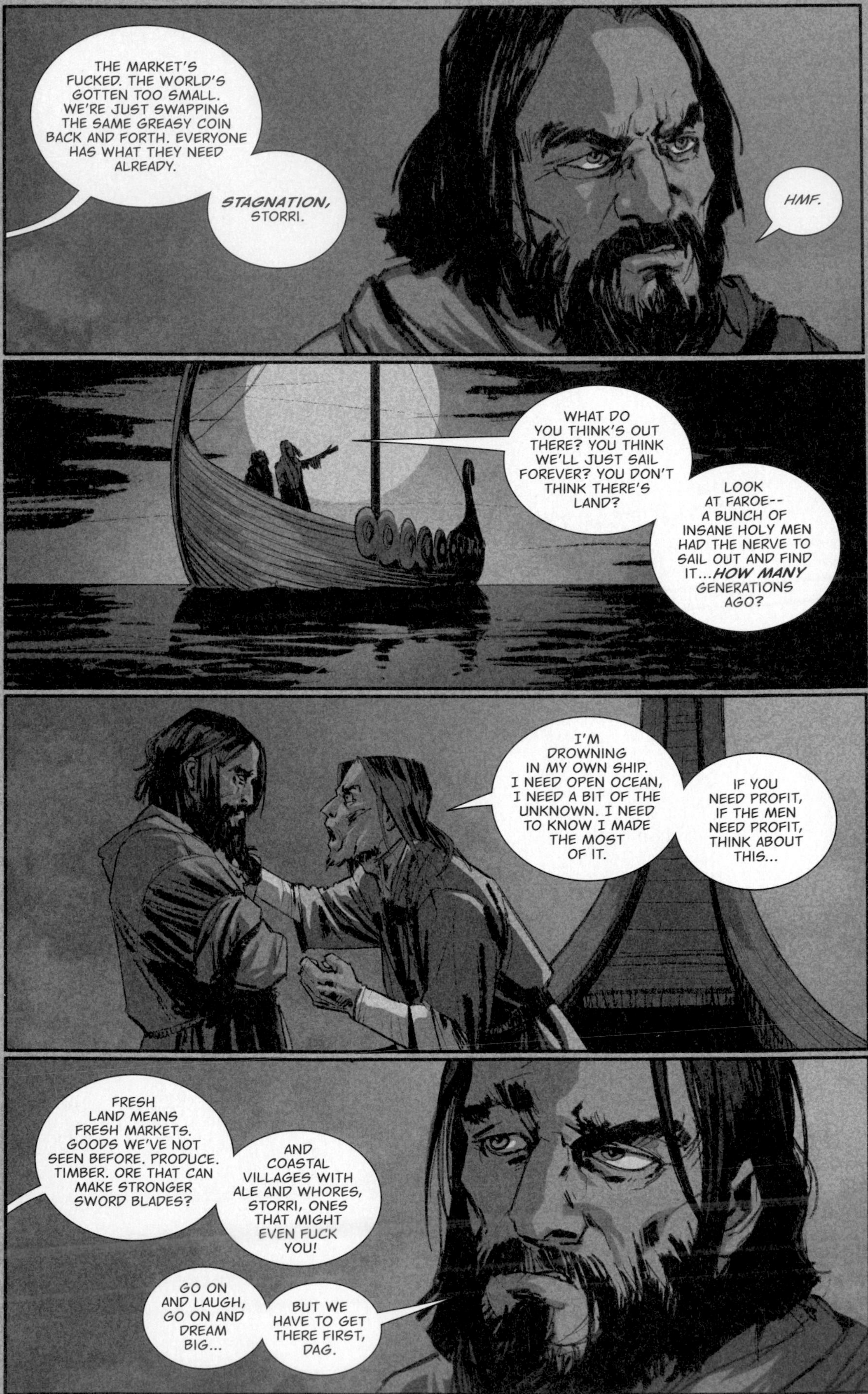
THE MARKET'S FUCKED. THE WORLD'S GOTTEN TOO SMALL. WE'RE JUST SWAPPING THE SAME GREASY COIN BACK AND FORTH. EVERYONE HAS WHAT THEY NEED ALREADY.
STAGNATION, STORRI.
HMF.
WHAT DO YOU THINK'S OUT THERE? YOU THINK WE'LL JUST SAIL FOREVER? YOU DON'T THINK THERE'S LAND?
LOOK AT FAROE-- A BUNCH OF INSANE HOLY MEN HAD THE NERVE TO SAIL OUT AND FIND IT...HOW MANY GENERATIONS AGO?
I'M DROWNING IN MY OWN SHIP. I NEED OPEN OCEAN, I NEED A BIT OF THE UNKNOWN. I NEED TO KNOW I MADE THE MOST OF IT.
IF YOU NEED PROFIT, IF THE MEN NEED PROFIT, THINK ABOUT THIS...
FRESH LAND MEANS FRESH MARKETS. GOODS WE'VE NOT SEEN BEFORE. PRODUCE. TIMBER. ORE THAT CAN MAKE STRONGER SWORD BLADES?
AND COASTAL VILLAGES WITH ALE AND WHORES, STORRI, ONES THAT MIGHT EVEN FUCK YOU!
GO ON AND LAUGH, GO ON AND DREAM BIG...
BUT WE HAVE TO GET THERE FIRST, DAG.

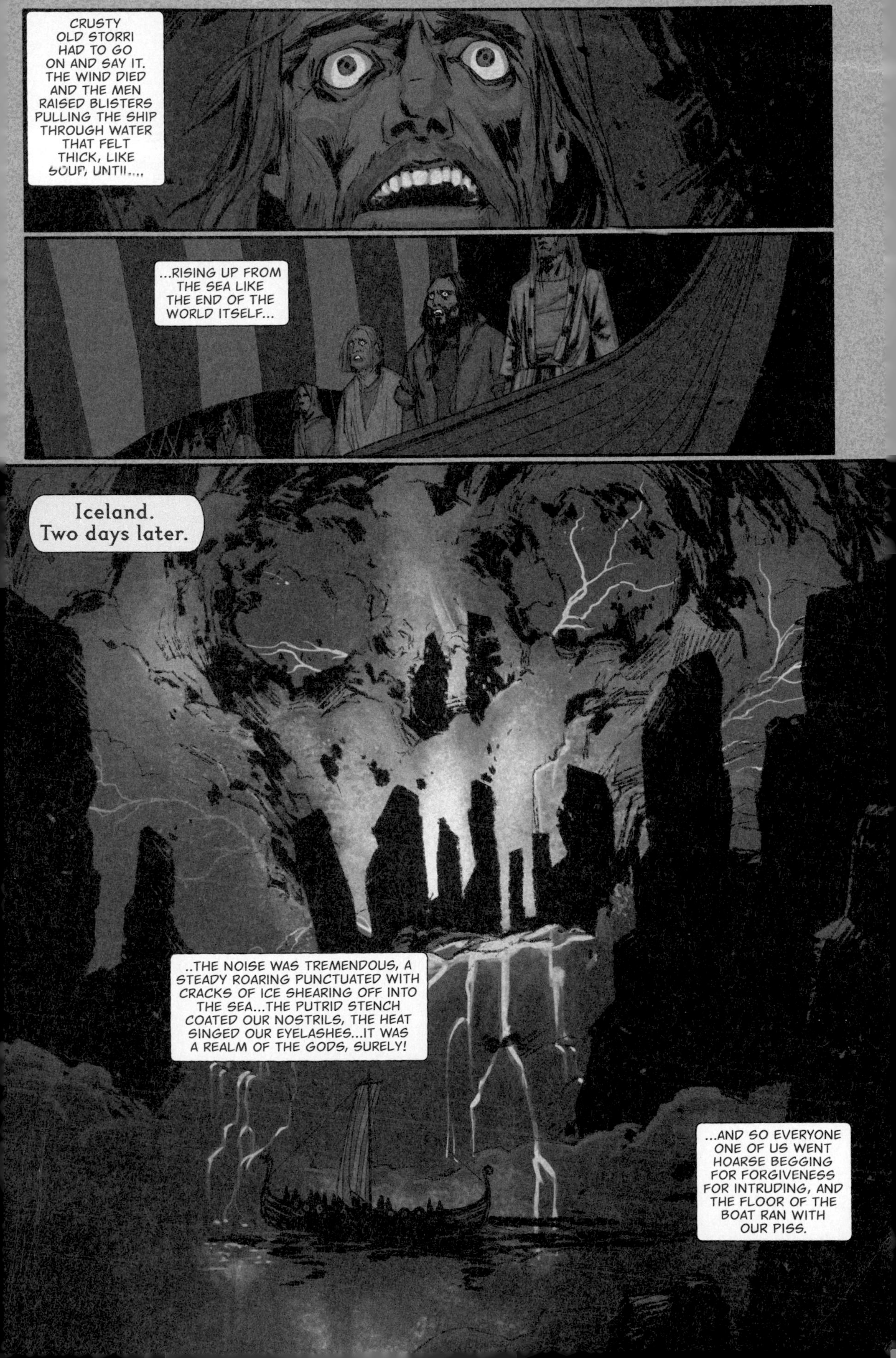
CRUSTY OLD STORRI HAD TO GO ON AND SAY IT. THE WIND DIED AND THE MEN RAISED BLISTERS PULLING THE SHIP THROUGH WATER THAT FELT THICK, LIKE SOUP, UNTIL...,
...RISING UP FROM THE SEA LIKE THE END OF THE WORLD ITSELF...
Iceland. Two days later.
..THE NOISE WAS TREMENDOUS, A STEADY ROARING PUNCTUATED WITH CRACKS OF ICE SHEARING OFF INTO THE SEA...THE PUTRID STENCH COATED OUR NOSTRILS, THE HEAT SINGED OUR EYELASHES...IT WAS A REALM OF THE GODS, SURELY!
...AND SO EVERYONE ONE OF US WENT HOARSE BEGGING FOR FORGIVENESS FOR INTRUDING, AND THE FLOOR OF THE BOAT RAN WITH OUR PISS.

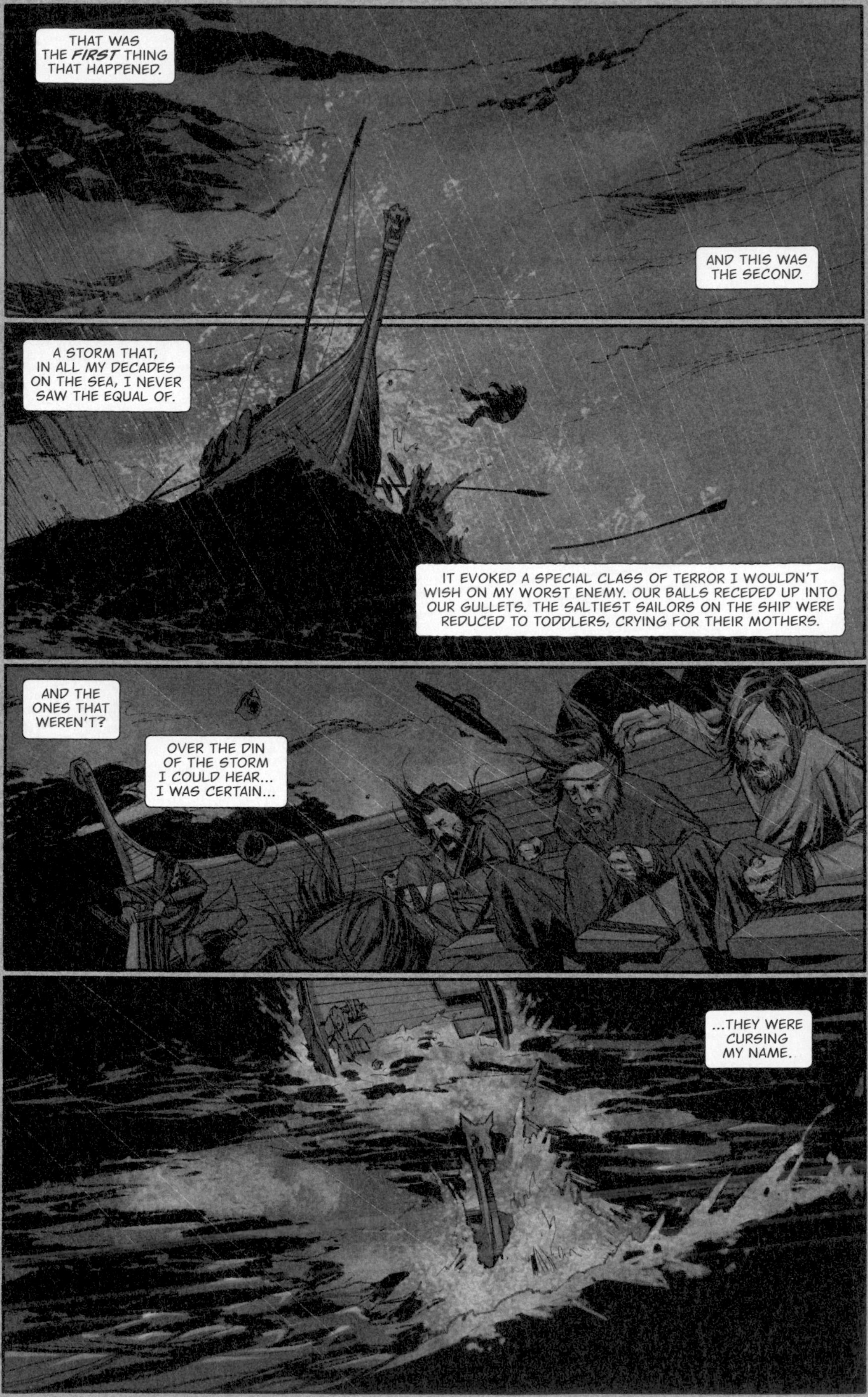
THAT WAS THE FIRST THING THAT HAPPENED.
AND THIS WAS THE SECOND.
A STORM THAT, IN ALL MY DECADES ON THE SEA, I NEVER SAW THE EQUAL OF.
IT EVOKED A SPECIAL CLASS OF TERROR I WOULDN'T WISH ON MY WORST ENEMY. OUR BALLS RECEDED UP INTO OUR GULLETS. THE SALTIEST SAILORS ON THE SHIP WERE REDUCED TO TODDLERS, CRYING FOR THEIR MOTHERS.
AND THE ONES THAT WEREN'T?
OVER THE DIN OF THE STORM I COULD HEAR... I WAS CERTAIN...
...THEY WERE CURSING MY NAME.

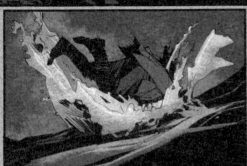

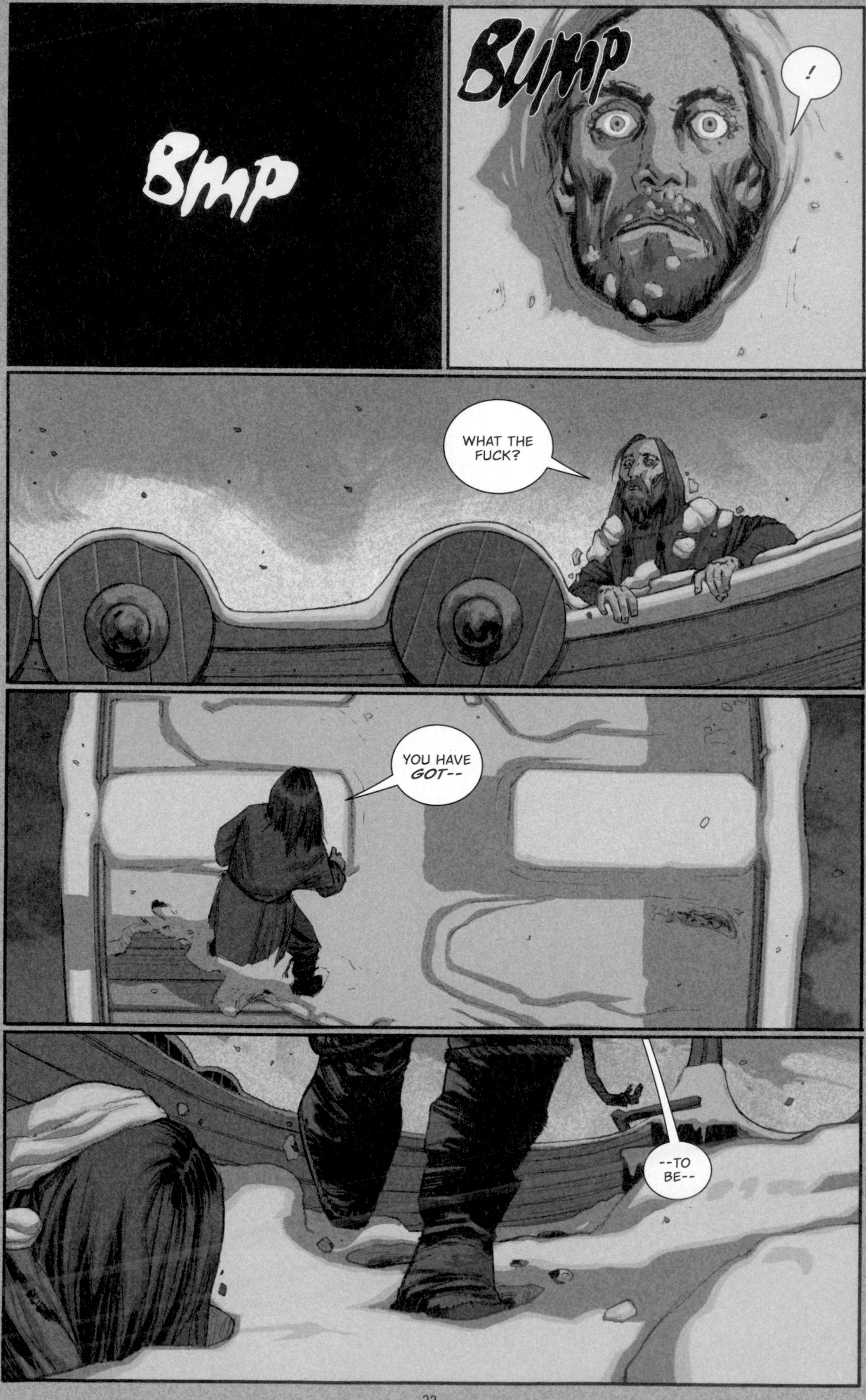
BMP
BUMP
!
WHAT THE FUCK?
YOU HAVE GOT--
--TO BE--

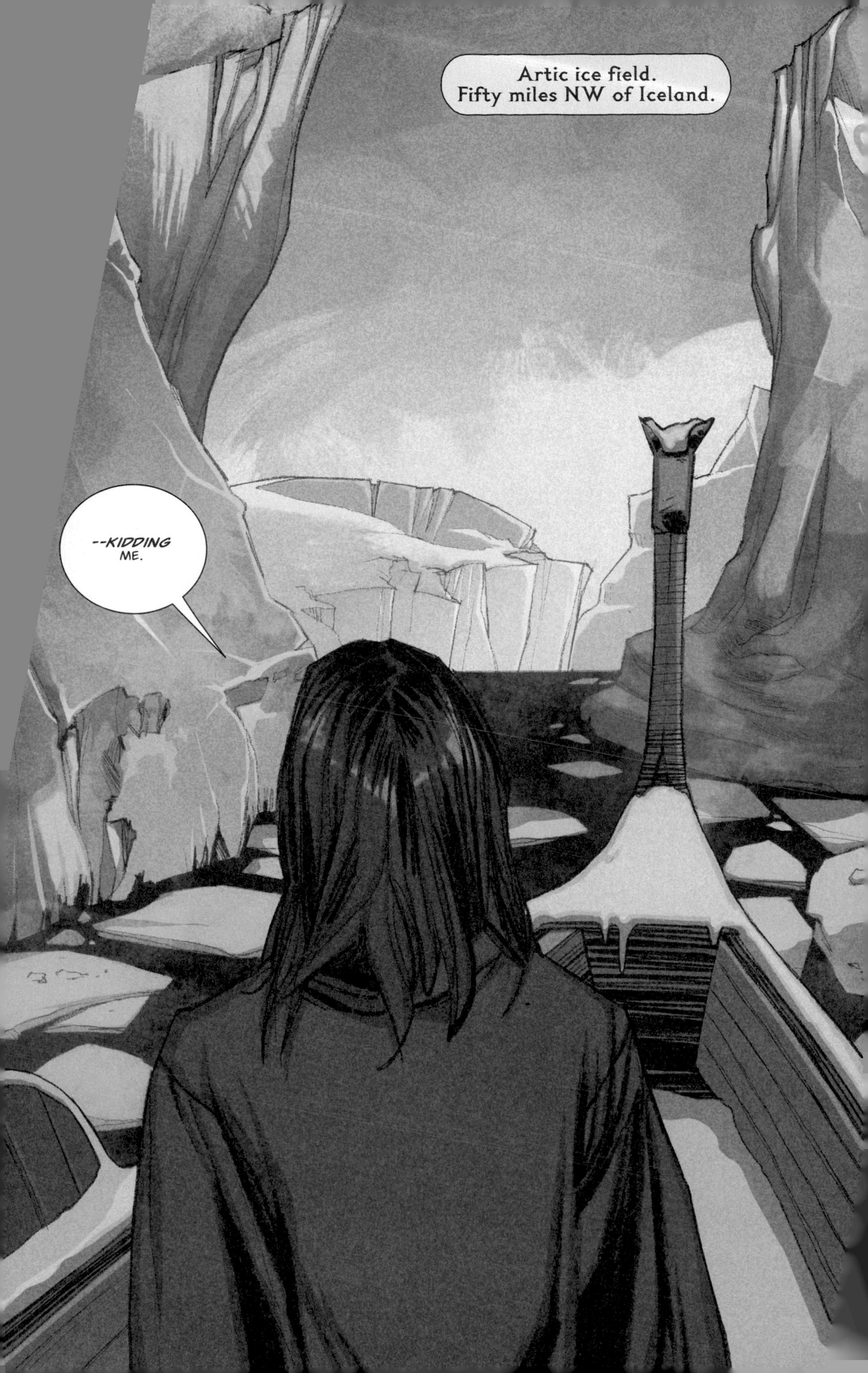
Artic ice field.
Fifty miles NW of Iceland.
--KIDDING ME.

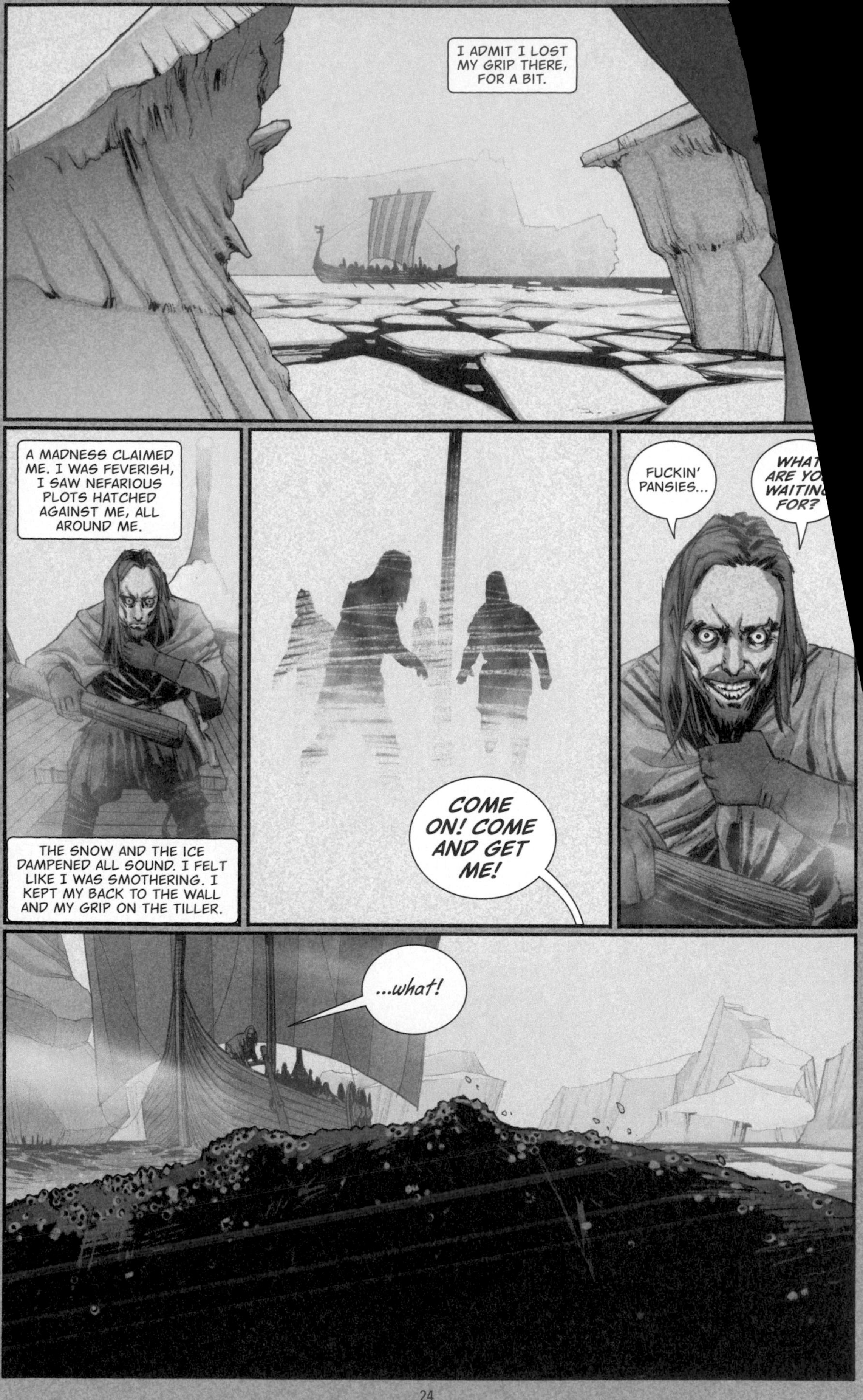
I ADMIT I LOST MY GRIP THERE, FOR A BIT.
A MADNESS CLAIMED ME. I WAS FEVERISH, I SAW NEFARIOUS PLOTS HATCHED AGAINST ME, ALL AROUND ME.
THE SNOW AND THE ICE DAMPENED ALL SOUND. I FELT LIKE I WAS SMOTHERING. I KEPT MY BACK TO THE WALL AND MY GRIP ON THE TILLER.
COME ON! COME AND GET ME!
FUCKIN' PANSIES...
WHAT ARE YO WAITIN FOR?
...what!

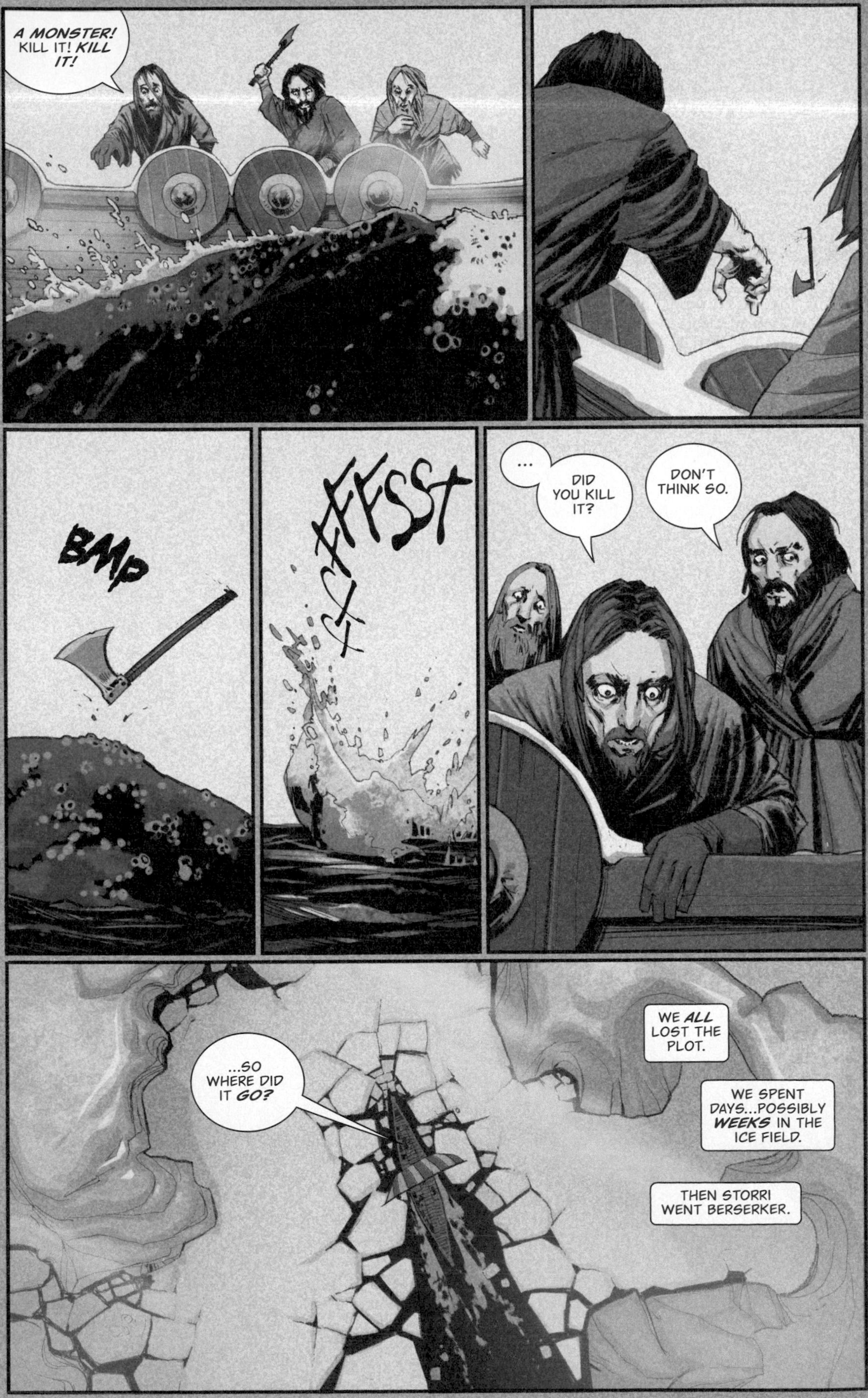
A MONSTER! KILL IT! KILL IT!
BMP
FFFSST
...
DID YOU KILL IT?
DON'T THINK SO.
...SO WHERE DID IT GO?
WE ALL LOST THE PLOT.
WE SPENT DAYS...POSSIBLY WEEKS IN THE ICE FIELD.
THEN STORRI WENT BERSERKER.

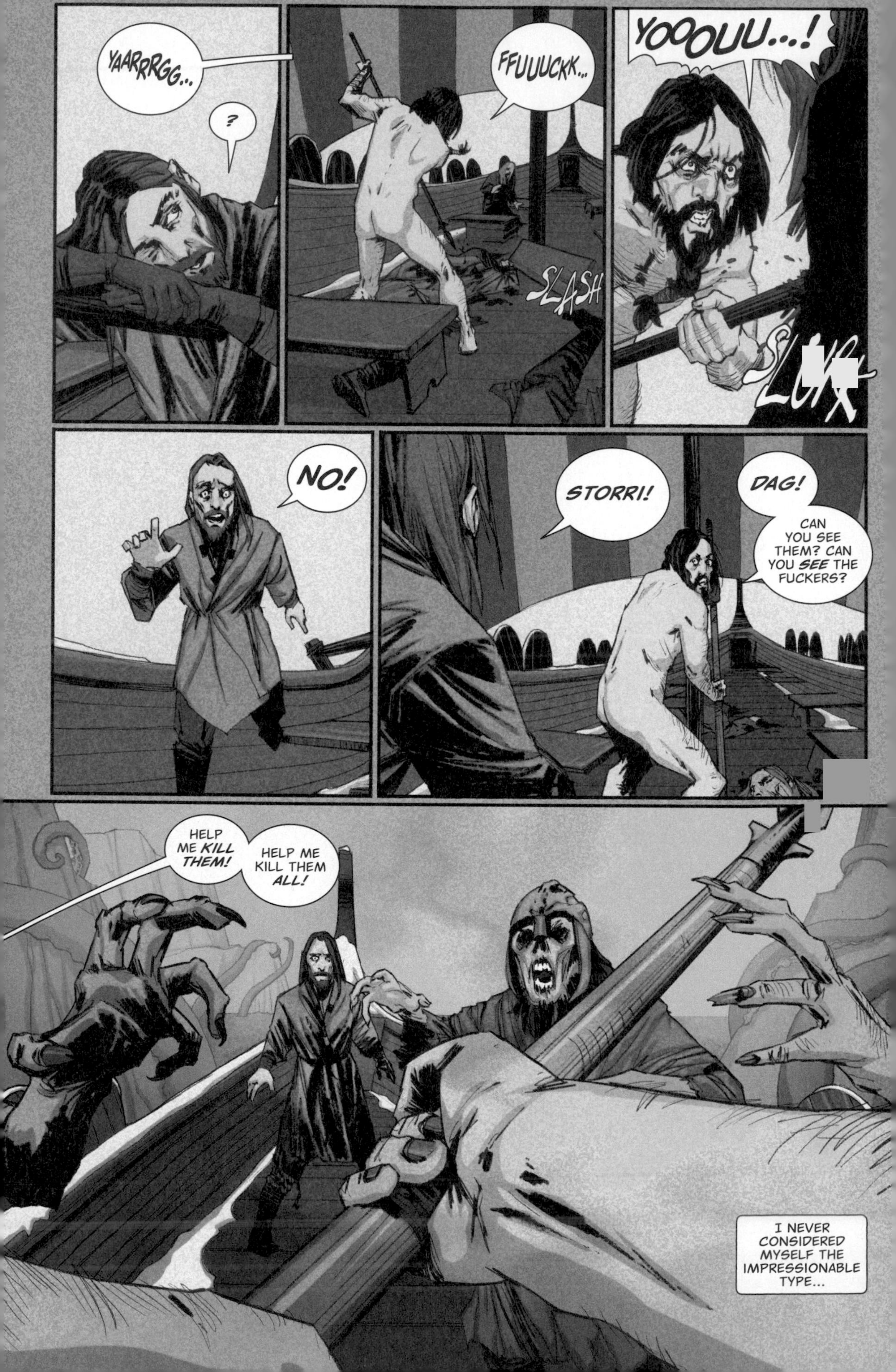
YAARRRGG...
?
FFUUUCKK...
SLASH
YOOOUU...!
NO!
STORRI!
DAG!
CAN YOU SEE THEM? CAN YOU *SEE* THE FUCKERS?
HELP ME *KILL THEM!*
HELP ME KILL THEM *ALL!*
I NEVER CONSIDERED MYSELF THE IMPRESSIONABLE TYPE...

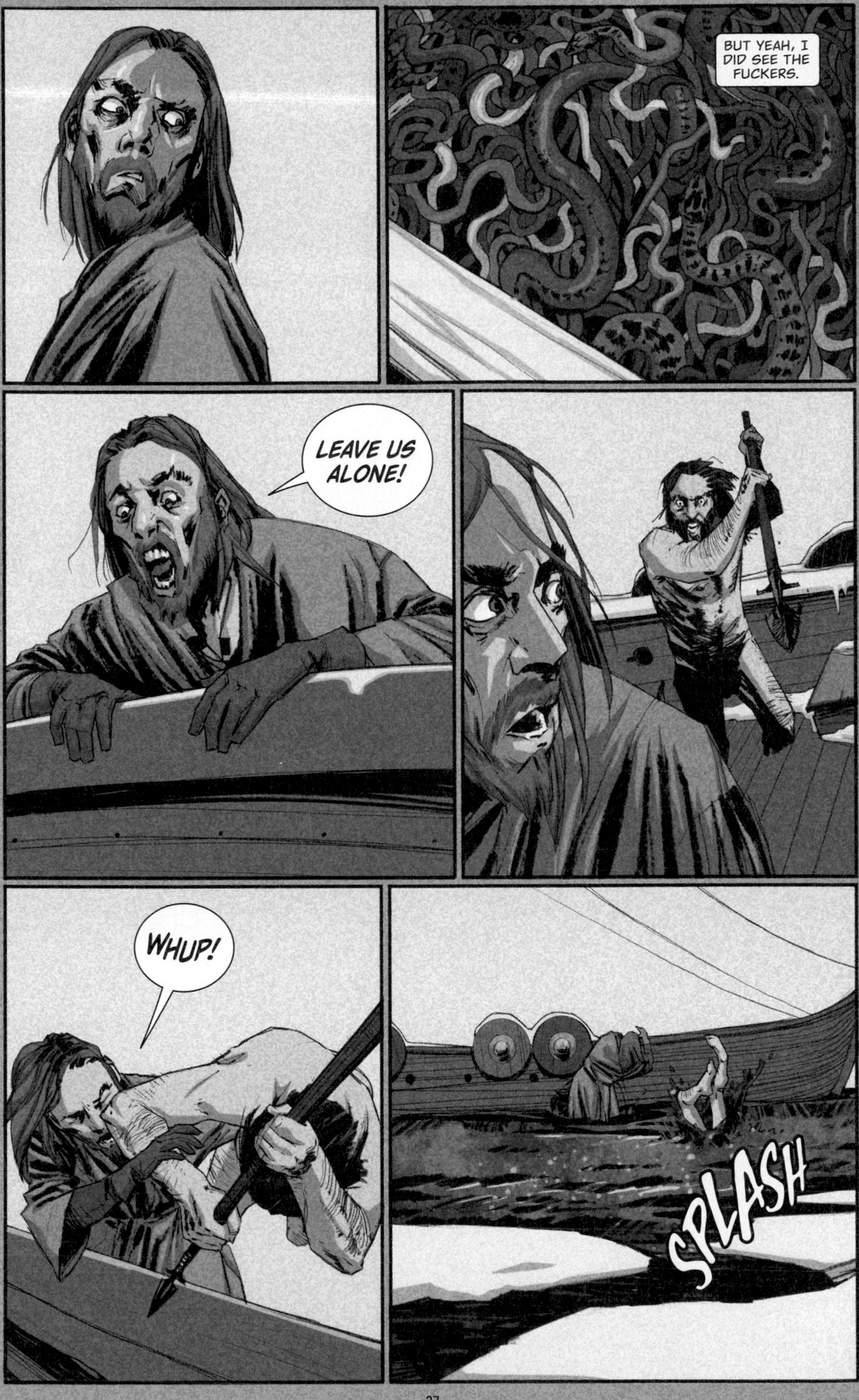
BUT YEAH, I DID SEE THE FUCKERS.
LEAVE US ALONE!
WHUP!
SPLASH

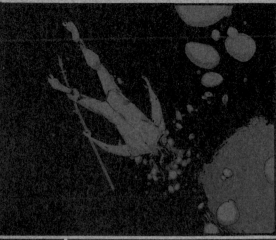

I'D FUCK YOUR MOTHER, YOU UGLY BASTARD FISHIE...

...TO BE BACK ON THE AARHUS/HEDEBY CORRIDOR, HAULING STINKING SHEEP PELTS.

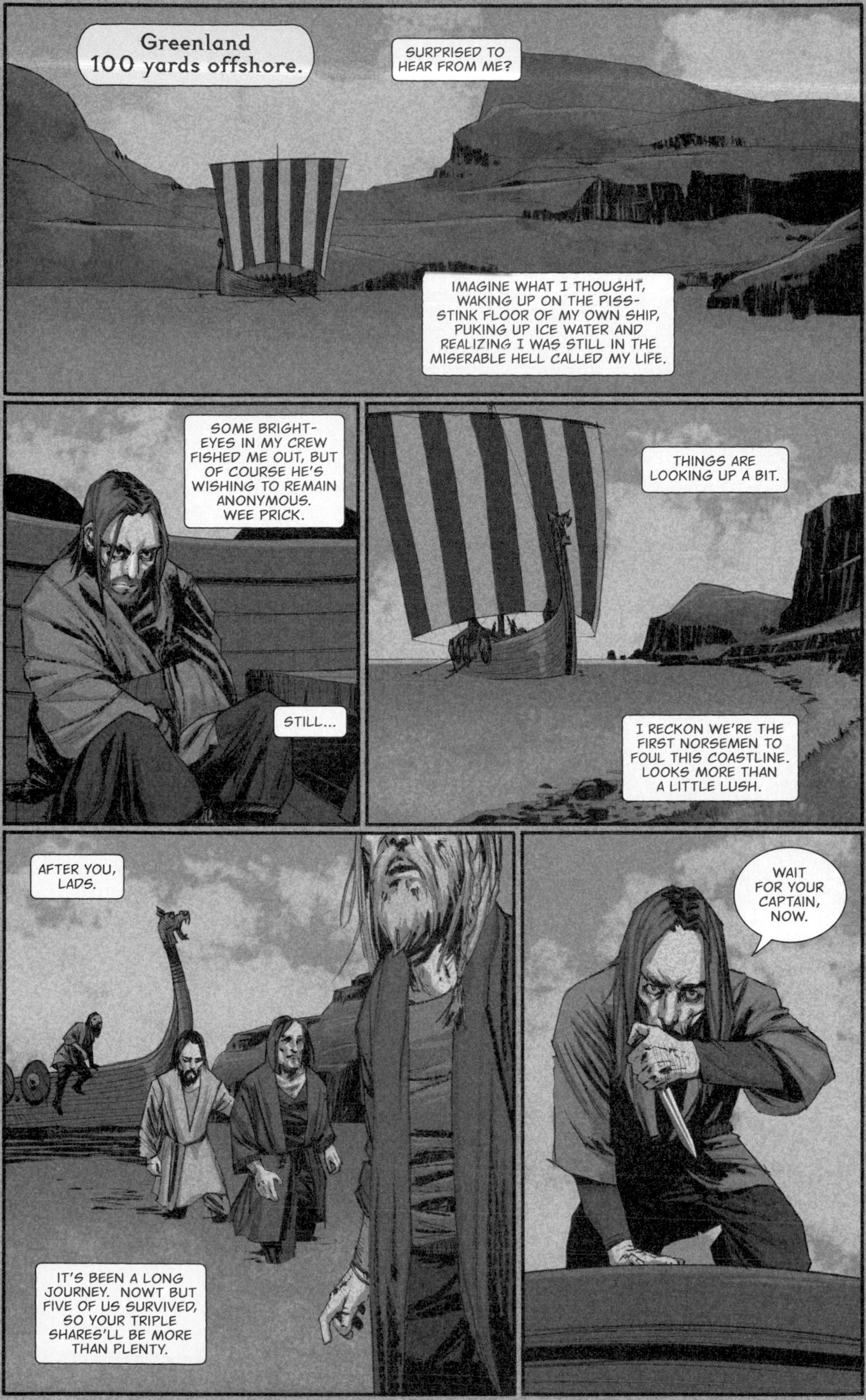
Greenland
100 yards offshore.
SURPRISED TO HEAR FROM ME?
IMAGINE WHAT I THOUGHT, WAKING UP ON THE PISS-STINK FLOOR OF MY OWN SHIP, PUKING UP ICE WATER AND REALIZING I WAS STILL IN THE MISERABLE HELL CALLED MY LIFE.
SOME BRIGHT-EYES IN MY CREW FISHED ME OUT, BUT OF COURSE HE'S WISHING TO REMAIN ANONYMOUS. WEE PRICK.
STILL...
THINGS ARE LOOKING UP A BIT.
I RECKON WE'RE THE FIRST NORSEMEN TO FOUL THIS COASTLINE. LOOKS MORE THAN A LITTLE LUSH.
AFTER YOU, LADS.
IT'S BEEN A LONG JOURNEY. NOWT BUT FIVE OF US SURVIVED, SO YOUR TRIPLE SHARES'LL BE MORE THAN PLENTY.
WAIT FOR YOUR CAPTAIN, NOW.

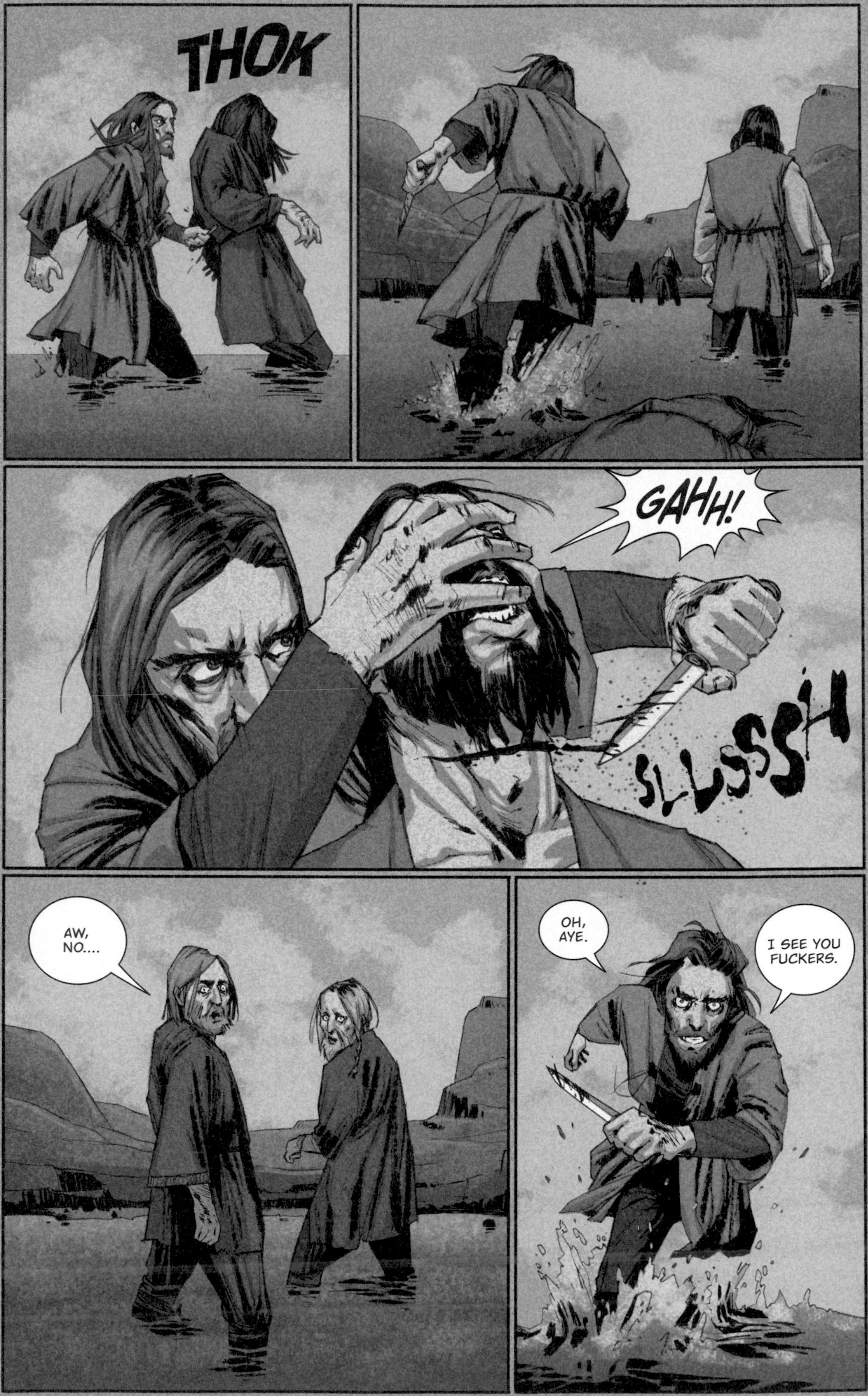
THOK
GAHH!
SLLSSSH
AW, NO....
OH, AYE.
I SEE YOU FUCKERS.

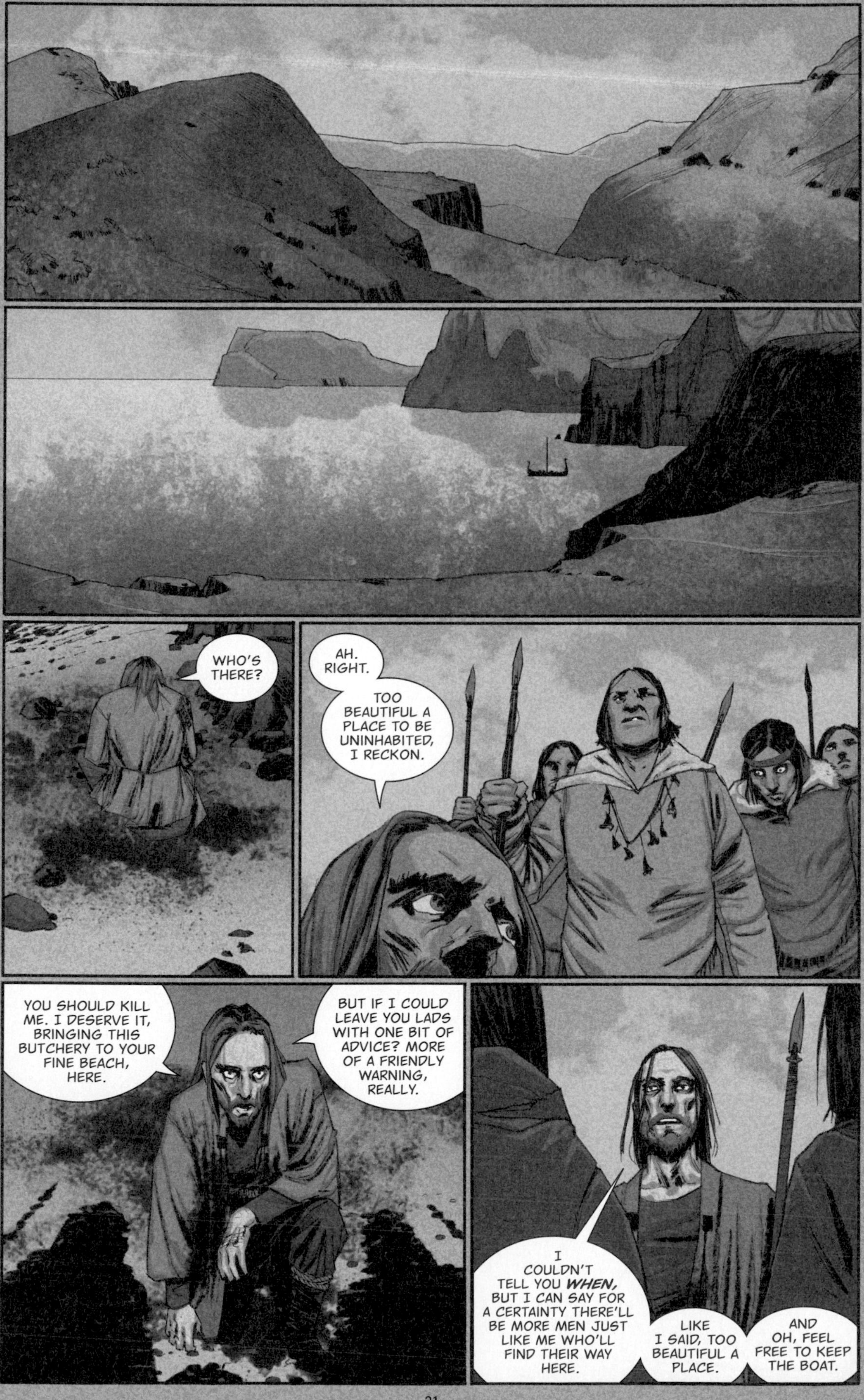

WHO'S THERE?
AH. RIGHT.
TOO BEAUTIFUL A PLACE TO BE UNINHABITED, I RECKON.
YOU SHOULD KILL ME. I DESERVE IT, BRINGING THIS BUTCHERY TO YOUR FINE BEACH, HERE.
BUT IF I COULD LEAVE YOU LADS WITH ONE BIT OF ADVICE? MORE OF A FRIENDLY WARNING, REALLY.
I COULDN'T TELL YOU ***WHEN,*** BUT I CAN SAY FOR A CERTAINTY THERE'LL BE MORE MEN JUST LIKE ME WHO'LL FIND THEIR WAY HERE.
LIKE I SAID, TOO BEAUTIFUL A PLACE.
AND OH, FEEL FREE TO KEEP THE BOAT.

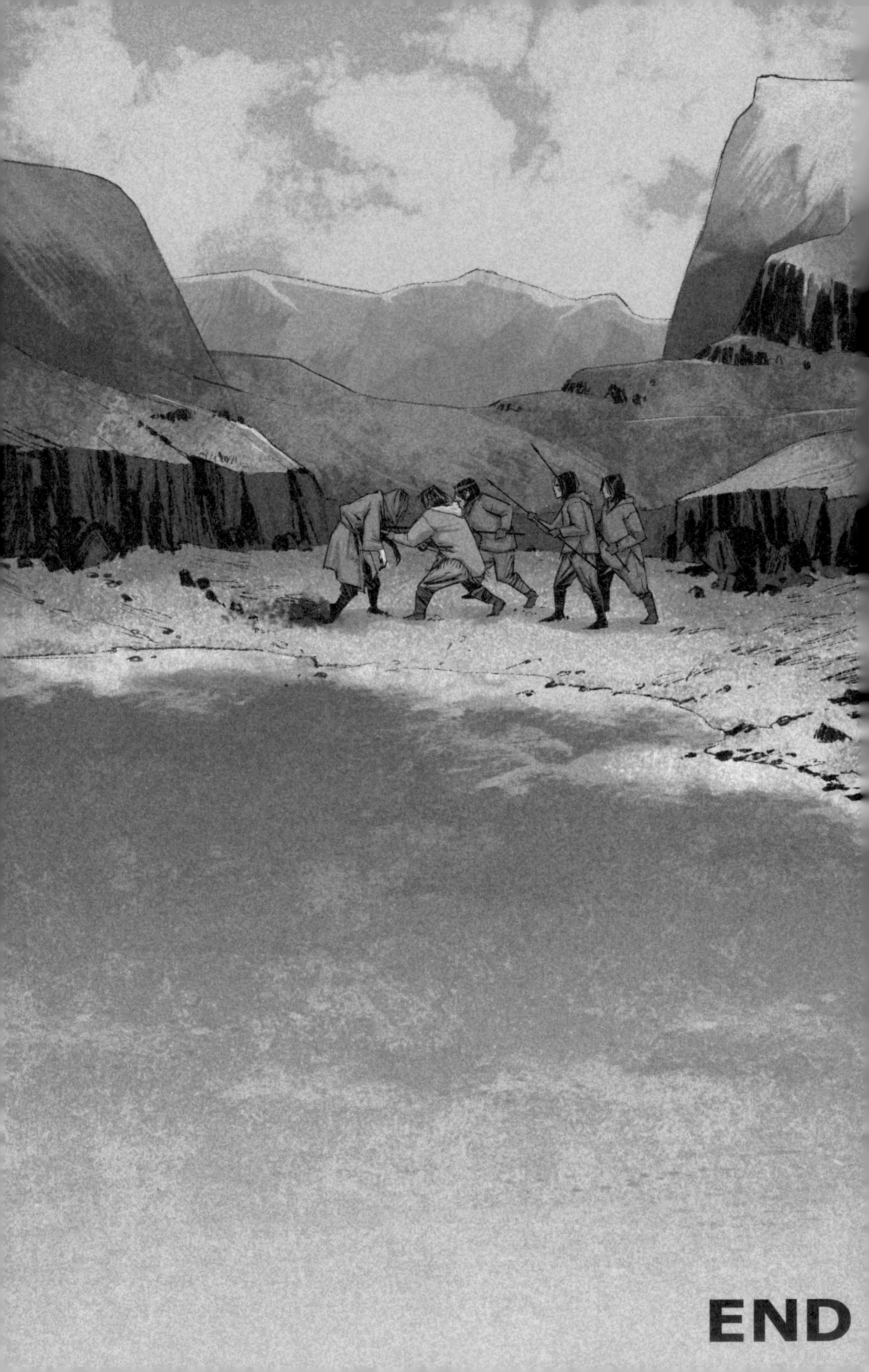
END

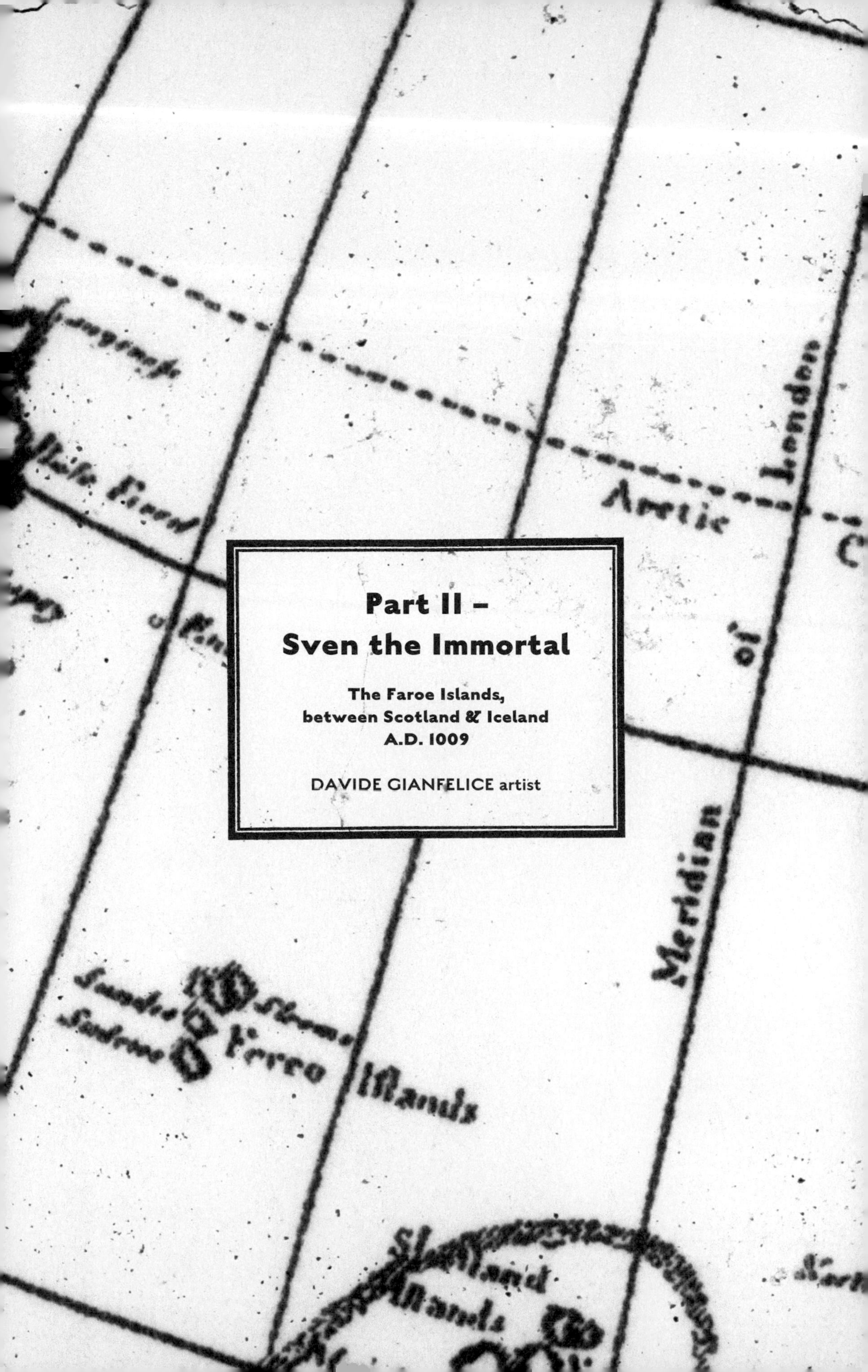
Arctic
Meridian of London
Ferro

Part II – Sven the Immortal

The Faroe Islands,
between Scotland & Iceland
A.D. 1009

DAVIDE GIANFELICE artist

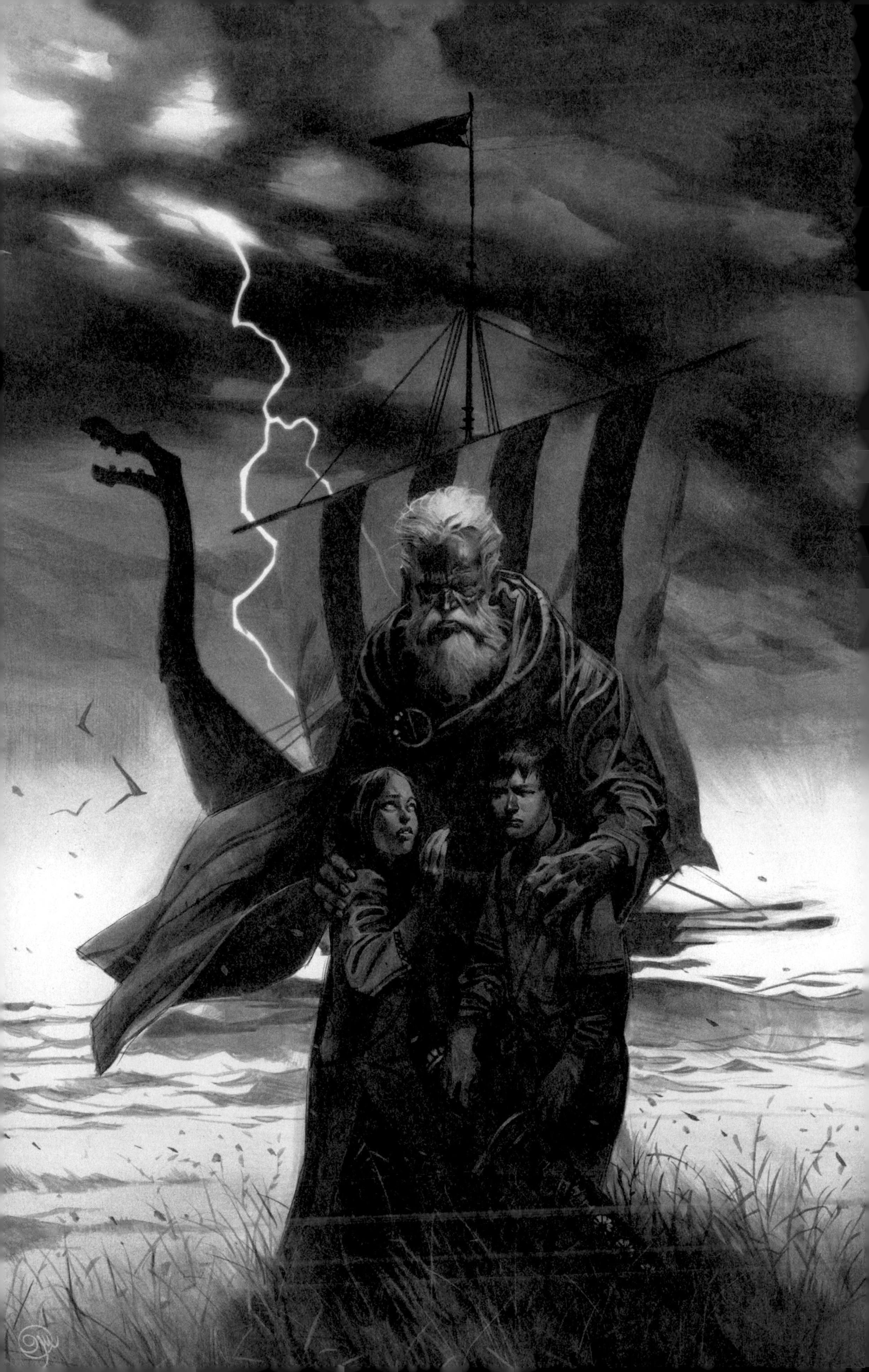

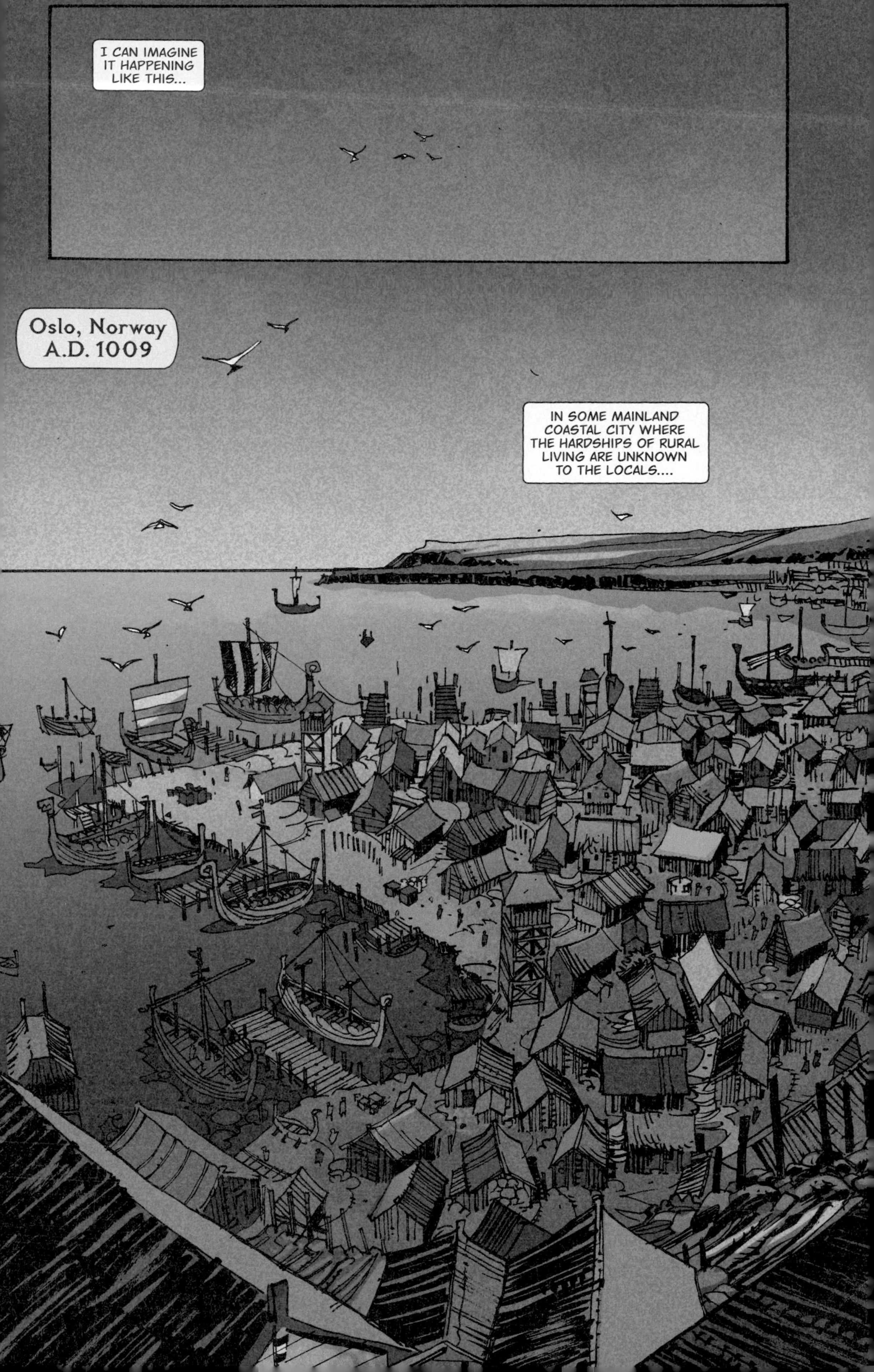
I CAN IMAGINE IT HAPPENING LIKE THIS...
Oslo, Norway A.D. 1009
IN SOME MAINLAND COASTAL CITY WHERE THE HARDSHIPS OF RURAL LIVING ARE UNKNOWN TO THE LOCALS....

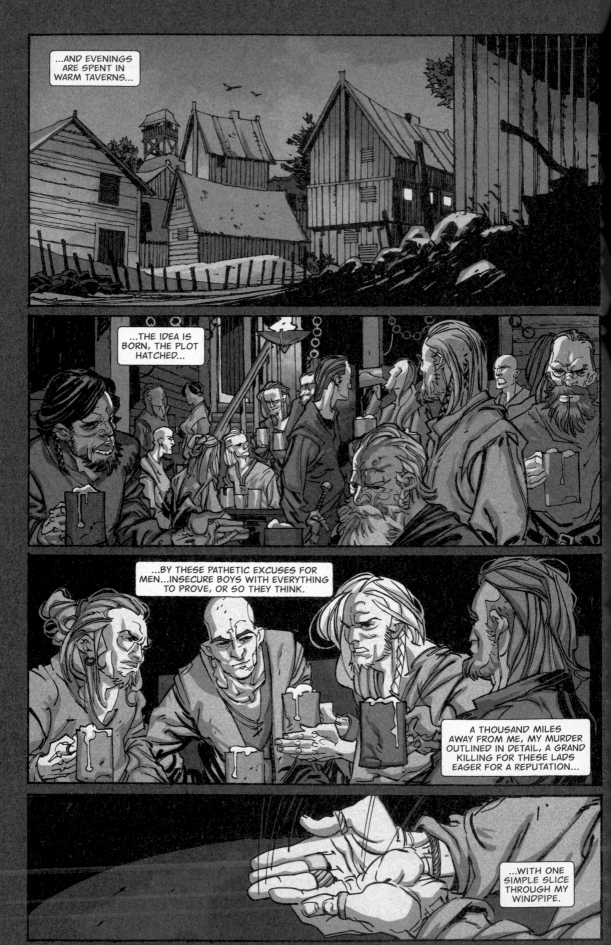

...AND EVENINGS ARE SPENT IN WARM TAVERNS...

...THE IDEA IS BORN, THE PLOT HATCHED...

...BY THESE PATHETIC EXCUSES FOR MEN...INSECURE BOYS WITH EVERYTHING TO PROVE, OR SO THEY THINK.

A THOUSAND MILES AWAY FROM ME, MY MURDER OUTLINED IN DETAIL, A GRAND KILLING FOR THESE LADS EAGER FOR A REPUTATION...

...WITH ONE SIMPLE SLICE THROUGH MY WINDPIPE.

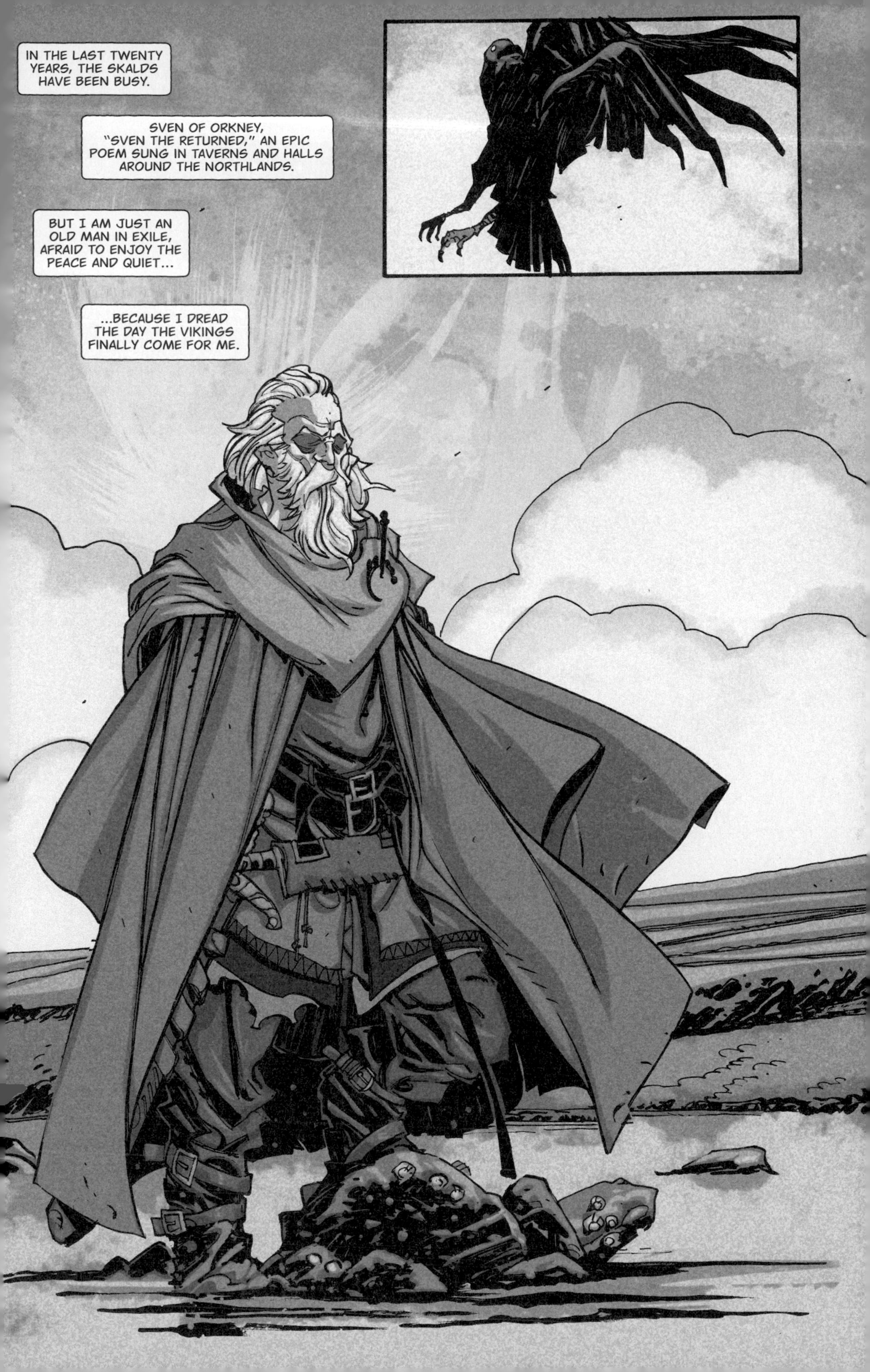
IN THE LAST TWENTY YEARS, THE SKALDS HAVE BEEN BUSY.
SVEN OF ORKNEY, "SVEN THE RETURNED," AN EPIC POEM SUNG IN TAVERNS AND HALLS AROUND THE NORTHLANDS.
BUT I AM JUST AN OLD MAN IN EXILE, AFRAID TO ENJOY THE PEACE AND QUIET...
...BECAUSE I DREAD THE DAY THE VIKINGS FINALLY COME FOR ME.

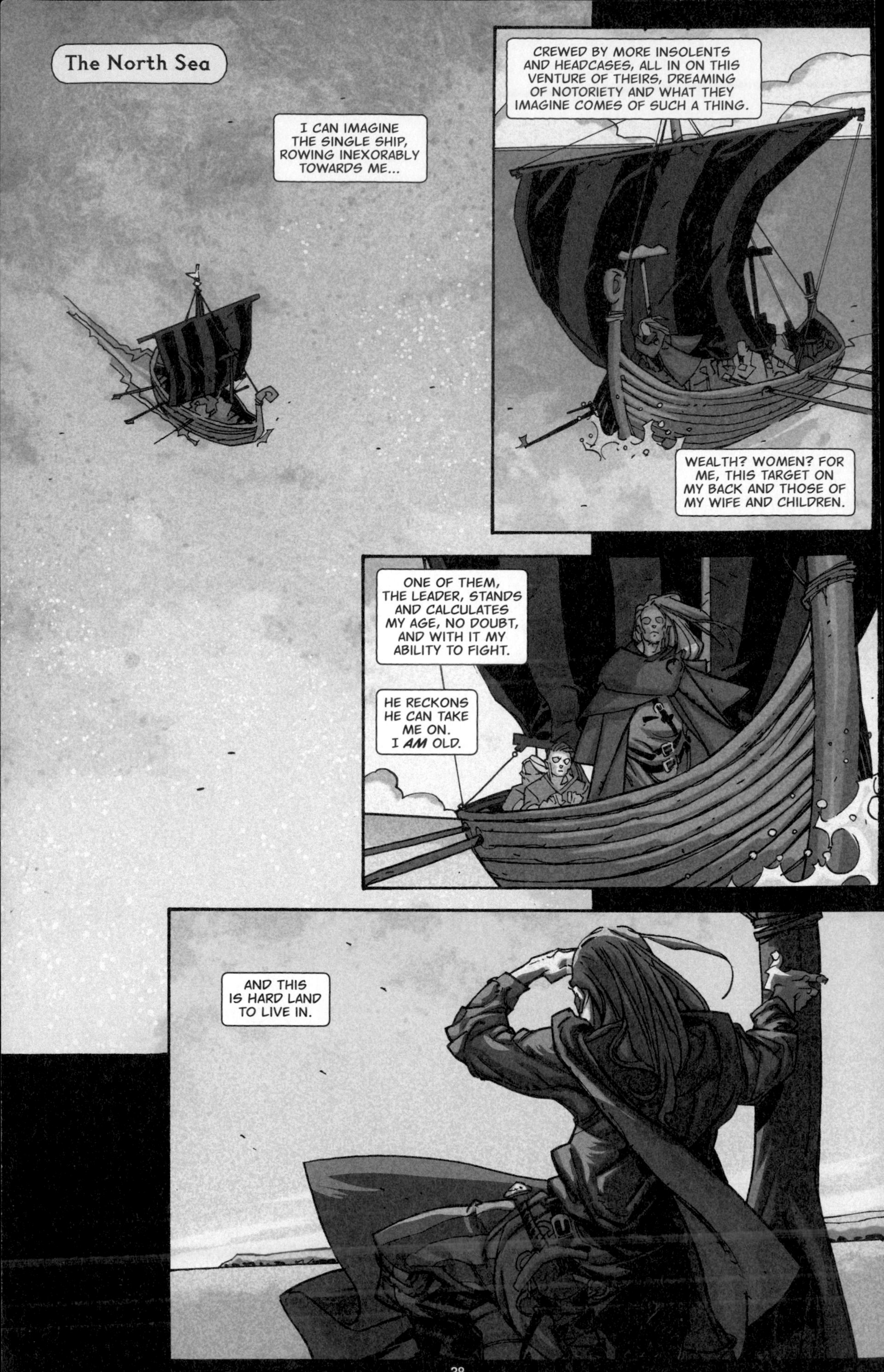
The North Sea
I CAN IMAGINE THE SINGLE SHIP, ROWING INEXORABLY TOWARDS ME...
CREWED BY MORE INSOLENTS AND HEADCASES, ALL IN ON THIS VENTURE OF THEIRS, DREAMING OF NOTORIETY AND WHAT THEY IMAGINE COMES OF SUCH A THING.
WEALTH? WOMEN? FOR ME, THIS TARGET ON MY BACK AND THOSE OF MY WIFE AND CHILDREN.
ONE OF THEM, THE LEADER, STANDS AND CALCULATES MY AGE, NO DOUBT, AND WITH IT MY ABILITY TO FIGHT.
HE RECKONS HE CAN TAKE ME ON. I ***AM*** OLD.
AND THIS IS HARD LAND TO LIVE IN.

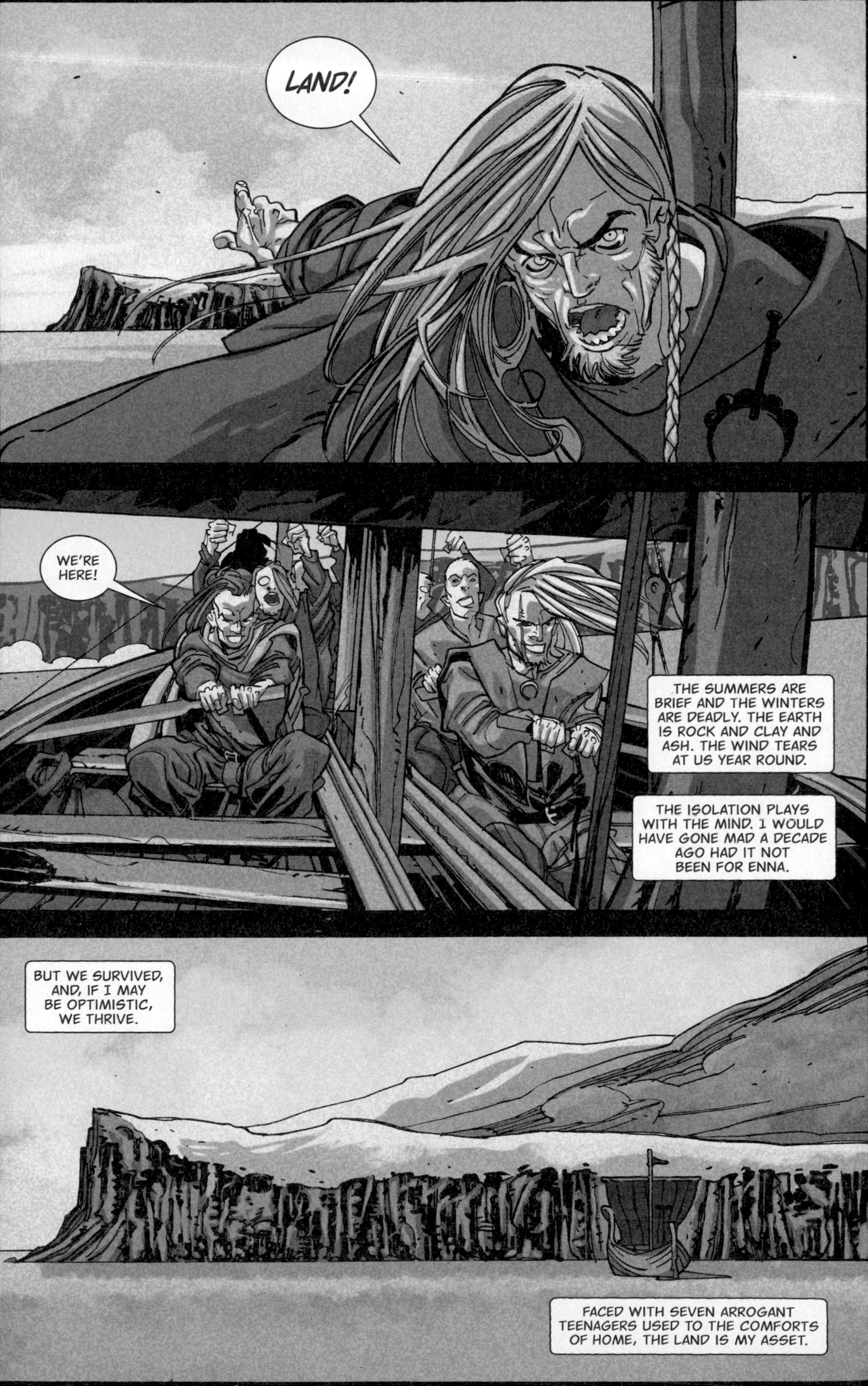
LAND!
WE'RE HERE!
THE SUMMERS ARE BRIEF AND THE WINTERS ARE DEADLY. THE EARTH IS ROCK AND CLAY AND ASH. THE WIND TEARS AT US YEAR ROUND.
THE ISOLATION PLAYS WITH THE MIND. I WOULD HAVE GONE MAD A DECADE AGO HAD IT NOT BEEN FOR ENNA.
BUT WE SURVIVED, AND, IF I MAY BE OPTIMISTIC, WE THRIVE.
FACED WITH SEVEN ARROGANT TEENAGERS USED TO THE COMFORTS OF HOME, THE LAND IS MY ASSET.

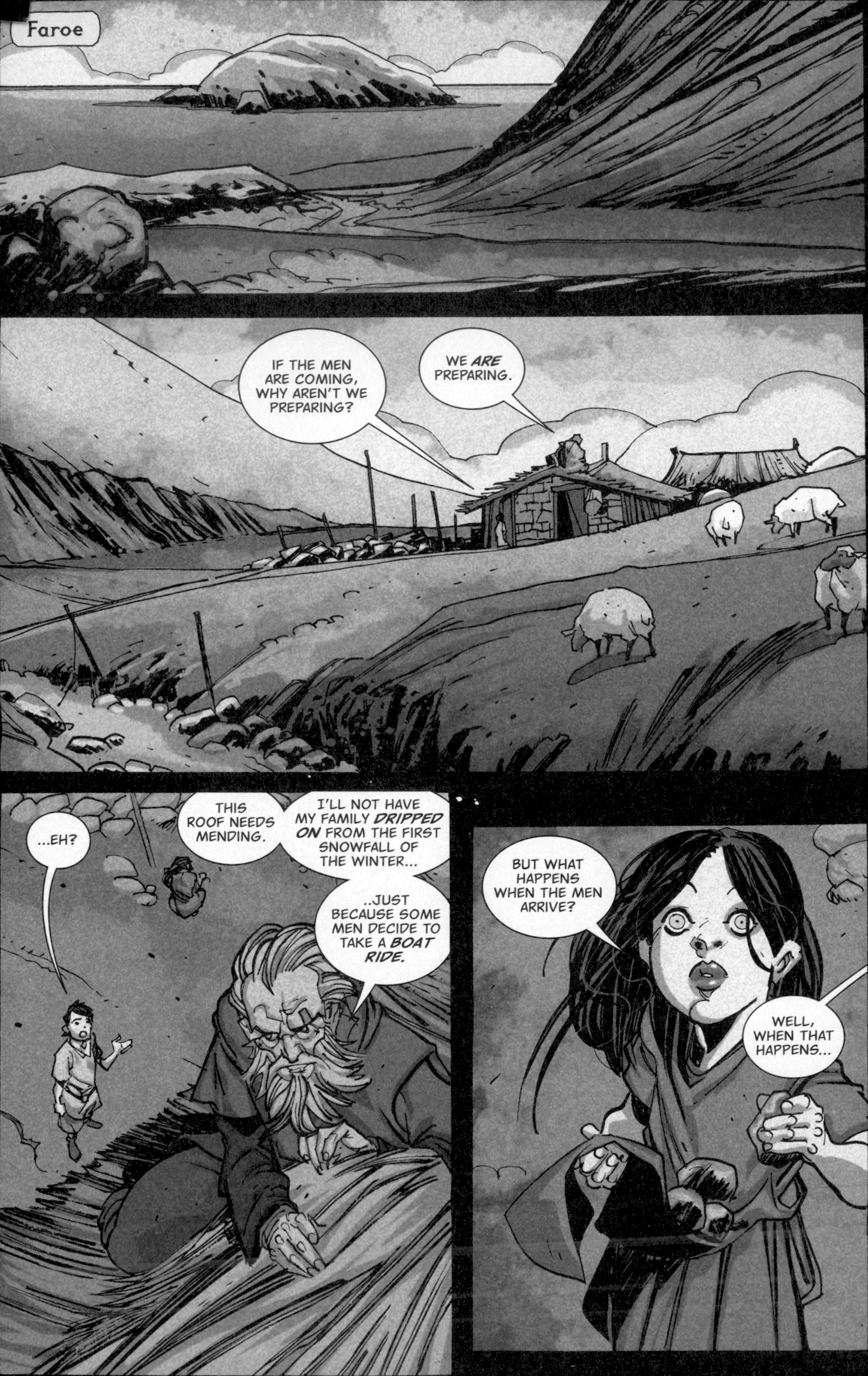
Faroe
IF THE MEN ARE COMING, WHY AREN'T WE PREPARING?
WE *ARE* PREPARING.
...EH?
THIS ROOF NEEDS MENDING.
I'LL NOT HAVE MY FAMILY *DRIPPED ON* FROM THE FIRST SNOWFALL OF THE WINTER...
..JUST BECAUSE SOME MEN DECIDE TO TAKE A *BOAT RIDE.*
BUT WHAT HAPPENS WHEN THE MEN ARRIVE?
WELL, WHEN THAT HAPPENS...

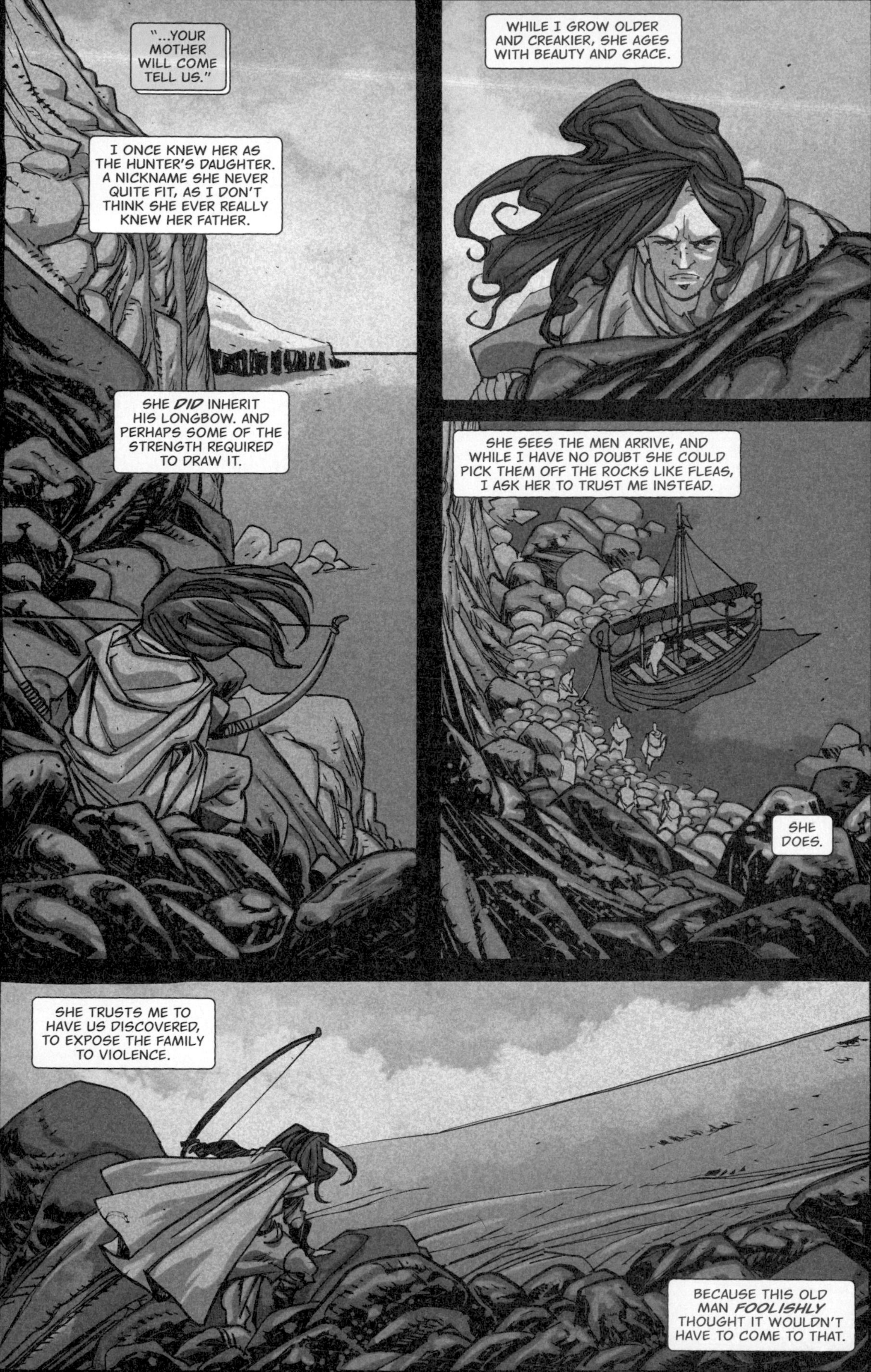
"...YOUR MOTHER WILL COME TELL US."
I ONCE KNEW HER AS THE HUNTER'S DAUGHTER. A NICKNAME SHE NEVER QUITE FIT, AS I DON'T THINK SHE EVER REALLY KNEW HER FATHER.
SHE *DID* INHERIT HIS LONGBOW. AND PERHAPS SOME OF THE STRENGTH REQUIRED TO DRAW IT.
WHILE I GROW OLDER AND CREAKIER, SHE AGES WITH BEAUTY AND GRACE.
SHE SEES THE MEN ARRIVE, AND WHILE I HAVE NO DOUBT SHE COULD PICK THEM OFF THE ROCKS LIKE FLEAS, I ASK HER TO TRUST ME INSTEAD.
SHE DOES.
SHE TRUSTS ME TO HAVE US DISCOVERED, TO EXPOSE THE FAMILY TO VIOLENCE.
BECAUSE THIS OLD MAN *FOOLISHLY* THOUGHT IT WOULDN'T HAVE TO COME TO THAT.

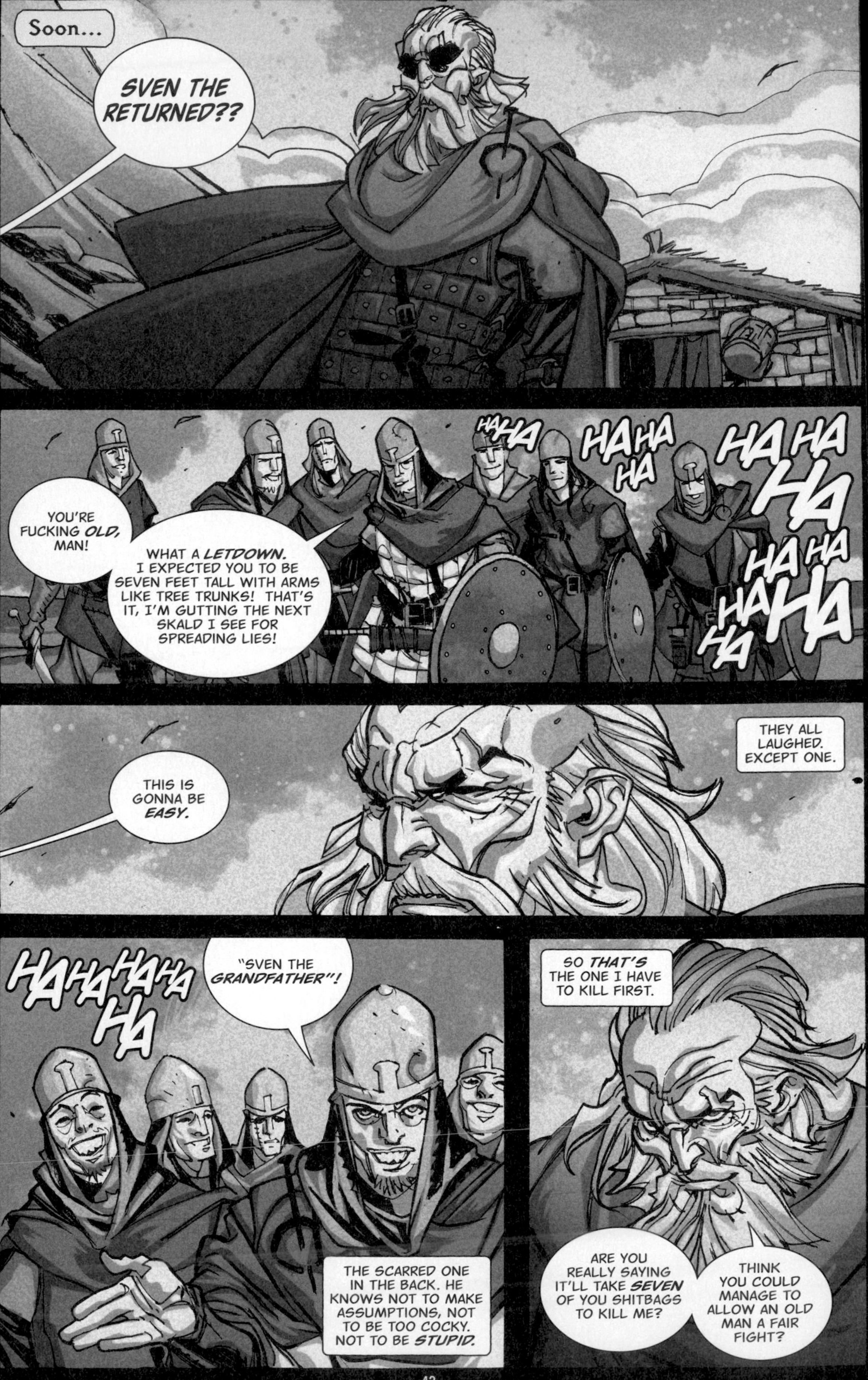

Soon...
SVEN THE RETURNED??
YOU'RE FUCKING OLD, MAN!
WHAT A LETDOWN. I EXPECTED YOU TO BE SEVEN FEET TALL WITH ARMS LIKE TREE TRUNKS! THAT'S IT, I'M GUTTING THE NEXT SKALD I SEE FOR SPREADING LIES!
HAHA
HA HA HA
HA HA HA
HA HA HA HA HA HA
THIS IS GONNA BE EASY.
THEY ALL LAUGHED. EXCEPT ONE.
HA HA HA HA HA
"SVEN THE GRANDFATHER"!
THE SCARRED ONE IN THE BACK. HE KNOWS NOT TO MAKE ASSUMPTIONS, NOT TO BE TOO COCKY. NOT TO BE STUPID.
SO THAT'S THE ONE I HAVE TO KILL FIRST.
ARE YOU REALLY SAYING IT'LL TAKE SEVEN OF YOU SHITBAGS TO KILL ME?
THINK YOU COULD MANAGE TO ALLOW AN OLD MAN A FAIR FIGHT?

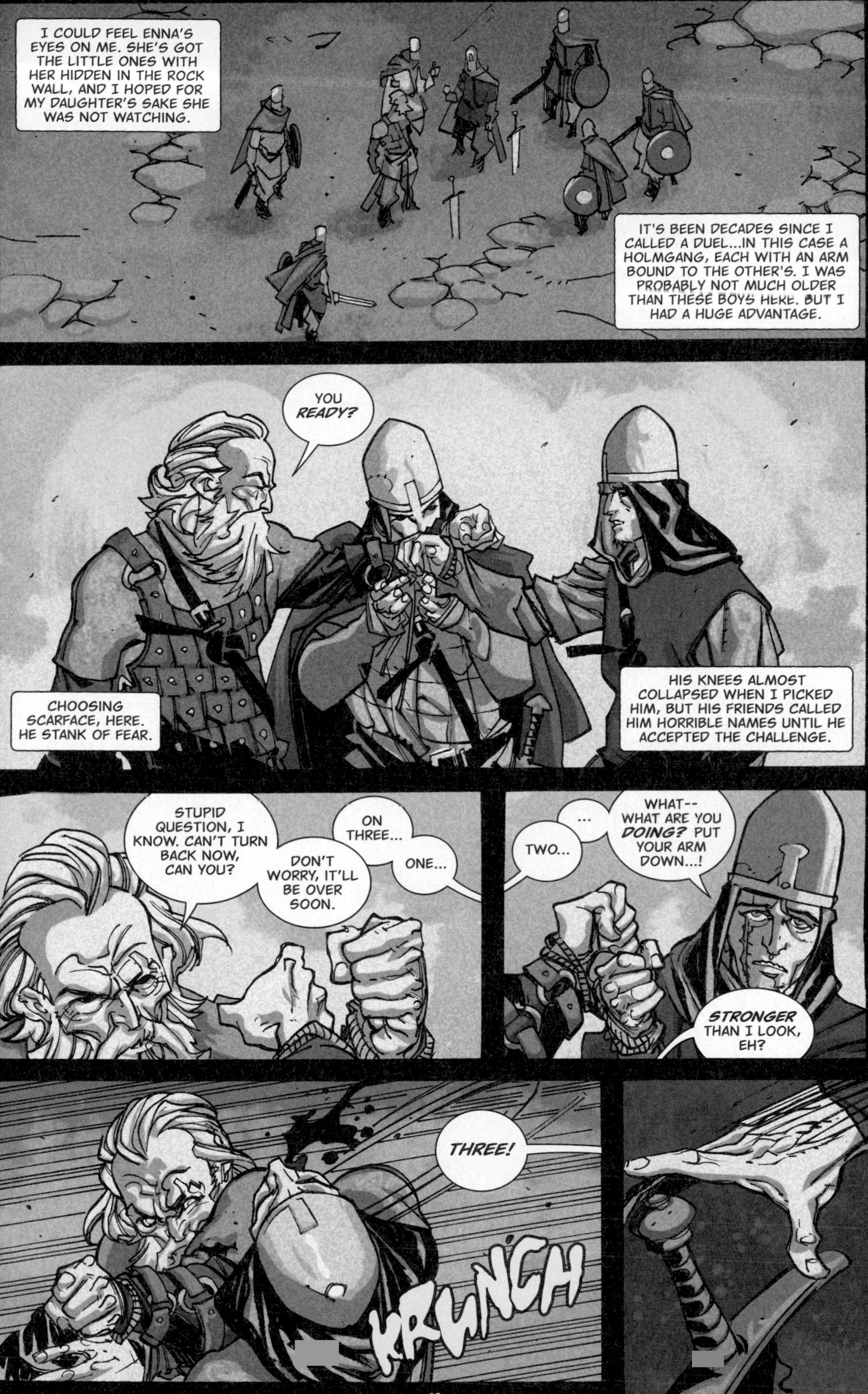
I COULD FEEL ENNA'S EYES ON ME. SHE'S GOT THE LITTLE ONES WITH HER HIDDEN IN THE ROCK WALL, AND I HOPED FOR MY DAUGHTER'S SAKE SHE WAS NOT WATCHING.
IT'S BEEN DECADES SINCE I CALLED A DUEL...IN THIS CASE A HOLMGANG, EACH WITH AN ARM BOUND TO THE OTHER'S. I WAS PROBABLY NOT MUCH OLDER THAN THESE BOYS HERE. BUT I HAD A HUGE ADVANTAGE.
YOU *READY?*
CHOOSING SCARFACE, HERE. HE STANK OF FEAR.
HIS KNEES ALMOST COLLAPSED WHEN I PICKED HIM, BUT HIS FRIENDS CALLED HIM HORRIBLE NAMES UNTIL HE ACCEPTED THE CHALLENGE.
STUPID QUESTION, I KNOW. CAN'T TURN BACK NOW, CAN YOU?
DON'T WORRY, IT'LL BE OVER SOON.
ON THREE...
ONE...
TWO...
...
WHAT-- WHAT ARE YOU *DOING?* PUT YOUR ARM DOWN...!
STRONGER THAN I LOOK, EH?
THREE!
KRUNCH

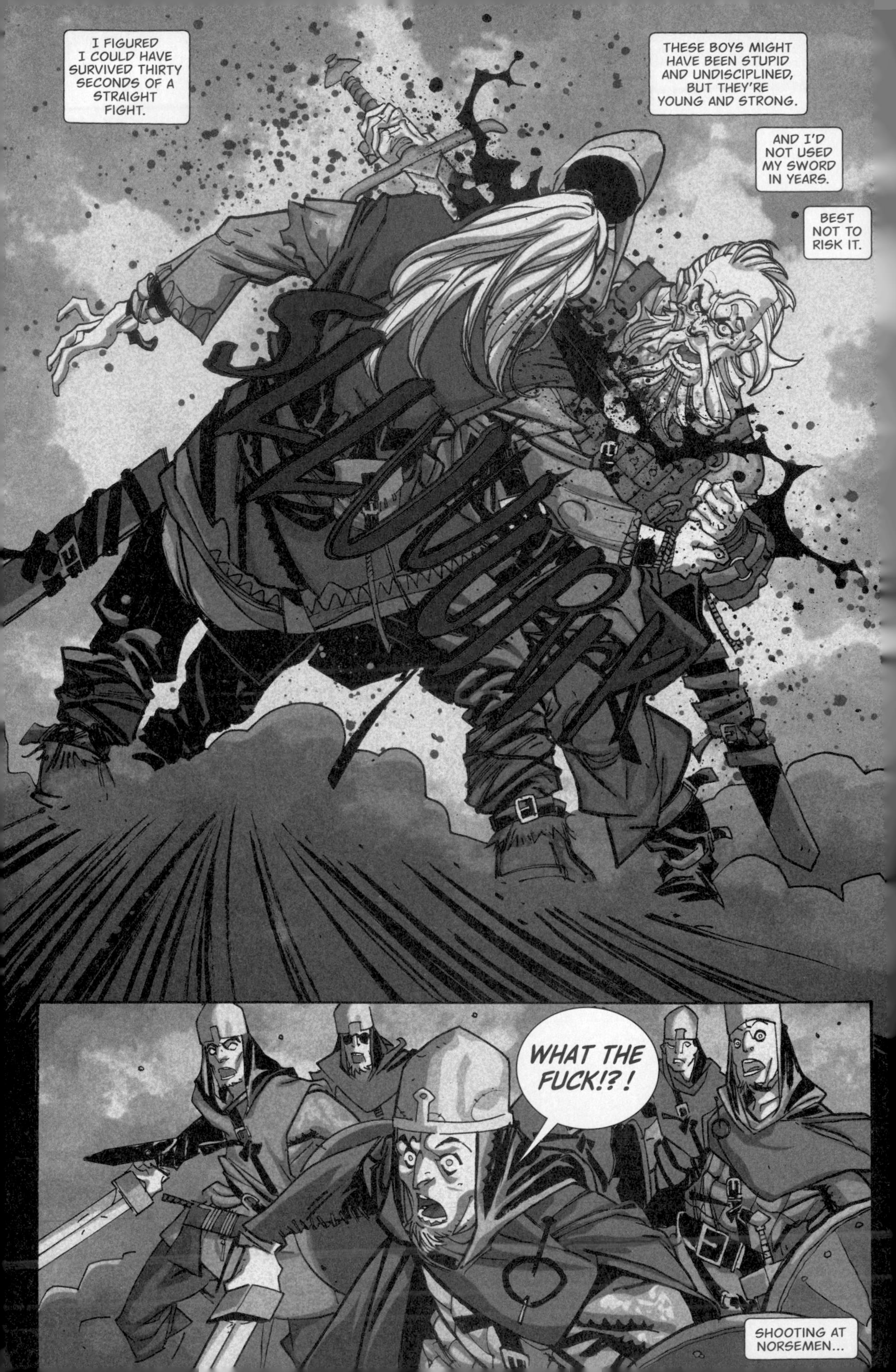
I FIGURED I COULD HAVE SURVIVED THIRTY SECONDS OF A STRAIGHT FIGHT.
THESE BOYS MIGHT HAVE BEEN STUPID AND UNDISCIPLINED, BUT THEY'RE YOUNG AND STRONG.
AND I'D NOT USED MY SWORD IN YEARS.
BEST NOT TO RISK IT.
WHAT THE FUCK!?!
SHOOTING AT NORSEMEN...

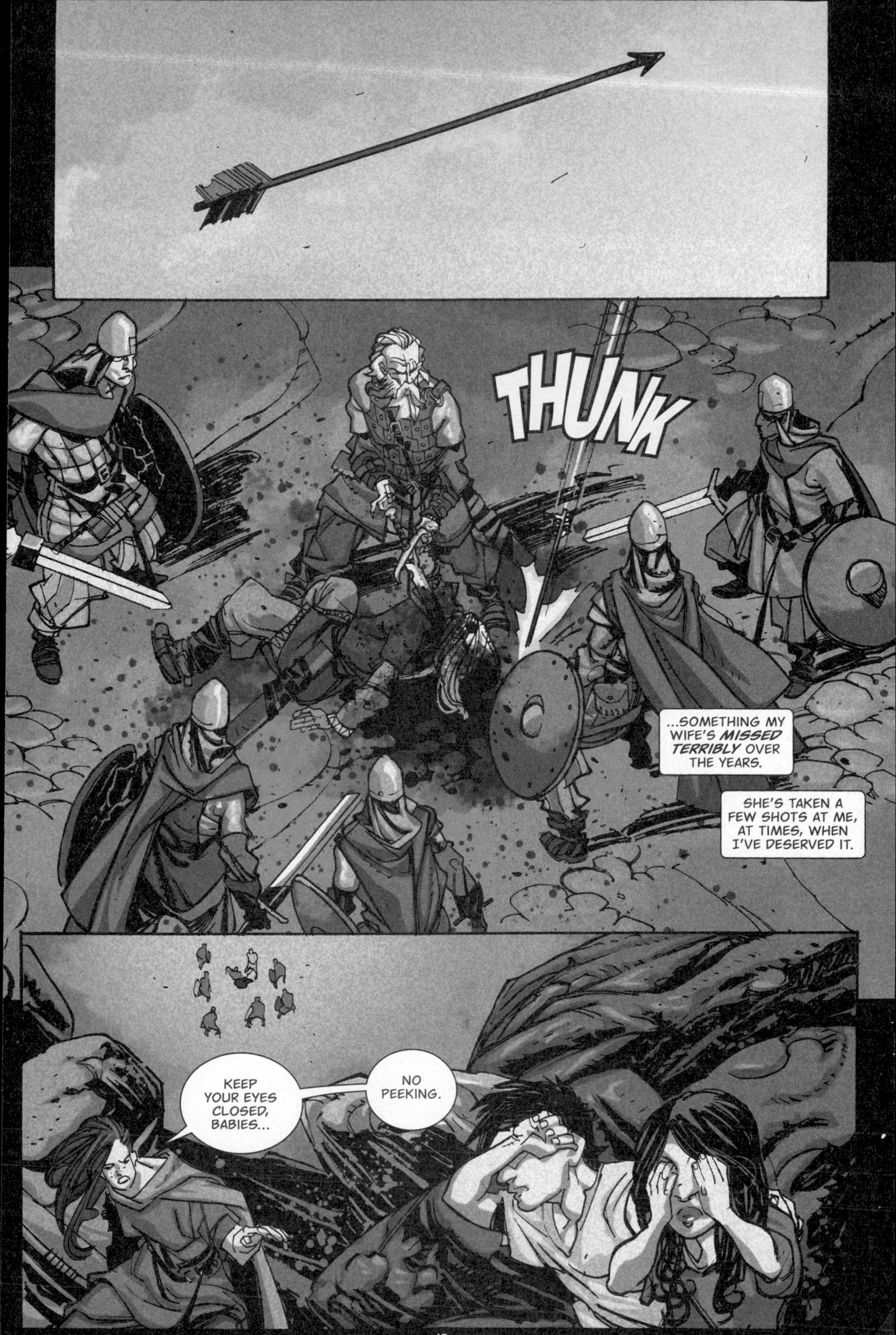
THUNK
...SOMETHING MY WIFE'S MISSED TERRIBLY OVER THE YEARS.
SHE'S TAKEN A FEW SHOTS AT ME, AT TIMES, WHEN I'VE DESERVED IT.
KEEP YOUR EYES CLOSED, BABIES...
NO PEEKING.

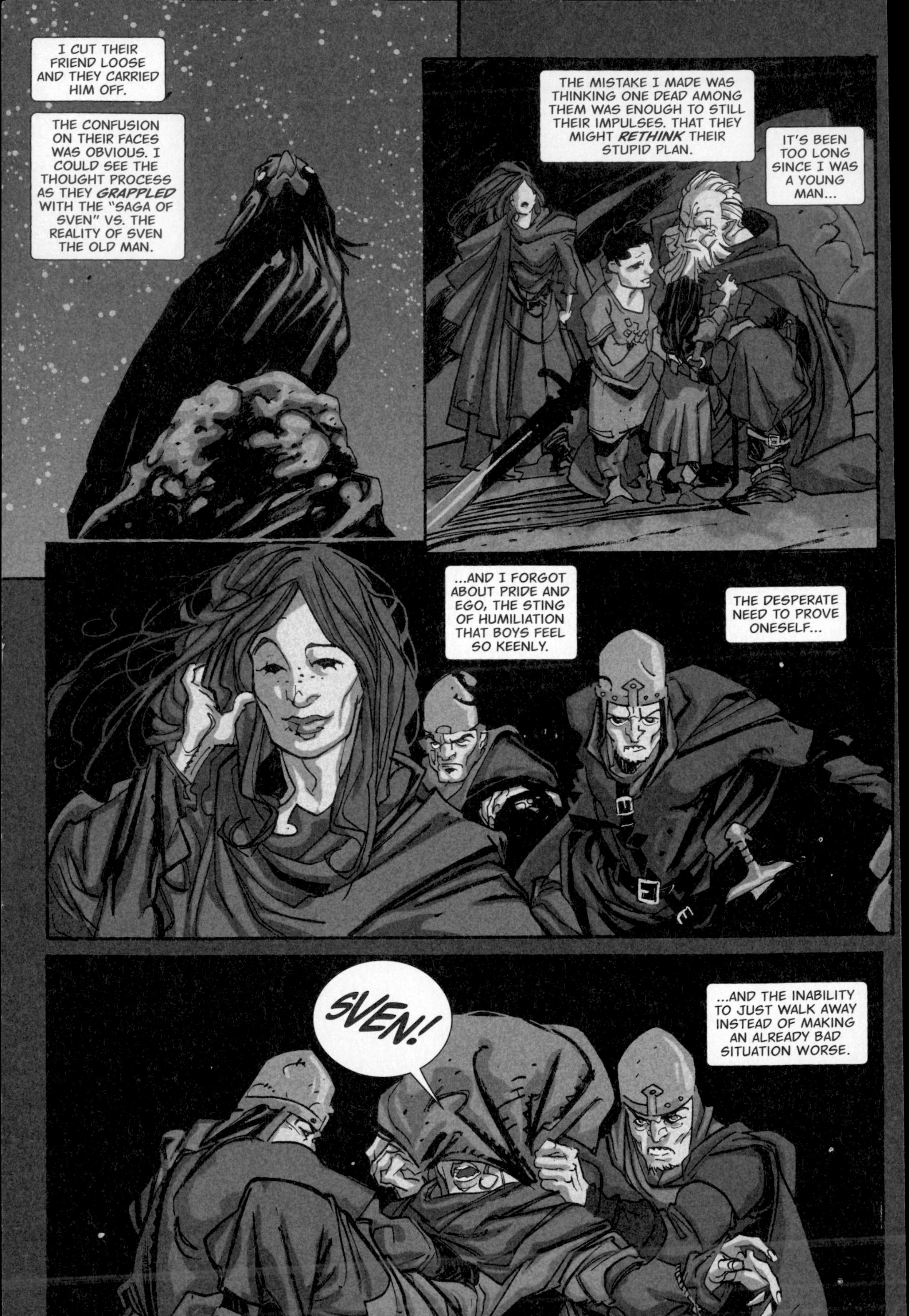
I CUT THEIR FRIEND LOOSE AND THEY CARRIED HIM OFF.
THE CONFUSION ON THEIR FACES WAS OBVIOUS. I COULD SEE THE THOUGHT PROCESS AS THEY GRAPPLED WITH THE "SAGA OF SVEN" VS. THE REALITY OF SVEN THE OLD MAN.
THE MISTAKE I MADE WAS THINKING ONE DEAD AMONG THEM WAS ENOUGH TO STILL THEIR IMPULSES. THAT THEY MIGHT RETHINK THEIR STUPID PLAN.
IT'S BEEN TOO LONG SINCE I WAS A YOUNG MAN...
...AND I FORGOT ABOUT PRIDE AND EGO, THE STING OF HUMILIATION THAT BOYS FEEL SO KEENLY.
THE DESPERATE NEED TO PROVE ONESELF...
SVEN!
...AND THE INABILITY TO JUST WALK AWAY INSTEAD OF MAKING AN ALREADY BAD SITUATION WORSE.

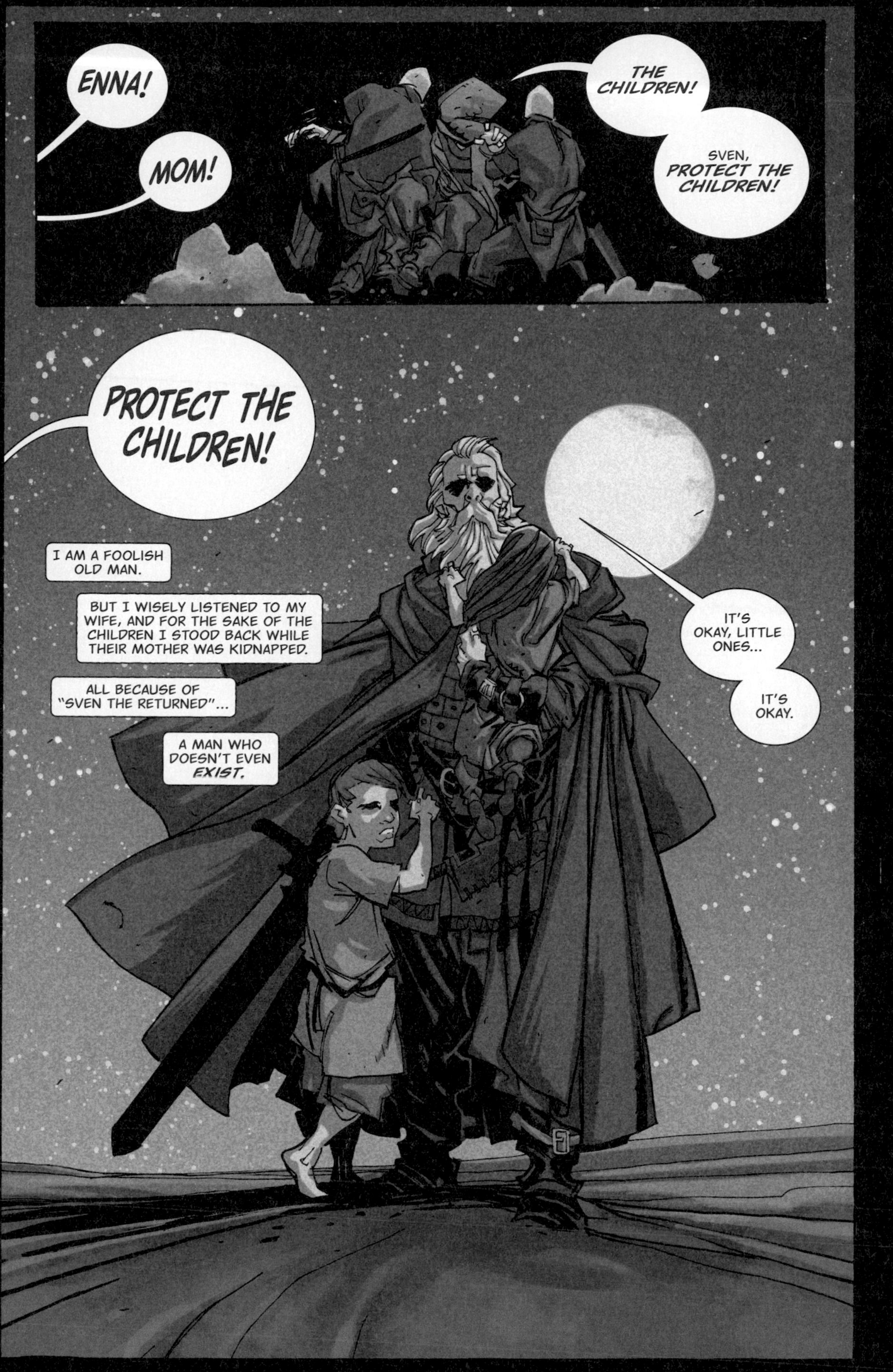
ENNA!
MOM!
THE CHILDREN!
SVEN, PROTECT THE CHILDREN!
PROTECT THE CHILDREN!
I AM A FOOLISH OLD MAN.
BUT I WISELY LISTENED TO MY WIFE, AND FOR THE SAKE OF THE CHILDREN I STOOD BACK WHILE THEIR MOTHER WAS KIDNAPPED.
ALL BECAUSE OF "SVEN THE RETURNED"...
A MAN WHO DOESN'T EVEN EXIST.
IT'S OKAY, LITTLE ONES...
IT'S OKAY.

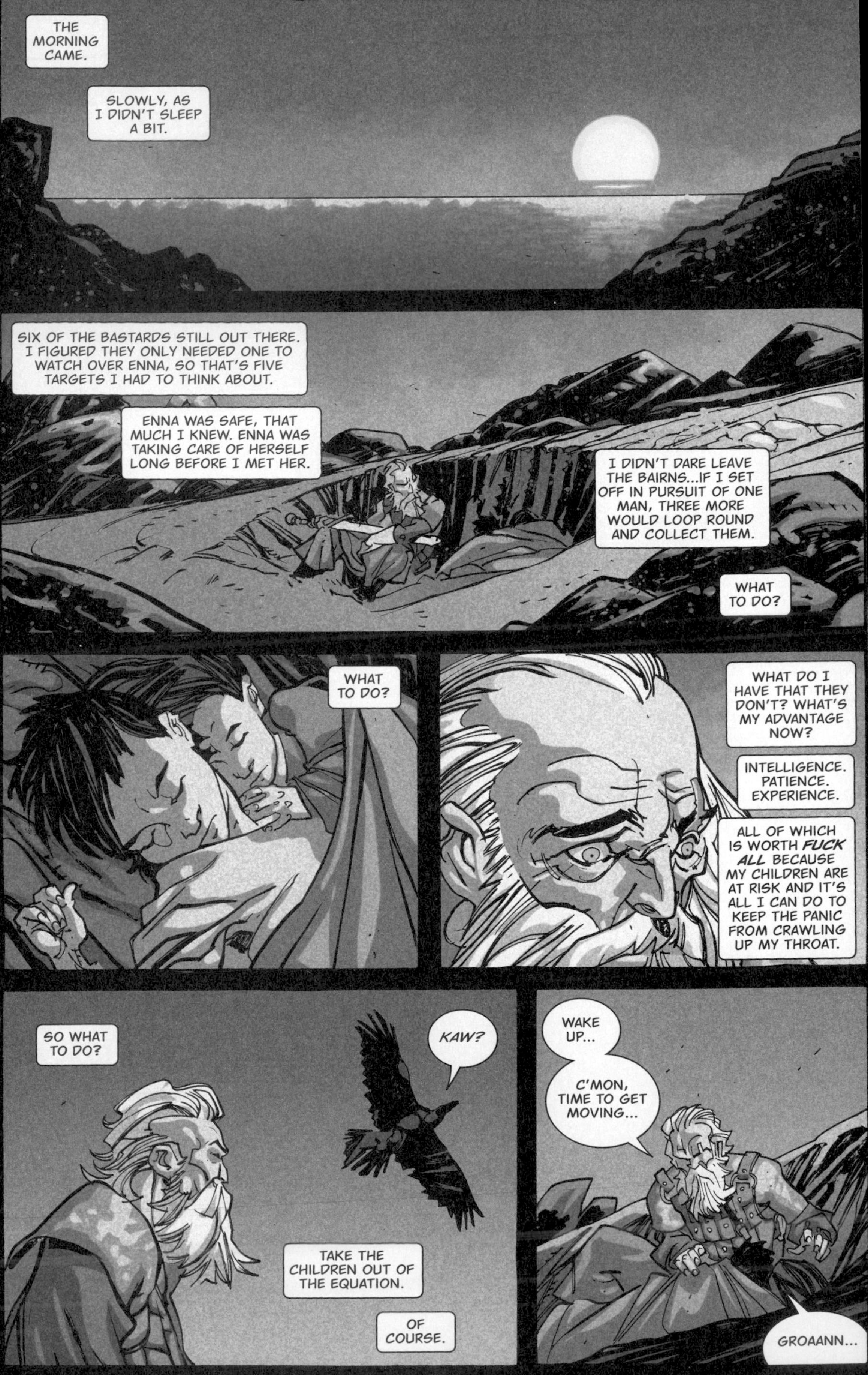
THE MORNING CAME.
SLOWLY, AS I DIDN'T SLEEP A BIT.
SIX OF THE BASTARDS STILL OUT THERE. I FIGURED THEY ONLY NEEDED ONE TO WATCH OVER ENNA, SO THAT'S FIVE TARGETS I HAD TO THINK ABOUT.
ENNA WAS SAFE, THAT MUCH I KNEW. ENNA WAS TAKING CARE OF HERSELF LONG BEFORE I MET HER.
I DIDN'T DARE LEAVE THE BAIRNS...IF I SET OFF IN PURSUIT OF ONE MAN, THREE MORE WOULD LOOP ROUND AND COLLECT THEM.
WHAT TO DO?
WHAT TO DO?
WHAT DO I HAVE THAT THEY DON'T? WHAT'S MY ADVANTAGE NOW?
INTELLIGENCE. PATIENCE. EXPERIENCE.
ALL OF WHICH IS WORTH *FUCK ALL* BECAUSE MY CHILDREN ARE AT RISK AND IT'S ALL I CAN DO TO KEEP THE PANIC FROM CRAWLING UP MY THROAT.
SO WHAT TO DO?
KAW?
TAKE THE CHILDREN OUT OF THE EQUATION.
OF COURSE.
WAKE UP...
C'MON, TIME TO GET MOVING...
GROAANN...

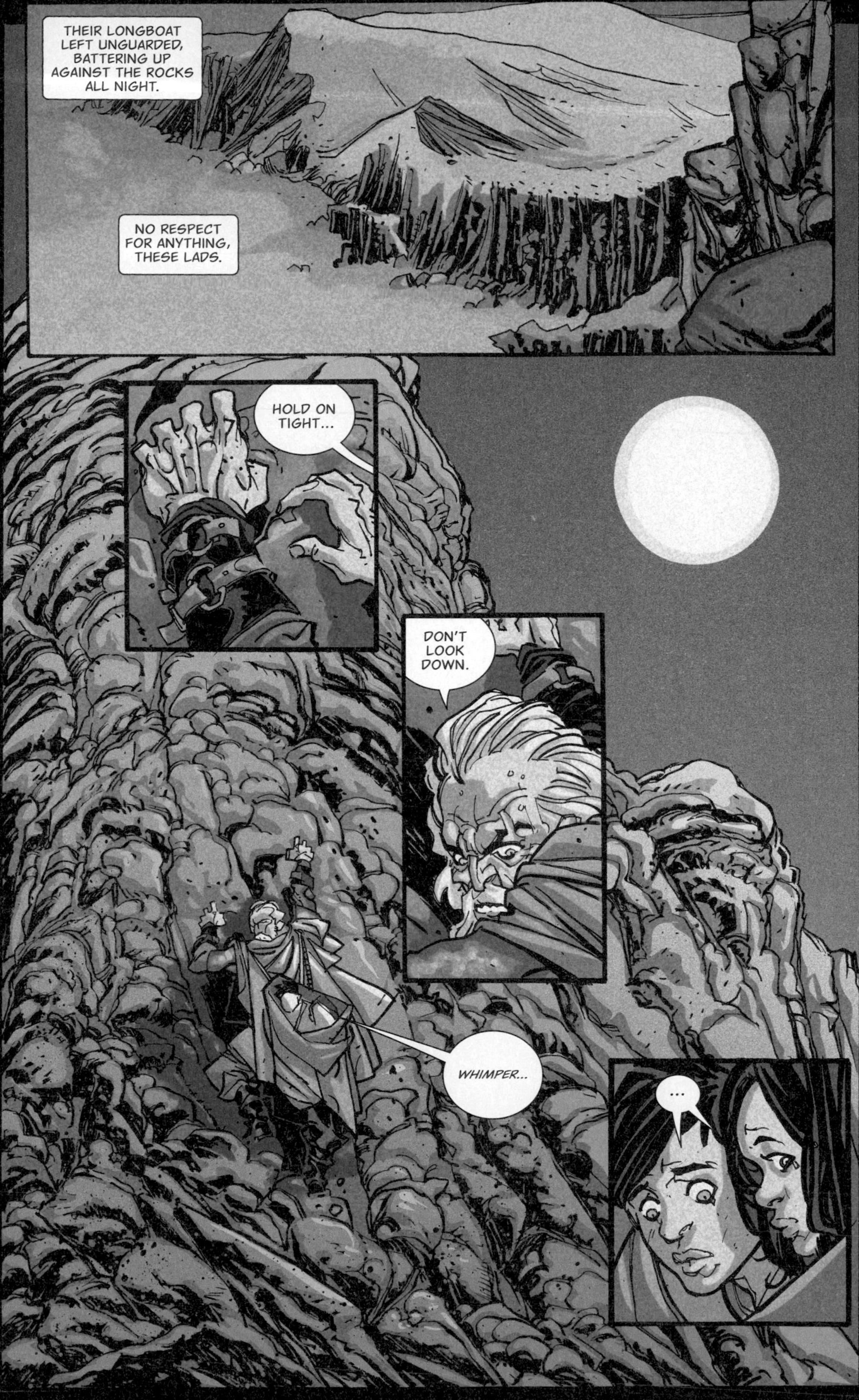
THEIR LONGBOAT LEFT UNGUARDED, BATTERING UP AGAINST THE ROCKS ALL NIGHT.
NO RESPECT FOR ANYTHING, THESE LADS.
HOLD ON TIGHT...
DON'T LOOK DOWN.
WHIMPER...
...

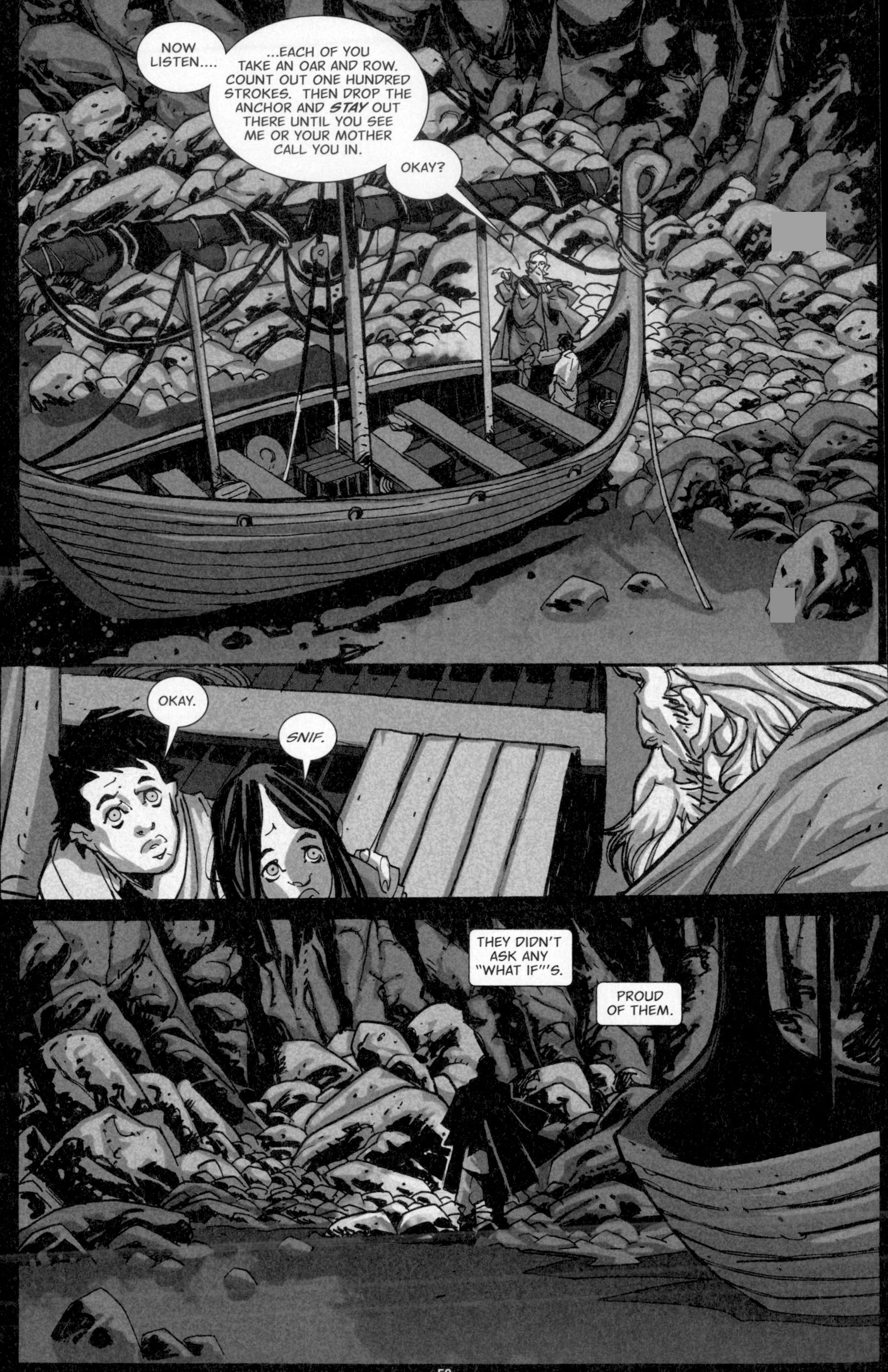
NOW LISTEN....
...EACH OF YOU TAKE AN OAR AND ROW. COUNT OUT ONE HUNDRED STROKES. THEN DROP THE ANCHOR AND STAY OUT THERE UNTIL YOU SEE ME OR YOUR MOTHER CALL YOU IN.
OKAY?
OKAY.
SNIF.
THEY DIDN'T ASK ANY "WHAT IF"'S.
PROUD OF THEM.

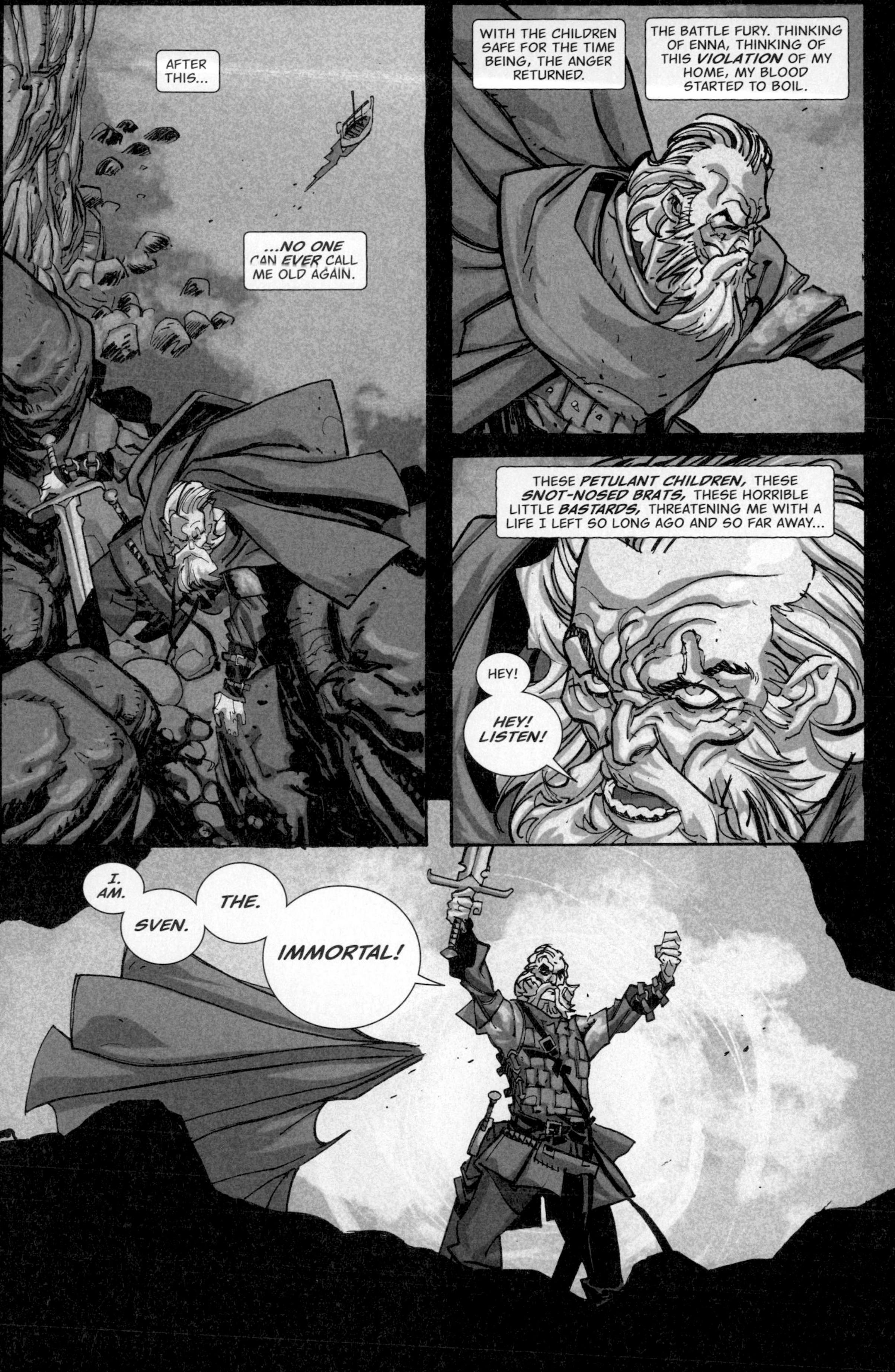
AFTER THIS...
...NO ONE CAN EVER CALL ME OLD AGAIN.
WITH THE CHILDREN SAFE FOR THE TIME BEING, THE ANGER RETURNED.
THE BATTLE FURY. THINKING OF ENNA, THINKING OF THIS VIOLATION OF MY HOME, MY BLOOD STARTED TO BOIL.
THESE PETULANT CHILDREN, THESE SNOT-NOSED BRATS, THESE HORRIBLE LITTLE BASTARDS, THREATENING ME WITH A LIFE I LEFT SO LONG AGO AND SO FAR AWAY...
HEY!
HEY! LISTEN!
I. AM.
SVEN.
THE.
IMMORTAL!

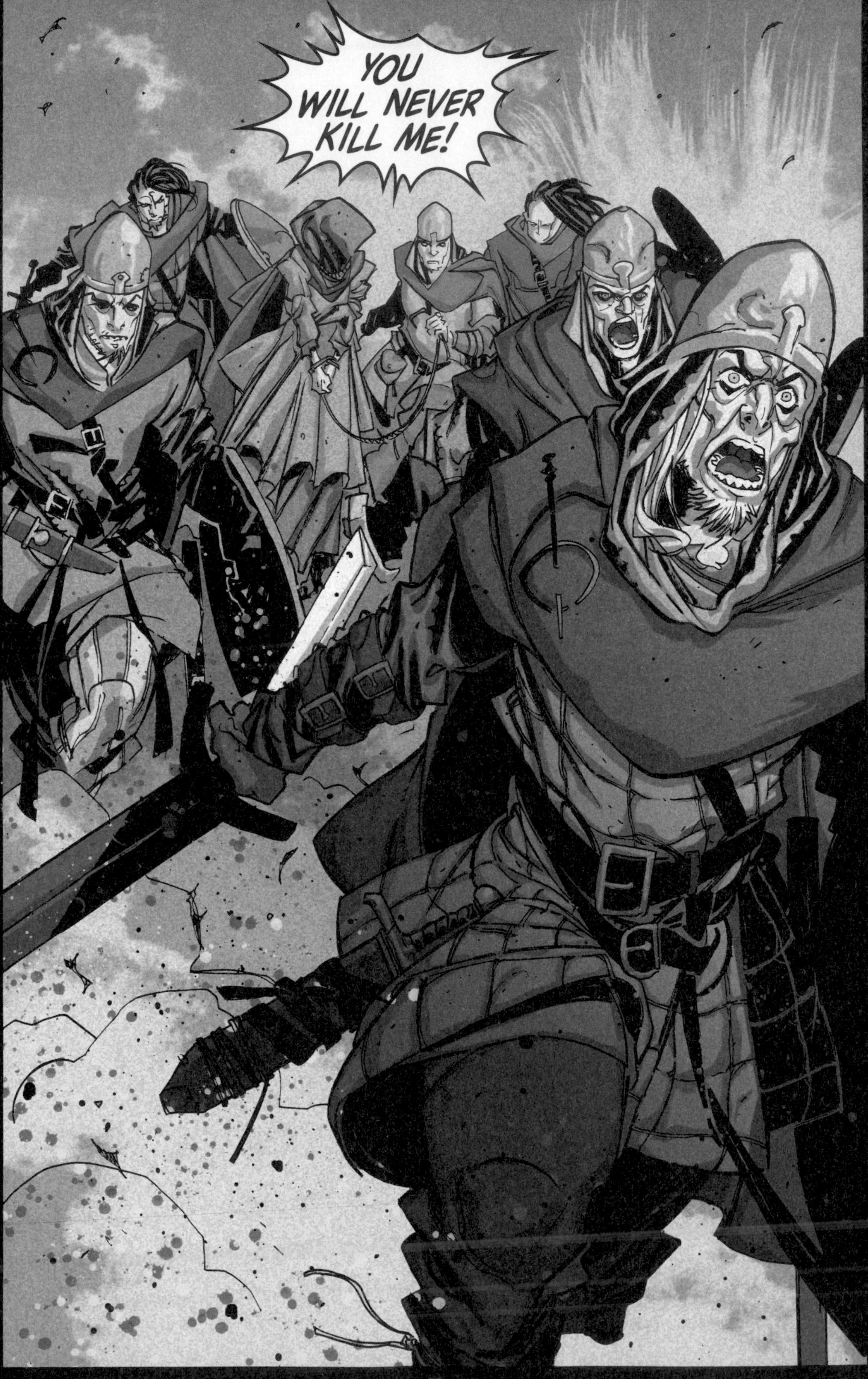
YOU WILL NEVER KILL ME!

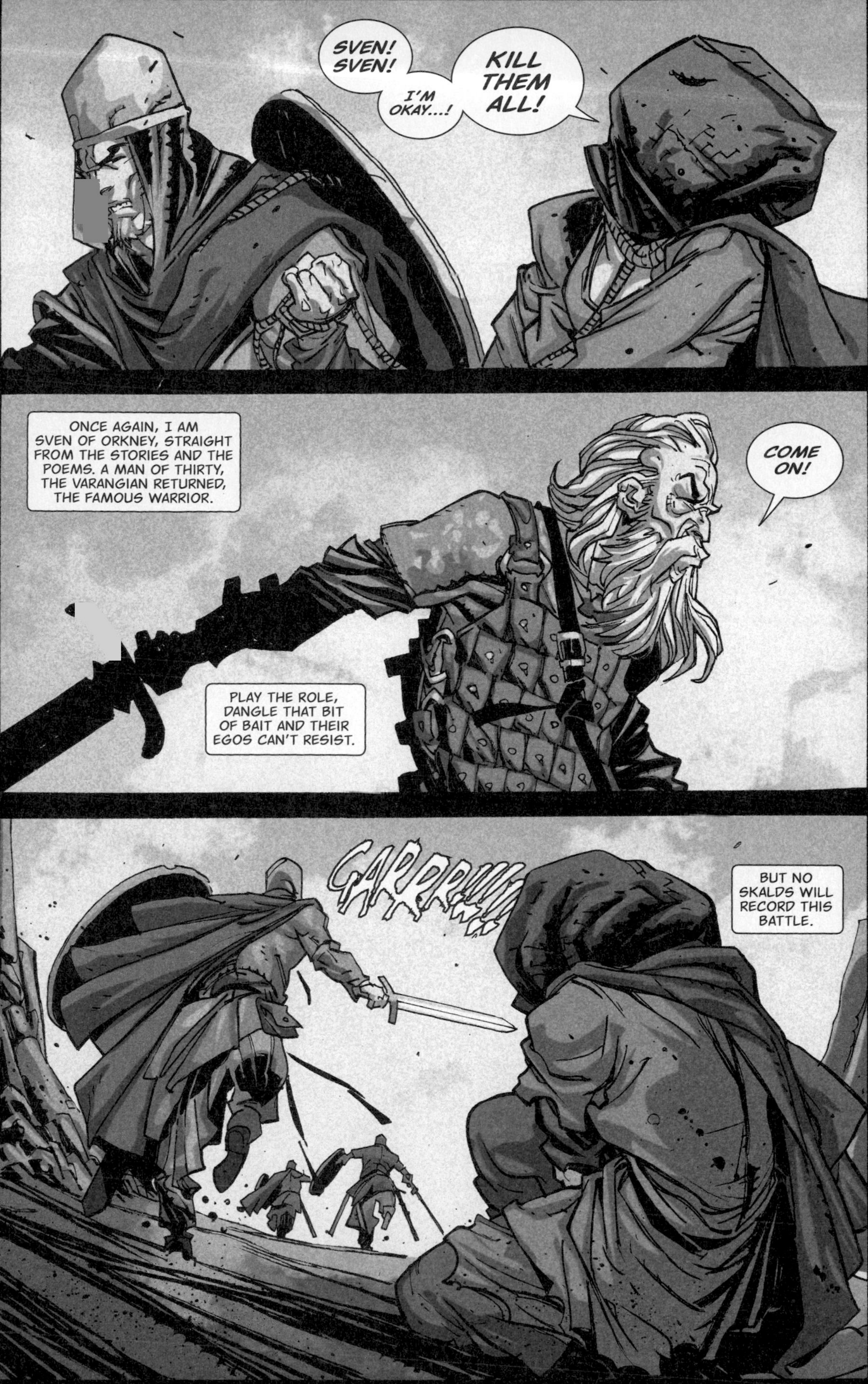
SVEN! SVEN!
I'M OKAY...!
KILL THEM ALL!
ONCE AGAIN, I AM SVEN OF ORKNEY, STRAIGHT FROM THE STORIES AND THE POEMS. A MAN OF THIRTY, THE VARANGIAN RETURNED, THE FAMOUS WARRIOR.
COME ON!
PLAY THE ROLE, DANGLE THAT BIT OF BAIT AND THEIR EGOS CAN'T RESIST.
GARRRUUU
BUT NO SKALDS WILL RECORD THIS BATTLE.

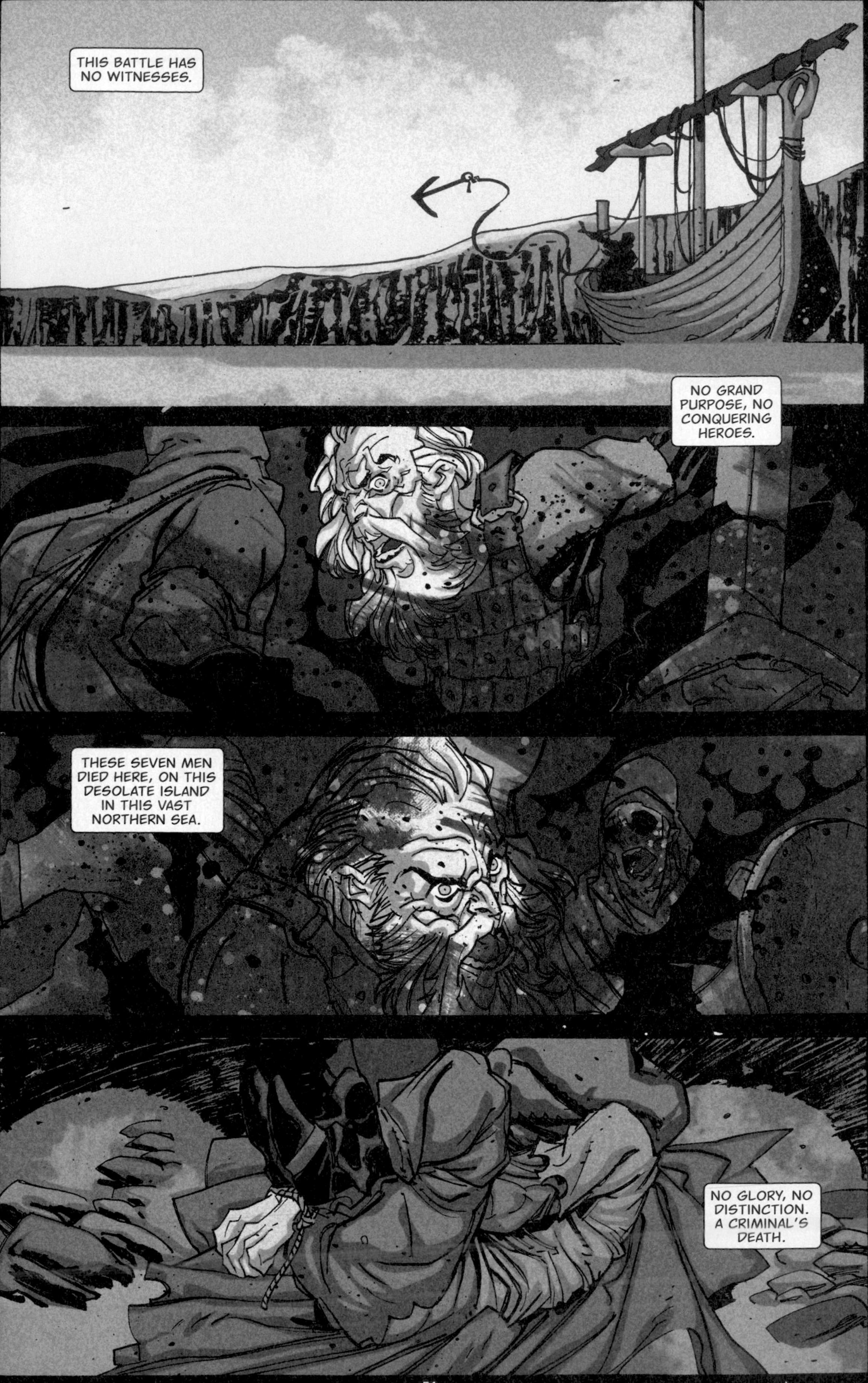
THIS BATTLE HAS NO WITNESSES.
NO GRAND PURPOSE, NO CONQUERING HEROES.
THESE SEVEN MEN DIED HERE, ON THIS DESOLATE ISLAND IN THIS VAST NORTHERN SEA.
NO GLORY, NO DISTINCTION. A CRIMINAL'S DEATH.

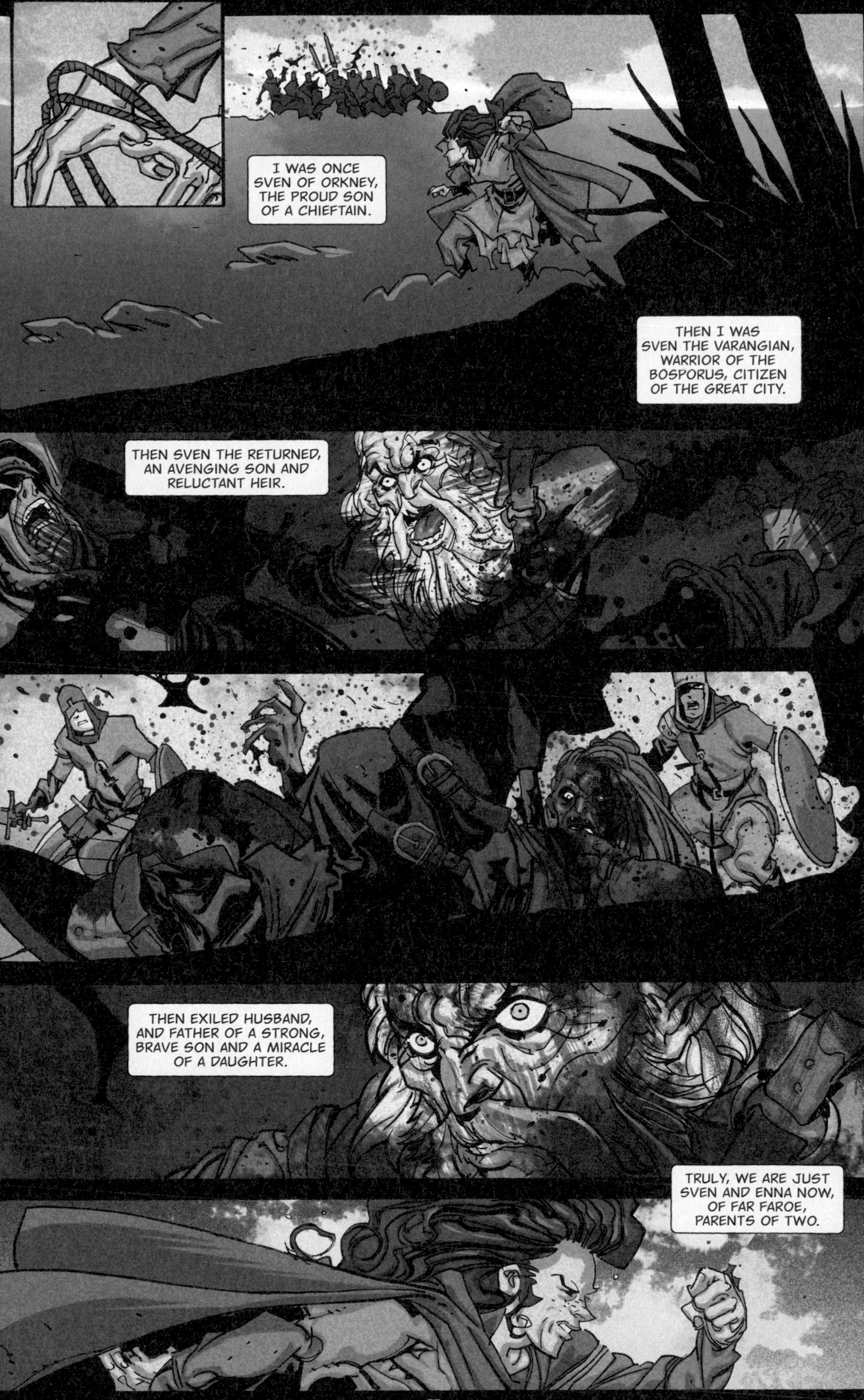
I WAS ONCE SVEN OF ORKNEY, THE PROUD SON OF A CHIEFTAIN.
THEN I WAS SVEN THE VARANGIAN, WARRIOR OF THE BOSPORUS, CITIZEN OF THE GREAT CITY.
THEN SVEN THE RETURNED, AN AVENGING SON AND RELUCTANT HEIR.
THEN EXILED HUSBAND, AND FATHER OF A STRONG, BRAVE SON AND A MIRACLE OF A DAUGHTER.
TRULY, WE ARE JUST SVEN AND ENNA NOW, OF FAR FAROE, PARENTS OF TWO.

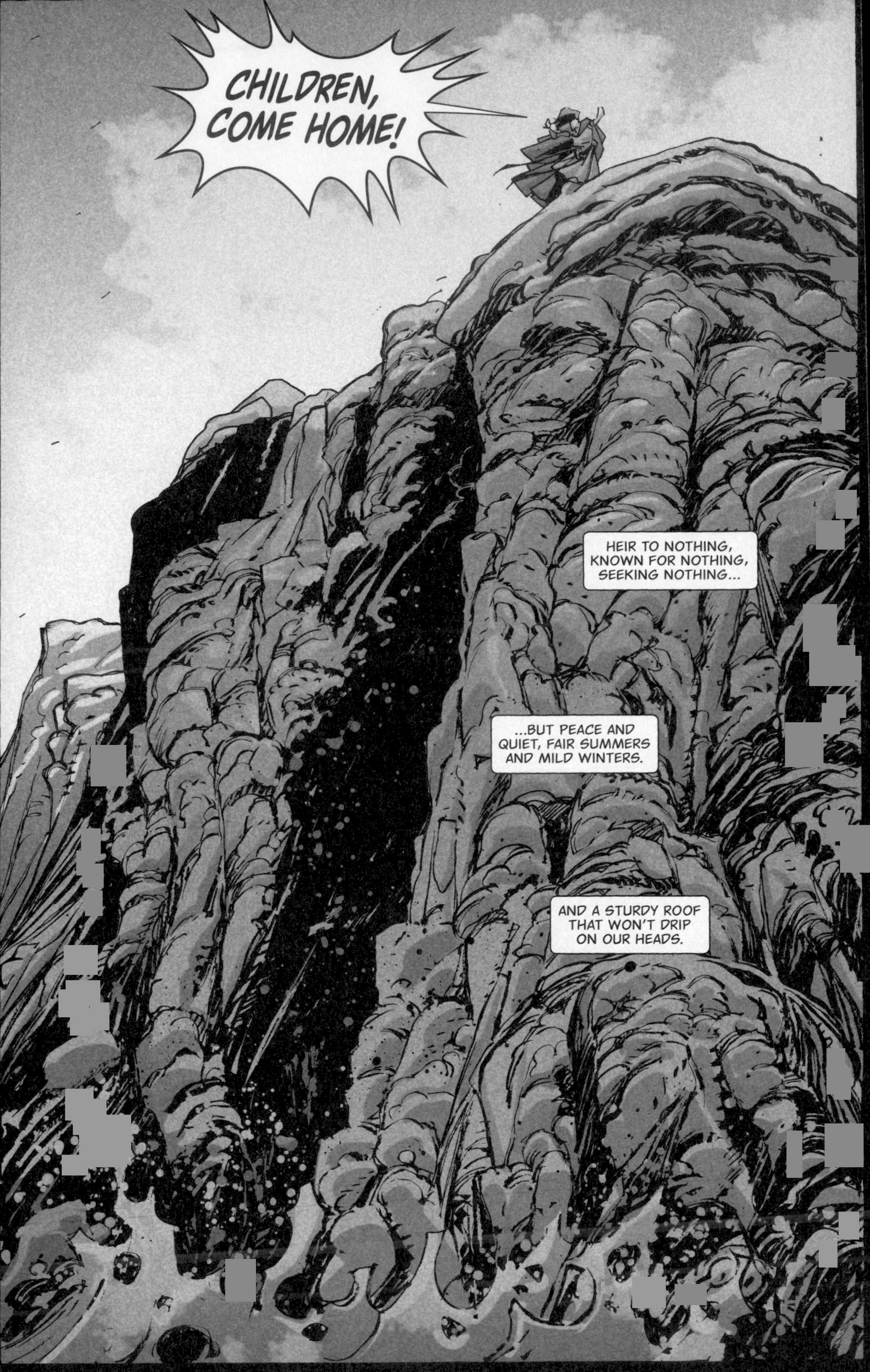
CHILDREN, COME HOME!
HEIR TO NOTHING, KNOWN FOR NOTHING, SEEKING NOTHING...
...BUT PEACE AND QUIET, FAIR SUMMERS AND MILD WINTERS.
AND A STURDY ROOF THAT WON'T DRIP ON OUR HEADS.

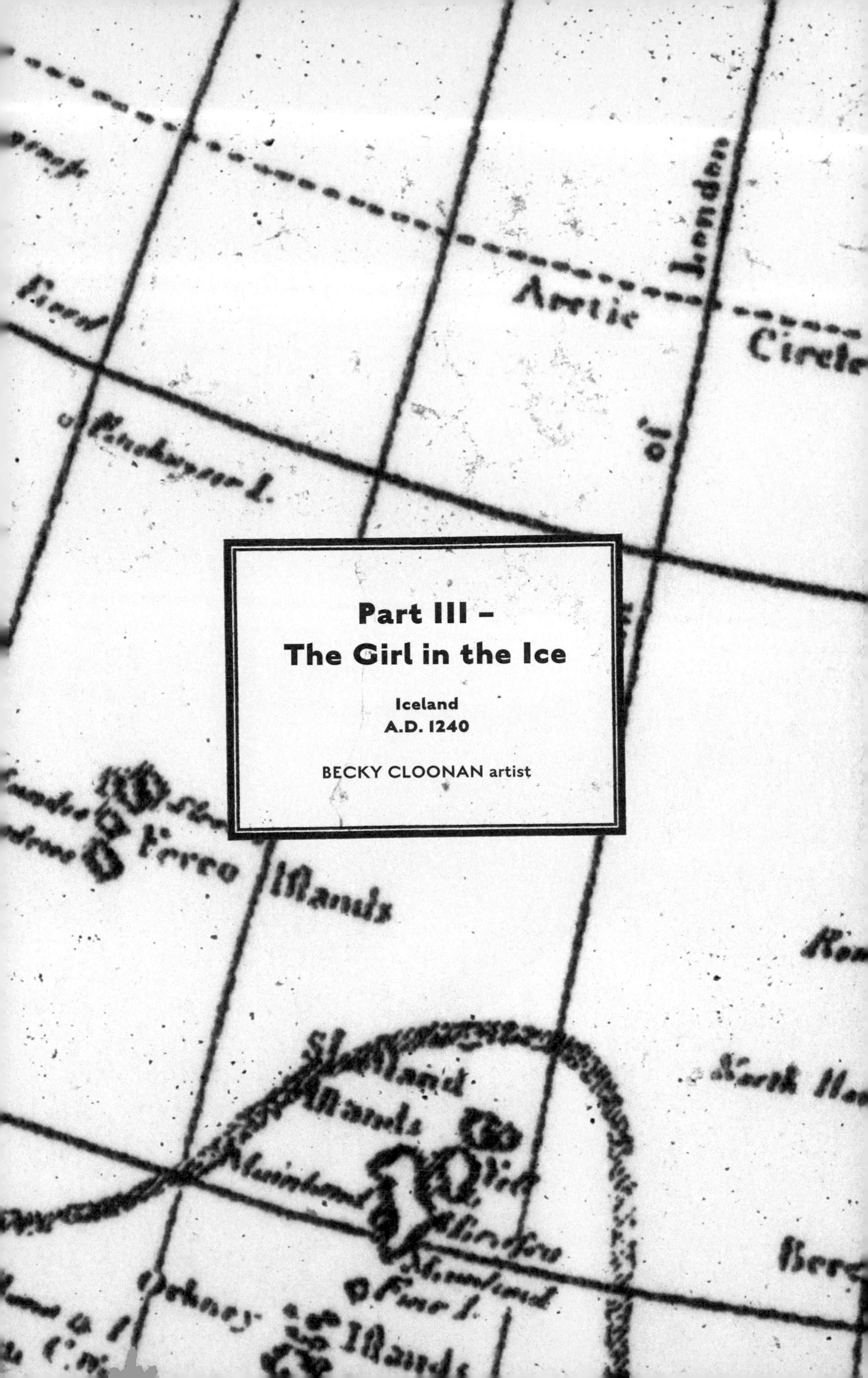
Arctic
Circle
of London
Ferro Islands
Shetland Islands
Orkney
Islands

Part III – The Girl in the Ice

Iceland
A.D. 1240

BECKY CLOONAN artist

Chapter I

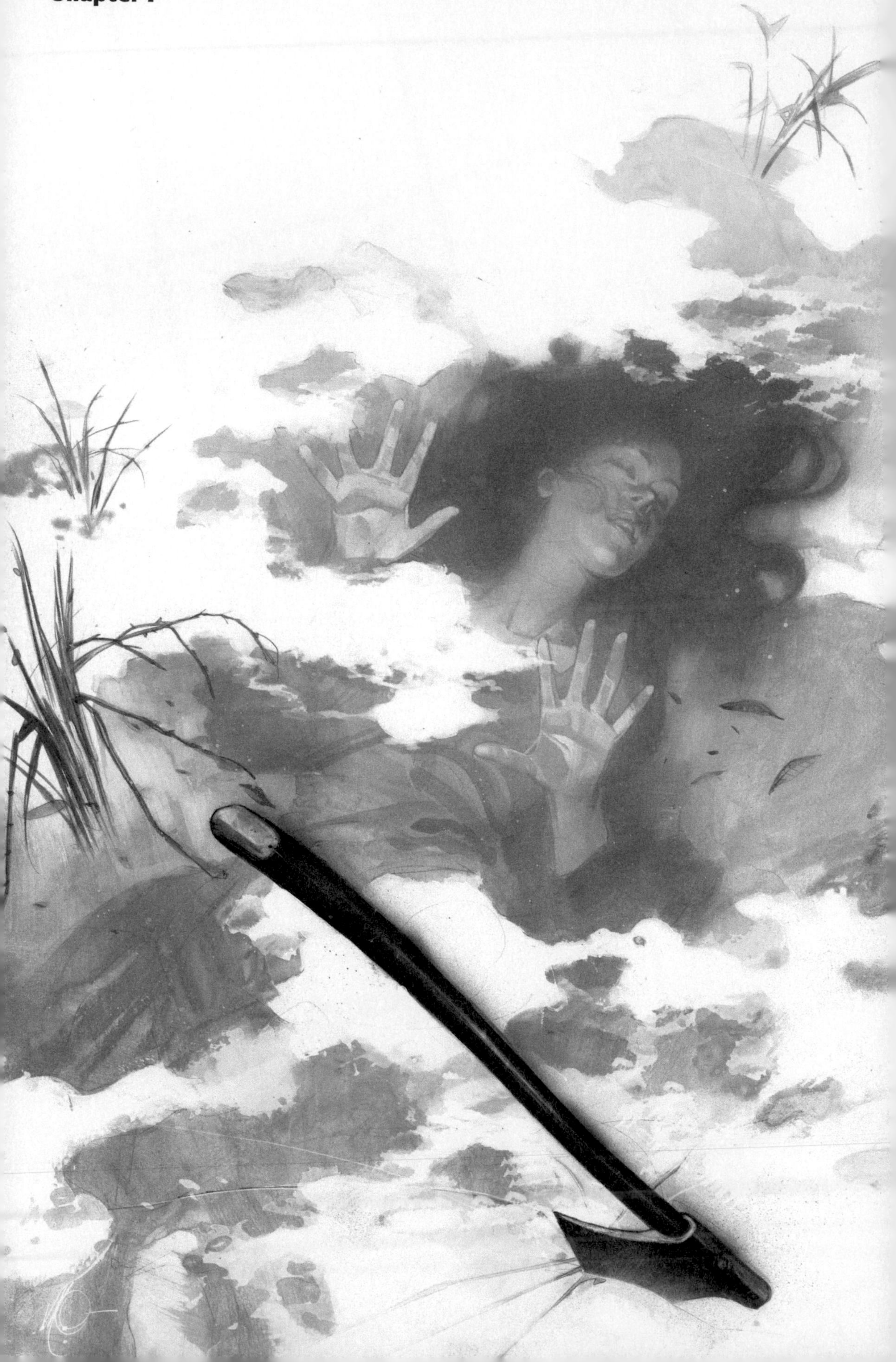

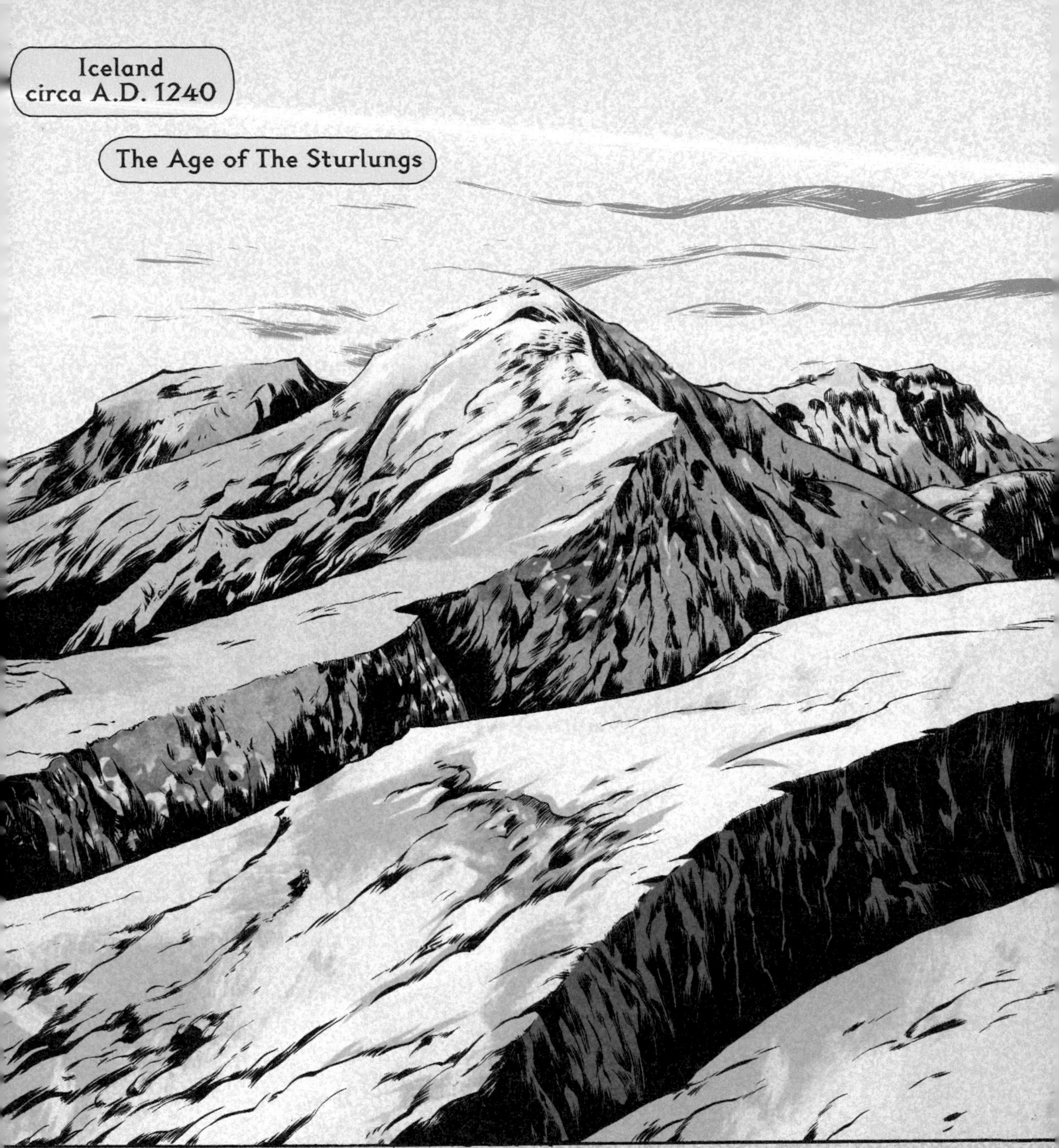
Iceland
circa A.D. 1240
The Age of The Sturlungs

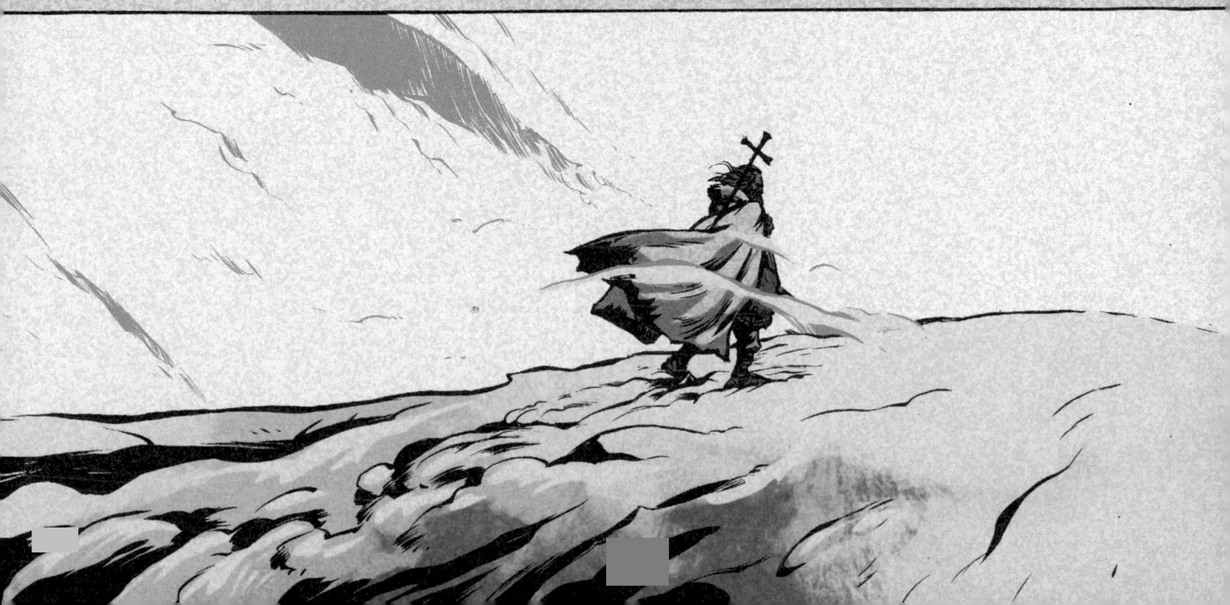

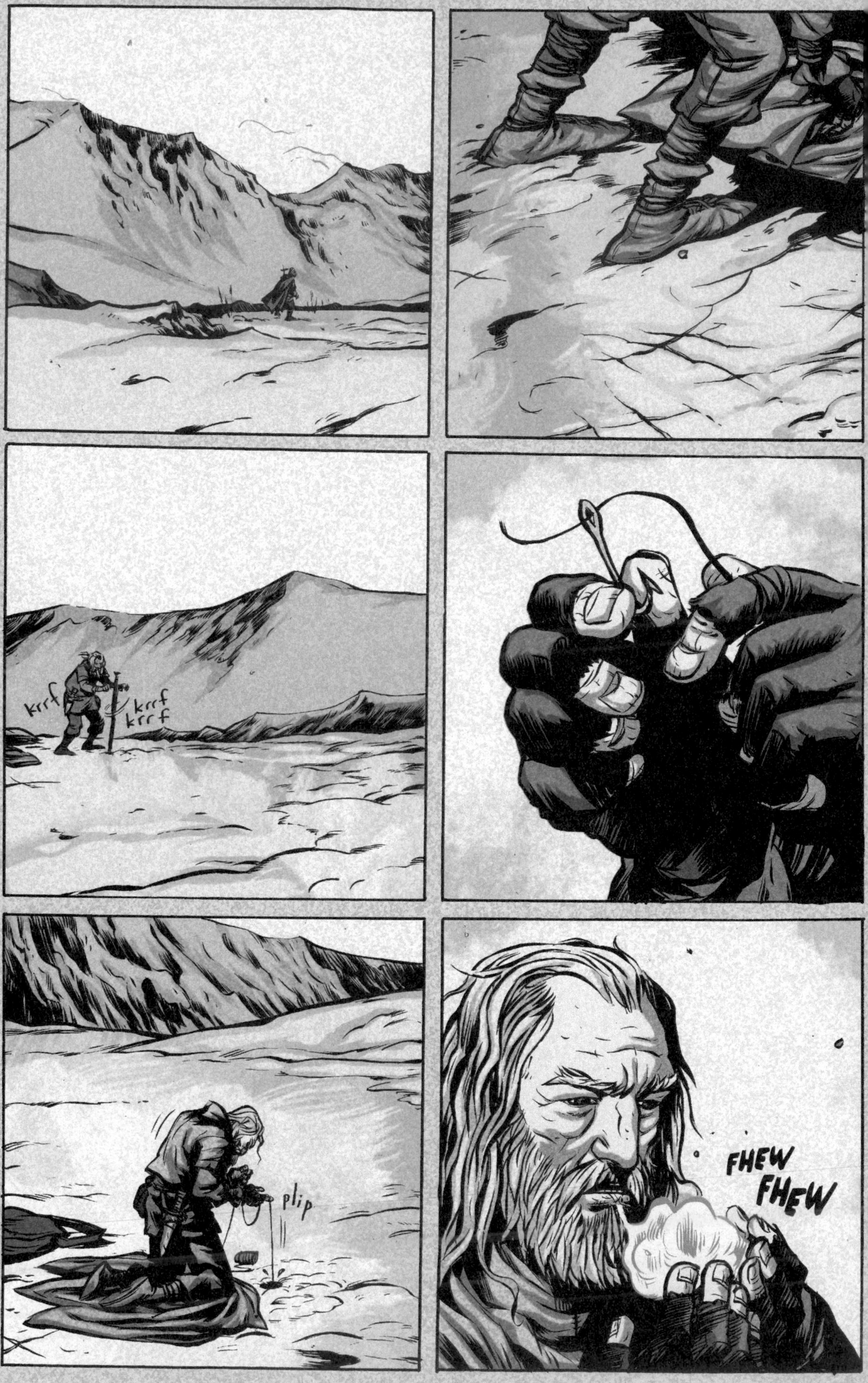
krrf
krrf
krrf
plip
FHEW
FHEW

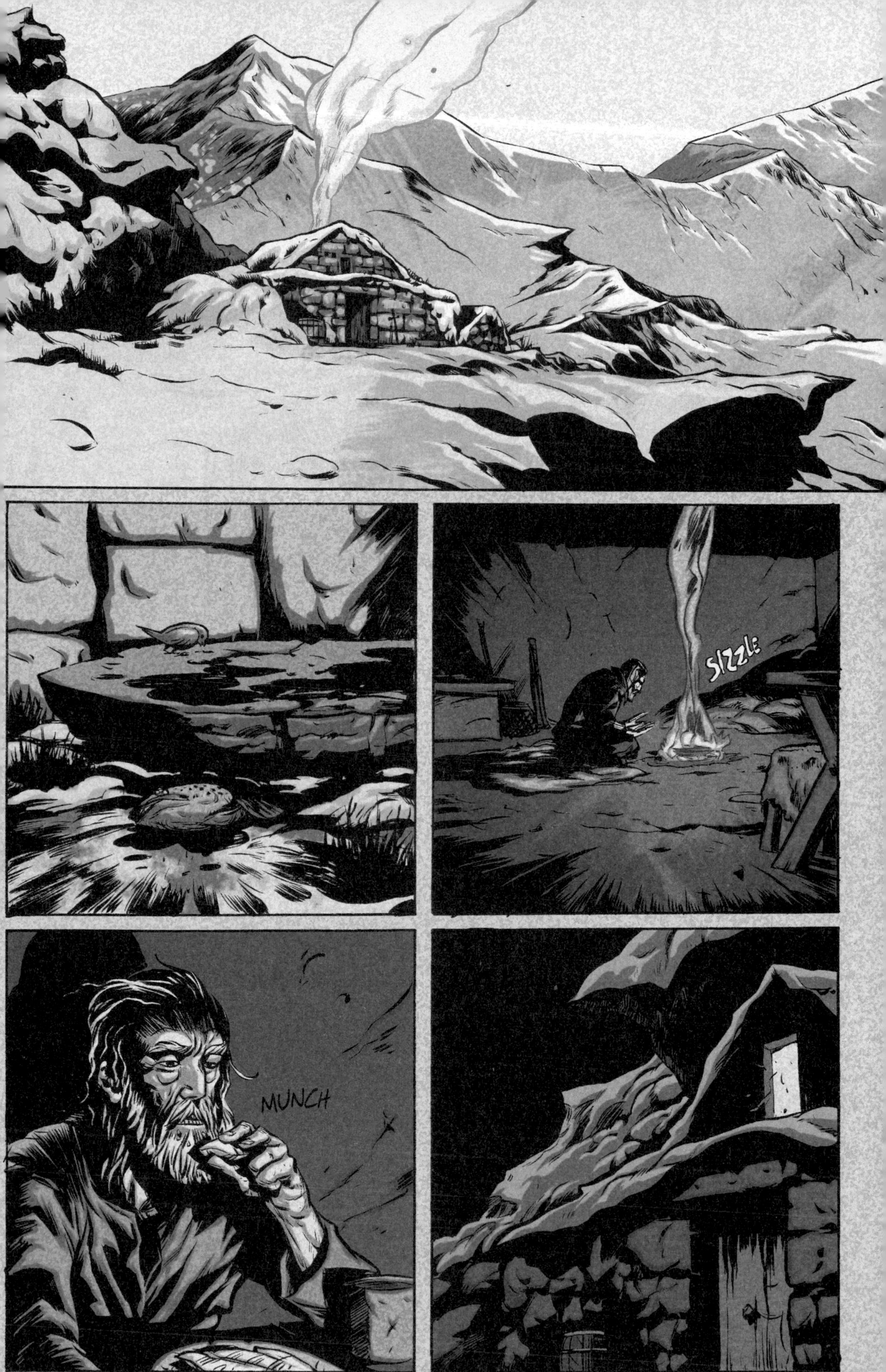
SIZZLE
MUNCH

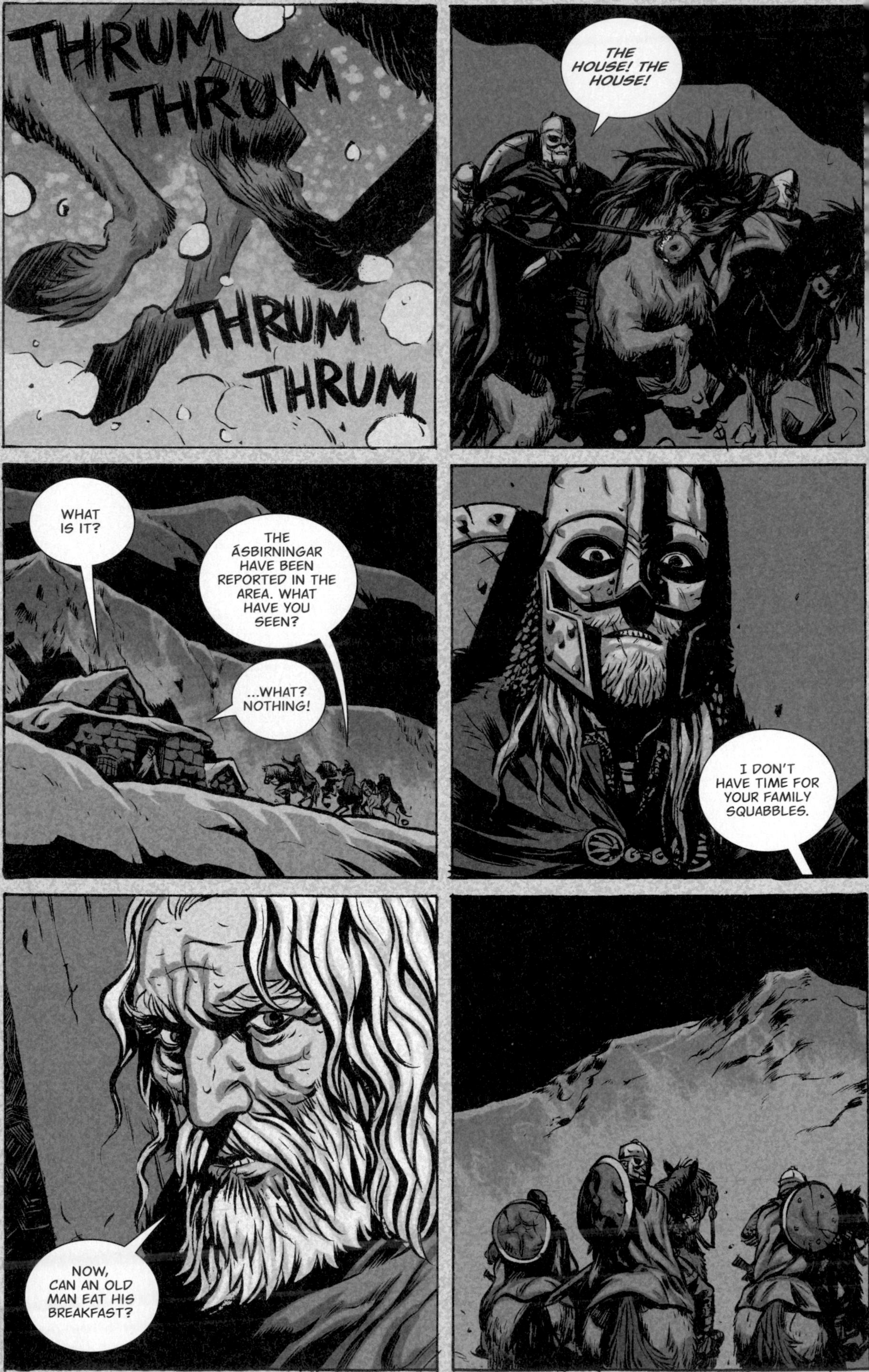
THRUM
THRUM
THRUM
THRUM
THE HOUSE! THE HOUSE!
WHAT IS IT?
THE ÁSBIRNINGAR HAVE BEEN REPORTED IN THE AREA. WHAT HAVE YOU SEEN?
...WHAT? NOTHING!
I DON'T HAVE TIME FOR YOUR FAMILY SQUABBLES.
NOW, CAN AN OLD MAN EAT HIS BREAKFAST?

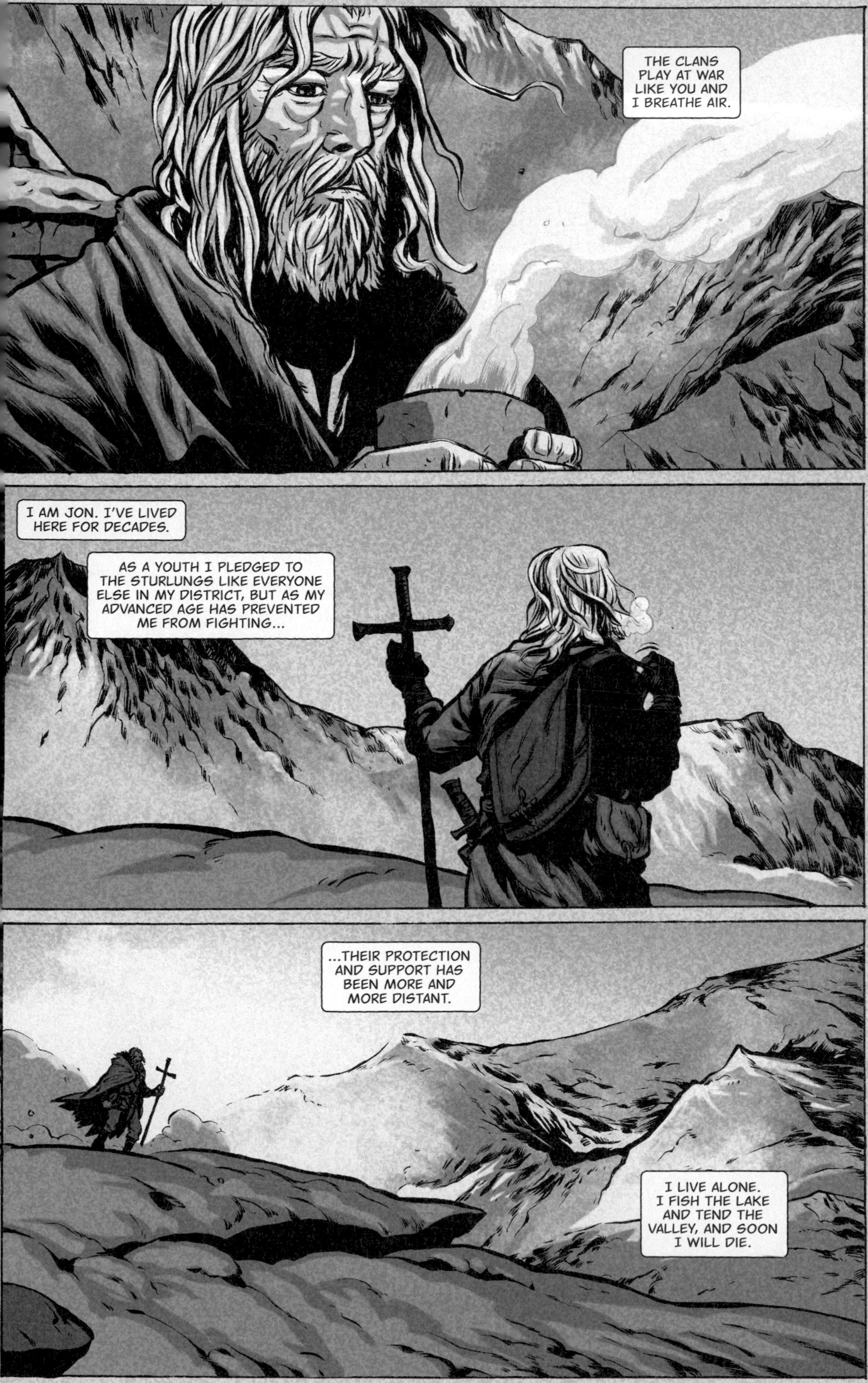
THE CLANS PLAY AT WAR LIKE YOU AND I BREATHE AIR.
I AM JON. I'VE LIVED HERE FOR DECADES.
AS A YOUTH I PLEDGED TO THE STURLUNGS LIKE EVERYONE ELSE IN MY DISTRICT, BUT AS MY ADVANCED AGE HAS PREVENTED ME FROM FIGHTING...
...THEIR PROTECTION AND SUPPORT HAS BEEN MORE AND MORE DISTANT.
I LIVE ALONE. I FISH THE LAKE AND TEND THE VALLEY, AND SOON I WILL DIE.

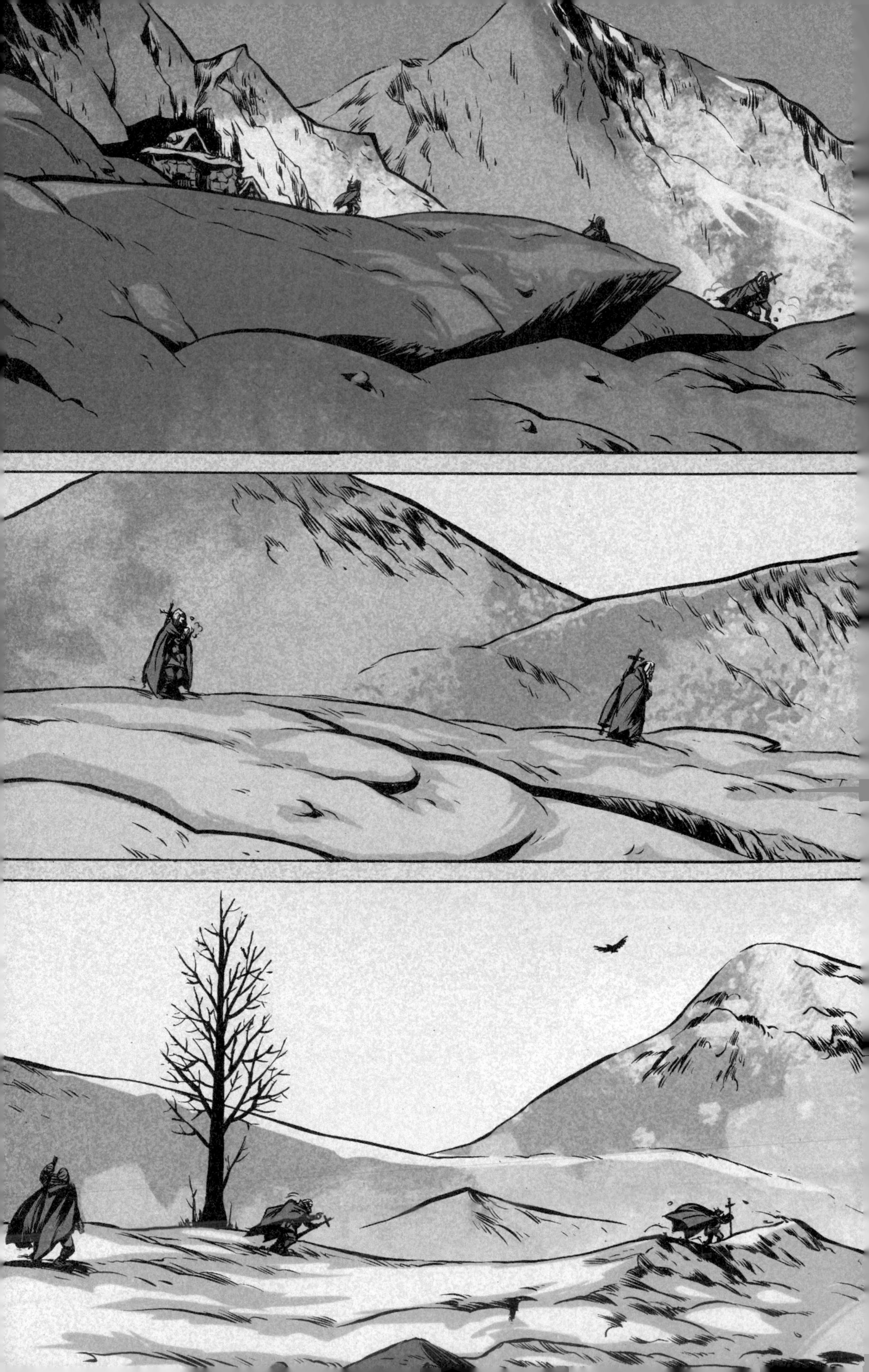

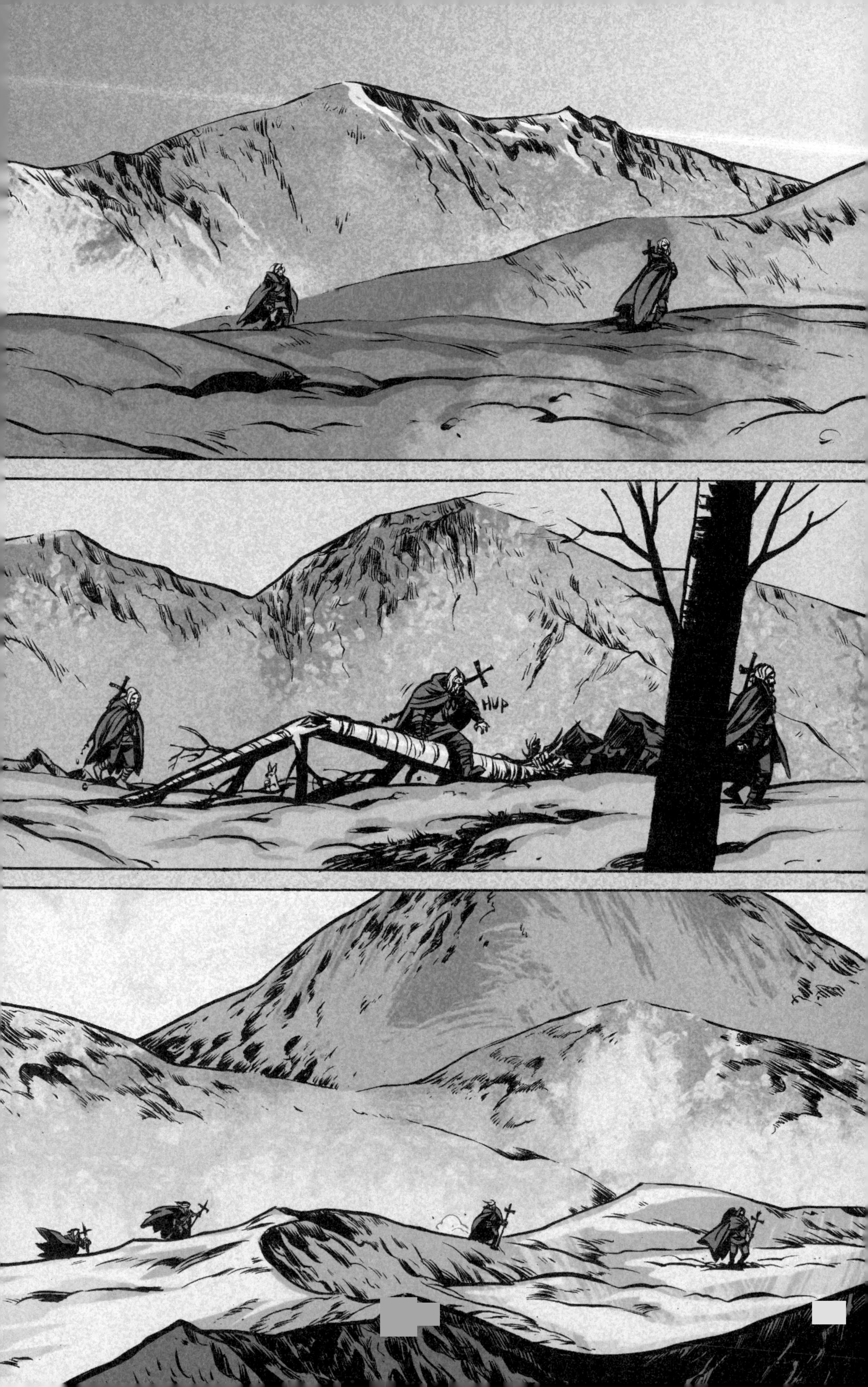
HUP

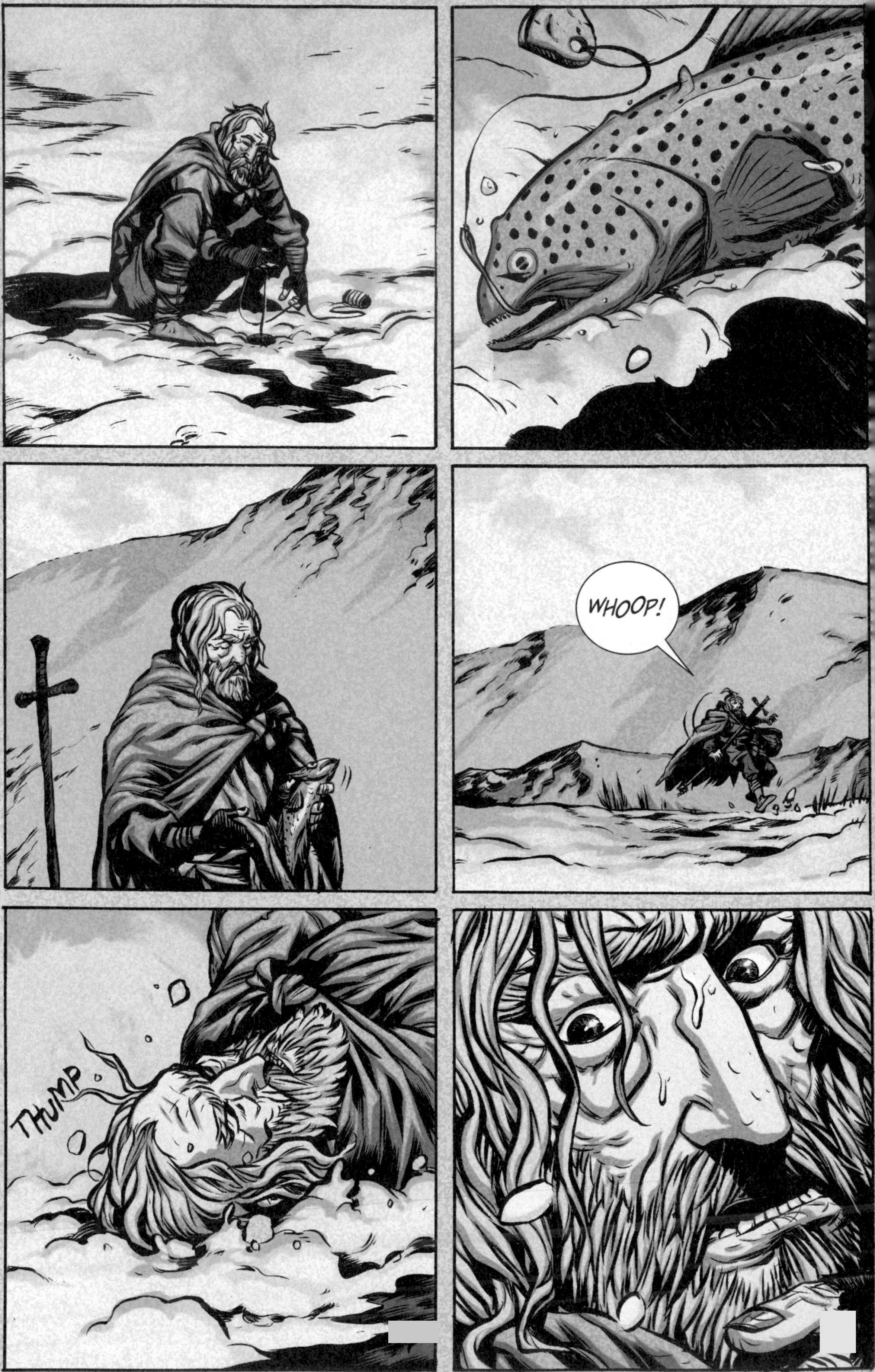
WHOOP!
THUMP

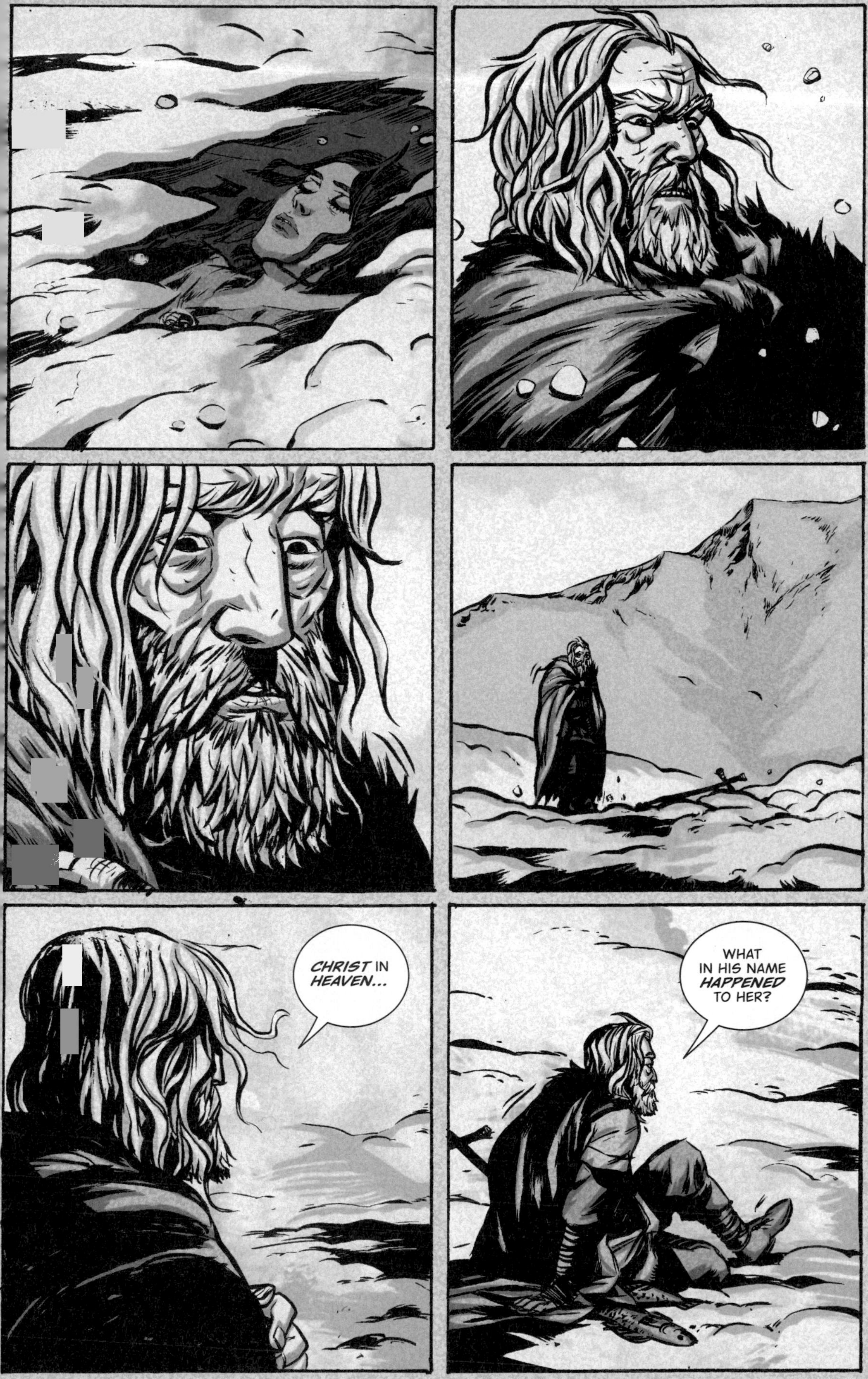
CHRIST IN *HEAVEN...*
WHAT IN HIS NAME *HAPPENED* TO HER?

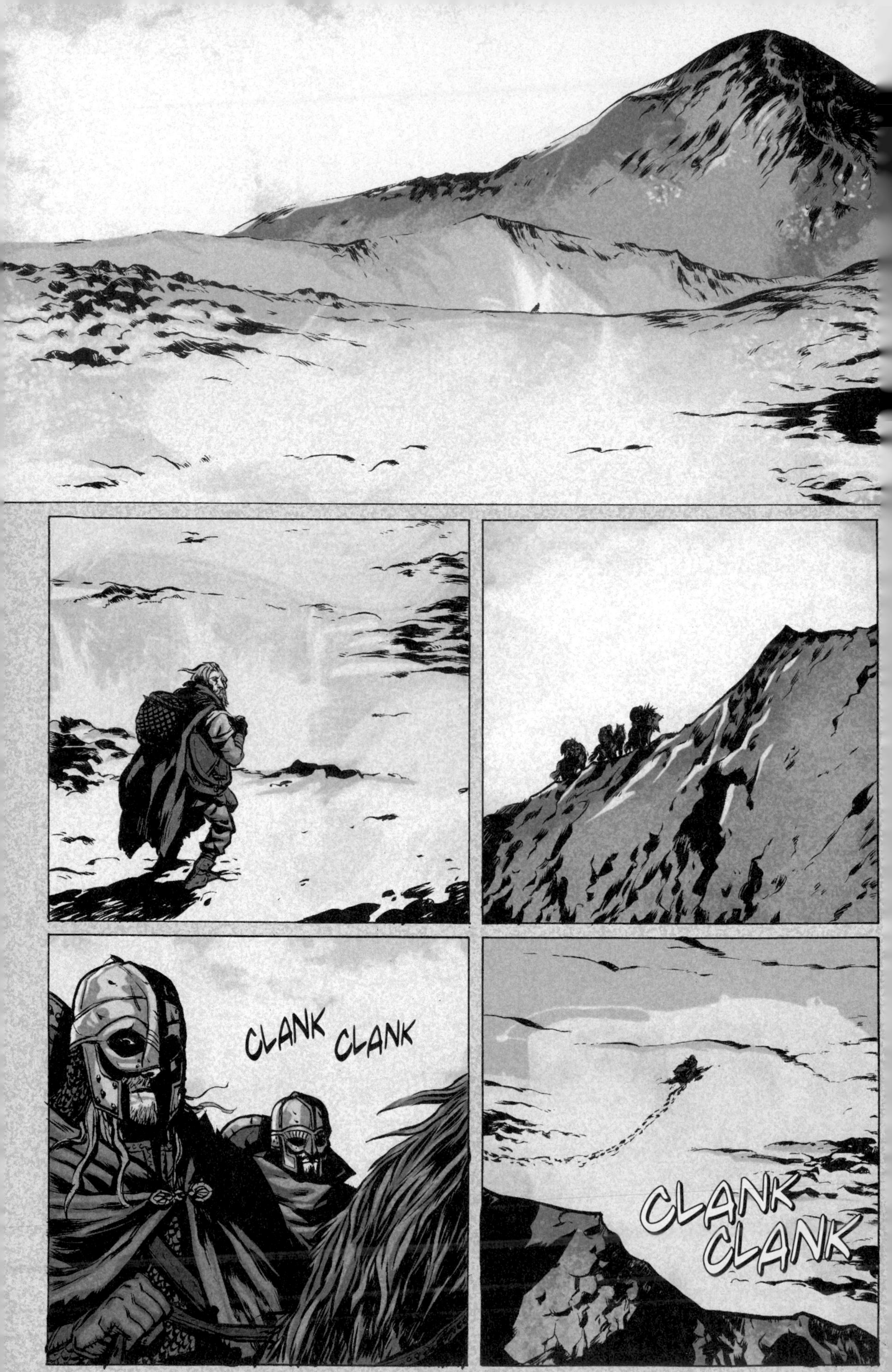
CLANK CLANK
CLANK
CLANK

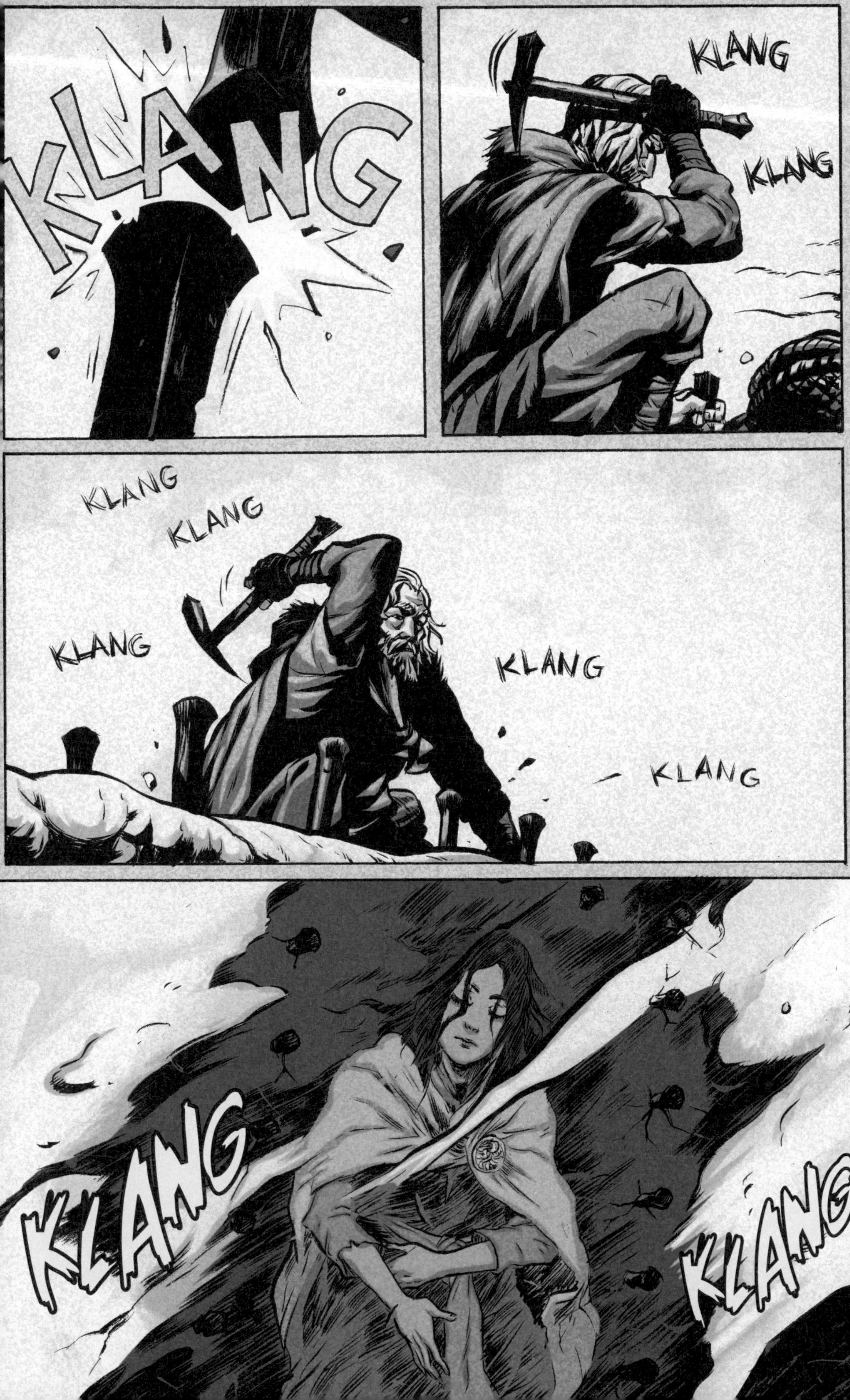
KLANG
KLANG
KLANG
KLANG
KLANG
KLANG
KLANG
KLANG
KLANG
KLANG

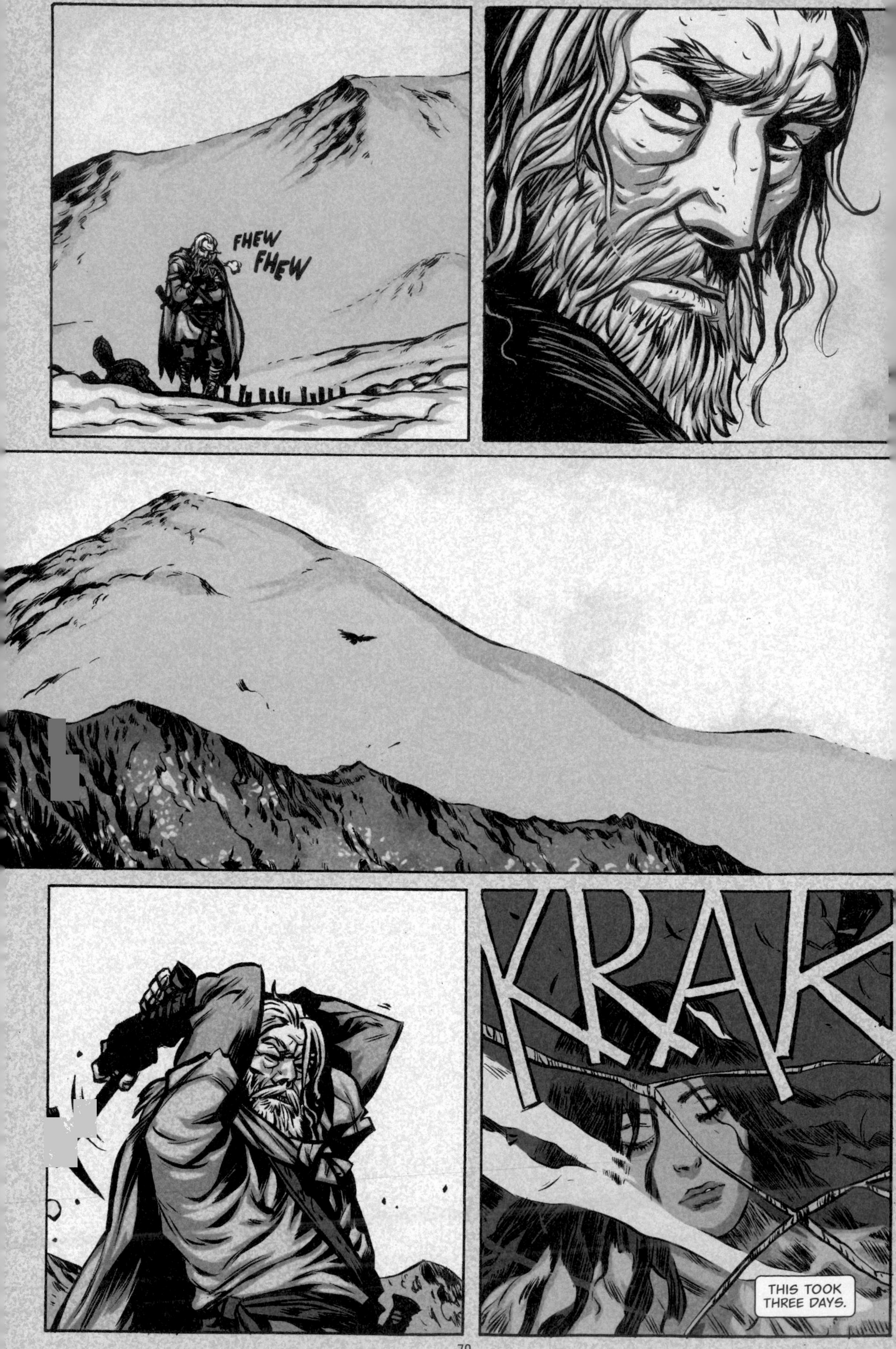
FHEW
FHEW
KRAK
THIS TOOK THREE DAYS.

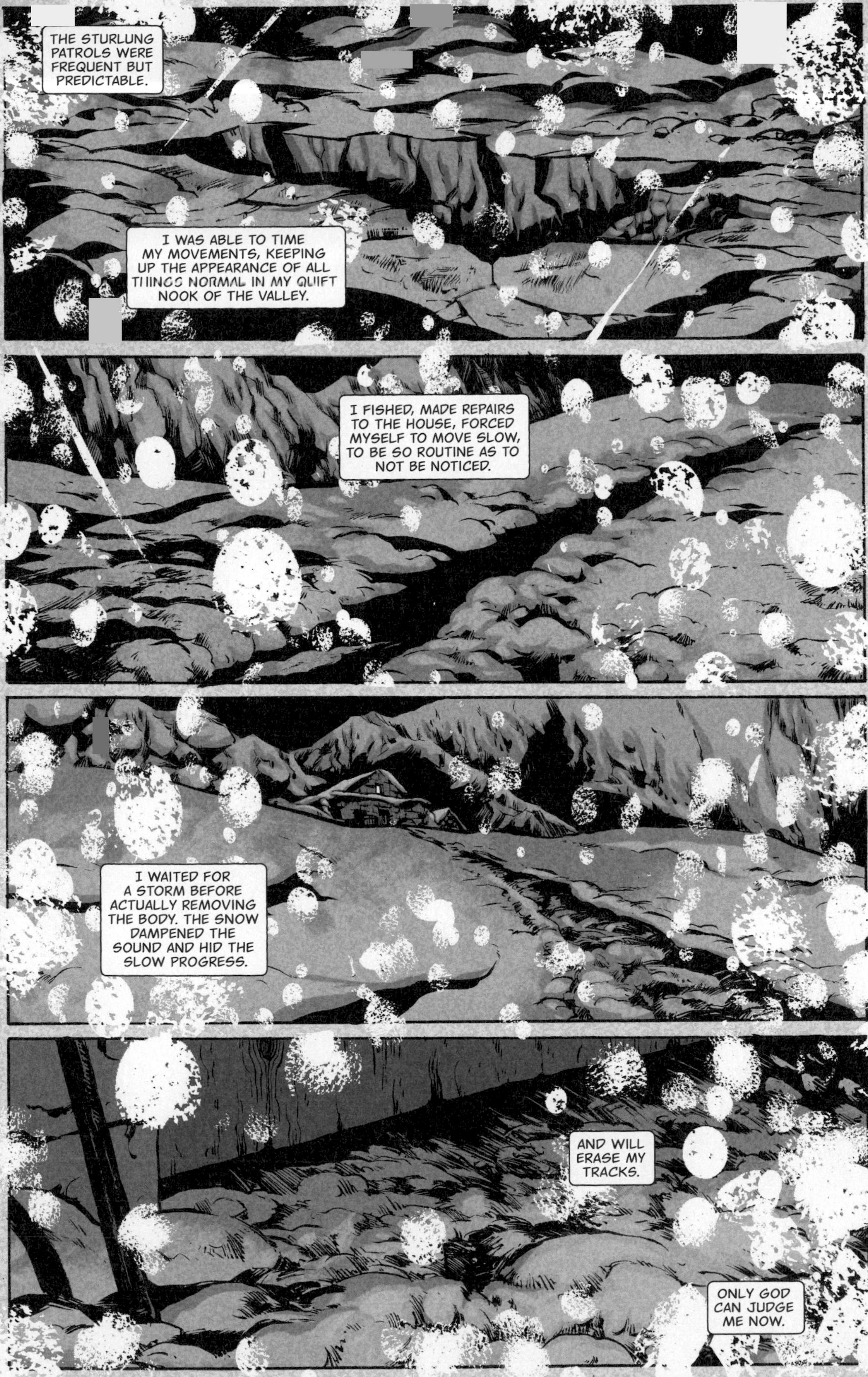
THE STURLUNG PATROLS WERE FREQUENT BUT PREDICTABLE.
I WAS ABLE TO TIME MY MOVEMENTS, KEEPING UP THE APPEARANCE OF ALL THINGS NORMAL IN MY QUIET NOOK OF THE VALLEY.
I FISHED, MADE REPAIRS TO THE HOUSE, FORCED MYSELF TO MOVE SLOW, TO BE SO ROUTINE AS TO NOT BE NOTICED.
I WAITED FOR A STORM BEFORE ACTUALLY REMOVING THE BODY. THE SNOW DAMPENED THE SOUND AND HID THE SLOW PROGRESS.
AND WILL ERASE MY TRACKS.
ONLY GOD CAN JUDGE ME NOW.

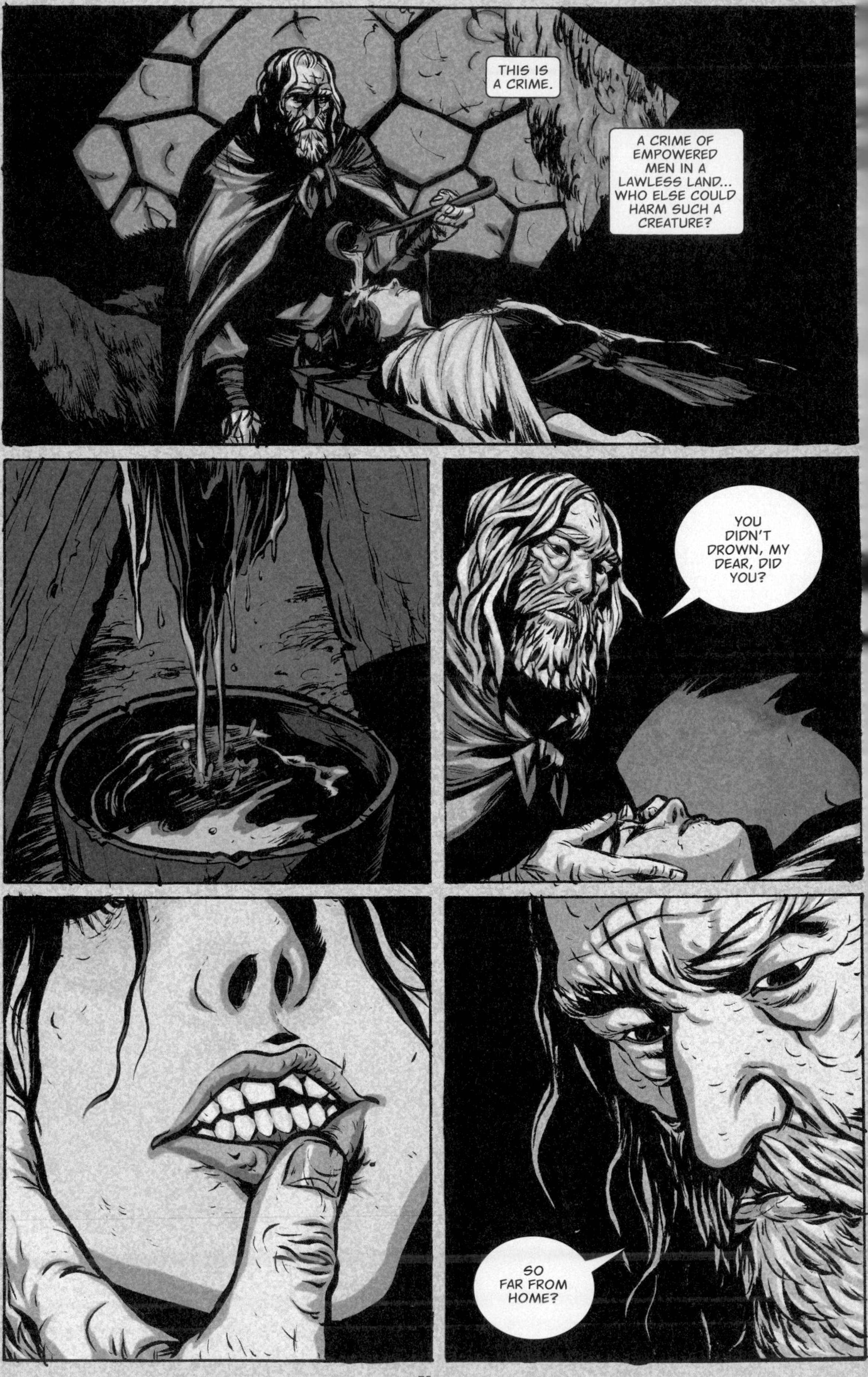
THIS IS A CRIME.
A CRIME OF EMPOWERED MEN IN A LAWLESS LAND... WHO ELSE COULD HARM SUCH A CREATURE?
YOU DIDN'T DROWN, MY DEAR, DID YOU?
SO FAR FROM HOME?

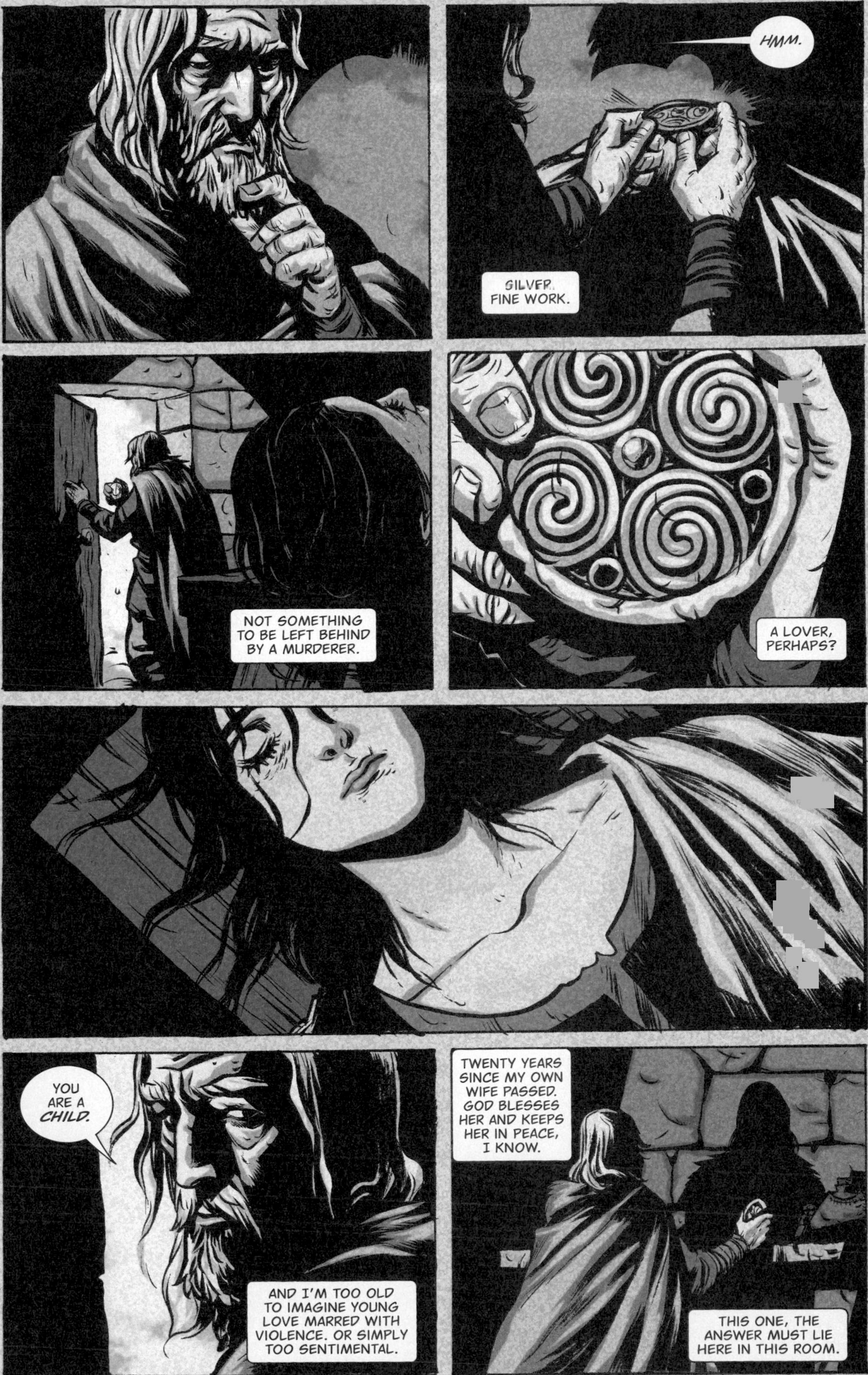
HMM.
SILVER. FINE WORK.
NOT SOMETHING TO BE LEFT BEHIND BY A MURDERER.
A LOVER, PERHAPS?
YOU ARE A CHILD.
AND I'M TOO OLD TO IMAGINE YOUNG LOVE MARRED WITH VIOLENCE. OR SIMPLY TOO SENTIMENTAL.
TWENTY YEARS SINCE MY OWN WIFE PASSED. GOD BLESSES HER AND KEEPS HER IN PEACE, I KNOW.
THIS ONE, THE ANSWER MUST LIE HERE IN THIS ROOM.

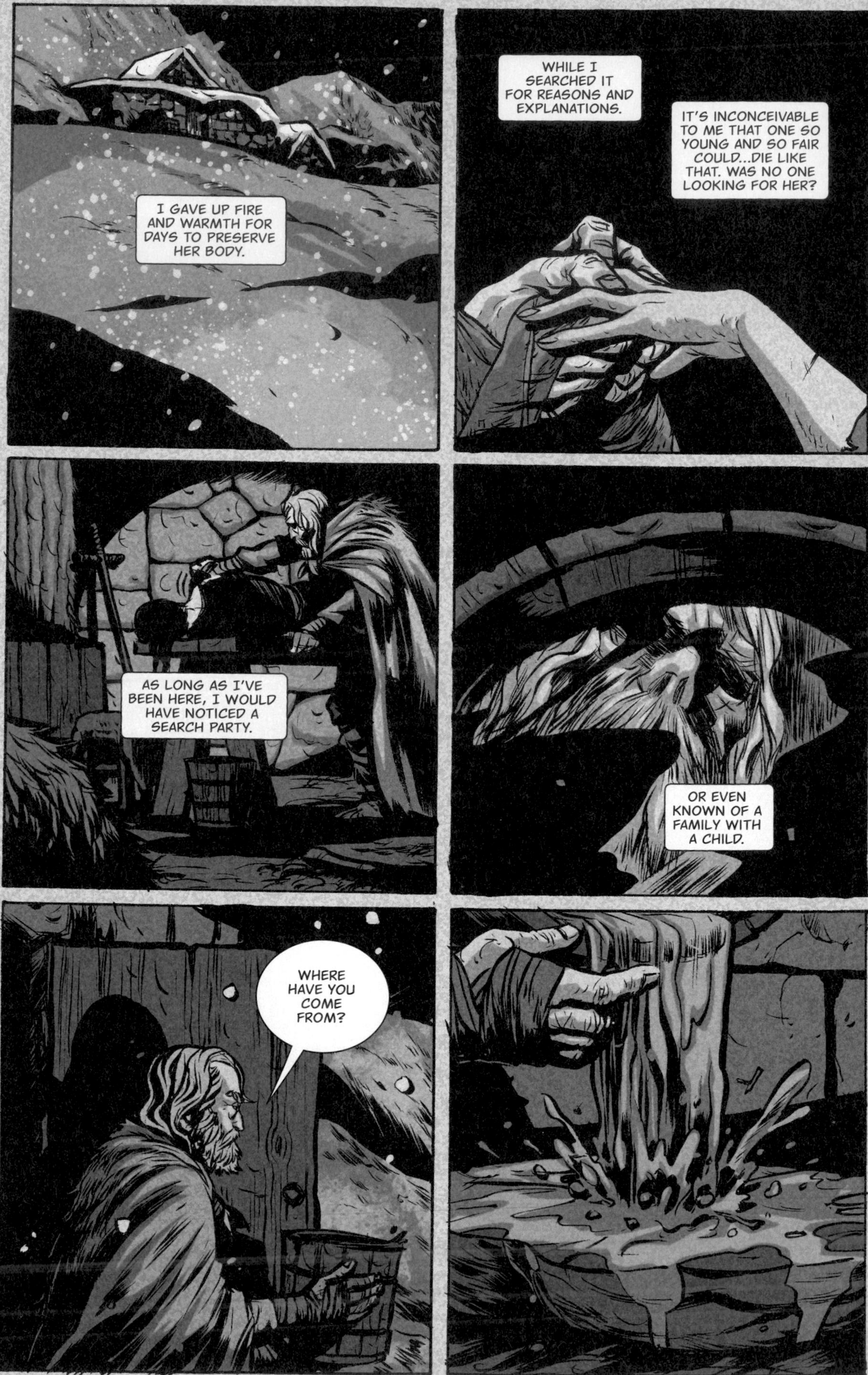
I GAVE UP FIRE AND WARMTH FOR DAYS TO PRESERVE HER BODY.
WHILE I SEARCHED IT FOR REASONS AND EXPLANATIONS.
IT'S INCONCEIVABLE TO ME THAT ONE SO YOUNG AND SO FAIR COULD...DIE LIKE THAT. WAS NO ONE LOOKING FOR HER?
AS LONG AS I'VE BEEN HERE, I WOULD HAVE NOTICED A SEARCH PARTY.
OR EVEN KNOWN OF A FAMILY WITH A CHILD.
WHERE HAVE YOU COME FROM?

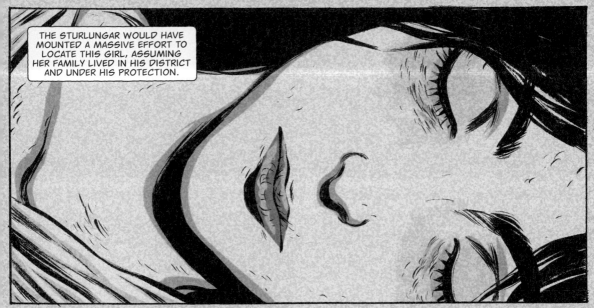

THE STURLUNGAR WOULD HAVE MOUNTED A MASSIVE EFFORT TO LOCATE THIS GIRL, ASSUMING HER FAMILY LIVED IN HIS DISTRICT AND UNDER HIS PROTECTION.

NOT TO DO SO WOULD BE AN UNTHINKABLE LAPSE IN RESPONSIBILITY.

HE WOULD NOT SURVIVE IT, POLITICALLY. ALL HIS ALLIES WOULD INSTANTLY LOSE FAITH. GOES AGAINST THE VERY FABRIC OF COMMONWEATH SOCIETY.

SO...THE GIRL IS EITHER FROM ANOTHER DISTRICT--WOULD HAVE TO BE QUITE FAR NOT TO CAUSE EVEN A MURMUR HERE--OR HER DEATH WAS KNOWN TO THE STURLUNGS.

AND... ALLOWED?

ORDERED?

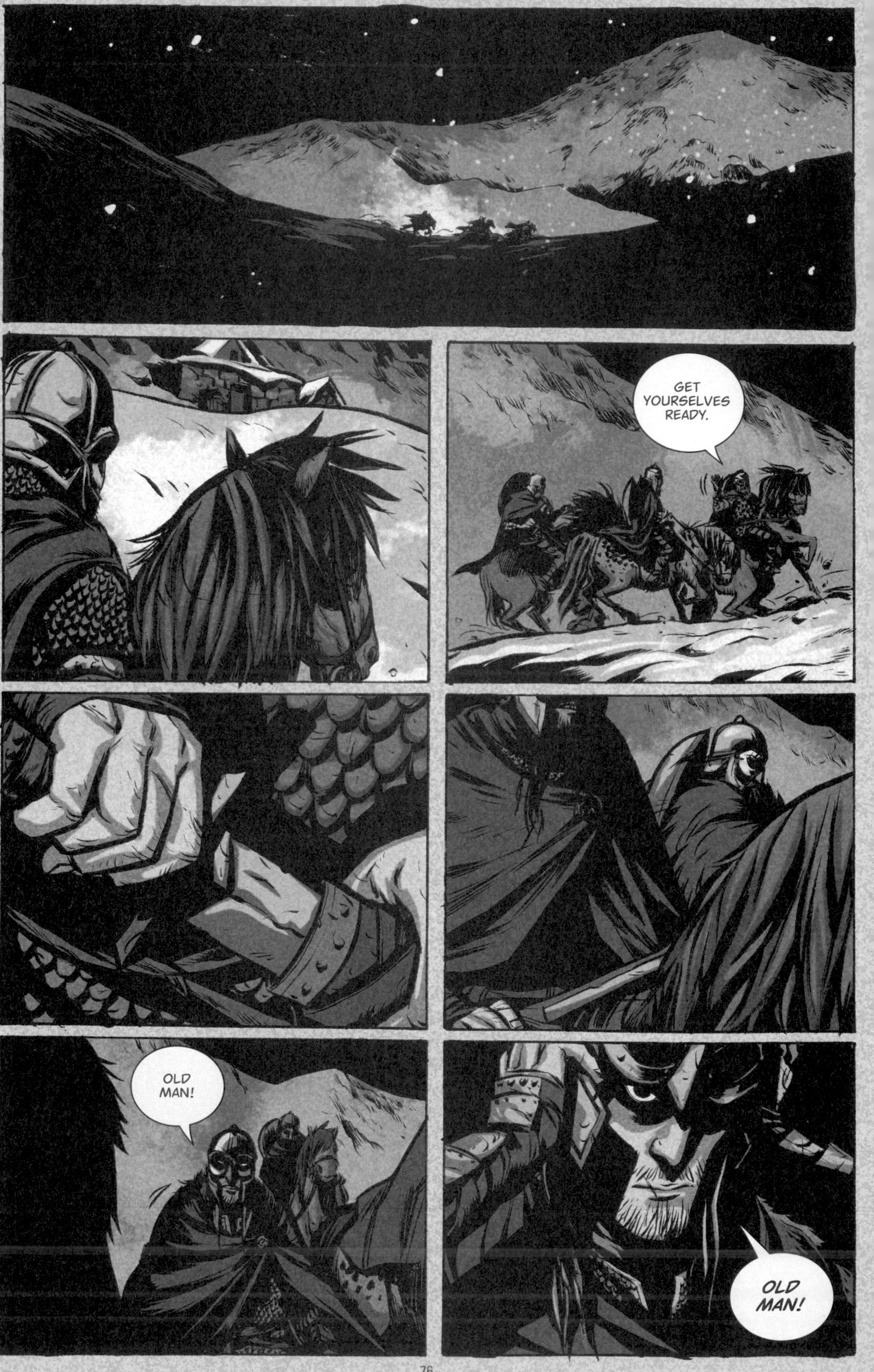
GET YOURSELVES READY.
OLD MAN!
OLD MAN!

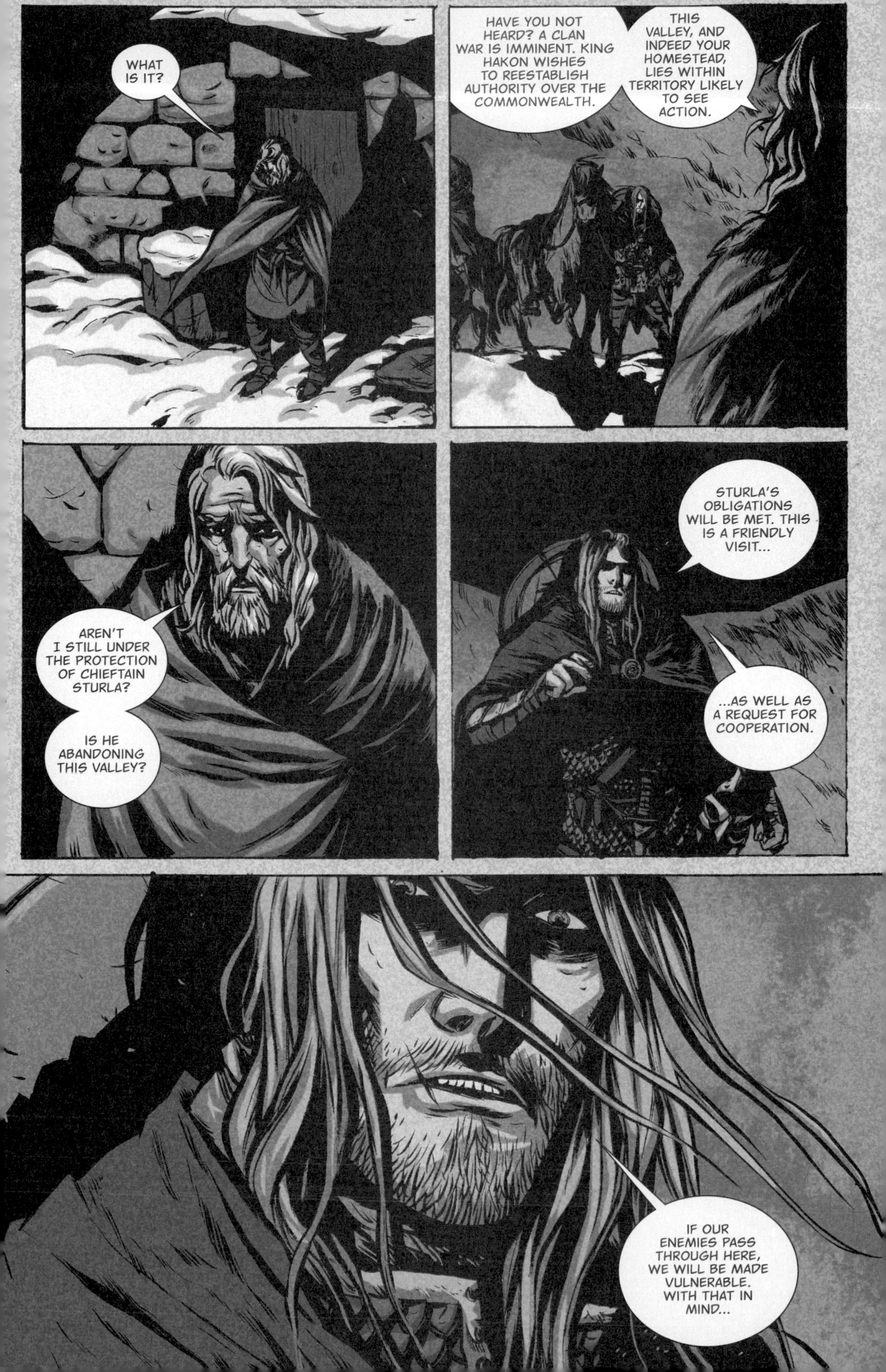
WHAT IS IT?
HAVE YOU NOT HEARD? A CLAN WAR IS IMMINENT. KING HAKON WISHES TO REESTABLISH AUTHORITY OVER THE COMMONWEALTH.
THIS VALLEY, AND INDEED YOUR HOMESTEAD, LIES WITHIN TERRITORY LIKELY TO SEE ACTION.
AREN'T I STILL UNDER THE PROTECTION OF CHIEFTAIN STURLA?
IS HE ABANDONING THIS VALLEY?
STURLA'S OBLIGATIONS WILL BE MET. THIS IS A FRIENDLY VISIT...
...AS WELL AS A REQUEST FOR COOPERATION.
IF OUR ENEMIES PASS THROUGH HERE, WE WILL BE MADE VULNERABLE. WITH THAT IN MIND...

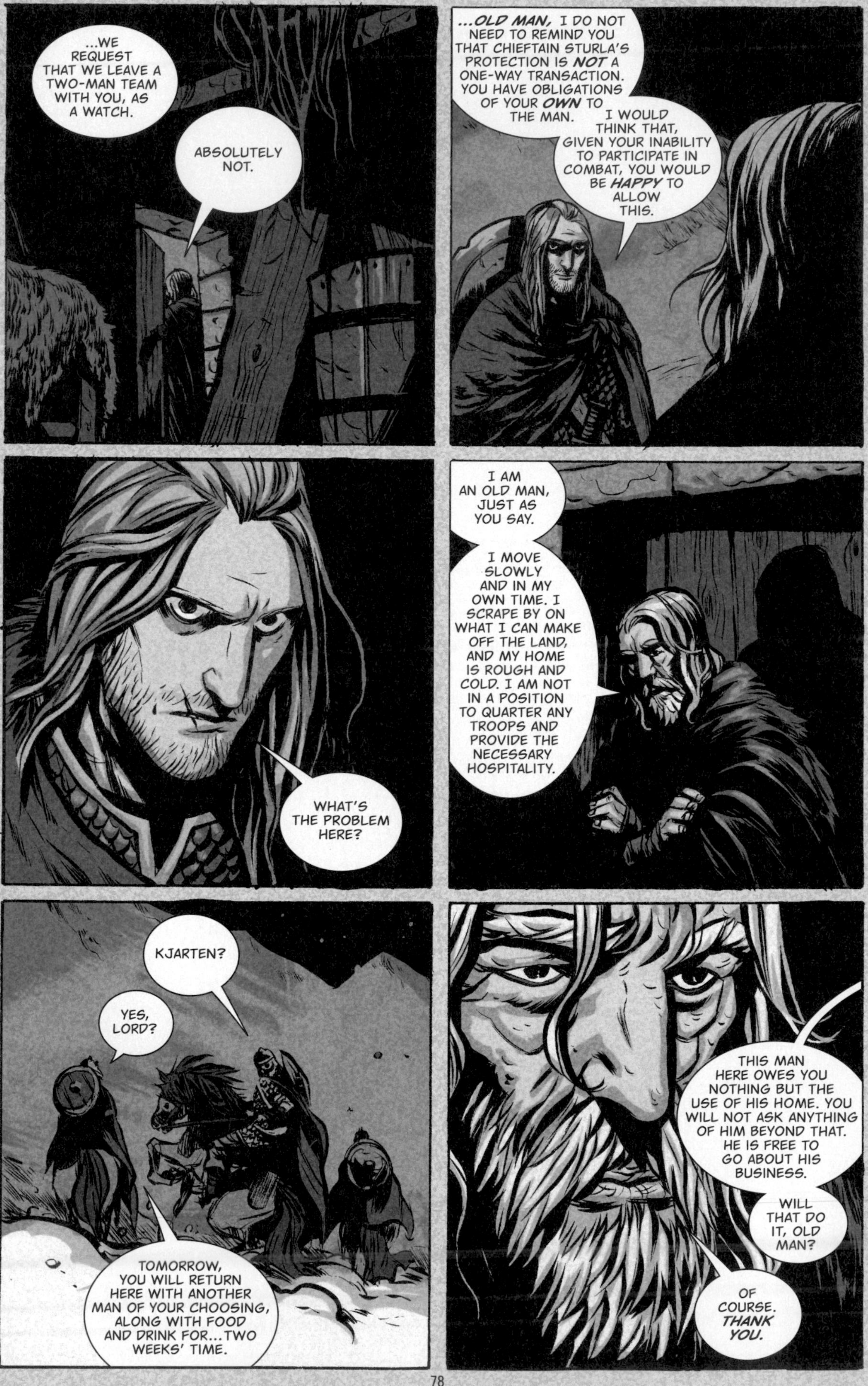
...WE REQUEST THAT WE LEAVE A TWO-MAN TEAM WITH YOU, AS A WATCH.
ABSOLUTELY NOT.
...OLD MAN, I DO NOT NEED TO REMIND YOU THAT CHIEFTAIN STURLA'S PROTECTION IS NOT A ONE-WAY TRANSACTION. YOU HAVE OBLIGATIONS OF YOUR OWN TO THE MAN.
I WOULD THINK THAT, GIVEN YOUR INABILITY TO PARTICIPATE IN COMBAT, YOU WOULD BE HAPPY TO ALLOW THIS.
WHAT'S THE PROBLEM HERE?
I AM AN OLD MAN, JUST AS YOU SAY.
I MOVE SLOWLY AND IN MY OWN TIME. I SCRAPE BY ON WHAT I CAN MAKE OFF THE LAND, AND MY HOME IS ROUGH AND COLD. I AM NOT IN A POSITION TO QUARTER ANY TROOPS AND PROVIDE THE NECESSARY HOSPITALITY.
KJARTEN?
YES, LORD?
TOMORROW, YOU WILL RETURN HERE WITH ANOTHER MAN OF YOUR CHOOSING, ALONG WITH FOOD AND DRINK FOR...TWO WEEKS' TIME.
THIS MAN HERE OWES YOU NOTHING BUT THE USE OF HIS HOME. YOU WILL NOT ASK ANYTHING OF HIM BEYOND THAT. HE IS FREE TO GO ABOUT HIS BUSINESS.
WILL THAT DO IT, OLD MAN?
OF COURSE. THANK YOU.

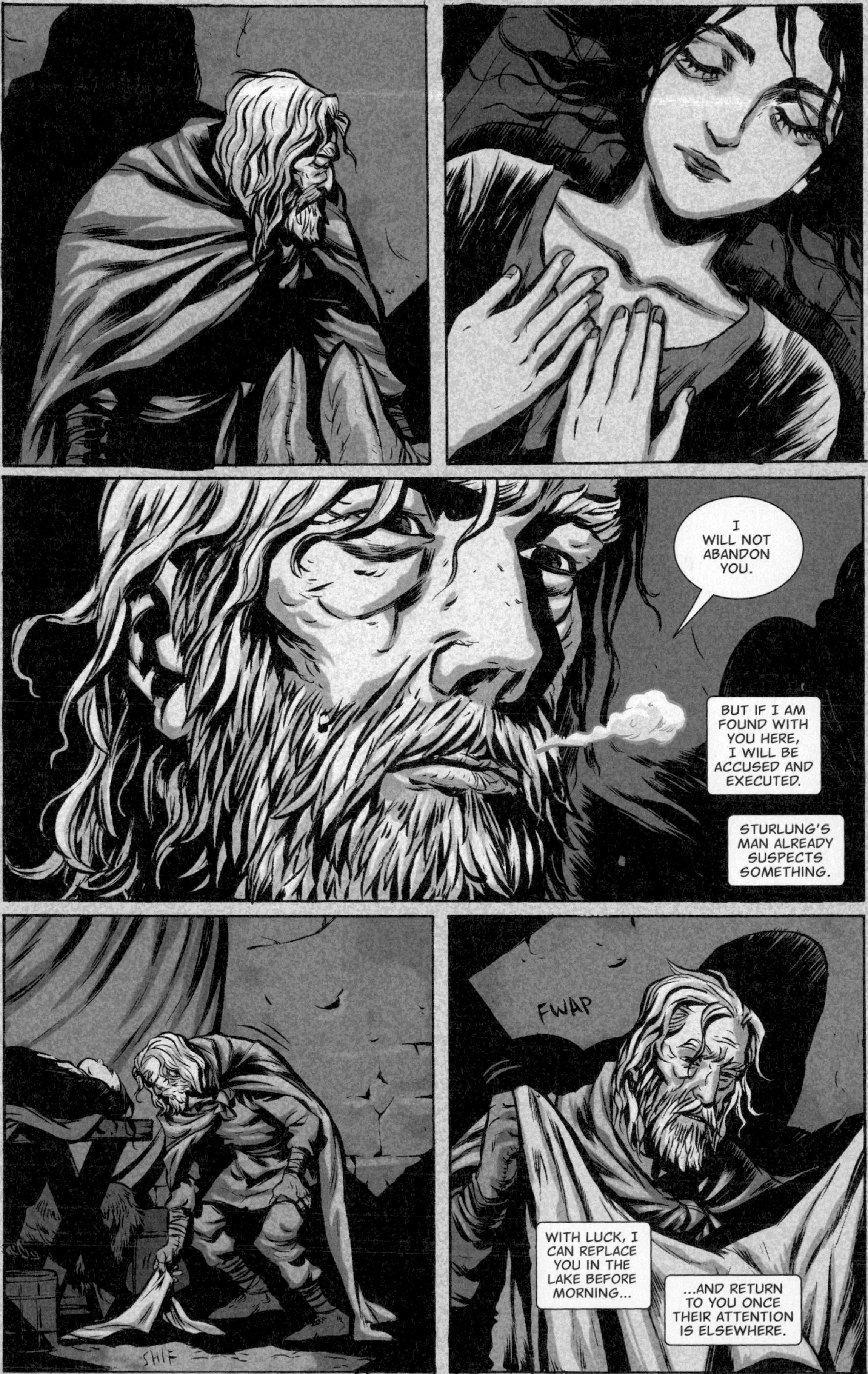
I WILL NOT ABANDON YOU.
BUT IF I AM FOUND WITH YOU HERE, I WILL BE ACCUSED AND EXECUTED.
STURLUNG'S MAN ALREADY SUSPECTS SOMETHING.
SHIF
FWAP
WITH LUCK, I CAN REPLACE YOU IN THE LAKE BEFORE MORNING...
...AND RETURN TO YOU ONCE THEIR ATTENTION IS ELSEWHERE.

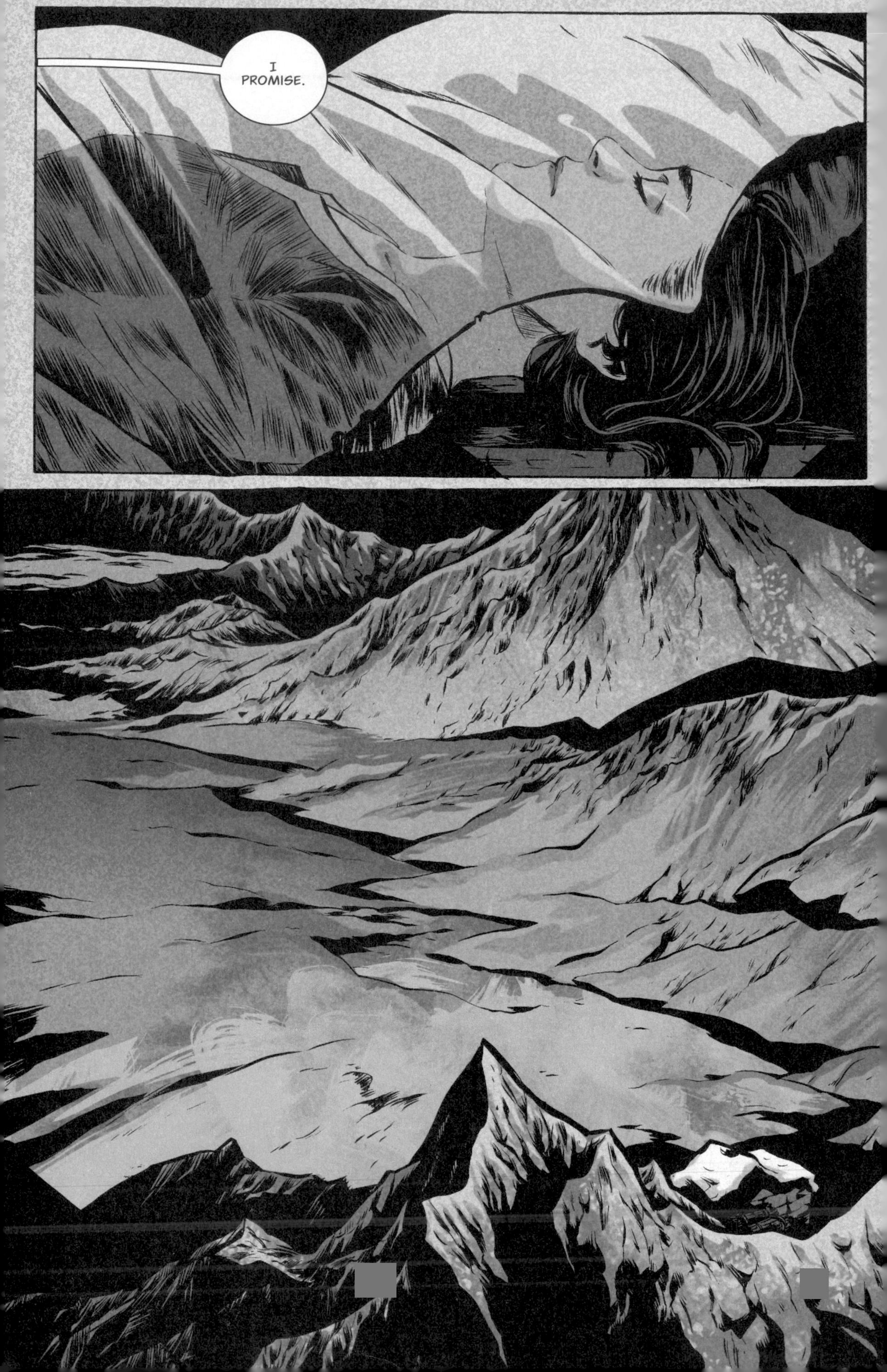
I PROMISE.

Chapter II

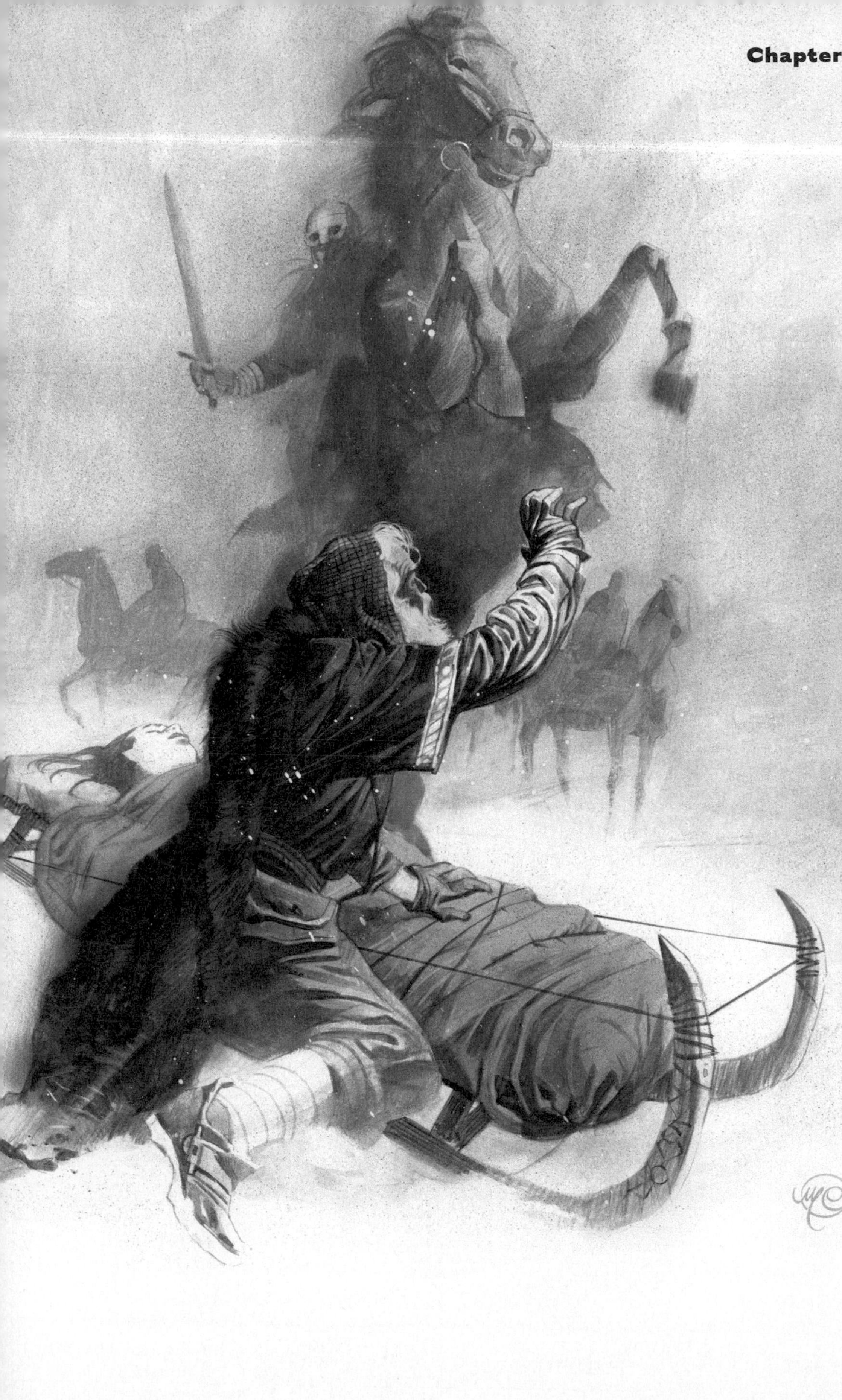

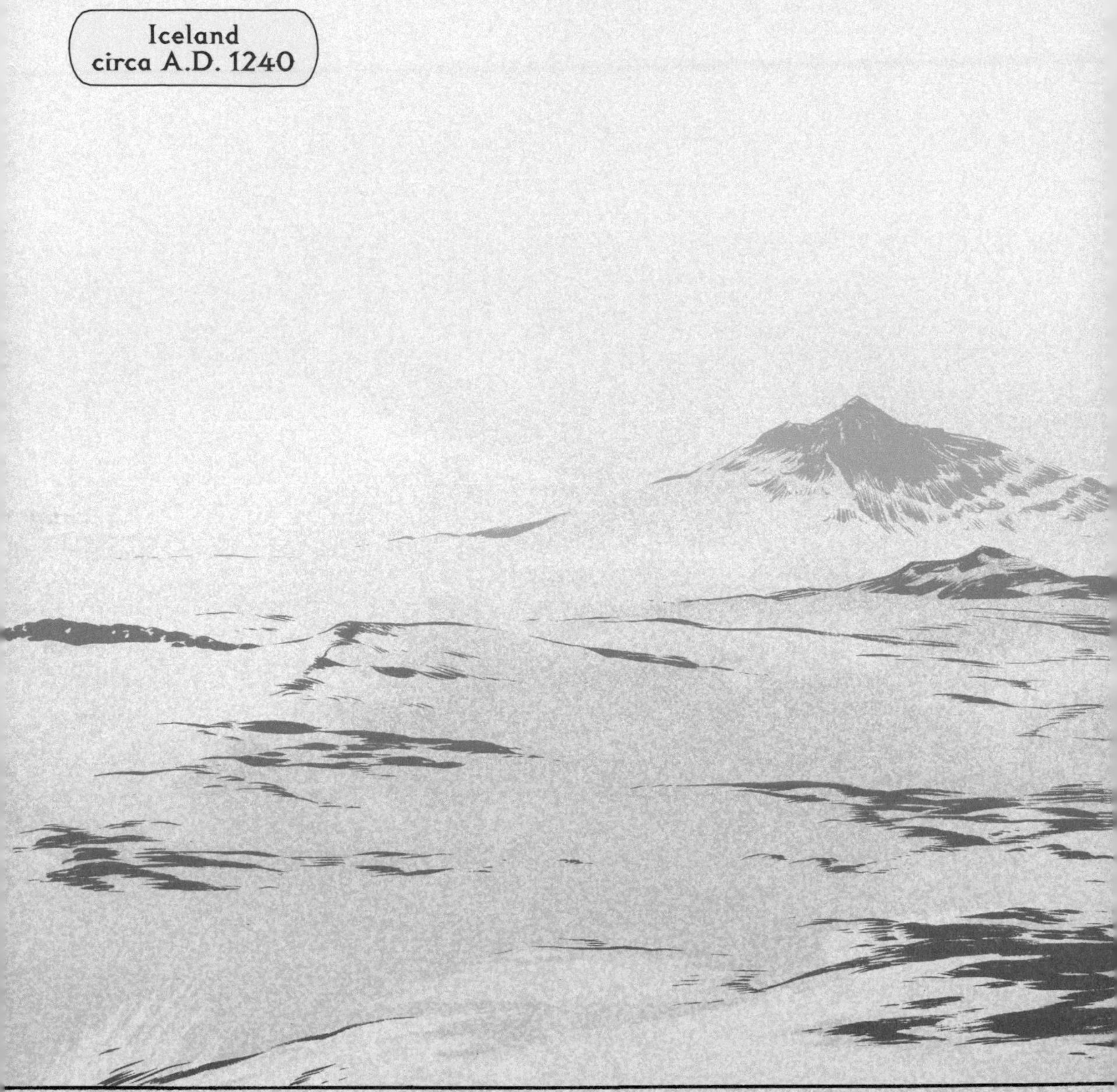
Iceland
circa A.D. 1240

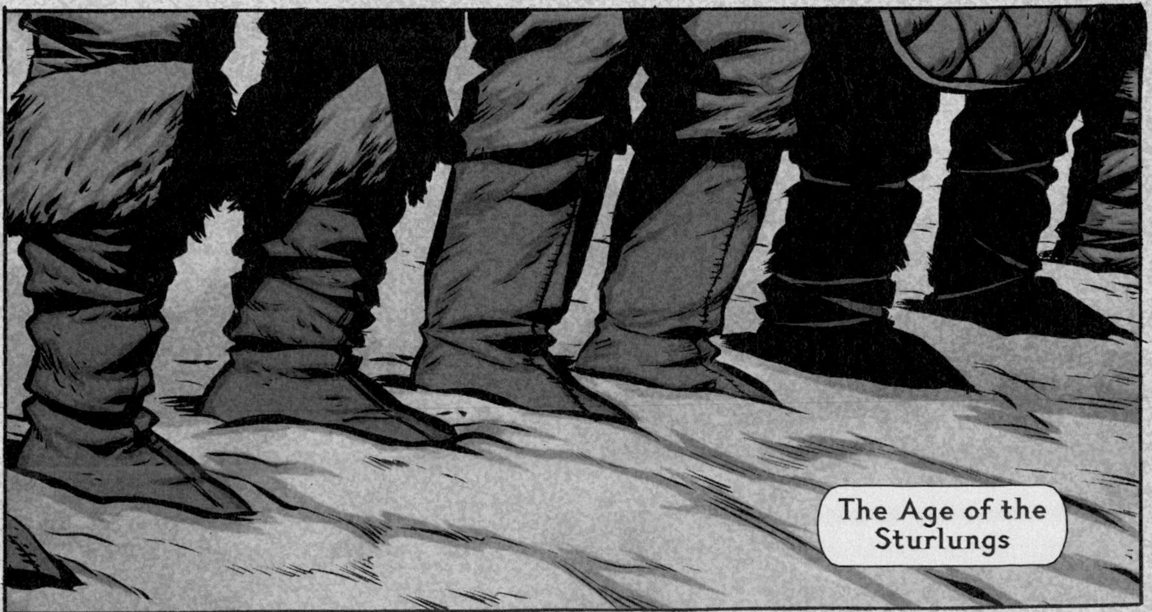
The Age of the Sturlungs

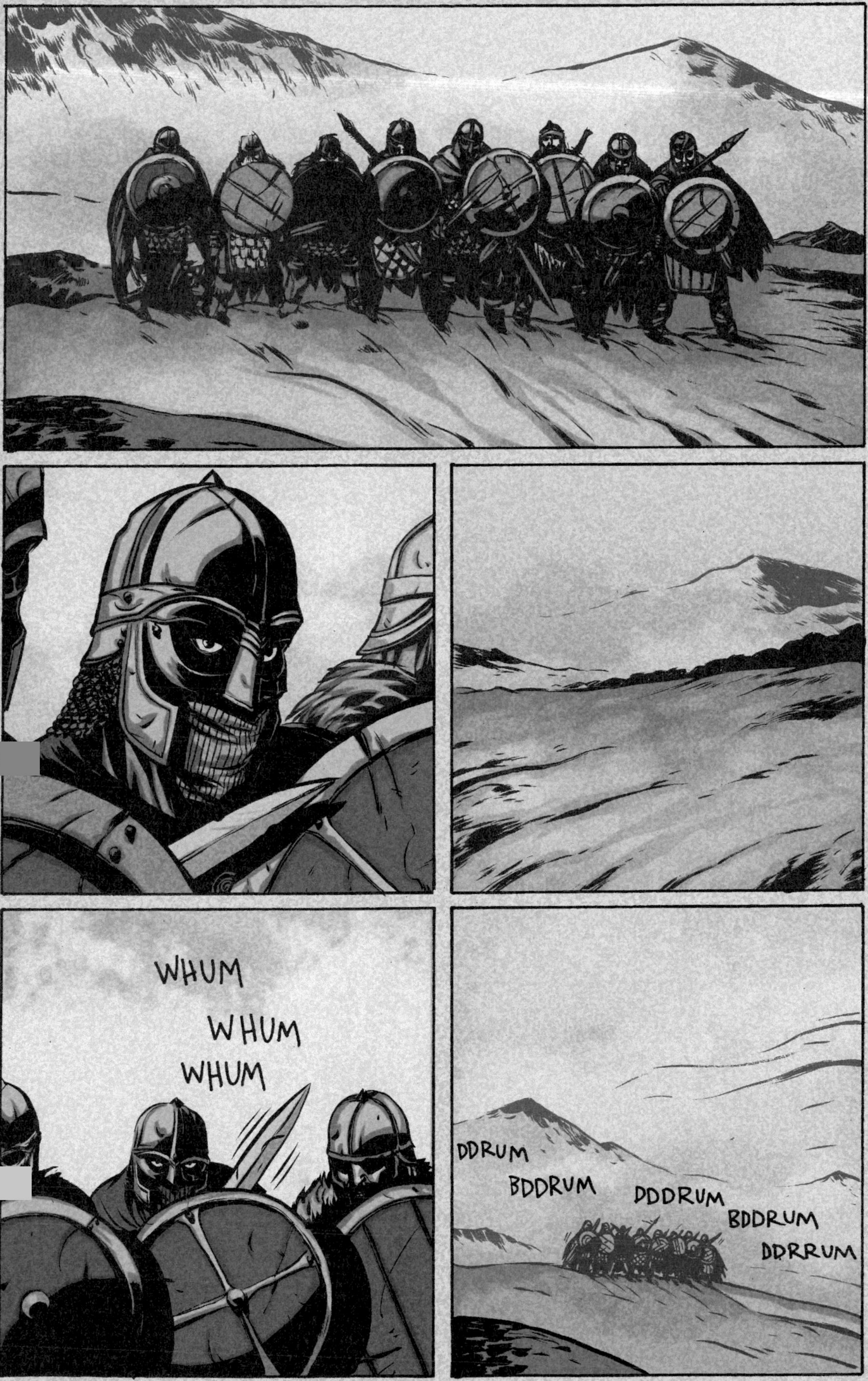
WHUM
WHUM
WHUM
DDRUM
BDDRUM
DDDRUM
BDDRUM
DDRRUM

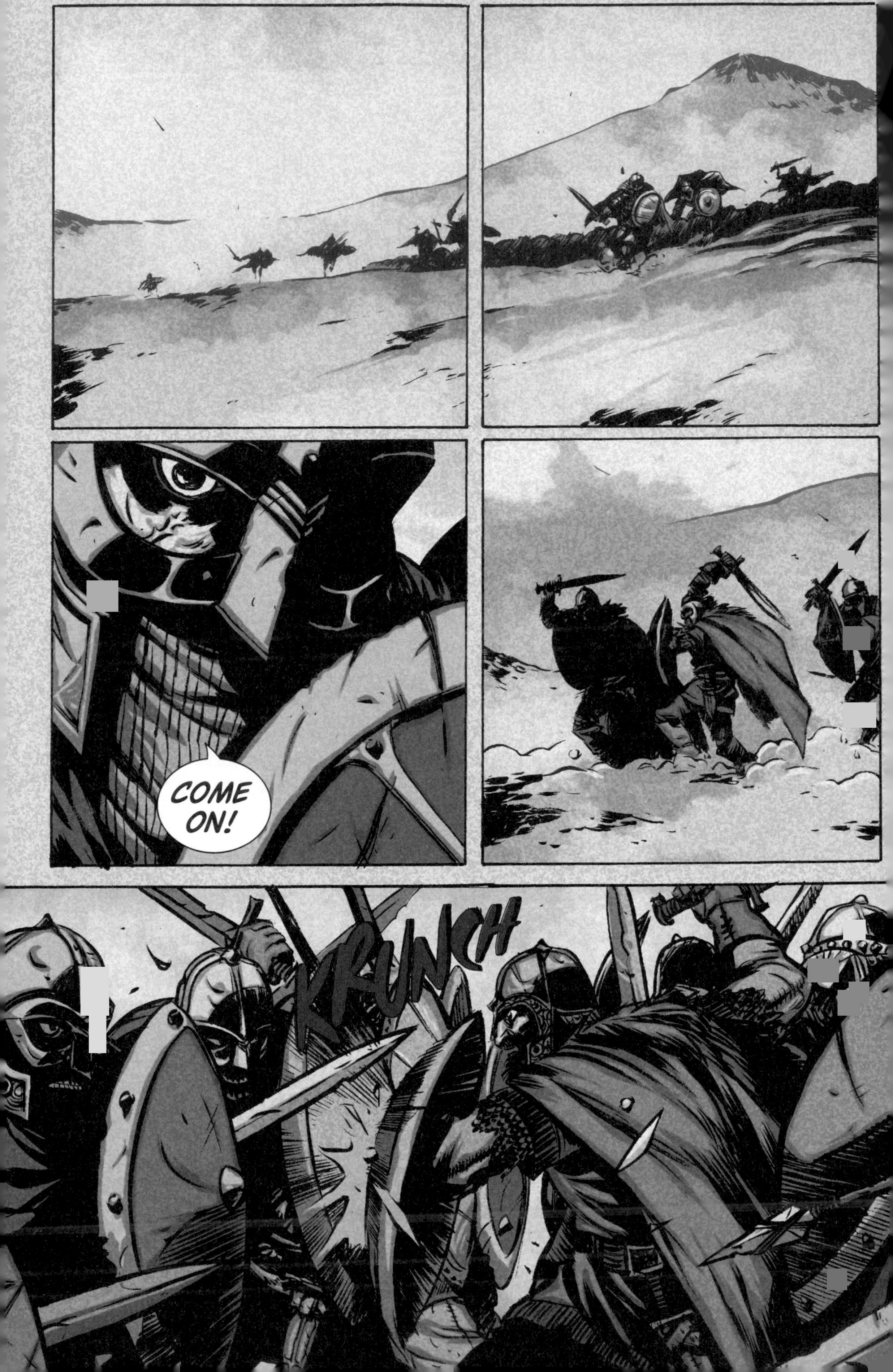
COME ON!
KRUNCH

SHLUK

KKRSCHH

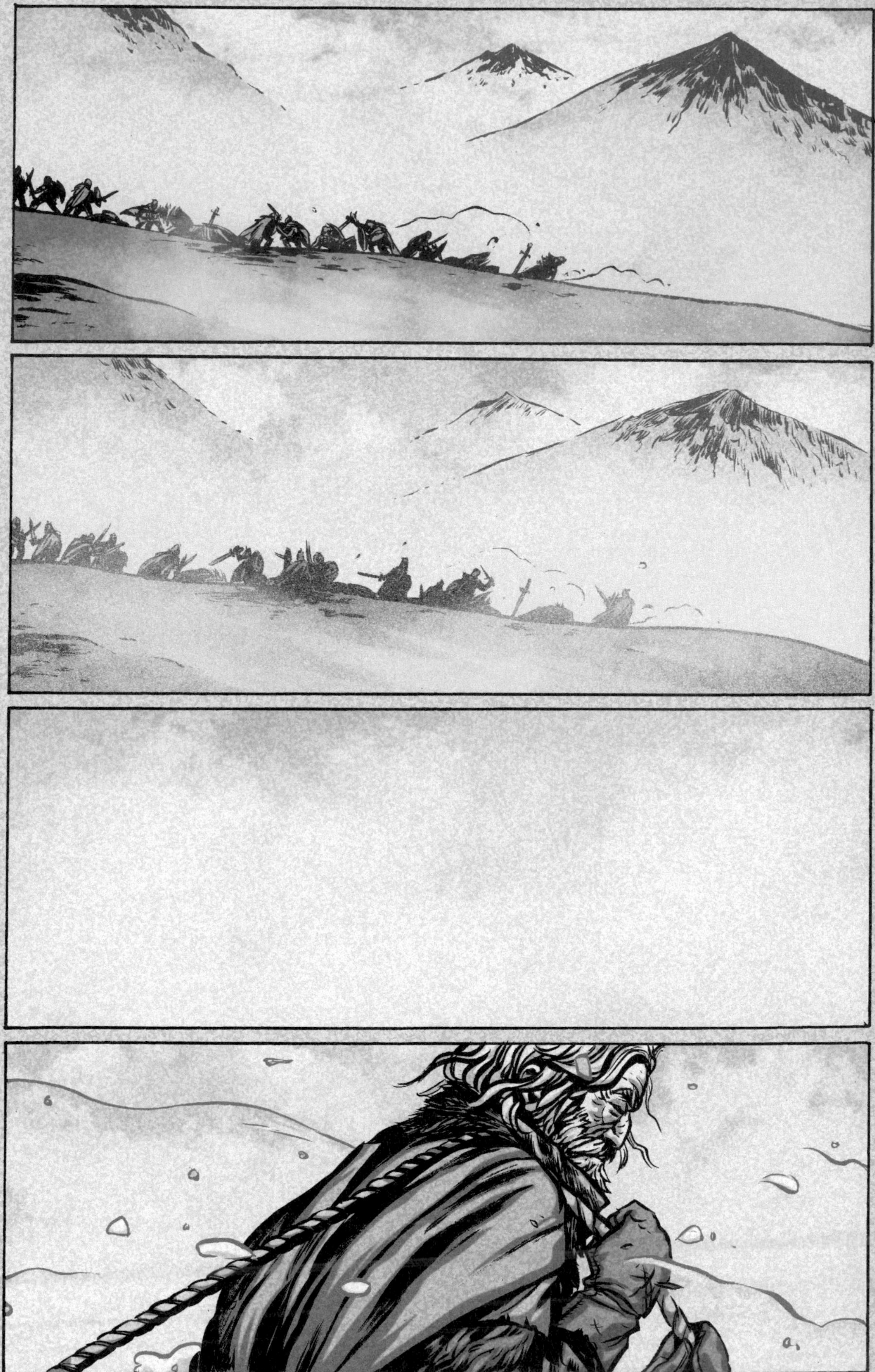

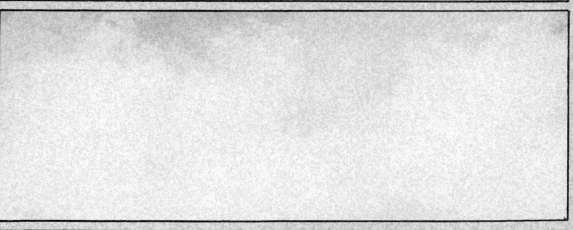

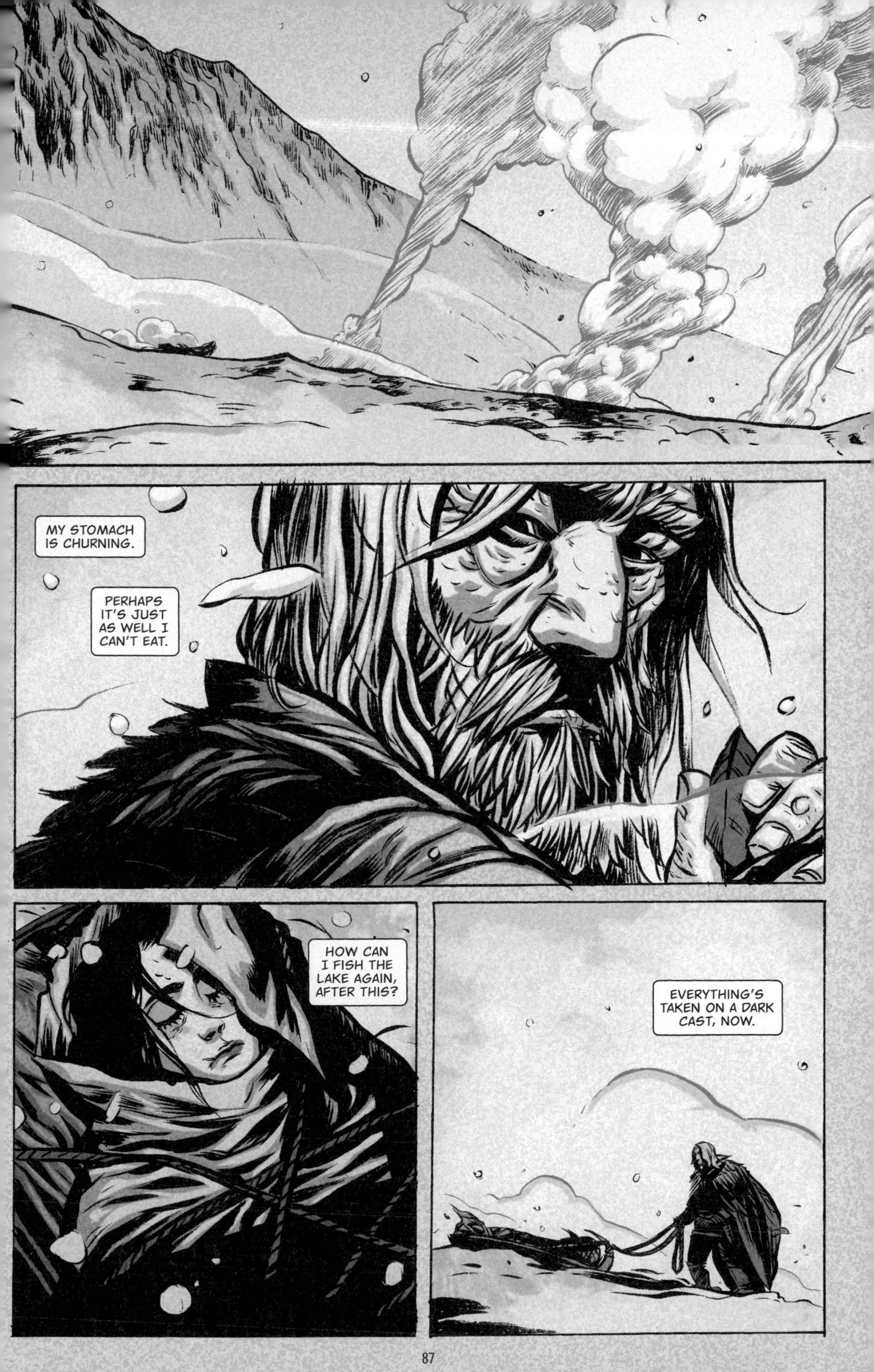
MY STOMACH IS CHURNING.
PERHAPS IT'S JUST AS WELL I CAN'T EAT.
HOW CAN I FISH THE LAKE AGAIN, AFTER THIS?
EVERYTHING'S TAKEN ON A DARK CAST, NOW.

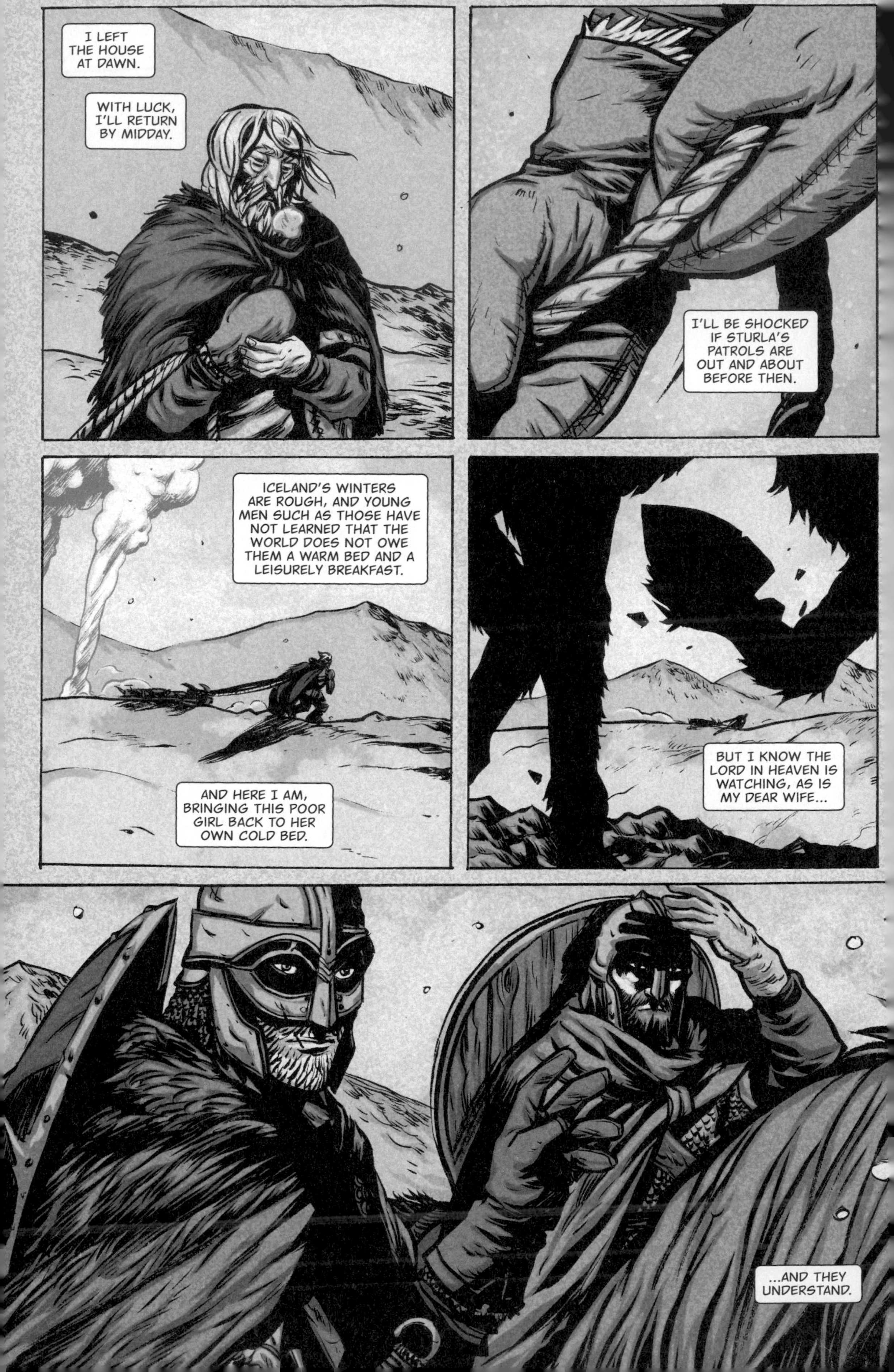
I LEFT THE HOUSE AT DAWN.
WITH LUCK, I'LL RETURN BY MIDDAY.
I'LL BE SHOCKED IF STURLA'S PATROLS ARE OUT AND ABOUT BEFORE THEN.
ICELAND'S WINTERS ARE ROUGH, AND YOUNG MEN SUCH AS THOSE HAVE NOT LEARNED THAT THE WORLD DOES NOT OWE THEM A WARM BED AND A LEISURELY BREAKFAST.
AND HERE I AM, BRINGING THIS POOR GIRL BACK TO HER OWN COLD BED.
BUT I KNOW THE LORD IN HEAVEN IS WATCHING, AS IS MY DEAR WIFE...
...AND THEY UNDERSTAND.

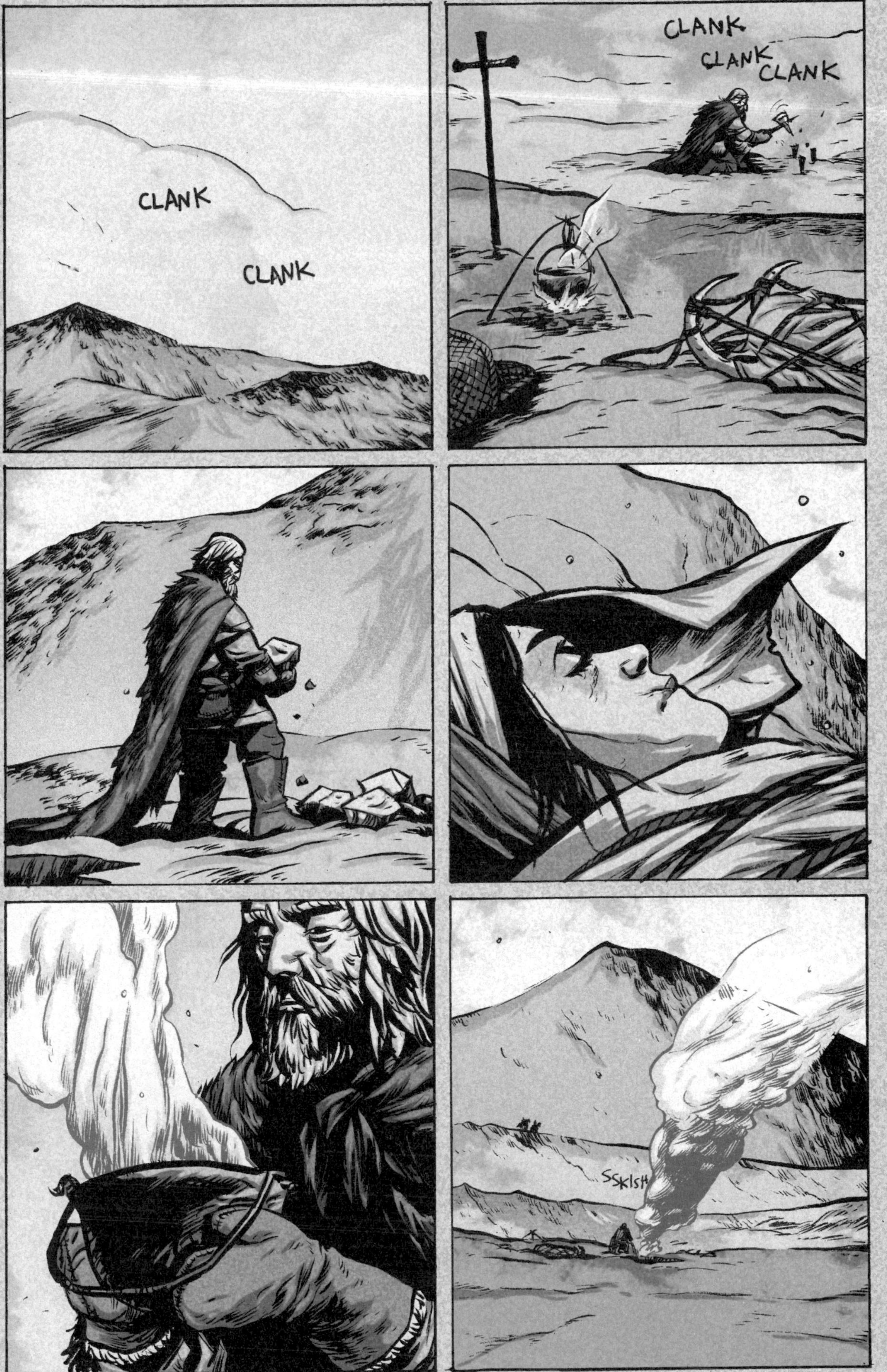
CLANK
CLANK
CLANK
CLANK
CLANK
SSKISH

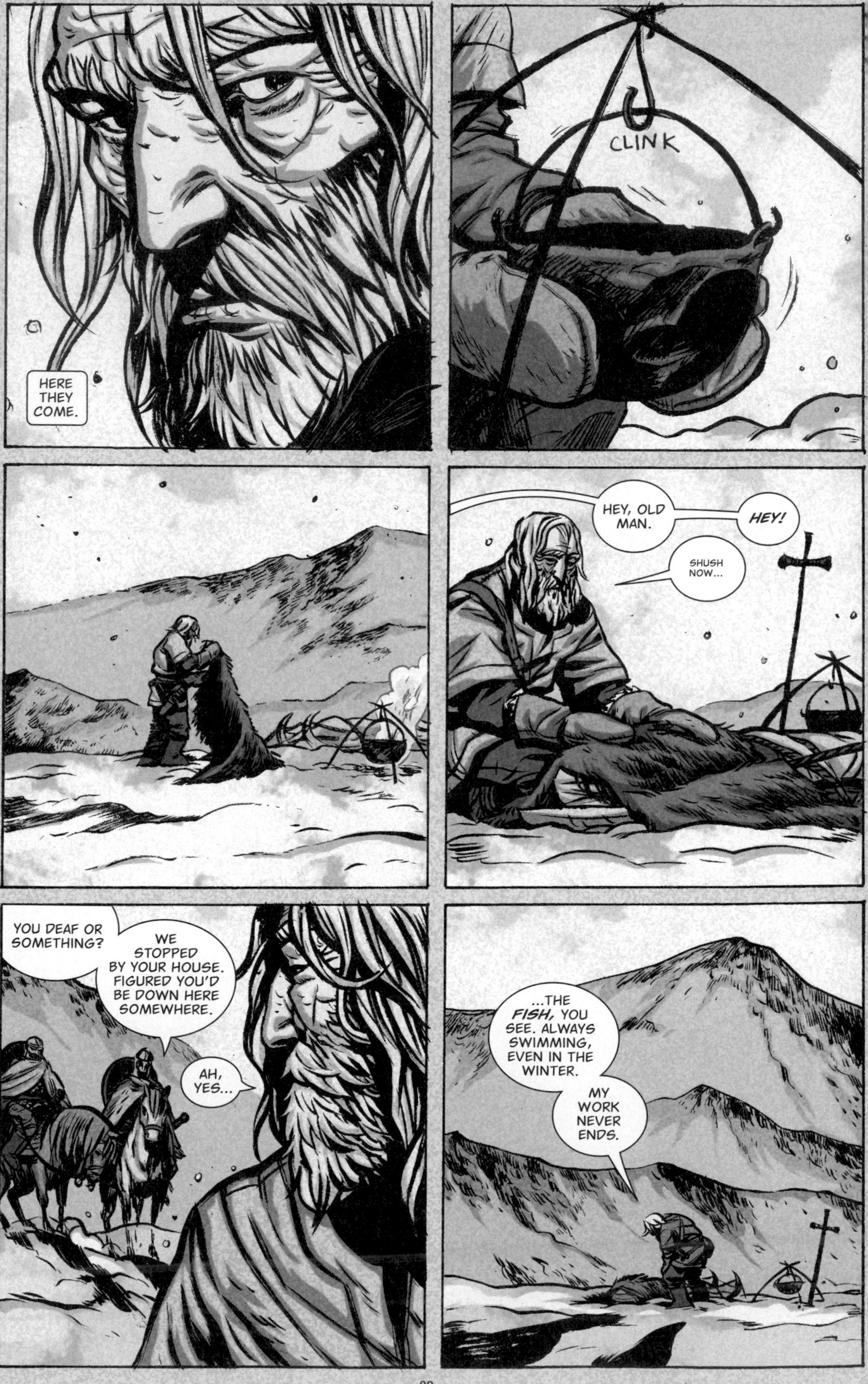
HERE THEY COME.
CLINK
HEY, OLD MAN.
HEY!
SHUSH NOW...
YOU DEAF OR SOMETHING?
WE STOPPED BY YOUR HOUSE. FIGURED YOU'D BE DOWN HERE SOMEWHERE.
AH, YES...
...THE FISH, YOU SEE. ALWAYS SWIMMING, EVEN IN THE WINTER.
MY WORK NEVER ENDS.

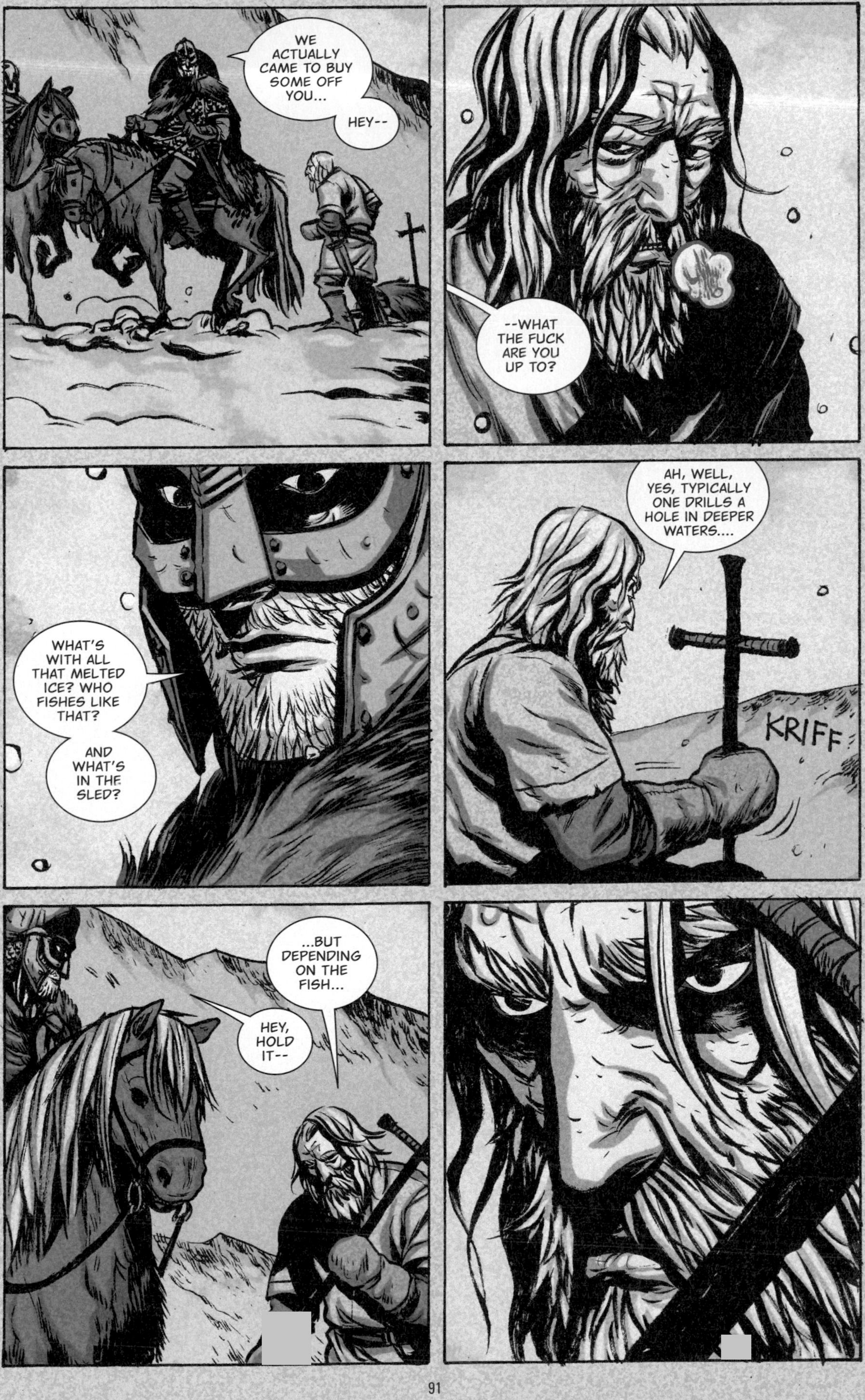
WE ACTUALLY CAME TO BUY SOME OFF YOU...
HEY--
--WHAT THE FUCK ARE YOU UP TO?
WHAT'S WITH ALL THAT MELTED ICE? WHO FISHES LIKE THAT?
AND WHAT'S IN THE SLED?
AH, WELL, YES, TYPICALLY ONE DRILLS A HOLE IN DEEPER WATERS....
KRIFF
...BUT DEPENDING ON THE FISH...
HEY, HOLD IT--

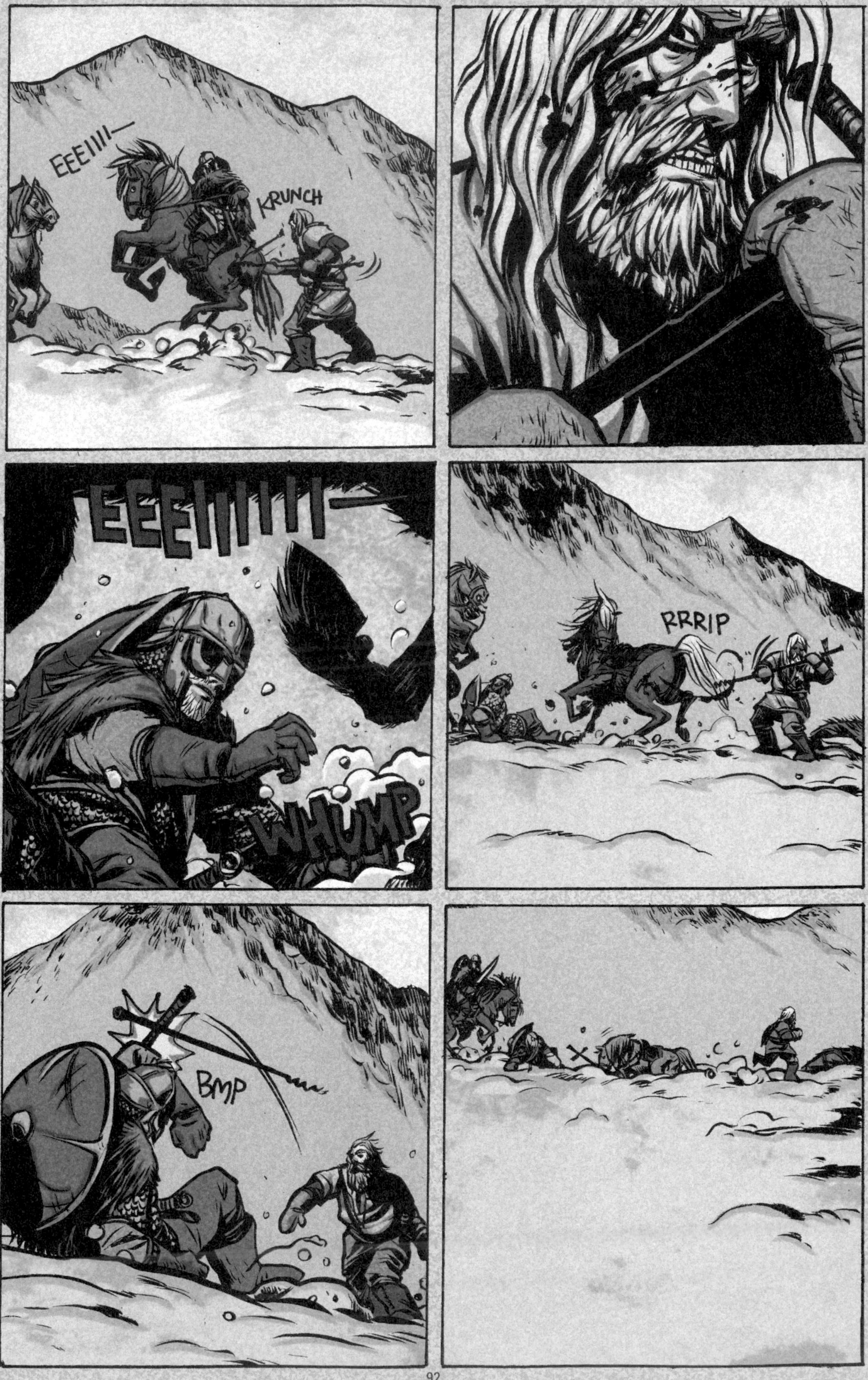
EEEIIII—
KRUNCH
EEEIIIIIIIII—
WHUMP
RRRIP
BMP

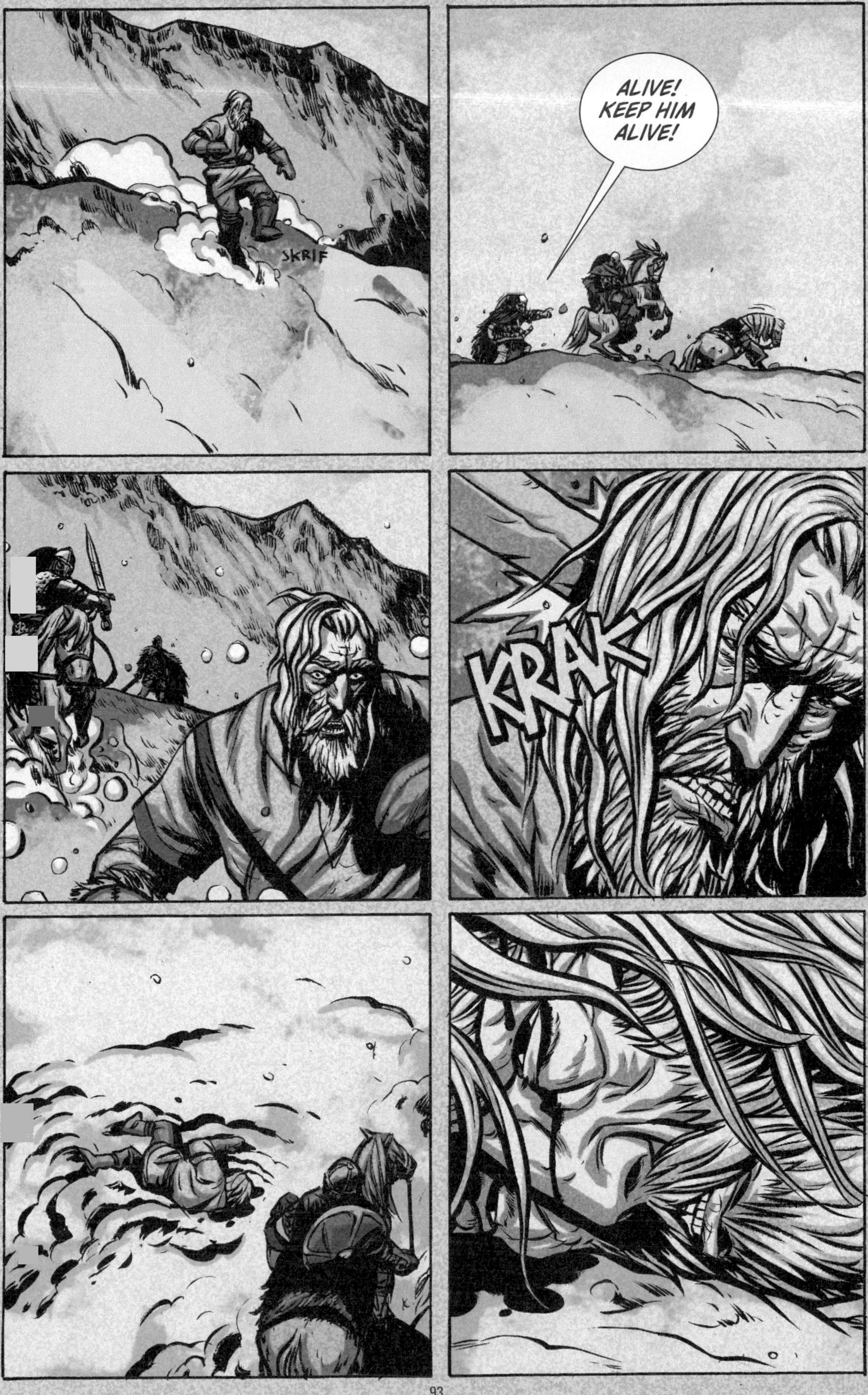
SKRIF
ALIVE! KEEP HIM ALIVE!
KRAK

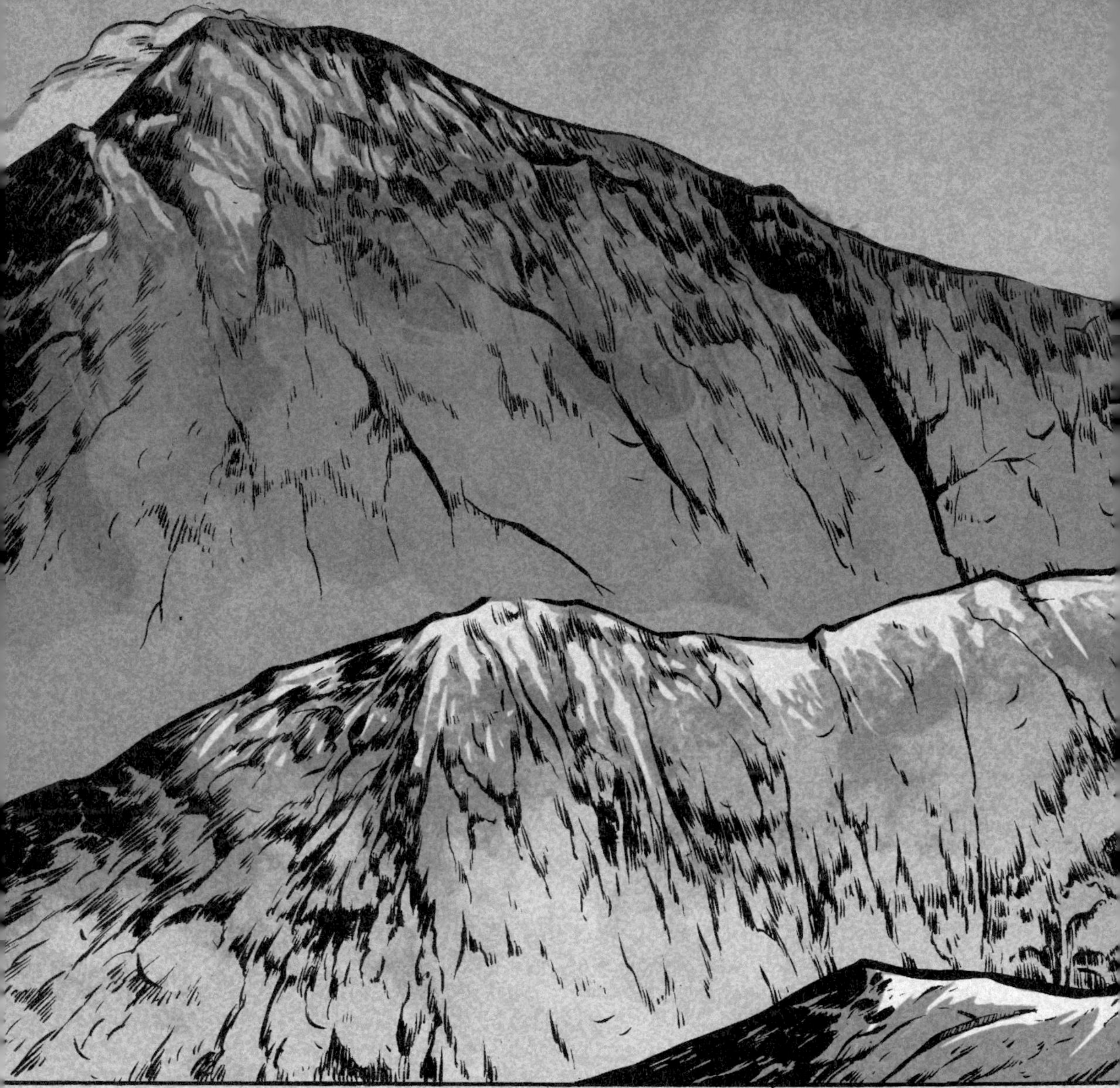

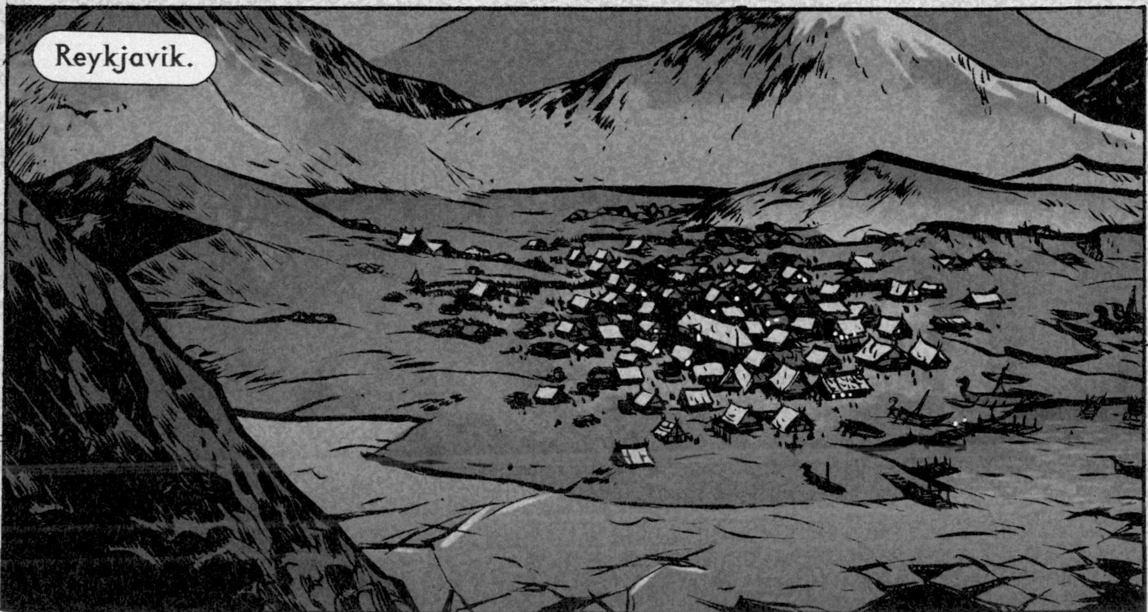
Reykjavik.

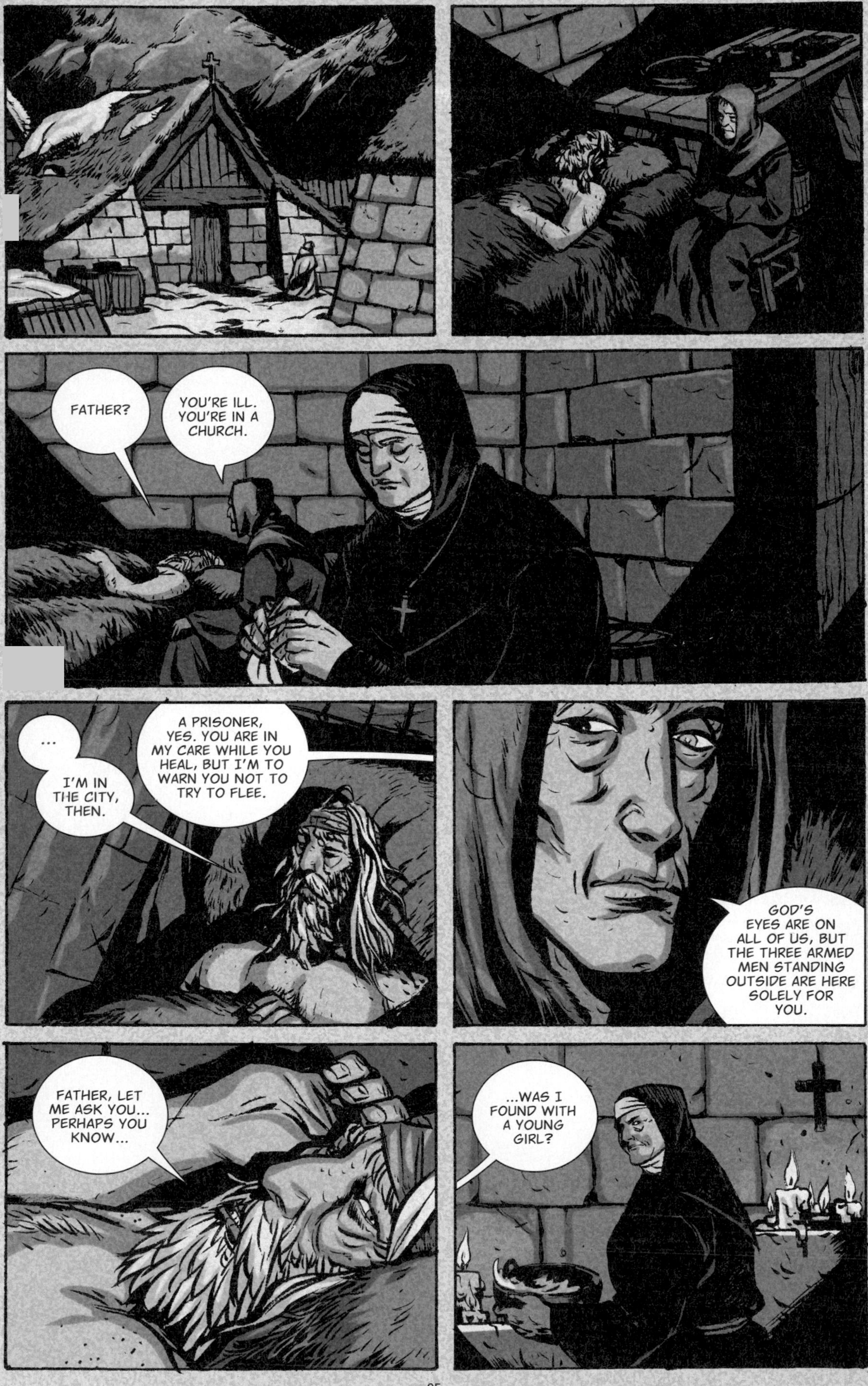
FATHER?
YOU'RE ILL. YOU'RE IN A CHURCH.
...
I'M IN THE CITY, THEN.
A PRISONER, YES. YOU ARE IN MY CARE WHILE YOU HEAL, BUT I'M TO WARN YOU NOT TO TRY TO FLEE.
GOD'S EYES ARE ON ALL OF US, BUT THE THREE ARMED MEN STANDING OUTSIDE ARE HERE SOLELY FOR YOU.
FATHER, LET ME ASK YOU... PERHAPS YOU KNOW...
...WAS I FOUND WITH A YOUNG GIRL?

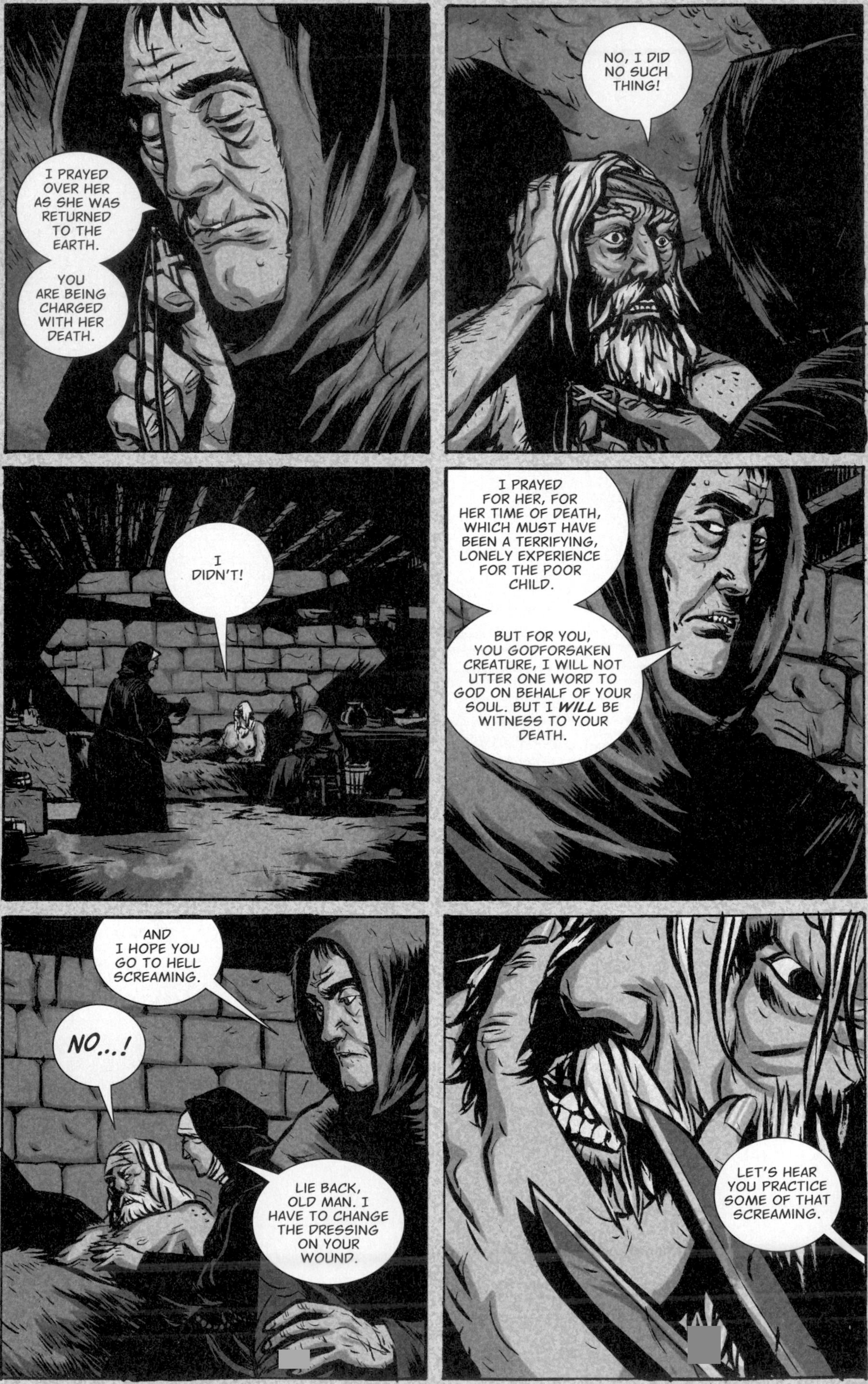

I PRAYED OVER HER AS SHE WAS RETURNED TO THE EARTH.
YOU ARE BEING CHARGED WITH HER DEATH.
NO, I DID NO SUCH THING!
I DIDN'T!
I PRAYED FOR HER, FOR HER TIME OF DEATH, WHICH MUST HAVE BEEN A TERRIFYING, LONELY EXPERIENCE FOR THE POOR CHILD.
BUT FOR YOU, YOU GODFORSAKEN CREATURE, I WILL NOT UTTER ONE WORD TO GOD ON BEHALF OF YOUR SOUL. BUT I *WILL* BE WITNESS TO YOUR DEATH.
AND I HOPE YOU GO TO HELL SCREAMING.
NO...!
LIE BACK, OLD MAN. I HAVE TO CHANGE THE DRESSING ON YOUR WOUND.
LET'S HEAR YOU PRACTICE SOME OF THAT SCREAMING.

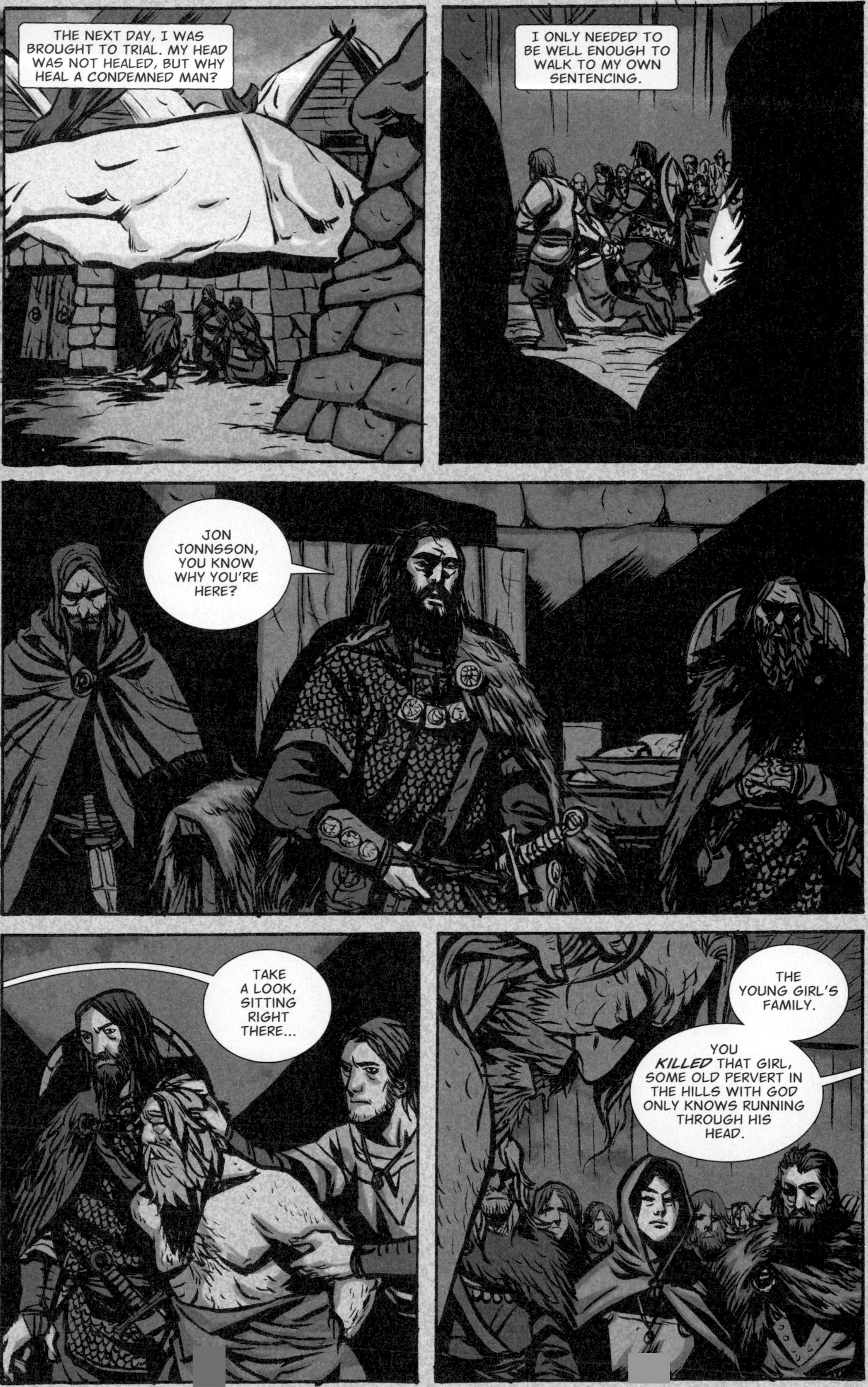
THE NEXT DAY, I WAS BROUGHT TO TRIAL. MY HEAD WAS NOT HEALED, BUT WHY HEAL A CONDEMNED MAN?
I ONLY NEEDED TO BE WELL ENOUGH TO WALK TO MY OWN SENTENCING.
JON JONNSSON, YOU KNOW WHY YOU'RE HERE?
TAKE A LOOK, SITTING RIGHT THERE...
THE YOUNG GIRL'S FAMILY.
YOU *KILLED* THAT GIRL, SOME OLD PERVERT IN THE HILLS WITH GOD ONLY KNOWS RUNNING THROUGH HIS HEAD.

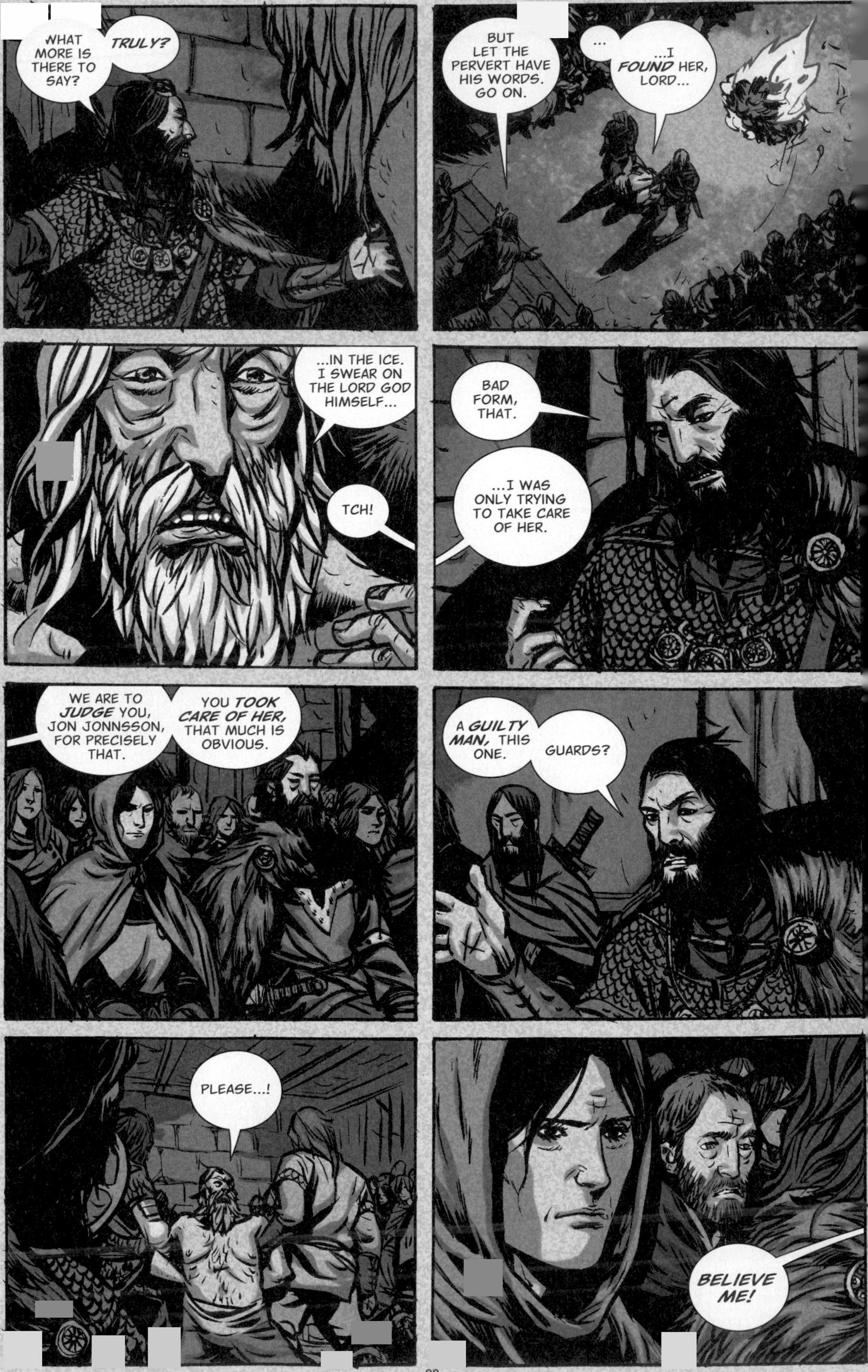
WHAT MORE IS THERE TO SAY?
TRULY?
BUT LET THE PERVERT HAVE HIS WORDS. GO ON.
...
...I FOUND HER, LORD...
...IN THE ICE. I SWEAR ON THE LORD GOD HIMSELF...
TCH!
BAD FORM, THAT.
...I WAS ONLY TRYING TO TAKE CARE OF HER.
WE ARE TO JUDGE YOU, JON JONNSSON, FOR PRECISELY THAT.
YOU TOOK CARE OF HER, THAT MUCH IS OBVIOUS.
A GUILTY MAN, THIS ONE.
GUARDS?
PLEASE...!
BELIEVE ME!

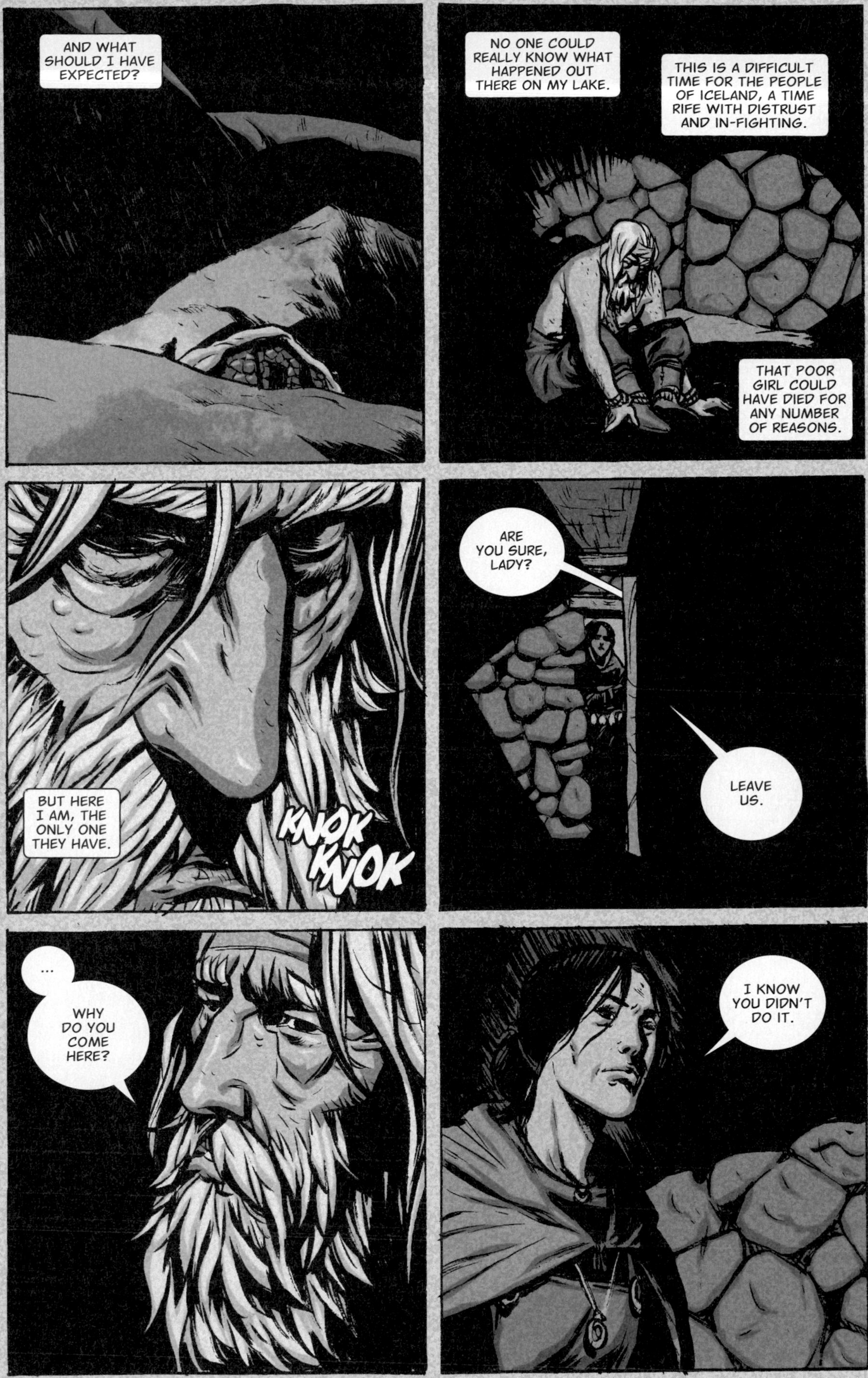
AND WHAT SHOULD I HAVE EXPECTED?
NO ONE COULD REALLY KNOW WHAT HAPPENED OUT THERE ON MY LAKE.
THIS IS A DIFFICULT TIME FOR THE PEOPLE OF ICELAND, A TIME RIFE WITH DISTRUST AND IN-FIGHTING.
THAT POOR GIRL COULD HAVE DIED FOR ANY NUMBER OF REASONS.
BUT HERE I AM, THE ONLY ONE THEY HAVE.
KNOK KNOK
ARE YOU SURE, LADY?
LEAVE US.
...
WHY DO YOU COME HERE?
I KNOW YOU DIDN'T DO IT.

THANK YOU.

TRULY. I NEEDED SOMEONE TO BELIEVE ME. I DON'T EVEN CARE ABOUT BEING FOUND GUILTY...

...I JUST NEEDED *SOMEONE* NOT TO THINK THOSE HORRIBLE THINGS ABOUT ME.

YES, WELL.

I JUST WANTED TO SAY THAT.

WAIT.

COME CLOSER.

PUT YOUR HAND INSIDE MY SHIRT.

NO, LISTEN TO ME. TRUST ME.

PINNED ON THE INSIDE, SEE IT? TAKE IT.

IT'S YOURS.

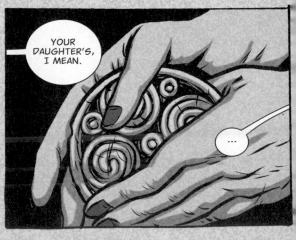

YOUR DAUGHTER'S, I MEAN.

...

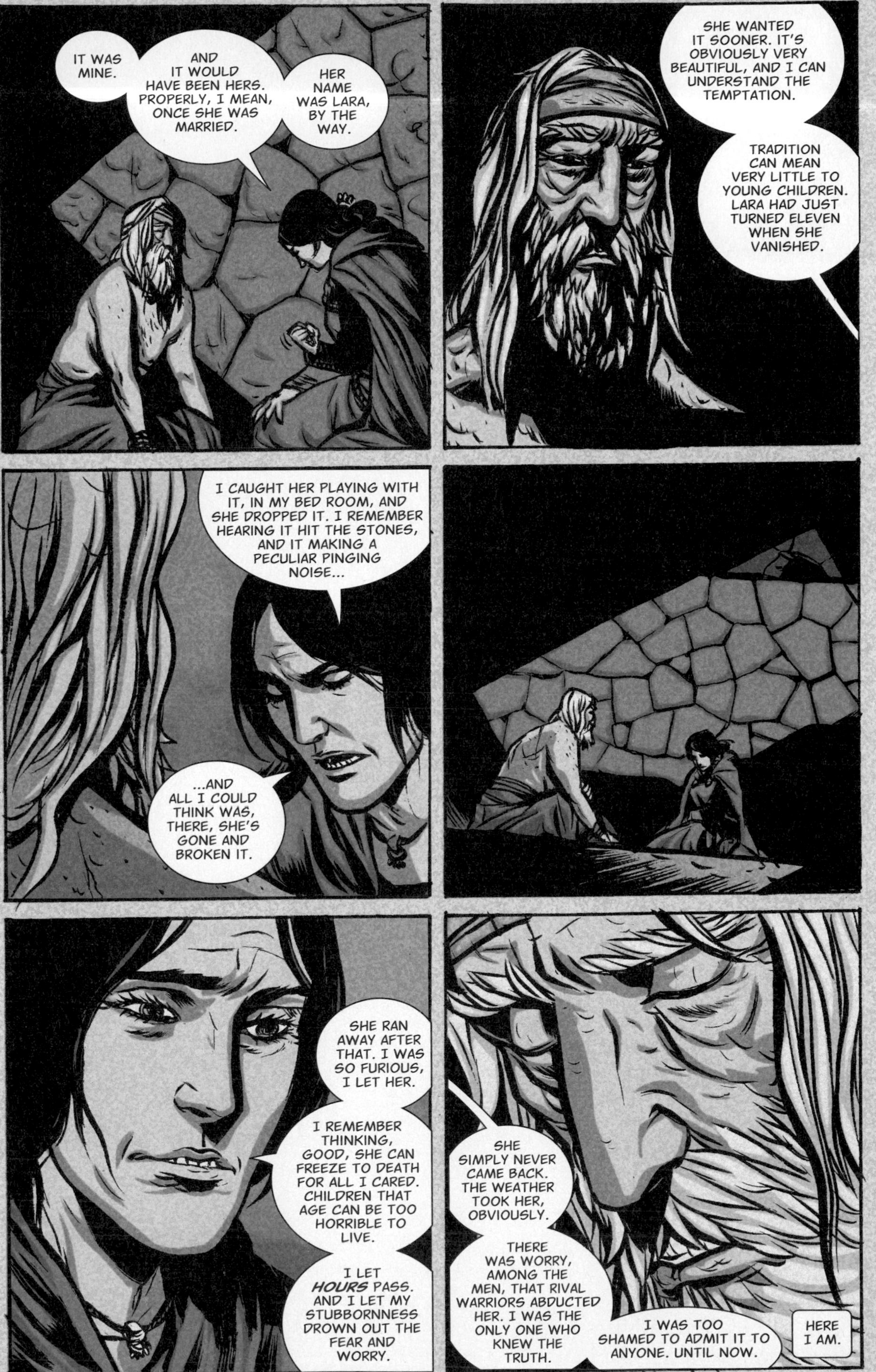
IT WAS MINE.
AND IT WOULD HAVE BEEN HERS. PROPERLY, I MEAN, ONCE SHE WAS MARRIED.
HER NAME WAS LARA, BY THE WAY.
SHE WANTED IT SOONER. IT'S OBVIOUSLY VERY BEAUTIFUL, AND I CAN UNDERSTAND THE TEMPTATION.
TRADITION CAN MEAN VERY LITTLE TO YOUNG CHILDREN. LARA HAD JUST TURNED ELEVEN WHEN SHE VANISHED.
I CAUGHT HER PLAYING WITH IT, IN MY BED ROOM, AND SHE DROPPED IT. I REMEMBER HEARING IT HIT THE STONES, AND IT MAKING A PECULIAR PINGING NOISE...
...AND ALL I COULD THINK WAS, THERE, SHE'S GONE AND BROKEN IT.
SHE RAN AWAY AFTER THAT. I WAS SO FURIOUS, I LET HER.
I REMEMBER THINKING, GOOD, SHE CAN FREEZE TO DEATH FOR ALL I CARED. CHILDREN THAT AGE CAN BE TOO HORRIBLE TO LIVE.
I LET HOURS PASS. AND I LET MY STUBBORNNESS DROWN OUT THE FEAR AND WORRY.
SHE SIMPLY NEVER CAME BACK. THE WEATHER TOOK HER, OBVIOUSLY.
THERE WAS WORRY, AMONG THE MEN, THAT RIVAL WARRIORS ABDUCTED HER. I WAS THE ONLY ONE WHO KNEW THE TRUTH.
I WAS TOO SHAMED TO ADMIT IT TO ANYONE. UNTIL NOW.
HERE I AM.

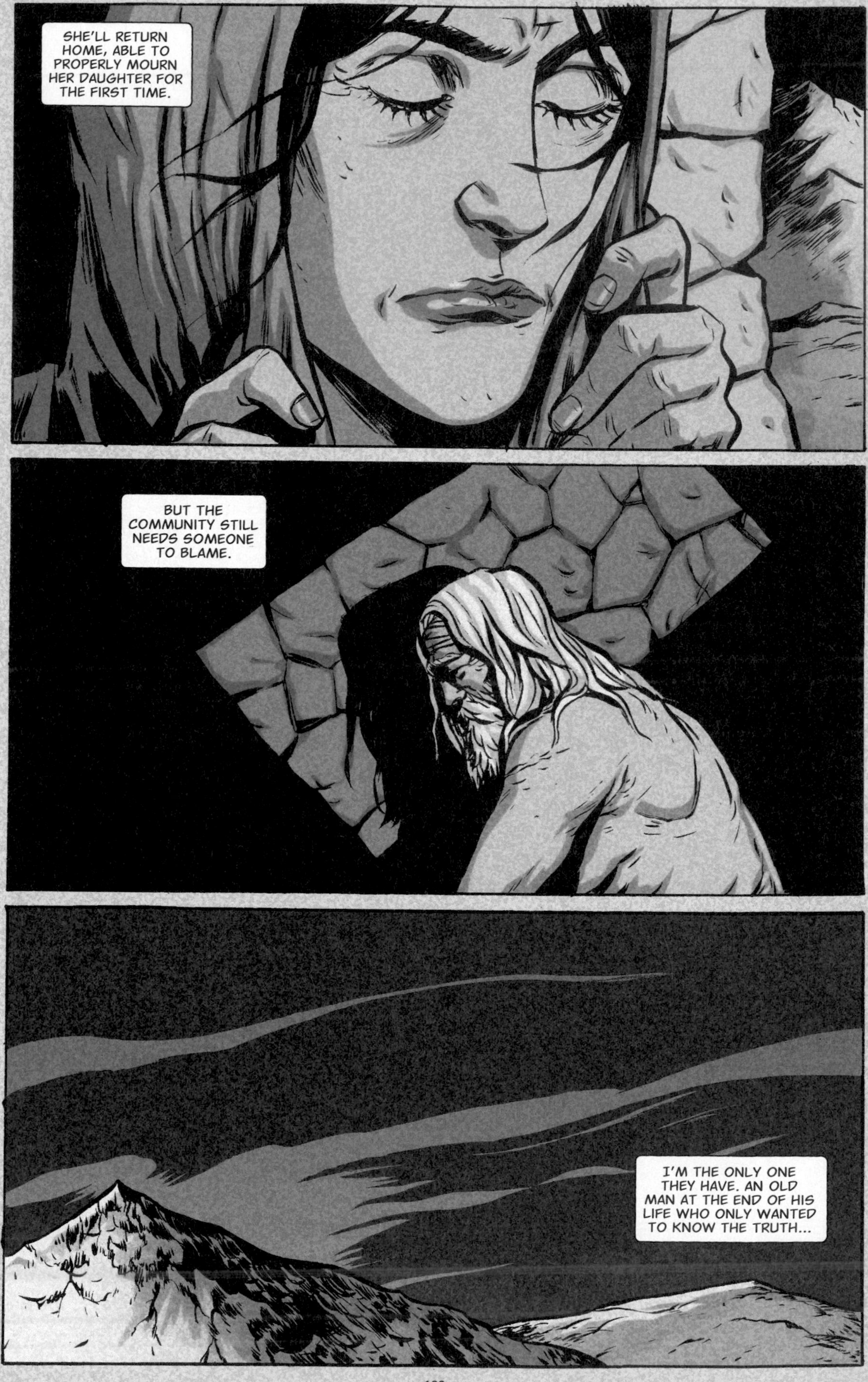
SHE'LL RETURN HOME, ABLE TO PROPERLY MOURN HER DAUGHTER FOR THE FIRST TIME.
BUT THE COMMUNITY STILL NEEDS SOMEONE TO BLAME.
I'M THE ONLY ONE THEY HAVE. AN OLD MAN AT THE END OF HIS LIFE WHO ONLY WANTED TO KNOW THE TRUTH...

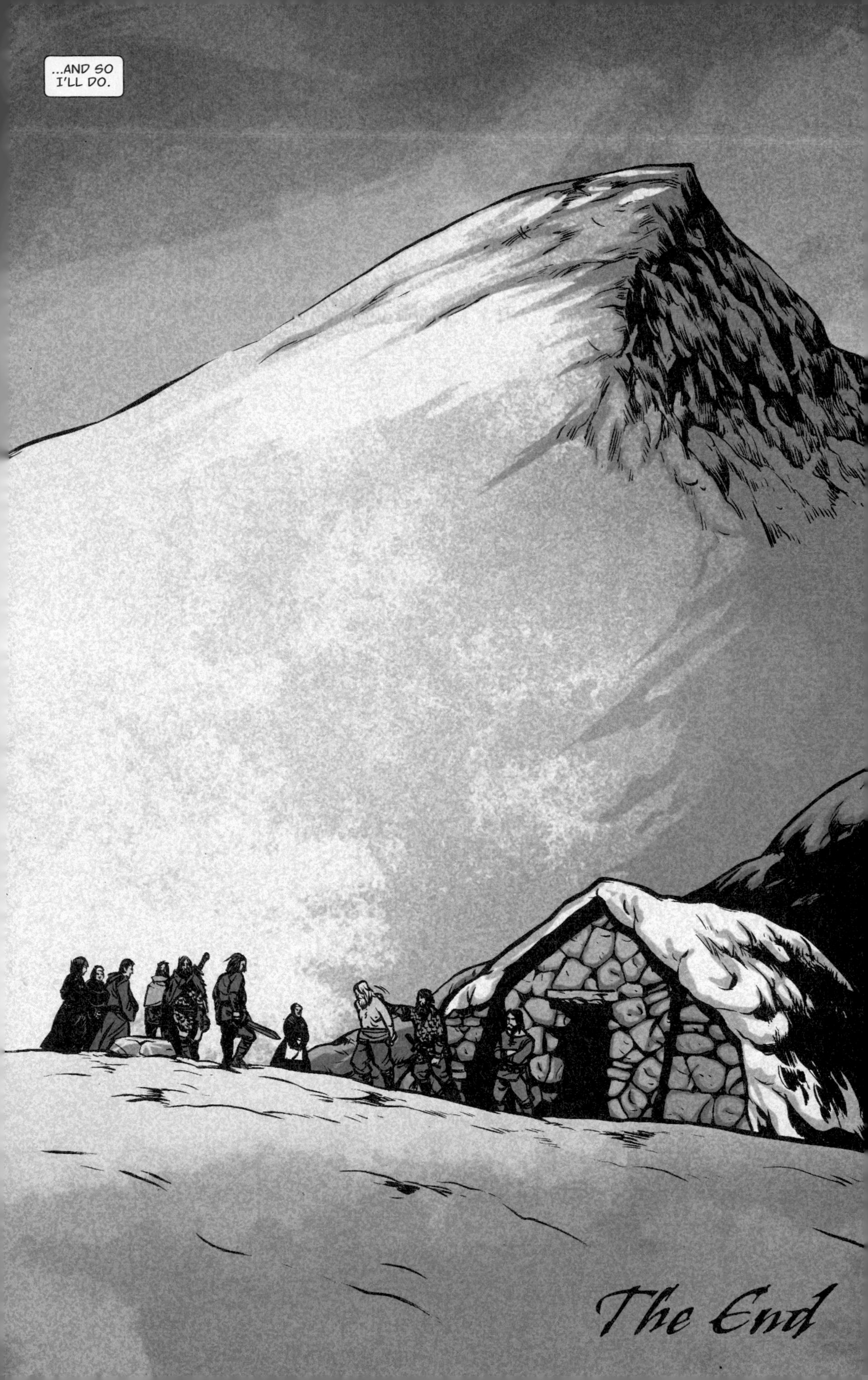
...AND SO I'LL DO.
The End

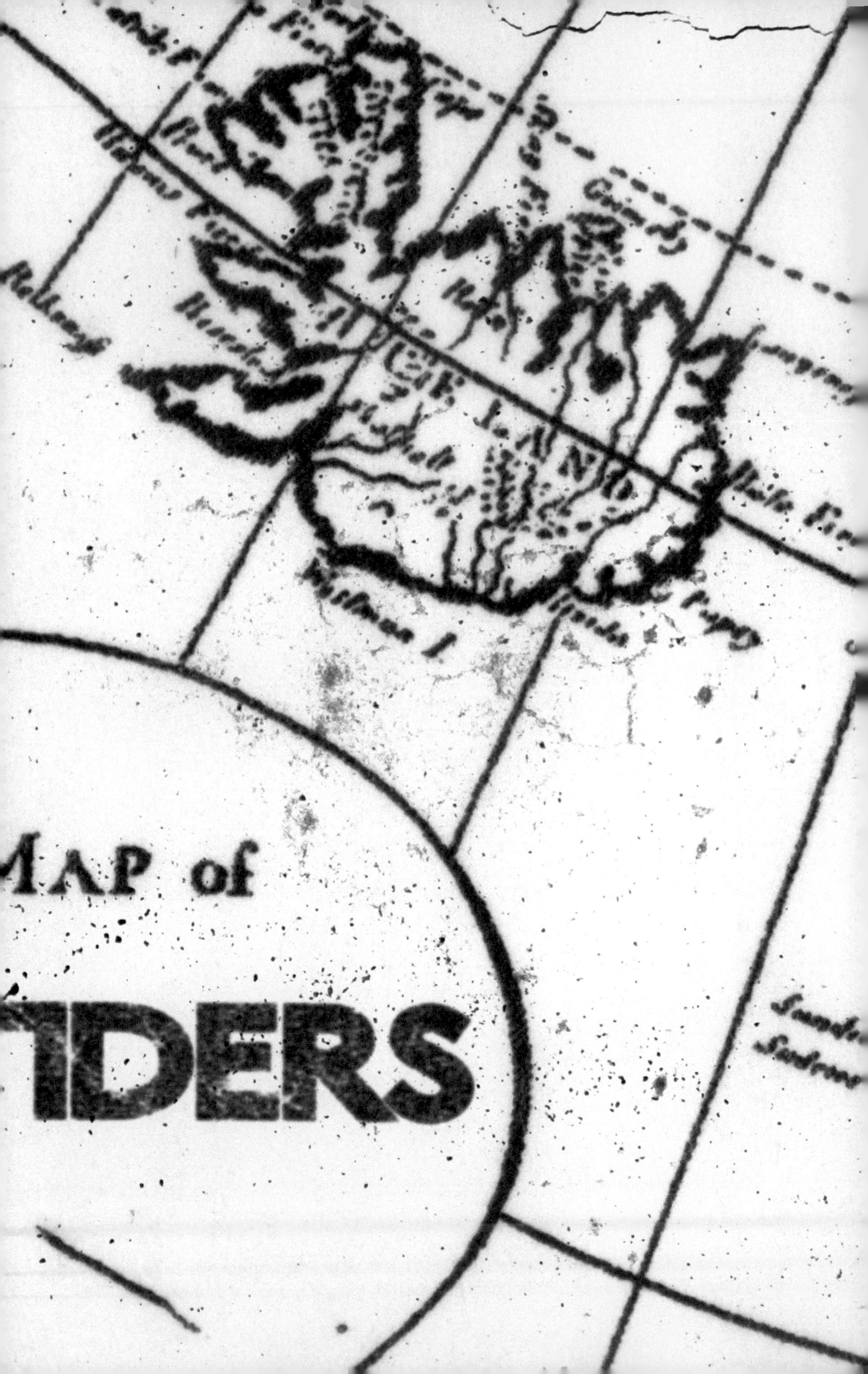
MAP of
IDERS

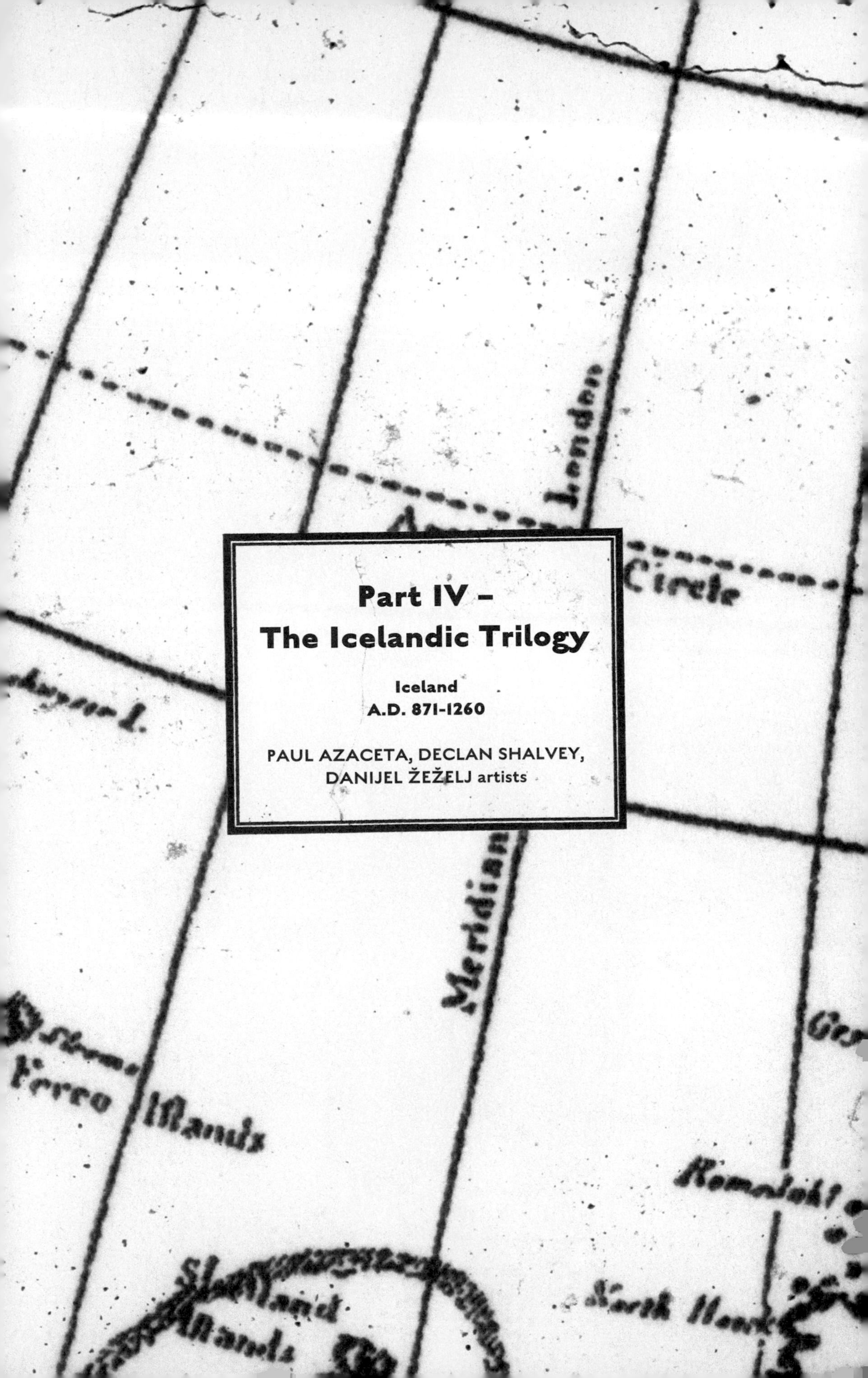
London
Circle
Meridian
Ferro Islands
North

Part IV –
The Icelandic Trilogy

Iceland
A.D. 871-1260

PAUL AZACETA, DECLAN SHALVEY,
DANIJEL ŽEŽELJ artists

Chapter I
Settlement
A.D. 871

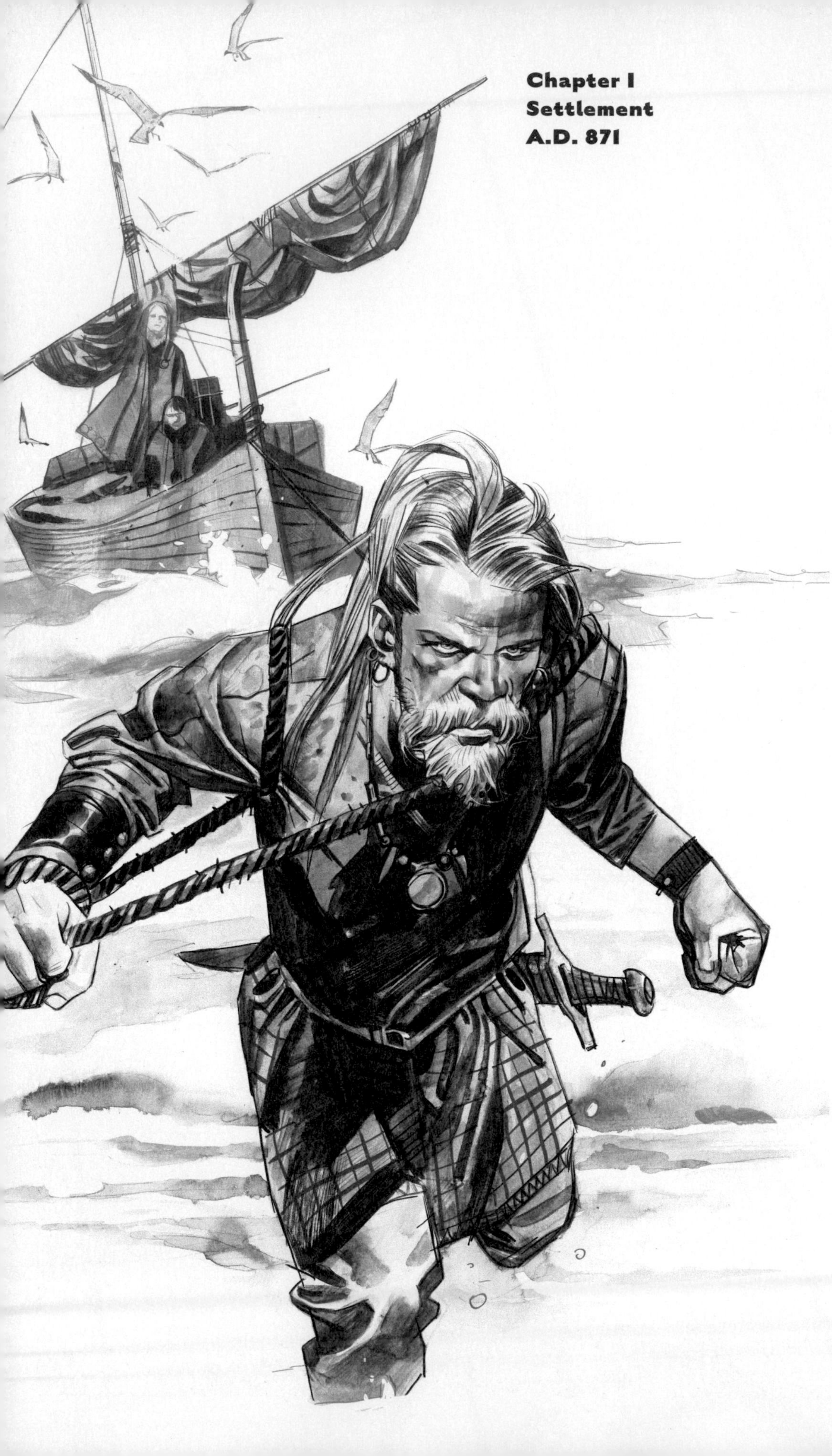

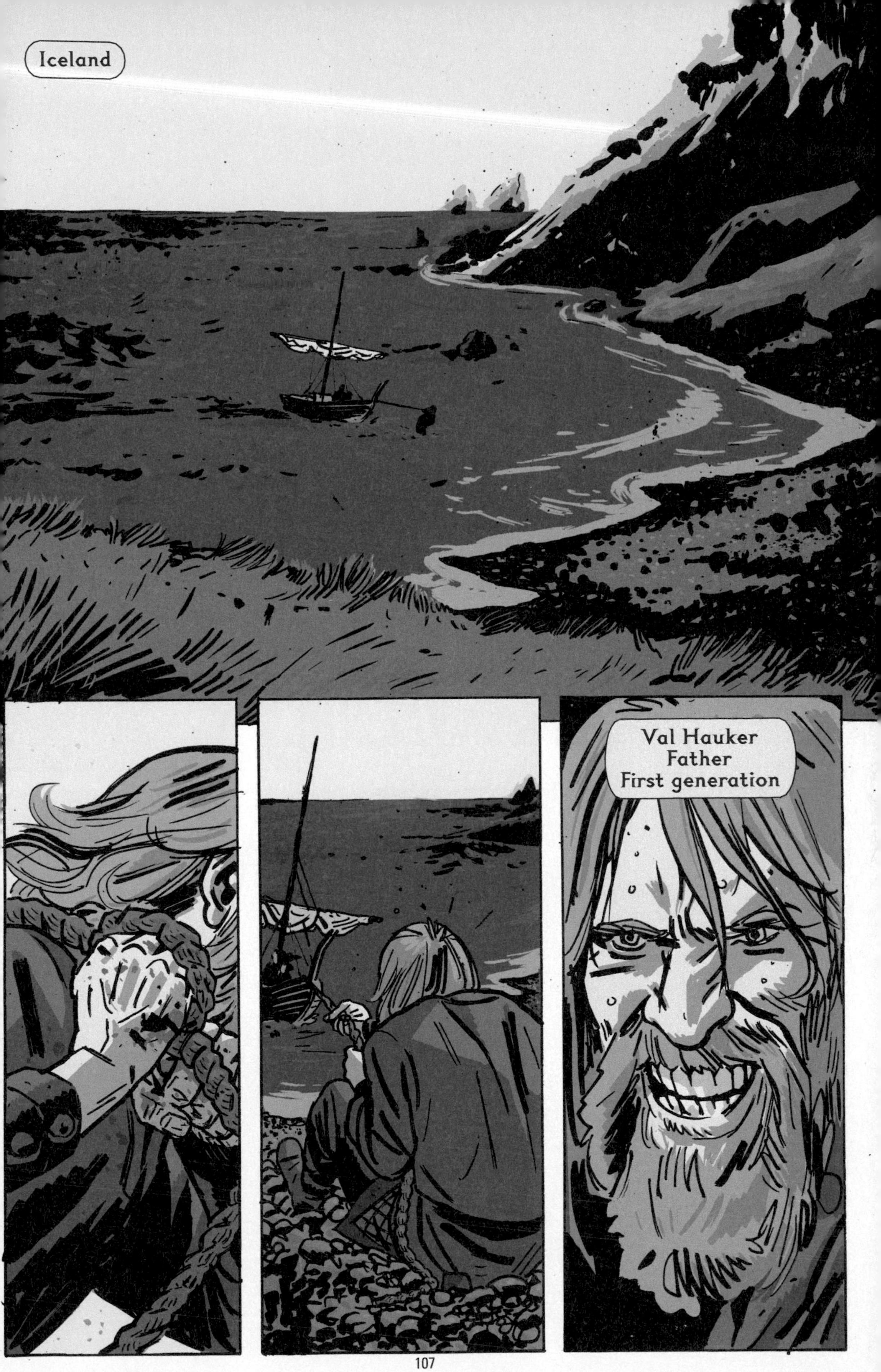
Iceland
Val Hauker
Father
First generation

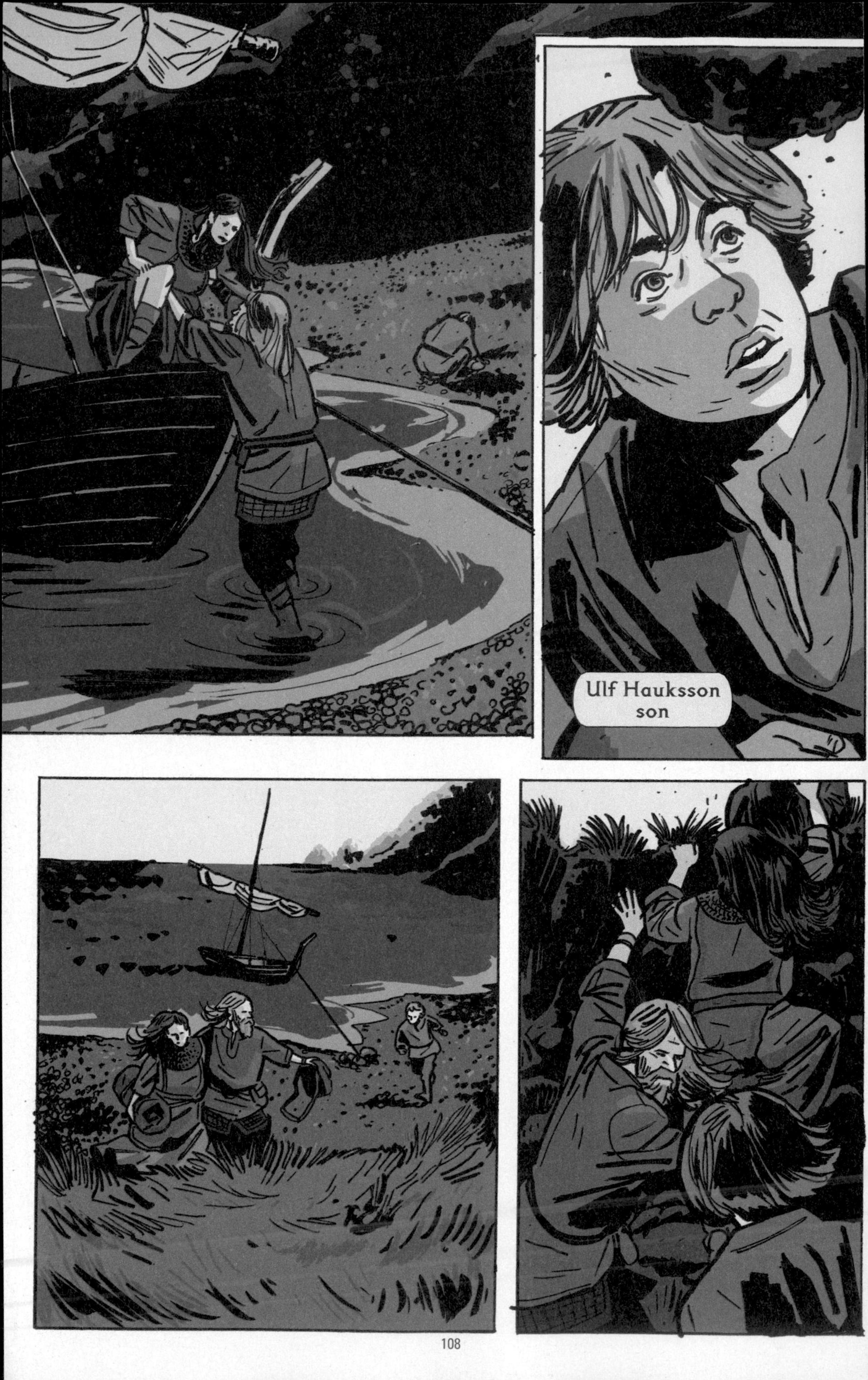
Ulf Hauksson
son

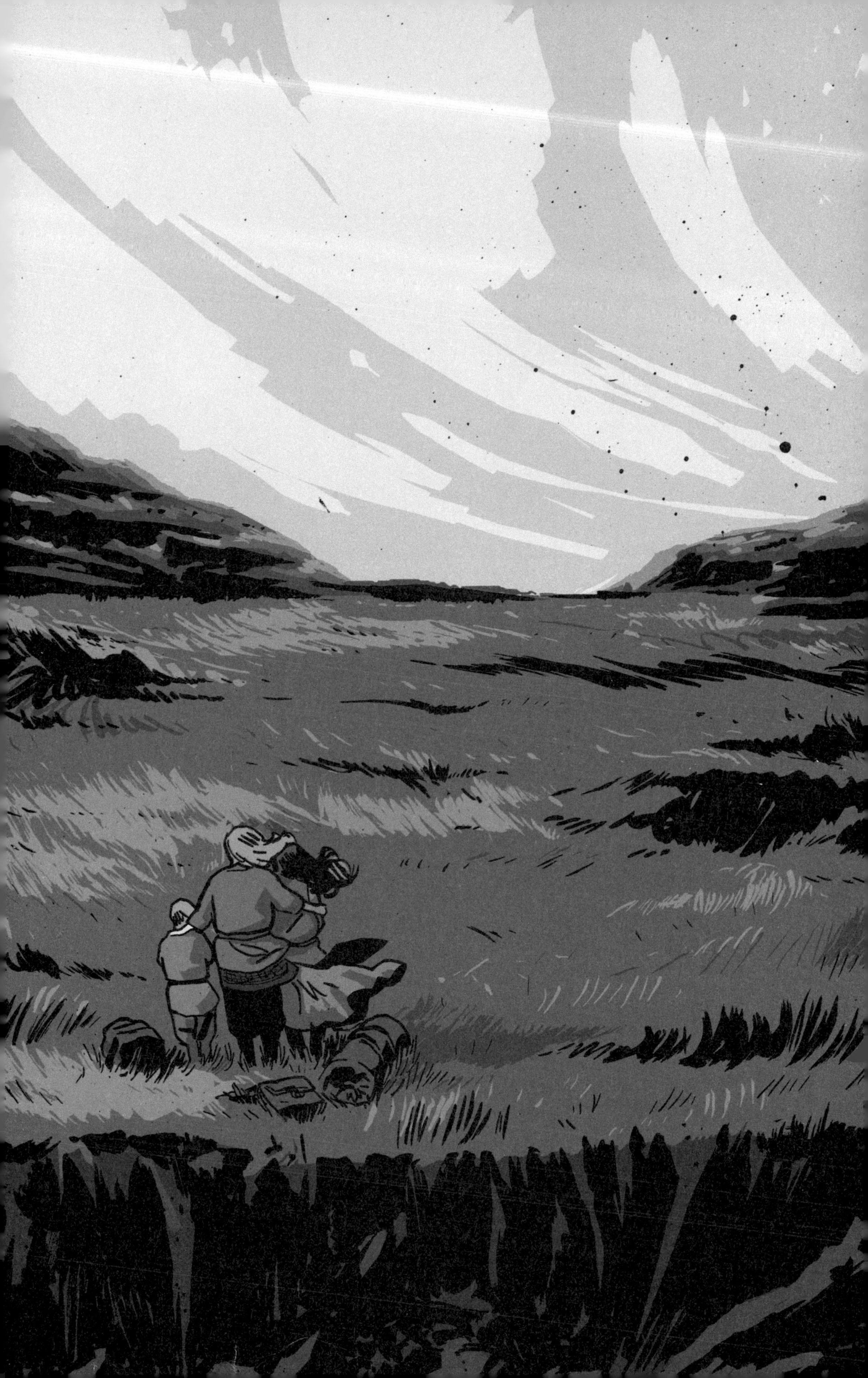

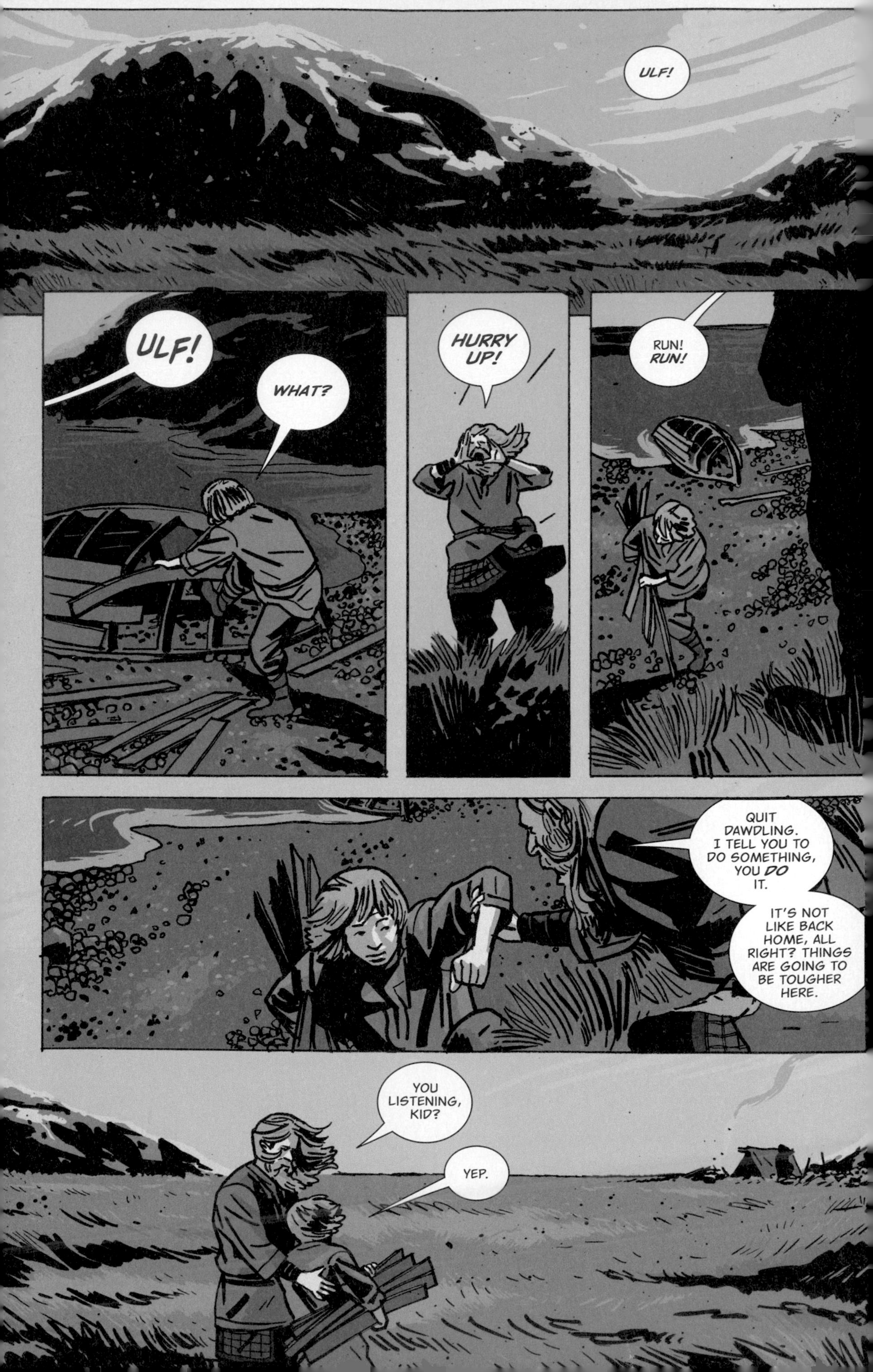
ULF!
ULF!
WHAT?
HURRY UP!
RUN! RUN!
QUIT DAWDLING. I TELL YOU TO DO SOMETHING, YOU DO IT.
IT'S NOT LIKE BACK HOME, ALL RIGHT? THINGS ARE GOING TO BE TOUGHER HERE.
YOU LISTENING, KID?
YEP.

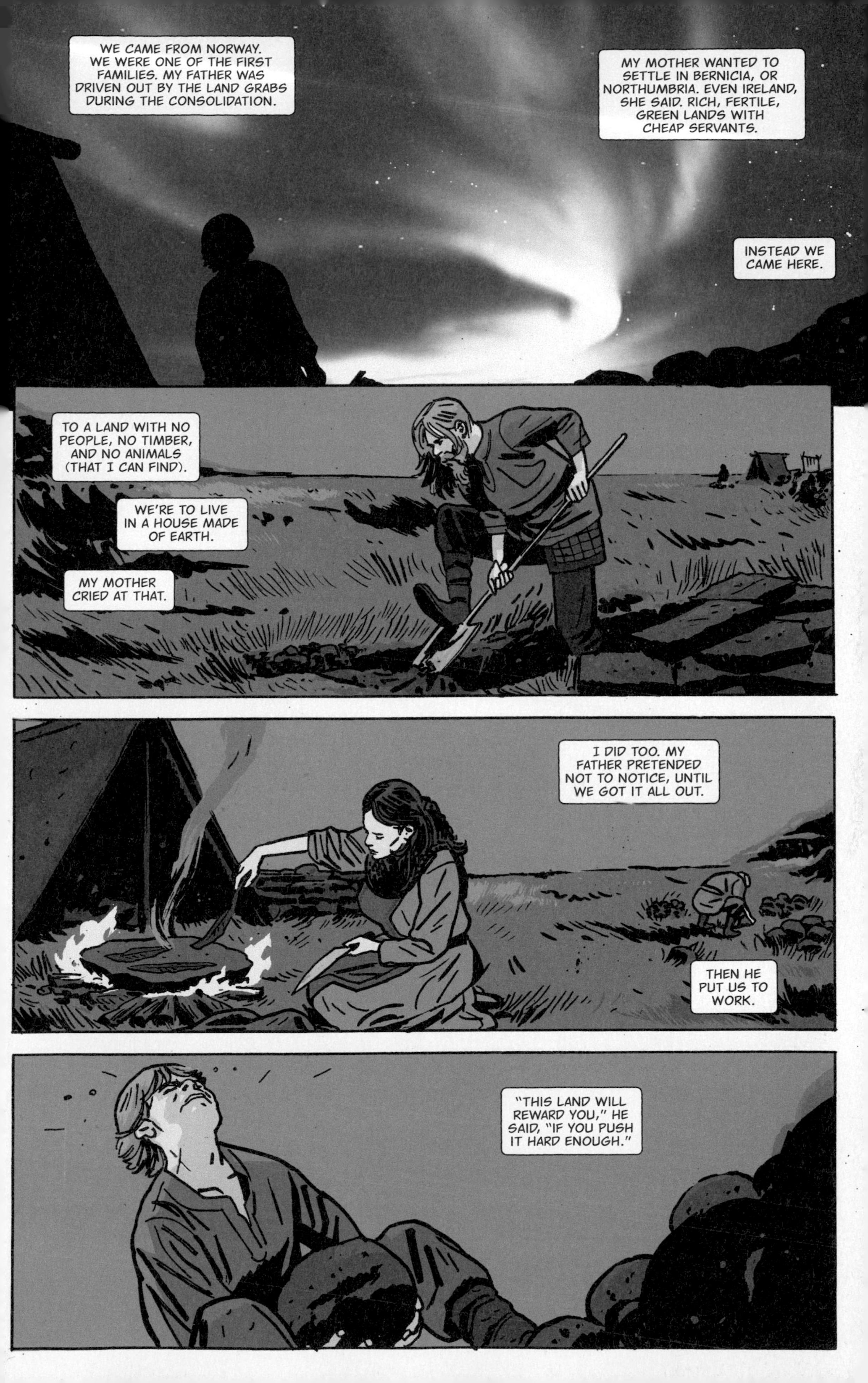
WE CAME FROM NORWAY. WE WERE ONE OF THE FIRST FAMILIES. MY FATHER WAS DRIVEN OUT BY THE LAND GRABS DURING THE CONSOLIDATION.
MY MOTHER WANTED TO SETTLE IN BERNICIA, OR NORTHUMBRIA. EVEN IRELAND, SHE SAID. RICH, FERTILE, GREEN LANDS WITH CHEAP SERVANTS.
INSTEAD WE CAME HERE.
TO A LAND WITH NO PEOPLE, NO TIMBER, AND NO ANIMALS (THAT I CAN FIND).
WE'RE TO LIVE IN A HOUSE MADE OF EARTH.
MY MOTHER CRIED AT THAT.
I DID TOO. MY FATHER PRETENDED NOT TO NOTICE, UNTIL WE GOT IT ALL OUT.
THEN HE PUT US TO WORK.
"THIS LAND WILL REWARD YOU," HE SAID, "IF YOU PUSH IT HARD ENOUGH."

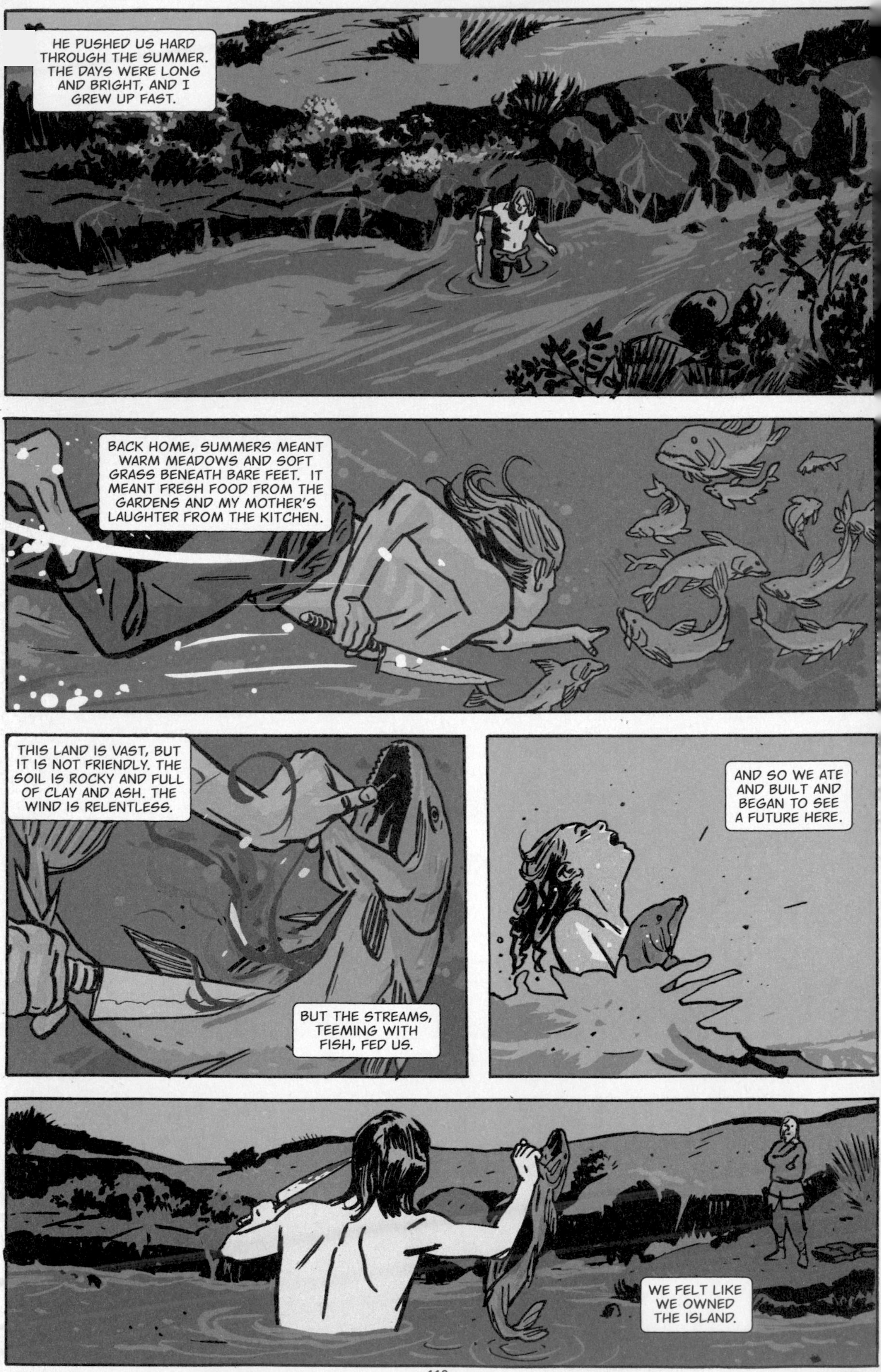
HE PUSHED US HARD THROUGH THE SUMMER. THE DAYS WERE LONG AND BRIGHT, AND I GREW UP FAST.
BACK HOME, SUMMERS MEANT WARM MEADOWS AND SOFT GRASS BENEATH BARE FEET. IT MEANT FRESH FOOD FROM THE GARDENS AND MY MOTHER'S LAUGHTER FROM THE KITCHEN.
THIS LAND IS VAST, BUT IT IS NOT FRIENDLY. THE SOIL IS ROCKY AND FULL OF CLAY AND ASH. THE WIND IS RELENTLESS.
BUT THE STREAMS, TEEMING WITH FISH, FED US.
AND SO WE ATE AND BUILT AND BEGAN TO SEE A FUTURE HERE.
WE FELT LIKE WE OWNED THE ISLAND.

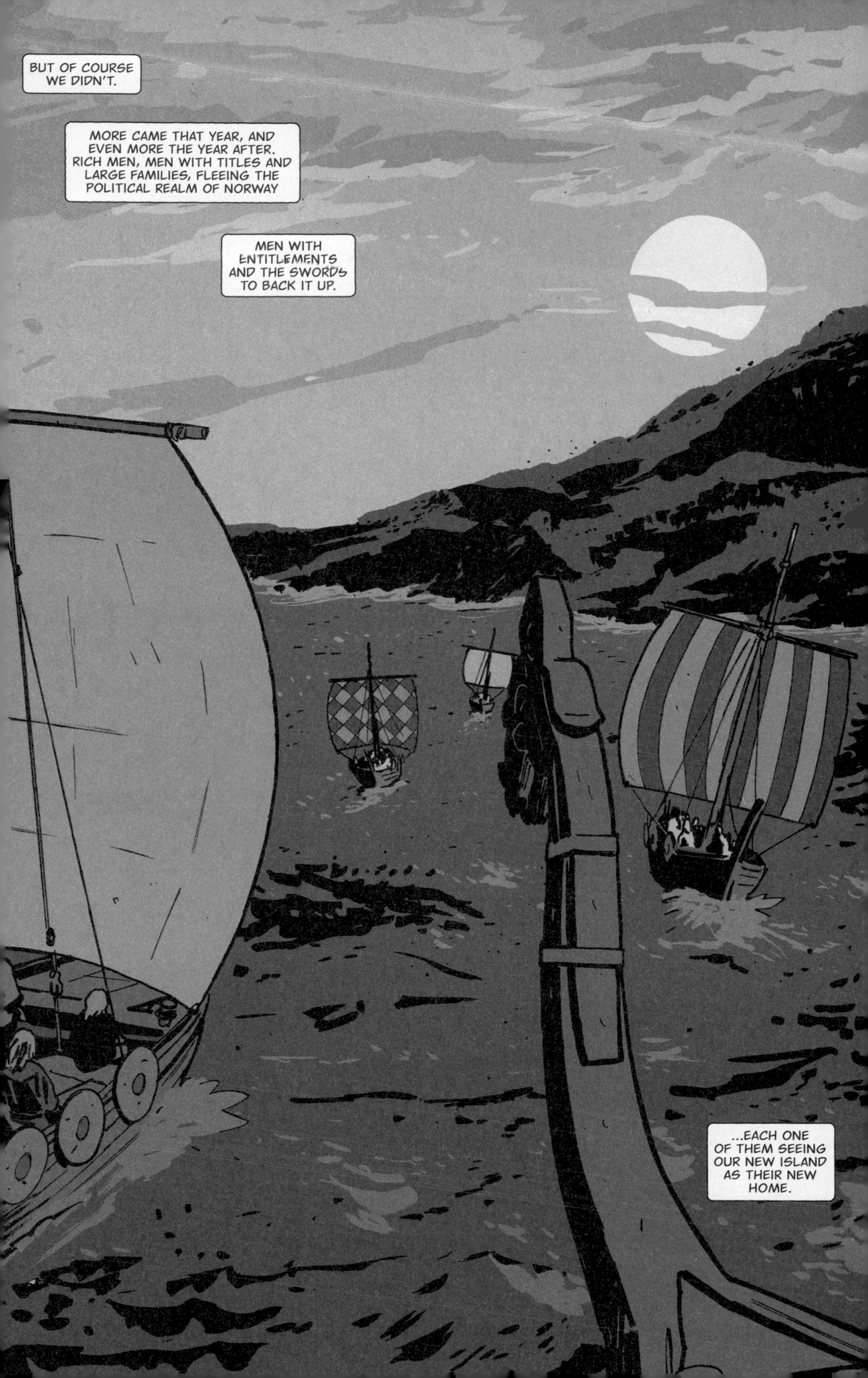
BUT OF COURSE WE DIDN'T.
MORE CAME THAT YEAR, AND EVEN MORE THE YEAR AFTER. RICH MEN, MEN WITH TITLES AND LARGE FAMILIES, FLEEING THE POLITICAL REALM OF NORWAY
MEN WITH ENTITLEMENTS AND THE SWORDS TO BACK IT UP.
...EACH ONE OF THEM SEEING OUR NEW ISLAND AS THEIR NEW HOME.

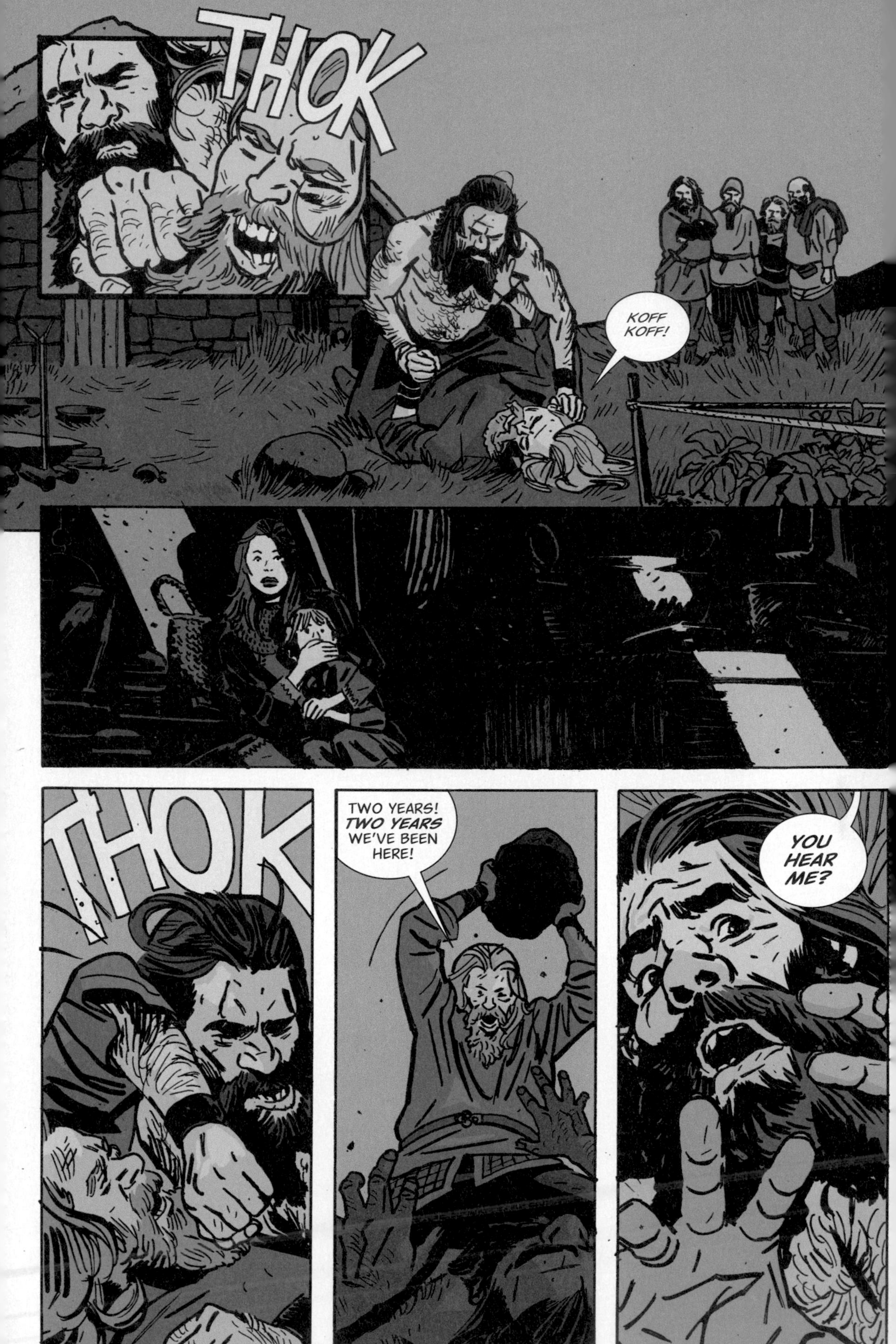
THOK
KOFF KOFF!
THOK
TWO YEARS! *TWO YEARS* WE'VE BEEN HERE!
YOU HEAR ME?

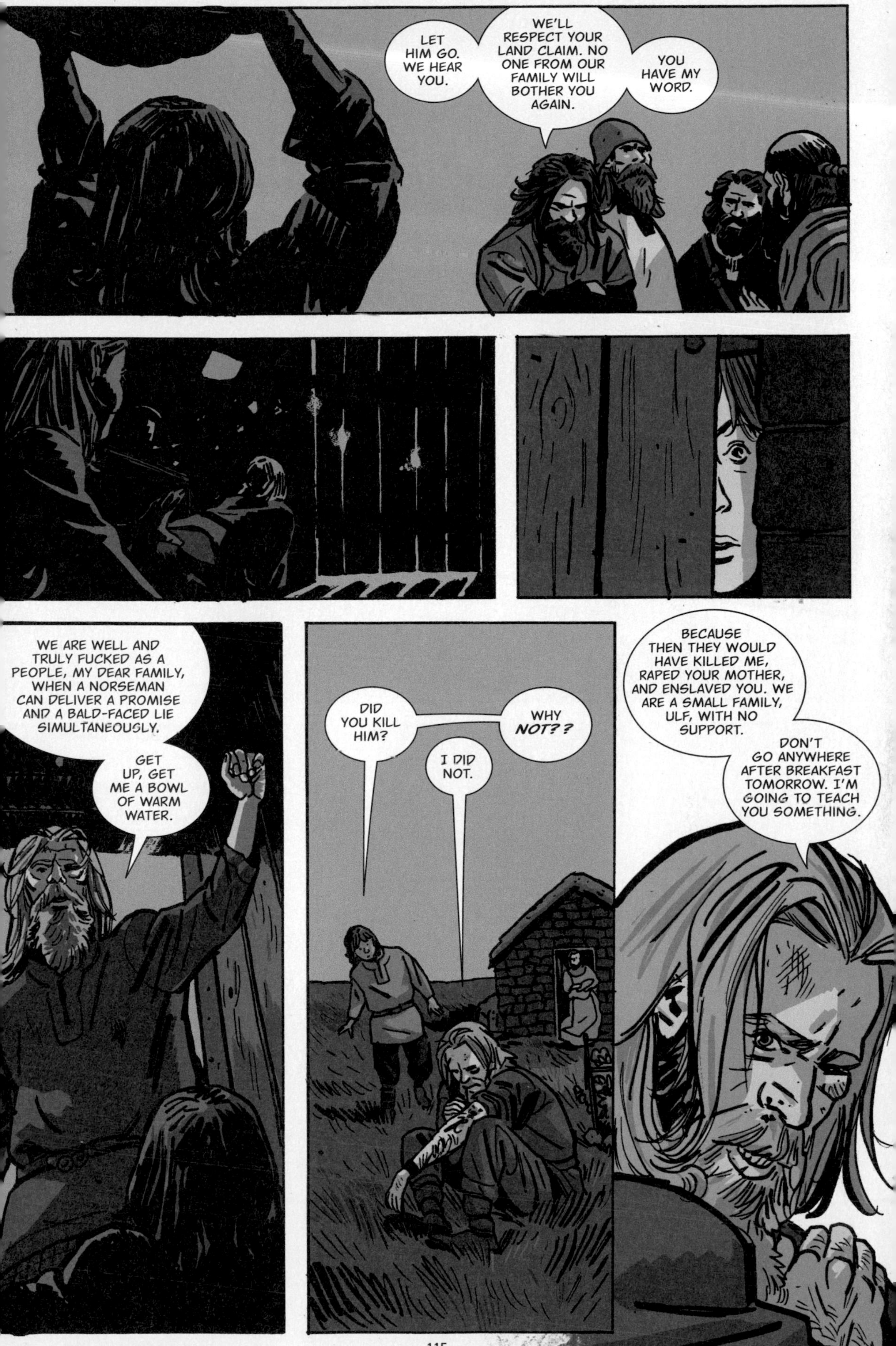
LET HIM GO. WE HEAR YOU.
WE'LL RESPECT YOUR LAND CLAIM. NO ONE FROM OUR FAMILY WILL BOTHER YOU AGAIN.
YOU HAVE MY WORD.
WE ARE WELL AND TRULY FUCKED AS A PEOPLE, MY DEAR FAMILY, WHEN A NORSEMAN CAN DELIVER A PROMISE AND A BALD-FACED LIE SIMULTANEOUSLY.
GET UP, GET ME A BOWL OF WARM WATER.
DID YOU KILL HIM?
I DID NOT.
WHY *NOT??*
BECAUSE THEN THEY WOULD HAVE KILLED ME, RAPED YOUR MOTHER, AND ENSLAVED YOU. WE ARE A SMALL FAMILY, ULF, WITH NO SUPPORT.
DON'T GO ANYWHERE AFTER BREAKFAST TOMORROW. I'M GOING TO TEACH YOU SOMETHING.

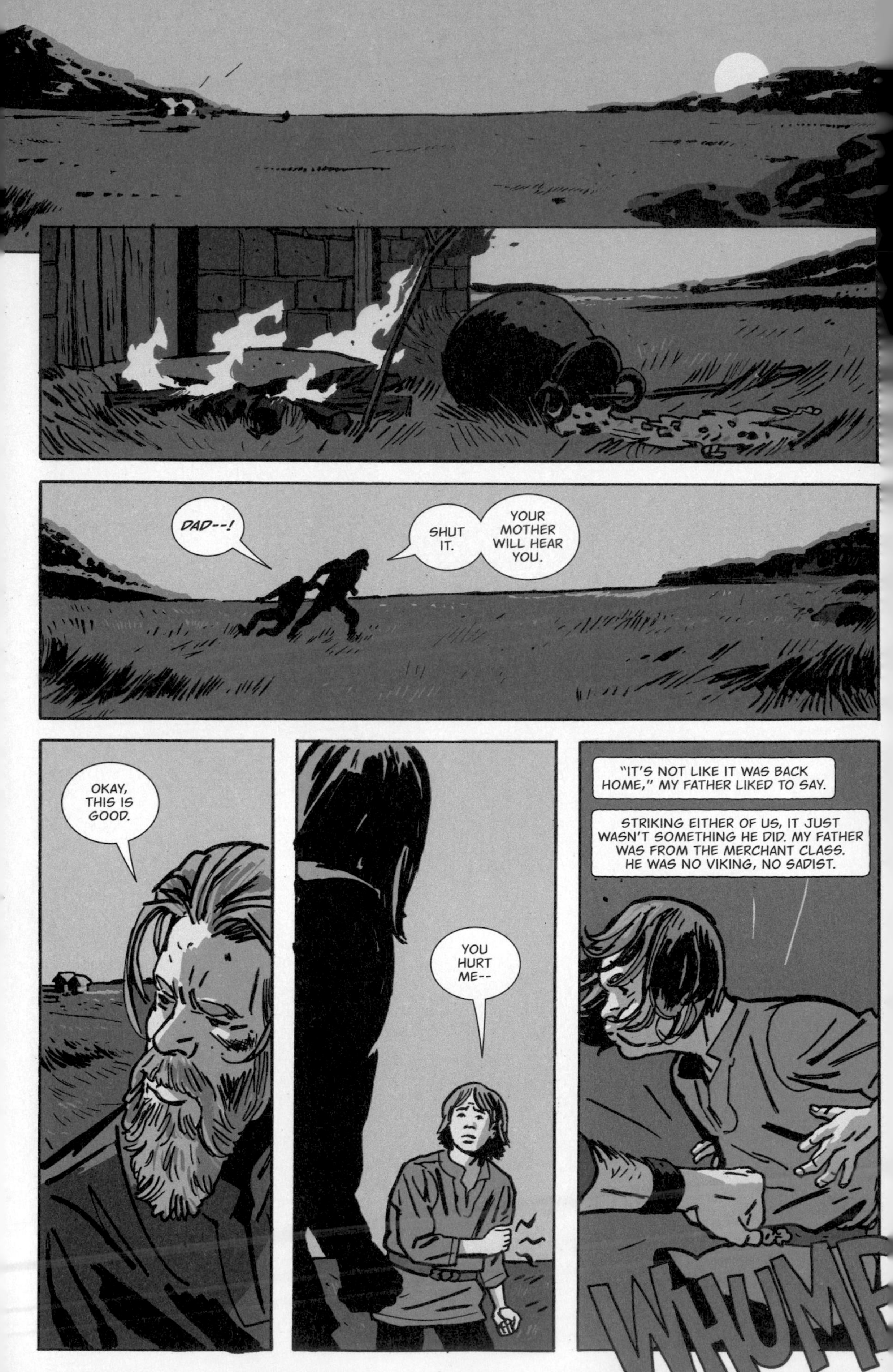
DAD--!
SHUT IT.
YOUR MOTHER WILL HEAR YOU.
OKAY, THIS IS GOOD.
YOU HURT ME--
"IT'S NOT LIKE IT WAS BACK HOME," MY FATHER LIKED TO SAY.
STRIKING EITHER OF US, IT JUST WASN'T SOMETHING HE DID. MY FATHER WAS FROM THE MERCHANT CLASS. HE WAS NO VIKING, NO SADIST.
WHUMP

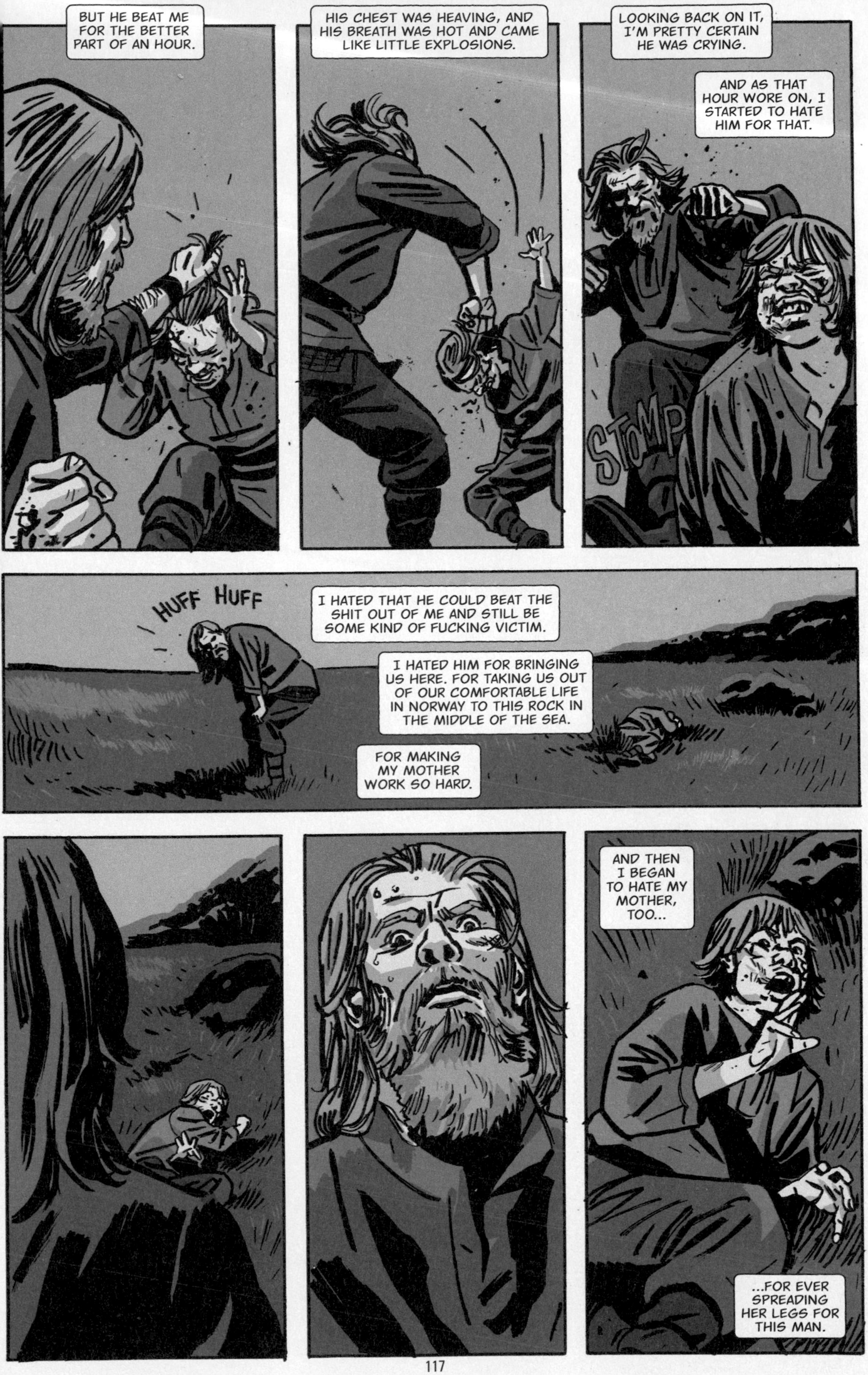
BUT HE BEAT ME FOR THE BETTER PART OF AN HOUR.
HIS CHEST WAS HEAVING, AND HIS BREATH WAS HOT AND CAME LIKE LITTLE EXPLOSIONS.
LOOKING BACK ON IT, I'M PRETTY CERTAIN HE WAS CRYING.
AND AS THAT HOUR WORE ON, I STARTED TO HATE HIM FOR THAT.
STOMP
HUFF HUFF
I HATED THAT HE COULD BEAT THE SHIT OUT OF ME AND STILL BE SOME KIND OF FUCKING VICTIM.
I HATED HIM FOR BRINGING US HERE. FOR TAKING US OUT OF OUR COMFORTABLE LIFE IN NORWAY TO THIS ROCK IN THE MIDDLE OF THE SEA.
FOR MAKING MY MOTHER WORK SO HARD.
AND THEN I BEGAN TO HATE MY MOTHER, TOO...
...FOR EVER SPREADING HER LEGS FOR THIS MAN.

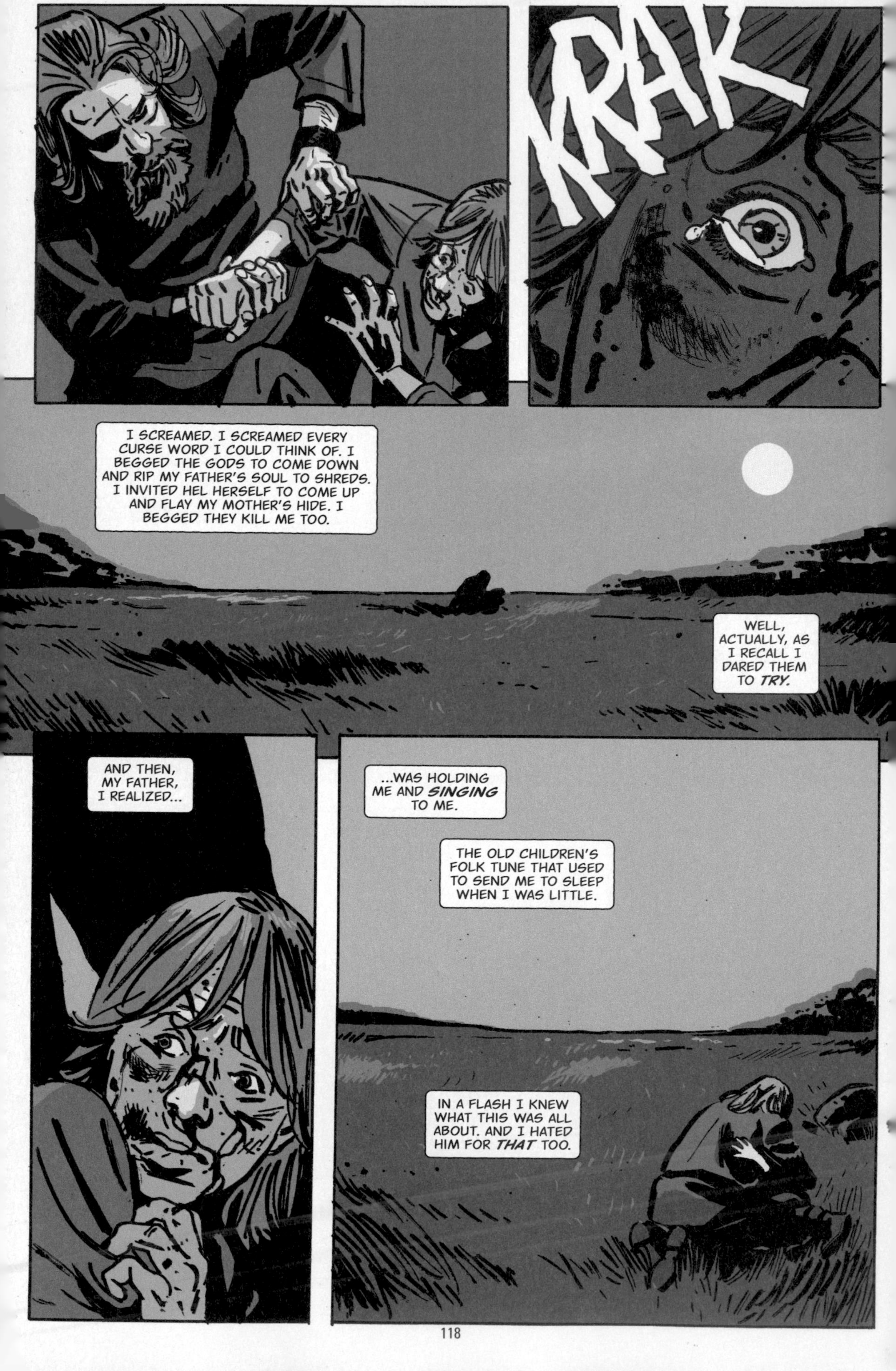
KRAK
I SCREAMED. I SCREAMED EVERY CURSE WORD I COULD THINK OF. I BEGGED THE GODS TO COME DOWN AND RIP MY FATHER'S SOUL TO SHREDS. I INVITED HEL HERSELF TO COME UP AND FLAY MY MOTHER'S HIDE. I BEGGED THEY KILL ME TOO.
WELL, ACTUALLY, AS I RECALL I DARED THEM TO *TRY.*
AND THEN, MY FATHER, I REALIZED...
...WAS HOLDING ME AND *SINGING* TO ME.
THE OLD CHILDREN'S FOLK TUNE THAT USED TO SEND ME TO SLEEP WHEN I WAS LITTLE.
IN A FLASH I KNEW WHAT THIS WAS ALL ABOUT. AND I HATED HIM FOR *THAT* TOO.

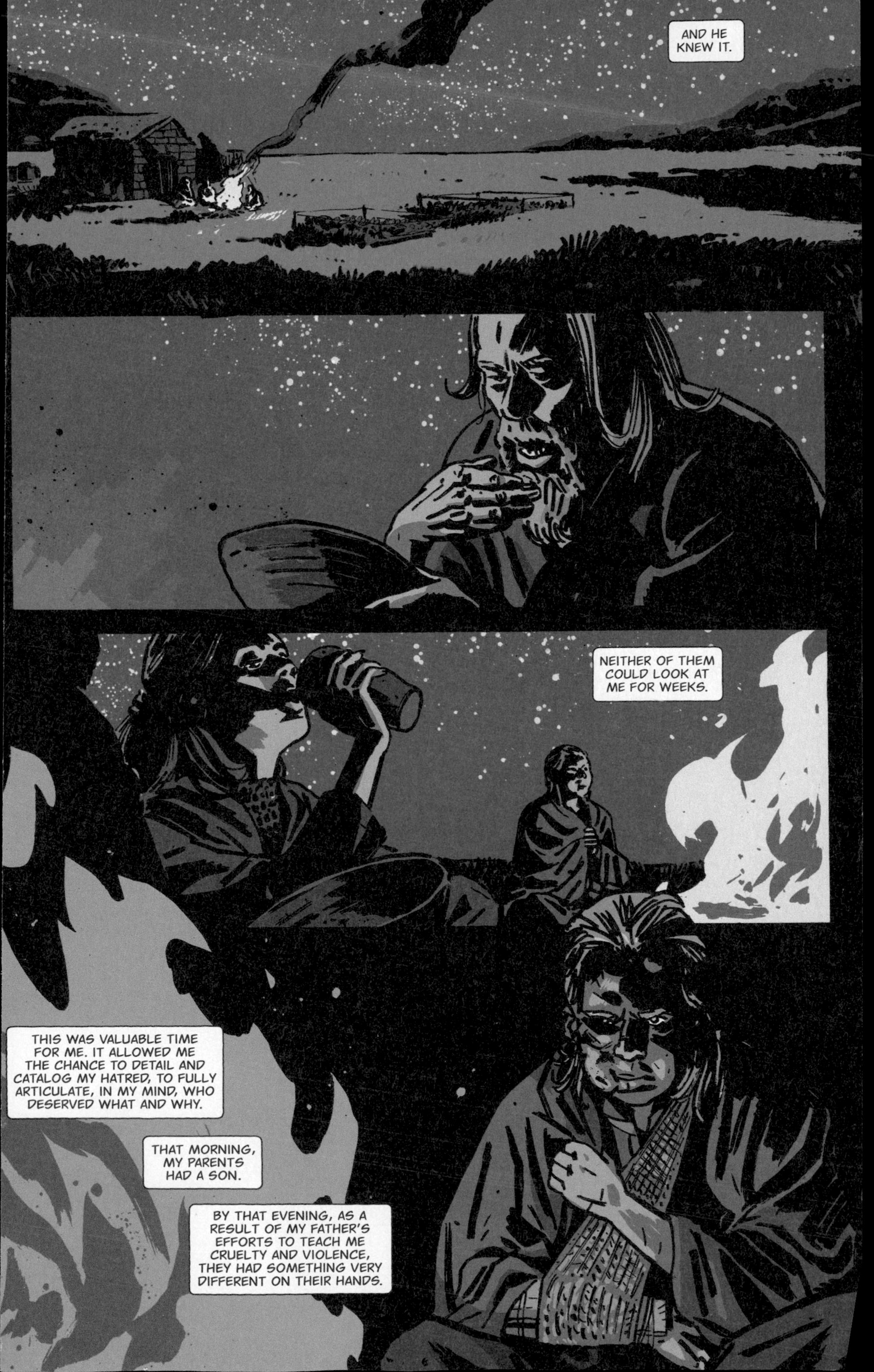
AND HE KNEW IT.
NEITHER OF THEM COULD LOOK AT ME FOR WEEKS.
THIS WAS VALUABLE TIME FOR ME. IT ALLOWED ME THE CHANCE TO DETAIL AND CATALOG MY HATRED, TO FULLY ARTICULATE, IN MY MIND, WHO DESERVED WHAT AND WHY.
THAT MORNING, MY PARENTS HAD A SON.
BY THAT EVENING, AS A RESULT OF MY FATHER'S EFFORTS TO TEACH ME CRUELTY AND VIOLENCE, THEY HAD SOMETHING VERY DIFFERENT ON THEIR HANDS.

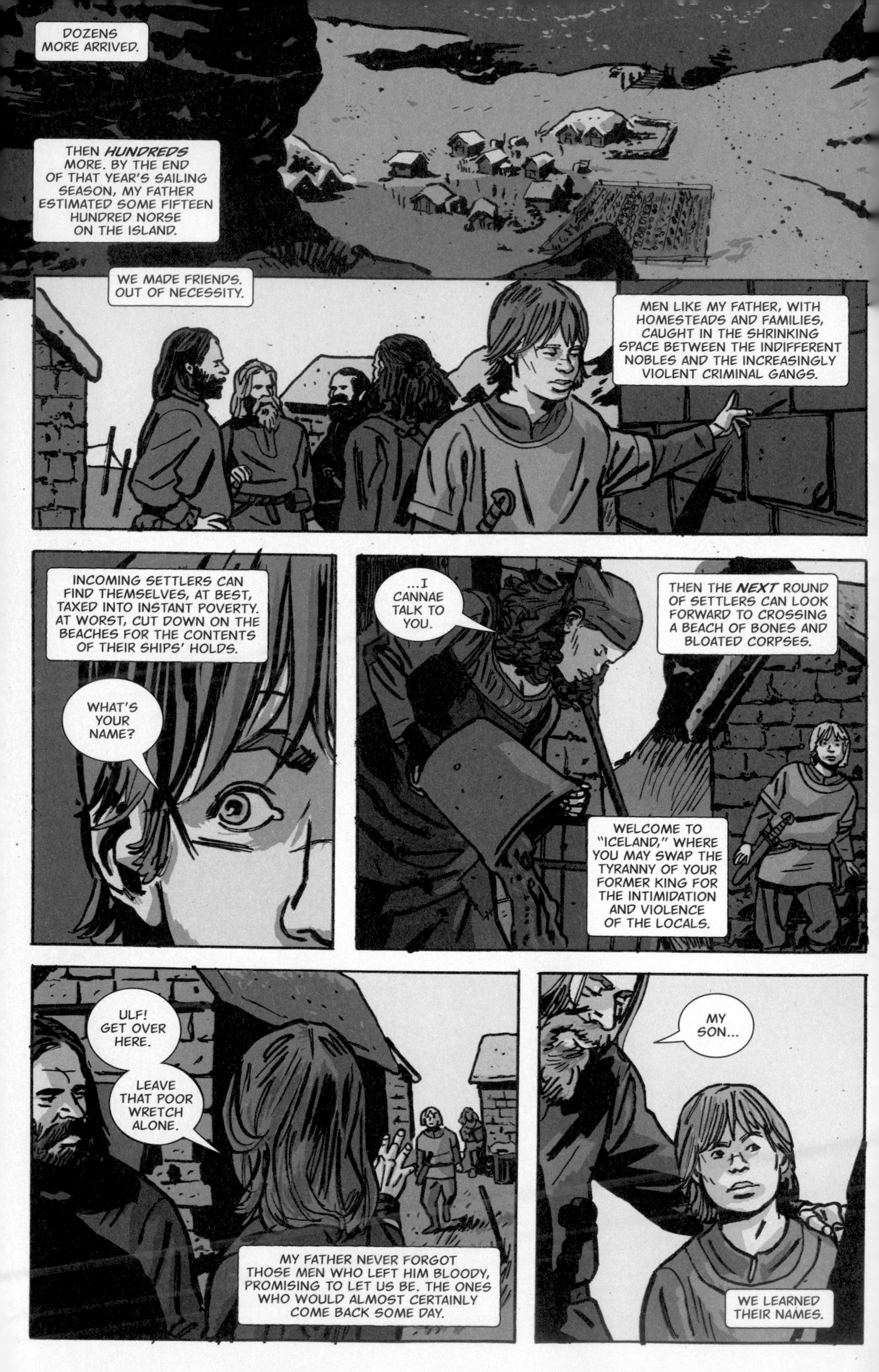
DOZENS MORE ARRIVED.
THEN *HUNDREDS* MORE. BY THE END OF THAT YEAR'S SAILING SEASON, MY FATHER ESTIMATED SOME FIFTEEN HUNDRED NORSE ON THE ISLAND.
WE MADE FRIENDS. OUT OF NECESSITY.
MEN LIKE MY FATHER, WITH HOMESTEADS AND FAMILIES, CAUGHT IN THE SHRINKING SPACE BETWEEN THE INDIFFERENT NOBLES AND THE INCREASINGLY VIOLENT CRIMINAL GANGS.
INCOMING SETTLERS CAN FIND THEMSELVES, AT BEST, TAXED INTO INSTANT POVERTY. AT WORST, CUT DOWN ON THE BEACHES FOR THE CONTENTS OF THEIR SHIPS' HOLDS.
WHAT'S YOUR NAME?
...I CANNAE TALK TO YOU.
THEN THE *NEXT* ROUND OF SETTLERS CAN LOOK FORWARD TO CROSSING A BEACH OF BONES AND BLOATED CORPSES.
WELCOME TO "ICELAND," WHERE YOU MAY SWAP THE TYRANNY OF YOUR FORMER KING FOR THE INTIMIDATION AND VIOLENCE OF THE LOCALS.
ULF! GET OVER HERE.
LEAVE THAT POOR WRETCH ALONE.
MY FATHER NEVER FORGOT THOSE MEN WHO LEFT HIM BLOODY, PROMISING TO LET US BE. THE ONES WHO WOULD ALMOST CERTAINLY COME BACK SOME DAY.
MY SON...
WE LEARNED THEIR NAMES.

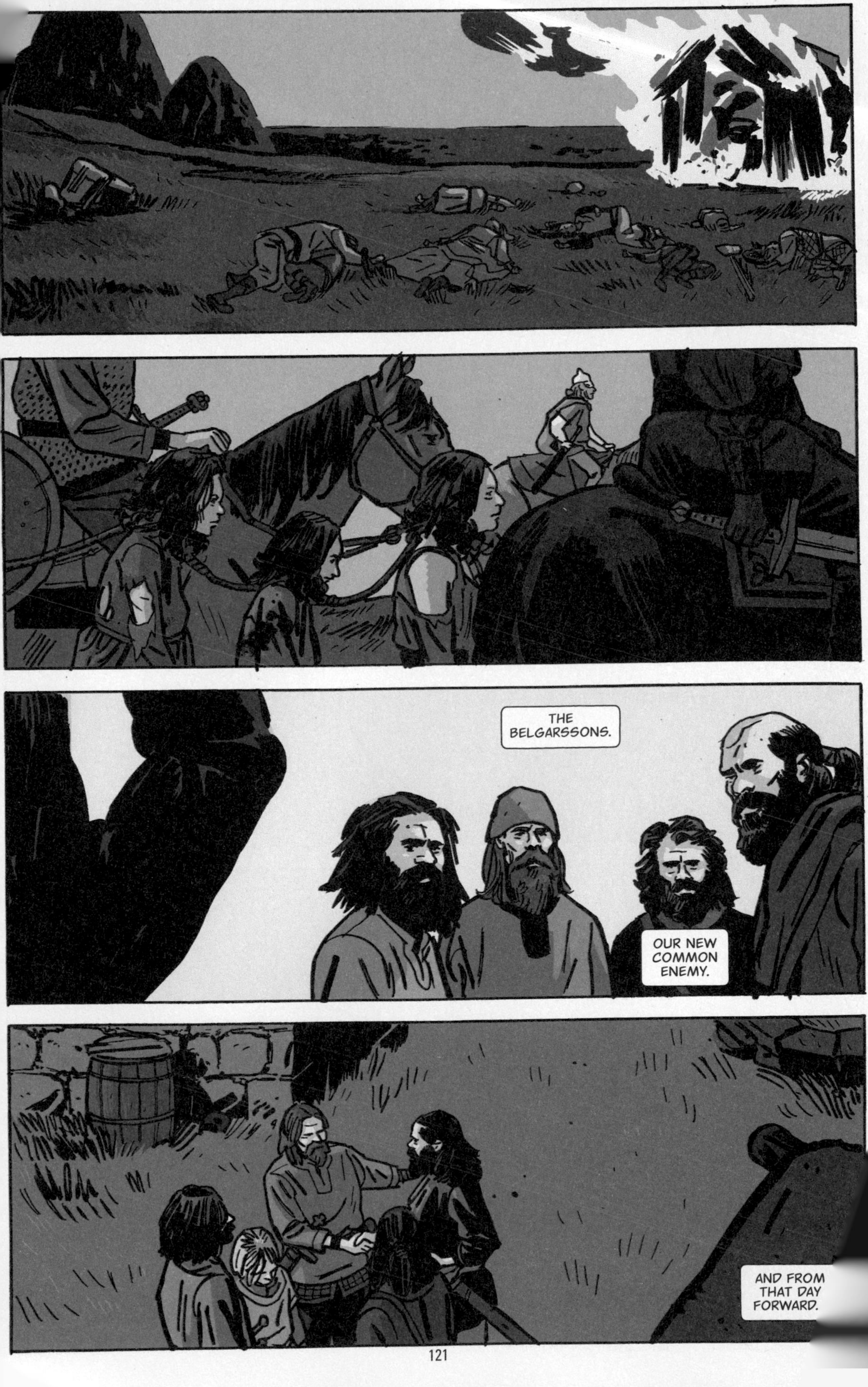
THE BELGARSSONS.
OUR NEW COMMON ENEMY.
AND FROM THAT DAY FORWARD.

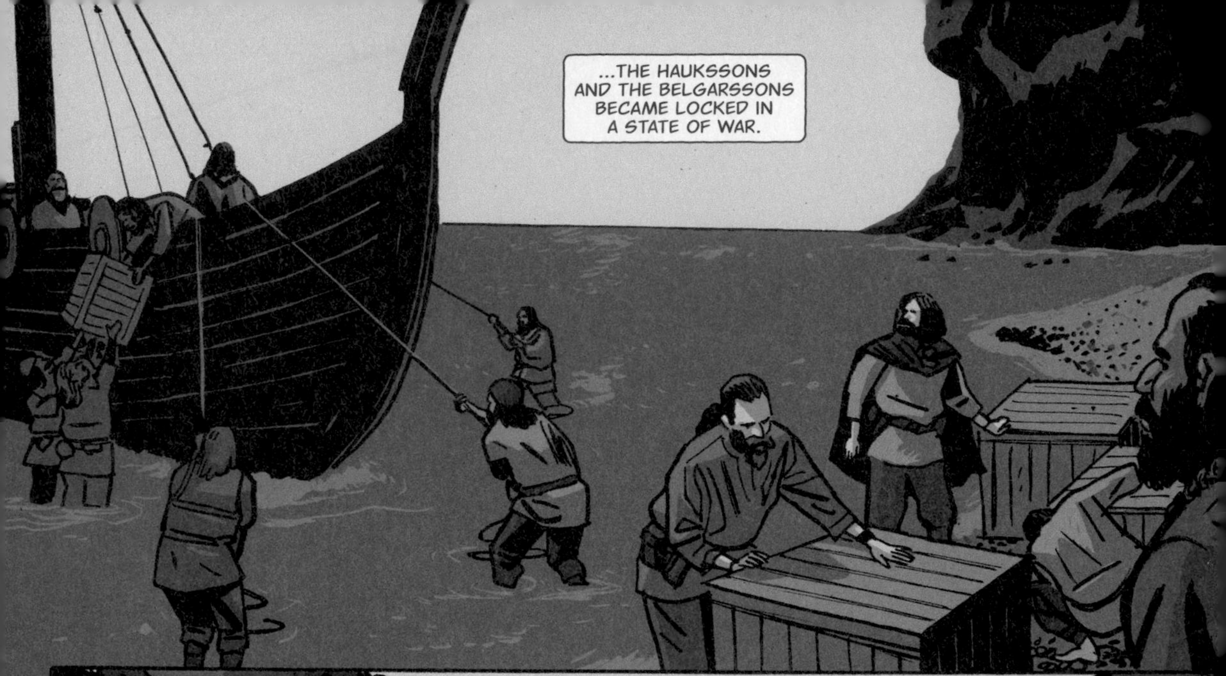
...THE HAUKSSONS AND THE BELGARSSONS BECAME LOCKED IN A STATE OF WAR.

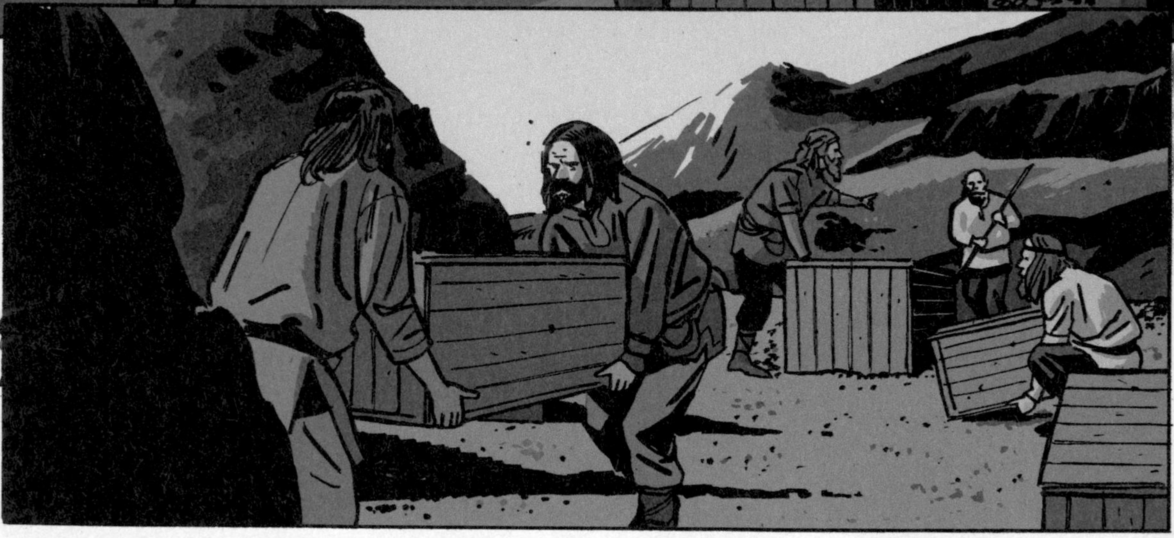

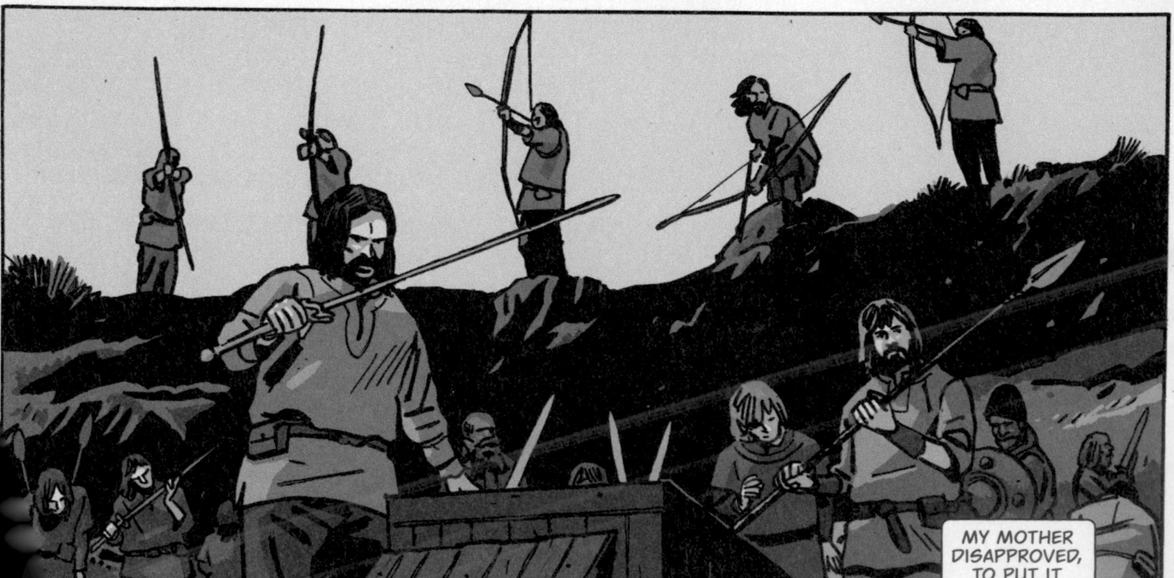
MY MOTHER DISAPPROVED, TO PUT IT MILDLY.

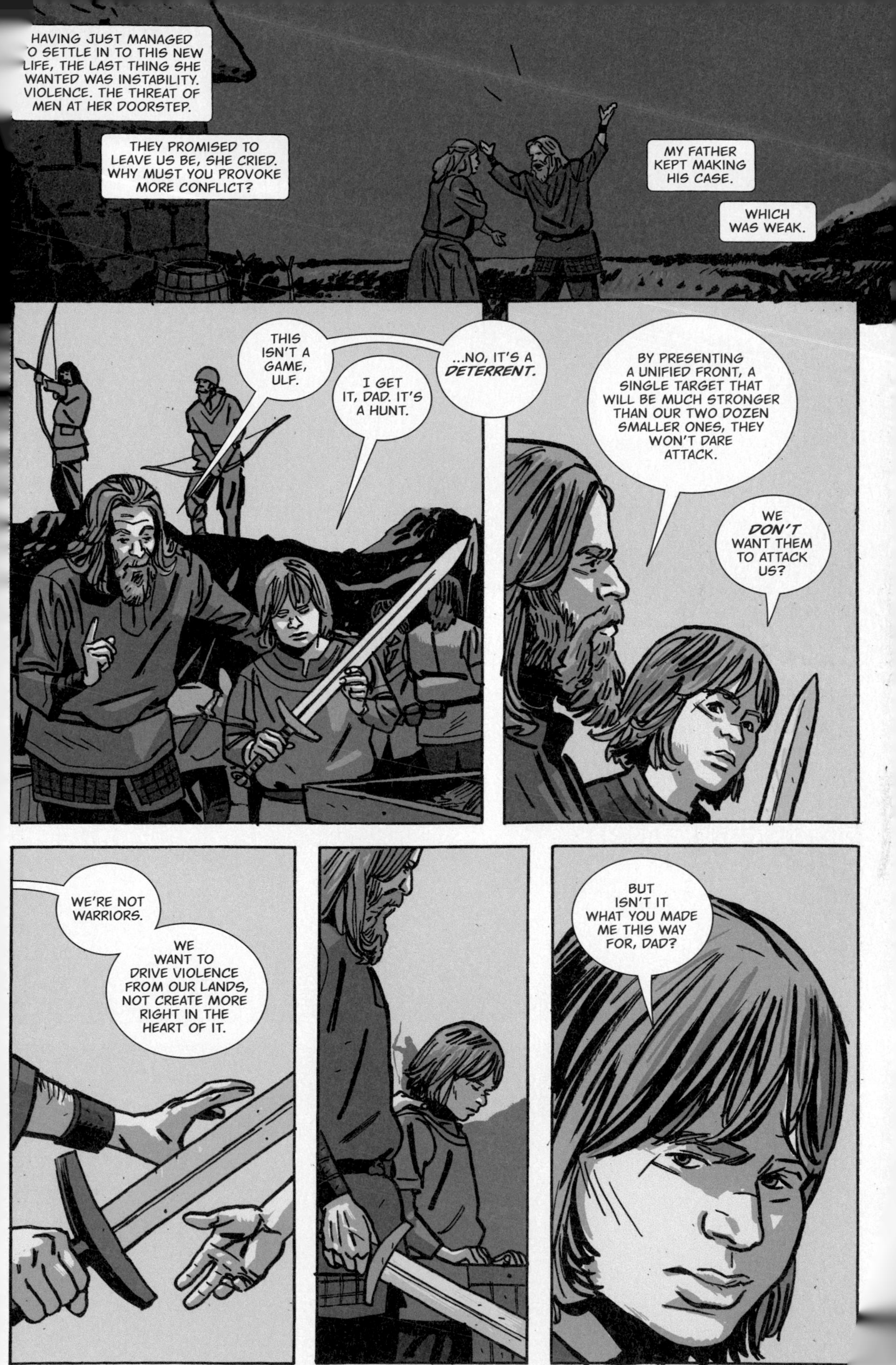
HAVING JUST MANAGED TO SETTLE IN TO THIS NEW LIFE, THE LAST THING SHE WANTED WAS INSTABILITY. VIOLENCE. THE THREAT OF MEN AT HER DOORSTEP.
THEY PROMISED TO LEAVE US BE, SHE CRIED. WHY MUST YOU PROVOKE MORE CONFLICT?
MY FATHER KEPT MAKING HIS CASE.
WHICH WAS WEAK.
THIS ISN'T A GAME, ULF.
I GET IT, DAD. IT'S A HUNT.
...NO, IT'S A *DETERRENT.*
BY PRESENTING A UNIFIED FRONT, A SINGLE TARGET THAT WILL BE MUCH STRONGER THAN OUR TWO DOZEN SMALLER ONES, THEY WON'T DARE ATTACK.
WE *DON'T* WANT THEM TO ATTACK US?
WE'RE NOT WARRIORS.
WE WANT TO DRIVE VIOLENCE FROM OUR LANDS, NOT CREATE MORE RIGHT IN THE HEART OF IT.
BUT ISN'T IT WHAT YOU MADE ME THIS WAY FOR, DAD?

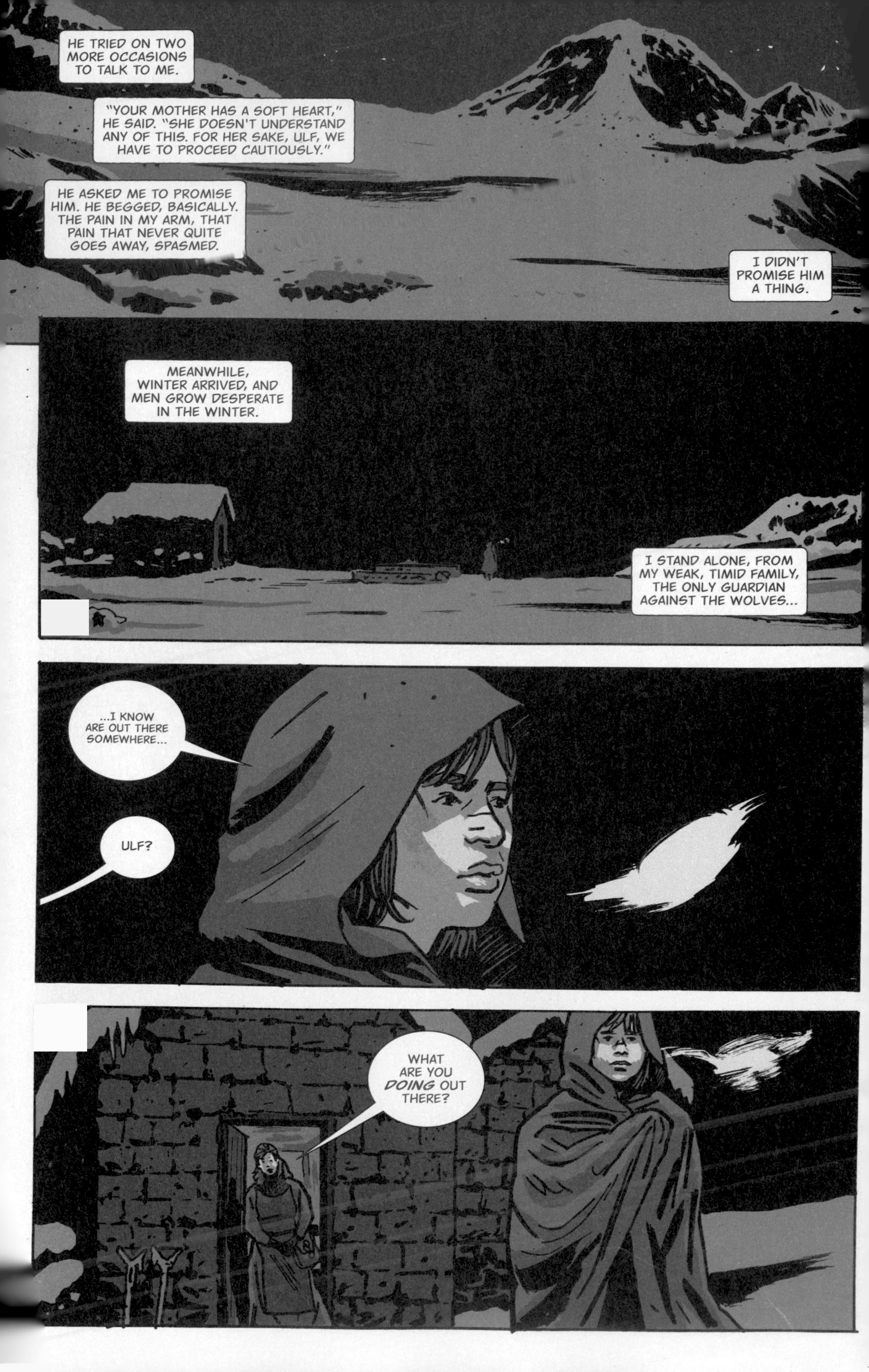

HE TRIED ON TWO MORE OCCASIONS TO TALK TO ME.
"YOUR MOTHER HAS A SOFT HEART," HE SAID. "SHE DOESN'T UNDERSTAND ANY OF THIS. FOR HER SAKE, ULF, WE HAVE TO PROCEED CAUTIOUSLY."
HE ASKED ME TO PROMISE HIM. HE BEGGED, BASICALLY. THE PAIN IN MY ARM, THAT PAIN THAT NEVER QUITE GOES AWAY, SPASMED.
I DIDN'T PROMISE HIM A THING.
MEANWHILE, WINTER ARRIVED, AND MEN GROW DESPERATE IN THE WINTER.
I STAND ALONE, FROM MY WEAK, TIMID FAMILY, THE ONLY GUARDIAN AGAINST THE WOLVES...
...I KNOW ARE OUT THERE SOMEWHERE...
ULF?
WHAT ARE YOU DOING OUT THERE?

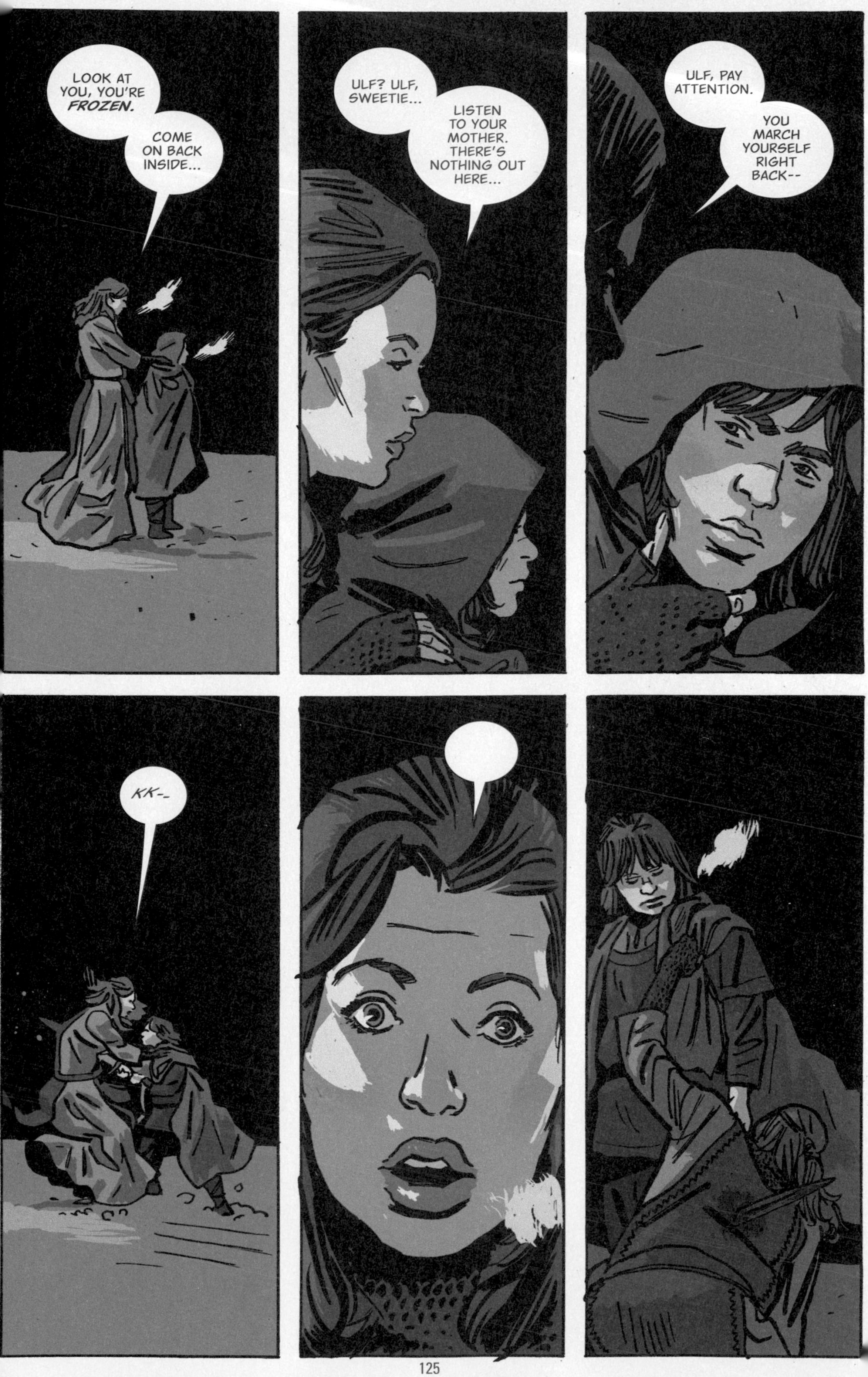
LOOK AT YOU, YOU'RE *FROZEN.*
COME ON BACK INSIDE...
ULF? ULF, SWEETIE...
LISTEN TO YOUR MOTHER. THERE'S NOTHING OUT HERE...
ULF, PAY ATTENTION.
YOU MARCH YOURSELF RIGHT BACK--
KK-_

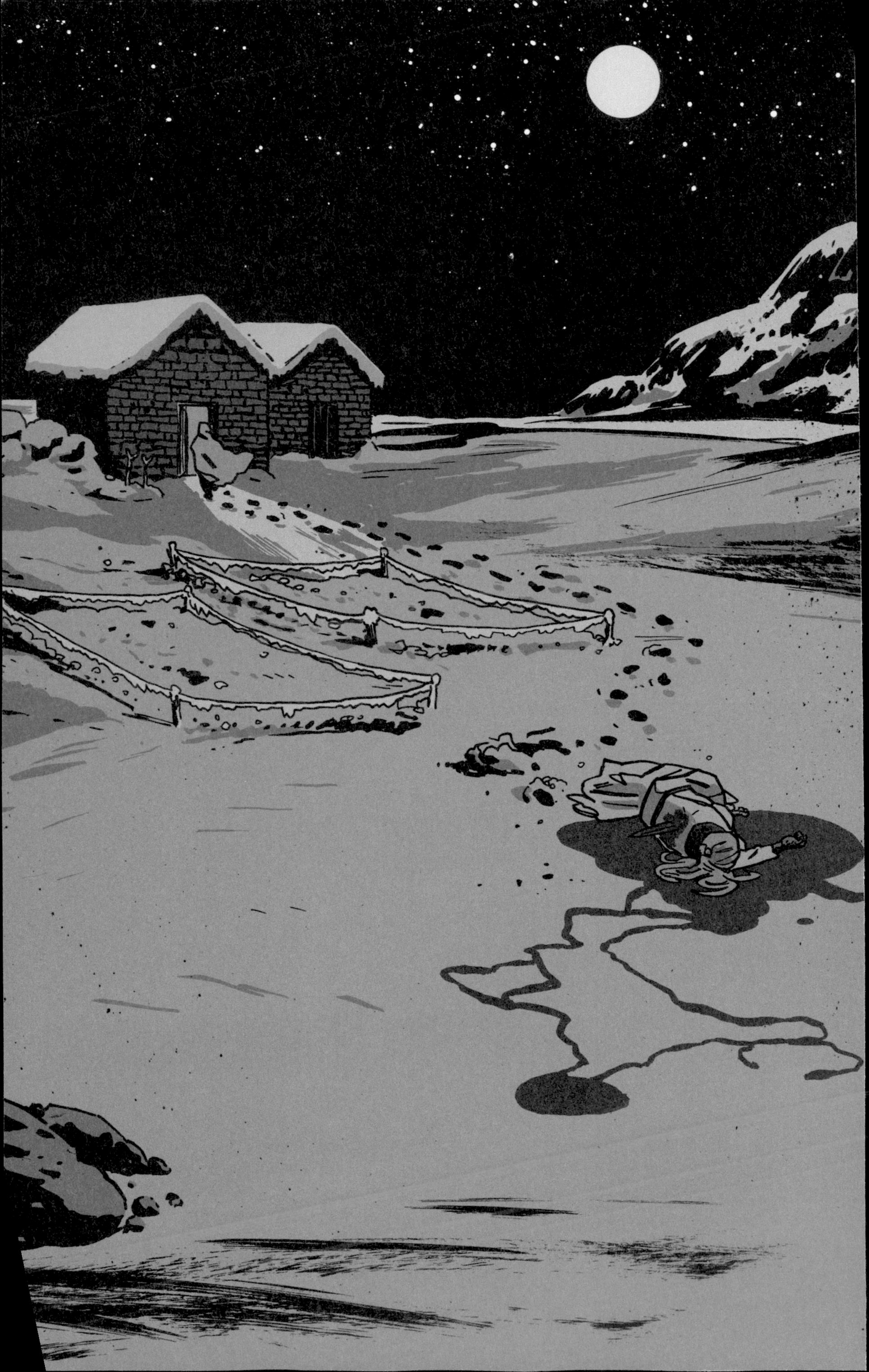

Chapter II
Security
A.D. 880

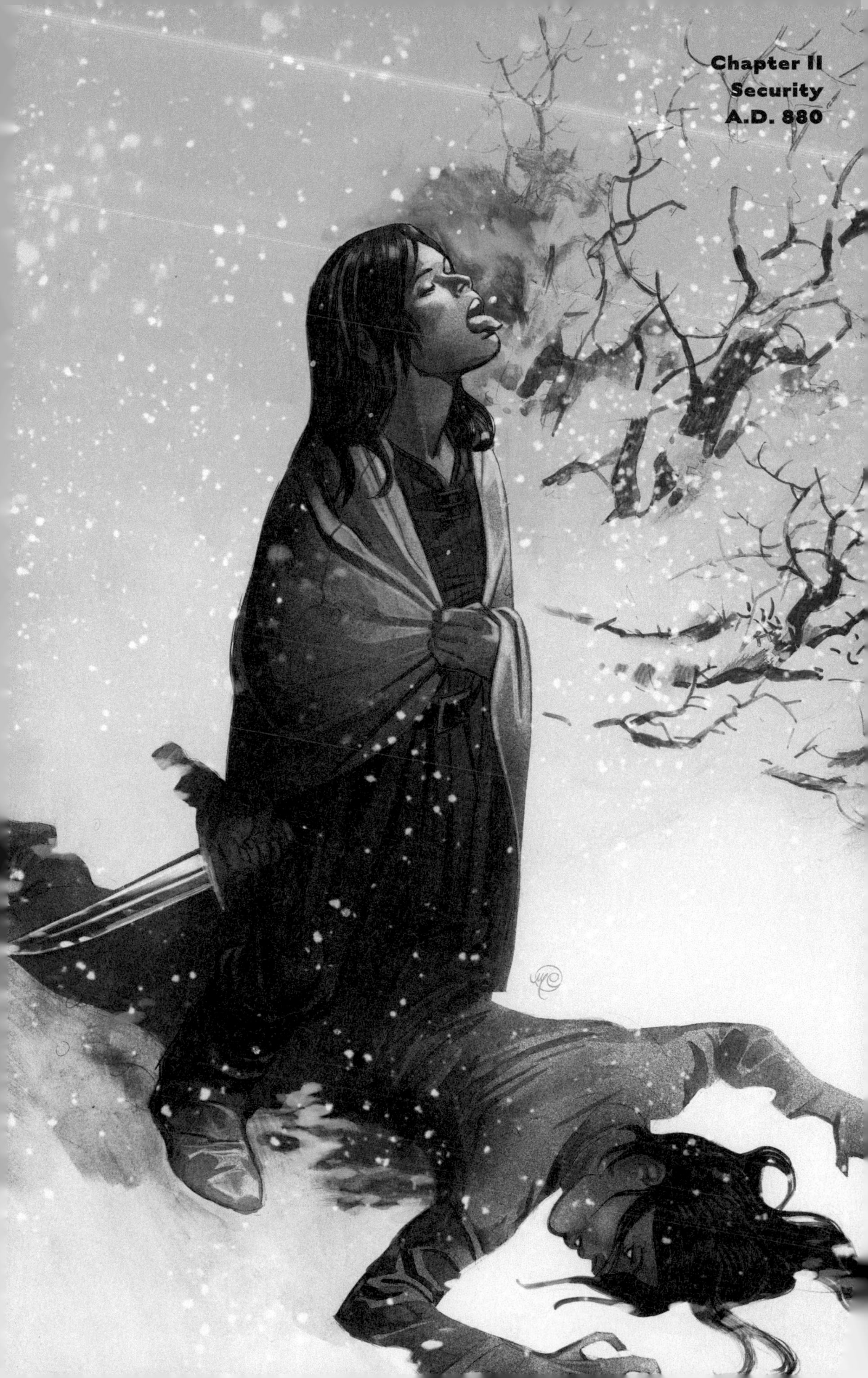

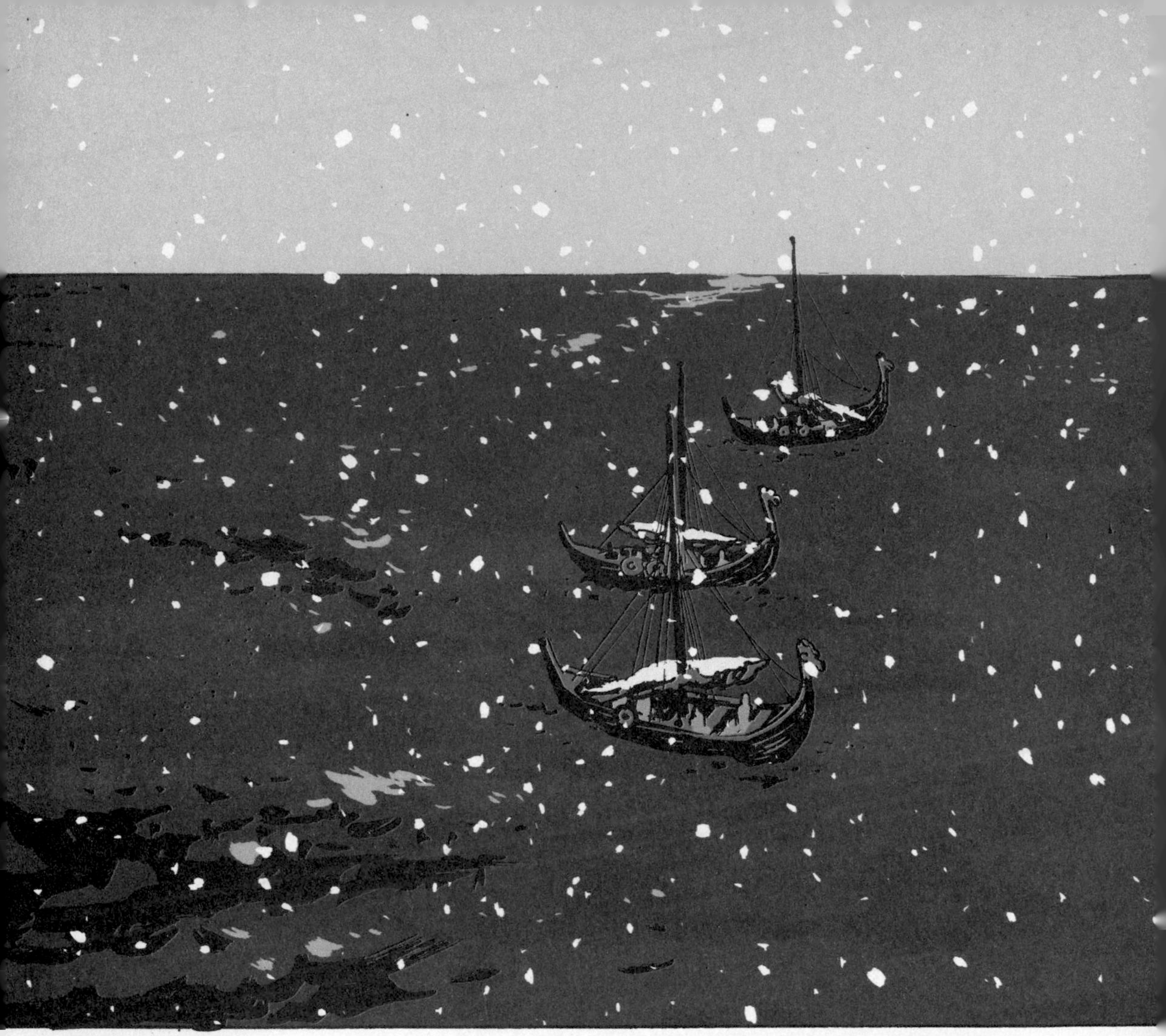

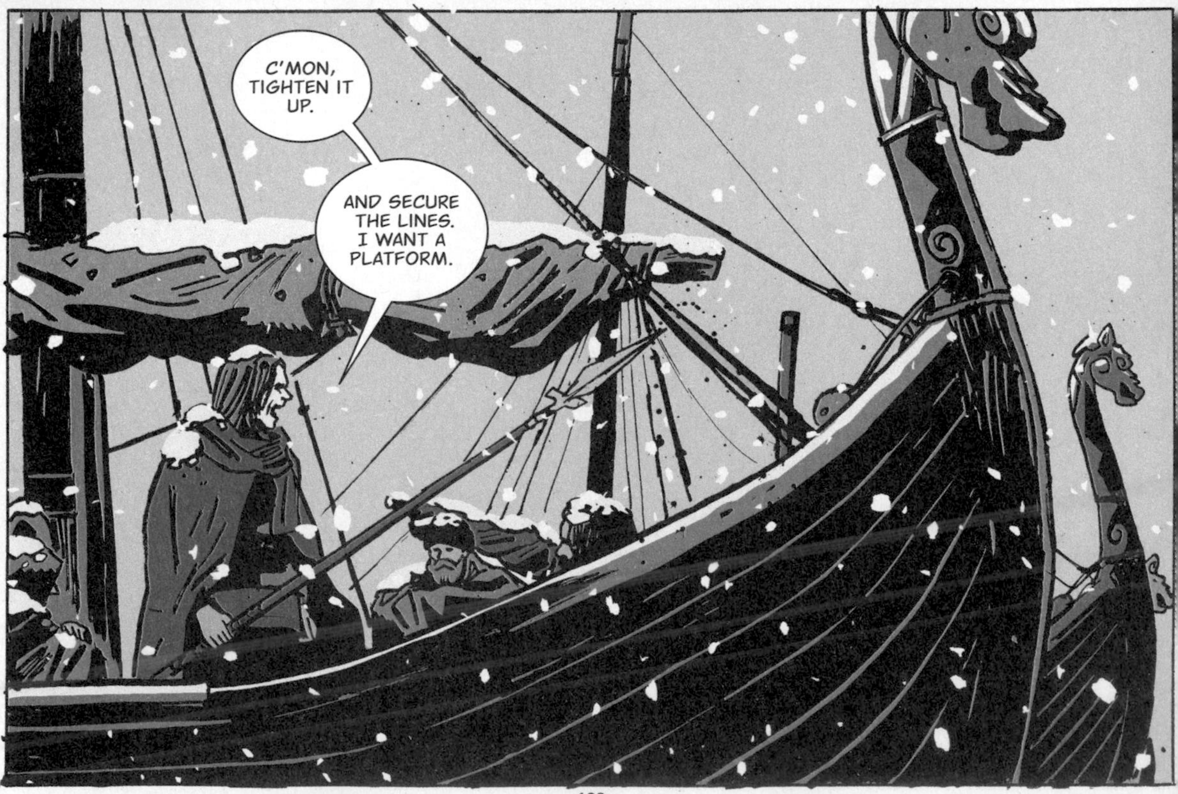
C'MON, TIGHTEN IT UP.
AND SECURE THE LINES. I WANT A PLATFORM.

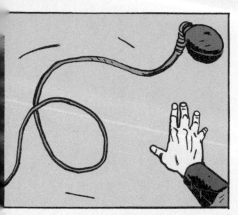

NO MATTER WHAT...

BUMP

...YOU HOLD THESE BOATS *STEADY.*

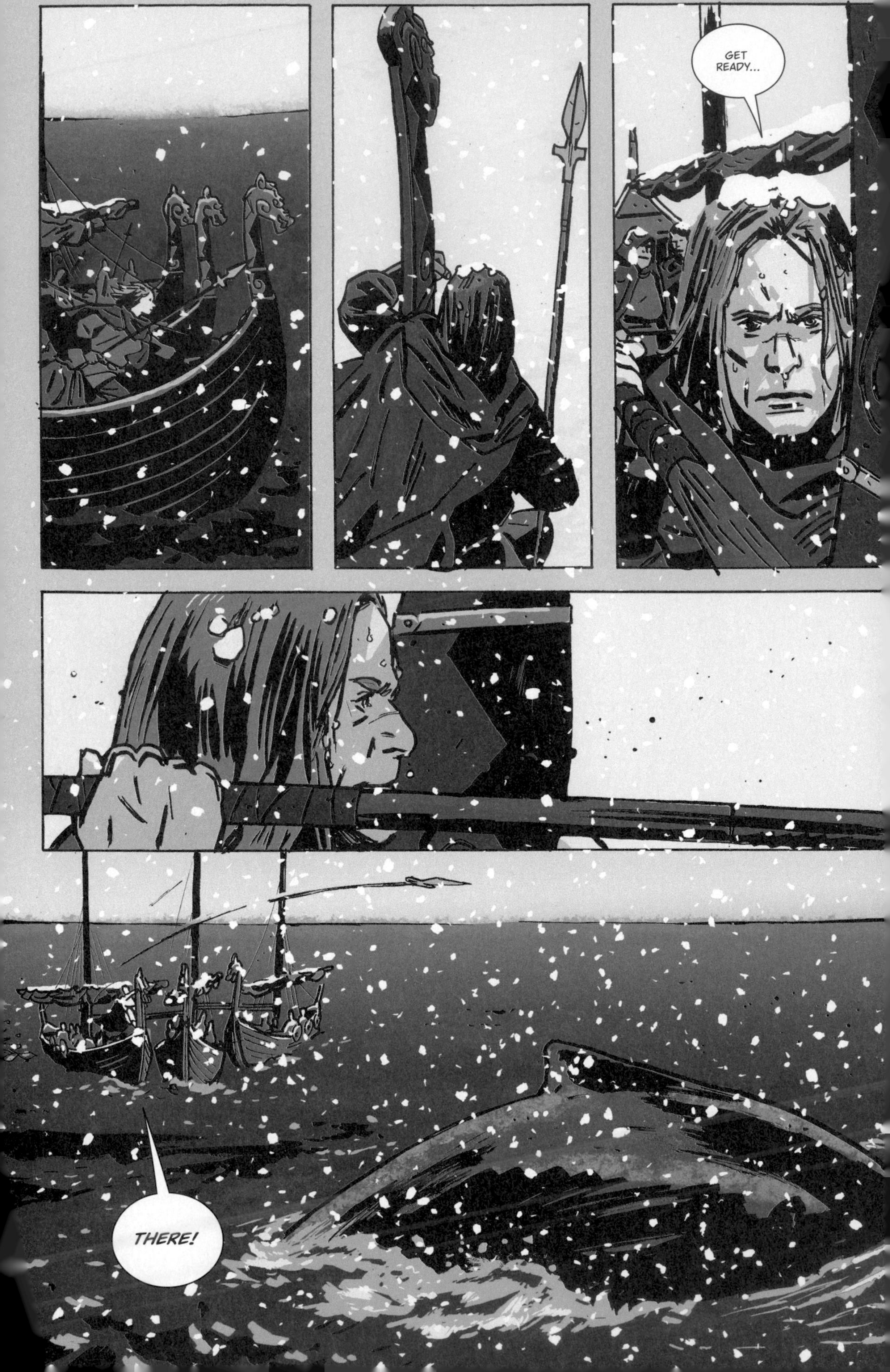
GET READY...
THERE!

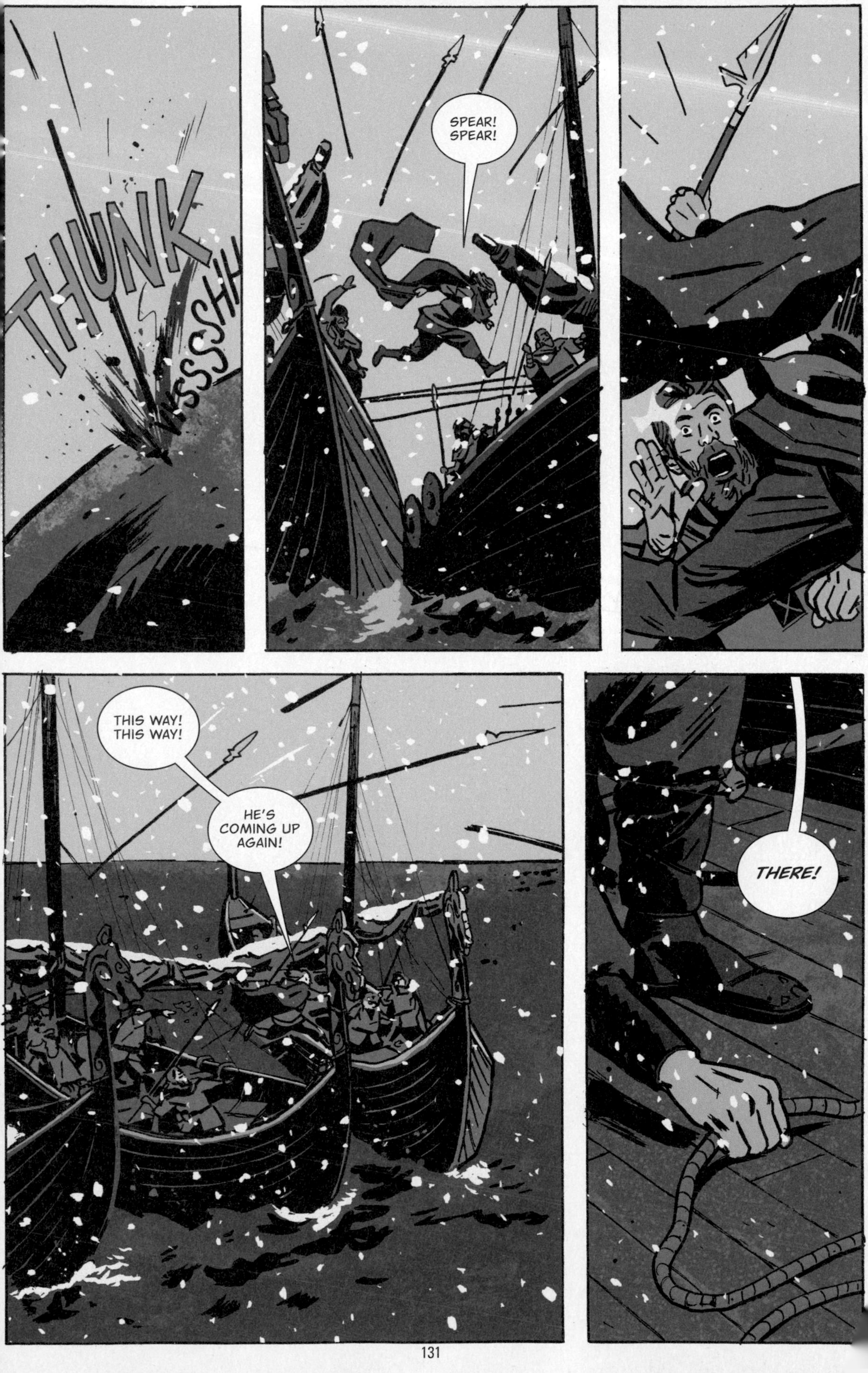
THUNK
WSSSHH
SPEAR! SPEAR!
THIS WAY! THIS WAY!
HE'S COMING UP AGAIN!
THERE!

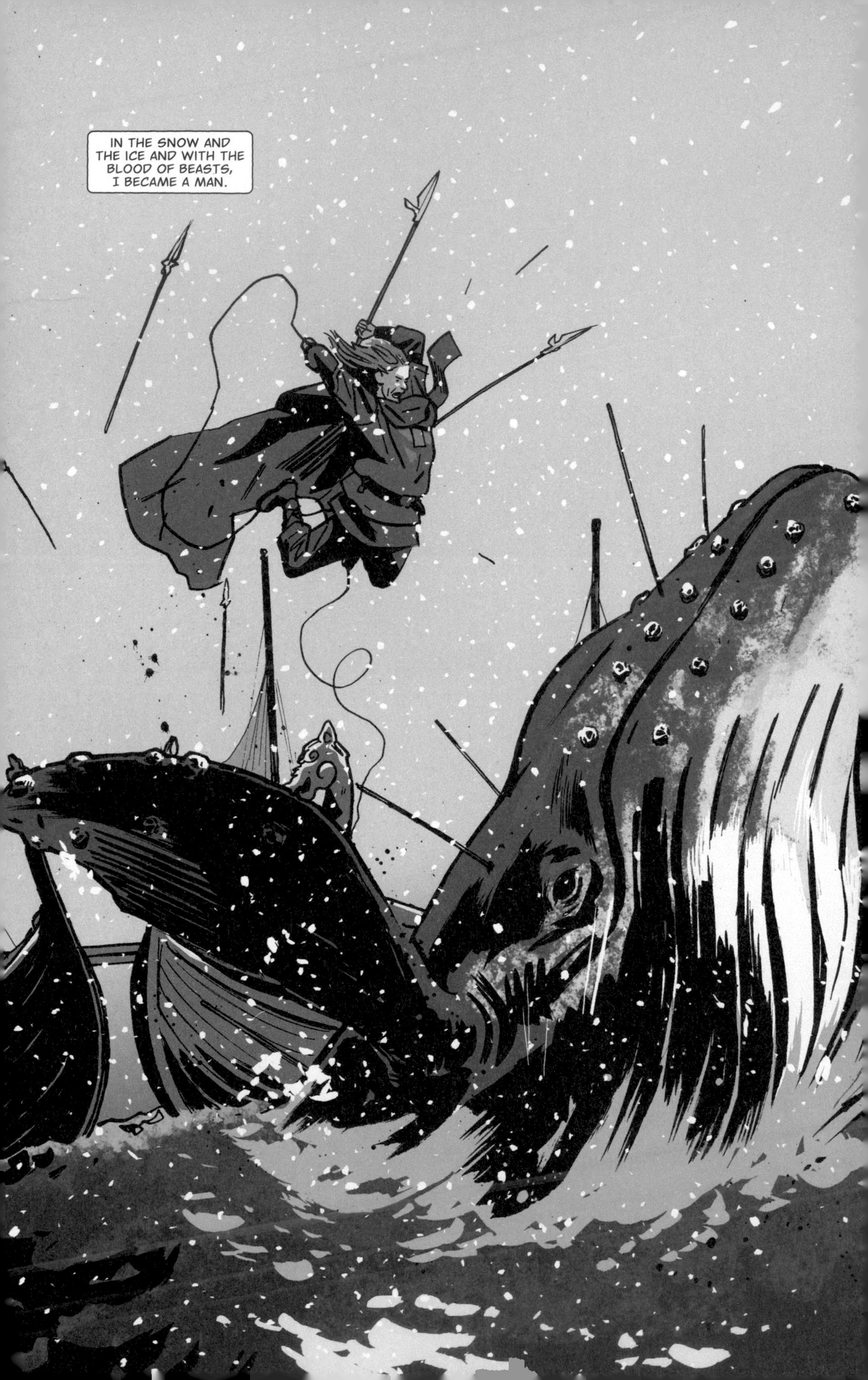
IN THE SNOW AND THE ICE AND WITH THE BLOOD OF BEASTS, I BECAME A MAN.

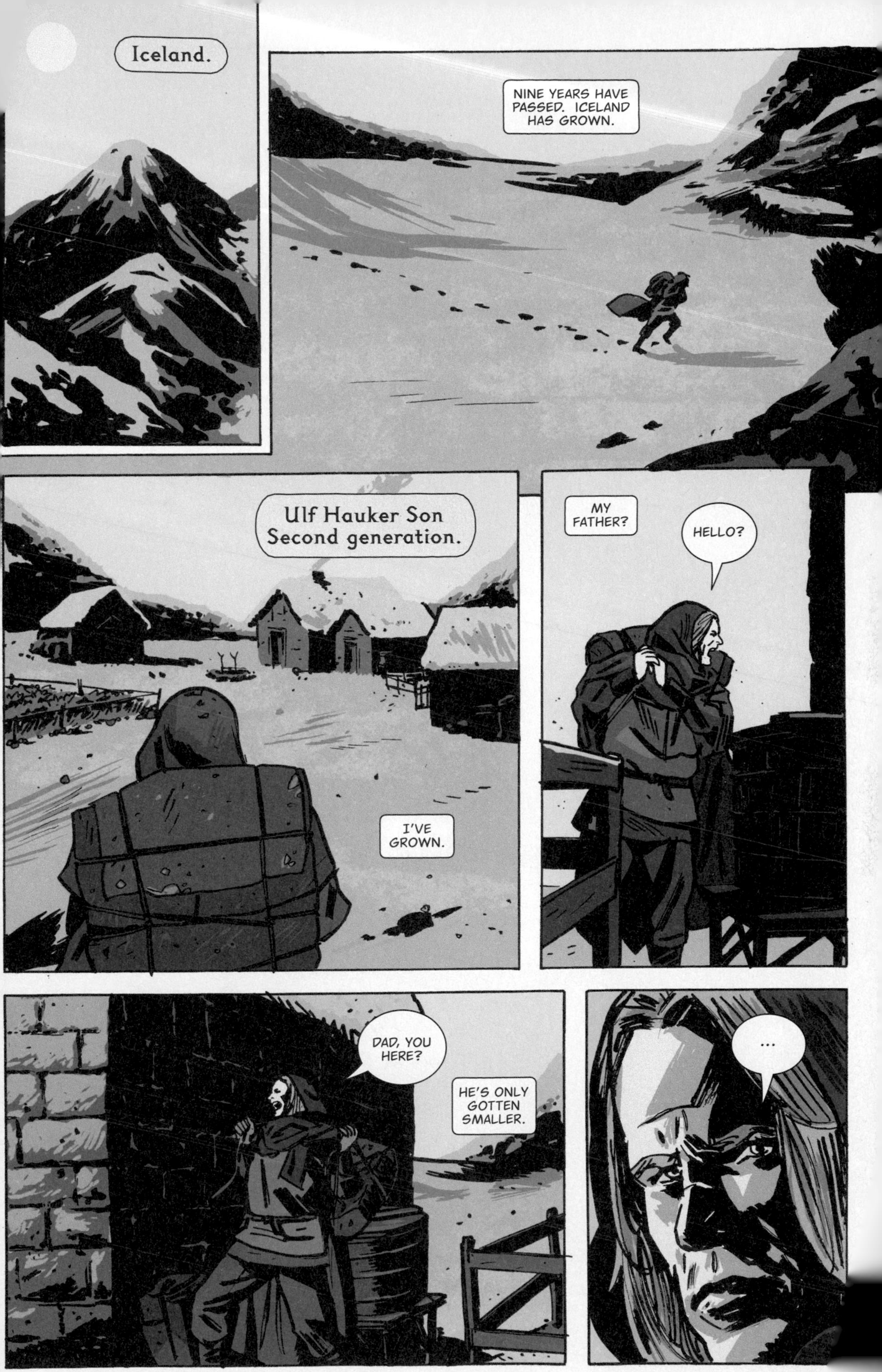
Iceland.
NINE YEARS HAVE PASSED. ICELAND HAS GROWN.
Ulf Hauker Son
Second generation.
I'VE GROWN.
MY FATHER?
HELLO?
DAD, YOU HERE?
HE'S ONLY GOTTEN SMALLER.
...

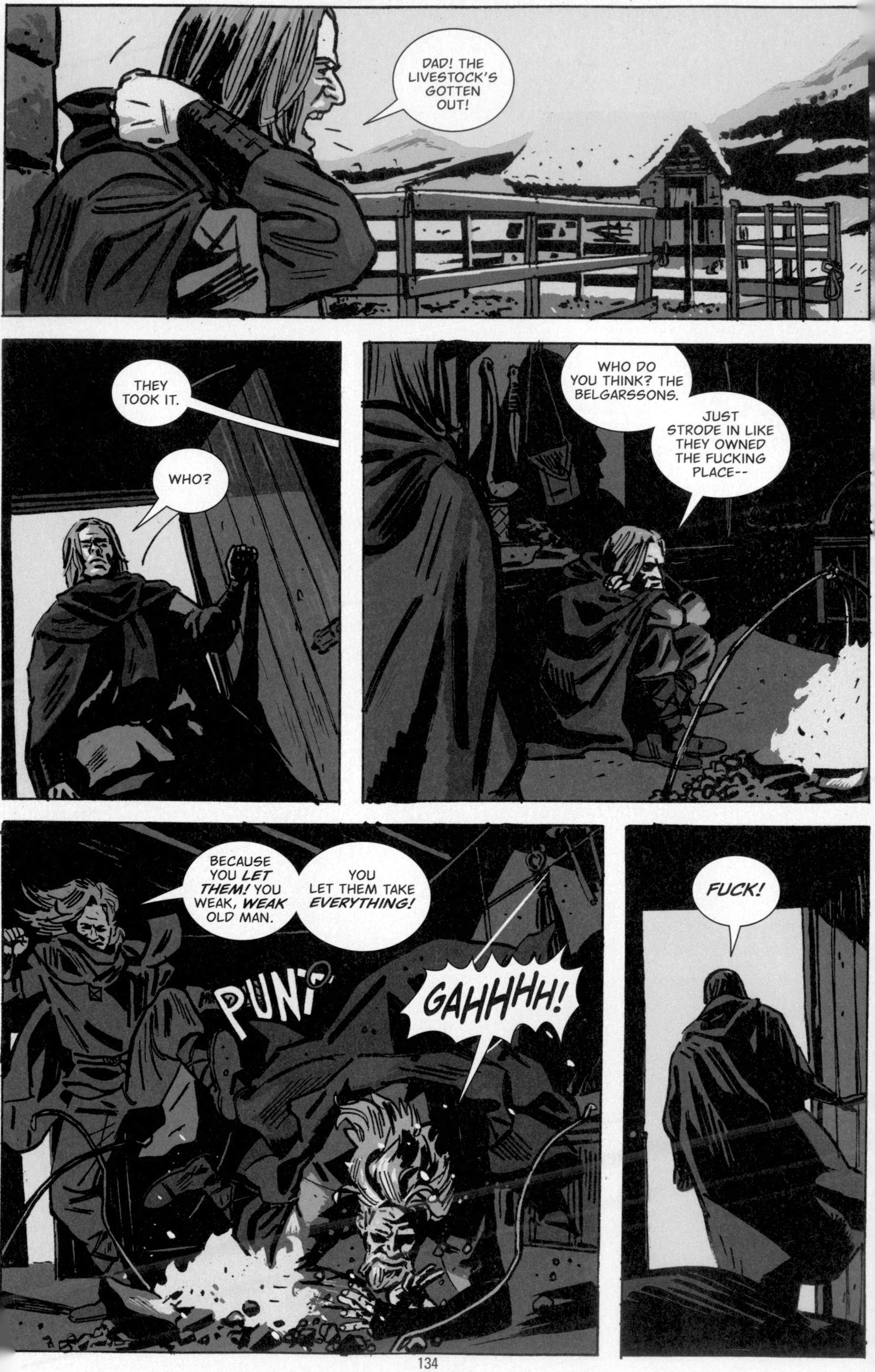
DAD! THE LIVESTOCK'S GOTTEN OUT!
THEY TOOK IT.
WHO?
WHO DO YOU THINK? THE BELGARSSONS.
JUST STRODE IN LIKE THEY OWNED THE FUCKING PLACE--
BECAUSE YOU *LET THEM!* YOU WEAK, *WEAK* OLD MAN.
YOU LET THEM TAKE *EVERYTHING!*
PUNT
GAHHHH!
FUCK!

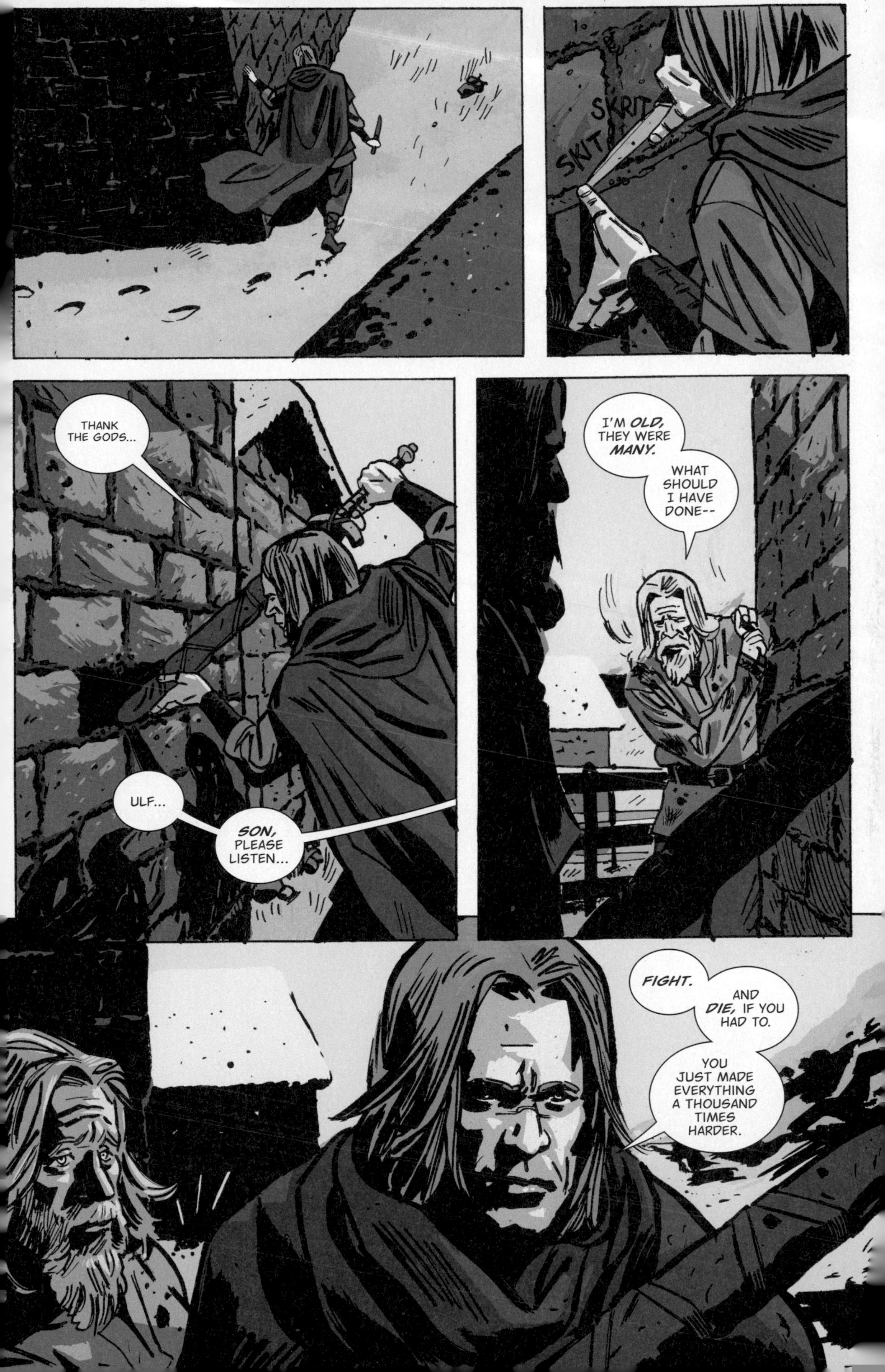
SKRIT
SKIT
THANK THE GODS...
ULF...
SON, PLEASE LISTEN...
I'M OLD, THEY WERE MANY.
WHAT SHOULD I HAVE DONE--
FIGHT.
AND DIE, IF YOU HAD TO.
YOU JUST MADE EVERYTHING A THOUSAND TIMES HARDER.

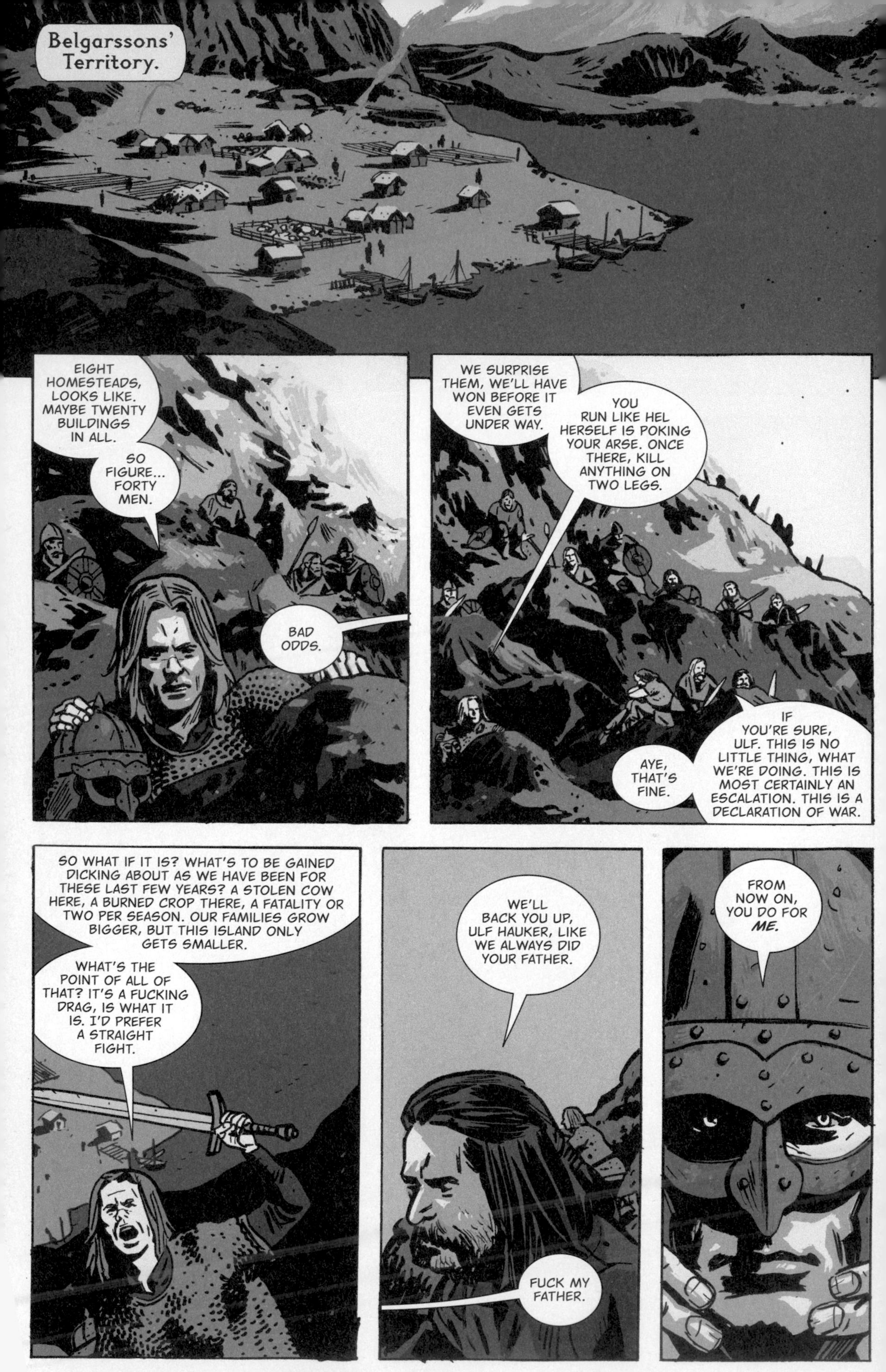
Belgarssons' Territory.
EIGHT HOMESTEADS, LOOKS LIKE. MAYBE TWENTY BUILDINGS IN ALL.
SO FIGURE... FORTY MEN.
BAD ODDS.
WE SURPRISE THEM, WE'LL HAVE WON BEFORE IT EVEN GETS UNDER WAY.
YOU RUN LIKE HEL HERSELF IS POKING YOUR ARSE. ONCE THERE, KILL ANYTHING ON TWO LEGS.
AYE, THAT'S FINE.
IF YOU'RE SURE, ULF. THIS IS NO LITTLE THING, WHAT WE'RE DOING. THIS IS MOST CERTAINLY AN ESCALATION. THIS IS A DECLARATION OF WAR.
SO WHAT IF IT IS? WHAT'S TO BE GAINED DICKING ABOUT AS WE HAVE BEEN FOR THESE LAST FEW YEARS? A STOLEN COW HERE, A BURNED CROP THERE, A FATALITY OR TWO PER SEASON. OUR FAMILIES GROW BIGGER, BUT THIS ISLAND ONLY GETS SMALLER.
WHAT'S THE POINT OF ALL OF THAT? IT'S A FUCKING DRAG, IS WHAT IT IS. I'D PREFER A STRAIGHT FIGHT.
WE'LL BACK YOU UP, ULF HAUKER, LIKE WE ALWAYS DID YOUR FATHER.
FUCK MY FATHER.
FROM NOW ON, YOU DO FOR ***ME.***

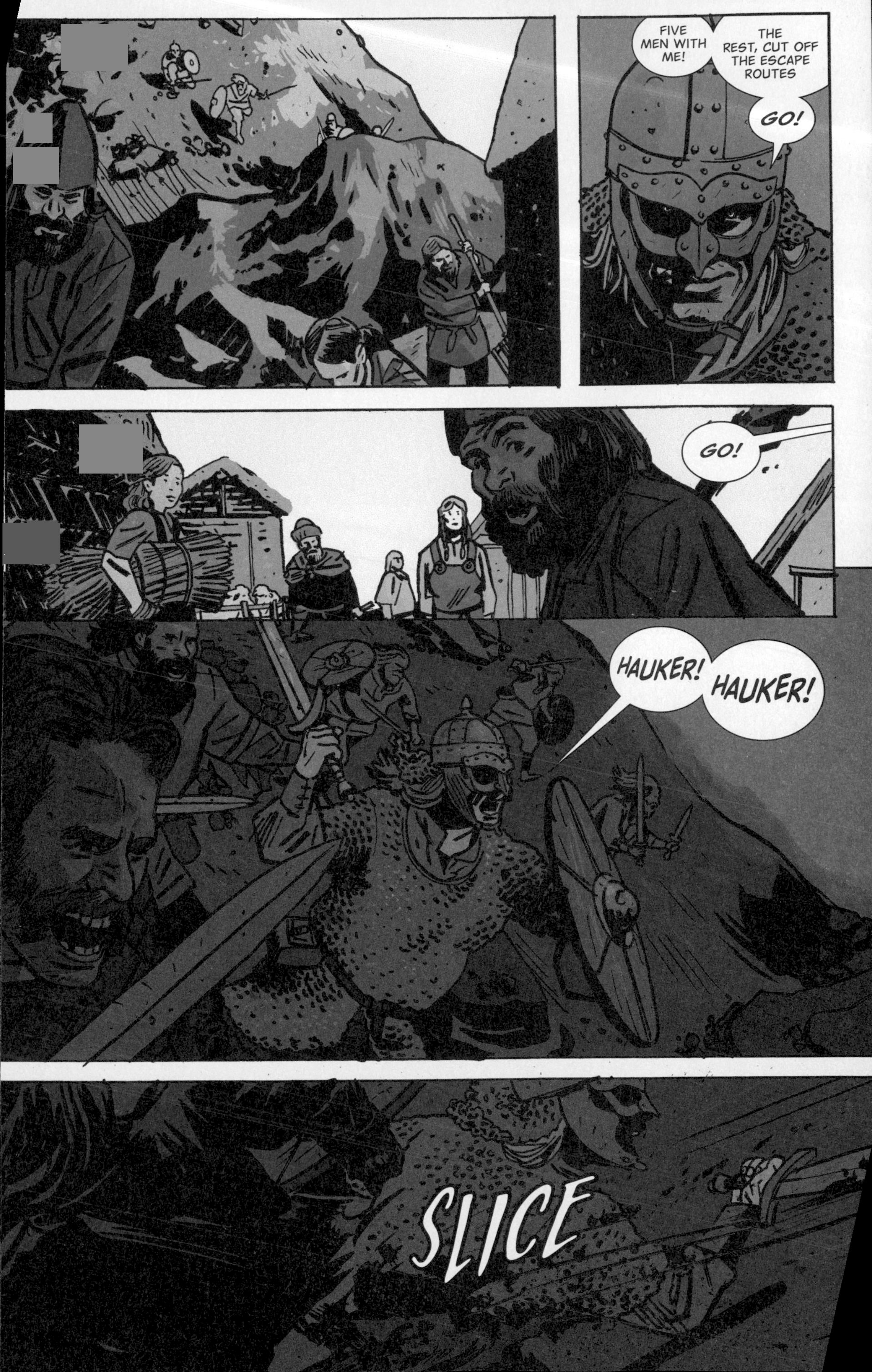
FIVE MEN WITH ME!
THE REST, CUT OFF THE ESCAPE ROUTES
GO!
GO!
HAUKER!
HAUKER!
SLICE

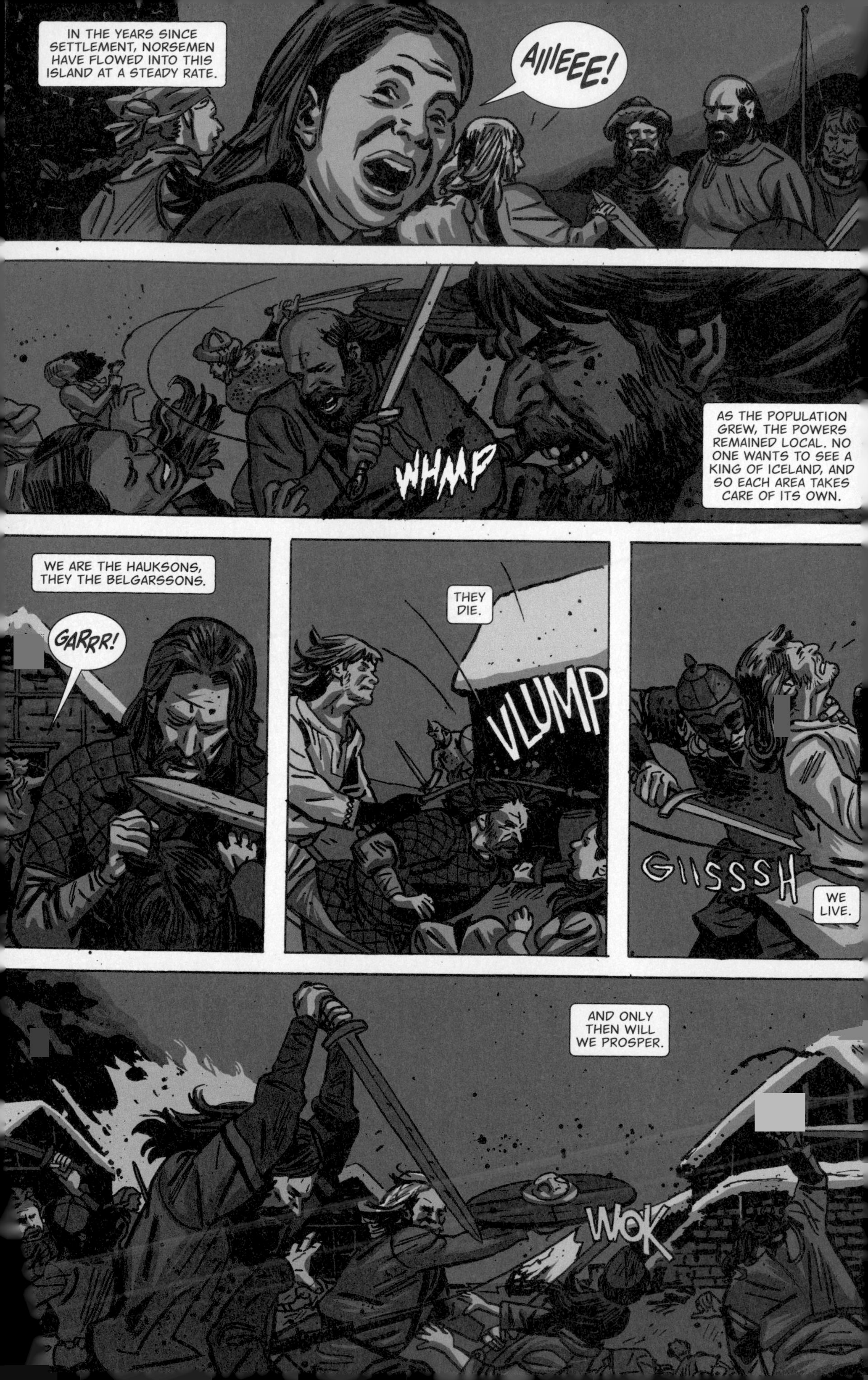
IN THE YEARS SINCE SETTLEMENT, NORSEMEN HAVE FLOWED INTO THIS ISLAND AT A STEADY RATE.
AIIIEEE!
WHMP
AS THE POPULATION GREW, THE POWERS REMAINED LOCAL. NO ONE WANTS TO SEE A KING OF ICELAND, AND SO EACH AREA TAKES CARE OF ITS OWN.
WE ARE THE HAUKSONS, THEY THE BELGARSSONS.
GARRR!
THEY DIE.
VLUMP
GIISSSH
WE LIVE.
AND ONLY THEN WILL WE PROSPER.
WOK

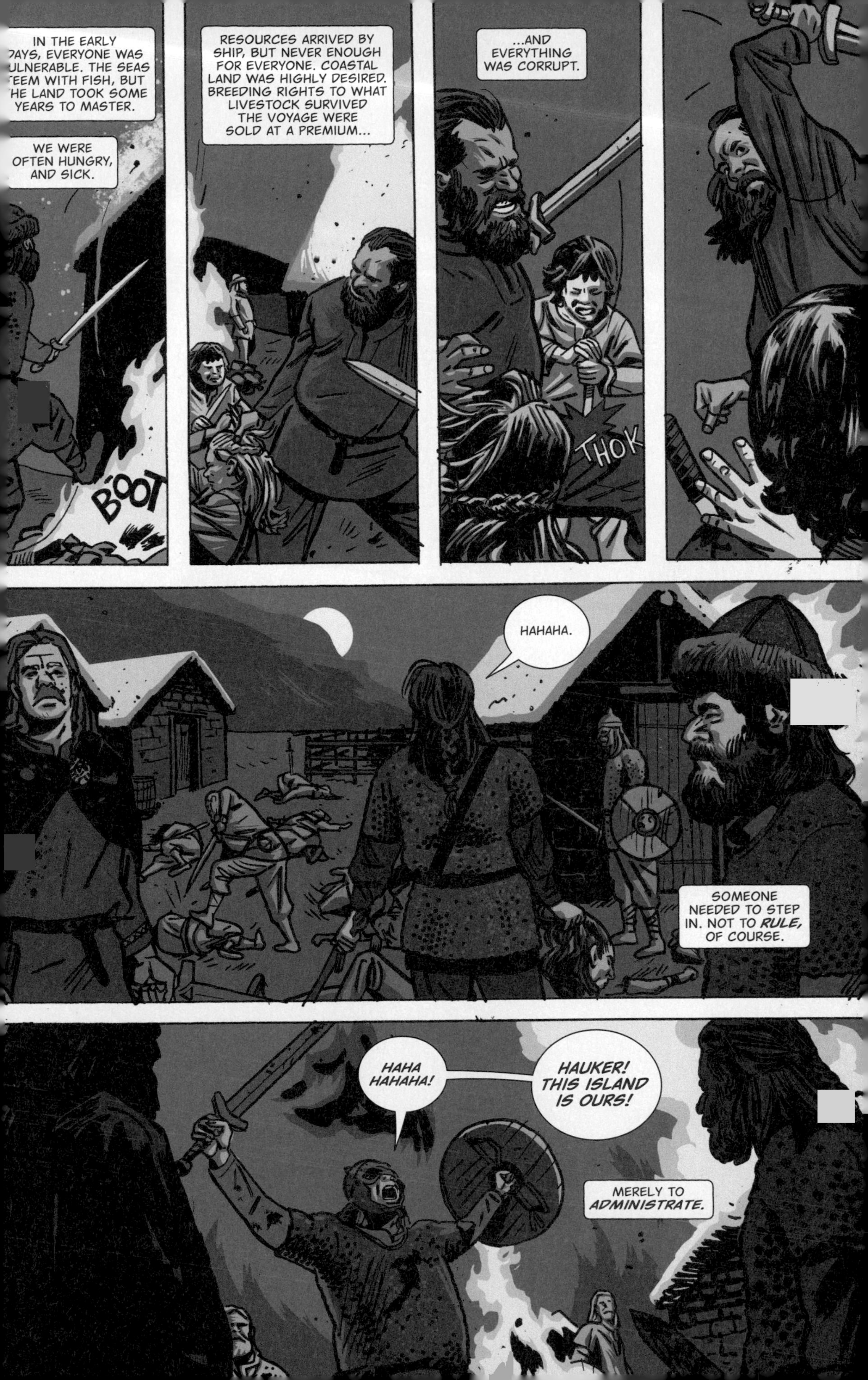

IN THE EARLY DAYS, EVERYONE WAS VULNERABLE. THE SEAS TEEM WITH FISH, BUT THE LAND TOOK SOME YEARS TO MASTER.
WE WERE OFTEN HUNGRY, AND SICK.
B'OOT
RESOURCES ARRIVED BY SHIP, BUT NEVER ENOUGH FOR EVERYONE. COASTAL LAND WAS HIGHLY DESIRED. BREEDING RIGHTS TO WHAT LIVESTOCK SURVIVED THE VOYAGE WERE SOLD AT A PREMIUM...
...AND EVERYTHING WAS CORRUPT.
THOK
HAHAHA.
SOMEONE NEEDED TO STEP IN. NOT TO *RULE,* OF COURSE.
HAHA HAHAHA!
HAUKER! THIS ISLAND IS OURS!
MERELY TO *ADMINISTRATE.*

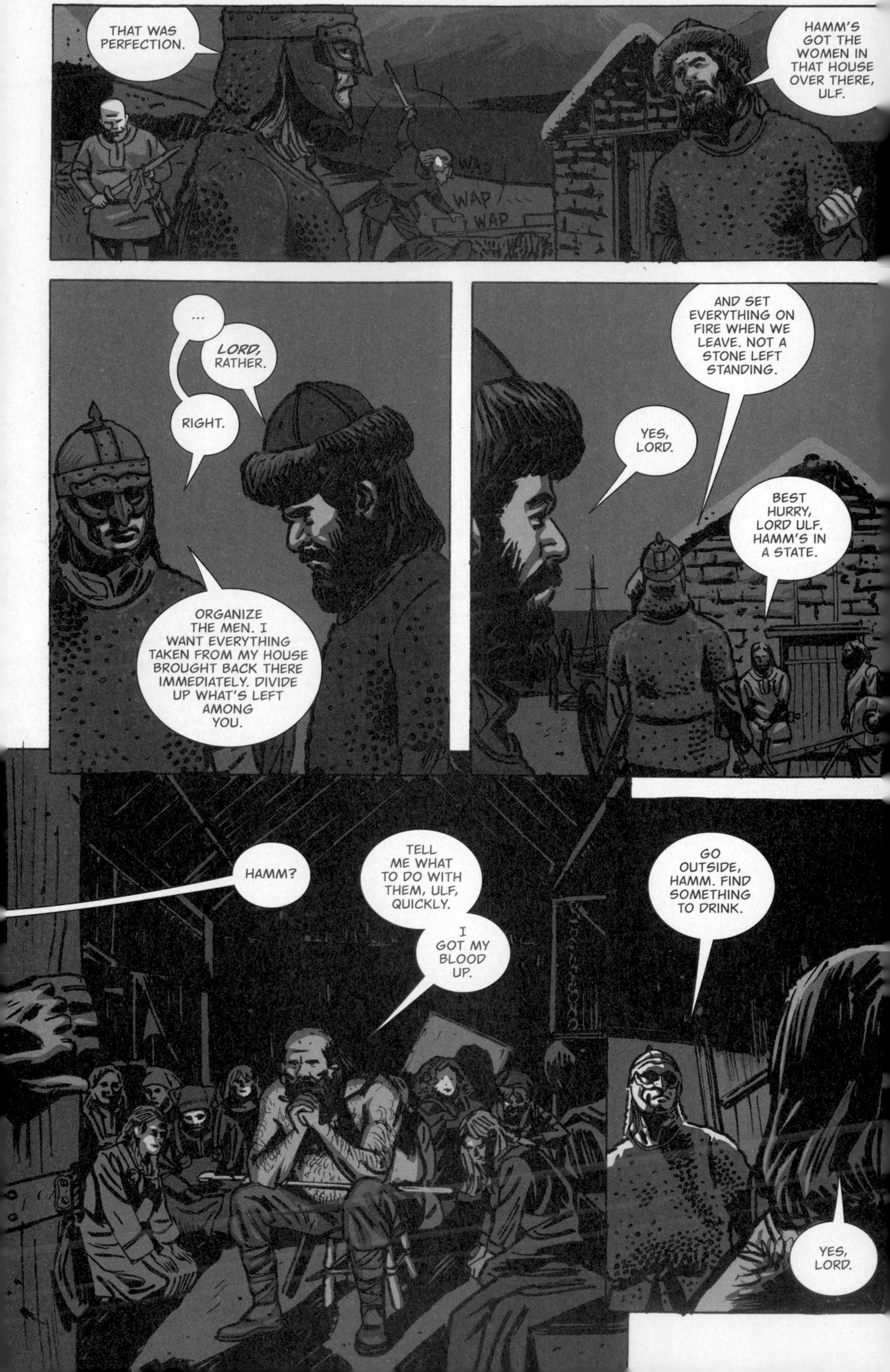
THAT WAS PERFECTION.
WAP
WAP
WAP
HAMM'S GOT THE WOMEN IN THAT HOUSE OVER THERE, ULF.
...
LORD, RATHER.
RIGHT.
ORGANIZE THE MEN. I WANT EVERYTHING TAKEN FROM MY HOUSE BROUGHT BACK THERE IMMEDIATELY. DIVIDE UP WHAT'S LEFT AMONG YOU.
AND SET EVERYTHING ON FIRE WHEN WE LEAVE. NOT A STONE LEFT STANDING.
YES, LORD.
BEST HURRY, LORD ULF. HAMM'S IN A STATE.
HAMM?
TELL ME WHAT TO DO WITH THEM, ULF, QUICKLY.
I GOT MY BLOOD UP.
GO OUTSIDE, HAMM. FIND SOMETHING TO DRINK.
YES, LORD.

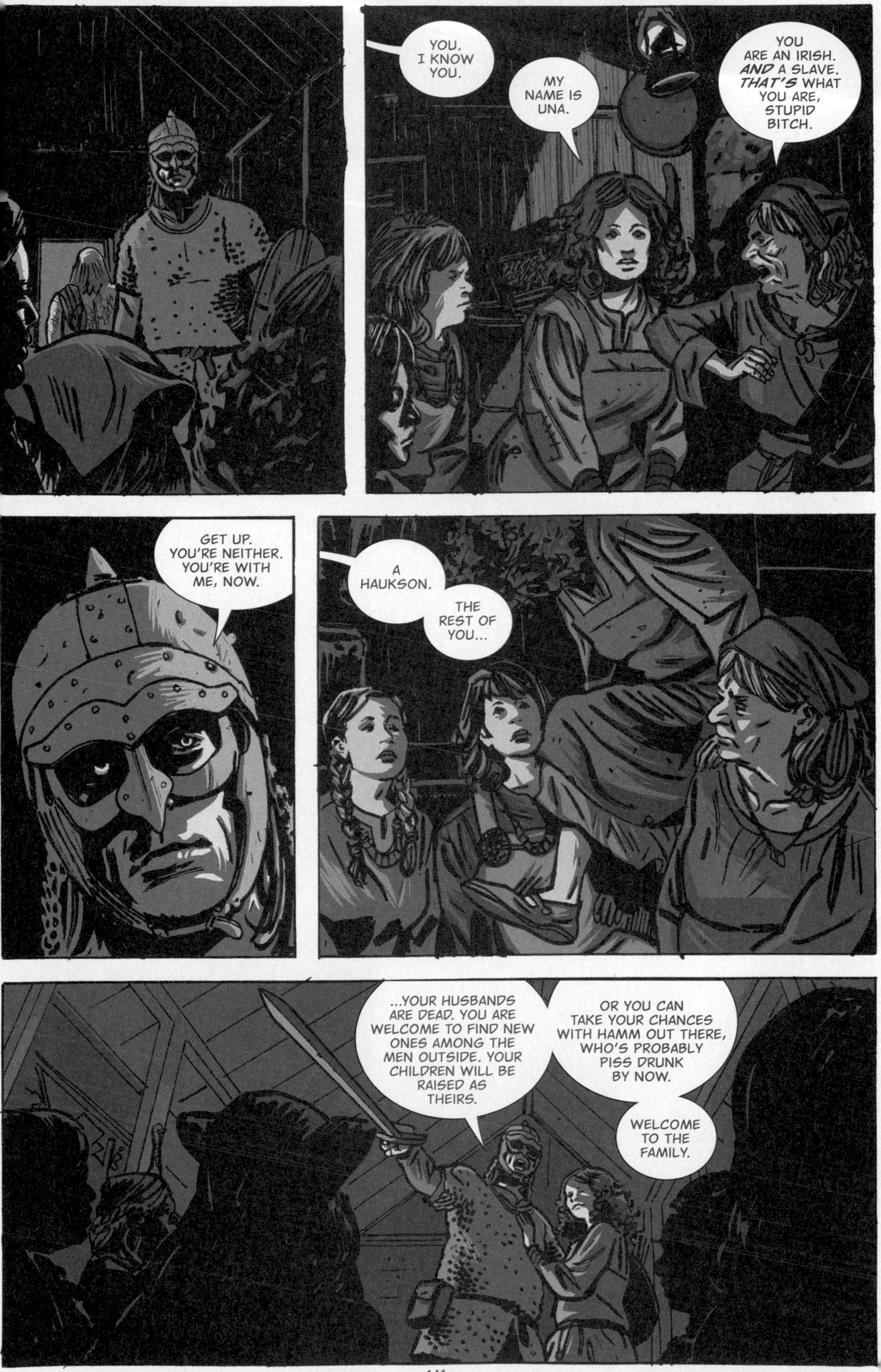
YOU. I KNOW YOU.
MY NAME IS UNA.
YOU ARE AN IRISH. AND A SLAVE. THAT'S WHAT YOU ARE, STUPID BITCH.
GET UP. YOU'RE NEITHER. YOU'RE WITH ME, NOW.
A HAUKSON.
THE REST OF YOU...
...YOUR HUSBANDS ARE DEAD. YOU ARE WELCOME TO FIND NEW ONES AMONG THE MEN OUTSIDE. YOUR CHILDREN WILL BE RAISED AS THEIRS.
OR YOU CAN TAKE YOUR CHANCES WITH HAMM OUT THERE, WHO'S PROBABLY PISS DRUNK BY NOW.
WELCOME TO THE FAMILY.

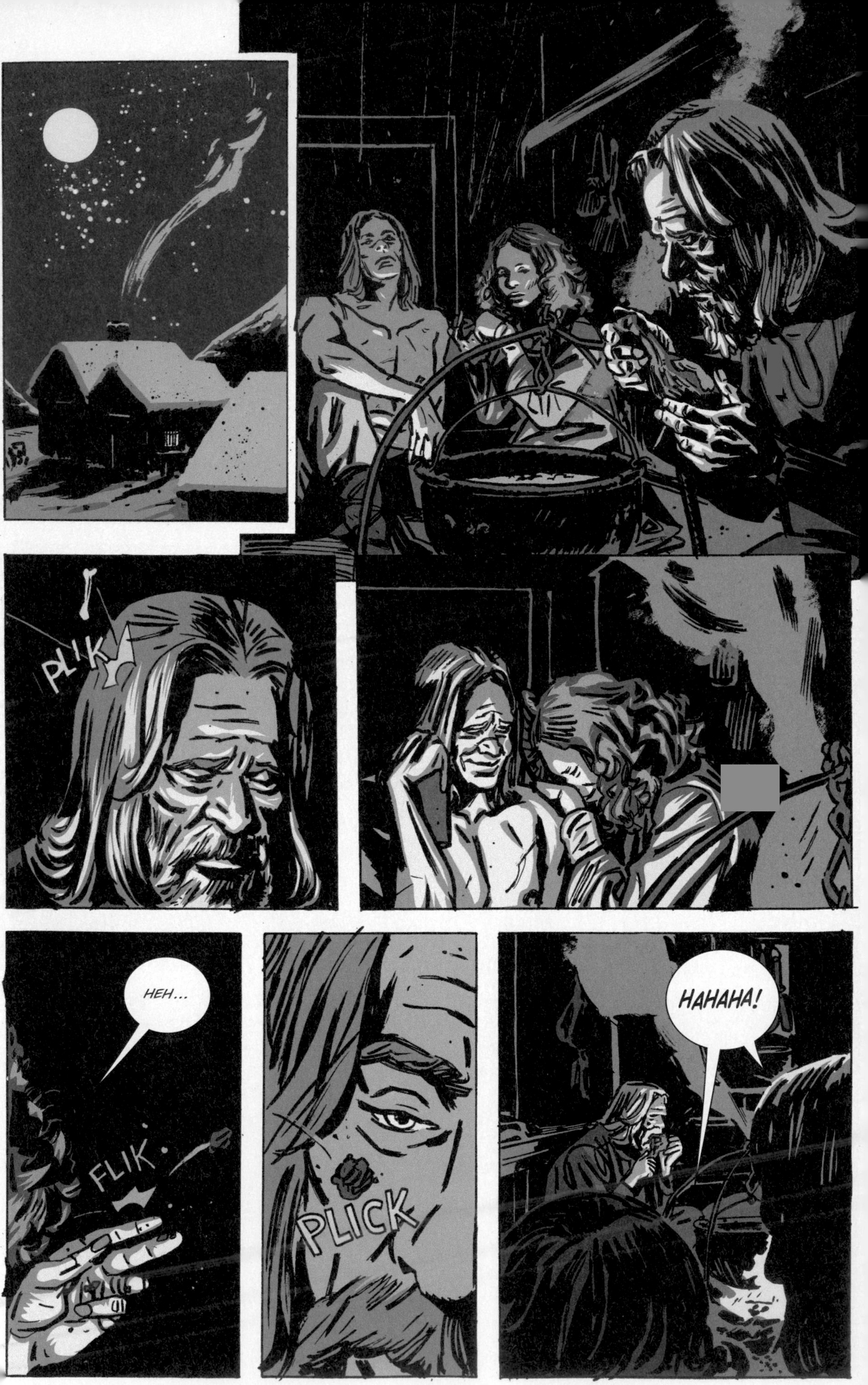

PLIK
HEH...
FLIK
PLICK
HAHAHA!

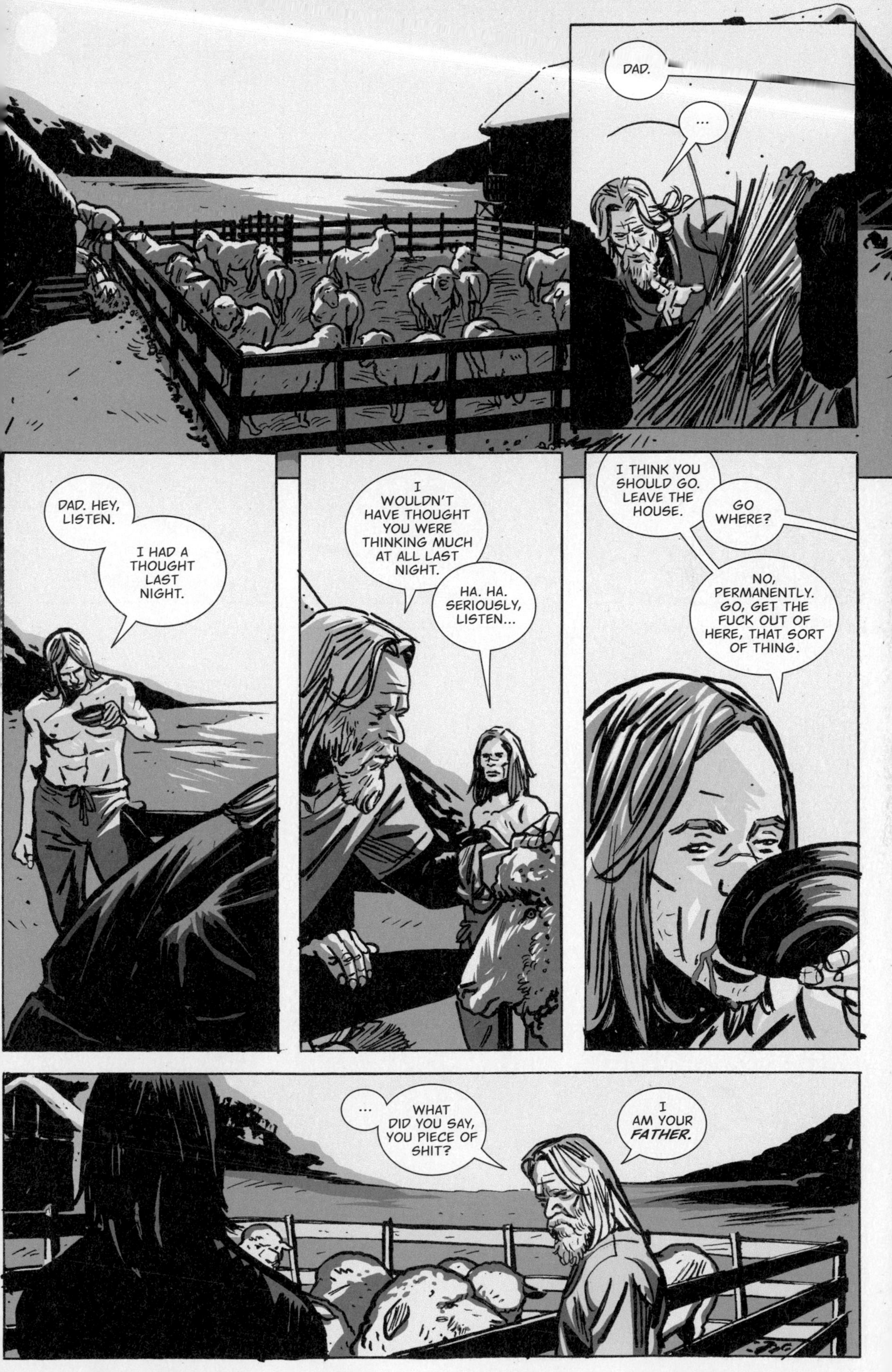
DAD.
...
DAD. HEY, LISTEN.
I HAD A THOUGHT LAST NIGHT.
I WOULDN'T HAVE THOUGHT YOU WERE THINKING MUCH AT ALL LAST NIGHT.
HA. HA. SERIOUSLY, LISTEN...
I THINK YOU SHOULD GO. LEAVE THE HOUSE.
GO WHERE?
NO, PERMANENTLY. GO, GET THE FUCK OUT OF HERE, THAT SORT OF THING.
...
WHAT DID YOU SAY, YOU PIECE OF SHIT?
I AM YOUR *FATHER.*

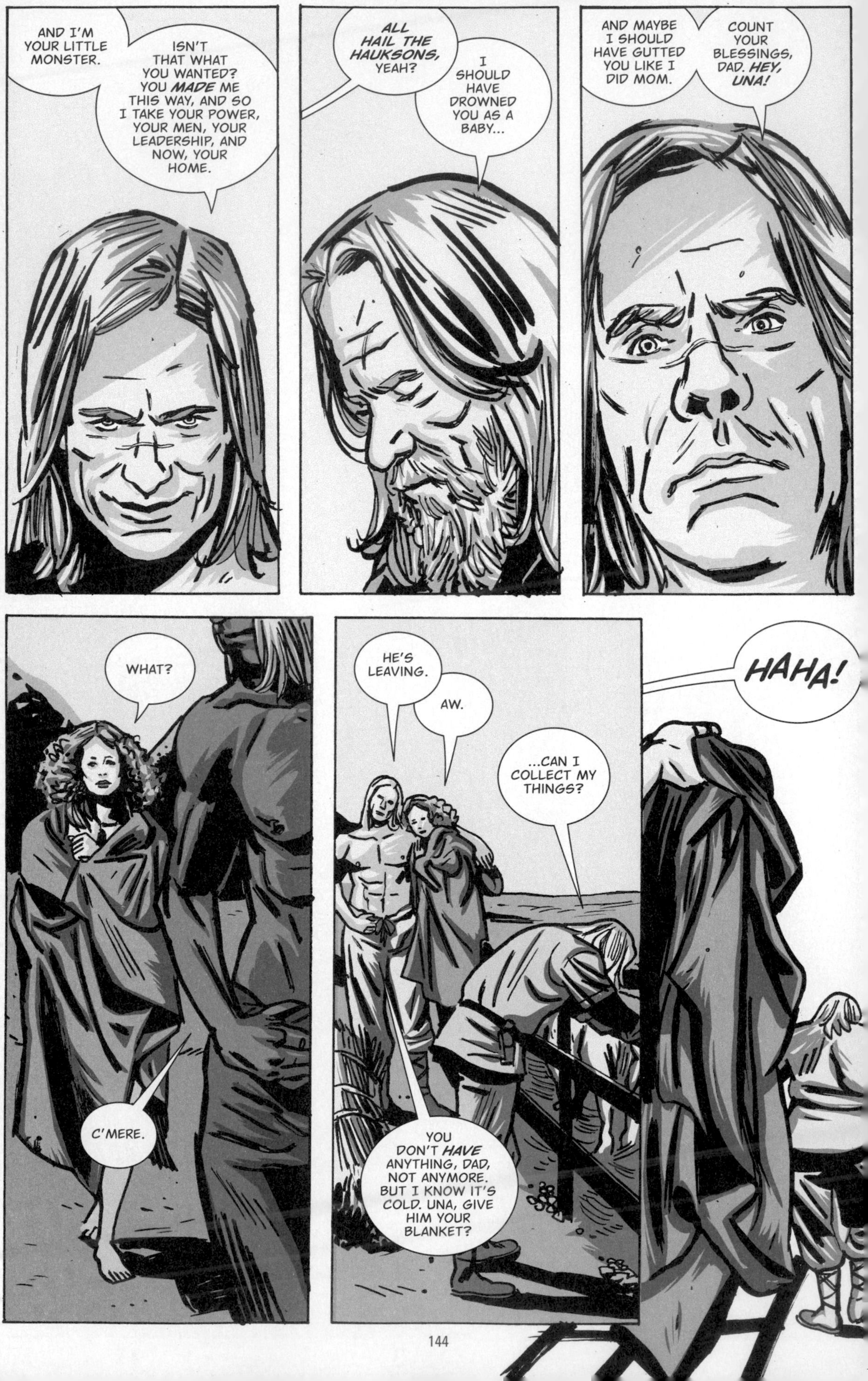
AND I'M YOUR LITTLE MONSTER.
ISN'T THAT WHAT YOU WANTED? YOU MADE ME THIS WAY, AND SO I TAKE YOUR POWER, YOUR MEN, YOUR LEADERSHIP, AND NOW, YOUR HOME.
ALL HAIL THE HAUKSONS, YEAH?
I SHOULD HAVE DROWNED YOU AS A BABY...
AND MAYBE I SHOULD HAVE GUTTED YOU LIKE I DID MOM.
COUNT YOUR BLESSINGS, DAD. HEY, UNA!
WHAT?
C'MERE.
HE'S LEAVING.
AW.
...CAN I COLLECT MY THINGS?
YOU DON'T HAVE ANYTHING, DAD, NOT ANYMORE. BUT I KNOW IT'S COLD. UNA, GIVE HIM YOUR BLANKET?
HAHA!

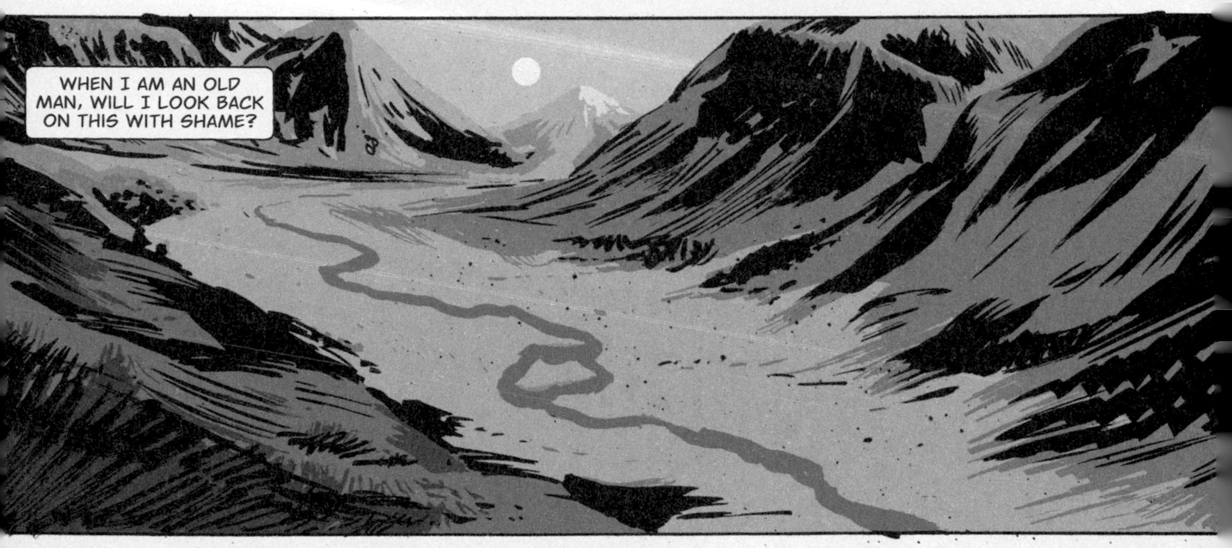
WHEN I AM AN OLD MAN, WILL I LOOK BACK ON THIS WITH SHAME?

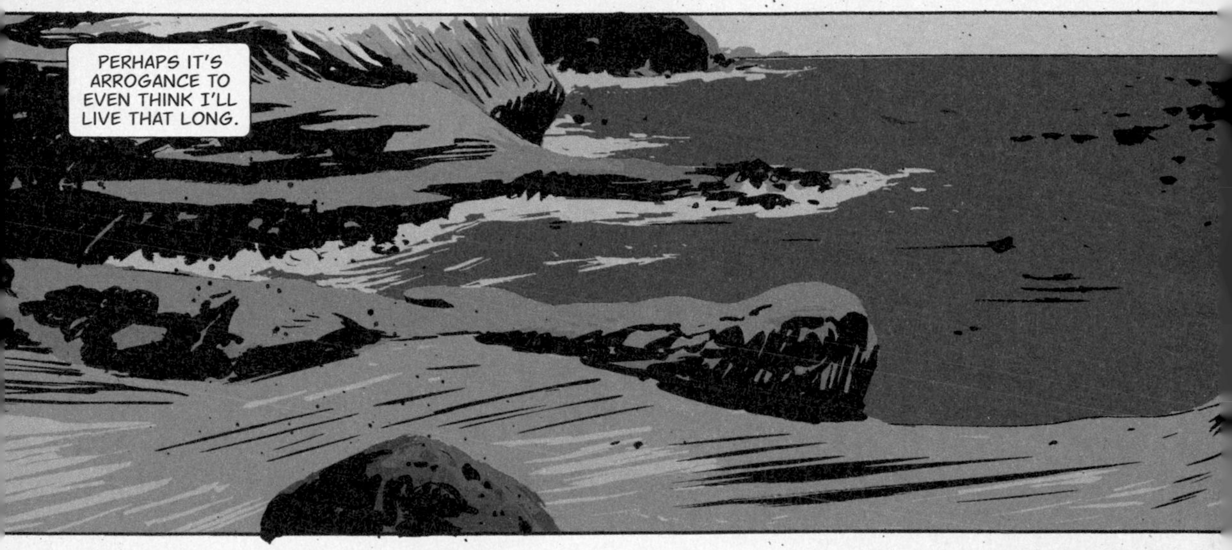
PERHAPS IT'S ARROGANCE TO EVEN THINK I'LL LIVE THAT LONG.

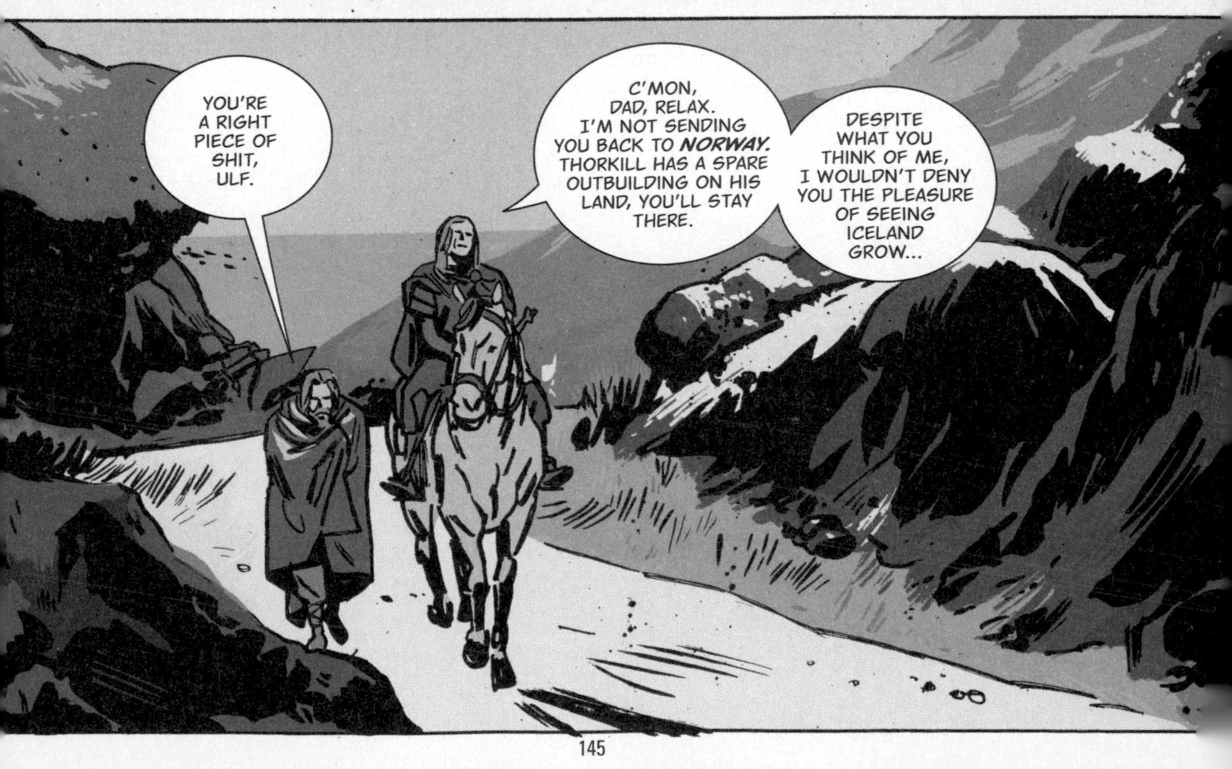
YOU'RE A RIGHT PIECE OF SHIT, ULF.
C'MON, DAD, RELAX. I'M NOT SENDING YOU BACK TO **NORWAY.** THORKILL HAS A SPARE OUTBUILDING ON HIS LAND, YOU'LL STAY THERE.
DESPITE WHAT YOU THINK OF ME, I WOULDN'T DENY YOU THE PLEASURE OF SEEING ICELAND GROW...

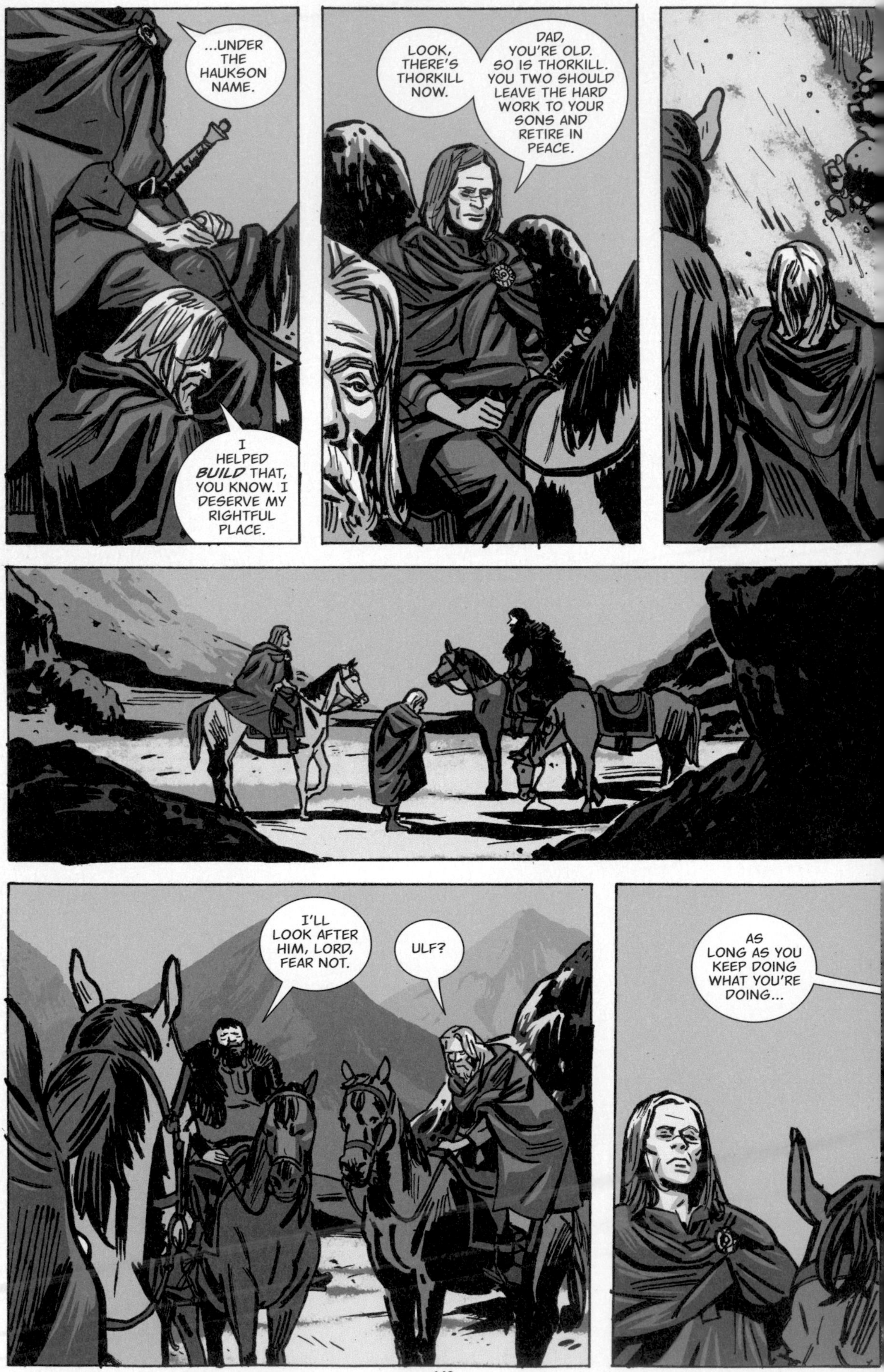

...UNDER THE HAUKSON NAME.
I HELPED BUILD THAT, YOU KNOW. I DESERVE MY RIGHTFUL PLACE.
LOOK, THERE'S THORKILL NOW.
DAD, YOU'RE OLD. SO IS THORKILL. YOU TWO SHOULD LEAVE THE HARD WORK TO YOUR SONS AND RETIRE IN PEACE.
I'LL LOOK AFTER HIM, LORD, FEAR NOT.
ULF?
AS LONG AS YOU KEEP DOING WHAT YOU'RE DOING...

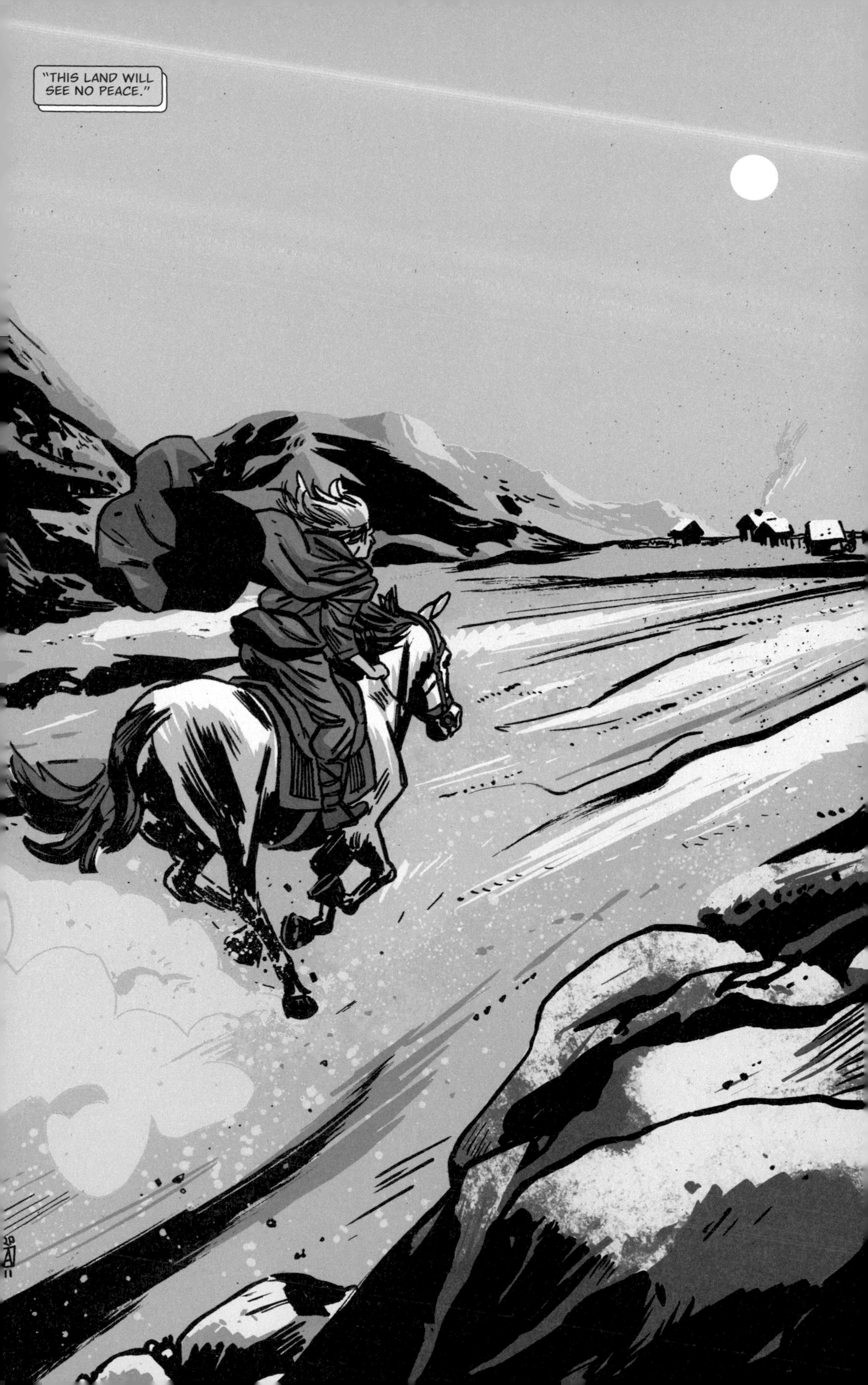
"THIS LAND WILL SEE NO PEACE."

Chapter III
Slavery
A.D. 886

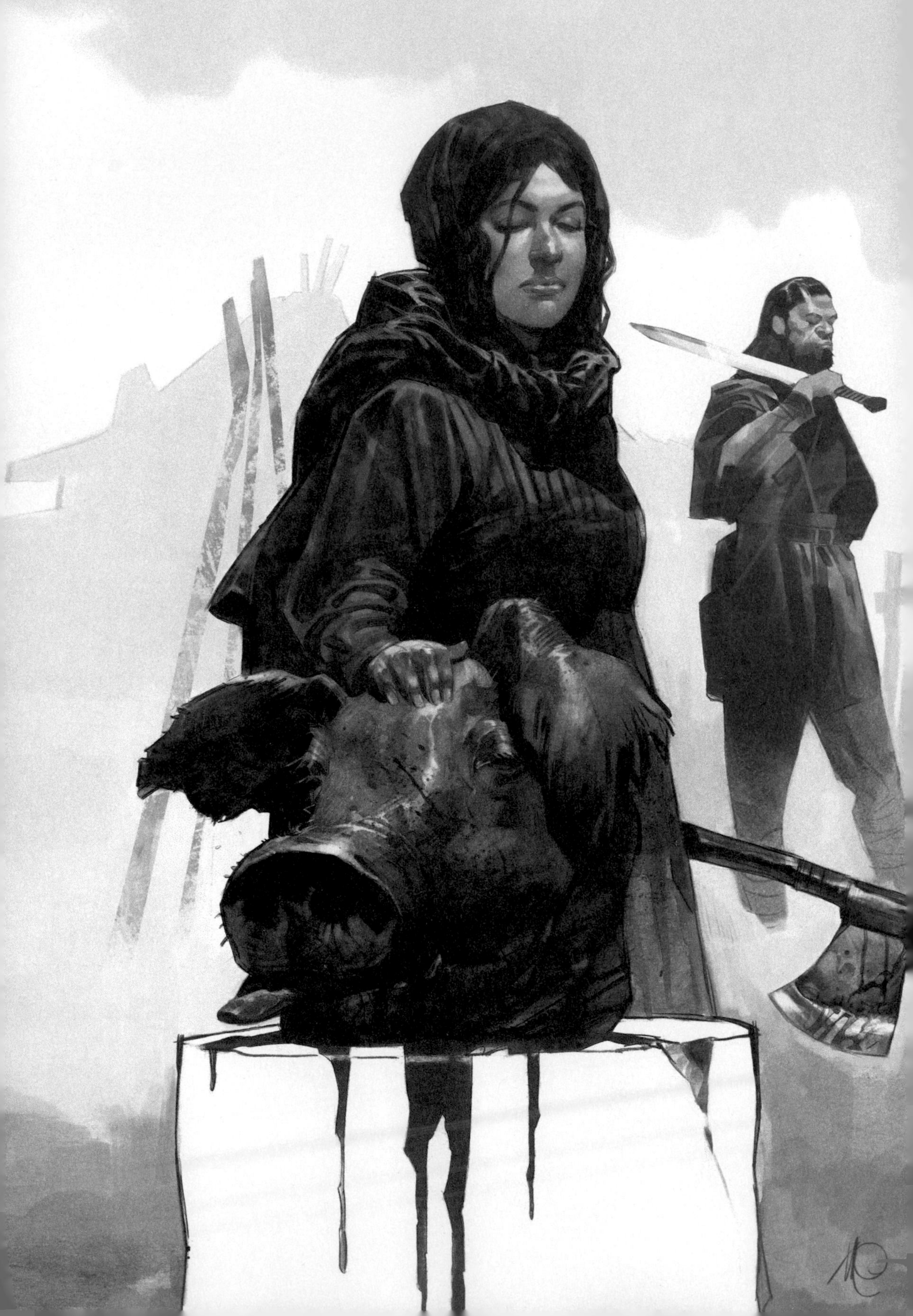

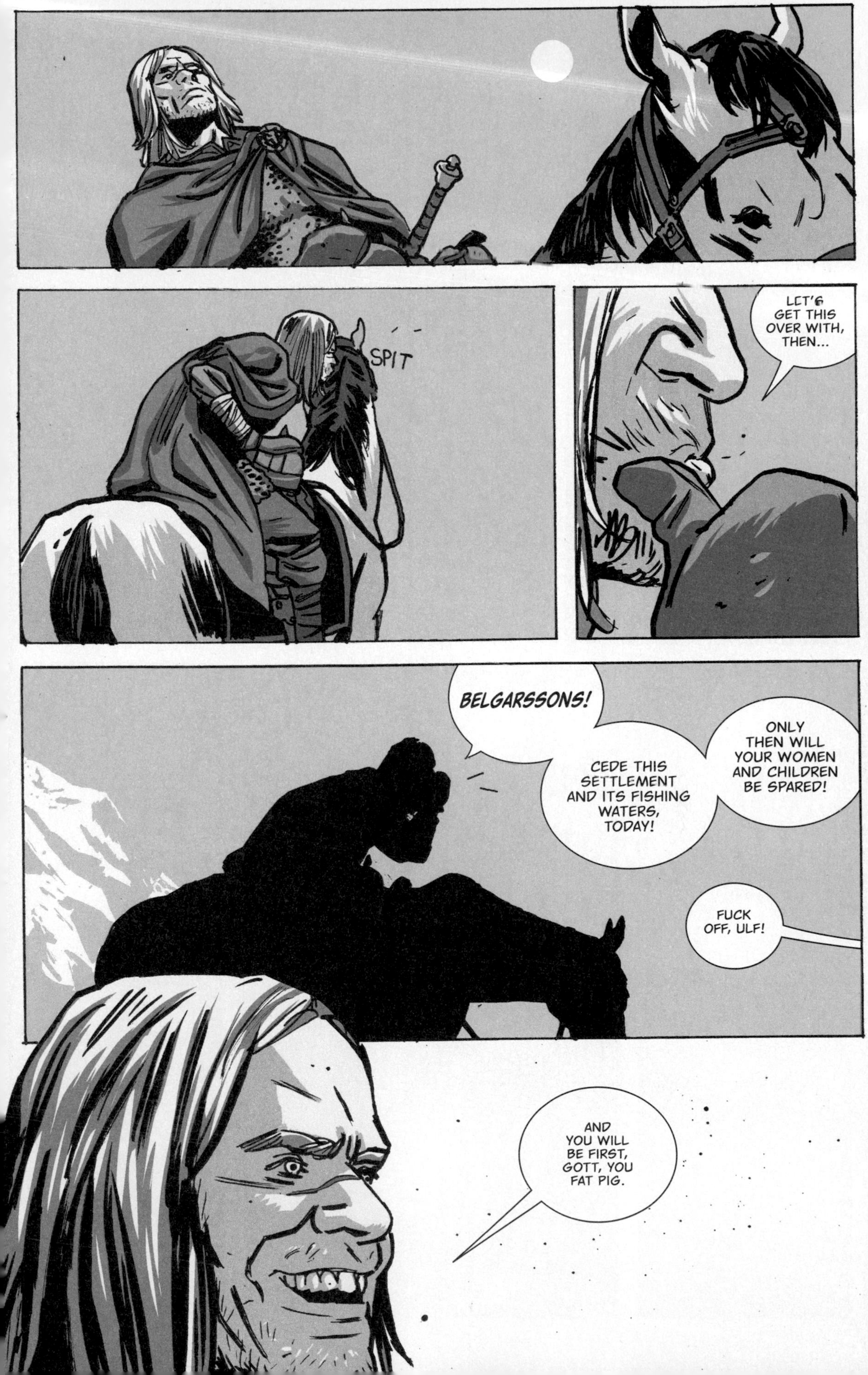
SPIT
LET'S GET THIS OVER WITH, THEN...
BELGARSSONS!
CEDE THIS SETTLEMENT AND ITS FISHING WATERS, TODAY!
ONLY THEN WILL YOUR WOMEN AND CHILDREN BE SPARED!
FUCK OFF, ULF!
AND YOU WILL BE FIRST, GOTT, YOU FAT PIG.

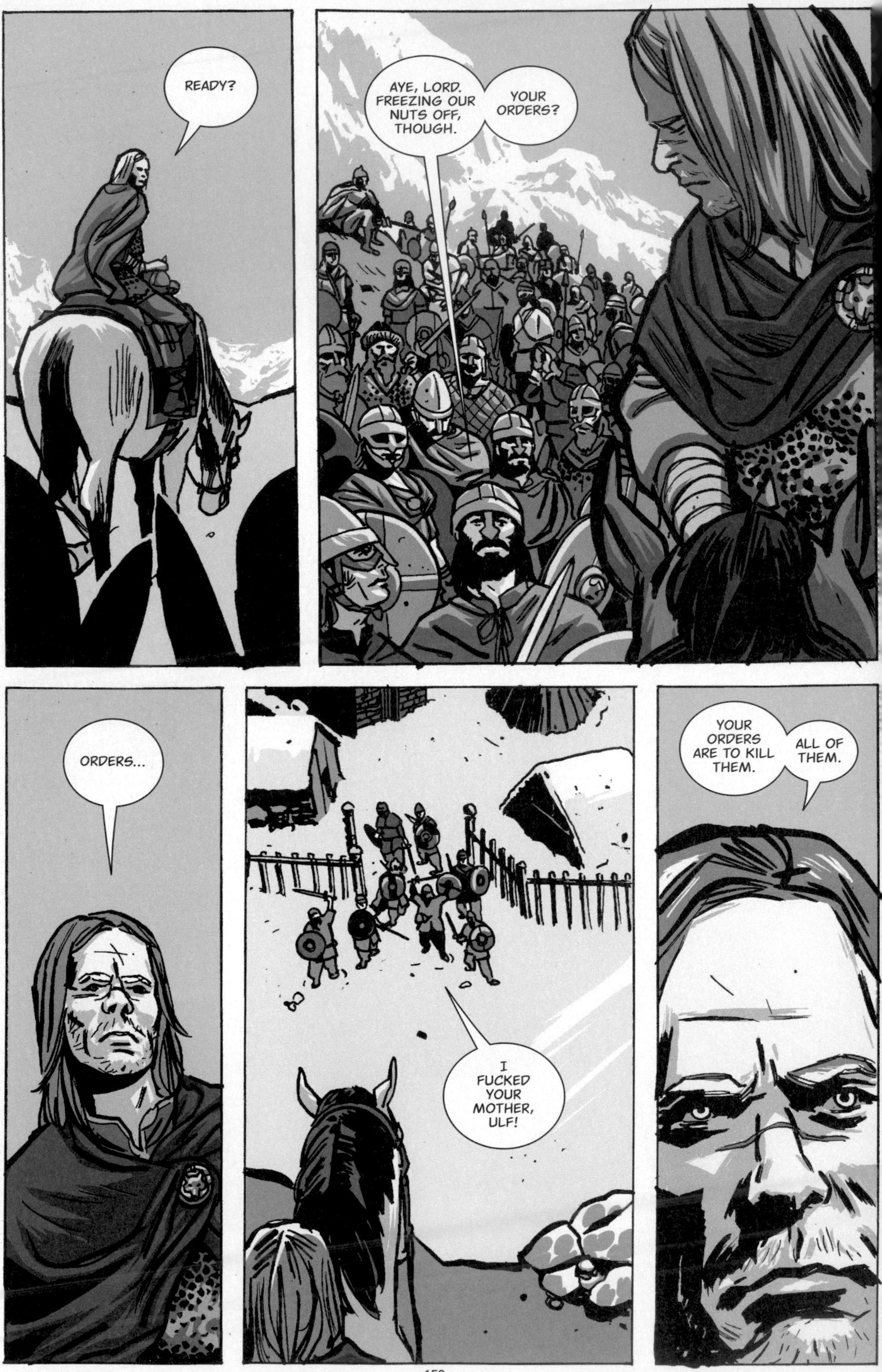
READY?
AYE, LORD. FREEZING OUR NUTS OFF, THOUGH.
YOUR ORDERS?
ORDERS...
I FUCKED YOUR MOTHER, ULF!
YOUR ORDERS ARE TO KILL THEM.
ALL OF THEM.

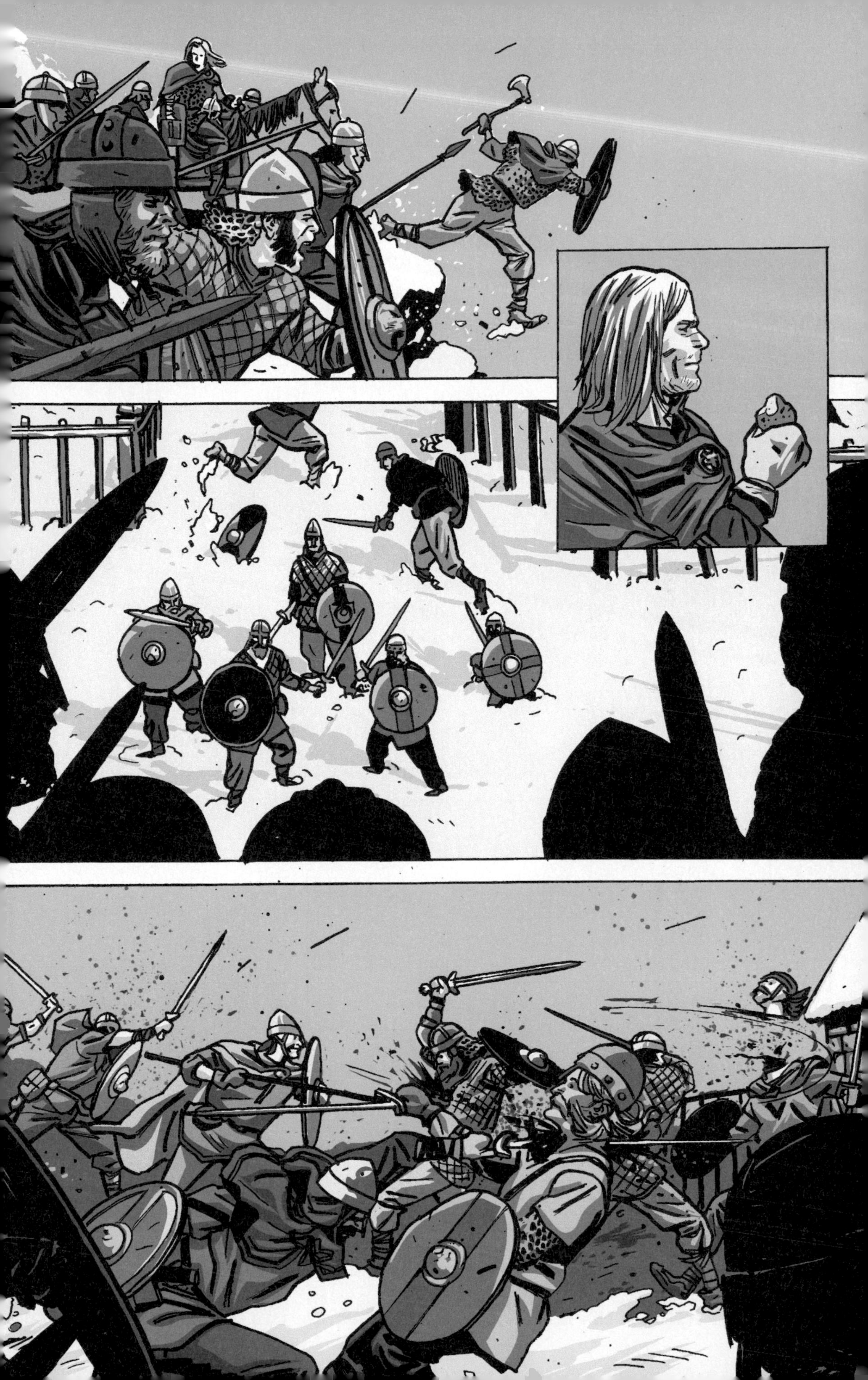

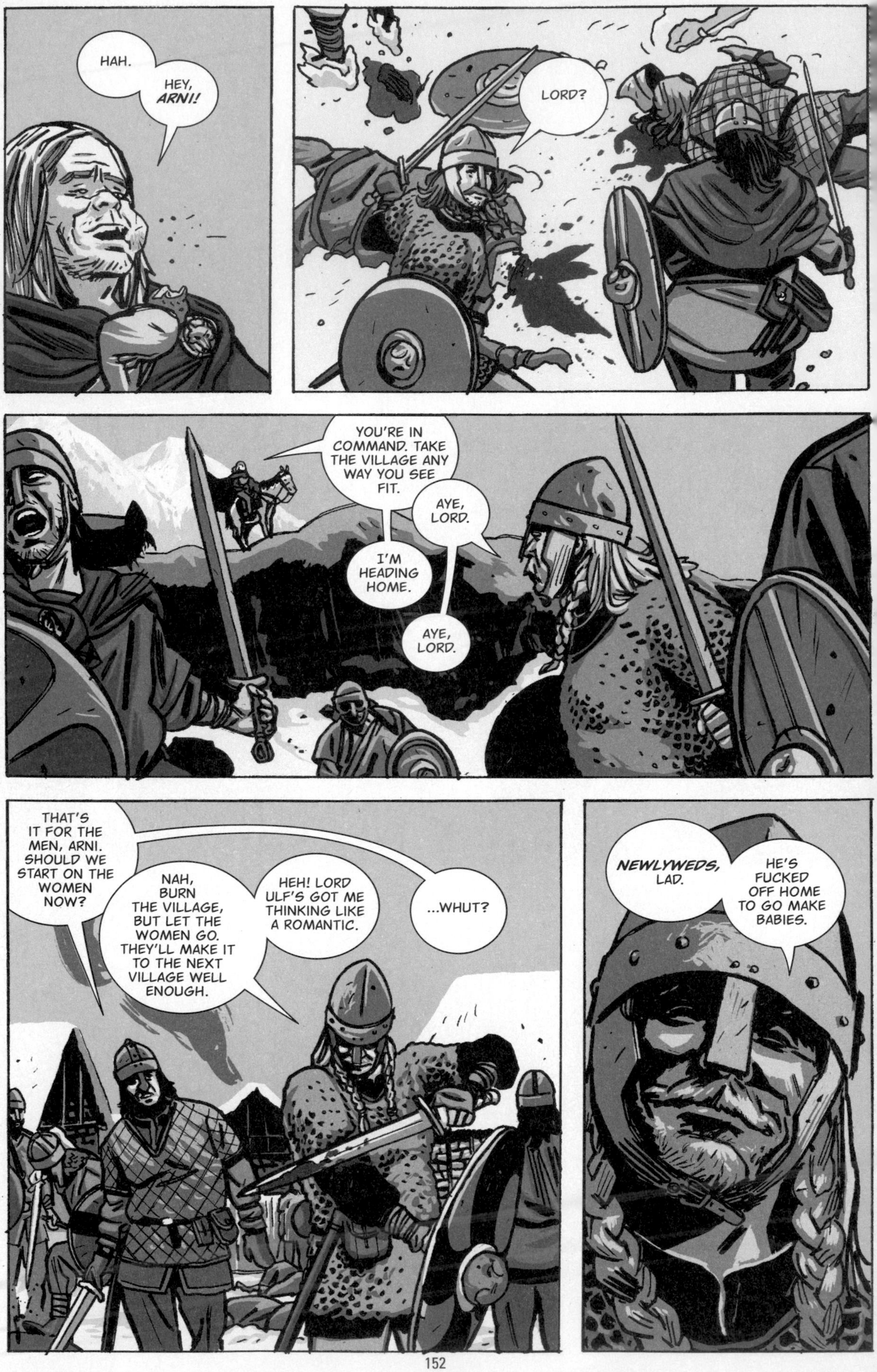
HAH.
HEY, ARNI!
LORD?
YOU'RE IN COMMAND. TAKE THE VILLAGE ANY WAY YOU SEE FIT.
AYE, LORD.
I'M HEADING HOME.
AYE, LORD.
THAT'S IT FOR THE MEN, ARNI. SHOULD WE START ON THE WOMEN NOW?
NAH, BURN THE VILLAGE, BUT LET THE WOMEN GO. THEY'LL MAKE IT TO THE NEXT VILLAGE WELL ENOUGH.
HEH! LORD ULF'S GOT ME THINKING LIKE A ROMANTIC.
...WHUT?
NEWLYWEDS, LAD.
HE'S FUCKED OFF HOME TO GO MAKE BABIES.

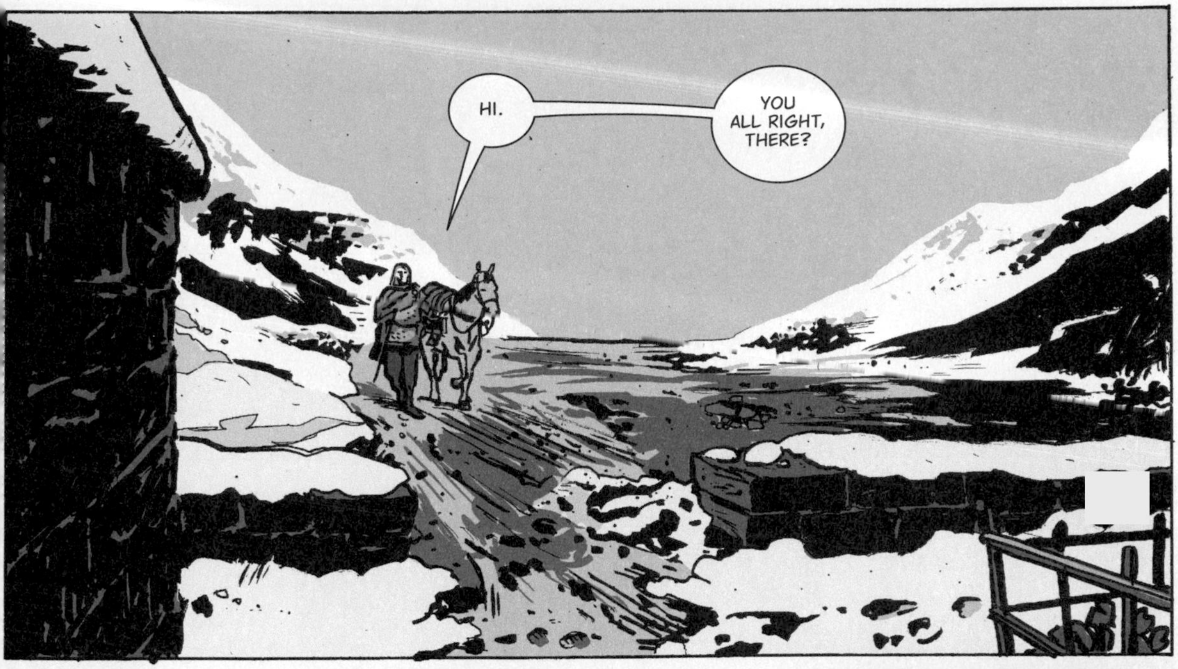
HI.
YOU ALL RIGHT, THERE?

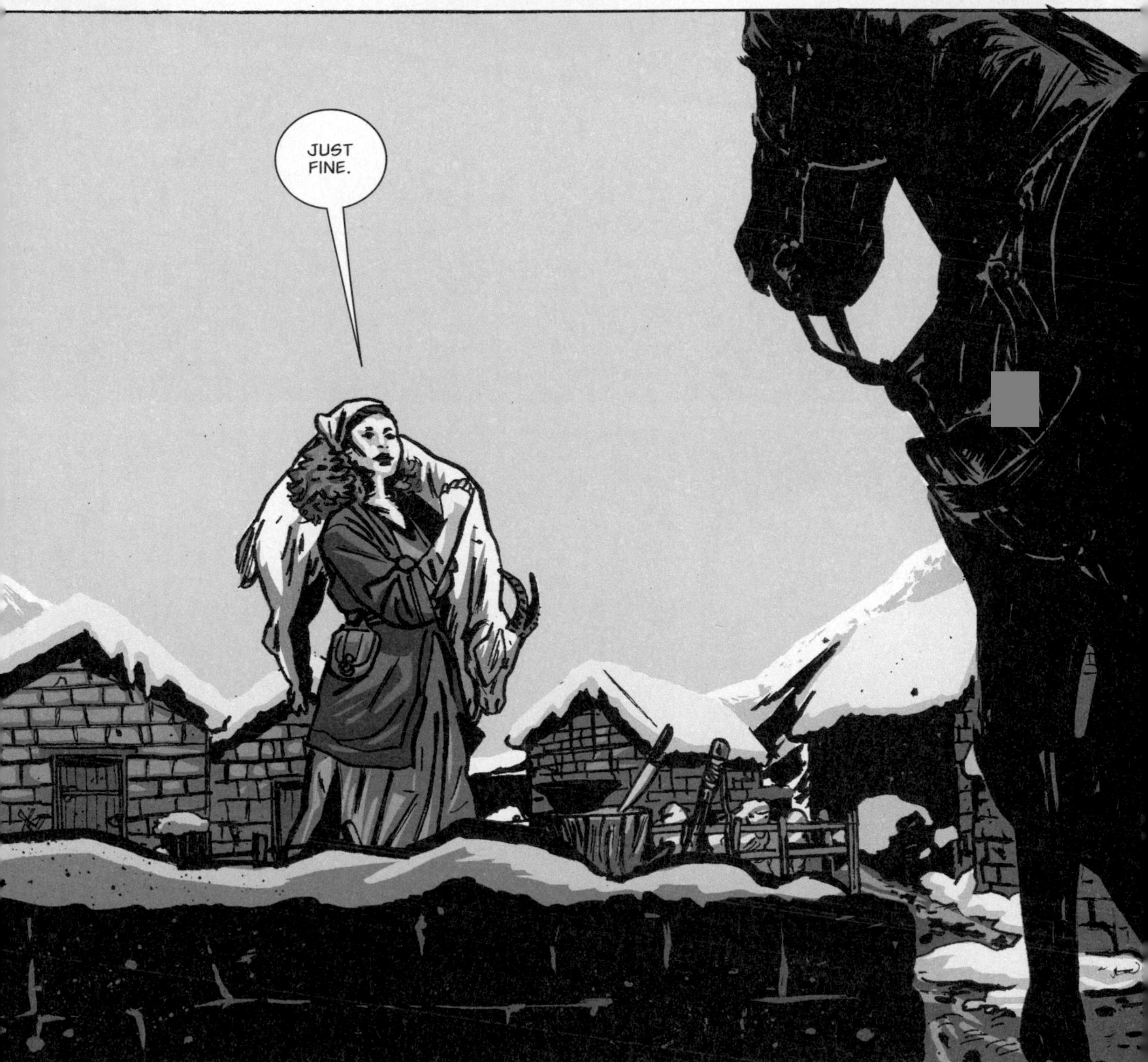
JUST FINE.

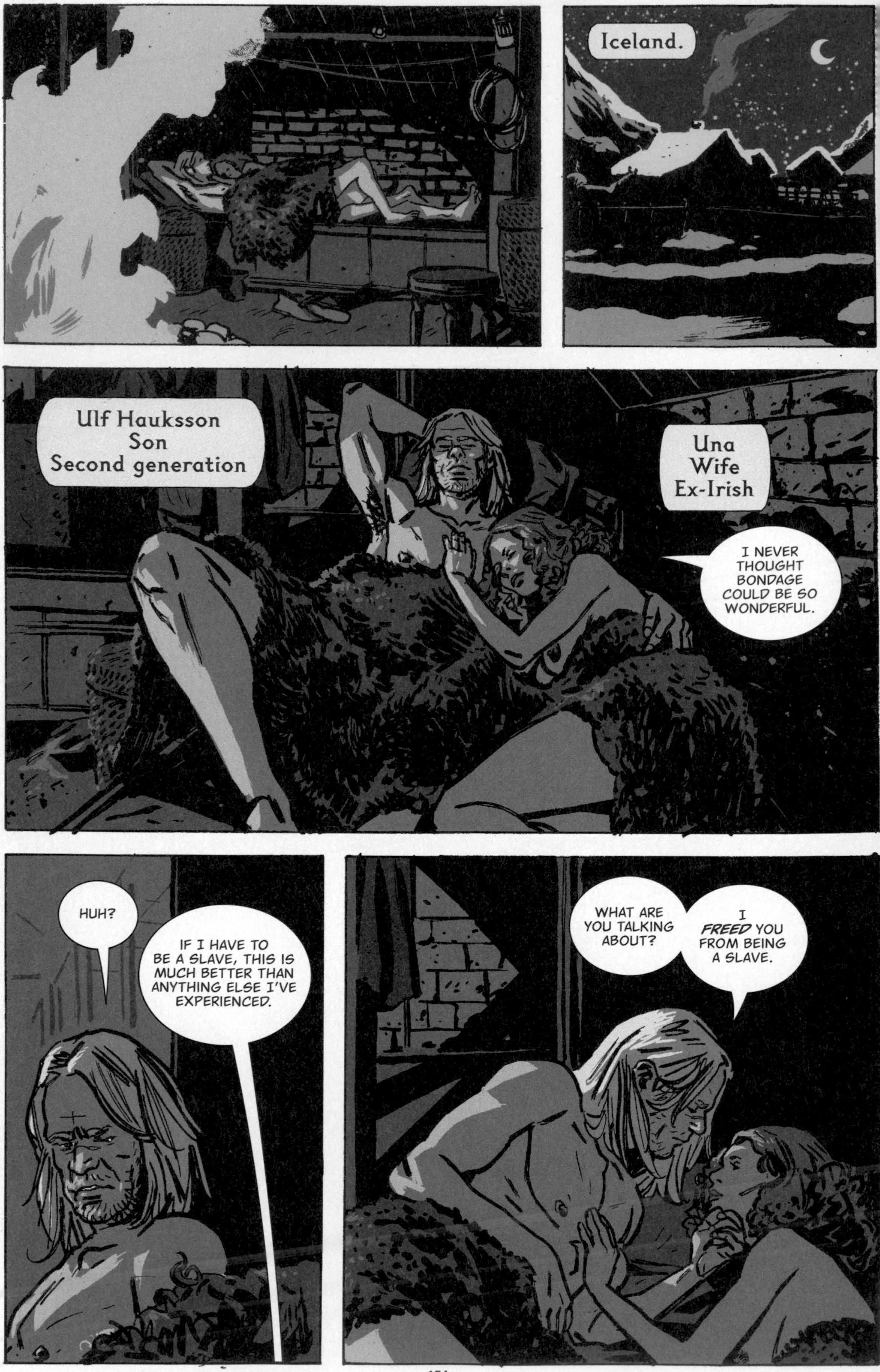
Iceland.
Ulf Hauksson
Son
Second generation
Una
Wife
Ex-Irish
I NEVER THOUGHT BONDAGE COULD BE SO WONDERFUL.
HUH?
IF I HAVE TO BE A SLAVE, THIS IS MUCH BETTER THAN ANYTHING ELSE I'VE EXPERIENCED.
WHAT ARE YOU TALKING ABOUT?
I *FREED* YOU FROM BEING A SLAVE.

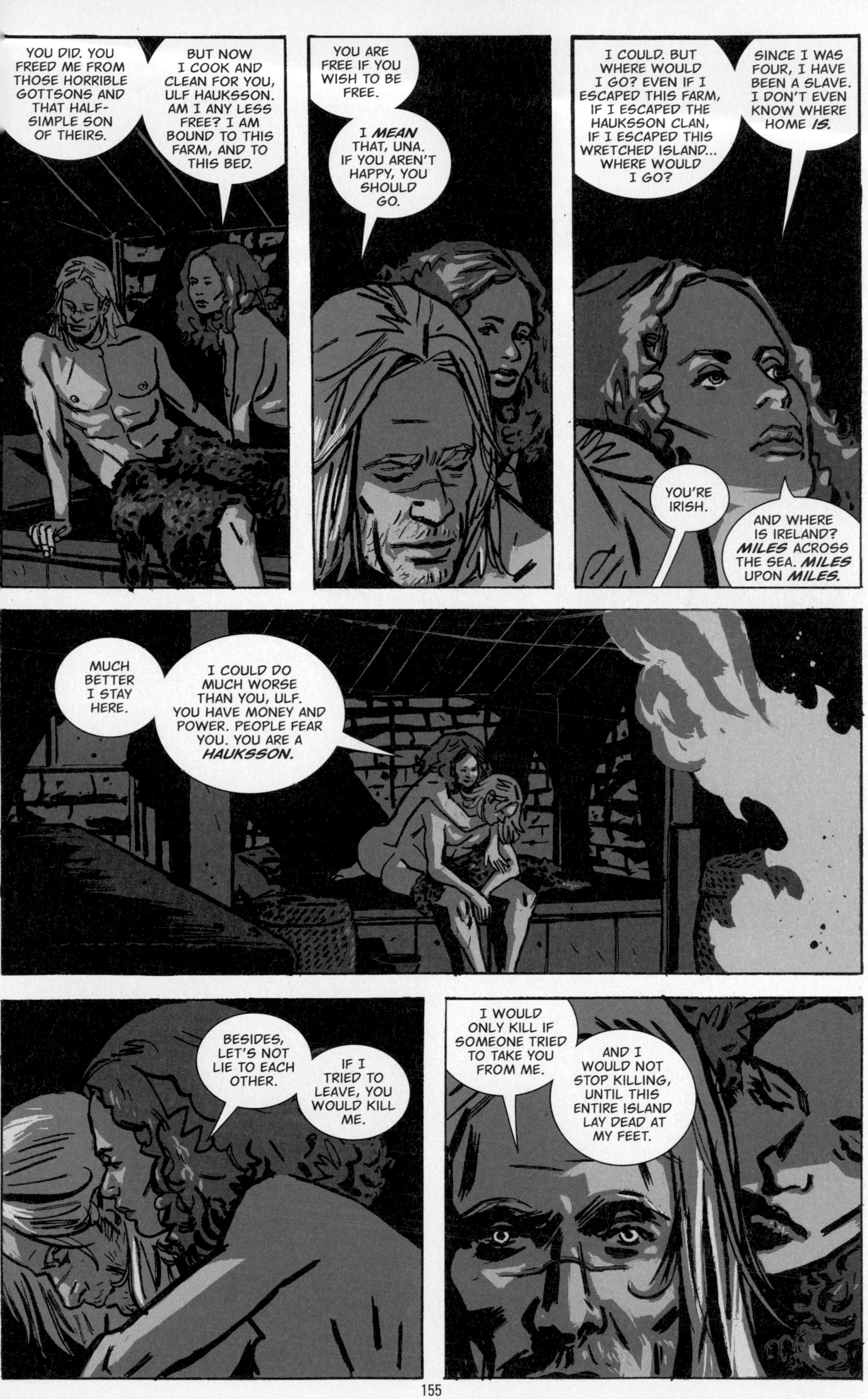
YOU DID. YOU FREED ME FROM THOSE HORRIBLE GOTTSONS AND THAT HALF-SIMPLE SON OF THEIRS.
BUT NOW I COOK AND CLEAN FOR YOU, ULF HAUKSSON. AM I ANY LESS FREE? I AM BOUND TO THIS FARM, AND TO THIS BED.
YOU ARE FREE IF YOU WISH TO BE FREE.
I MEAN THAT, UNA. IF YOU AREN'T HAPPY, YOU SHOULD GO.
I COULD. BUT WHERE WOULD I GO? EVEN IF I ESCAPED THIS FARM, IF I ESCAPED THE HAUKSSON CLAN, IF I ESCAPED THIS WRETCHED ISLAND... WHERE WOULD I GO?
SINCE I WAS FOUR, I HAVE BEEN A SLAVE. I DON'T EVEN KNOW WHERE HOME IS.
YOU'RE IRISH.
AND WHERE IS IRELAND? MILES ACROSS THE SEA. MILES UPON MILES.
MUCH BETTER I STAY HERE.
I COULD DO MUCH WORSE THAN YOU, ULF. YOU HAVE MONEY AND POWER. PEOPLE FEAR YOU. YOU ARE A HAUKSSON.
BESIDES, LET'S NOT LIE TO EACH OTHER.
IF I TRIED TO LEAVE, YOU WOULD KILL ME.
I WOULD ONLY KILL IF SOMEONE TRIED TO TAKE YOU FROM ME.
AND I WOULD NOT STOP KILLING, UNTIL THIS ENTIRE ISLAND LAY DEAD AT MY FEET.

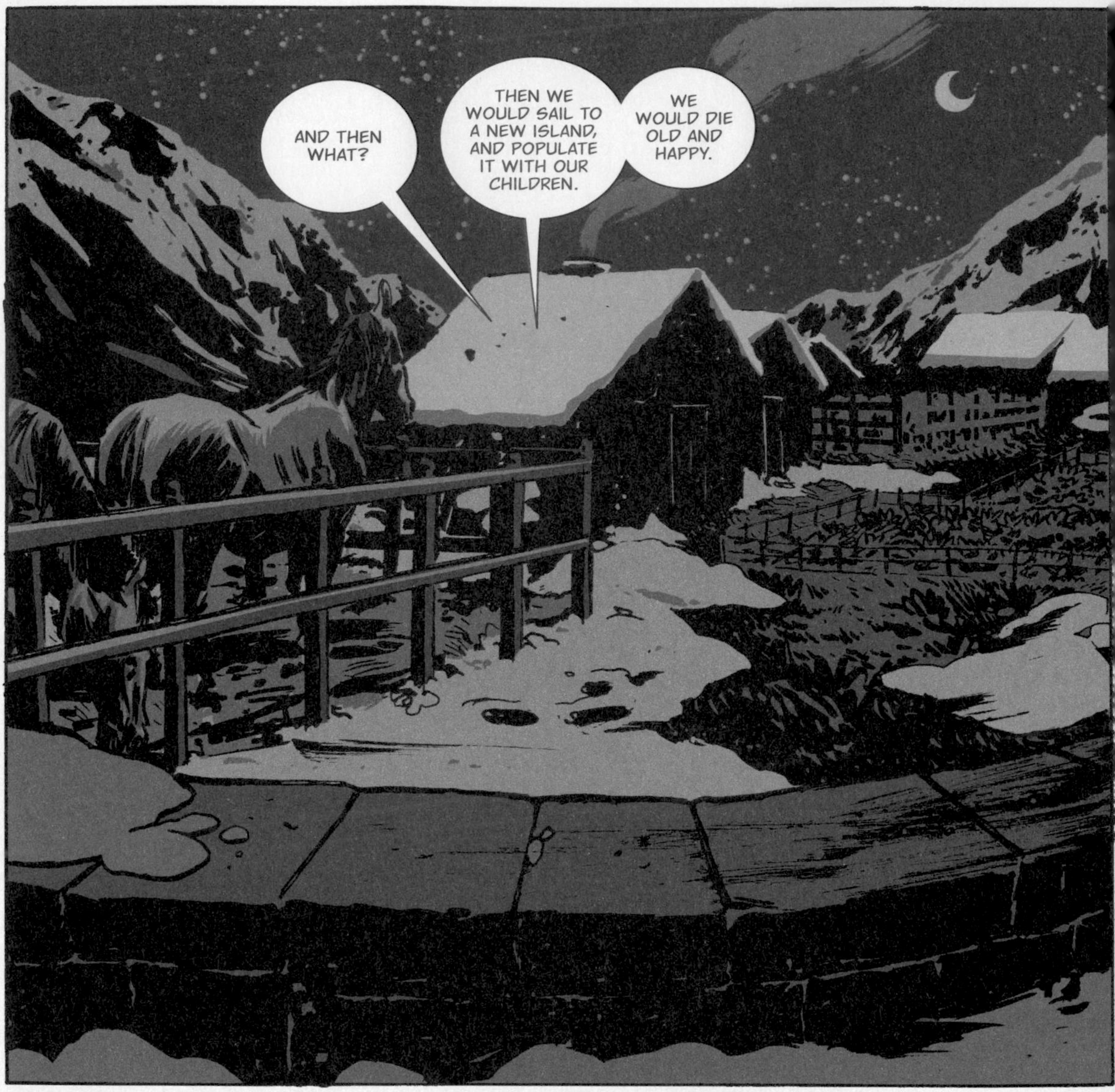
AND THEN WHAT?
THEN WE WOULD SAIL TO A NEW ISLAND, AND POPULATE IT WITH OUR CHILDREN.
WE WOULD DIE OLD AND HAPPY.

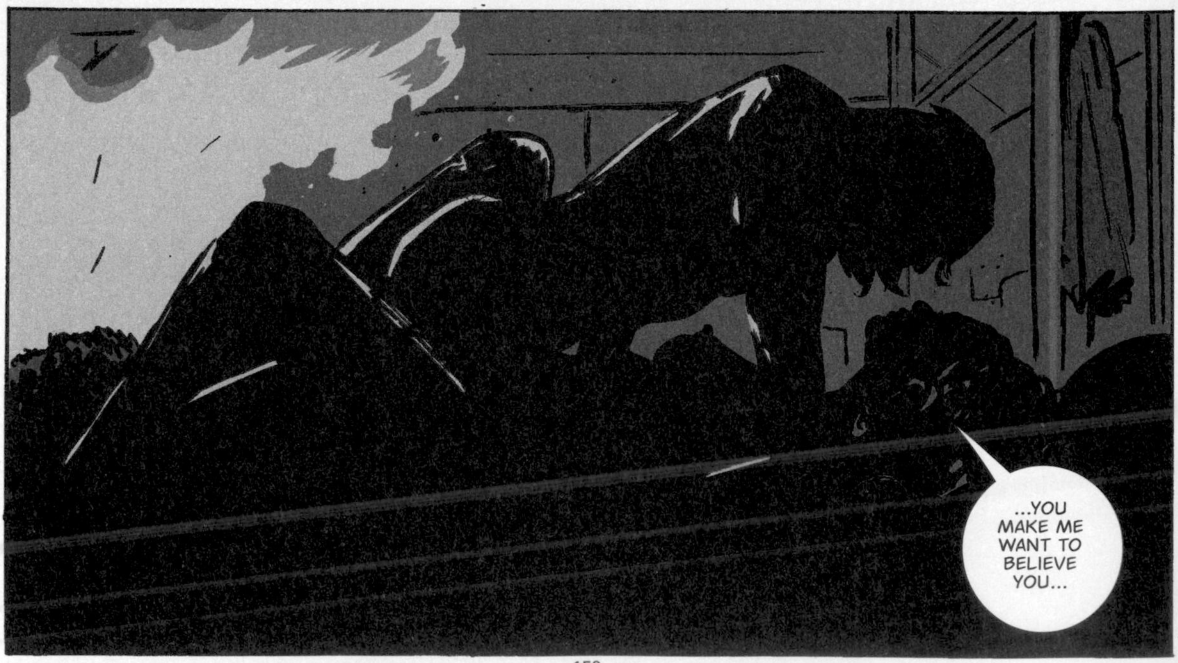
...YOU MAKE ME WANT TO BELIEVE YOU...

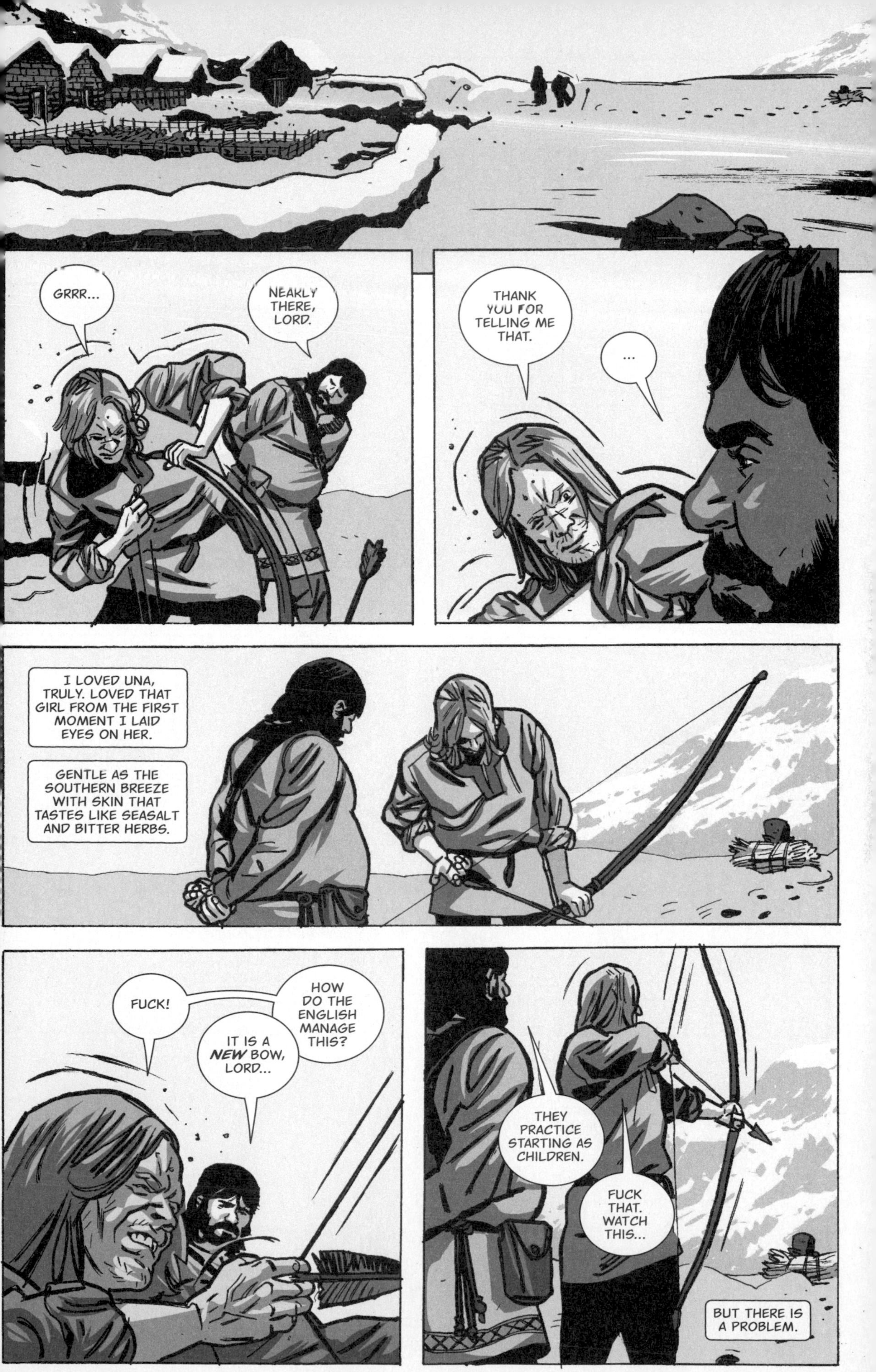
GRRR...
NEARLY THERE, LORD.
THANK YOU FOR TELLING ME THAT.
...
I LOVED UNA, TRULY. LOVED THAT GIRL FROM THE FIRST MOMENT I LAID EYES ON HER.
GENTLE AS THE SOUTHERN BREEZE WITH SKIN THAT TASTES LIKE SEASALT AND BITTER HERBS.
FUCK!
HOW DO THE ENGLISH MANAGE THIS?
IT IS A *NEW* BOW, LORD...
THEY PRACTICE STARTING AS CHILDREN.
FUCK THAT. WATCH THIS...
BUT THERE IS A PROBLEM.

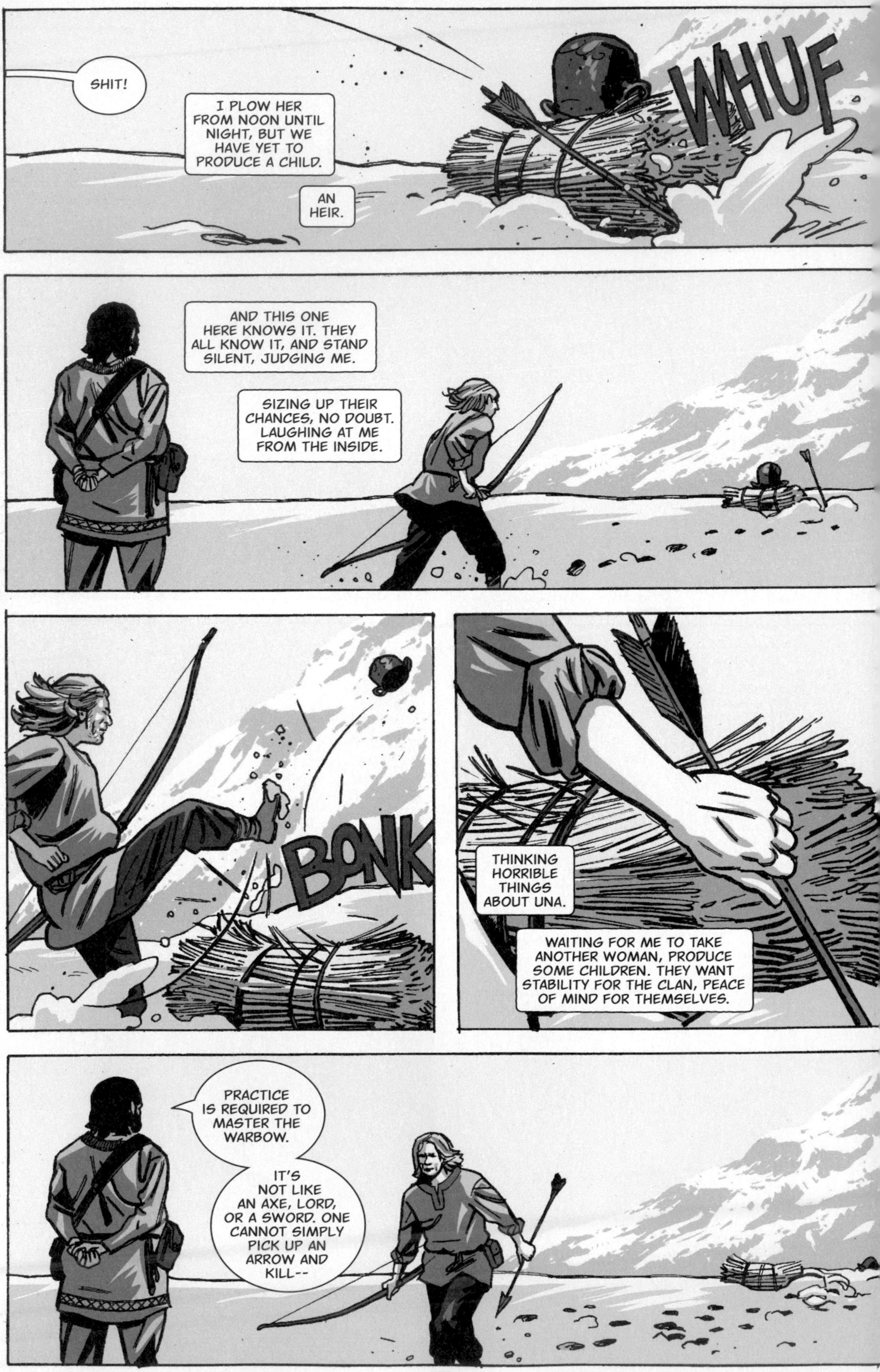
SHIT!
I PLOW HER FROM NOON UNTIL NIGHT, BUT WE HAVE YET TO PRODUCE A CHILD.
AN HEIR.
WHUF
AND THIS ONE HERE KNOWS IT. THEY ALL KNOW IT, AND STAND SILENT, JUDGING ME.
SIZING UP THEIR CHANCES, NO DOUBT. LAUGHING AT ME FROM THE INSIDE.
BONK
THINKING HORRIBLE THINGS ABOUT UNA.
WAITING FOR ME TO TAKE ANOTHER WOMAN, PRODUCE SOME CHILDREN. THEY WANT STABILITY FOR THE CLAN, PEACE OF MIND FOR THEMSELVES.
PRACTICE IS REQUIRED TO MASTER THE WARBOW.
IT'S NOT LIKE AN AXE, LORD, OR A SWORD. ONE CANNOT SIMPLY PICK UP AN ARROW AND KILL--

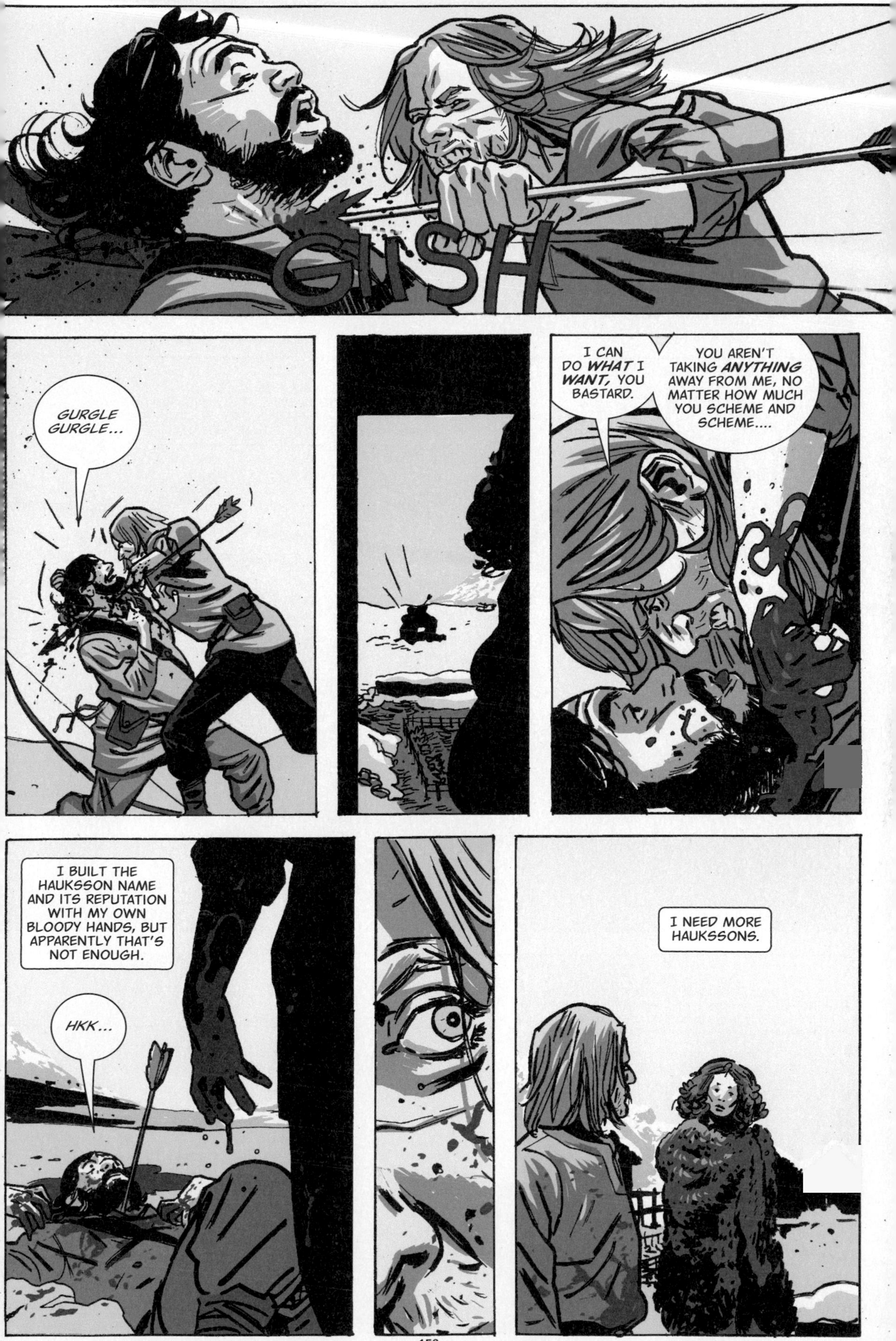
GUSH
GURGLE GURGLE...
I CAN DO WHAT I WANT, YOU BASTARD.
YOU AREN'T TAKING ANYTHING AWAY FROM ME, NO MATTER HOW MUCH YOU SCHEME AND SCHEME....
I BUILT THE HAUKSSON NAME AND ITS REPUTATION WITH MY OWN BLOODY HANDS, BUT APPARENTLY THAT'S NOT ENOUGH.
HKK...
I NEED MORE HAUKSSONS.

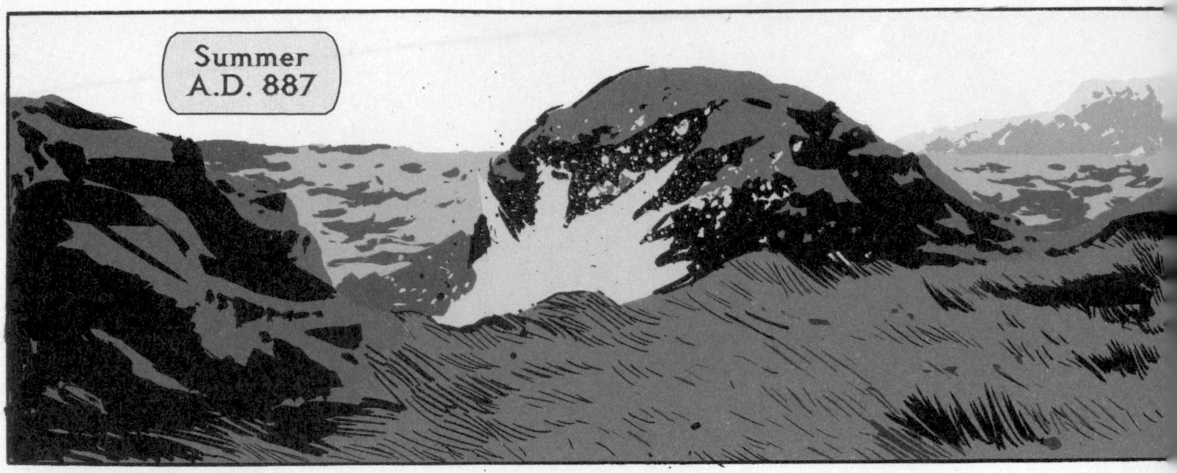
Summer
A.D. 887

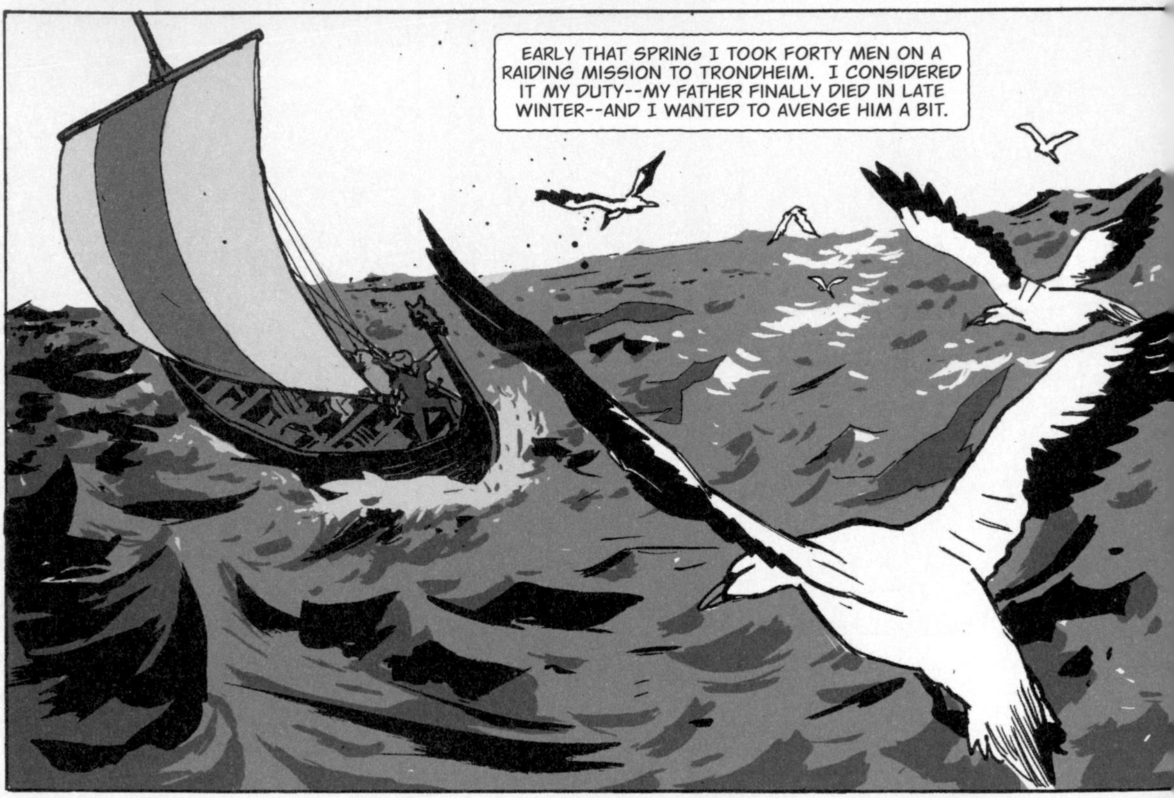
EARLY THAT SPRING I TOOK FORTY MEN ON A RAIDING MISSION TO TRONDHEIM. I CONSIDERED IT MY DUTY--MY FATHER FINALLY DIED IN LATE WINTER--AND I WANTED TO AVENGE HIM A BIT.

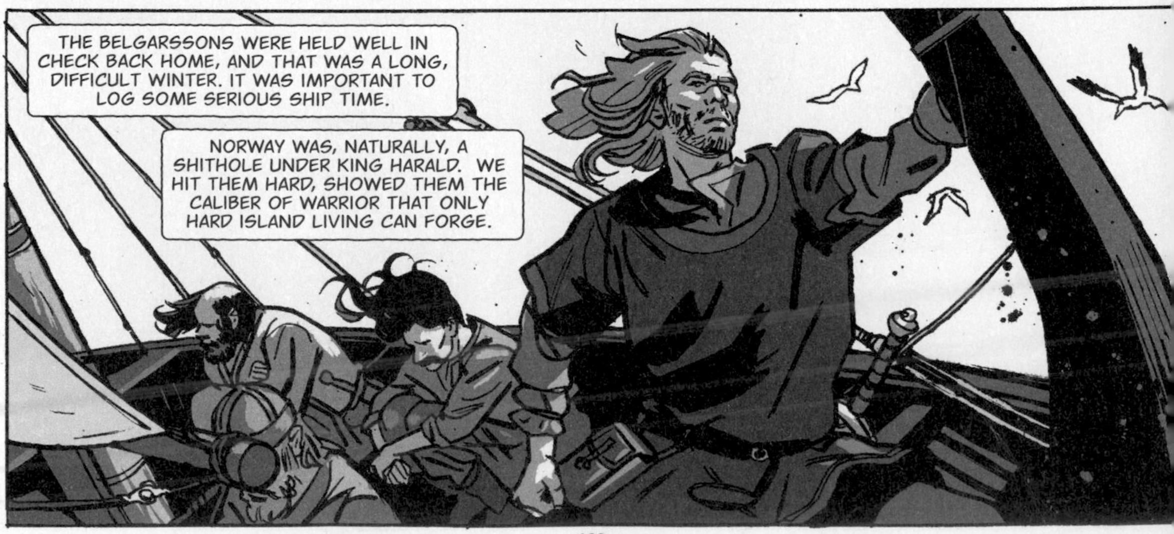
THE BELGARSSONS WERE HELD WELL IN CHECK BACK HOME, AND THAT WAS A LONG, DIFFICULT WINTER. IT WAS IMPORTANT TO LOG SOME SERIOUS SHIP TIME.
NORWAY WAS, NATURALLY, A SHITHOLE UNDER KING HARALD. WE HIT THEM HARD, SHOWED THEM THE CALIBER OF WARRIOR THAT ONLY HARD ISLAND LIVING CAN FORGE.

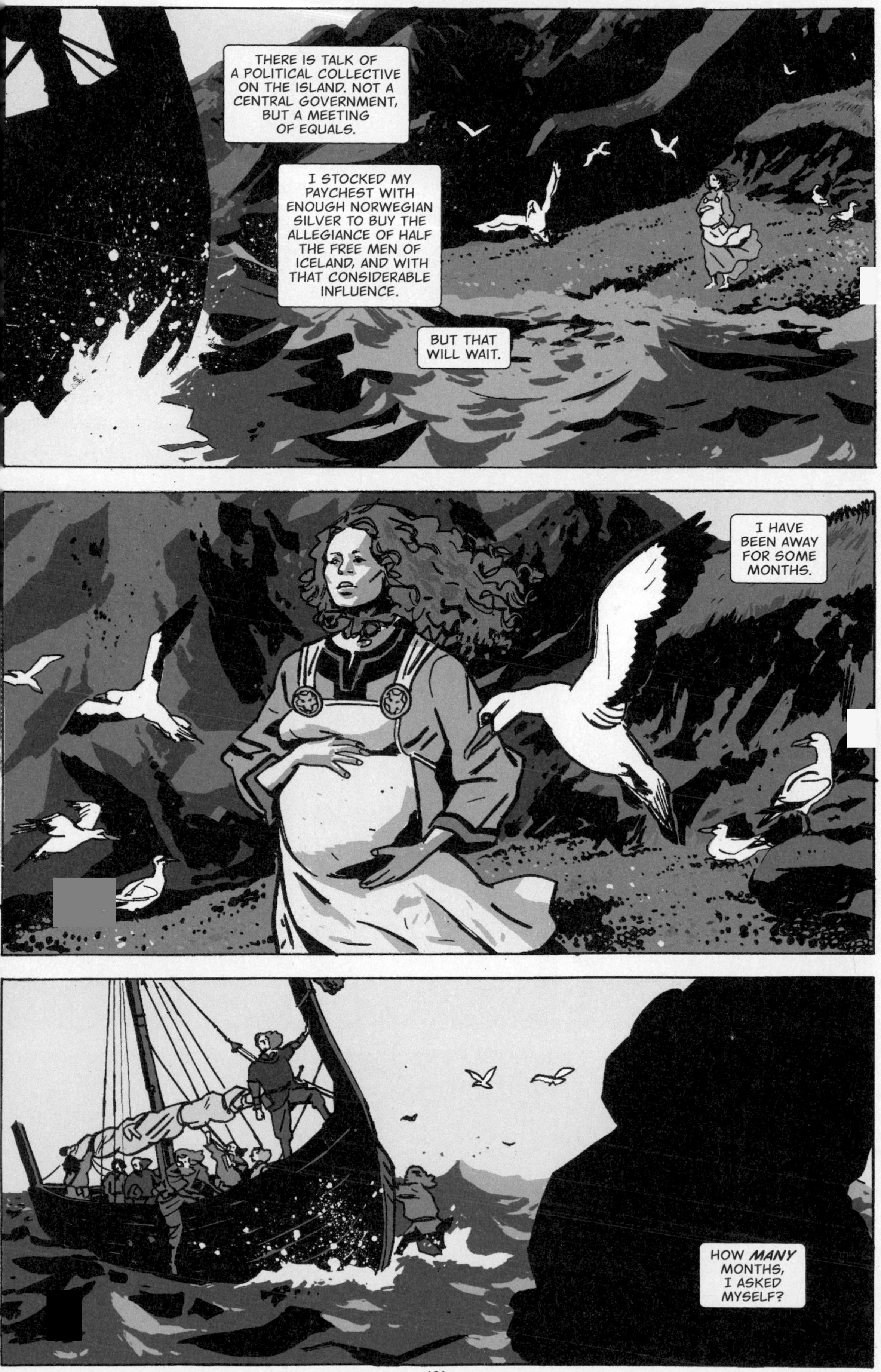
THERE IS TALK OF A POLITICAL COLLECTIVE ON THE ISLAND. NOT A CENTRAL GOVERNMENT, BUT A MEETING OF EQUALS.
I STOCKED MY PAYCHEST WITH ENOUGH NORWEGIAN SILVER TO BUY THE ALLEGIANCE OF HALF THE FREE MEN OF ICELAND, AND WITH THAT CONSIDERABLE INFLUENCE.
BUT THAT WILL WAIT.
I HAVE BEEN AWAY FOR SOME MONTHS.
HOW *MANY* MONTHS, I ASKED MYSELF?

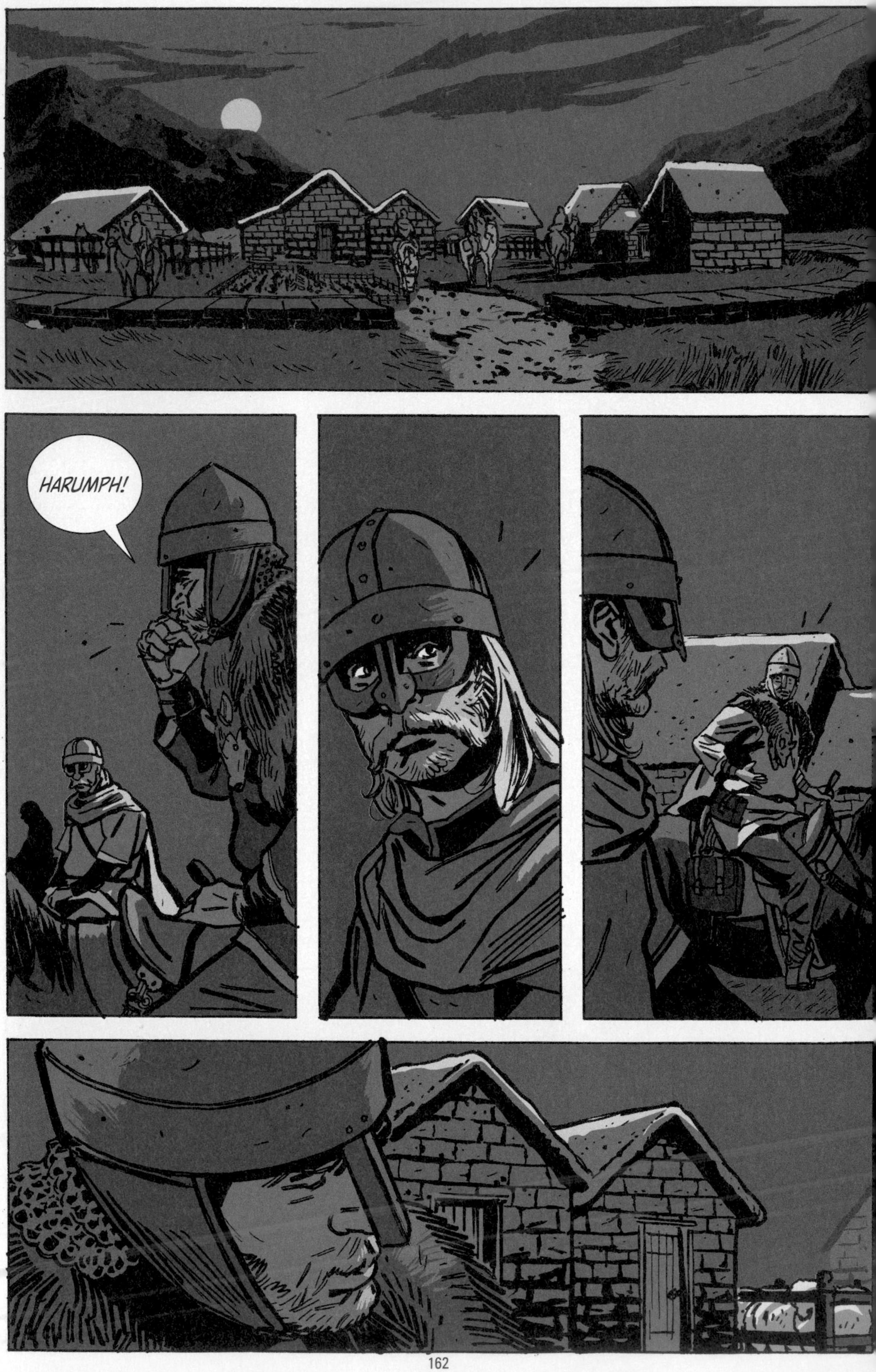
HARUMPH!

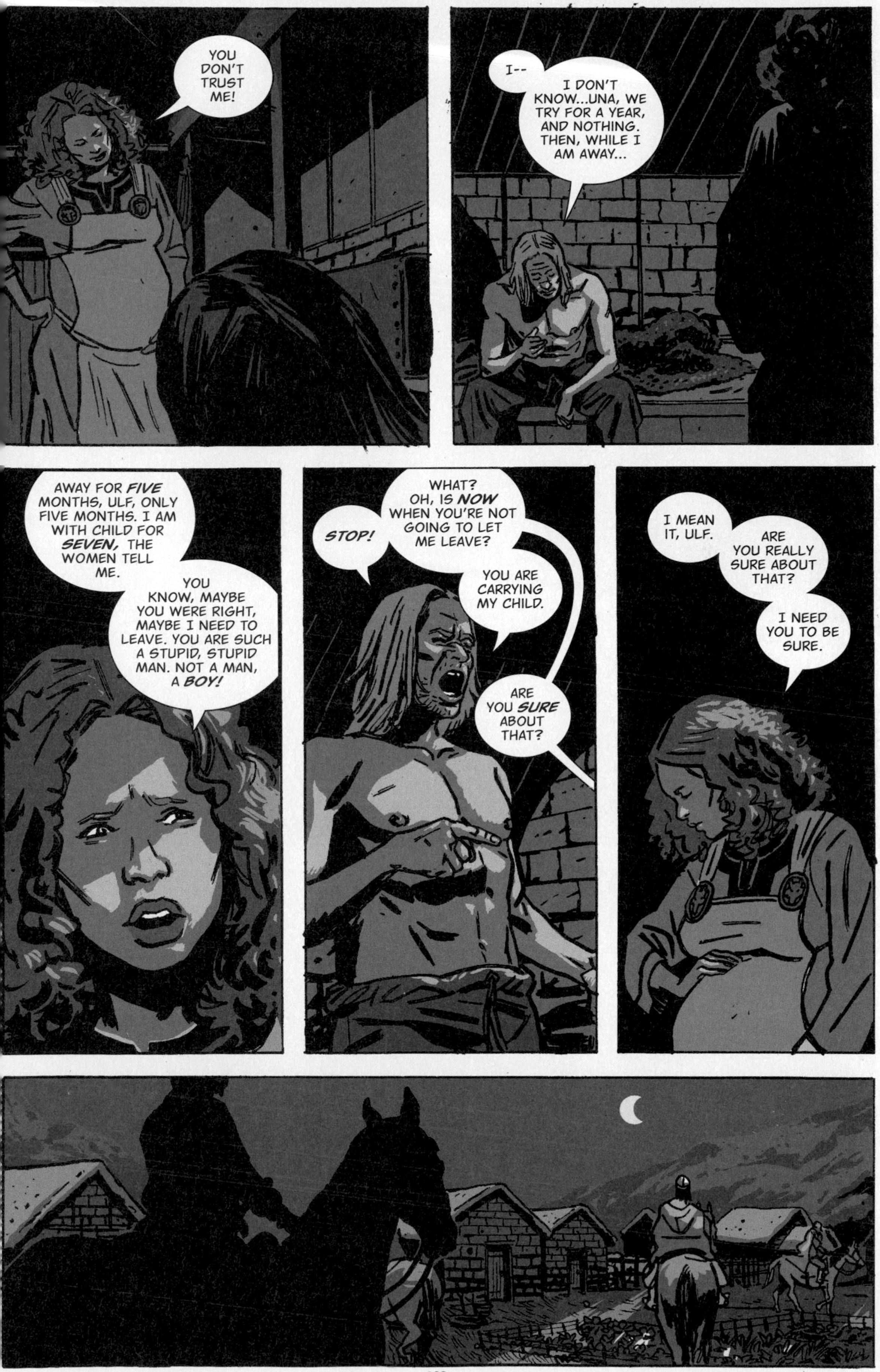
YOU DON'T TRUST ME!
I--
I DON'T KNOW...UNA, WE TRY FOR A YEAR, AND NOTHING. THEN, WHILE I AM AWAY...
AWAY FOR FIVE MONTHS, ULF, ONLY FIVE MONTHS. I AM WITH CHILD FOR SEVEN, THE WOMEN TELL ME.
YOU KNOW, MAYBE YOU WERE RIGHT, MAYBE I NEED TO LEAVE. YOU ARE SUCH A STUPID, STUPID MAN. NOT A MAN, A BOY!
STOP!
WHAT? OH, IS NOW WHEN YOU'RE NOT GOING TO LET ME LEAVE?
YOU ARE CARRYING MY CHILD.
ARE YOU SURE ABOUT THAT?
I MEAN IT, ULF.
ARE YOU REALLY SURE ABOUT THAT?
I NEED YOU TO BE SURE.

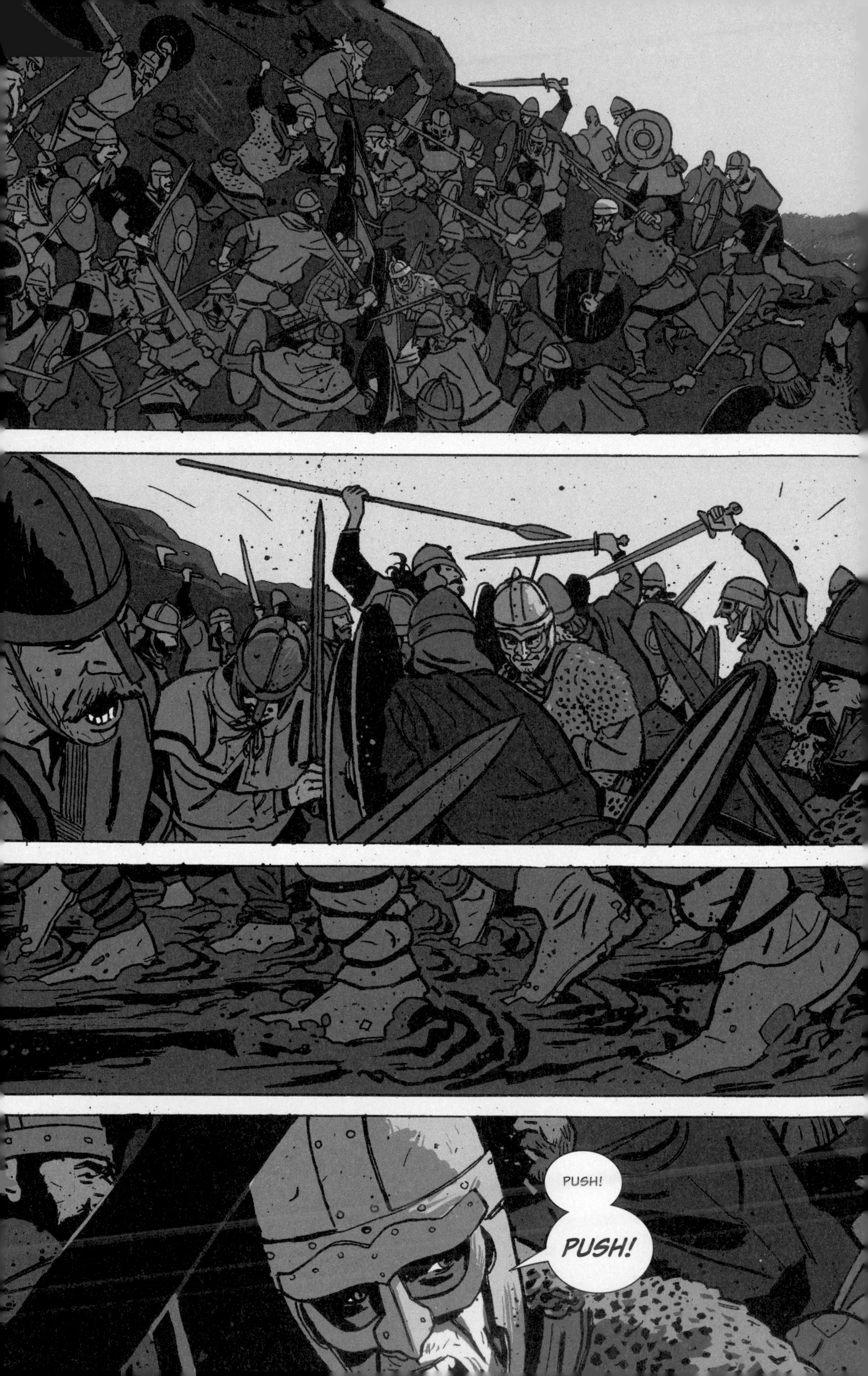
PUSH!
PUSH!

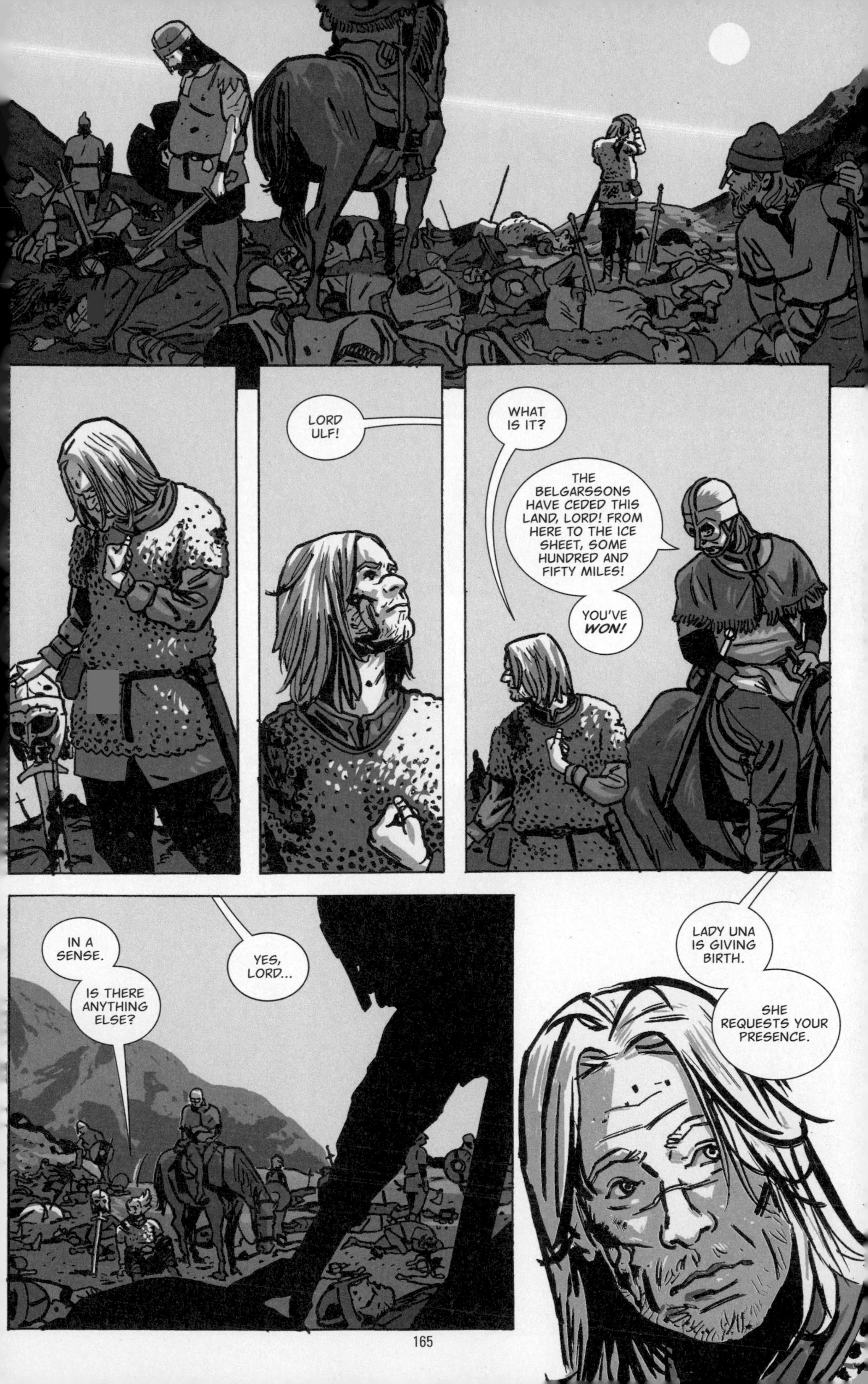
LORD ULF!
WHAT IS IT?
THE BELGARSSONS HAVE CEDED THIS LAND, LORD! FROM HERE TO THE ICE SHEET, SOME HUNDRED AND FIFTY MILES!
YOU'VE *WON!*
IN A SENSE.
IS THERE ANYTHING ELSE?
YES, LORD...
LADY UNA IS GIVING BIRTH.
SHE REQUESTS YOUR PRESENCE.

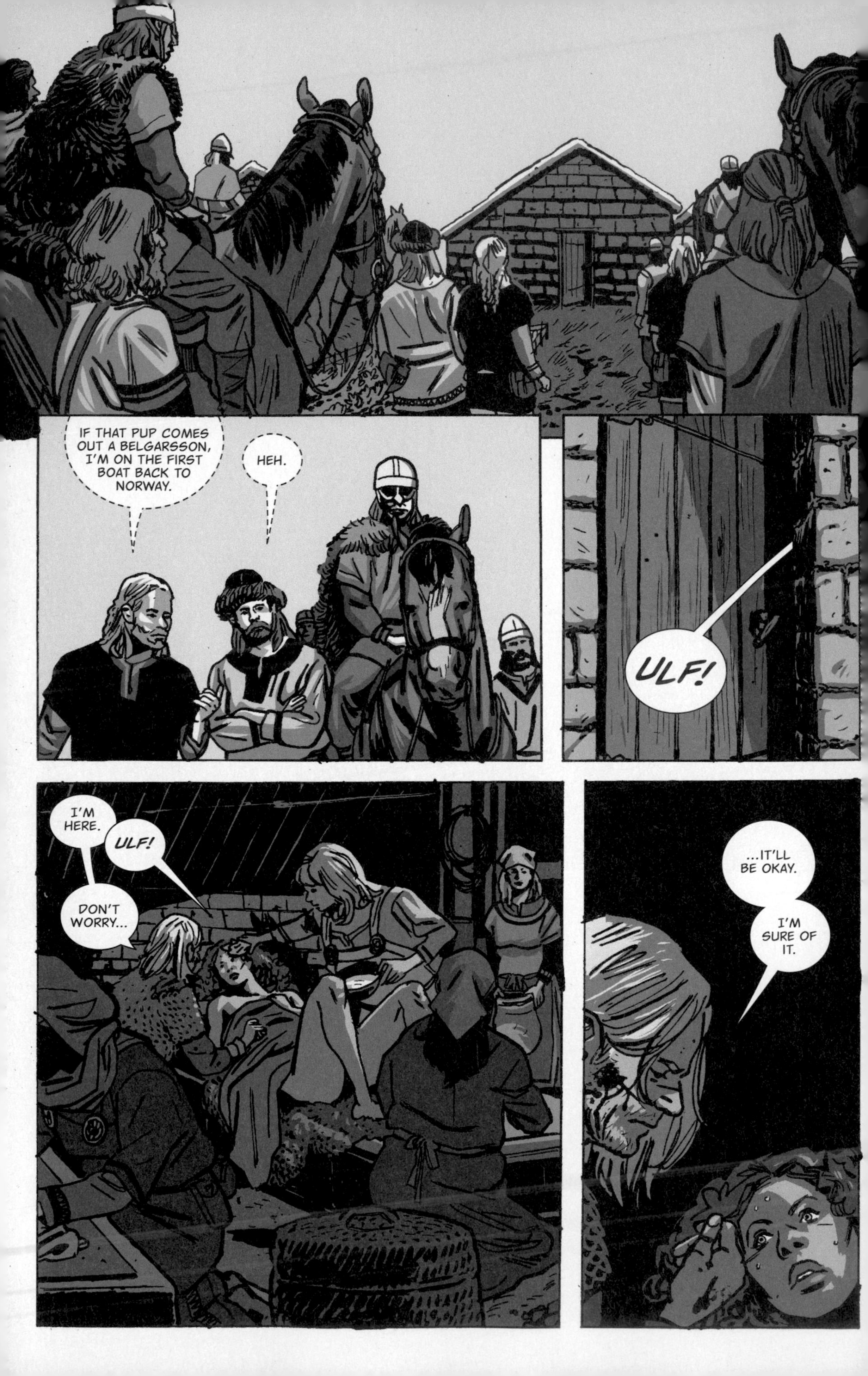

IF THAT PUP COMES OUT A BELGARSSON, I'M ON THE FIRST BOAT BACK TO NORWAY.
HEH.
ULF!
I'M HERE.
ULF!
DON'T WORRY...
...IT'LL BE OKAY.
I'M SURE OF IT.

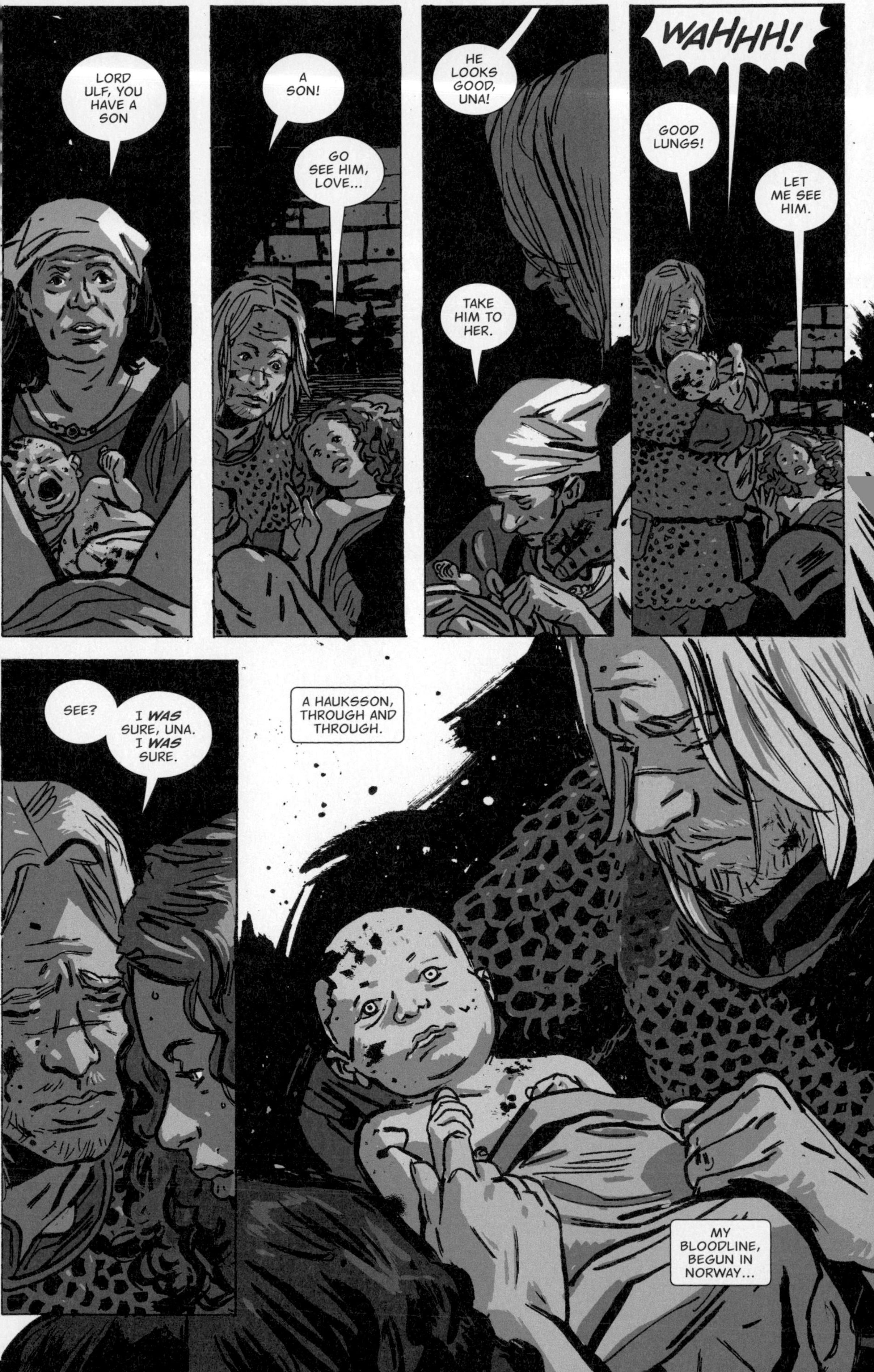

LORD ULF, YOU HAVE A SON
A SON!
GO SEE HIM, LOVE...
HE LOOKS GOOD, UNA!
TAKE HIM TO HER.
WAHHH!
GOOD LUNGS!
LET ME SEE HIM.
SEE?
I **WAS** SURE, UNA. I **WAS** SURE.
A HAUKSSON, THROUGH AND THROUGH.
MY BLOODLINE, BEGUN IN NORWAY...

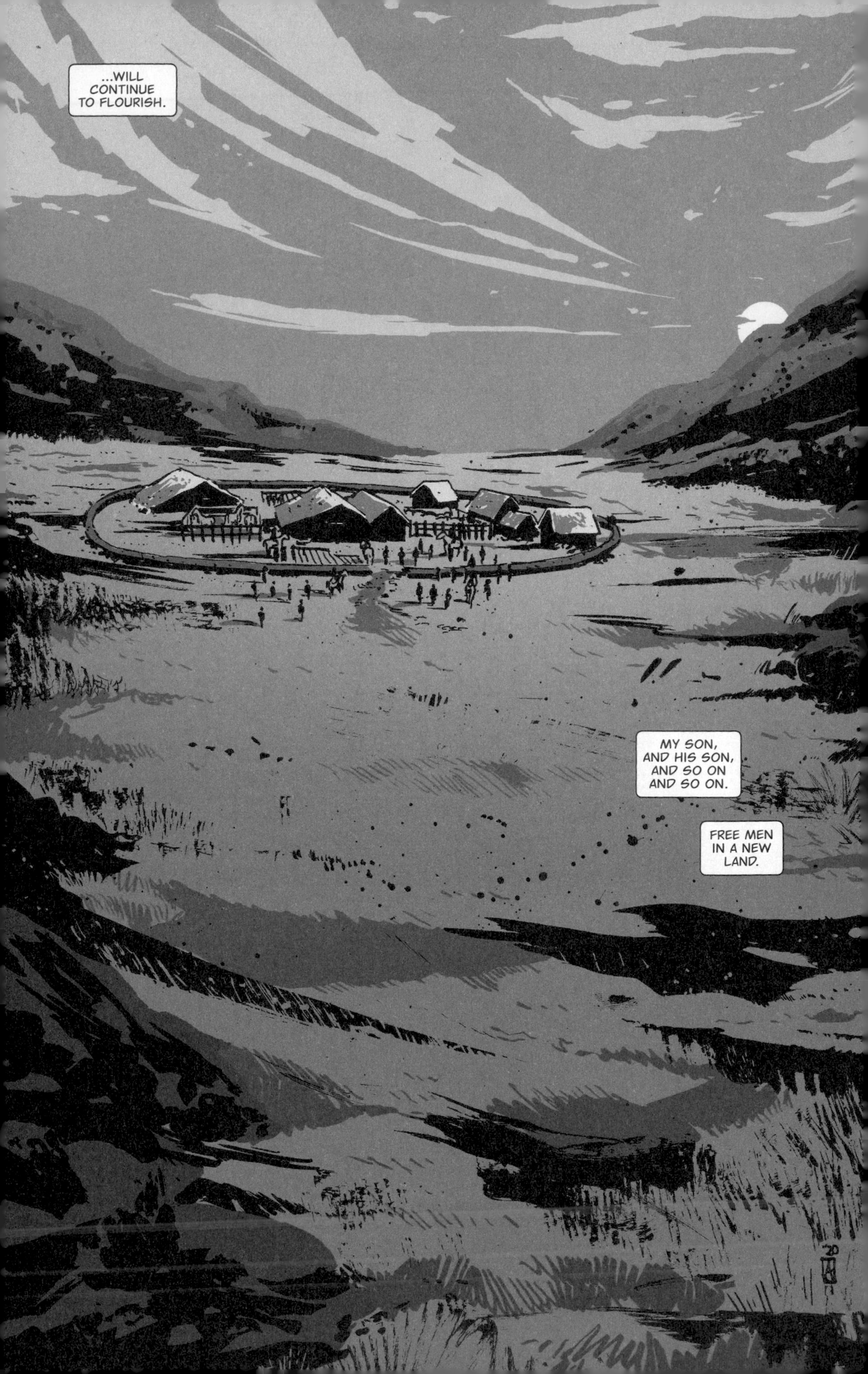
...WILL CONTINUE TO FLOURISH.
MY SON, AND HIS SON, AND SO ON AND SO ON.
FREE MEN IN A NEW LAND.

Chapter IV
Conversion
A.D. 999

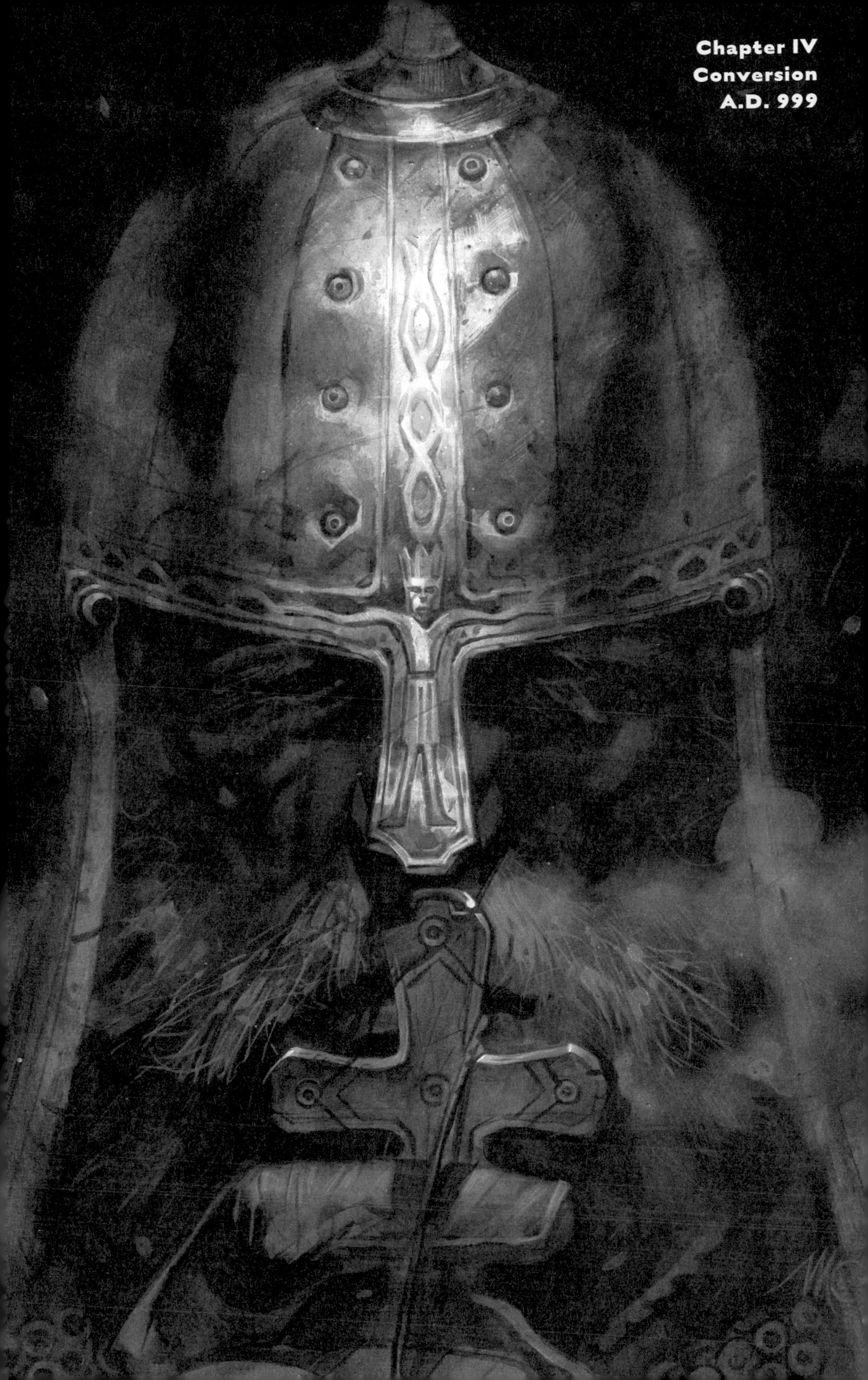

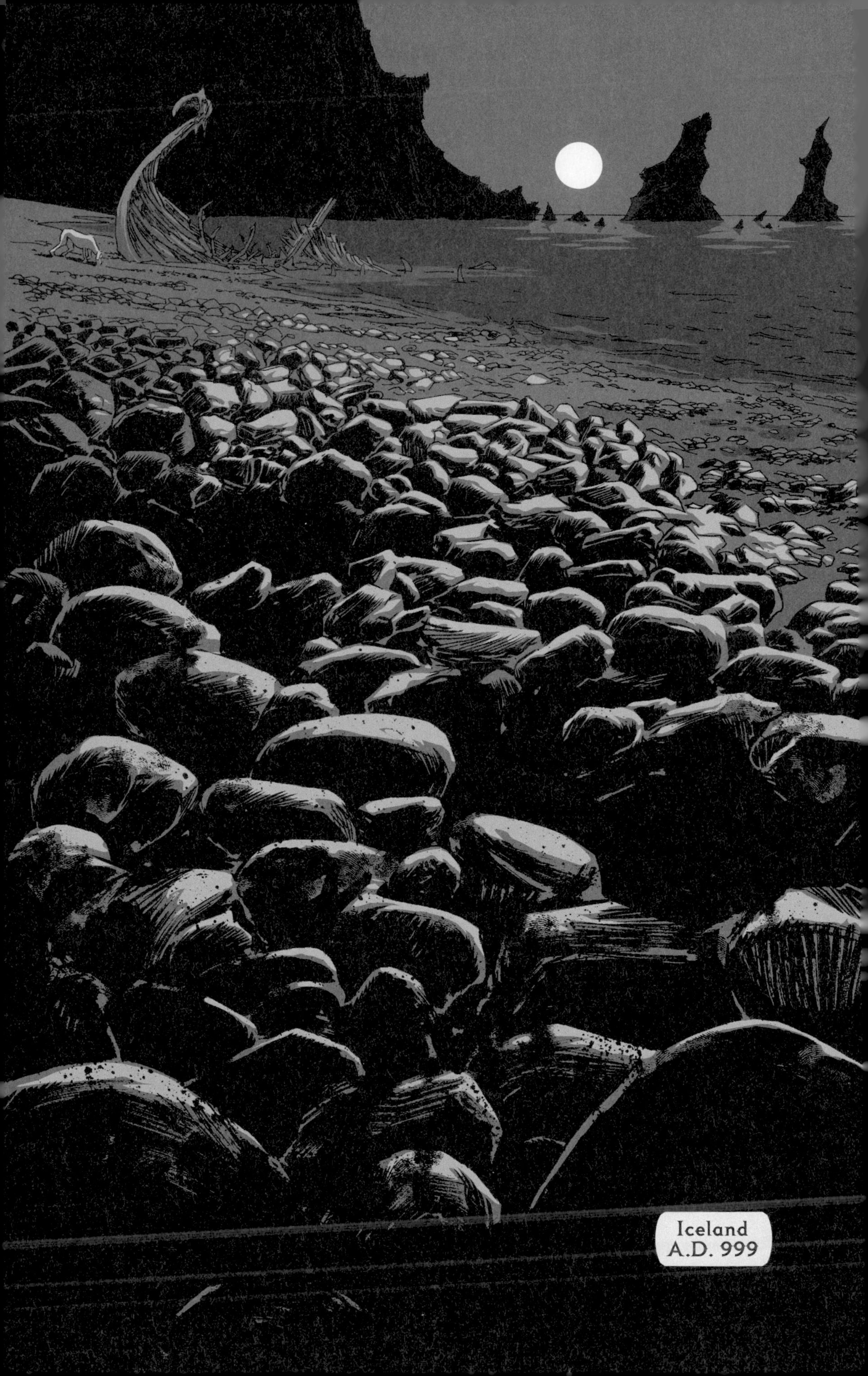
Iceland
A.D. 999

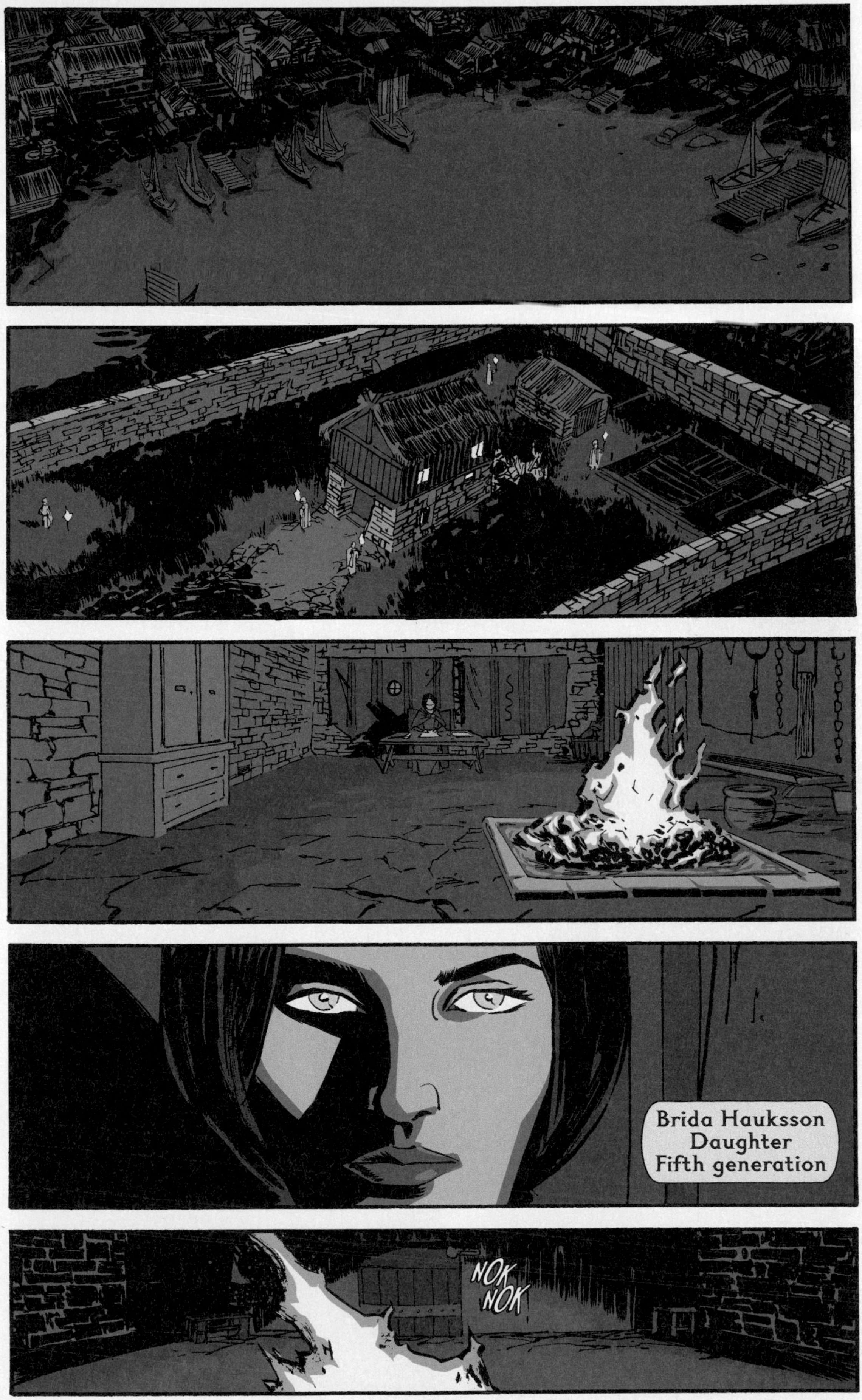
Brida Hauksson
Daughter
Fifth generation
NOK
NOK

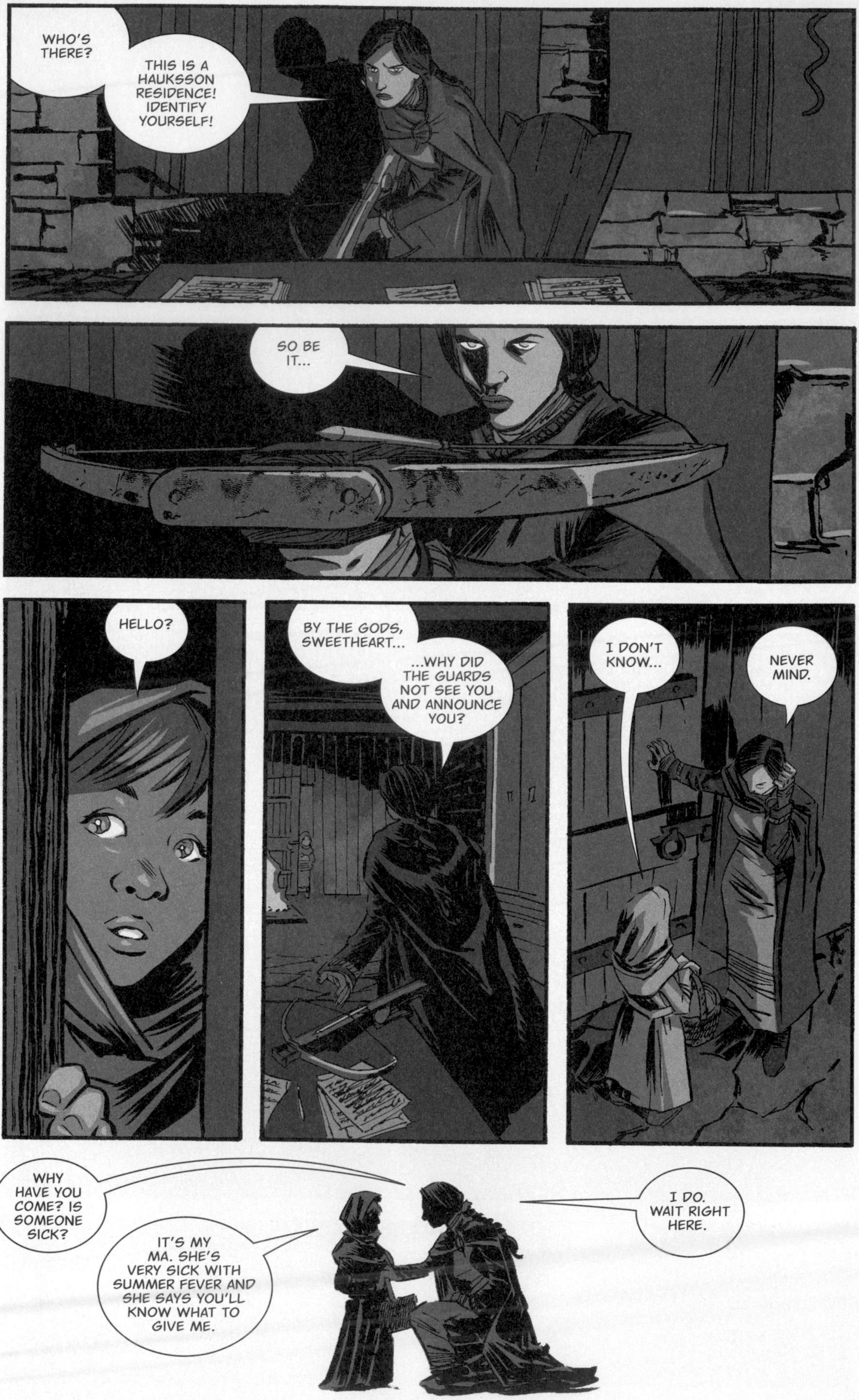
WHO'S THERE?
THIS IS A HAUKSSON RESIDENCE! IDENTIFY YOURSELF!
SO BE IT...
HELLO?
BY THE GODS, SWEETHEART...
...WHY DID THE GUARDS NOT SEE YOU AND ANNOUNCE YOU?
I DON'T KNOW...
NEVER MIND.
WHY HAVE YOU COME? IS SOMEONE SICK?
IT'S MY MA. SHE'S VERY SICK WITH SUMMER FEVER AND SHE SAYS YOU'LL KNOW WHAT TO GIVE ME.
I DO. WAIT RIGHT HERE.

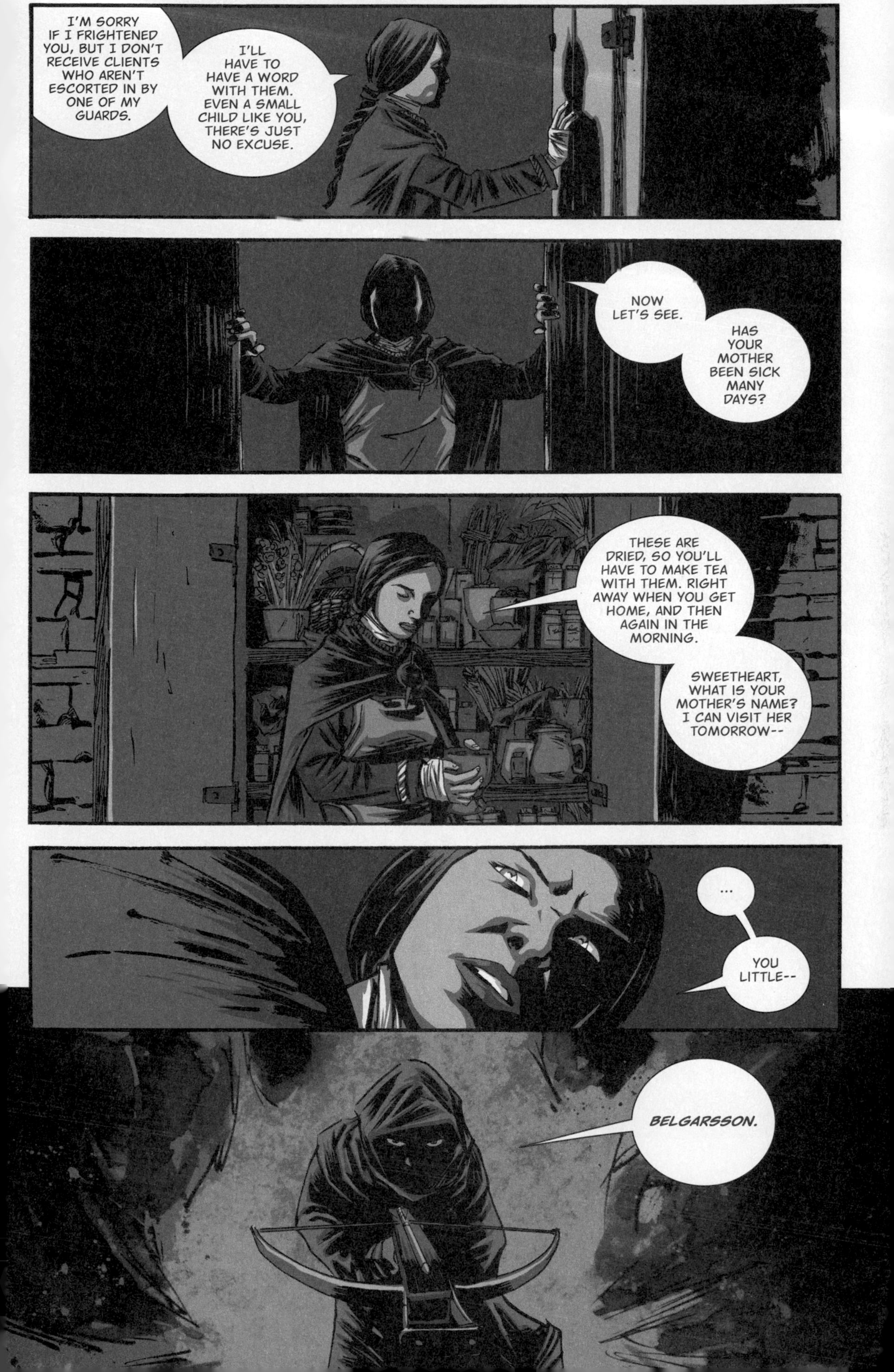
I'M SORRY IF I FRIGHTENED YOU, BUT I DON'T RECEIVE CLIENTS WHO AREN'T ESCORTED IN BY ONE OF MY GUARDS.
I'LL HAVE TO HAVE A WORD WITH THEM. EVEN A SMALL CHILD LIKE YOU, THERE'S JUST NO EXCUSE.
NOW LET'S SEE.
HAS YOUR MOTHER BEEN SICK MANY DAYS?
THESE ARE DRIED, SO YOU'LL HAVE TO MAKE TEA WITH THEM. RIGHT AWAY WHEN YOU GET HOME, AND THEN AGAIN IN THE MORNING.
SWEETHEART, WHAT IS YOUR MOTHER'S NAME? I CAN VISIT HER TOMORROW--
...
YOU LITTLE--
BELGARSSON.

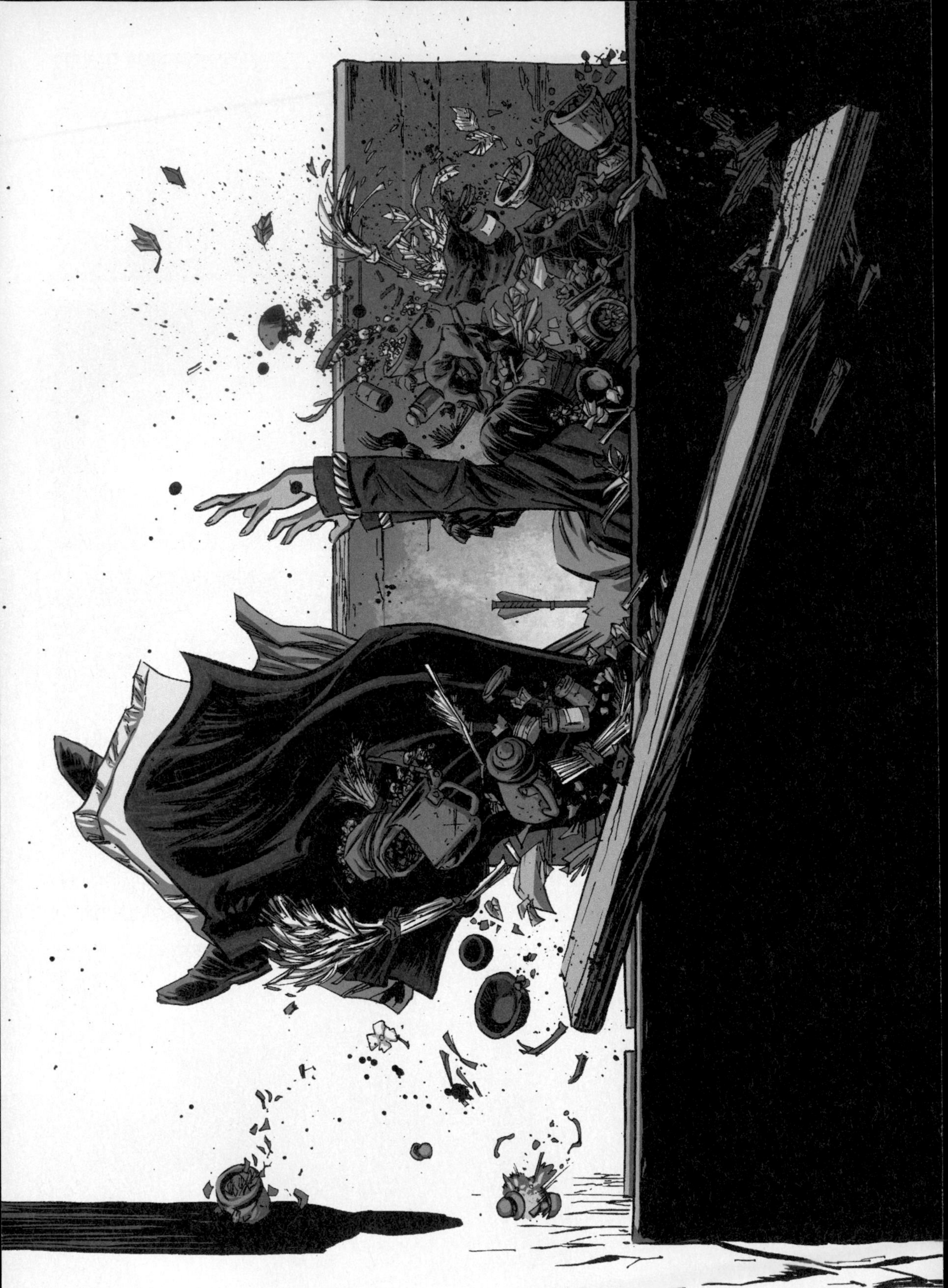

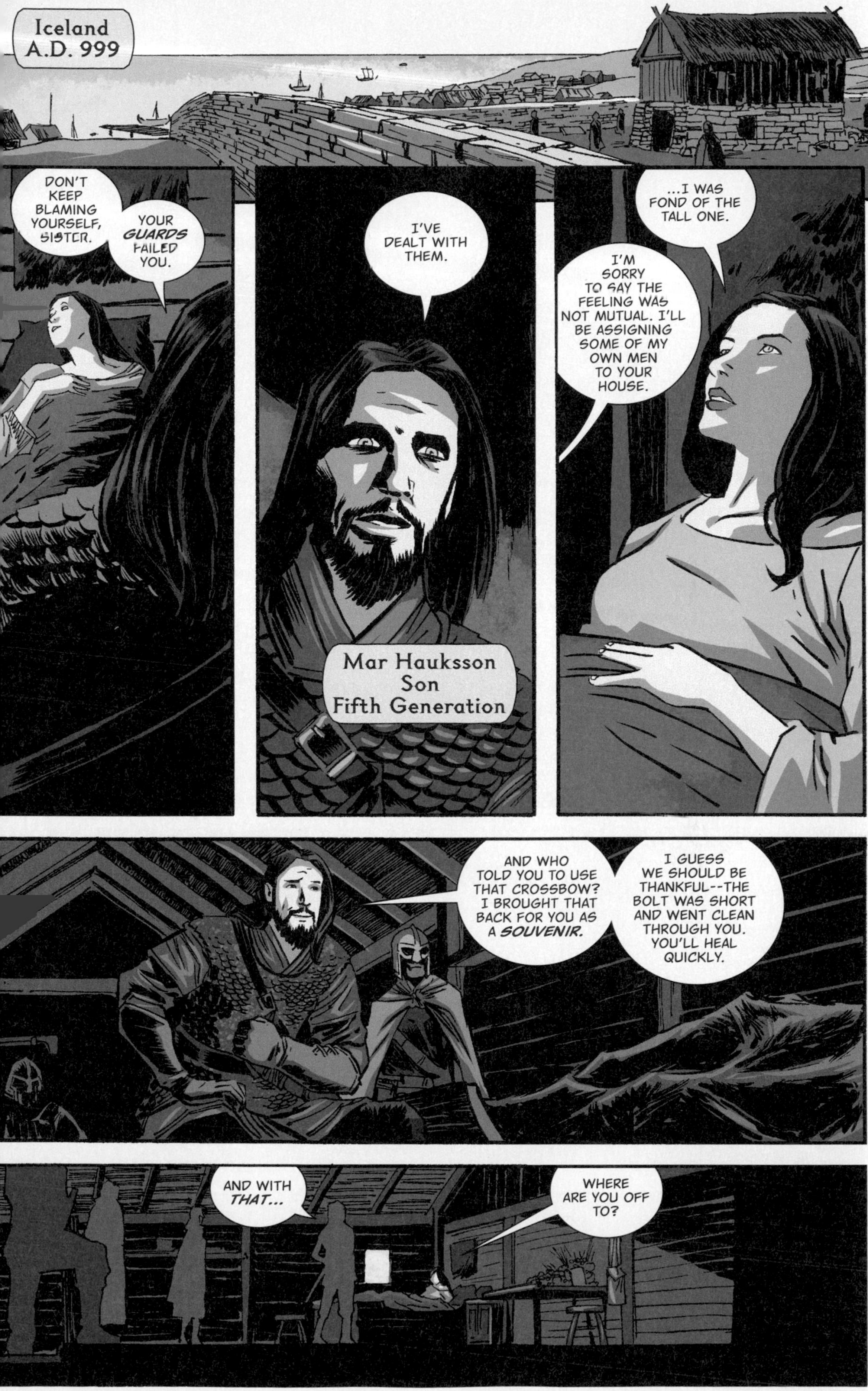
Iceland A.D. 999
DON'T KEEP BLAMING YOURSELF, SISTER.
YOUR GUARDS FAILED YOU.
I'VE DEALT WITH THEM.
Mar Hauksson Son Fifth Generation
...I WAS FOND OF THE TALL ONE.
I'M SORRY TO SAY THE FEELING WAS NOT MUTUAL. I'LL BE ASSIGNING SOME OF MY OWN MEN TO YOUR HOUSE.
AND WHO TOLD YOU TO USE THAT CROSSBOW? I BROUGHT THAT BACK FOR YOU AS A SOUVENIR.
I GUESS WE SHOULD BE THANKFUL--THE BOLT WAS SHORT AND WENT CLEAN THROUGH YOU. YOU'LL HEAL QUICKLY.
AND WITH THAT...
WHERE ARE YOU OFF TO?

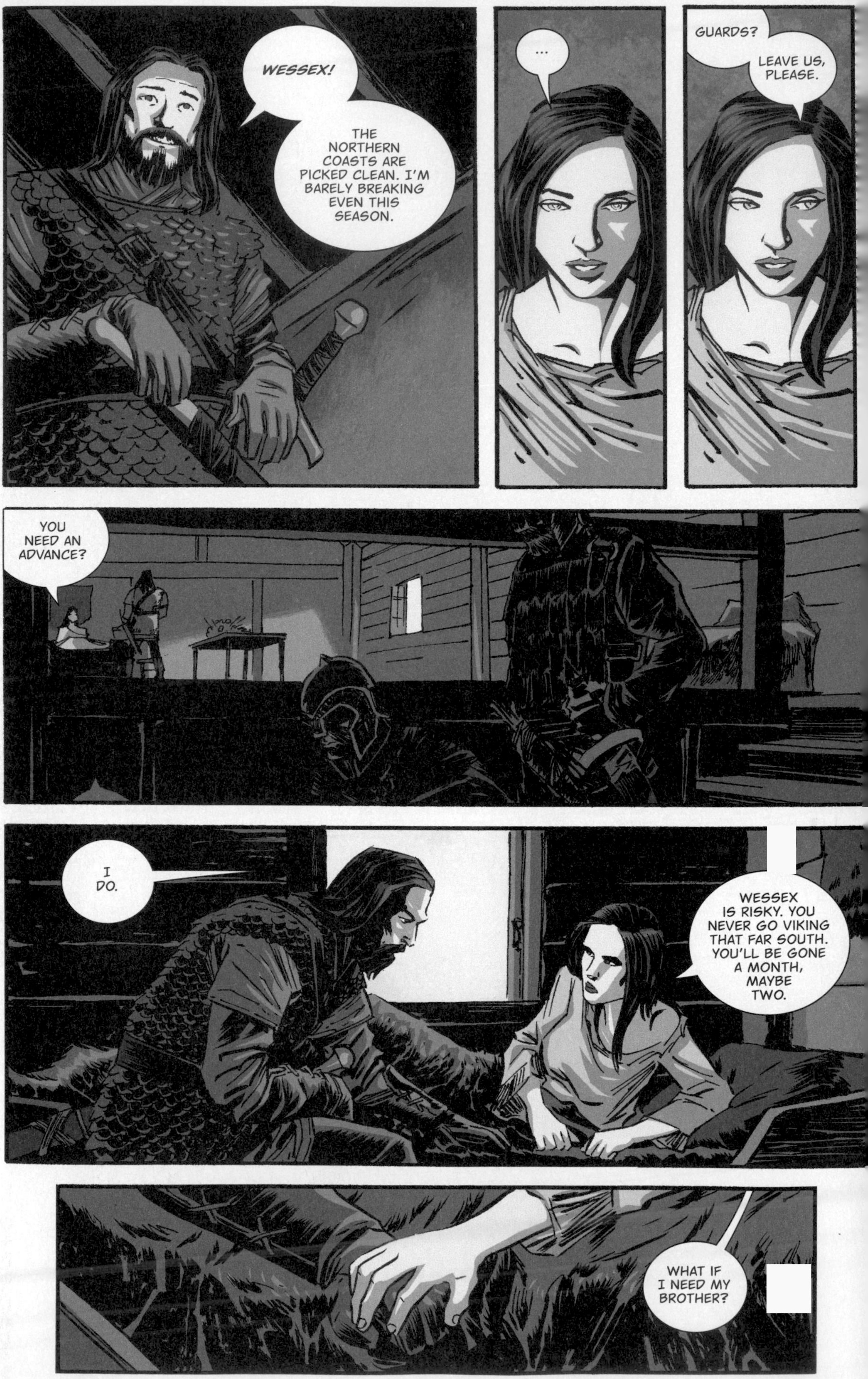

WESSEX!
THE NORTHERN COASTS ARE PICKED CLEAN. I'M BARELY BREAKING EVEN THIS SEASON.
...
GUARDS?
LEAVE US, PLEASE.
YOU NEED AN ADVANCE?
I DO.
WESSEX IS RISKY. YOU NEVER GO VIKING THAT FAR SOUTH. YOU'LL BE GONE A MONTH, MAYBE TWO.
WHAT IF I NEED MY BROTHER?

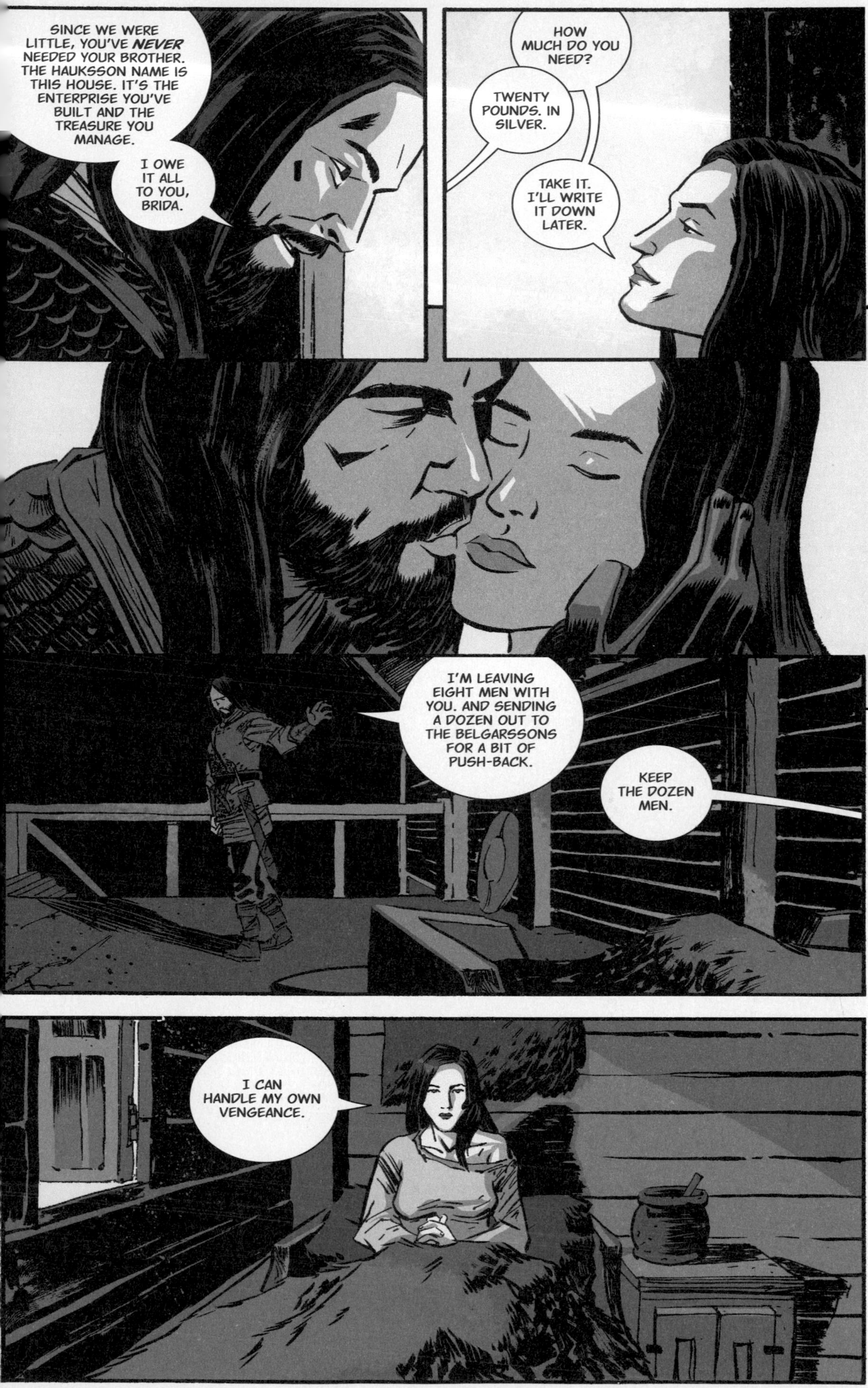
SINCE WE WERE LITTLE, YOU'VE *NEVER* NEEDED YOUR BROTHER. THE HAUKSSON NAME IS THIS HOUSE. IT'S THE ENTERPRISE YOU'VE BUILT AND THE TREASURE YOU MANAGE.
I OWE IT ALL TO YOU, BRIDA.
HOW MUCH DO YOU NEED?
TWENTY POUNDS. IN SILVER.
TAKE IT. I'LL WRITE IT DOWN LATER.
I'M LEAVING EIGHT MEN WITH YOU. AND SENDING A DOZEN OUT TO THE BELGARSSONS FOR A BIT OF PUSH-BACK.
KEEP THE DOZEN MEN.
I CAN HANDLE MY OWN VENGEANCE.

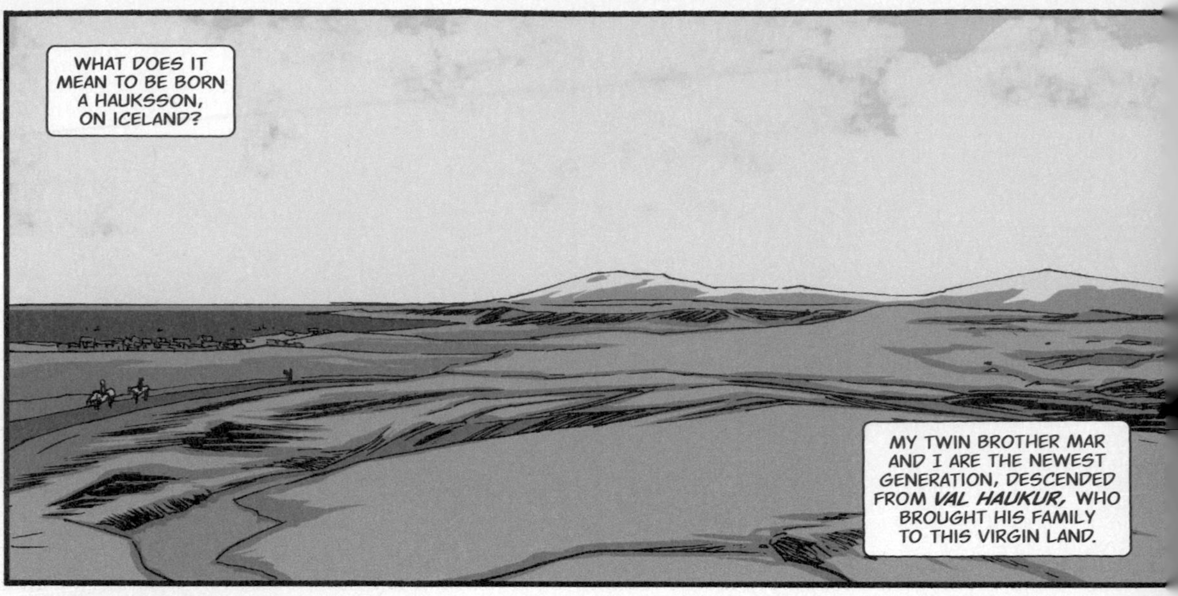
WHAT DOES IT MEAN TO BE BORN A HAUKSSON, ON ICELAND?
MY TWIN BROTHER MAR AND I ARE THE NEWEST GENERATION, DESCENDED FROM *VAL HAUKUR,* WHO BROUGHT HIS FAMILY TO THIS VIRGIN LAND.
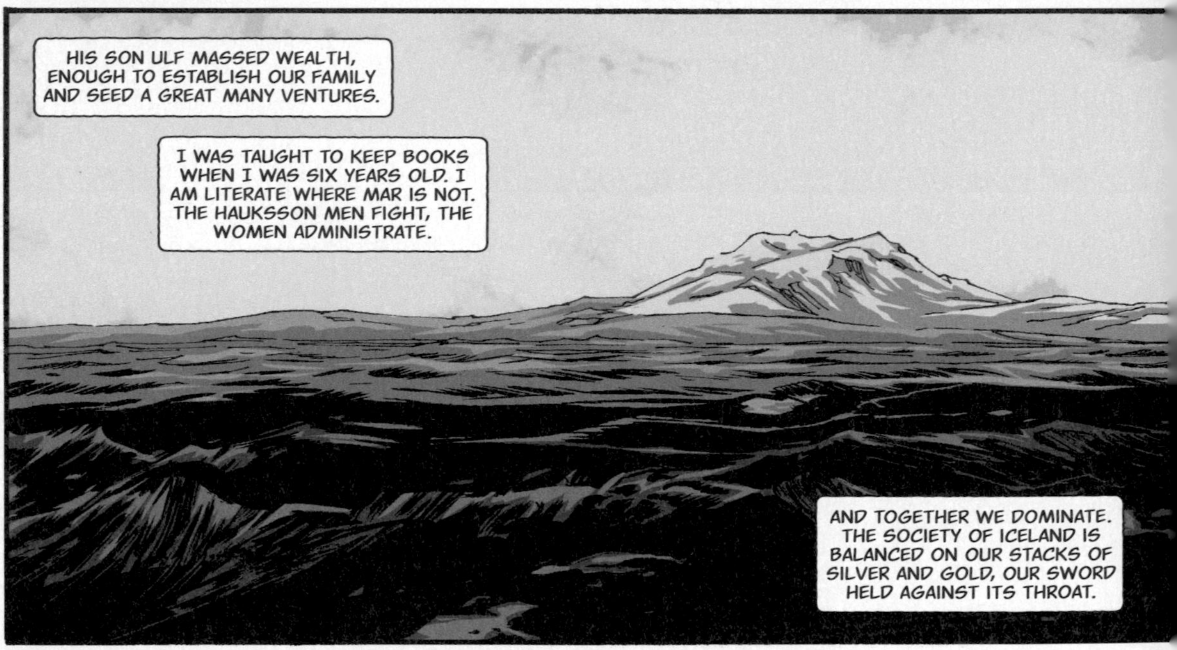
HIS SON ULF MASSED WEALTH, ENOUGH TO ESTABLISH OUR FAMILY AND SEED A GREAT MANY VENTURES.
I WAS TAUGHT TO KEEP BOOKS WHEN I WAS SIX YEARS OLD. I AM LITERATE WHERE MAR IS NOT. THE HAUKSSON MEN FIGHT, THE WOMEN ADMINISTRATE.
AND TOGETHER WE DOMINATE. THE SOCIETY OF ICELAND IS BALANCED ON OUR STACKS OF SILVER AND GOLD, OUR SWORD HELD AGAINST ITS THROAT.
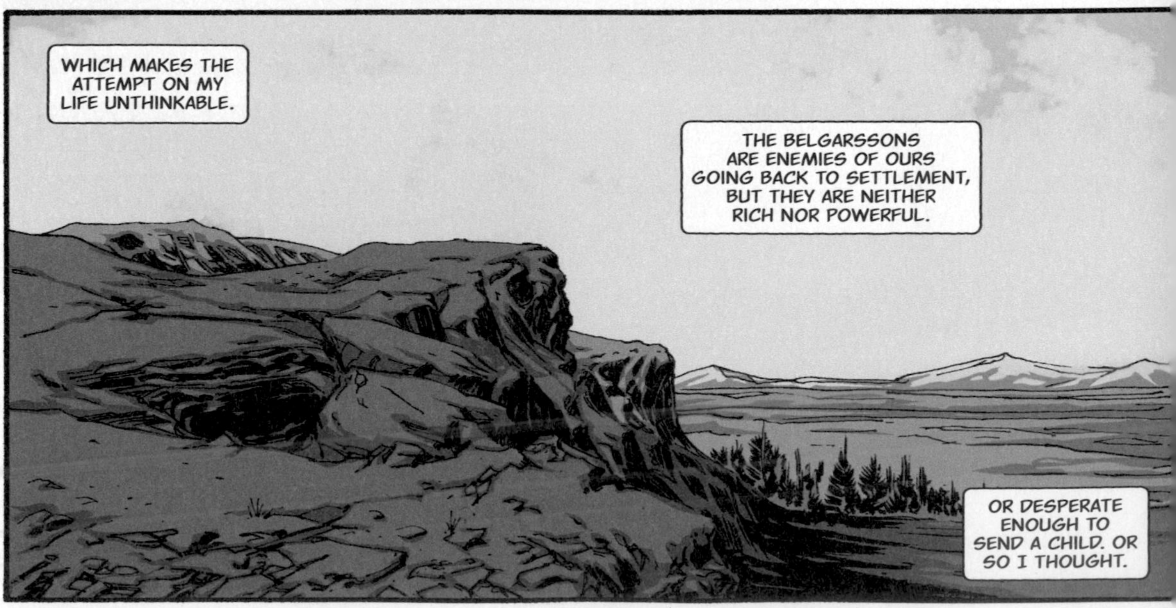
WHICH MAKES THE ATTEMPT ON MY LIFE UNTHINKABLE.
THE BELGARSSONS ARE ENEMIES OF OURS GOING BACK TO SETTLEMENT, BUT THEY ARE NEITHER RICH NOR POWERFUL.
OR DESPERATE ENOUGH TO SEND A CHILD. OR SO I THOUGHT.

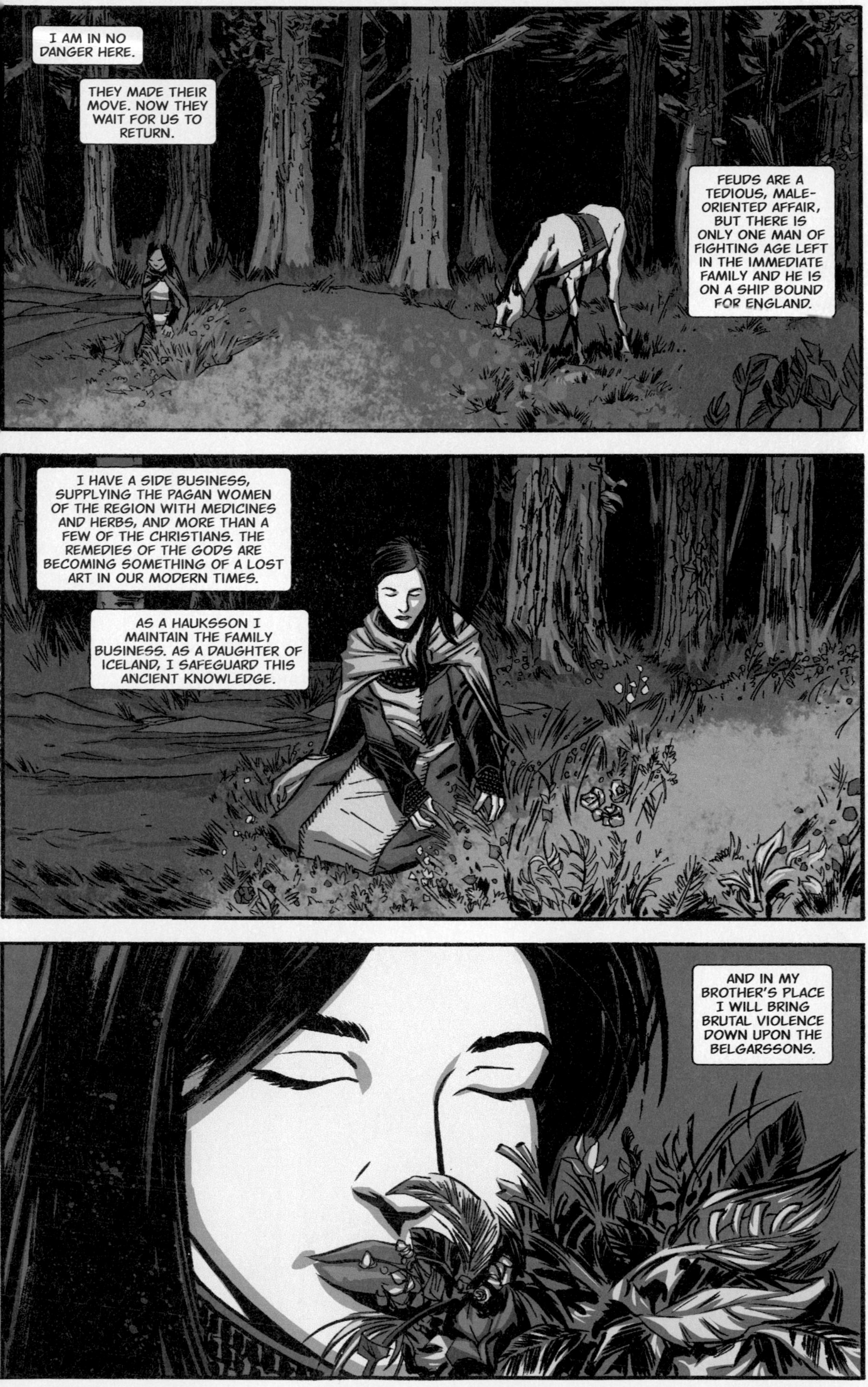
I AM IN NO DANGER HERE.
THEY MADE THEIR MOVE. NOW THEY WAIT FOR US TO RETURN.
FEUDS ARE A TEDIOUS, MALE-ORIENTED AFFAIR, BUT THERE IS ONLY ONE MAN OF FIGHTING AGE LEFT IN THE IMMEDIATE FAMILY AND HE IS ON A SHIP BOUND FOR ENGLAND.
I HAVE A SIDE BUSINESS, SUPPLYING THE PAGAN WOMEN OF THE REGION WITH MEDICINES AND HERBS, AND MORE THAN A FEW OF THE CHRISTIANS. THE REMEDIES OF THE GODS ARE BECOMING SOMETHING OF A LOST ART IN OUR MODERN TIMES.
AS A HAUKSSON I MAINTAIN THE FAMILY BUSINESS. AS A DAUGHTER OF ICELAND, I SAFEGUARD THIS ANCIENT KNOWLEDGE.
AND IN MY BROTHER'S PLACE I WILL BRING BRUTAL VIOLENCE DOWN UPON THE BELGARSSONS.

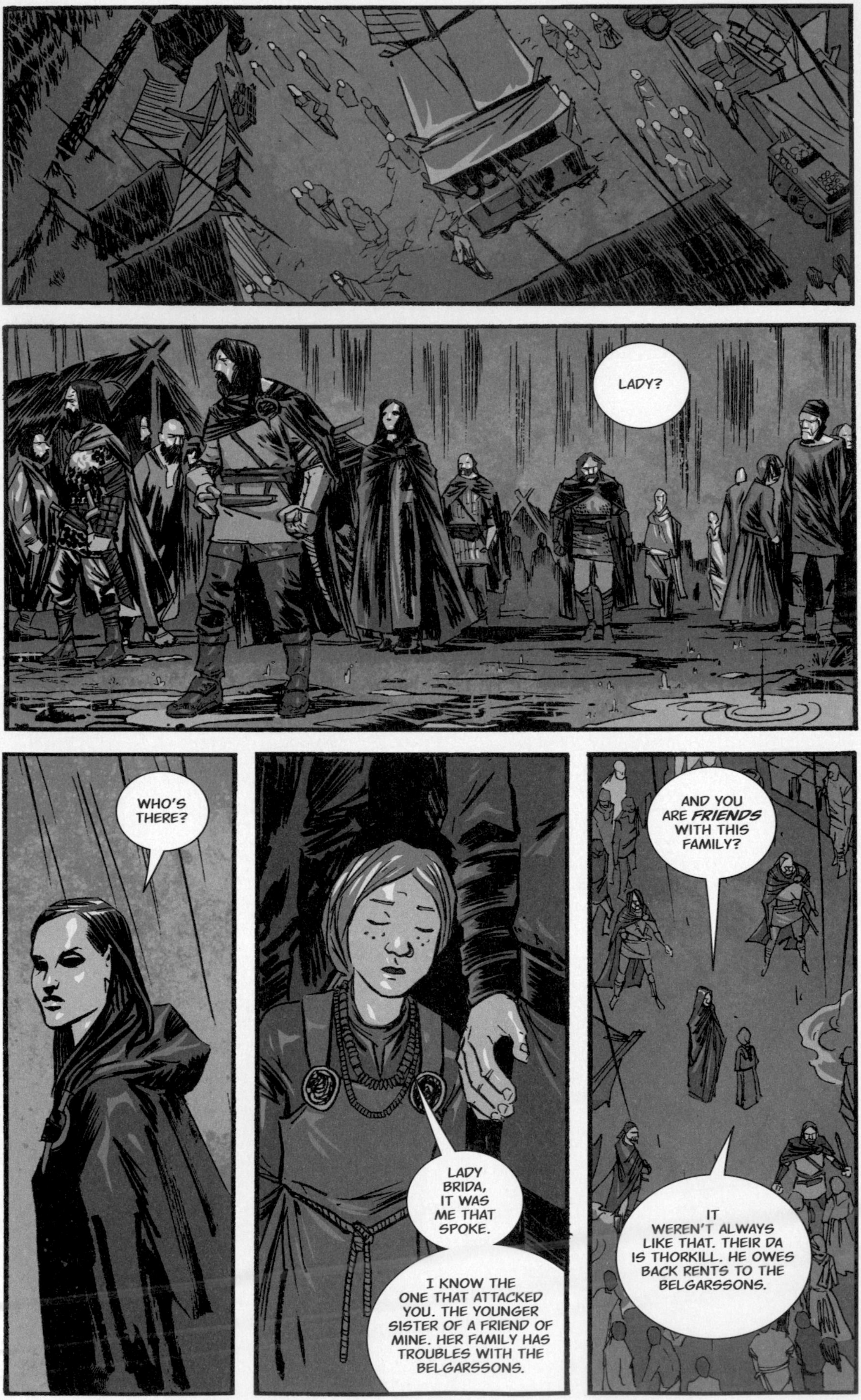
LADY?
WHO'S THERE?
LADY BRIDA, IT WAS ME THAT SPOKE.
I KNOW THE ONE THAT ATTACKED YOU. THE YOUNGER SISTER OF A FRIEND OF MINE. HER FAMILY HAS TROUBLES WITH THE BELGARSSONS.
AND YOU ARE *FRIENDS* WITH THIS FAMILY?
IT WEREN'T ALWAYS LIKE THAT. THEIR DA IS THORKILL. HE OWES BACK RENTS TO THE BELGARSSONS.

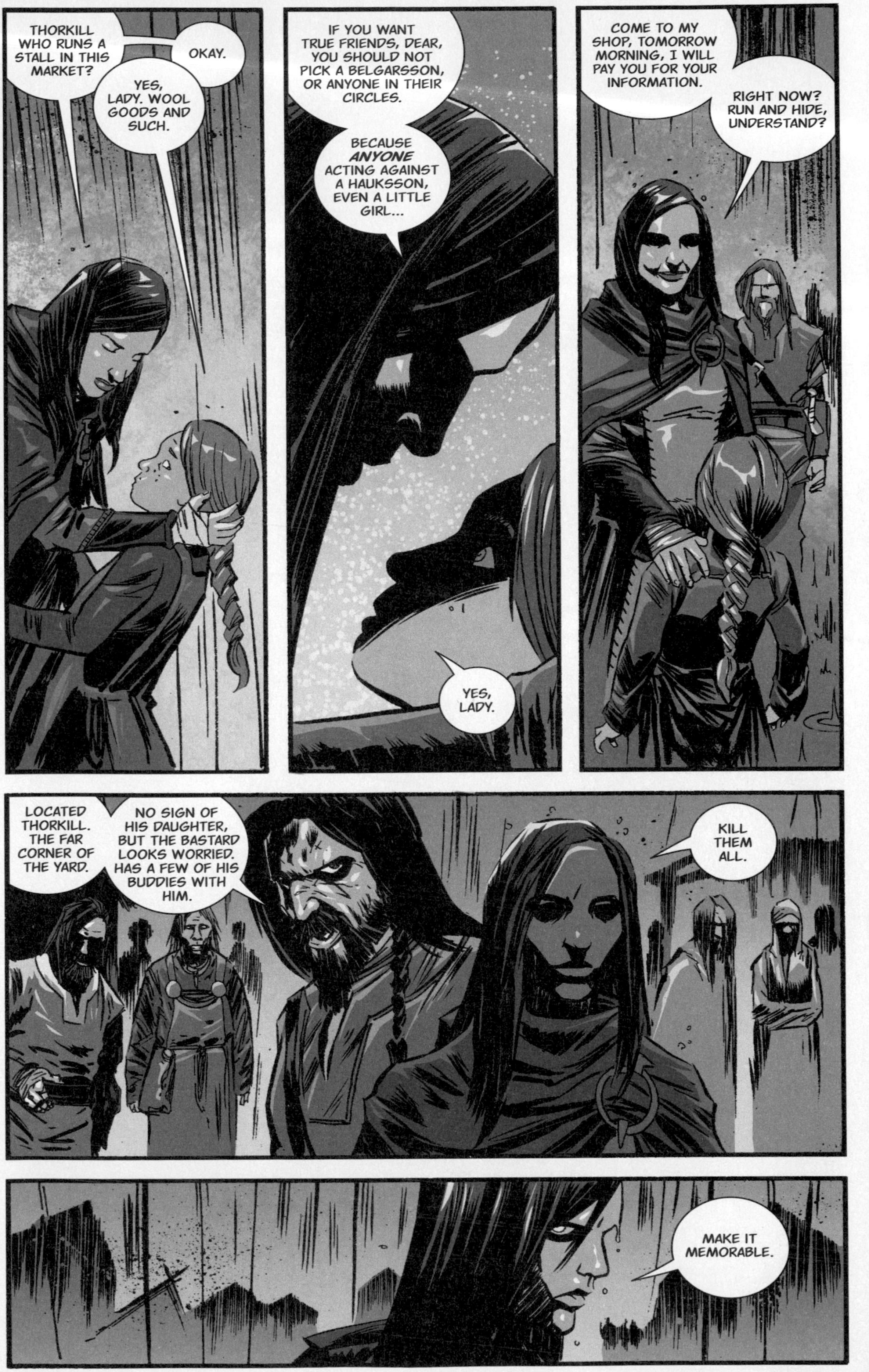
THORKILL WHO RUNS A STALL IN THIS MARKET?
YES, LADY. WOOL GOODS AND SUCH.
OKAY.
IF YOU WANT TRUE FRIENDS, DEAR, YOU SHOULD NOT PICK A BELGARSSON, OR ANYONE IN THEIR CIRCLES.
BECAUSE *ANYONE* ACTING AGAINST A HAUKSSON, EVEN A LITTLE GIRL...
YES, LADY.
COME TO MY SHOP, TOMORROW MORNING, I WILL PAY YOU FOR YOUR INFORMATION.
RIGHT NOW? RUN AND HIDE, UNDERSTAND?
LOCATED THORKILL. THE FAR CORNER OF THE YARD.
NO SIGN OF HIS DAUGHTER, BUT THE BASTARD LOOKS WORRIED. HAS A FEW OF HIS BUDDIES WITH HIM.
KILL THEM ALL.
MAKE IT MEMORABLE.

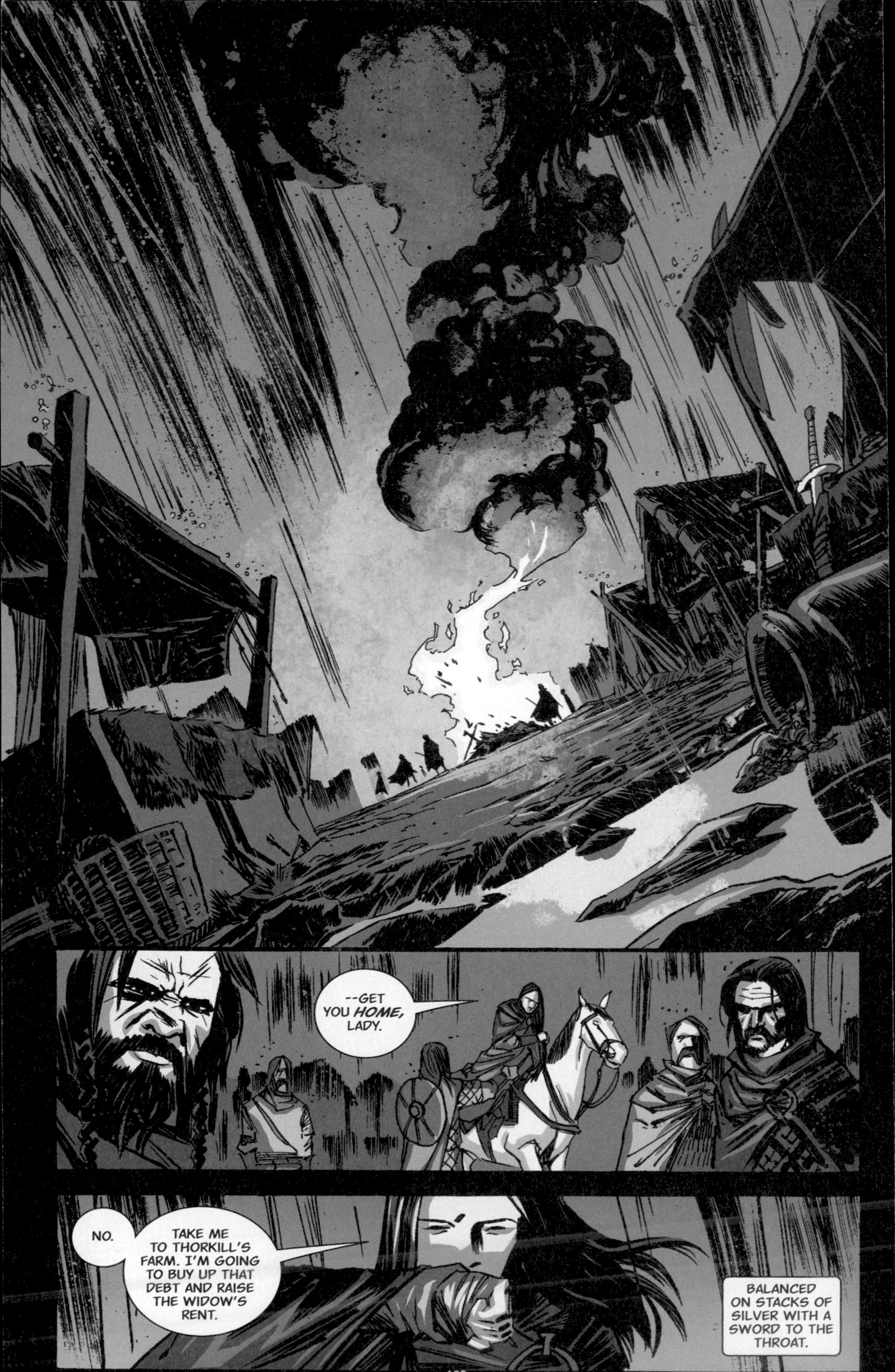
--GET YOU *HOME*, LADY.
NO.
TAKE ME TO THORKILL'S FARM. I'M GOING TO BUY UP THAT DEBT AND RAISE THE WIDOW'S RENT.
BALANCED ON STACKS OF SILVER WITH A SWORD TO THE THROAT.

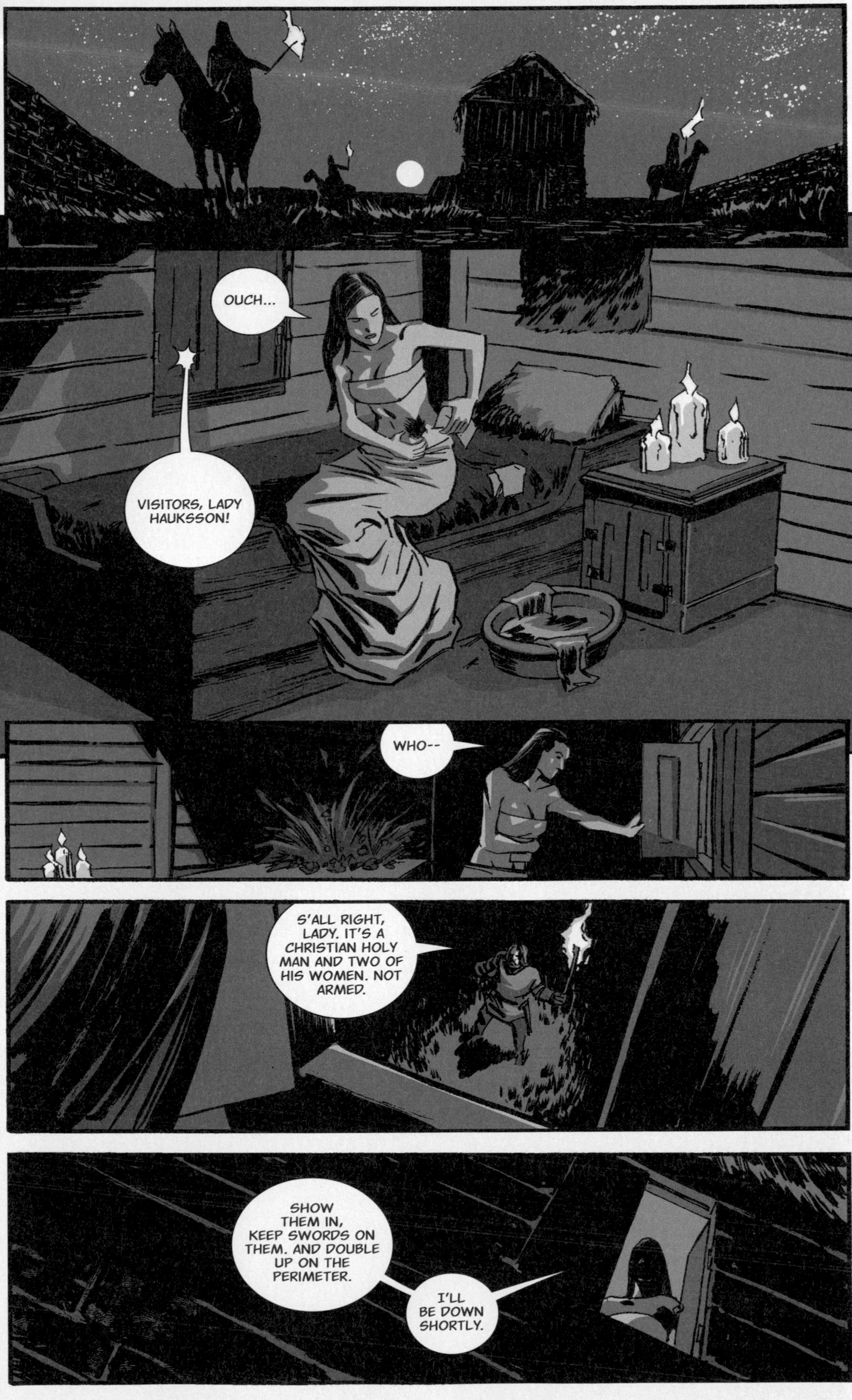
OUCH...
VISITORS, LADY HAUKSSON!
WHO--
S'ALL RIGHT, LADY. IT'S A CHRISTIAN HOLY MAN AND TWO OF HIS WOMEN. NOT ARMED.
SHOW THEM IN, KEEP SWORDS ON THEM. AND DOUBLE UP ON THE PERIMETER.
I'LL BE DOWN SHORTLY.

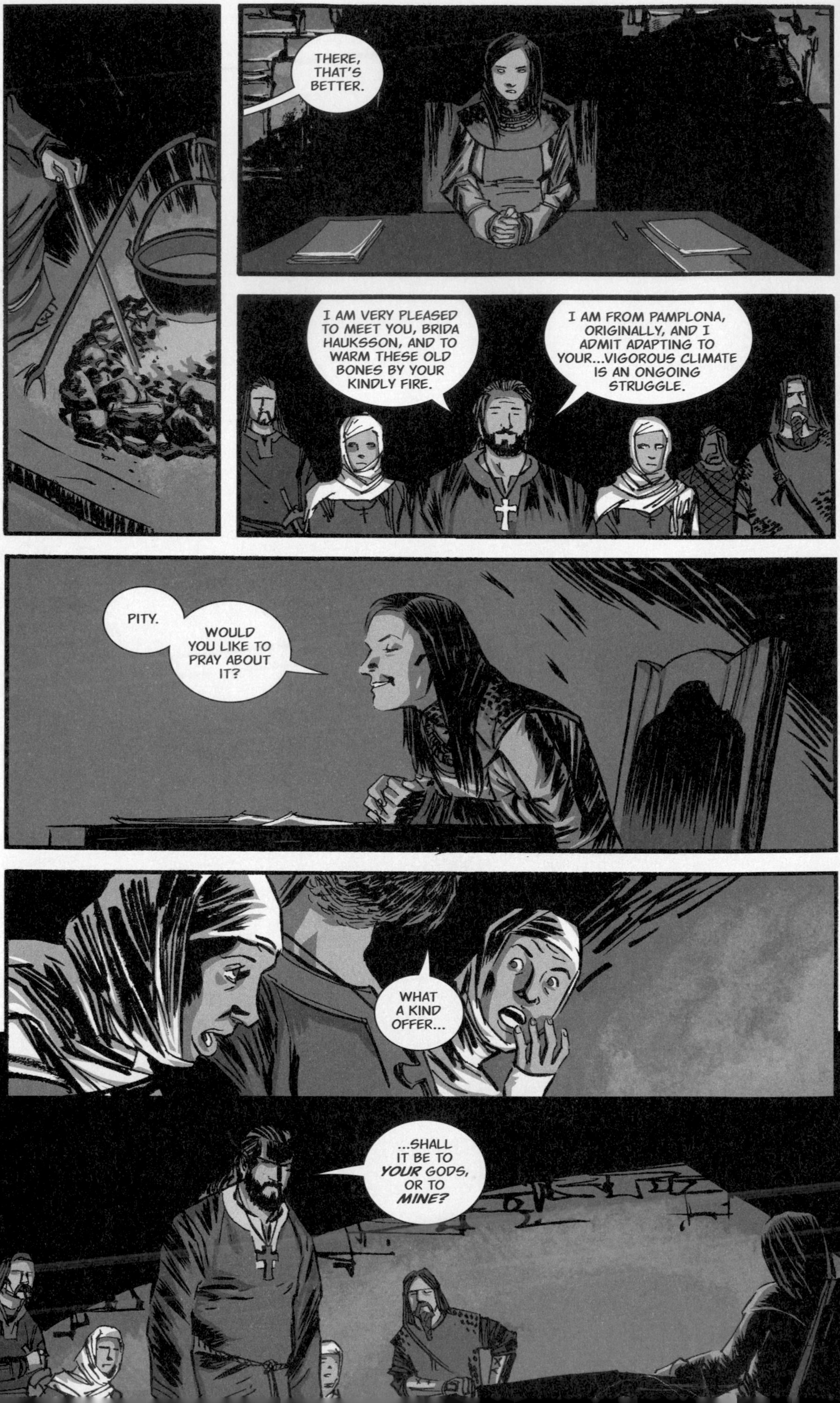

THERE, THAT'S BETTER.
I AM VERY PLEASED TO MEET YOU, BRIDA HAUKSSON, AND TO WARM THESE OLD BONES BY YOUR KINDLY FIRE.
I AM FROM PAMPLONA, ORIGINALLY, AND I ADMIT ADAPTING TO YOUR...VIGOROUS CLIMATE IS AN ONGOING STRUGGLE.
PITY.
WOULD YOU LIKE TO PRAY ABOUT IT?
WHAT A KIND OFFER...
...SHALL IT BE TO *YOUR* GODS, OR TO *MINE?*

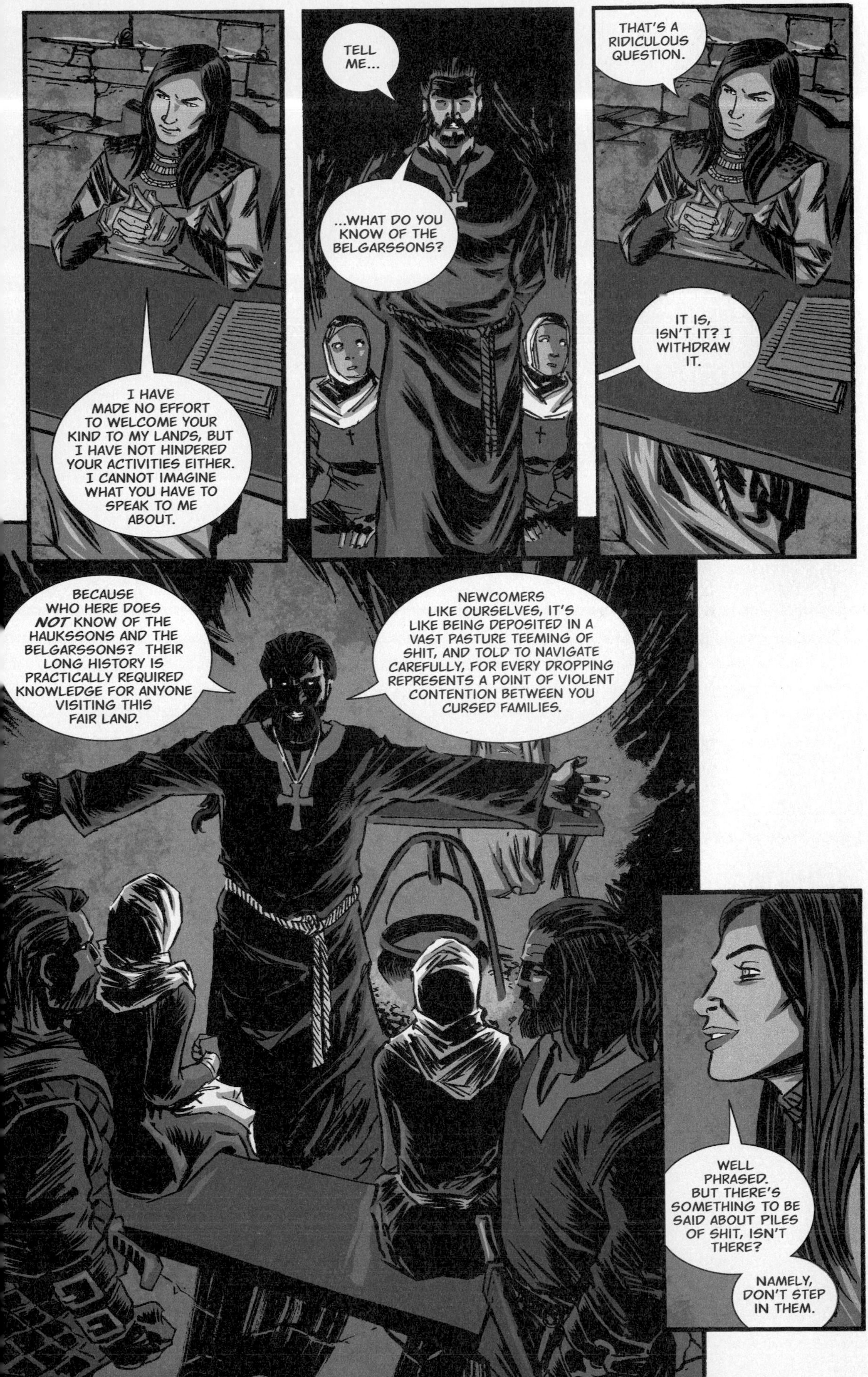

I HAVE MADE NO EFFORT TO WELCOME YOUR KIND TO MY LANDS, BUT I HAVE NOT HINDERED YOUR ACTIVITIES EITHER. I CANNOT IMAGINE WHAT YOU HAVE TO SPEAK TO ME ABOUT.
TELL ME...
...WHAT DO YOU KNOW OF THE BELGARSSONS?
THAT'S A RIDICULOUS QUESTION.
IT IS, ISN'T IT? I WITHDRAW IT.
BECAUSE WHO HERE DOES ***NOT*** KNOW OF THE HAUKSSONS AND THE BELGARSSONS? THEIR LONG HISTORY IS PRACTICALLY REQUIRED KNOWLEDGE FOR ANYONE VISITING THIS FAIR LAND.
NEWCOMERS LIKE OURSELVES, IT'S LIKE BEING DEPOSITED IN A VAST PASTURE TEEMING OF SHIT, AND TOLD TO NAVIGATE CAREFULLY, FOR EVERY DROPPING REPRESENTS A POINT OF VIOLENT CONTENTION BETWEEN YOU CURSED FAMILIES.
WELL PHRASED. BUT THERE'S SOMETHING TO BE SAID ABOUT PILES OF SHIT, ISN'T THERE?
NAMELY, DON'T STEP IN THEM.

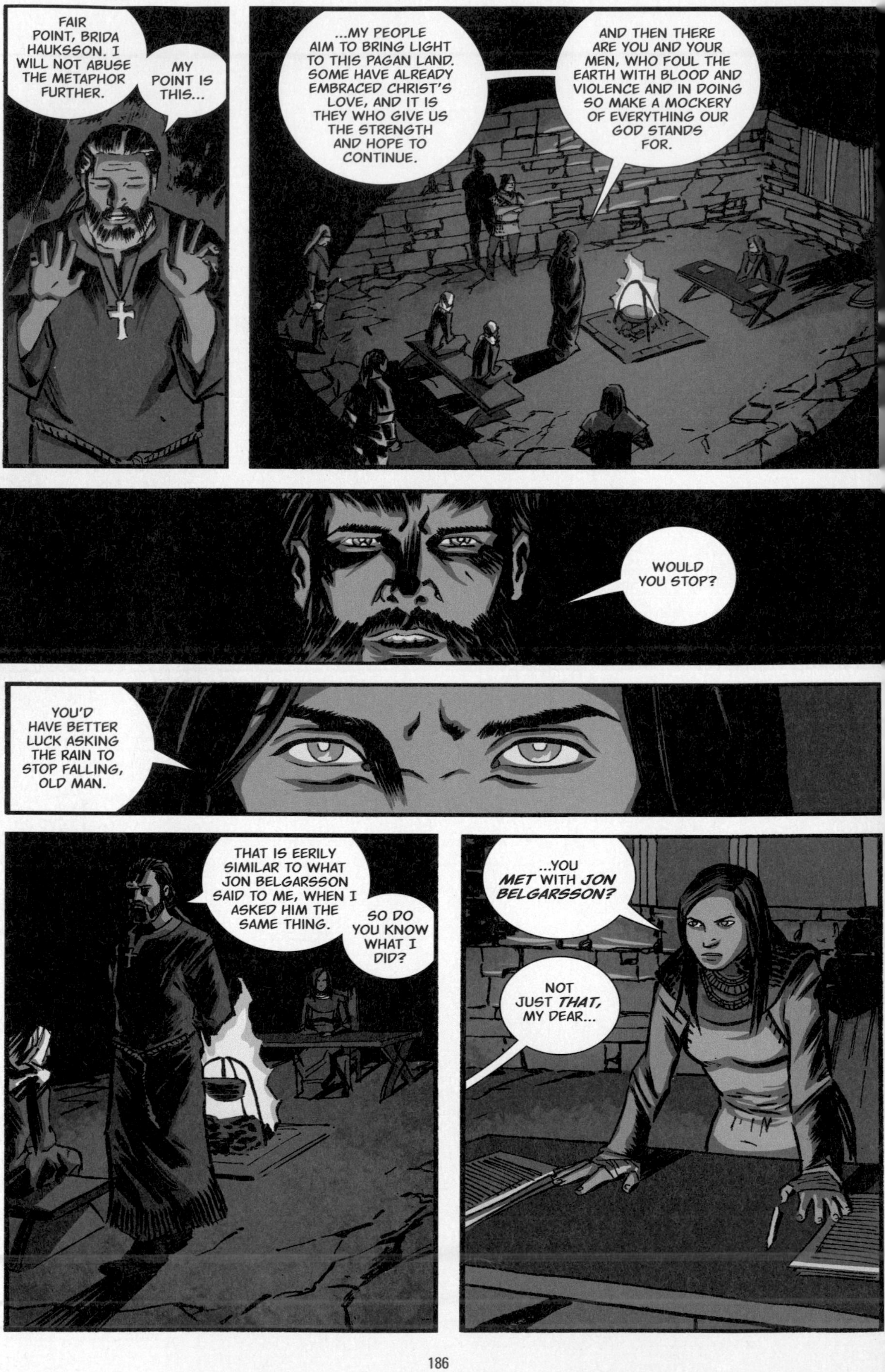
FAIR POINT, BRIDA HAUKSSON. I WILL NOT ABUSE THE METAPHOR FURTHER.
MY POINT IS THIS...
...MY PEOPLE AIM TO BRING LIGHT TO THIS PAGAN LAND. SOME HAVE ALREADY EMBRACED CHRIST'S LOVE, AND IT IS THEY WHO GIVE US THE STRENGTH AND HOPE TO CONTINUE.
AND THEN THERE ARE YOU AND YOUR MEN, WHO FOUL THE EARTH WITH BLOOD AND VIOLENCE AND IN DOING SO MAKE A MOCKERY OF EVERYTHING OUR GOD STANDS FOR.
WOULD YOU STOP?
YOU'D HAVE BETTER LUCK ASKING THE RAIN TO STOP FALLING, OLD MAN.
THAT IS EERILY SIMILAR TO WHAT JON BELGARSSON SAID TO ME, WHEN I ASKED HIM THE SAME THING.
SO DO YOU KNOW WHAT I DID?
...YOU *MET* WITH *JON BELGARSSON?*
NOT JUST *THAT,* MY DEAR...

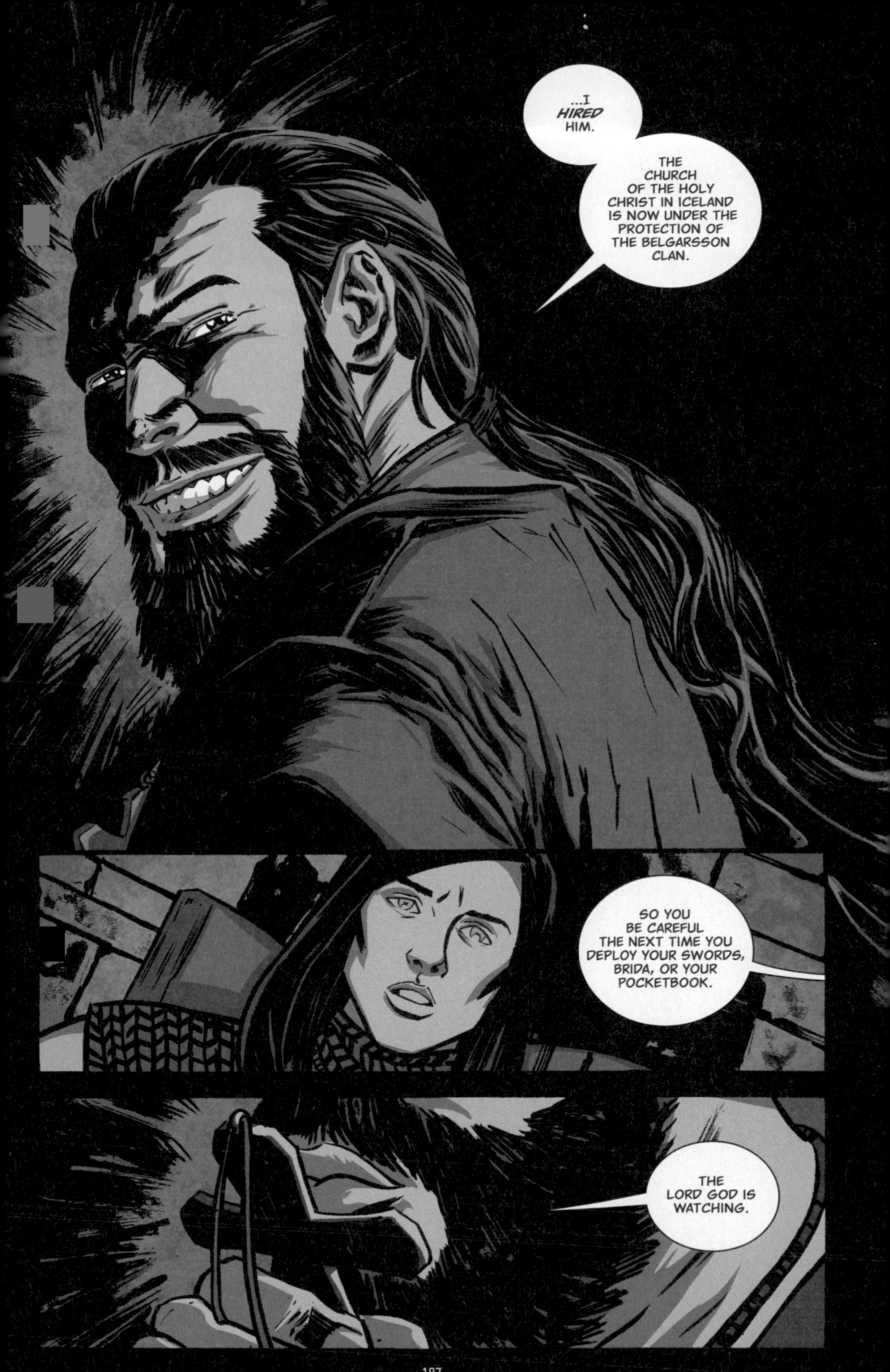
...I *HIRED* HIM.
THE CHURCH OF THE HOLY CHRIST IN ICELAND IS NOW UNDER THE PROTECTION OF THE BELGARSSON CLAN.
SO YOU BE CAREFUL THE NEXT TIME YOU DEPLOY YOUR SWORDS, BRIDA, OR YOUR POCKETBOOK.
THE LORD GOD IS WATCHING.

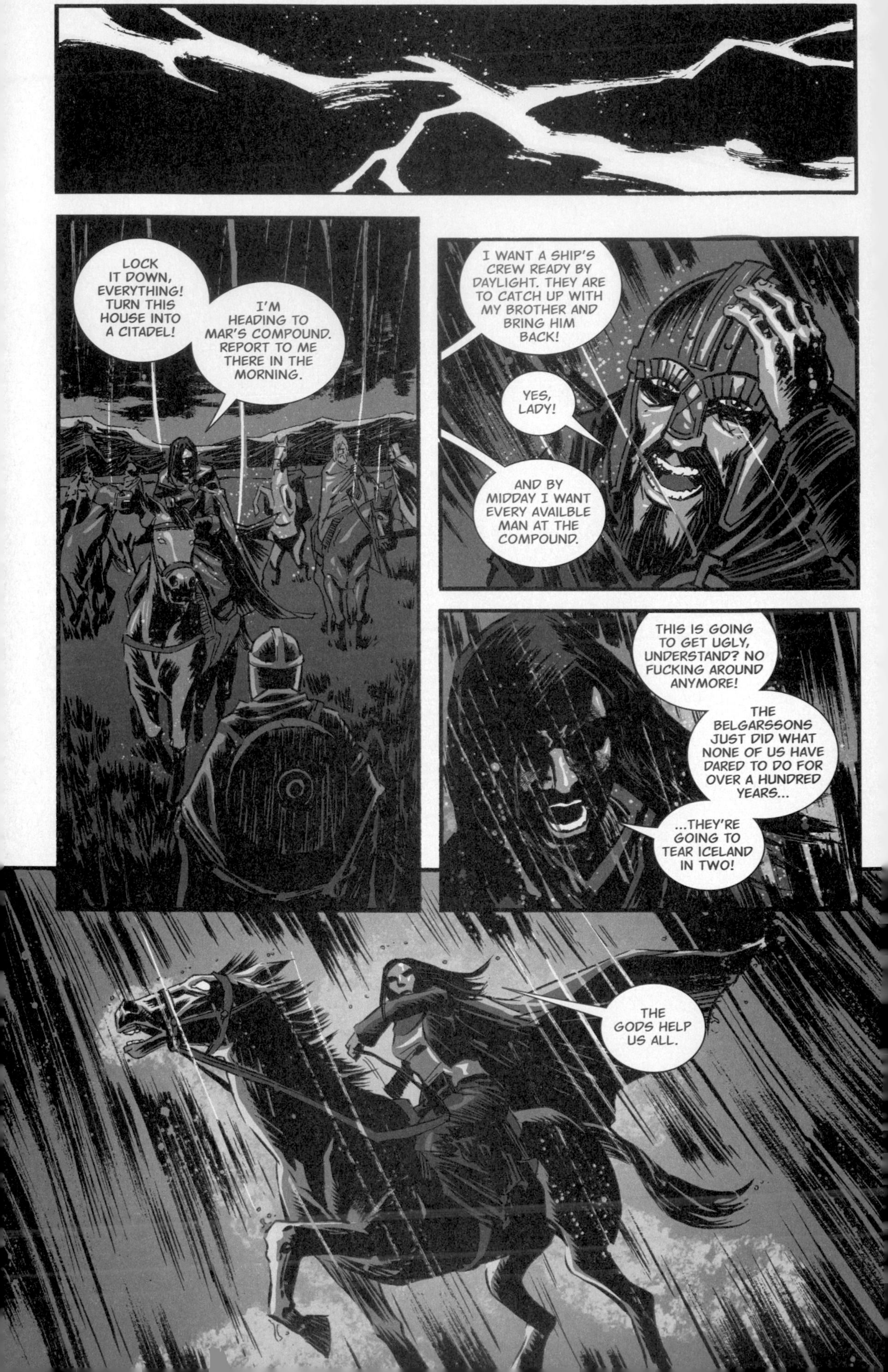
LOCK IT DOWN, EVERYTHING! TURN THIS HOUSE INTO A CITADEL!
I'M HEADING TO MAR'S COMPOUND. REPORT TO ME THERE IN THE MORNING.
I WANT A SHIP'S CREW READY BY DAYLIGHT. THEY ARE TO CATCH UP WITH MY BROTHER AND BRING HIM BACK!
YES, LADY!
AND BY MIDDAY I WANT EVERY AVAILBLE MAN AT THE COMPOUND.
THIS IS GOING TO GET UGLY, UNDERSTAND? NO FUCKING AROUND ANYMORE!
THE BELGARSSONS JUST DID WHAT NONE OF US HAVE DARED TO DO FOR OVER A HUNDRED YEARS...
...THEY'RE GOING TO TEAR ICELAND IN TWO!
THE GODS HELP US ALL.

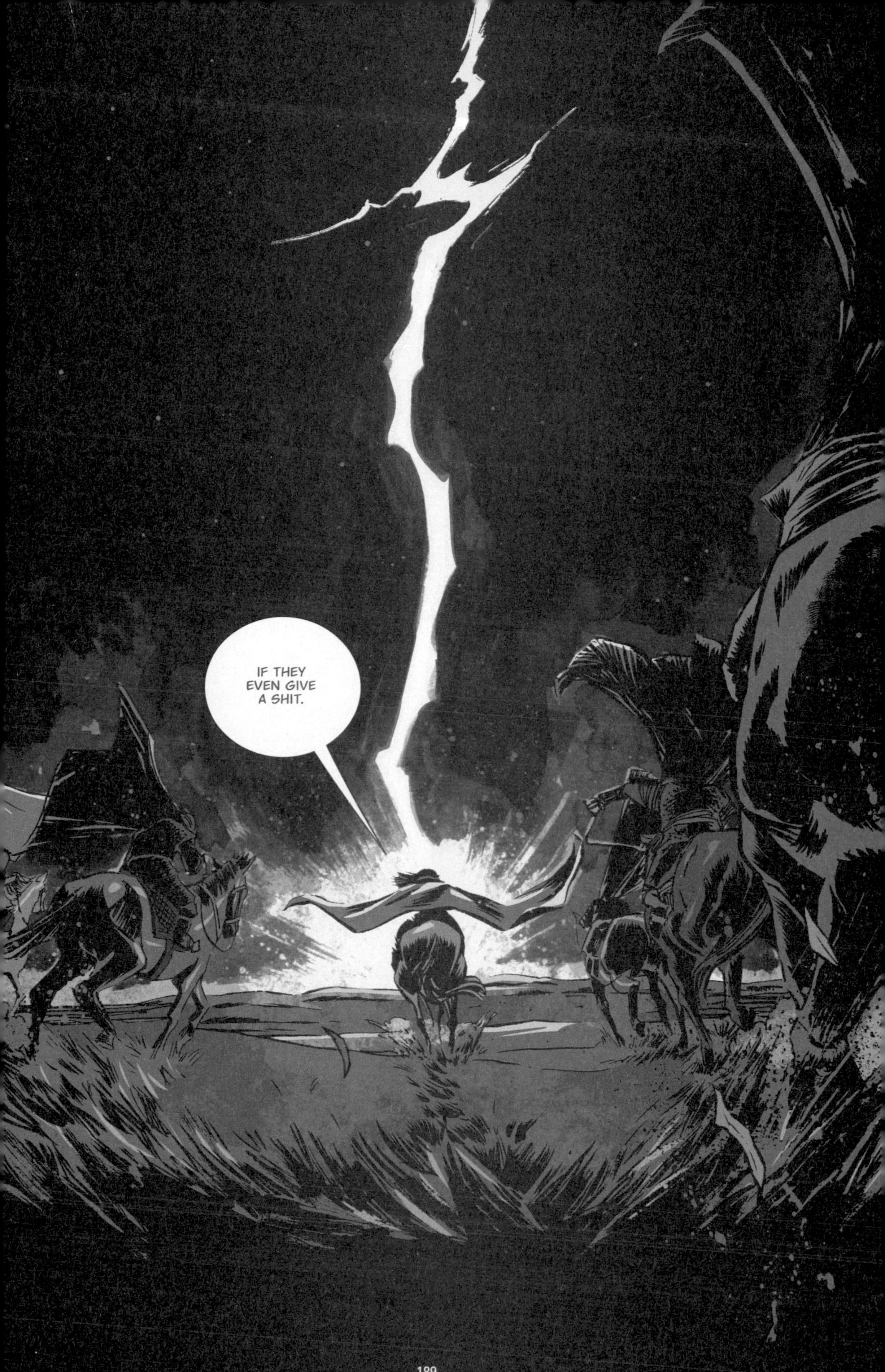
IF THEY EVEN GIVE A SHIT.

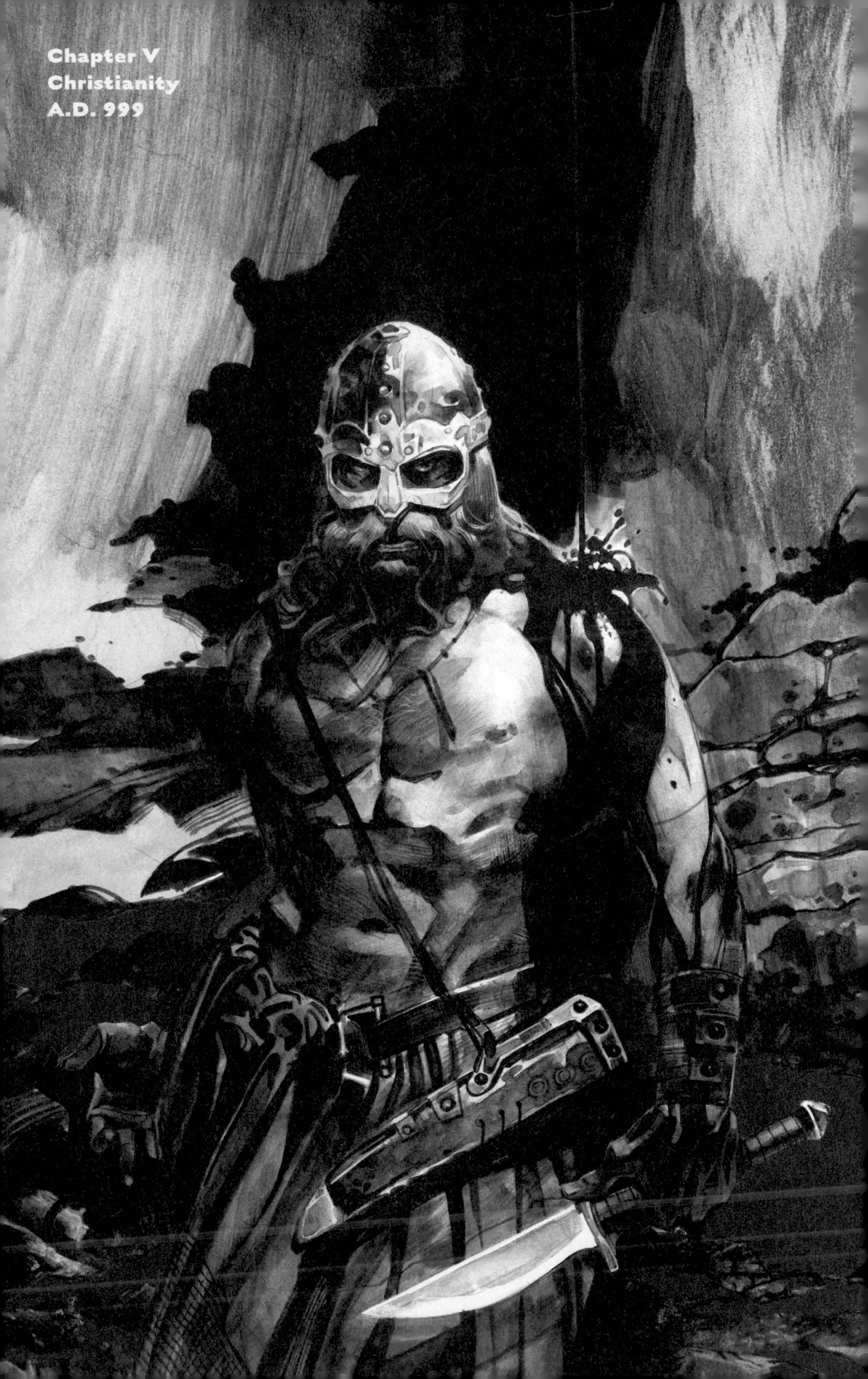
Chapter V
Christianity
A.D. 999

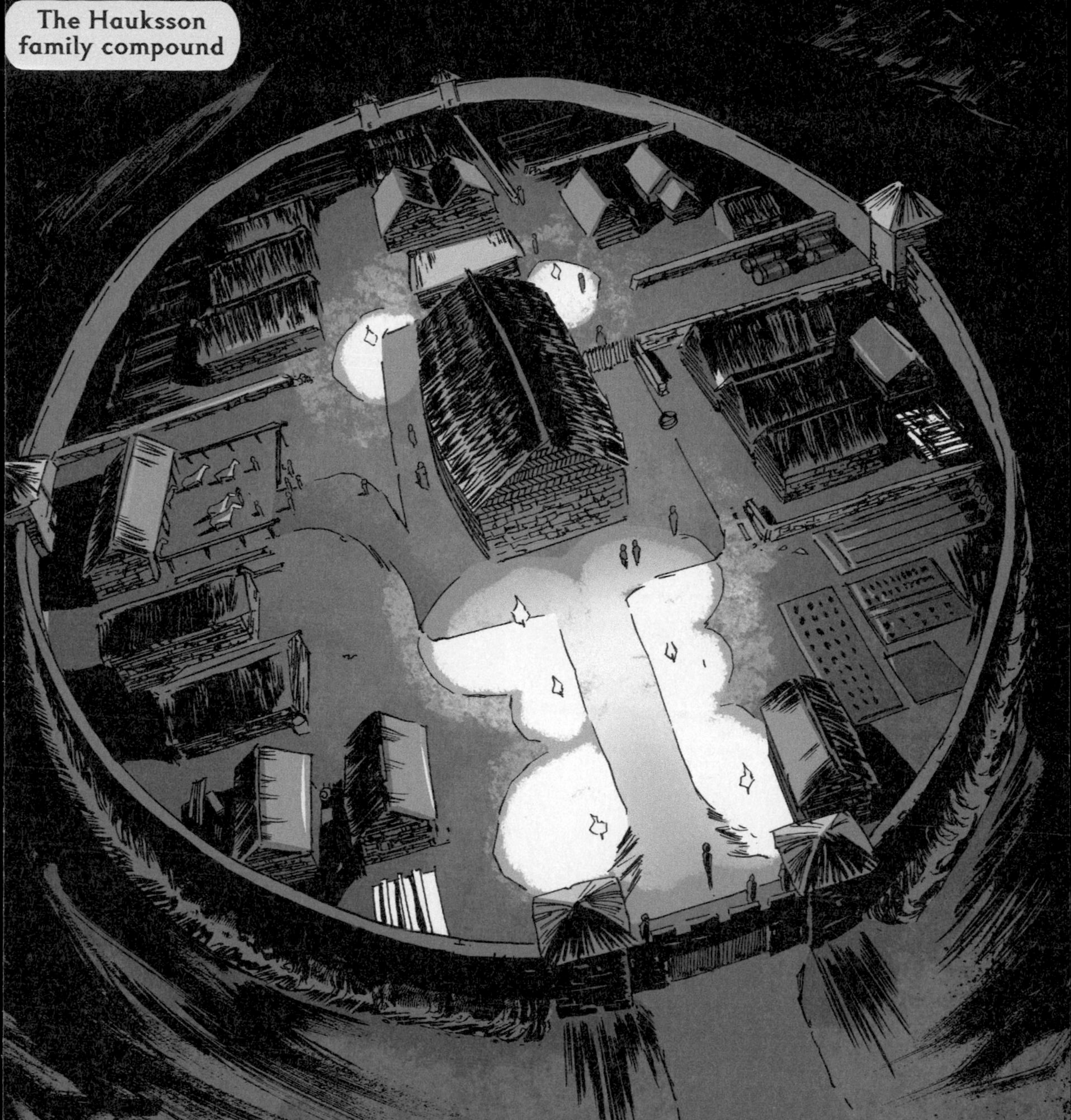
The Hauksson
family compound

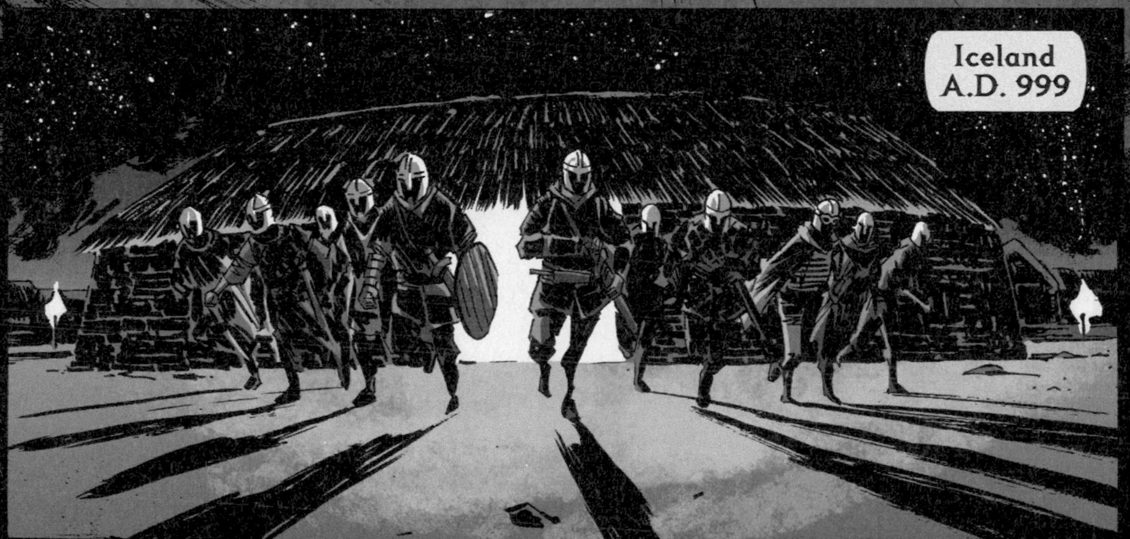
Iceland
A.D. 999

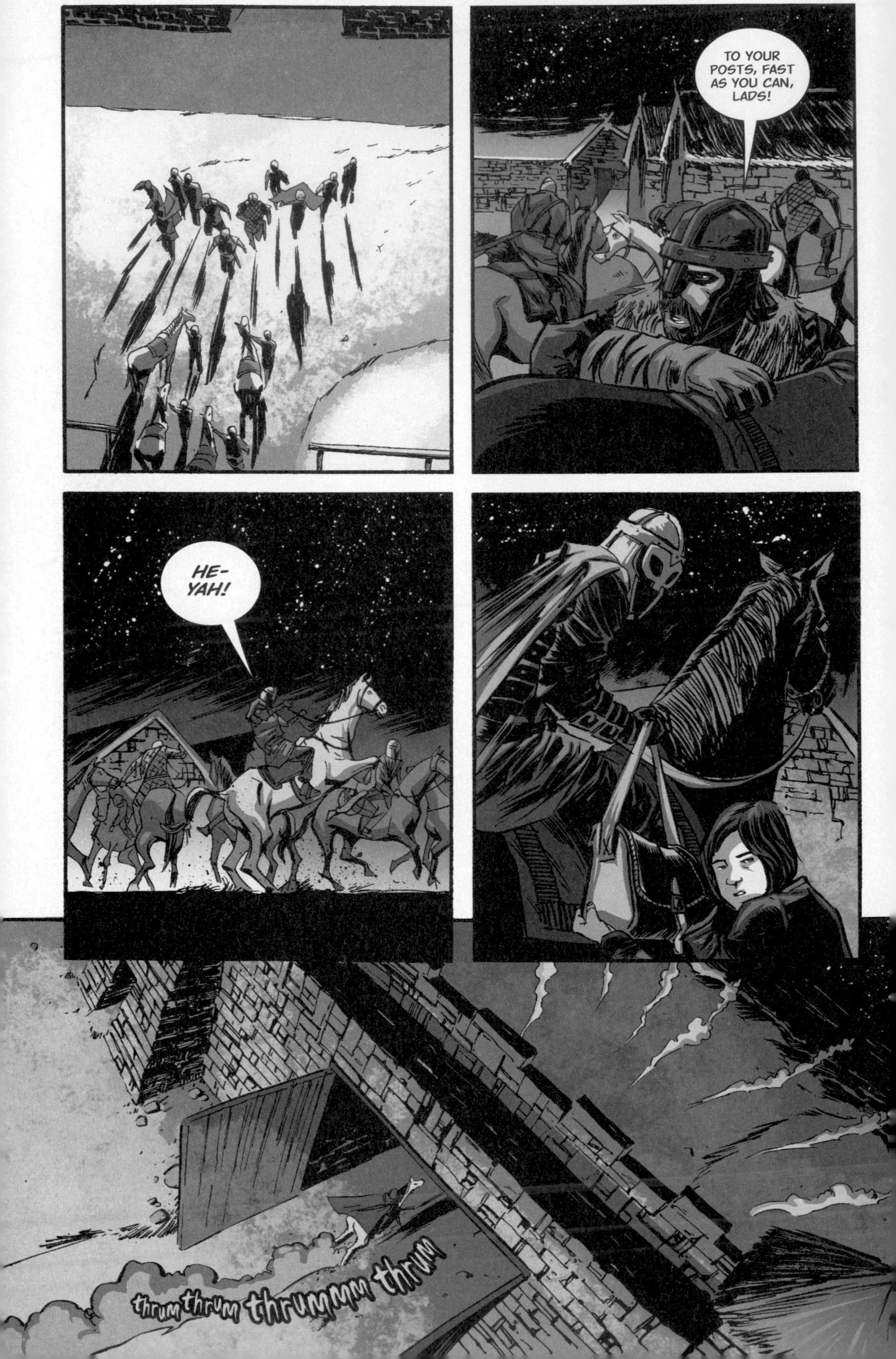

TO YOUR POSTS, FAST AS YOU CAN, LADS!
HE-YAH!
thrum thrum thrummm thrum

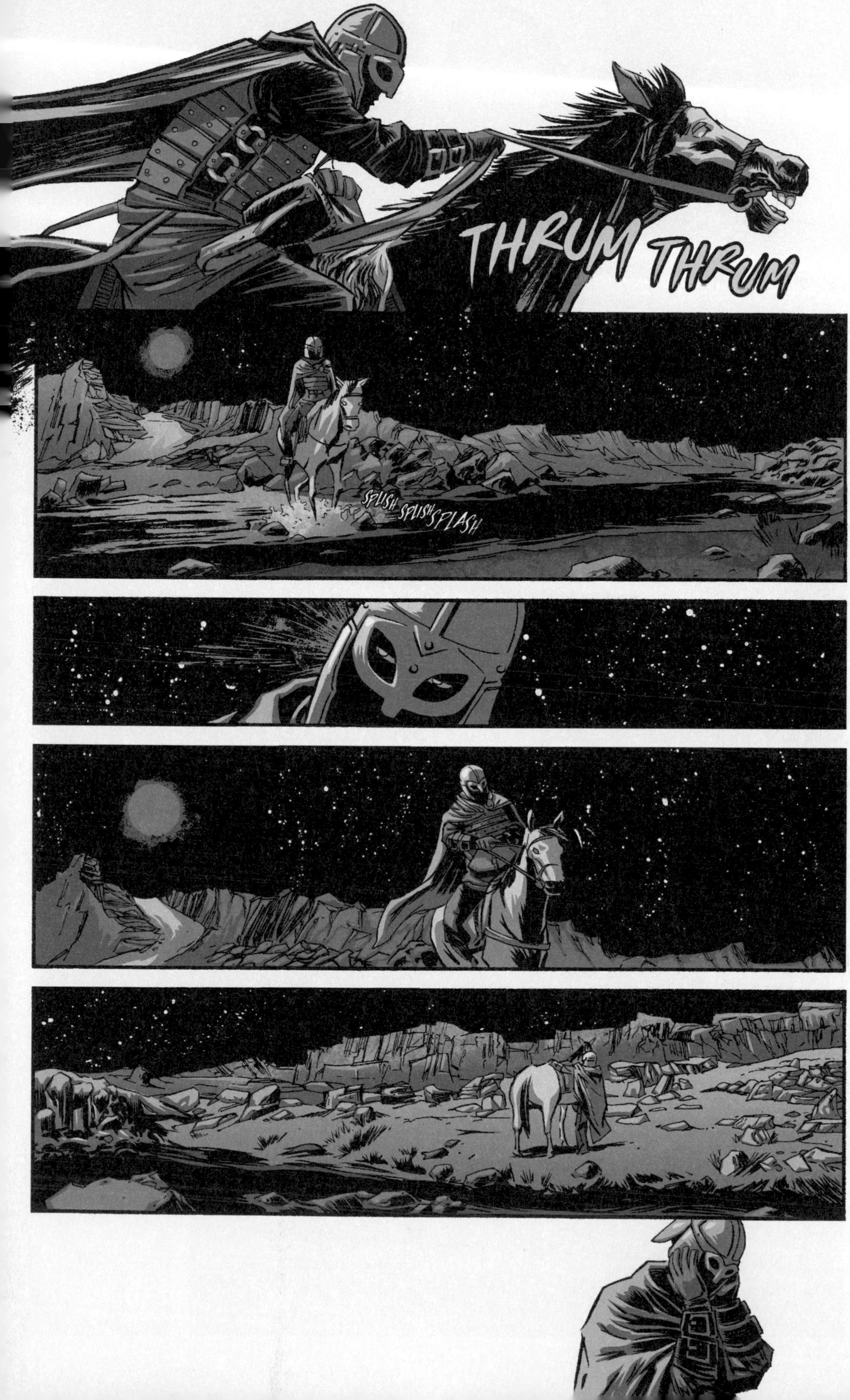
THRUM THRUM
SPLISH SPLISH SPLASH

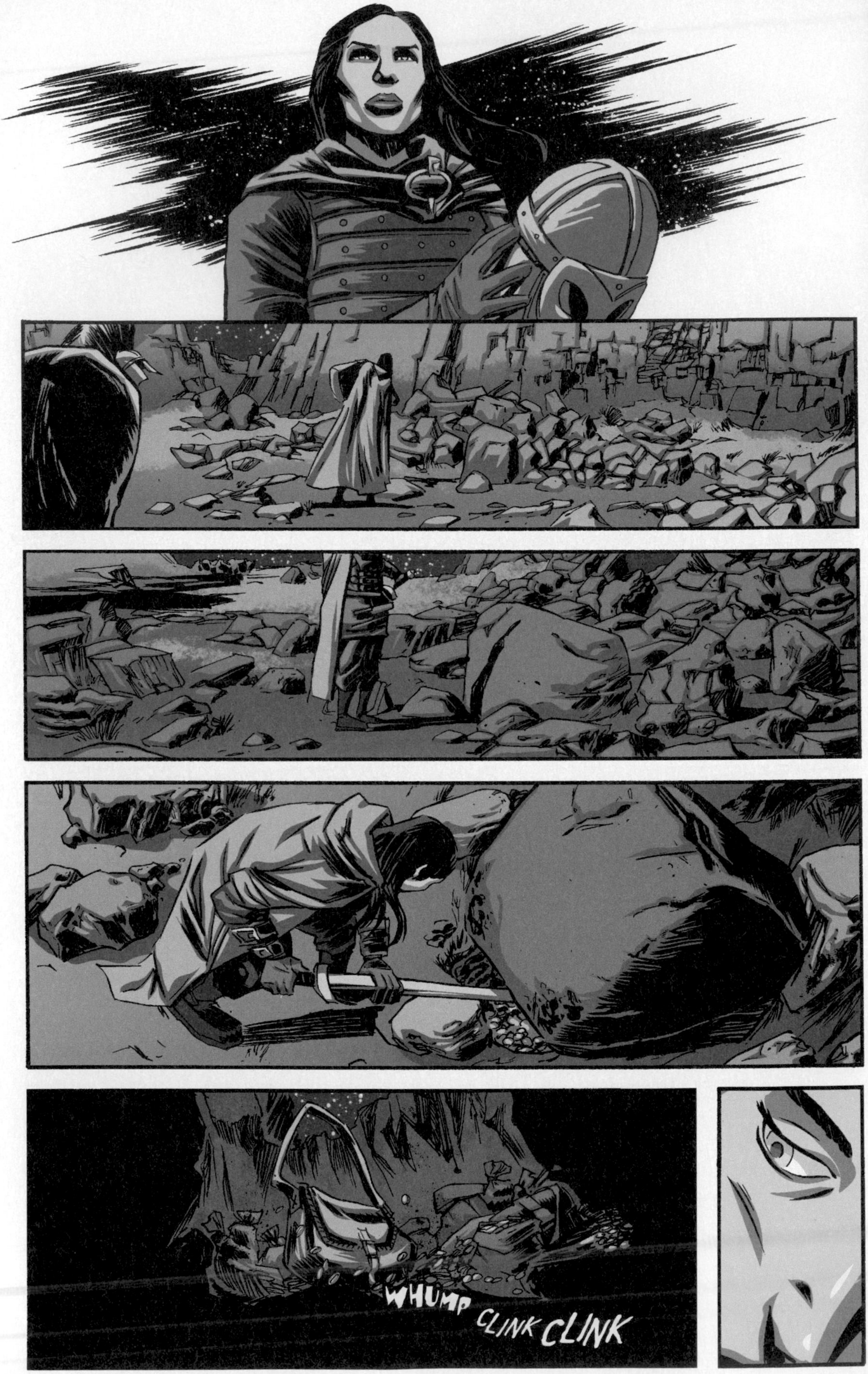
WHUMP
CLINK CLINK

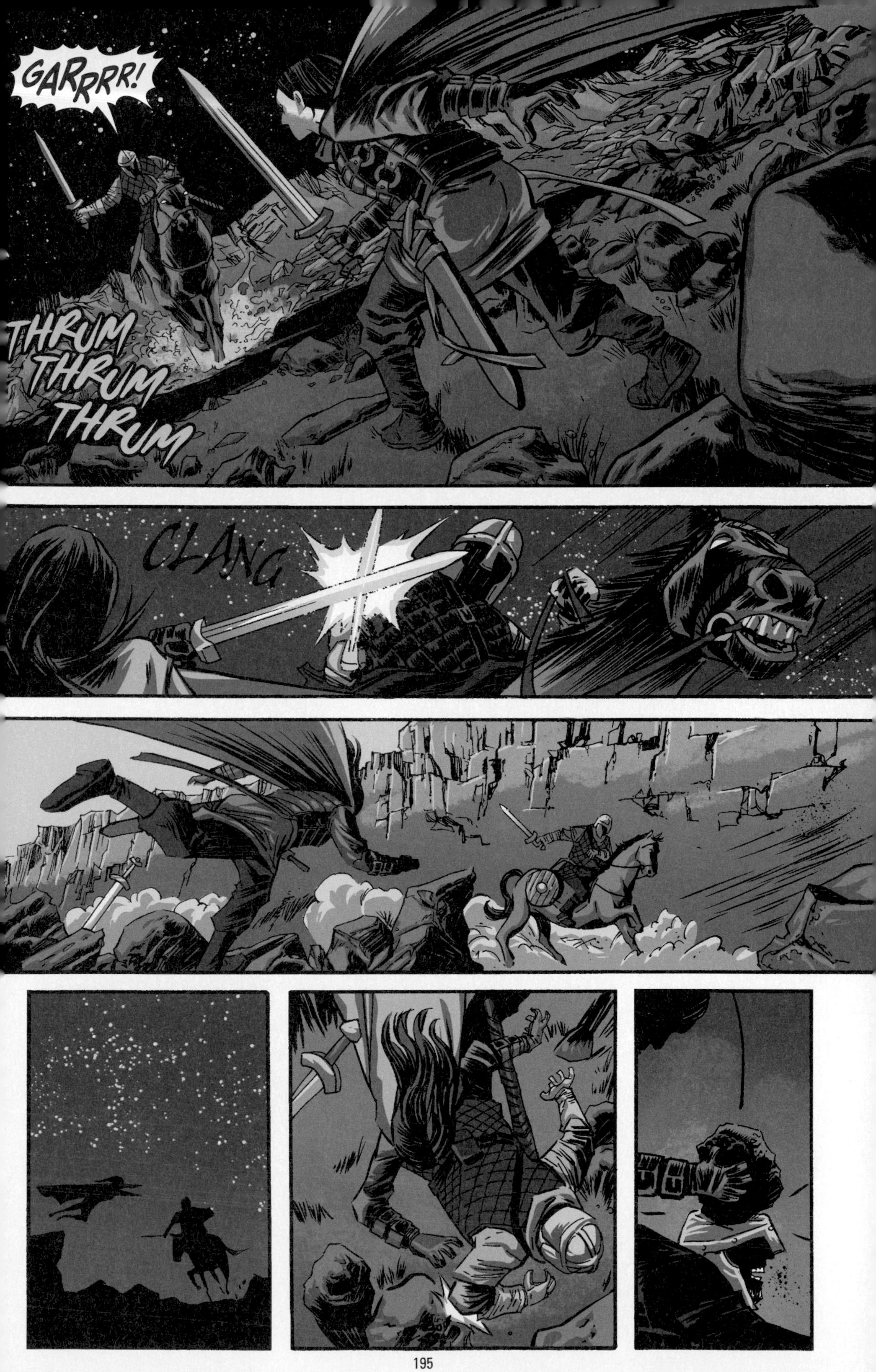
GARRRR!
THRUM THRUM THRUM
CLANG

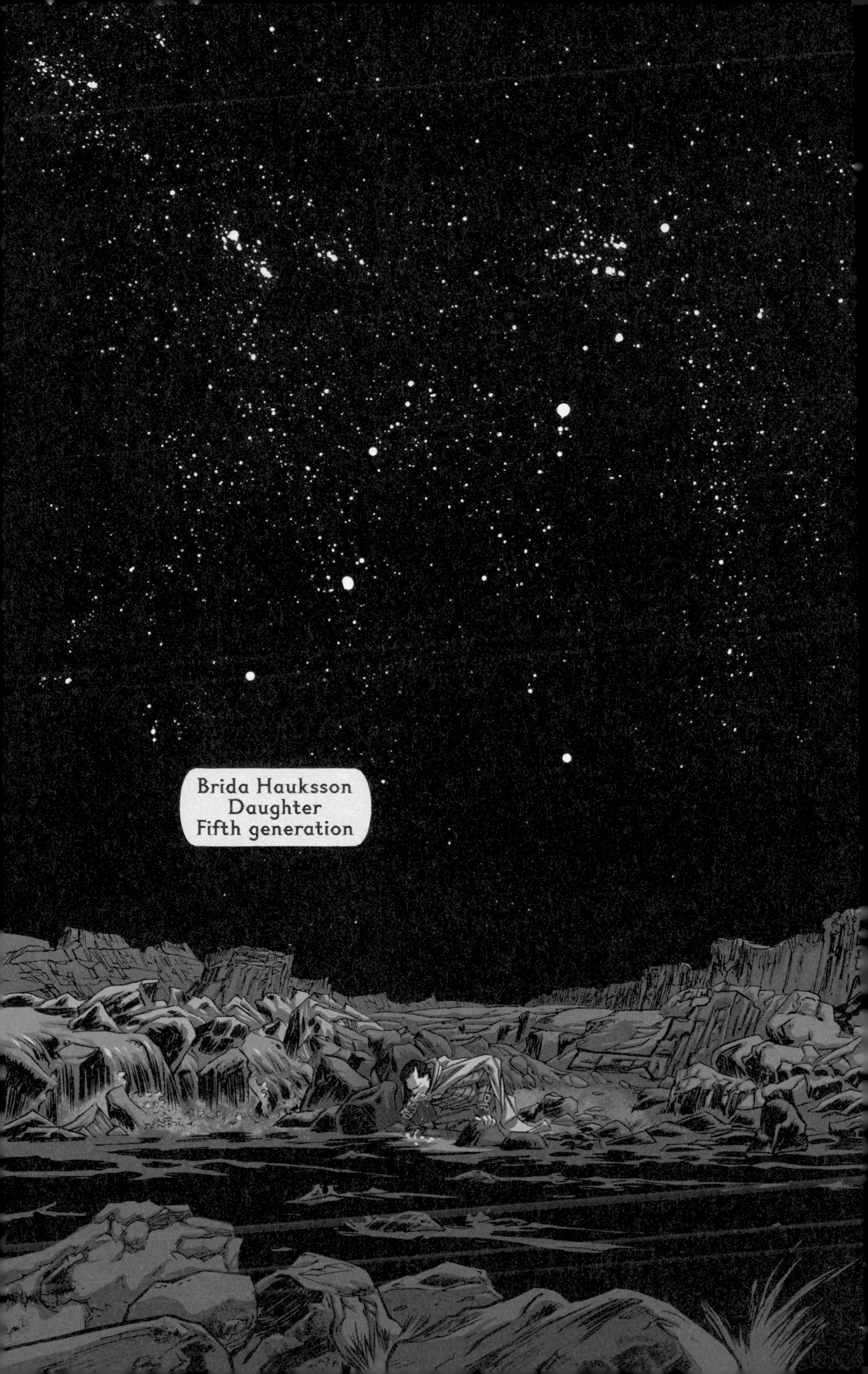
Brida Hauksson
Daughter
Fifth generation

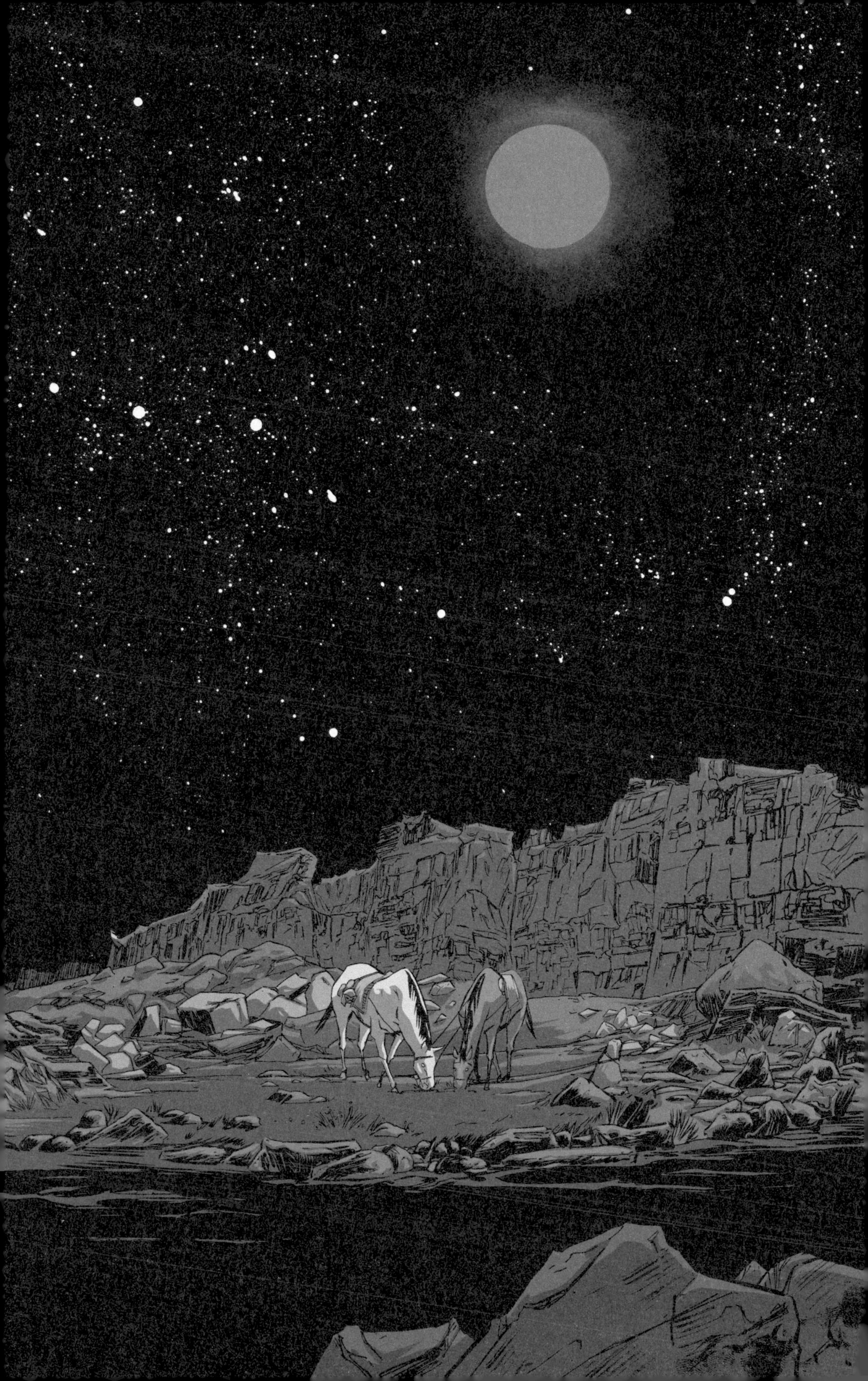

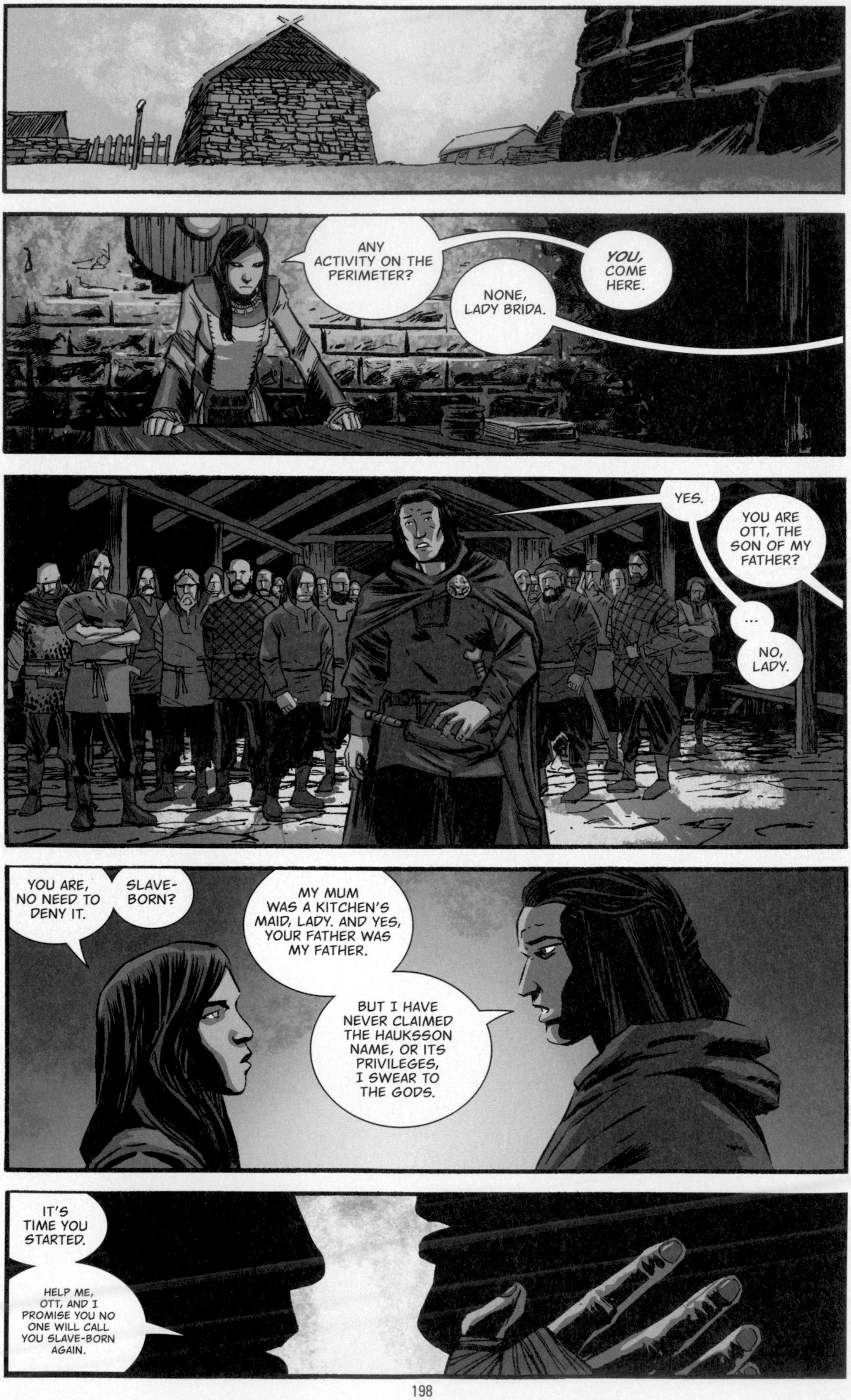

ANY ACTIVITY ON THE PERIMETER?
NONE, LADY BRIDA.
YOU, COME HERE.
YES.
YOU ARE OTT, THE SON OF MY FATHER?
...
NO, LADY.
YOU ARE, NO NEED TO DENY IT.
SLAVE-BORN?
MY MUM WAS A KITCHEN'S MAID, LADY. AND YES, YOUR FATHER WAS MY FATHER.
BUT I HAVE NEVER CLAIMED THE HAUKSSON NAME, OR ITS PRIVILEGES, I SWEAR TO THE GODS.
IT'S TIME YOU STARTED.
HELP ME, OTT, AND I PROMISE YOU NO ONE WILL CALL YOU SLAVE-BORN AGAIN.

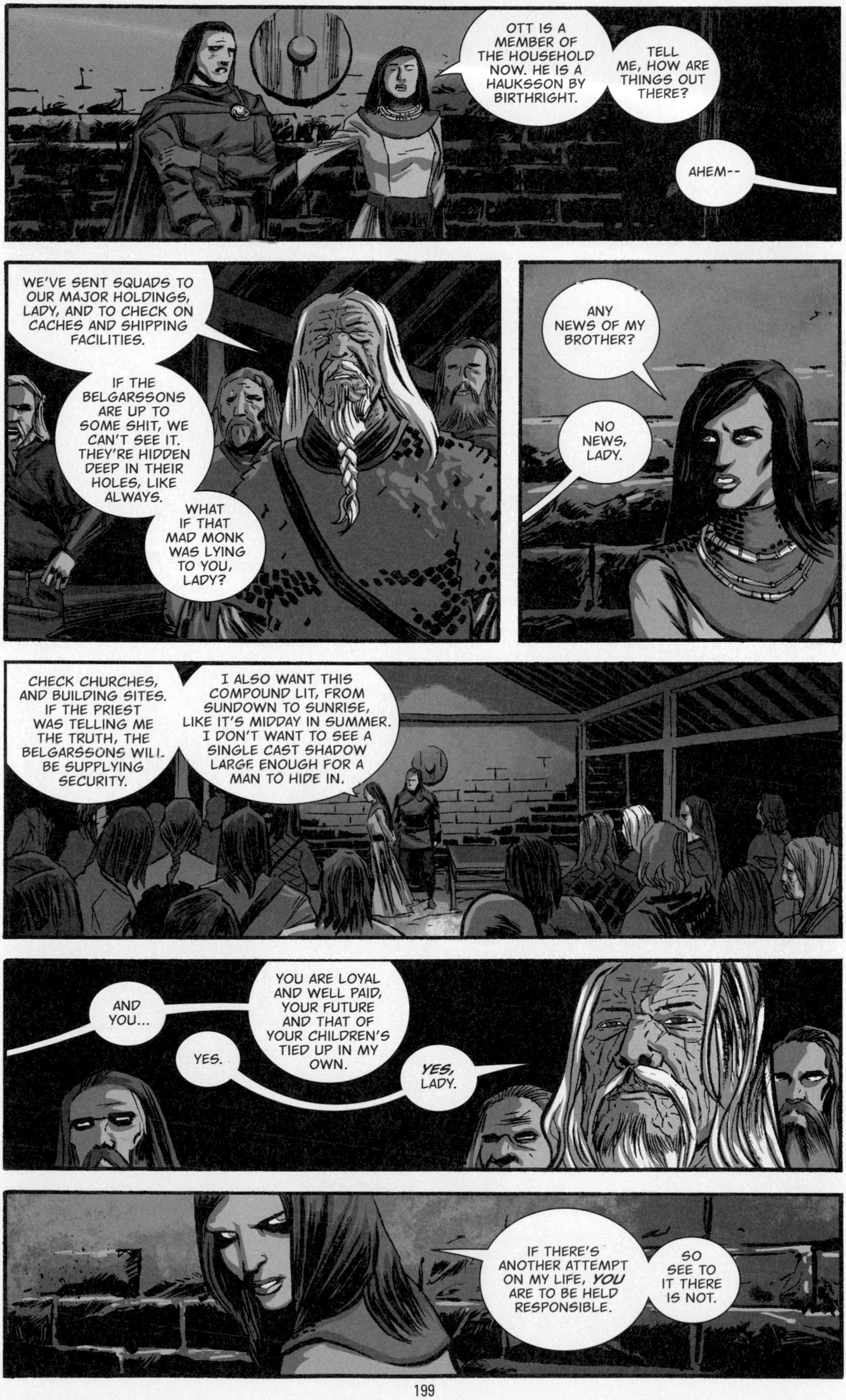

OTT IS A MEMBER OF THE HOUSEHOLD NOW. HE IS A HAUKSSON BY BIRTHRIGHT.
TELL ME, HOW ARE THINGS OUT THERE?
AHEM--
WE'VE SENT SQUADS TO OUR MAJOR HOLDINGS, LADY, AND TO CHECK ON CACHES AND SHIPPING FACILITIES.
IF THE BELGARSSONS ARE UP TO SOME SHIT, WE CAN'T SEE IT. THEY'RE HIDDEN DEEP IN THEIR HOLES, LIKE ALWAYS.
WHAT IF THAT MAD MONK WAS LYING TO YOU, LADY?
ANY NEWS OF MY BROTHER?
NO NEWS, LADY.
CHECK CHURCHES, AND BUILDING SITES. IF THE PRIEST WAS TELLING ME THE TRUTH, THE BELGARSSONS WILL BE SUPPLYING SECURITY.
I ALSO WANT THIS COMPOUND LIT, FROM SUNDOWN TO SUNRISE, LIKE IT'S MIDDAY IN SUMMER. I DON'T WANT TO SEE A SINGLE CAST SHADOW LARGE ENOUGH FOR A MAN TO HIDE IN.
AND YOU...
YOU ARE LOYAL AND WELL PAID, YOUR FUTURE AND THAT OF YOUR CHILDREN'S TIED UP IN MY OWN.
YES.
YES, LADY.
IF THERE'S ANOTHER ATTEMPT ON MY LIFE, YOU ARE TO BE HELD RESPONSIBLE.
SO SEE TO IT THERE IS NOT.

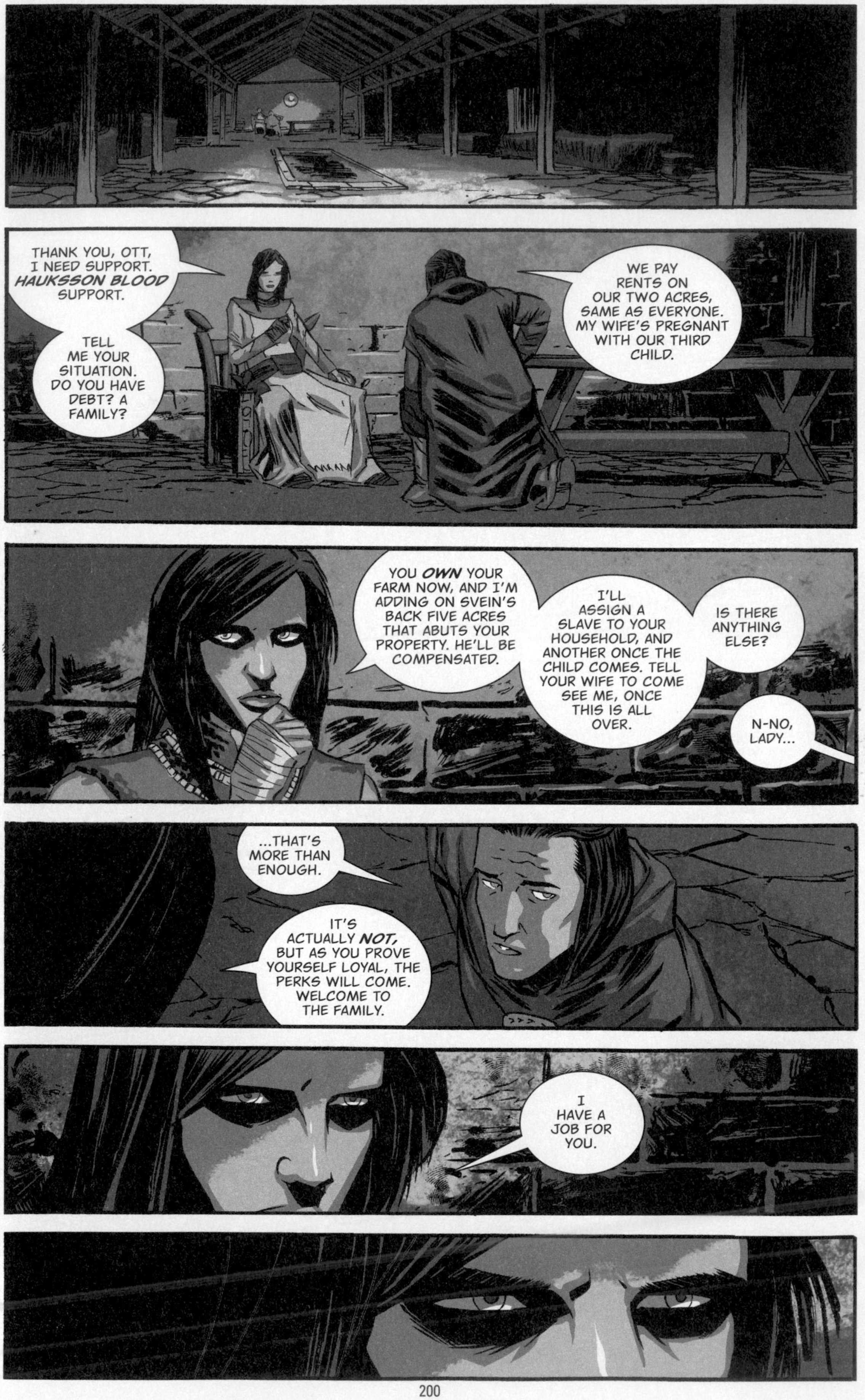
THANK YOU, OTT, I NEED SUPPORT. HAUKSSON BLOOD SUPPORT.
TELL ME YOUR SITUATION. DO YOU HAVE DEBT? A FAMILY?
WE PAY RENTS ON OUR TWO ACRES, SAME AS EVERYONE. MY WIFE'S PREGNANT WITH OUR THIRD CHILD.
YOU OWN YOUR FARM NOW, AND I'M ADDING ON SVEIN'S BACK FIVE ACRES THAT ABUTS YOUR PROPERTY. HE'LL BE COMPENSATED.
I'LL ASSIGN A SLAVE TO YOUR HOUSEHOLD, AND ANOTHER ONCE THE CHILD COMES. TELL YOUR WIFE TO COME SEE ME, ONCE THIS IS ALL OVER.
IS THERE ANYTHING ELSE?
N-NO, LADY...
...THAT'S MORE THAN ENOUGH.
IT'S ACTUALLY NOT, BUT AS YOU PROVE YOURSELF LOYAL, THE PERKS WILL COME. WELCOME TO THE FAMILY.
I HAVE A JOB FOR YOU.

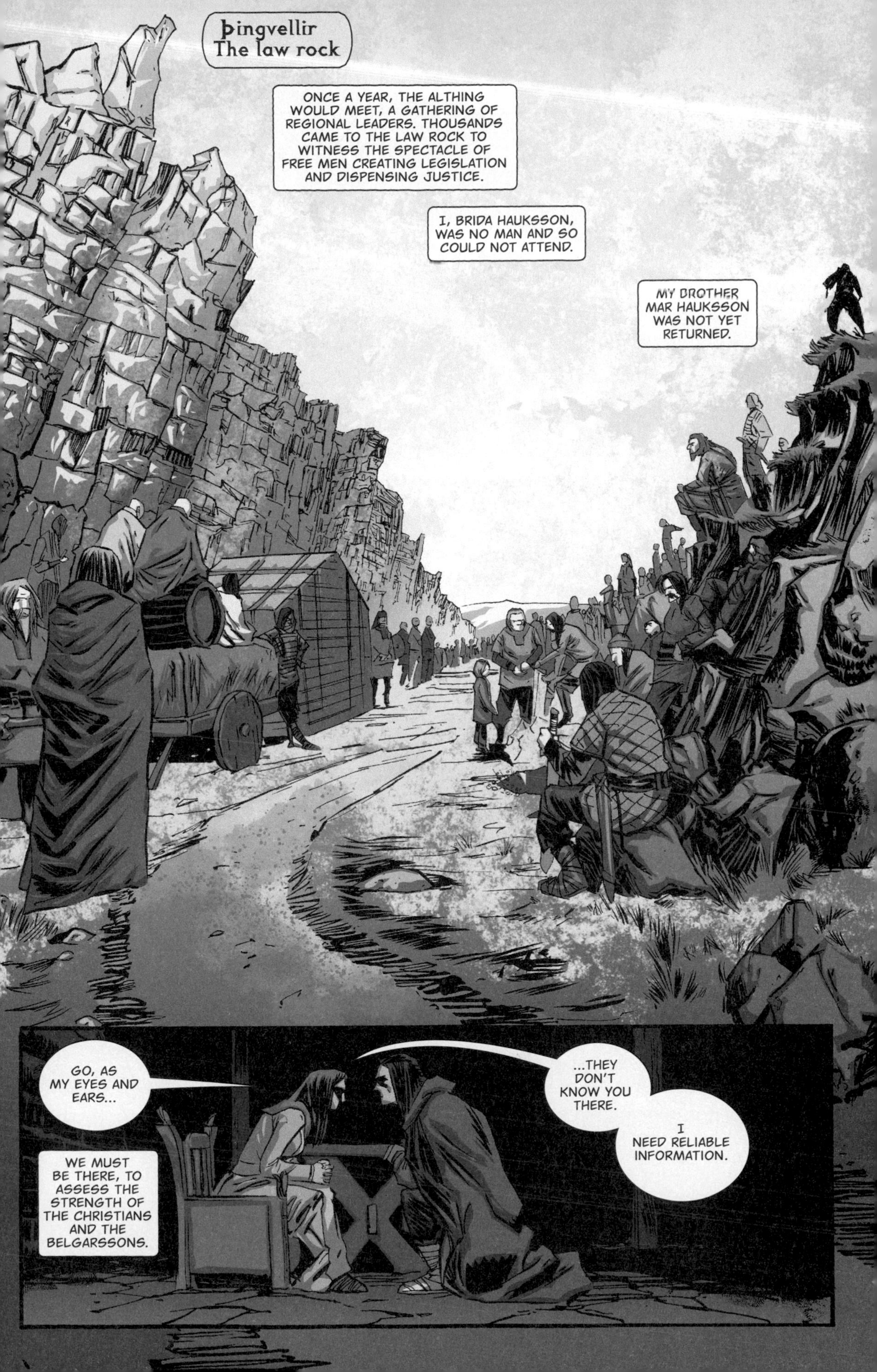
Þingvellir
The law rock
ONCE A YEAR, THE ALTHING WOULD MEET, A GATHERING OF REGIONAL LEADERS. THOUSANDS CAME TO THE LAW ROCK TO WITNESS THE SPECTACLE OF FREE MEN CREATING LEGISLATION AND DISPENSING JUSTICE.
I, BRIDA HAUKSSON, WAS NO MAN AND SO COULD NOT ATTEND.
MY BROTHER MAR HAUKSSON WAS NOT YET RETURNED.
GO, AS MY EYES AND EARS...
...THEY DON'T KNOW YOU THERE.
I NEED RELIABLE INFORMATION.
WE MUST BE THERE, TO ASSESS THE STRENGTH OF THE CHRISTIANS AND THE BELGARSSONS.

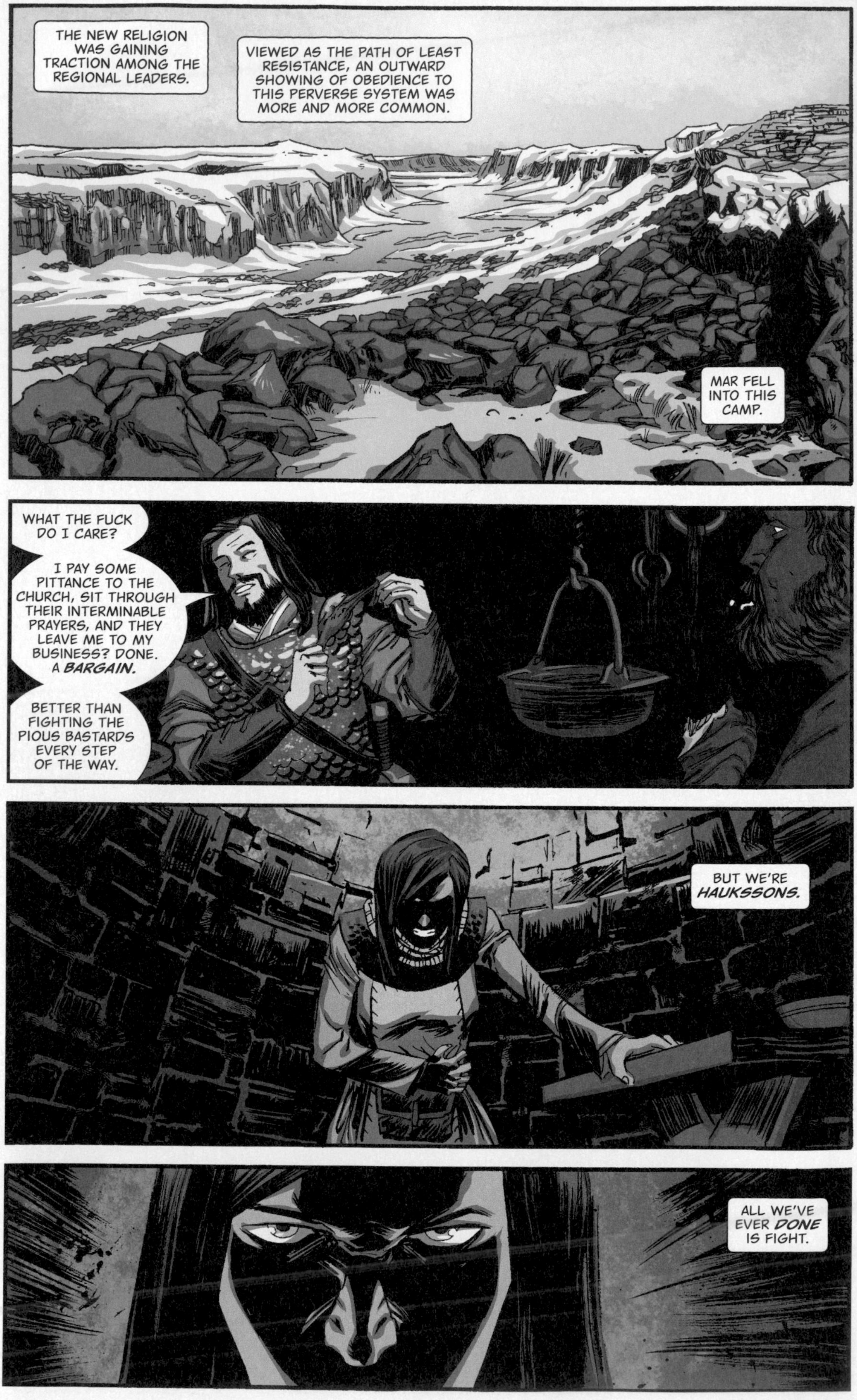
THE NEW RELIGION WAS GAINING TRACTION AMONG THE REGIONAL LEADERS.
VIEWED AS THE PATH OF LEAST RESISTANCE, AN OUTWARD SHOWING OF OBEDIENCE TO THIS PERVERSE SYSTEM WAS MORE AND MORE COMMON.
MAR FELL INTO THIS CAMP.
WHAT THE FUCK DO I CARE?
I PAY SOME PITTANCE TO THE CHURCH, SIT THROUGH THEIR INTERMINABLE PRAYERS, AND THEY LEAVE ME TO MY BUSINESS? DONE. A *BARGAIN.*
BETTER THAN FIGHTING THE PIOUS BASTARDS EVERY STEP OF THE WAY.
BUT WE'RE *HAUKSSONS.*
ALL WE'VE EVER *DONE* IS FIGHT.

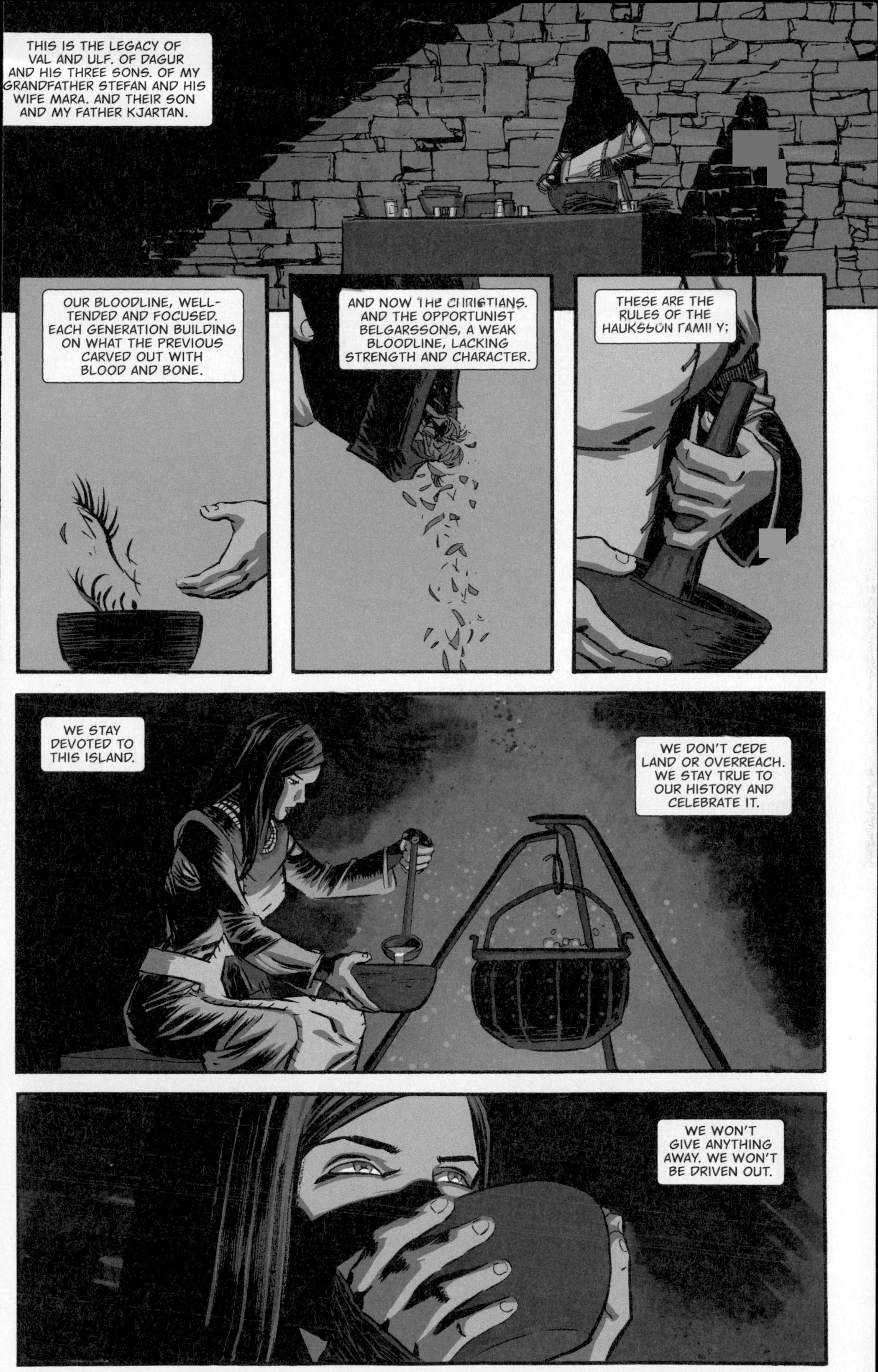
THIS IS THE LEGACY OF VAL AND ULF. OF DAGUR AND HIS THREE SONS. OF MY GRANDFATHER STEFAN AND HIS WIFE MARA. AND THEIR SON AND MY FATHER KJARTAN.
OUR BLOODLINE, WELL-TENDED AND FOCUSED. EACH GENERATION BUILDING ON WHAT THE PREVIOUS CARVED OUT WITH BLOOD AND BONE.
AND NOW THE CHRISTIANS. AND THE OPPORTUNIST BELGARSSONS, A WEAK BLOODLINE, LACKING STRENGTH AND CHARACTER.
THESE ARE THE RULES OF THE HAUKSSON FAMILY;
WE STAY DEVOTED TO THIS ISLAND.
WE DON'T CEDE LAND OR OVERREACH. WE STAY TRUE TO OUR HISTORY AND CELEBRATE IT.
WE WON'T GIVE ANYTHING AWAY. WE WON'T BE DRIVEN OUT.

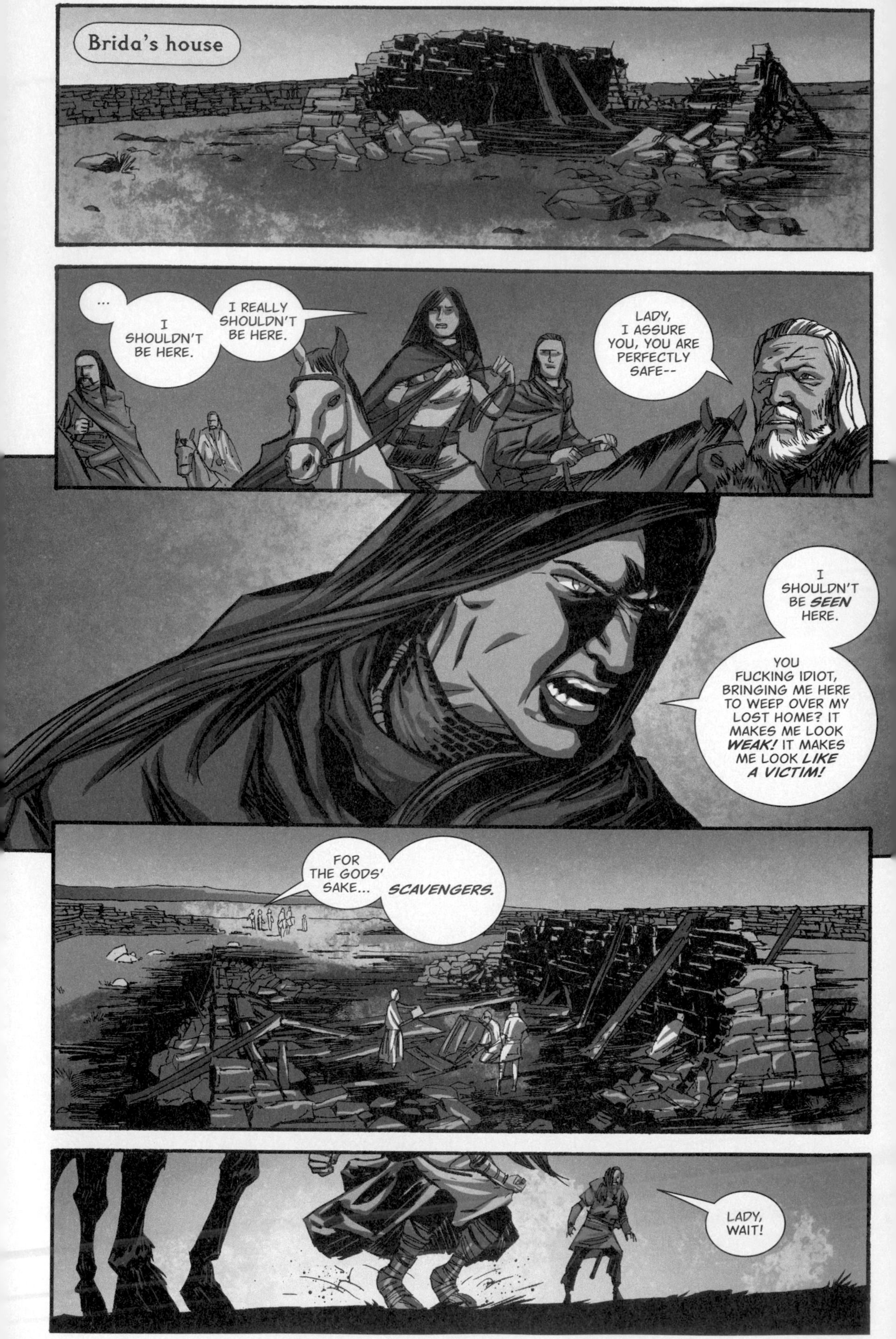

Brida's house
...
I SHOULDN'T BE HERE.
I REALLY SHOULDN'T BE HERE.
LADY, I ASSURE YOU, YOU ARE PERFECTLY SAFE--
I SHOULDN'T BE *SEEN* HERE.
YOU FUCKING IDIOT, BRINGING ME HERE TO WEEP OVER MY LOST HOME? IT MAKES ME LOOK ***WEAK!*** IT MAKES ME LOOK ***LIKE A VICTIM!***
FOR THE GODS' SAKE...
SCAVENGERS.
LADY, WAIT!

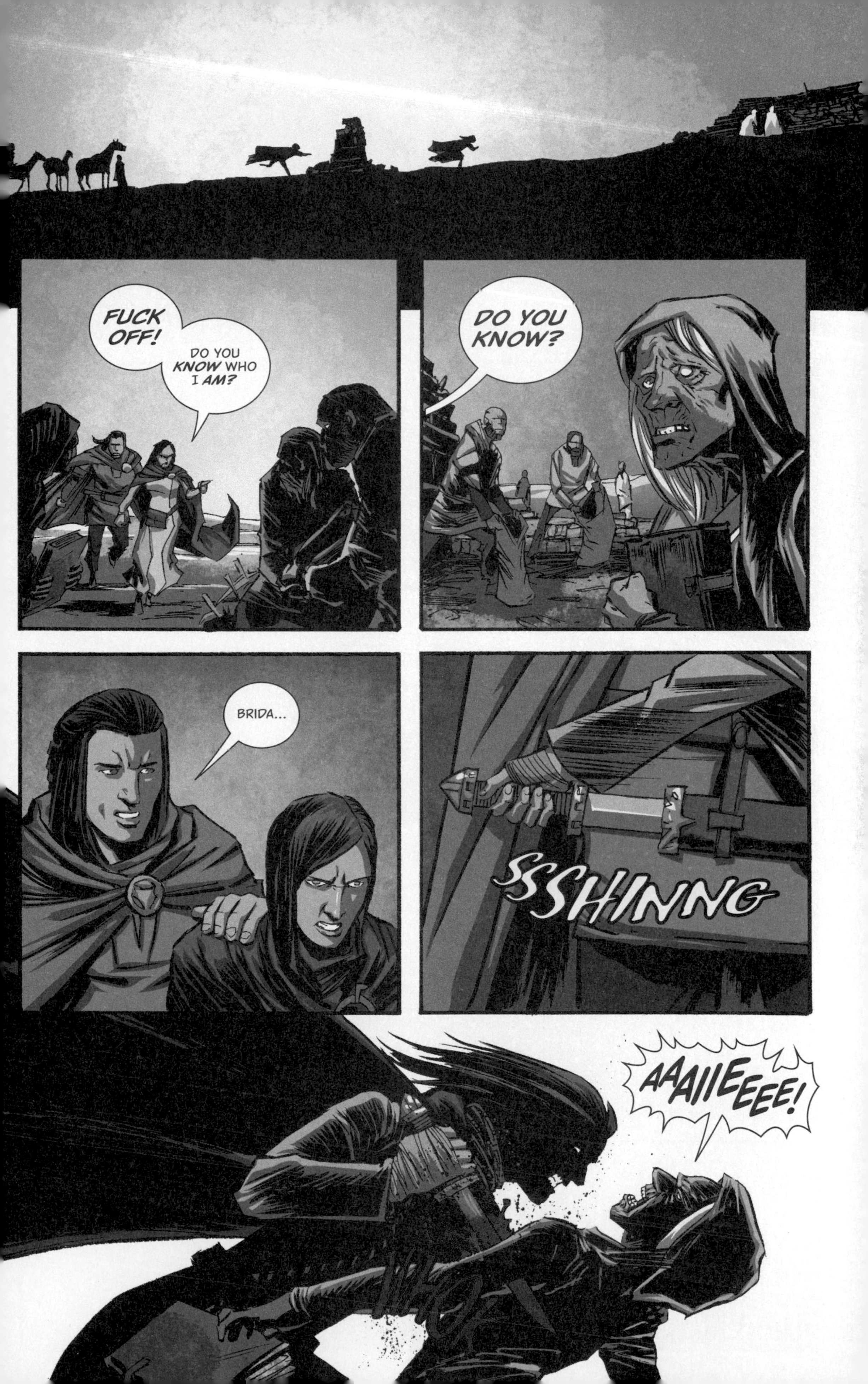
FUCK OFF!
DO YOU KNOW WHO I AM?
DO YOU KNOW?
BRIDA...
SSSHINNG
AAAIIIEEEE!

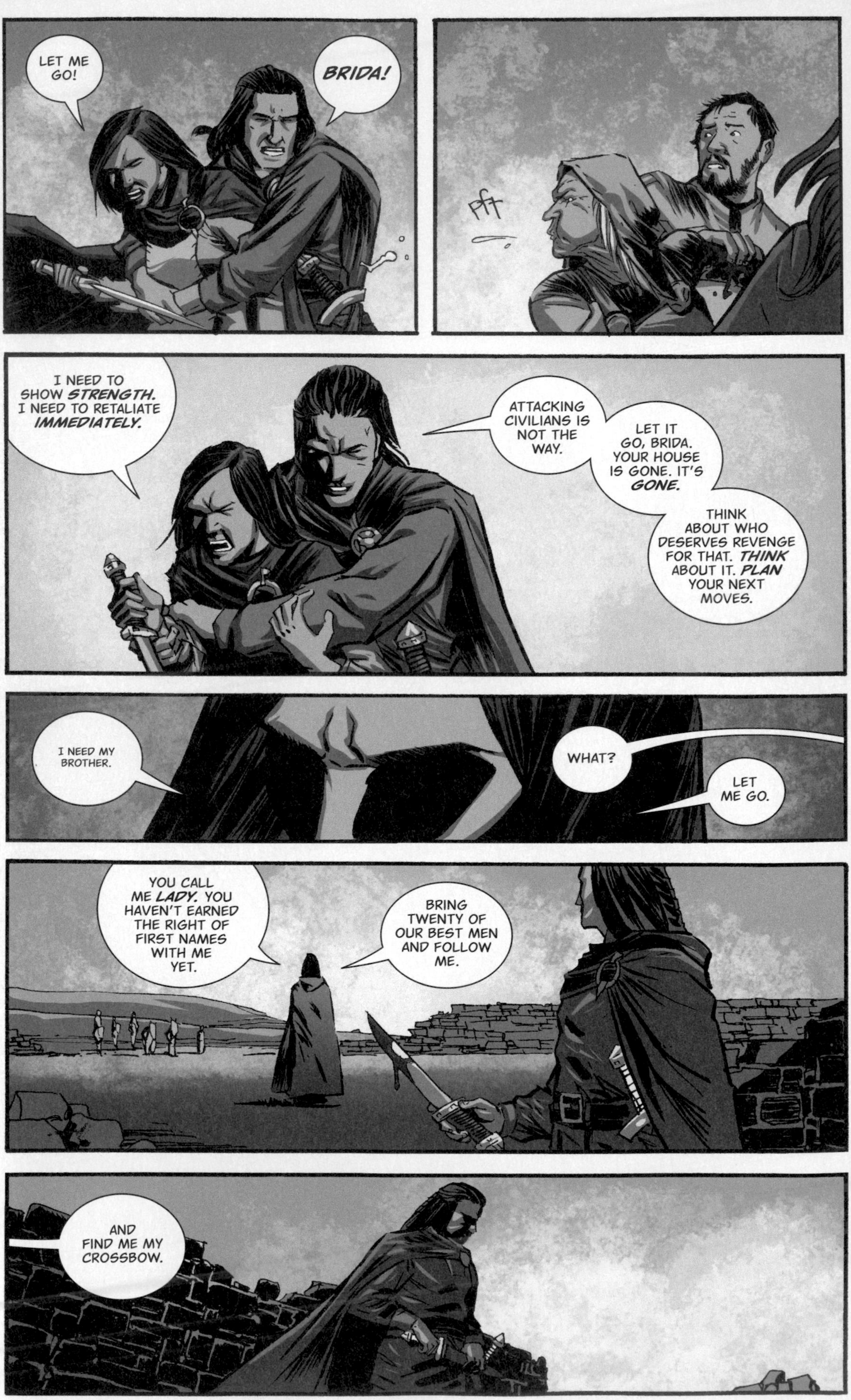
LET ME GO!
BRIDA!
pft
I NEED TO SHOW STRENGTH. I NEED TO RETALIATE IMMEDIATELY.
ATTACKING CIVILIANS IS NOT THE WAY.
LET IT GO, BRIDA. YOUR HOUSE IS GONE. IT'S GONE.
THINK ABOUT WHO DESERVES REVENGE FOR THAT. THINK ABOUT IT. PLAN YOUR NEXT MOVES.
I NEED MY BROTHER.
WHAT?
LET ME GO.
YOU CALL ME LADY. YOU HAVEN'T EARNED THE RIGHT OF FIRST NAMES WITH ME YET.
BRING TWENTY OF OUR BEST MEN AND FOLLOW ME.
AND FIND ME MY CROSSBOW.

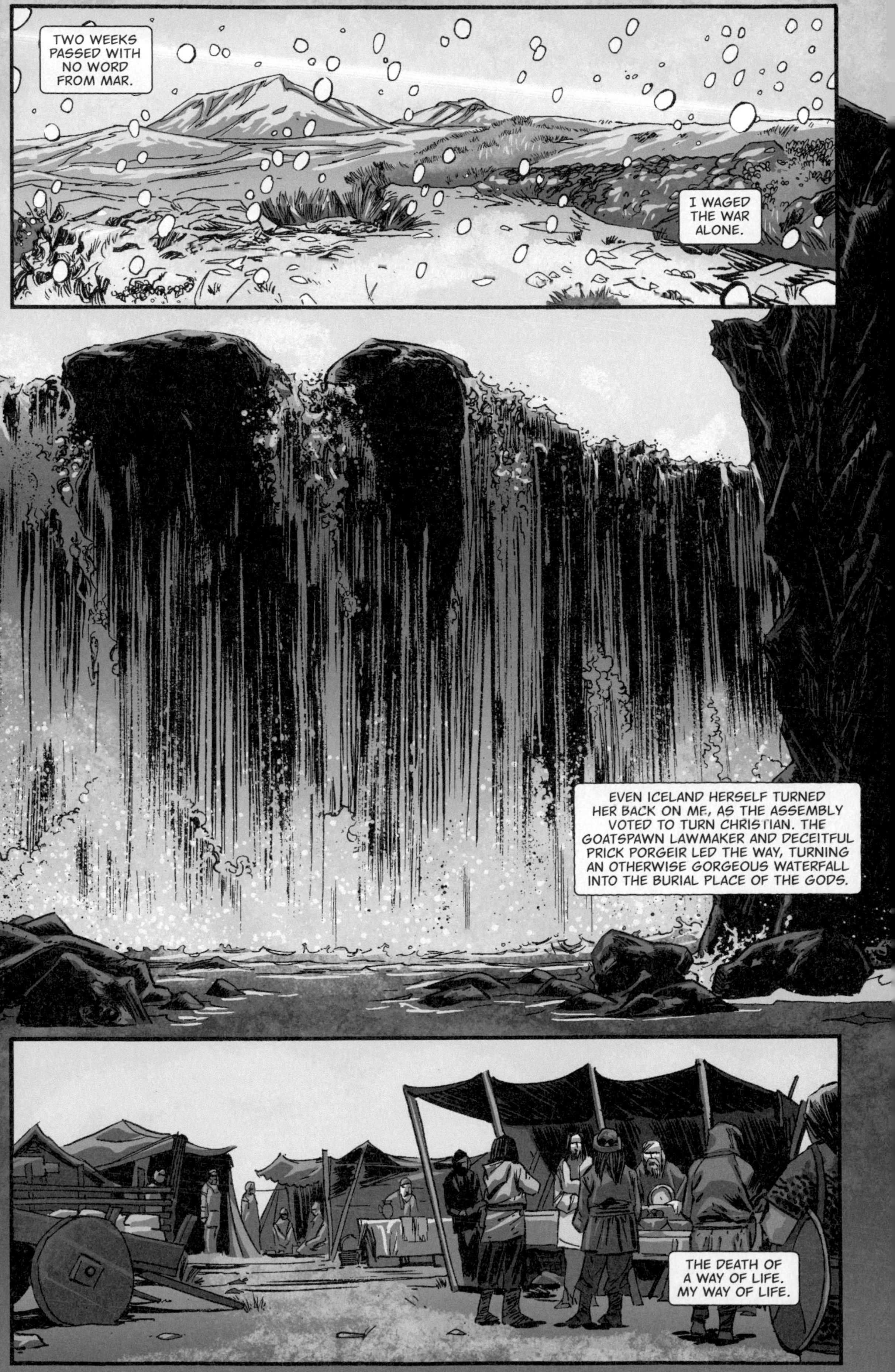
TWO WEEKS PASSED WITH NO WORD FROM MAR.
I WAGED THE WAR ALONE.
EVEN ICELAND HERSELF TURNED HER BACK ON ME, AS THE ASSEMBLY VOTED TO TURN CHRISTIAN. THE GOATSPAWN LAWMAKER AND DECEITFUL PRICK PORGEIR LED THE WAY, TURNING AN OTHERWISE GORGEOUS WATERFALL INTO THE BURIAL PLACE OF THE GODS.
THE DEATH OF A WAY OF LIFE. MY WAY OF LIFE.

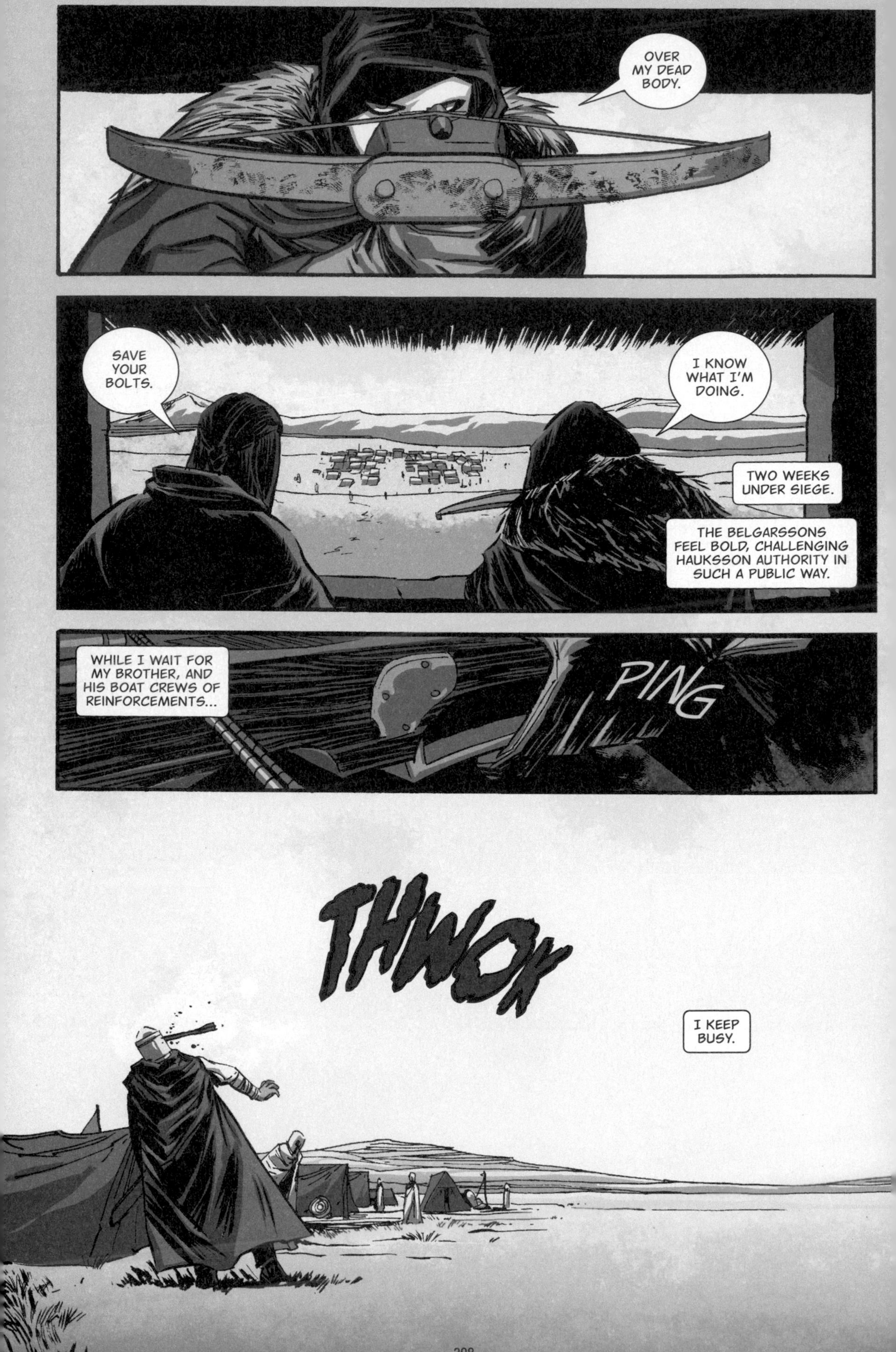
OVER MY DEAD BODY.
SAVE YOUR BOLTS.
I KNOW WHAT I'M DOING.
TWO WEEKS UNDER SIEGE.
THE BELGARSSONS FEEL BOLD, CHALLENGING HAUKSSON AUTHORITY IN SUCH A PUBLIC WAY.
WHILE I WAIT FOR MY BROTHER, AND HIS BOAT CREWS OF REINFORCEMENTS...
PING
THWOK
I KEEP BUSY.

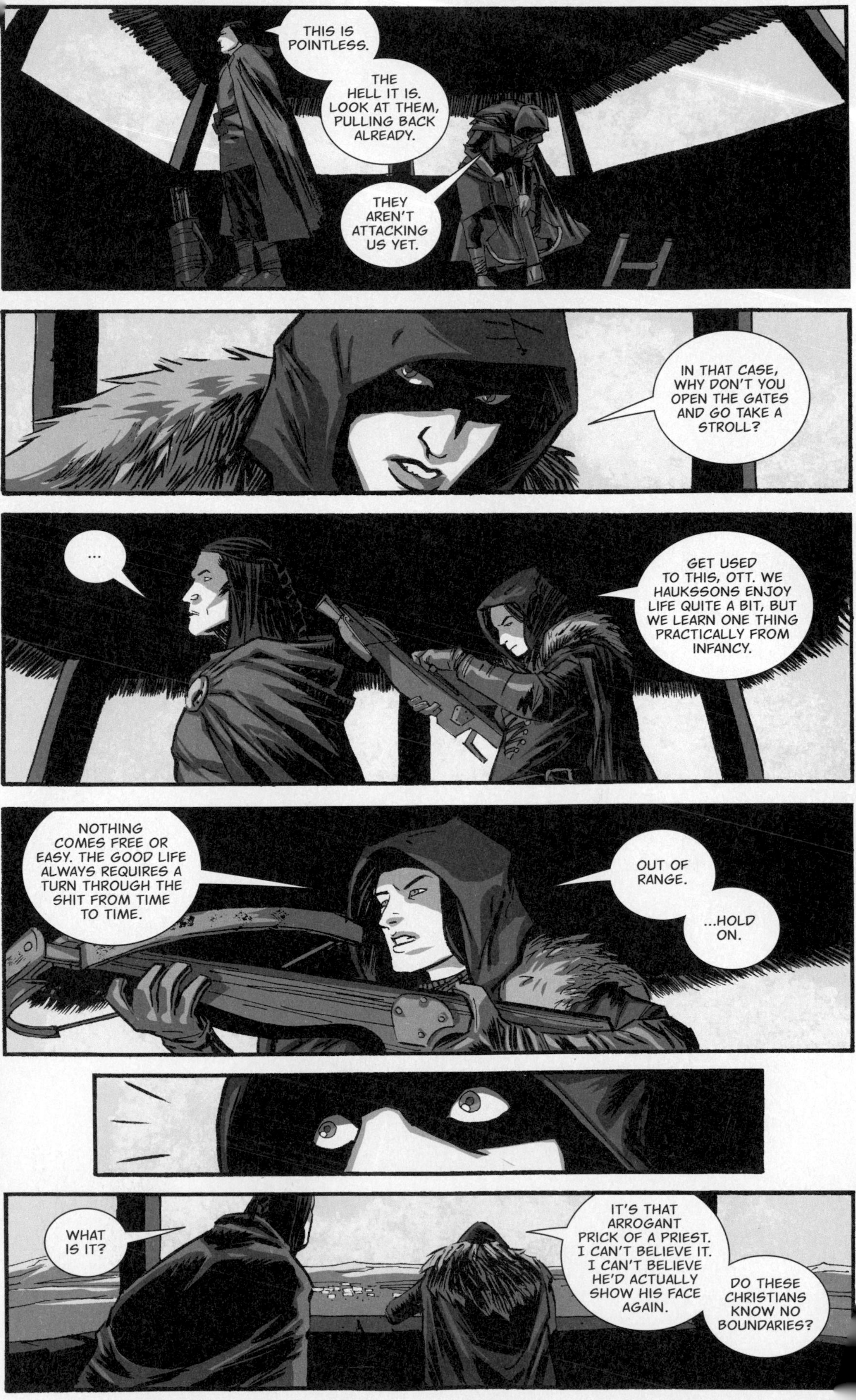
THIS IS POINTLESS.
THE HELL IT IS. LOOK AT THEM, PULLING BACK ALREADY.
THEY AREN'T ATTACKING US YET.
IN THAT CASE, WHY DON'T YOU OPEN THE GATES AND GO TAKE A STROLL?
...
GET USED TO THIS, OTT. WE HAUKSSONS ENJOY LIFE QUITE A BIT, BUT WE LEARN ONE THING PRACTICALLY FROM INFANCY.
NOTHING COMES FREE OR EASY. THE GOOD LIFE ALWAYS REQUIRES A TURN THROUGH THE SHIT FROM TIME TO TIME.
OUT OF RANGE.
...HOLD ON.
WHAT IS IT?
IT'S THAT ARROGANT PRICK OF A PRIEST. I CAN'T BELIEVE IT. I CAN'T BELIEVE HE'D ACTUALLY SHOW HIS FACE AGAIN.
DO THESE CHRISTIANS KNOW NO BOUNDARIES?

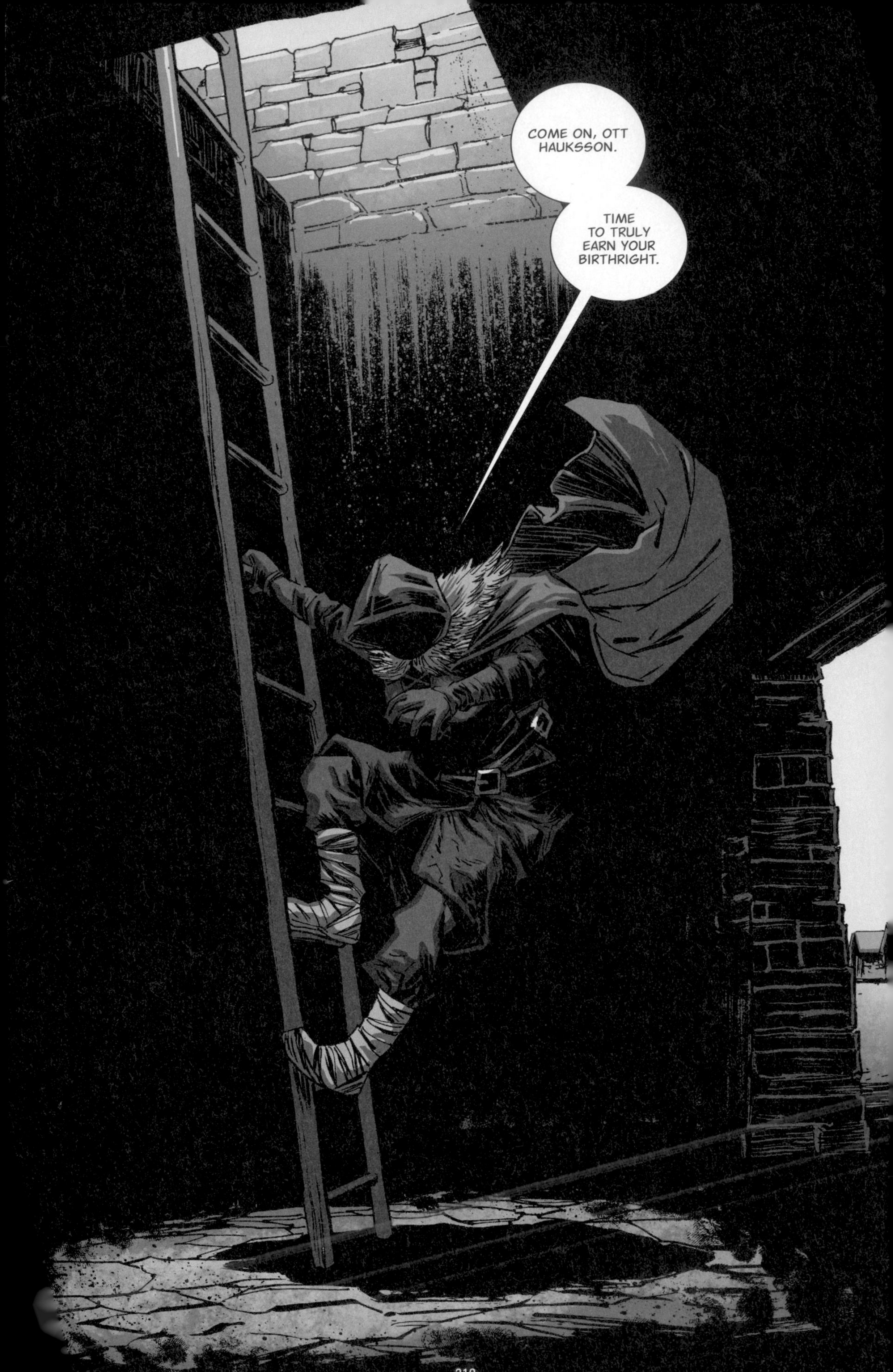
COME ON, OTT HAUKSSON.
TIME TO TRULY EARN YOUR BIRTHRIGHT.

Chapter VI
Commerce
A.D. 1000

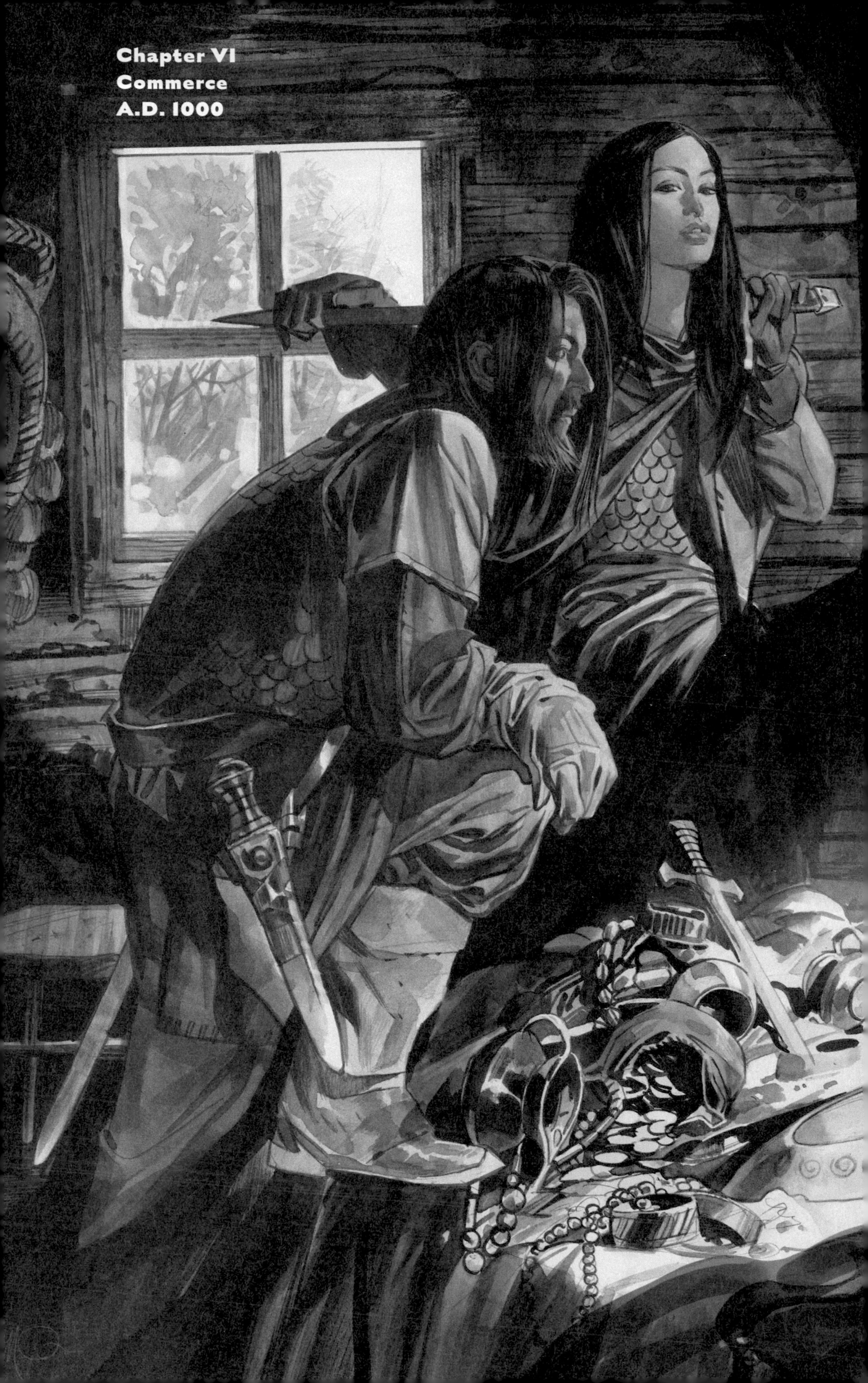

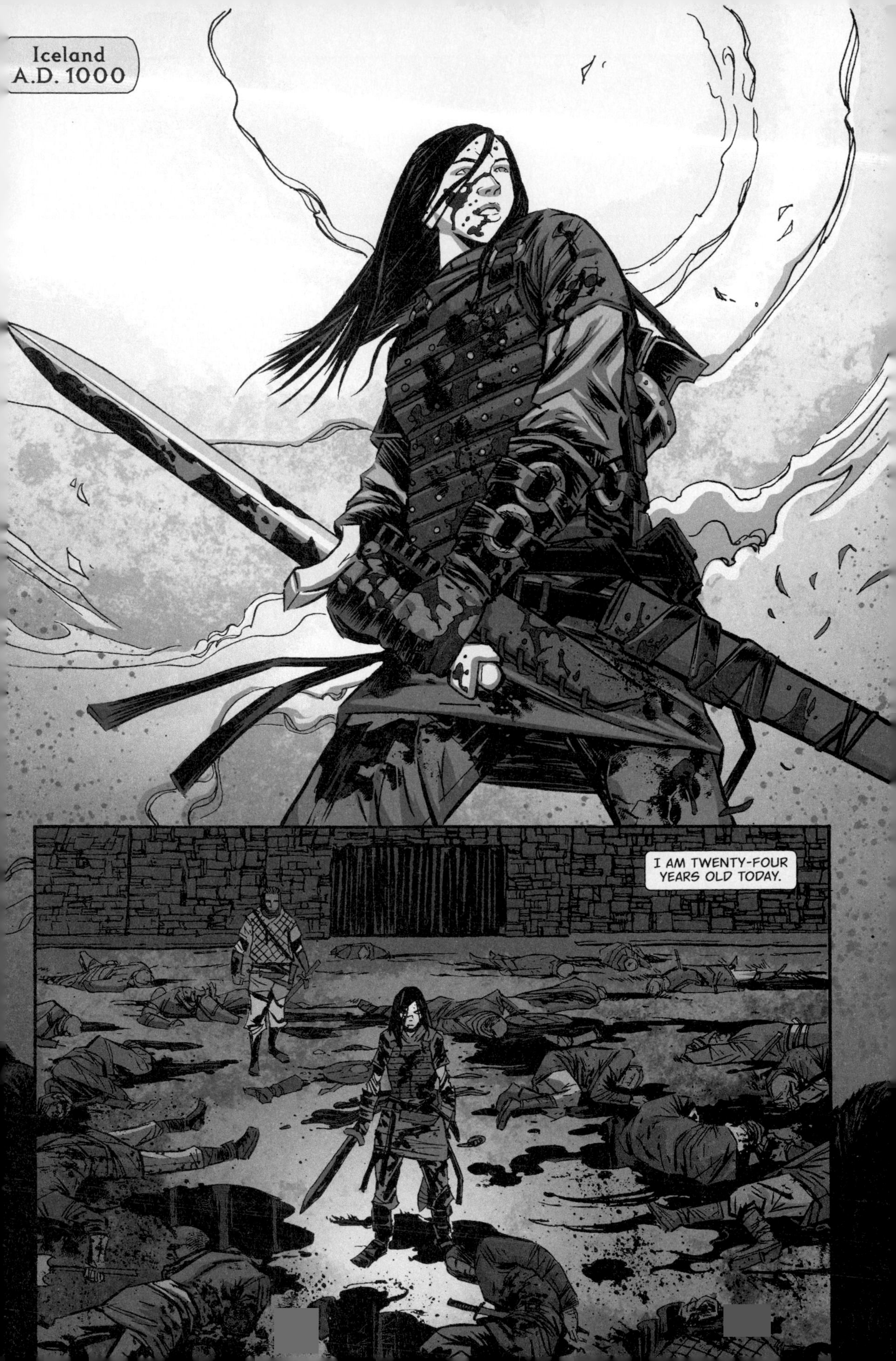
Iceland
A.D. 1000
I AM TWENTY-FOUR YEARS OLD TODAY.

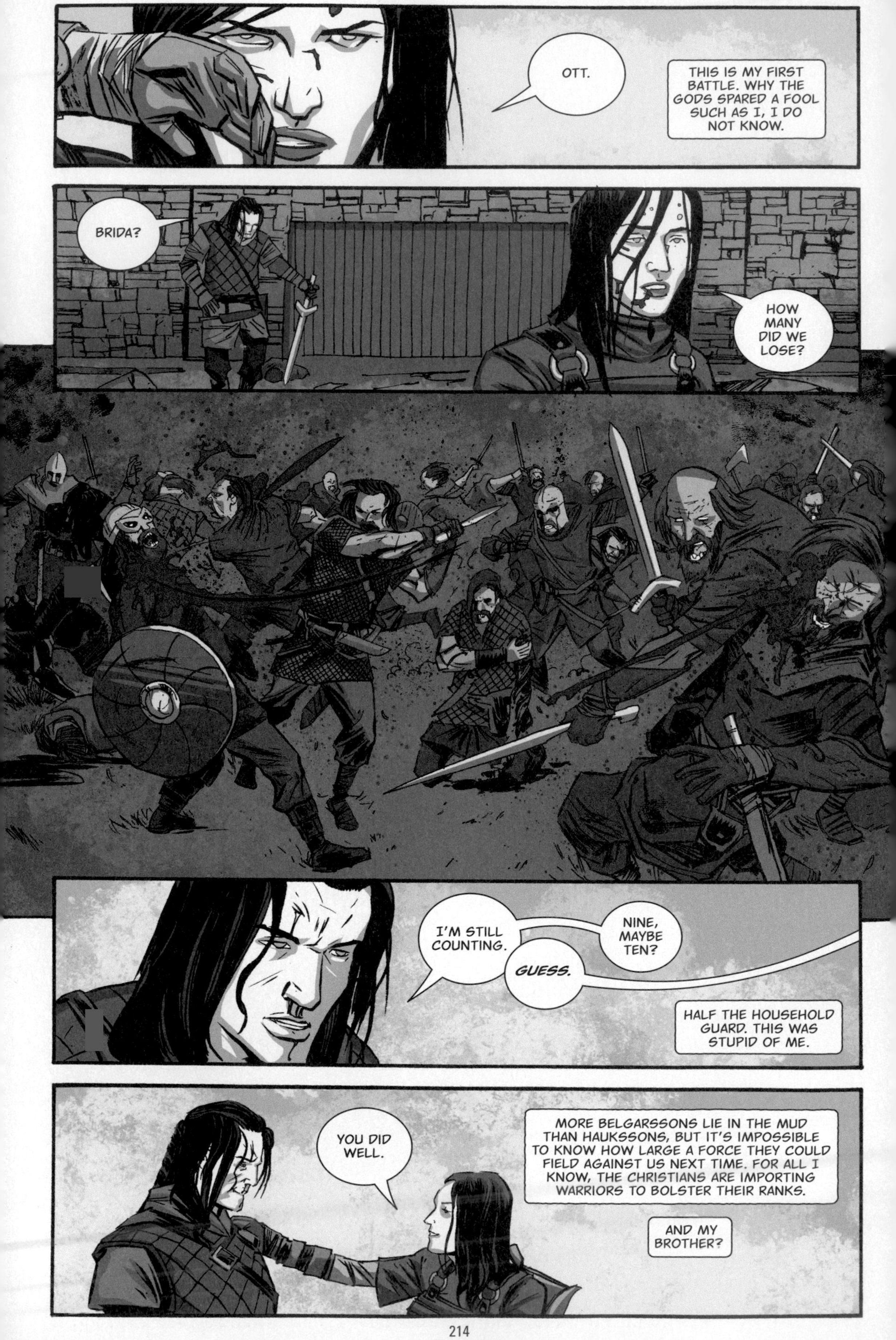
OTT.
THIS IS MY FIRST BATTLE. WHY THE GODS SPARED A FOOL SUCH AS I, I DO NOT KNOW.
BRIDA?
HOW MANY DID WE LOSE?
I'M STILL COUNTING.
GUESS.
NINE, MAYBE TEN?
HALF THE HOUSEHOLD GUARD. THIS WAS STUPID OF ME.
YOU DID WELL.
MORE BELGARSSONS LIE IN THE MUD THAN HAUKSSONS, BUT IT'S IMPOSSIBLE TO KNOW HOW LARGE A FORCE THEY COULD FIELD AGAINST US NEXT TIME. FOR ALL I KNOW, THE CHRISTIANS ARE IMPORTING WARRIORS TO BOLSTER THEIR RANKS.
AND MY BROTHER?

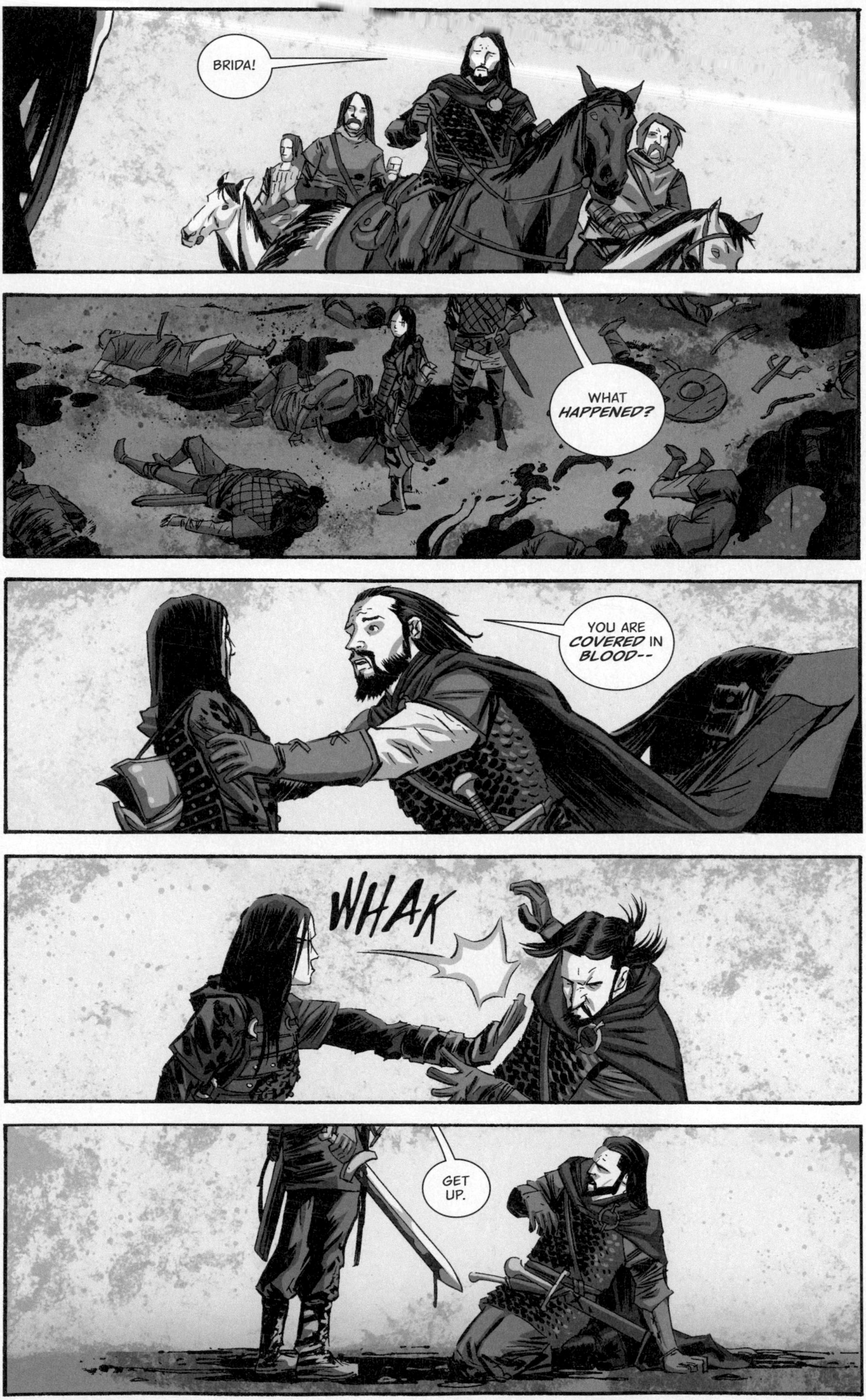
BRIDA!
WHAT HAPPENED?
YOU ARE COVERED IN BLOOD--
WHAK
GET UP.

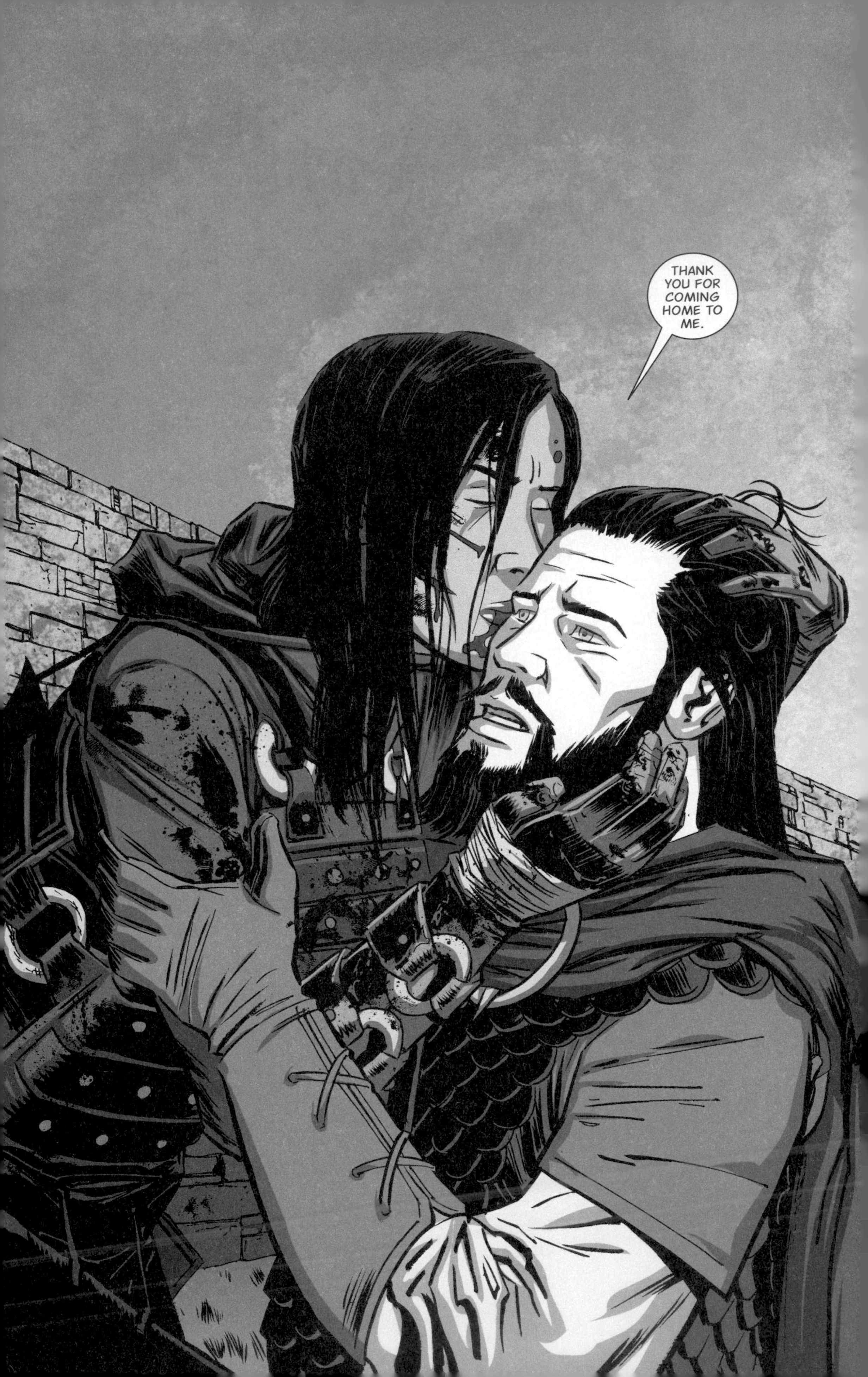
THANK YOU FOR COMING HOME TO ME.

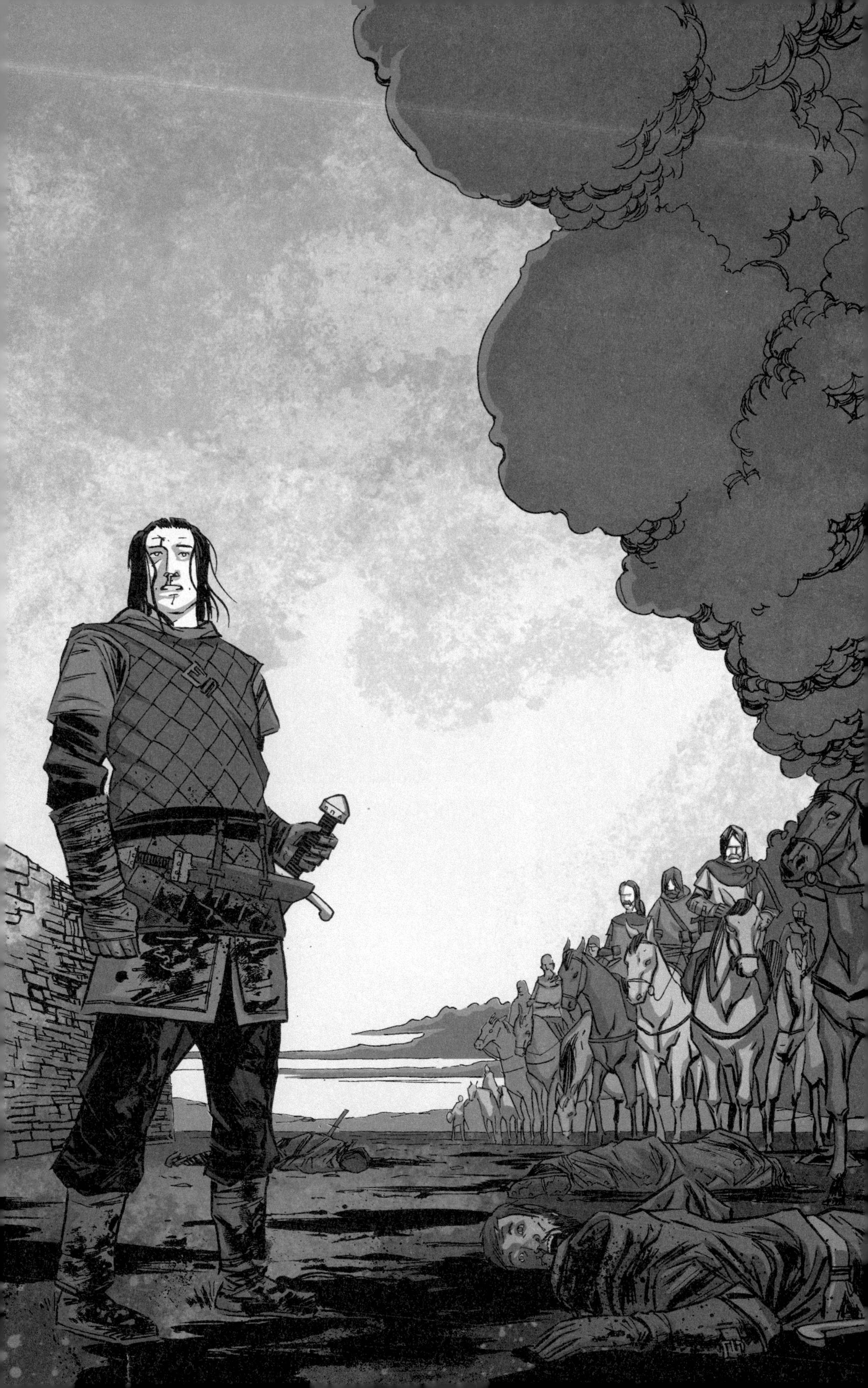

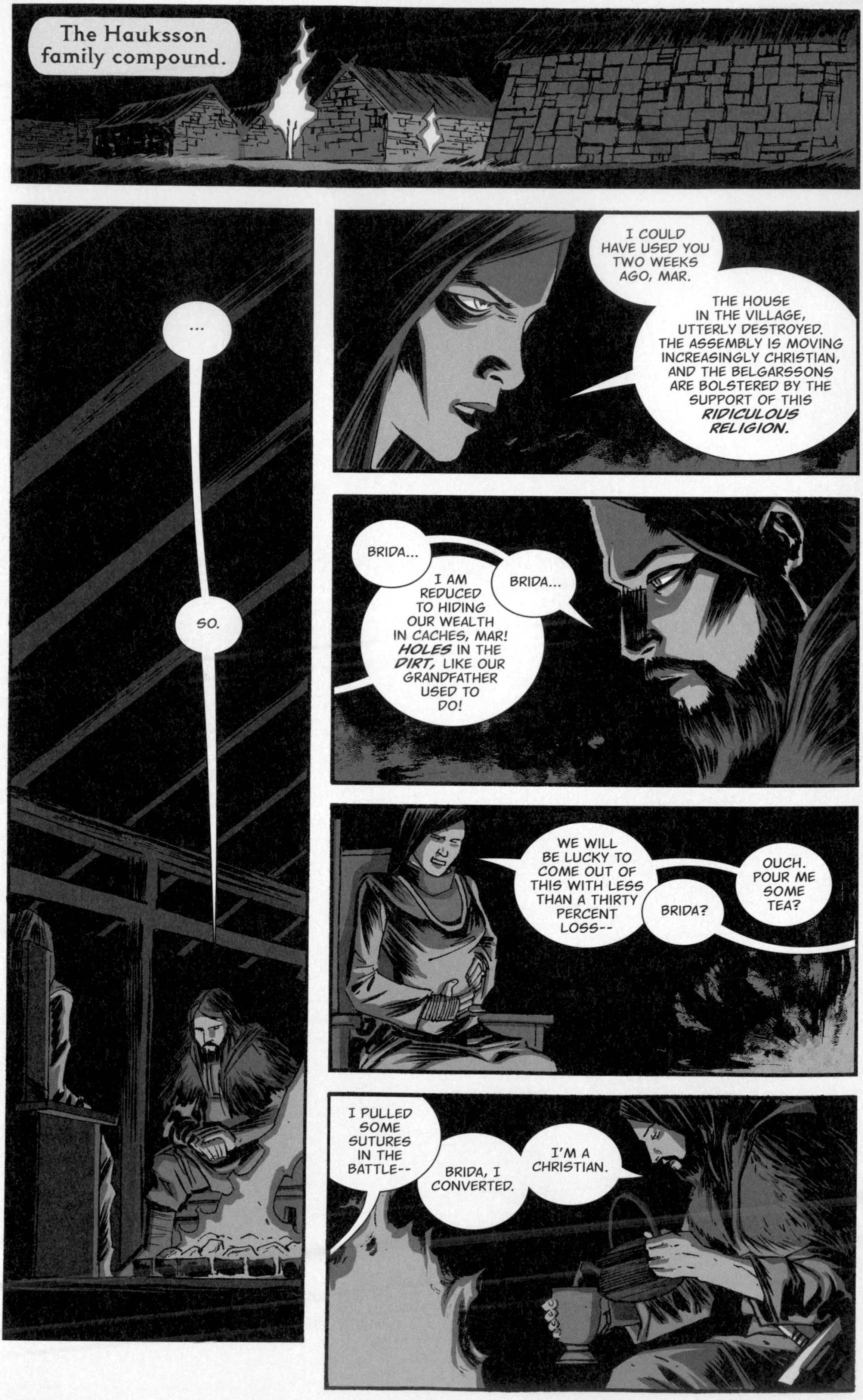
The Hauksson family compound.
...
SO.
I COULD HAVE USED YOU TWO WEEKS AGO, MAR.
THE HOUSE IN THE VILLAGE, UTTERLY DESTROYED. THE ASSEMBLY IS MOVING INCREASINGLY CHRISTIAN, AND THE BELGARSSONS ARE BOLSTERED BY THE SUPPORT OF THIS RIDICULOUS RELIGION.
BRIDA...
I AM REDUCED TO HIDING OUR WEALTH IN CACHES, MAR! HOLES IN THE DIRT, LIKE OUR GRANDFATHER USED TO DO!
BRIDA...
WE WILL BE LUCKY TO COME OUT OF THIS WITH LESS THAN A THIRTY PERCENT LOSS--
BRIDA?
OUCH. POUR ME SOME TEA?
I PULLED SOME SUTURES IN THE BATTLE--
BRIDA, I CONVERTED.
I'M A CHRISTIAN.

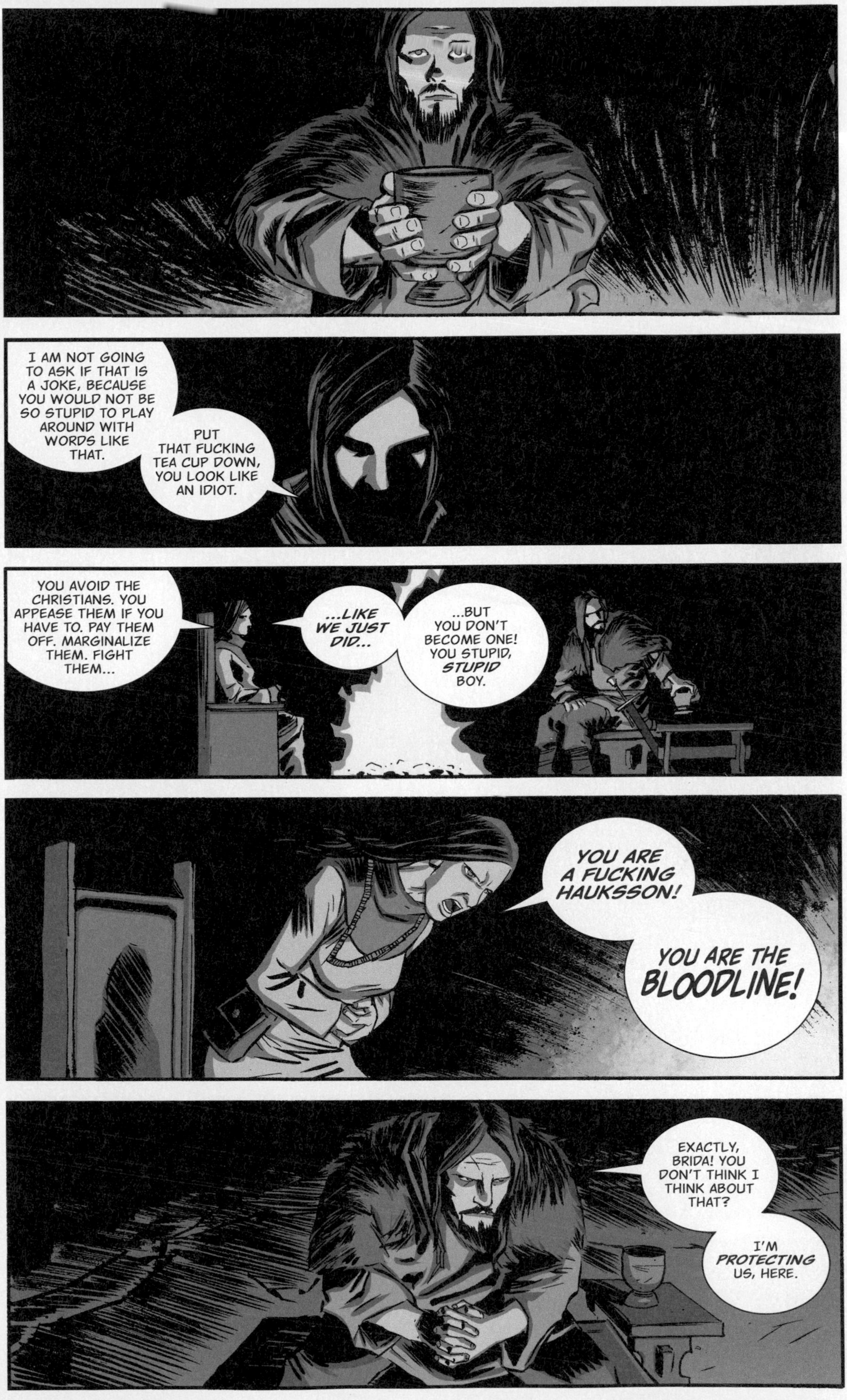
I AM NOT GOING TO ASK IF THAT IS A JOKE, BECAUSE YOU WOULD NOT BE SO STUPID TO PLAY AROUND WITH WORDS LIKE THAT.
PUT THAT FUCKING TEA CUP DOWN, YOU LOOK LIKE AN IDIOT.
YOU AVOID THE CHRISTIANS. YOU APPEASE THEM IF YOU HAVE TO. PAY THEM OFF. MARGINALIZE THEM. FIGHT THEM...
...LIKE WE JUST DID...
...BUT YOU DON'T BECOME ONE! YOU STUPID, *STUPID* BOY.
YOU ARE A FUCKING HAUKSSON!
YOU ARE THE BLOODLINE!
EXACTLY, BRIDA! YOU DON'T THINK I THINK ABOUT THAT?
I'M *PROTECTING* US, HERE.

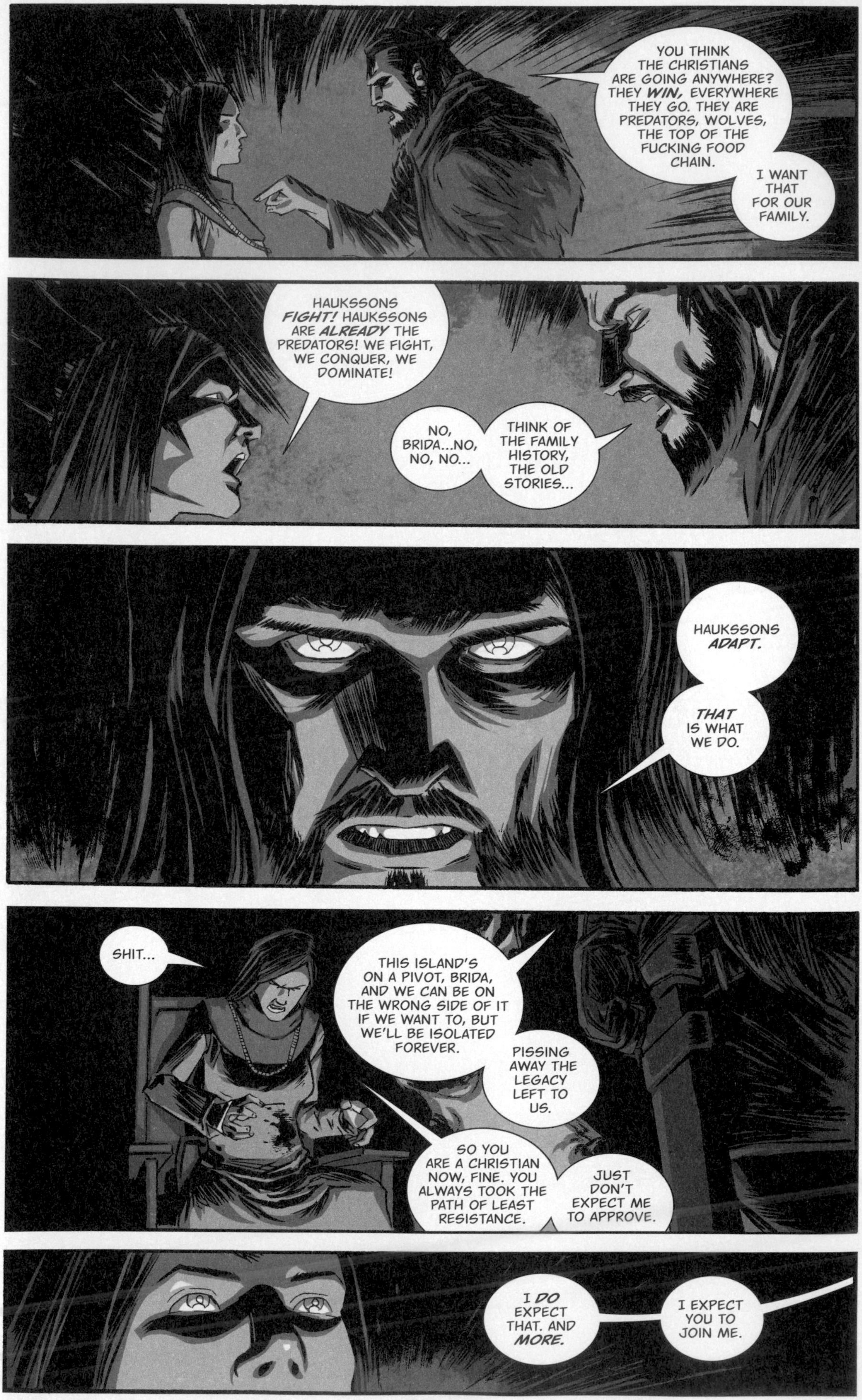
YOU THINK THE CHRISTIANS ARE GOING ANYWHERE? THEY WIN, EVERYWHERE THEY GO. THEY ARE PREDATORS, WOLVES, THE TOP OF THE FUCKING FOOD CHAIN.
I WANT THAT FOR OUR FAMILY.
HAUKSSONS FIGHT! HAUKSSONS ARE ALREADY THE PREDATORS! WE FIGHT, WE CONQUER, WE DOMINATE!
NO, BRIDA...NO, NO, NO...
THINK OF THE FAMILY HISTORY, THE OLD STORIES...
HAUKSSONS ADAPT.
THAT IS WHAT WE DO.
SHIT...
THIS ISLAND'S ON A PIVOT, BRIDA, AND WE CAN BE ON THE WRONG SIDE OF IT IF WE WANT TO, BUT WE'LL BE ISOLATED FOREVER.
PISSING AWAY THE LEGACY LEFT TO US.
SO YOU ARE A CHRISTIAN NOW, FINE. YOU ALWAYS TOOK THE PATH OF LEAST RESISTANCE.
JUST DON'T EXPECT ME TO APPROVE.
I DO EXPECT THAT. AND MORE.
I EXPECT YOU TO JOIN ME.

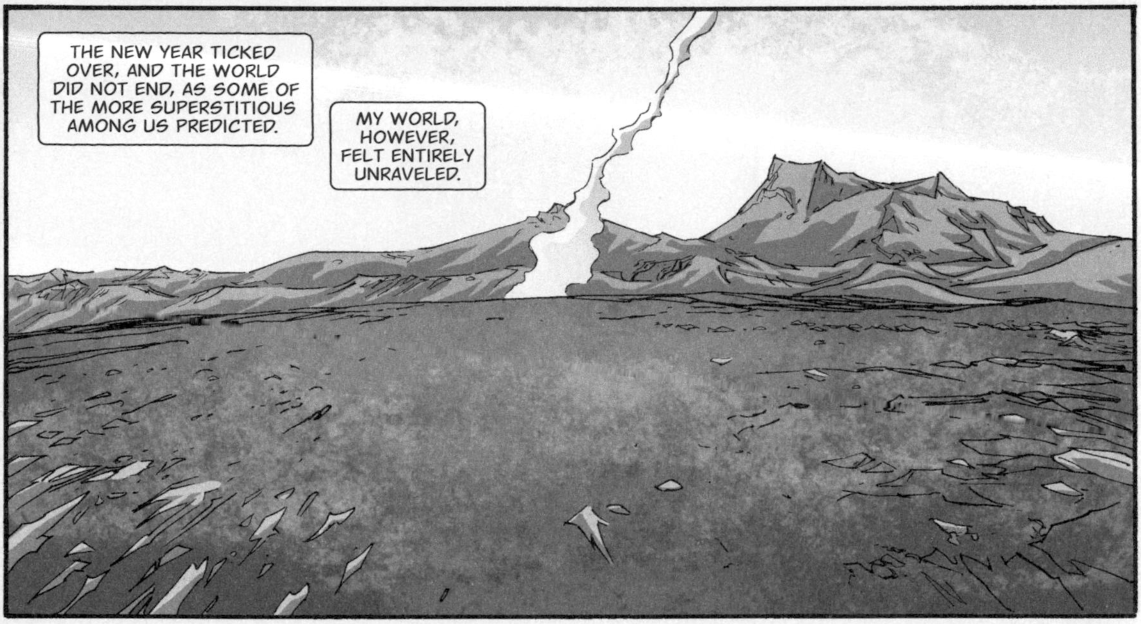
THE NEW YEAR TICKED OVER, AND THE WORLD DID NOT END, AS SOME OF THE MORE SUPERSTITIOUS AMONG US PREDICTED.
MY WORLD, HOWEVER, FELT ENTIRELY UNRAVELED.
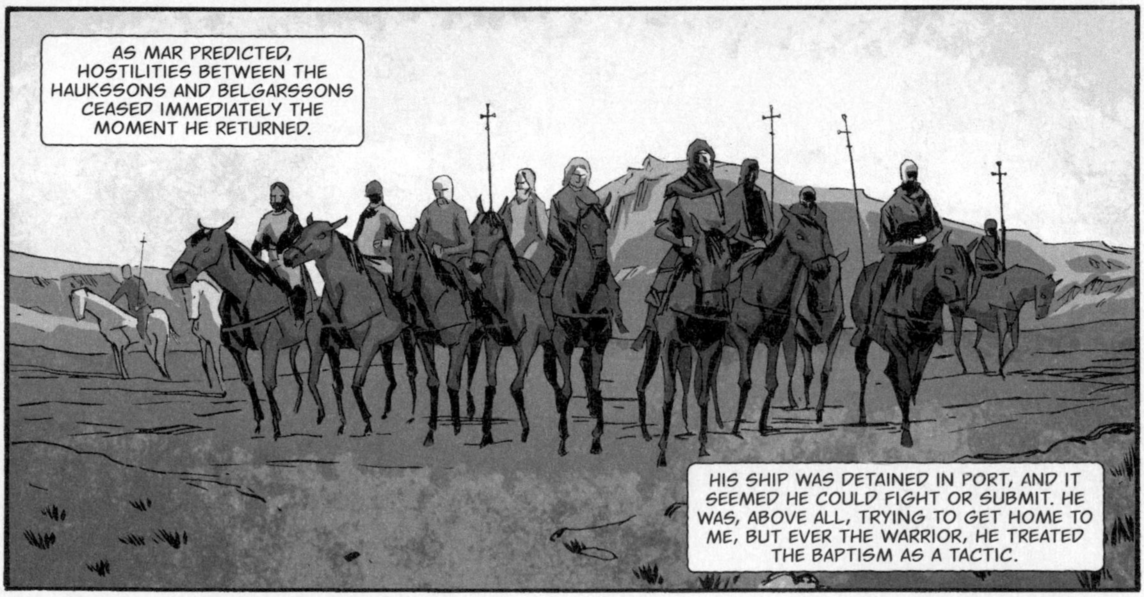
AS MAR PREDICTED, HOSTILITIES BETWEEN THE HAUKSSONS AND BELGARSSONS CEASED IMMEDIATELY THE MOMENT HE RETURNED.
HIS SHIP WAS DETAINED IN PORT, AND IT SEEMED HE COULD FIGHT OR SUBMIT. HE WAS, ABOVE ALL, TRYING TO GET HOME TO ME, BUT EVER THE WARRIOR, HE TREATED THE BAPTISM AS A TACTIC.
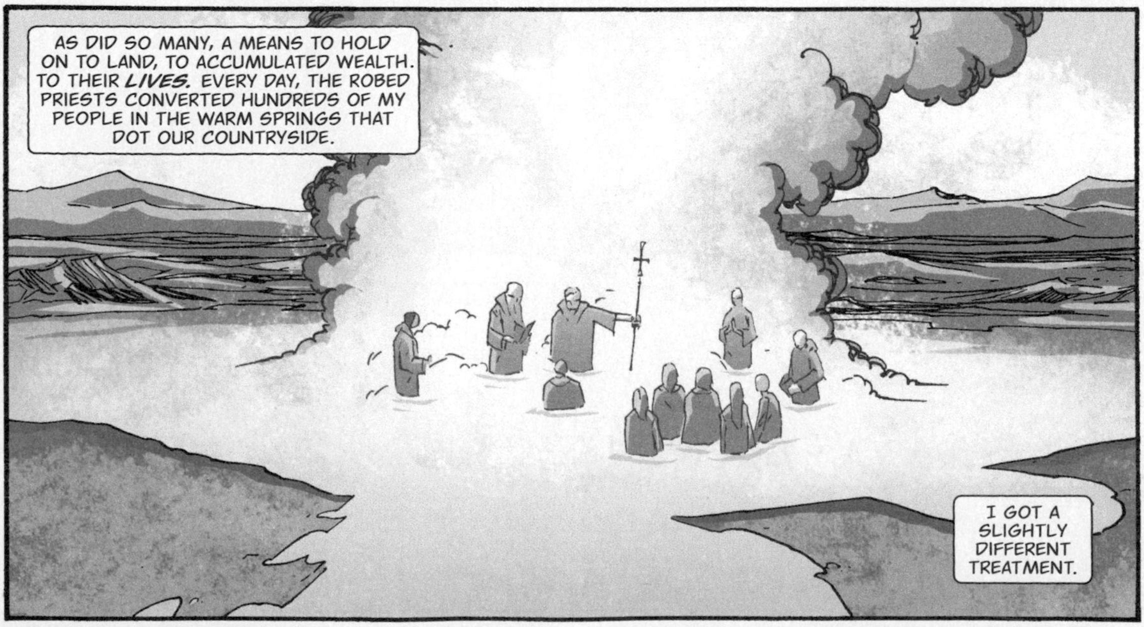
AS DID SO MANY, A MEANS TO HOLD ON TO LAND, TO ACCUMULATED WEALTH. TO THEIR *LIVES.* EVERY DAY, THE ROBED PRIESTS CONVERTED HUNDREDS OF MY PEOPLE IN THE WARM SPRINGS THAT DOT OUR COUNTRYSIDE.
I GOT A SLIGHTLY DIFFERENT TREATMENT.

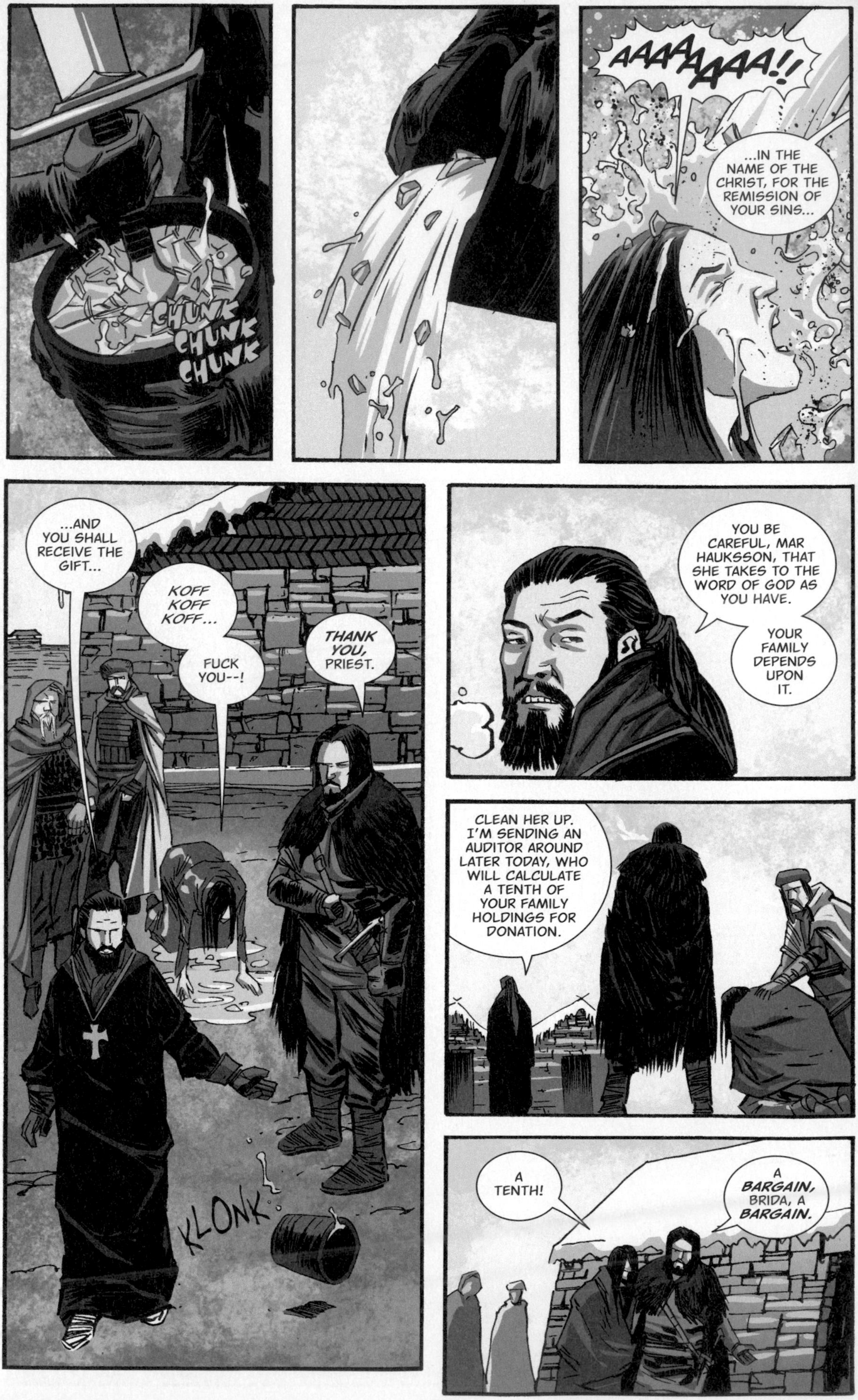
CHUNK
CHUNK
CHUNK
AAAAAAAA!!
...IN THE NAME OF THE CHRIST, FOR THE REMISSION OF YOUR SINS...
...AND YOU SHALL RECEIVE THE GIFT...
KOFF KOFF KOFF...
FUCK YOU--!
THANK YOU, PRIEST.
KLONK
YOU BE CAREFUL, MAR HAUKSSON, THAT SHE TAKES TO THE WORD OF GOD AS YOU HAVE.
YOUR FAMILY DEPENDS UPON IT.
CLEAN HER UP. I'M SENDING AN AUDITOR AROUND LATER TODAY, WHO WILL CALCULATE A TENTH OF YOUR FAMILY HOLDINGS FOR DONATION.
A TENTH!
A BARGAIN, BRIDA, A BARGAIN.

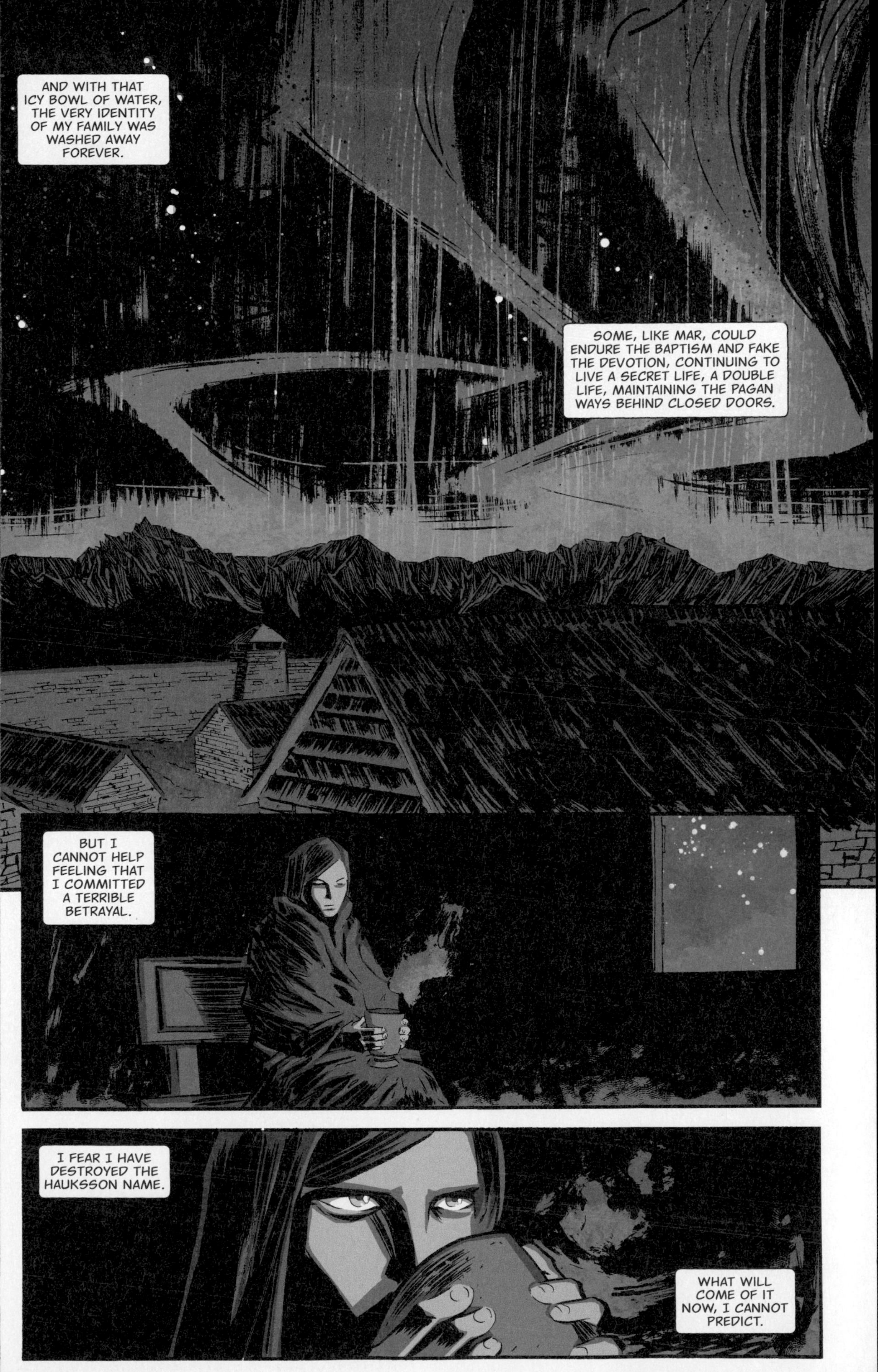
AND WITH THAT ICY BOWL OF WATER, THE VERY IDENTITY OF MY FAMILY WAS WASHED AWAY FOREVER.
SOME, LIKE MAR, COULD ENDURE THE BAPTISM AND FAKE THE DEVOTION, CONTINUING TO LIVE A SECRET LIFE, A DOUBLE LIFE, MAINTAINING THE PAGAN WAYS BEHIND CLOSED DOORS.
BUT I CANNOT HELP FEELING THAT I COMMITTED A TERRIBLE BETRAYAL.
I FEAR I HAVE DESTROYED THE HAUKSSON NAME.
WHAT WILL COME OF IT NOW, I CANNOT PREDICT.

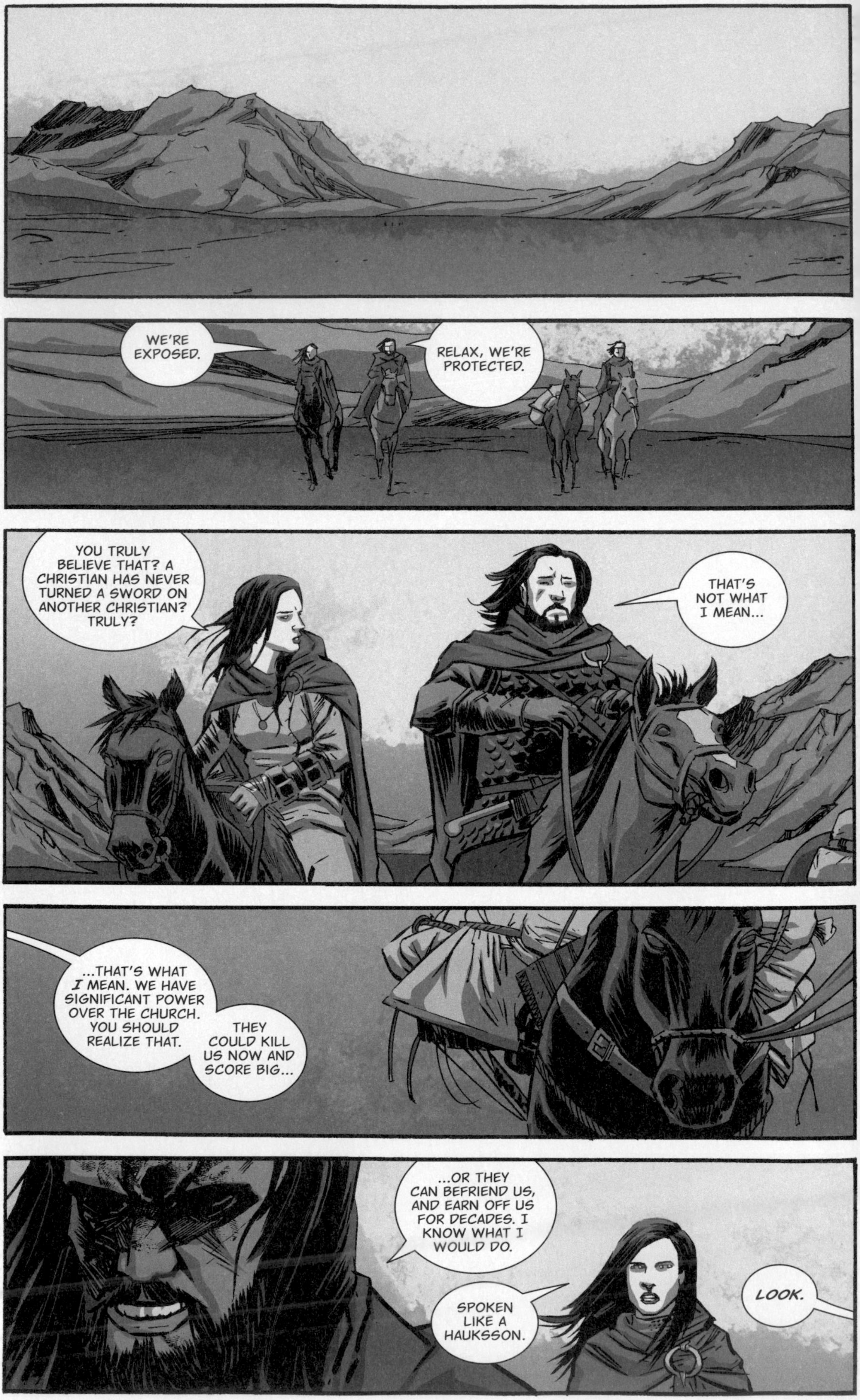

WE'RE EXPOSED.
RELAX, WE'RE PROTECTED.
YOU TRULY BELIEVE THAT? A CHRISTIAN HAS NEVER TURNED A SWORD ON ANOTHER CHRISTIAN? TRULY?
THAT'S NOT WHAT I MEAN...
...THAT'S WHAT I MEAN. WE HAVE SIGNIFICANT POWER OVER THE CHURCH. YOU SHOULD REALIZE THAT.
THEY COULD KILL US NOW AND SCORE BIG...
...OR THEY CAN BEFRIEND US, AND EARN OFF US FOR DECADES. I KNOW WHAT I WOULD DO.
SPOKEN LIKE A HAUKSSON.
LOOK.

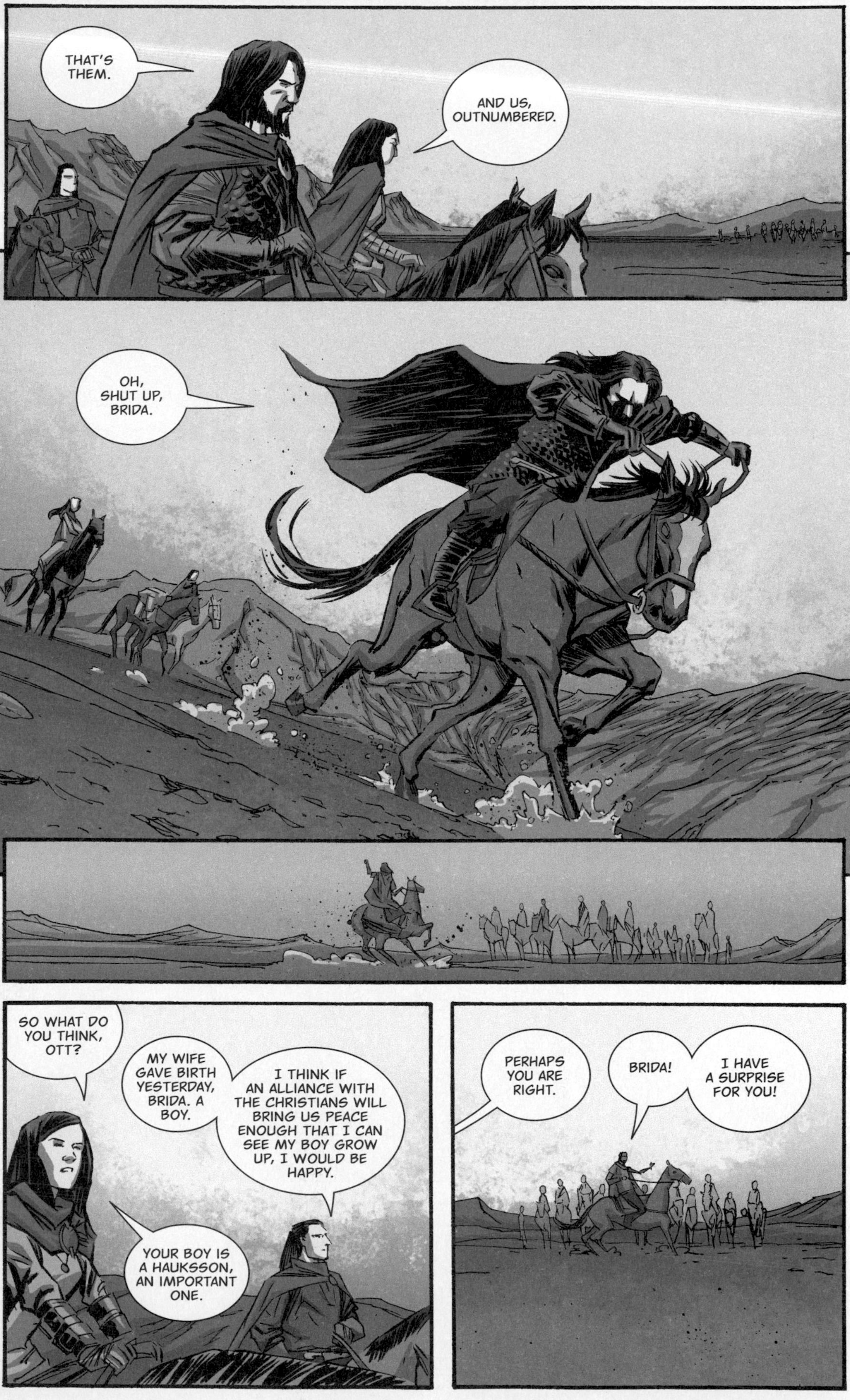
THAT'S THEM.
AND US, OUTNUMBERED.
OH, SHUT UP, BRIDA.
SO WHAT DO YOU THINK, OTT?
MY WIFE GAVE BIRTH YESTERDAY, BRIDA. A BOY.
I THINK IF AN ALLIANCE WITH THE CHRISTIANS WILL BRING US PEACE ENOUGH THAT I CAN SEE MY BOY GROW UP, I WOULD BE HAPPY.
YOUR BOY IS A HAUKSSON, AN IMPORTANT ONE.
PERHAPS YOU ARE RIGHT.
BRIDA!
I HAVE A SURPRISE FOR YOU!

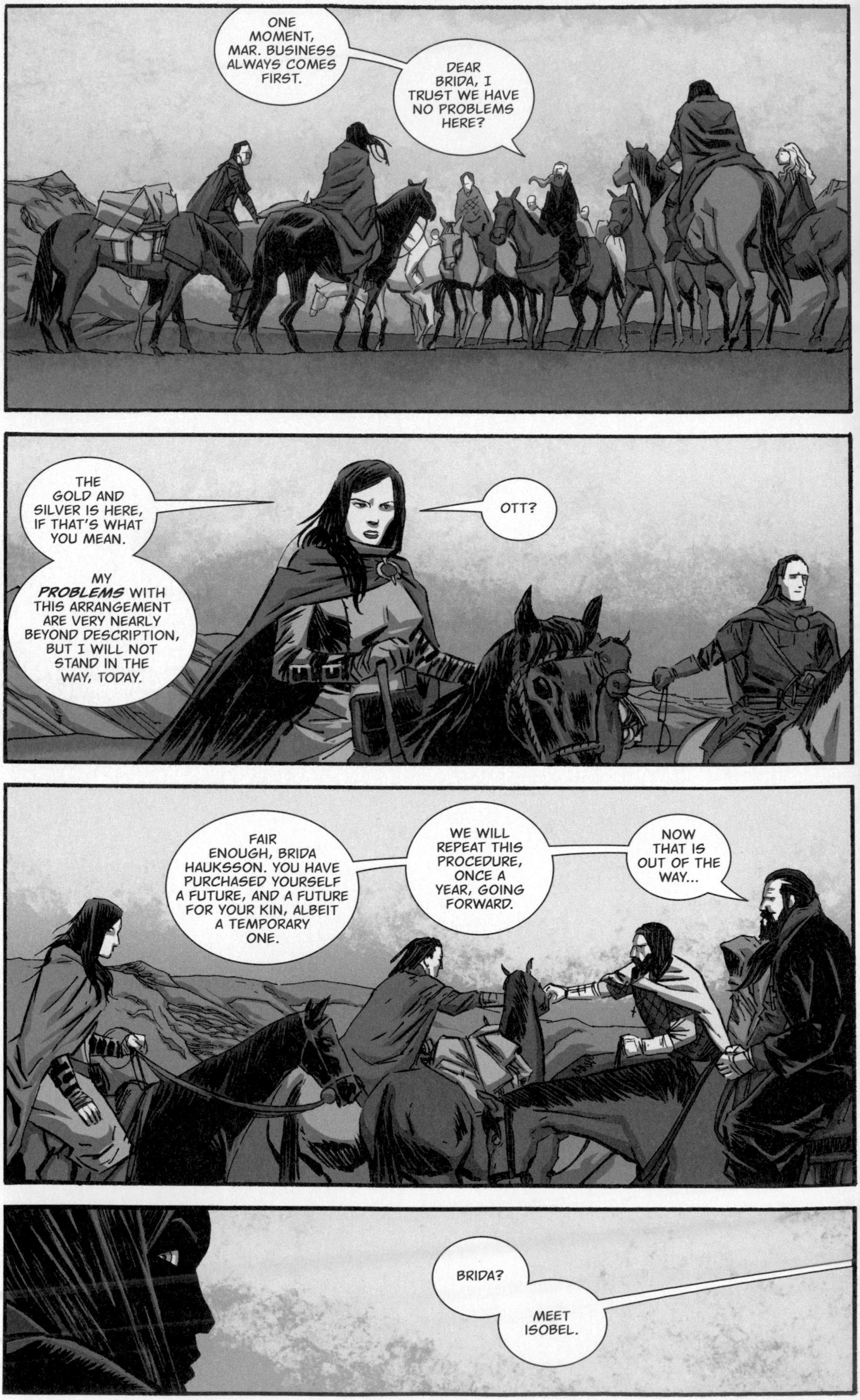
ONE MOMENT, MAR. BUSINESS ALWAYS COMES FIRST.
DEAR BRIDA, I TRUST WE HAVE NO PROBLEMS HERE?
THE GOLD AND SILVER IS HERE, IF THAT'S WHAT YOU MEAN.
MY *PROBLEMS* WITH THIS ARRANGEMENT ARE VERY NEARLY BEYOND DESCRIPTION, BUT I WILL NOT STAND IN THE WAY, TODAY.
OTT?
FAIR ENOUGH, BRIDA HAUKSSON. YOU HAVE PURCHASED YOURSELF A FUTURE, AND A FUTURE FOR YOUR KIN, ALBEIT A TEMPORARY ONE.
WE WILL REPEAT THIS PROCEDURE, ONCE A YEAR, GOING FORWARD.
NOW THAT IS OUT OF THE WAY...
BRIDA?
MEET ISOBEL.

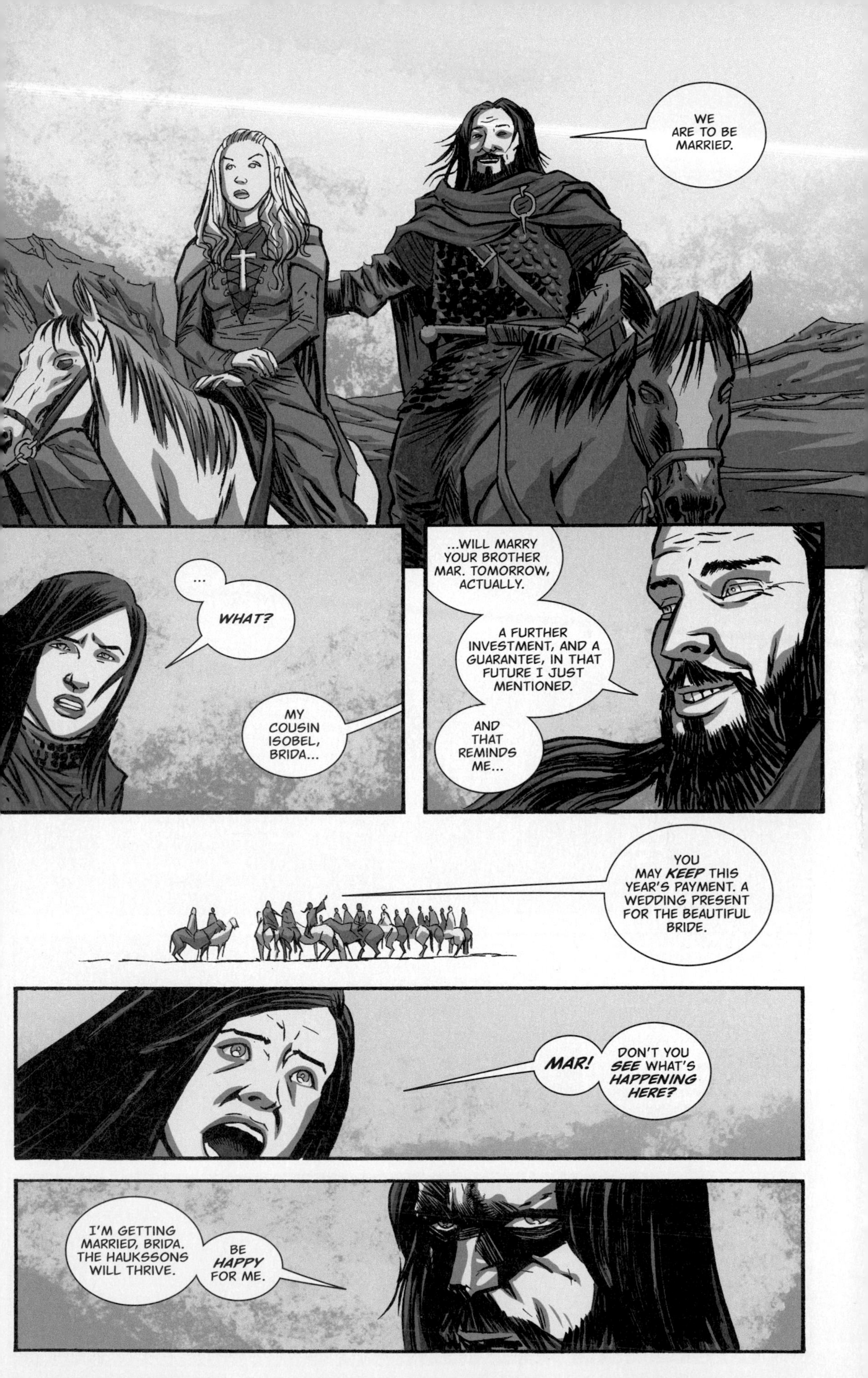
WE ARE TO BE MARRIED.
...
WHAT?
MY COUSIN ISOBEL, BRIDA...
...WILL MARRY YOUR BROTHER MAR. TOMORROW, ACTUALLY.
A FURTHER INVESTMENT, AND A GUARANTEE, IN THAT FUTURE I JUST MENTIONED.
AND THAT REMINDS ME...
YOU MAY KEEP THIS YEAR'S PAYMENT. A WEDDING PRESENT FOR THE BEAUTIFUL BRIDE.
MAR!
DON'T YOU SEE WHAT'S HAPPENING HERE?
I'M GETTING MARRIED, BRIDA. THE HAUKSSONS WILL THRIVE.
BE HAPPY FOR ME.

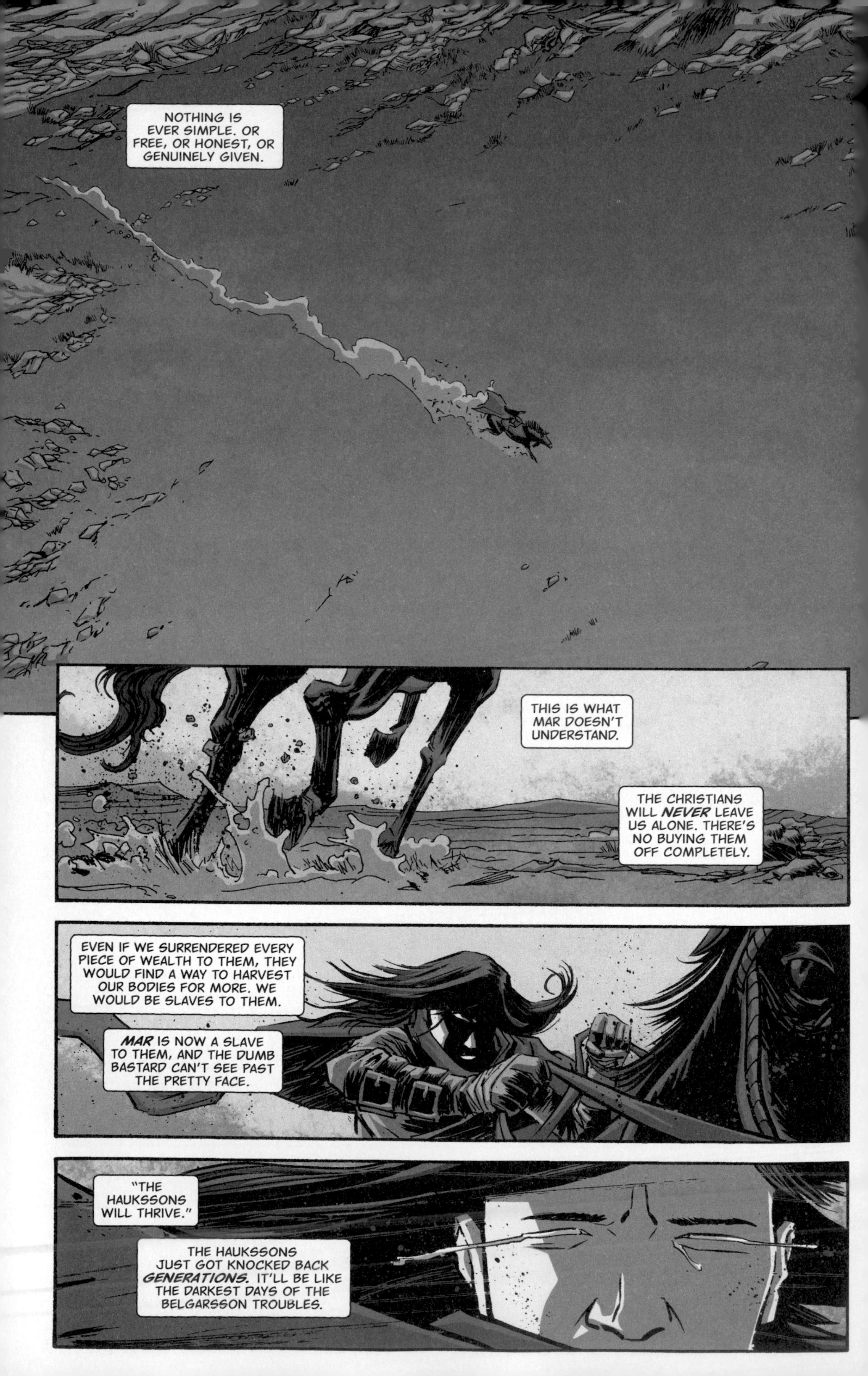

NOTHING IS EVER SIMPLE. OR FREE, OR HONEST, OR GENUINELY GIVEN.
THIS IS WHAT MAR DOESN'T UNDERSTAND.
THE CHRISTIANS WILL NEVER LEAVE US ALONE. THERE'S NO BUYING THEM OFF COMPLETELY.
EVEN IF WE SURRENDERED EVERY PIECE OF WEALTH TO THEM, THEY WOULD FIND A WAY TO HARVEST OUR BODIES FOR MORE. WE WOULD BE SLAVES TO THEM.
MAR IS NOW A SLAVE TO THEM, AND THE DUMB BASTARD CAN'T SEE PAST THE PRETTY FACE.
"THE HAUKSSONS WILL THRIVE."
THE HAUKSSONS JUST GOT KNOCKED BACK GENERATIONS. IT'LL BE LIKE THE DARKEST DAYS OF THE BELGARSSON TROUBLES.

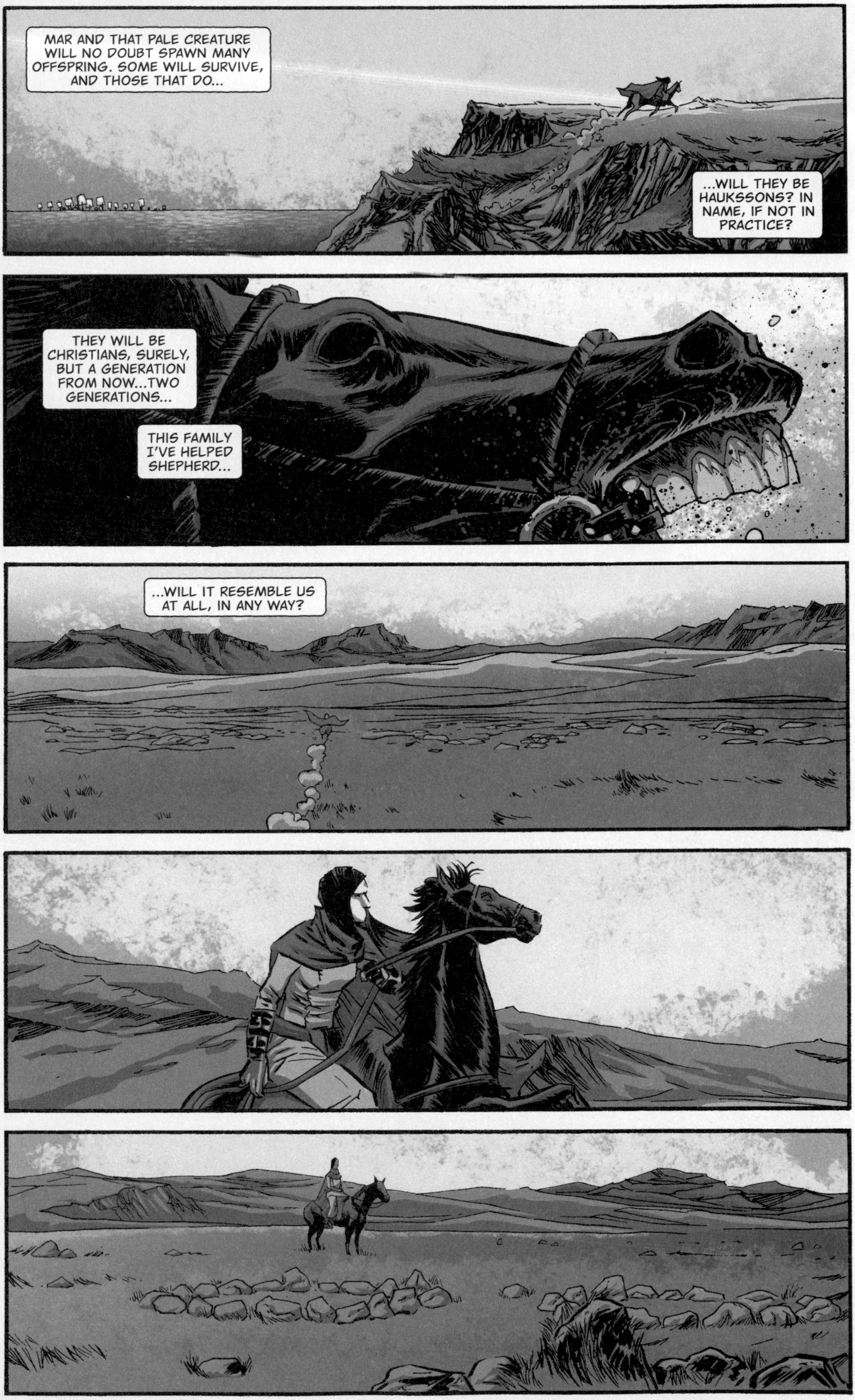
MAR AND THAT PALE CREATURE WILL NO DOUBT SPAWN MANY OFFSPRING. SOME WILL SURVIVE, AND THOSE THAT DO...
...WILL THEY BE HAUKSSONS? IN NAME, IF NOT IN PRACTICE?
THEY WILL BE CHRISTIANS, SURELY, BUT A GENERATION FROM NOW...TWO GENERATIONS...
THIS FAMILY I'VE HELPED SHEPHERD...
...WILL IT RESEMBLE US AT ALL, IN ANY WAY?

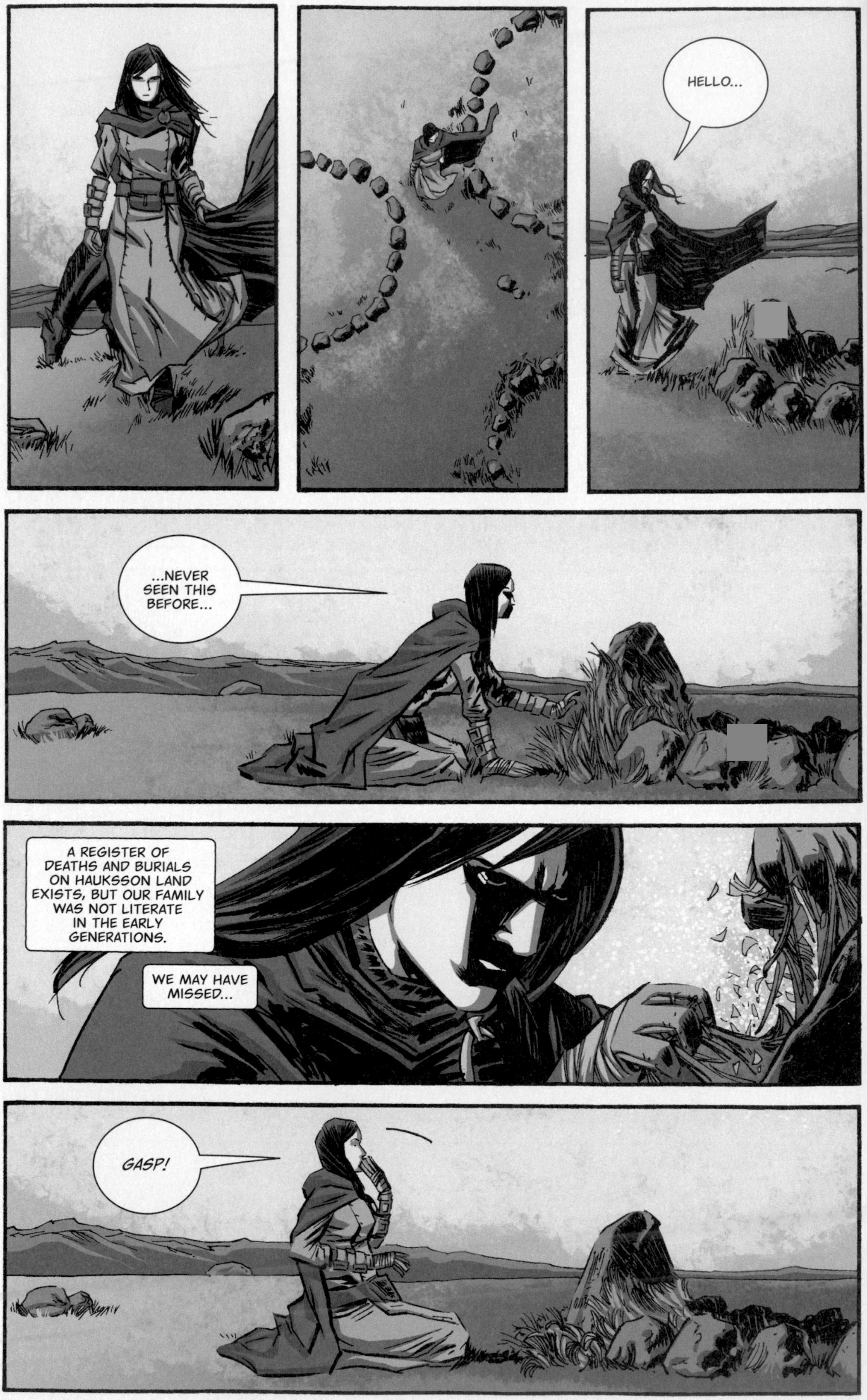
HELLO...
...NEVER SEEN THIS BEFORE...
A REGISTER OF DEATHS AND BURIALS ON HAUKSSON LAND EXISTS, BUT OUR FAMILY WAS NOT LITERATE IN THE EARLY GENERATIONS.
WE MAY HAVE MISSED...
GASP!

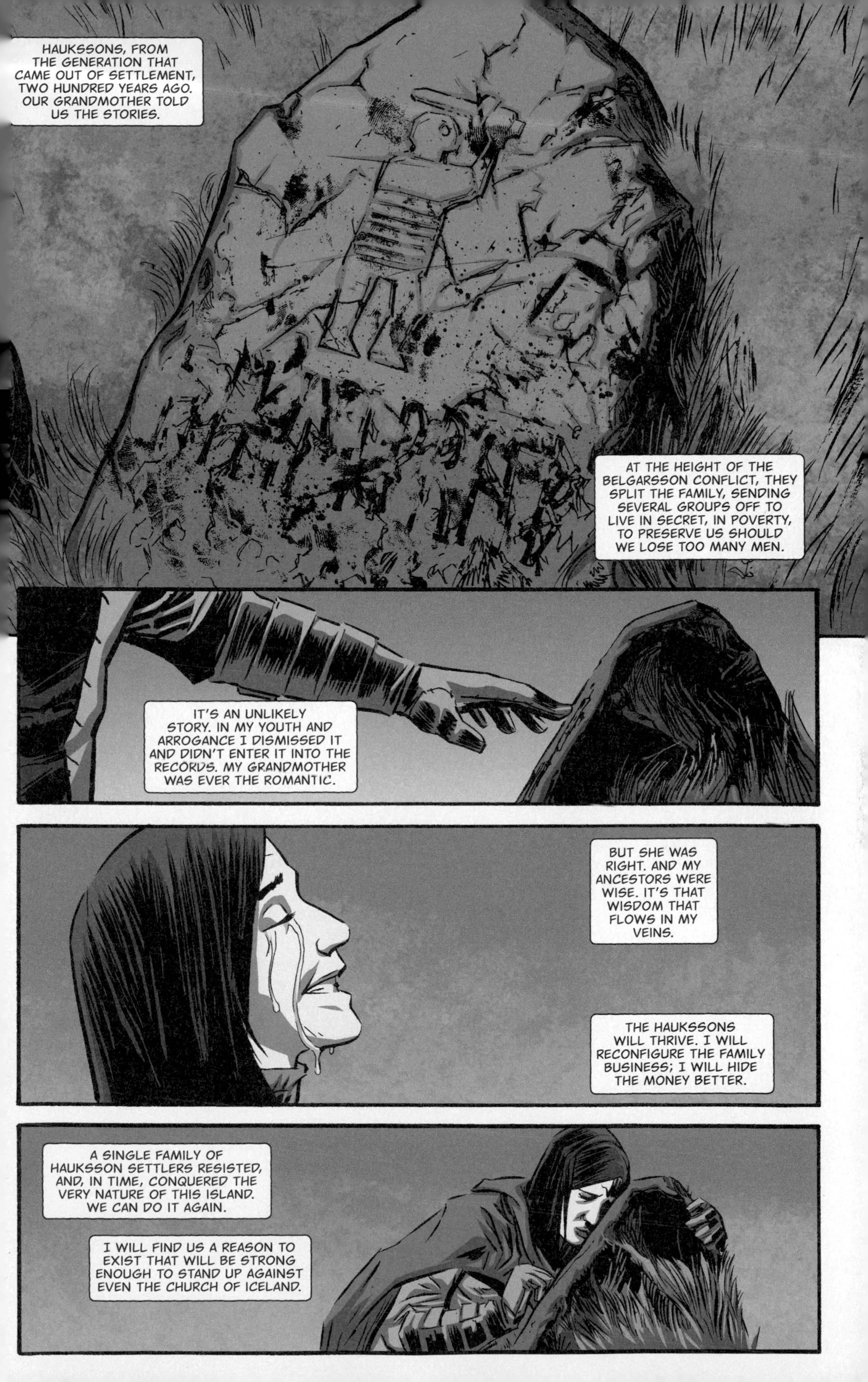
HAUKSSONS, FROM THE GENERATION THAT CAME OUT OF SETTLEMENT, TWO HUNDRED YEARS AGO. OUR GRANDMOTHER TOLD US THE STORIES.
AT THE HEIGHT OF THE BELGARSSON CONFLICT, THEY SPLIT THE FAMILY, SENDING SEVERAL GROUPS OFF TO LIVE IN SECRET, IN POVERTY, TO PRESERVE US SHOULD WE LOSE TOO MANY MEN.
IT'S AN UNLIKELY STORY. IN MY YOUTH AND ARROGANCE I DISMISSED IT AND DIDN'T ENTER IT INTO THE RECORDS. MY GRANDMOTHER WAS EVER THE ROMANTIC.
BUT SHE WAS RIGHT. AND MY ANCESTORS WERE WISE. IT'S THAT WISDOM THAT FLOWS IN MY VEINS.
THE HAUKSSONS WILL THRIVE. I WILL RECONFIGURE THE FAMILY BUSINESS; I WILL HIDE THE MONEY BETTER.
A SINGLE FAMILY OF HAUKSSON SETTLERS RESISTED, AND, IN TIME, CONQUERED THE VERY NATURE OF THIS ISLAND. WE CAN DO IT AGAIN.
I WILL FIND US A REASON TO EXIST THAT WILL BE STRONG ENOUGH TO STAND UP AGAINST EVEN THE CHURCH OF ICELAND.

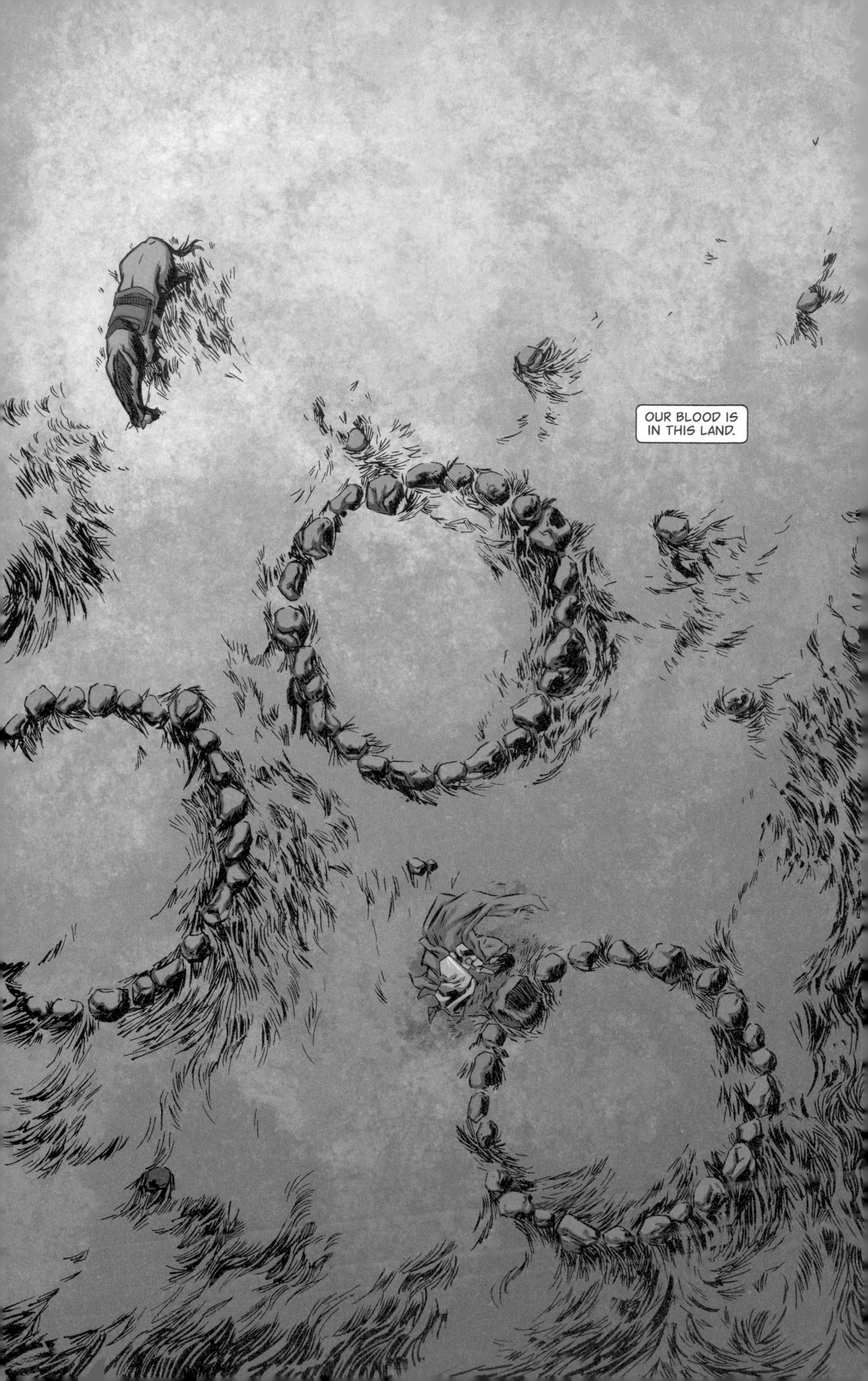
OUR BLOOD IS
IN THIS LAND.

Chapter VII
War
A.D. 1260

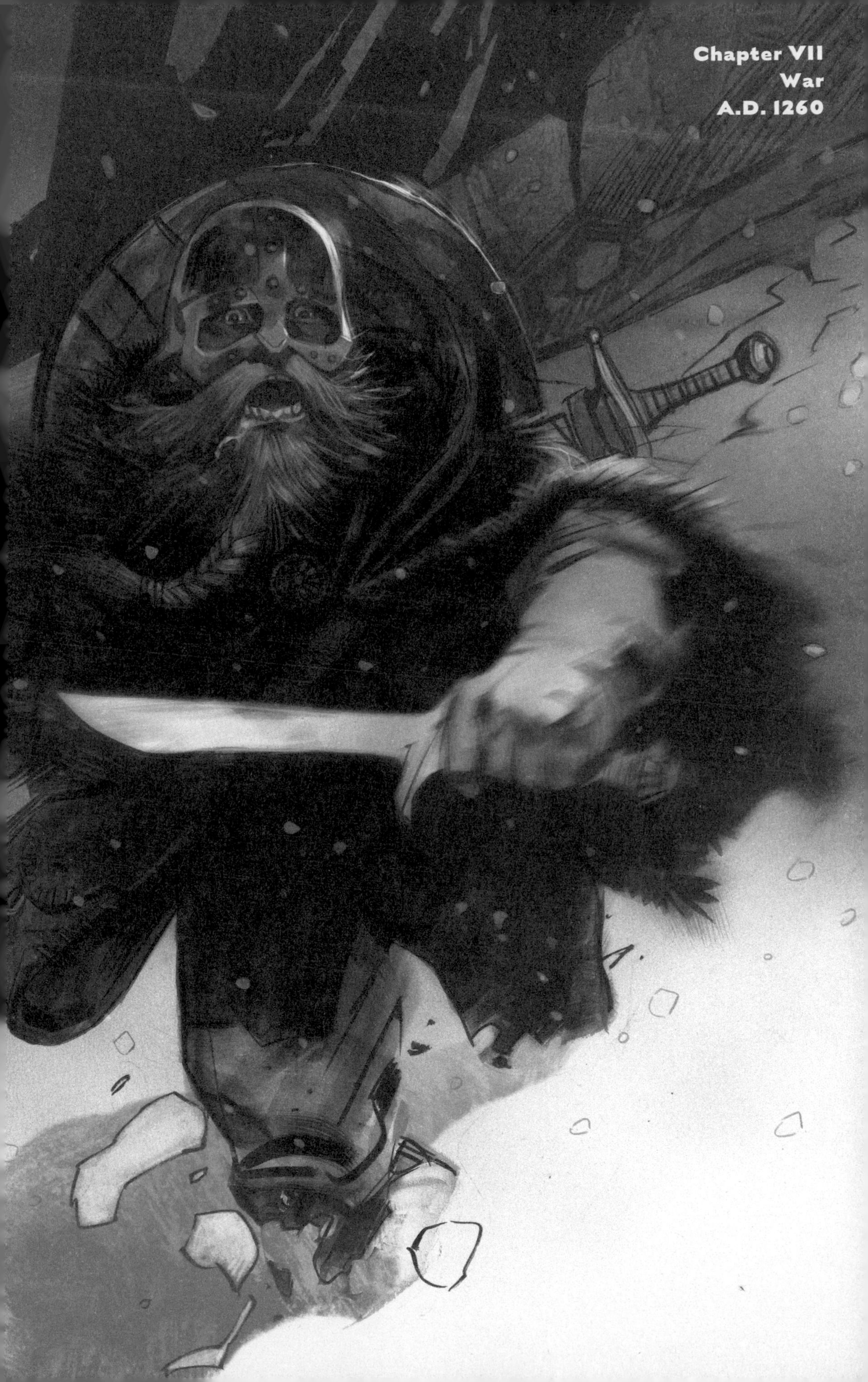

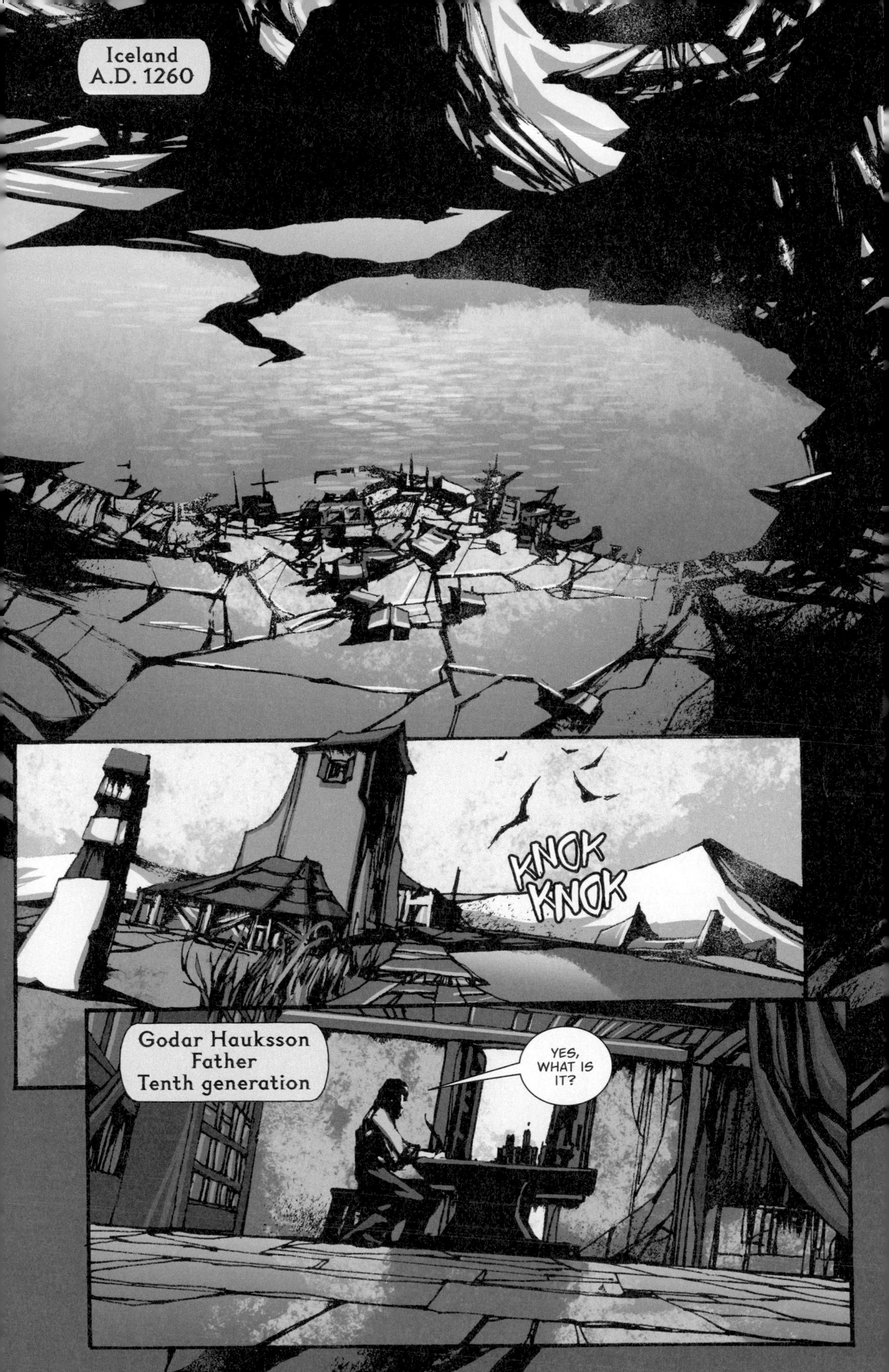
Iceland
A.D. 1260
KNOK KNOK
Godar Hauksson
Father
Tenth generation
YES, WHAT IS IT?

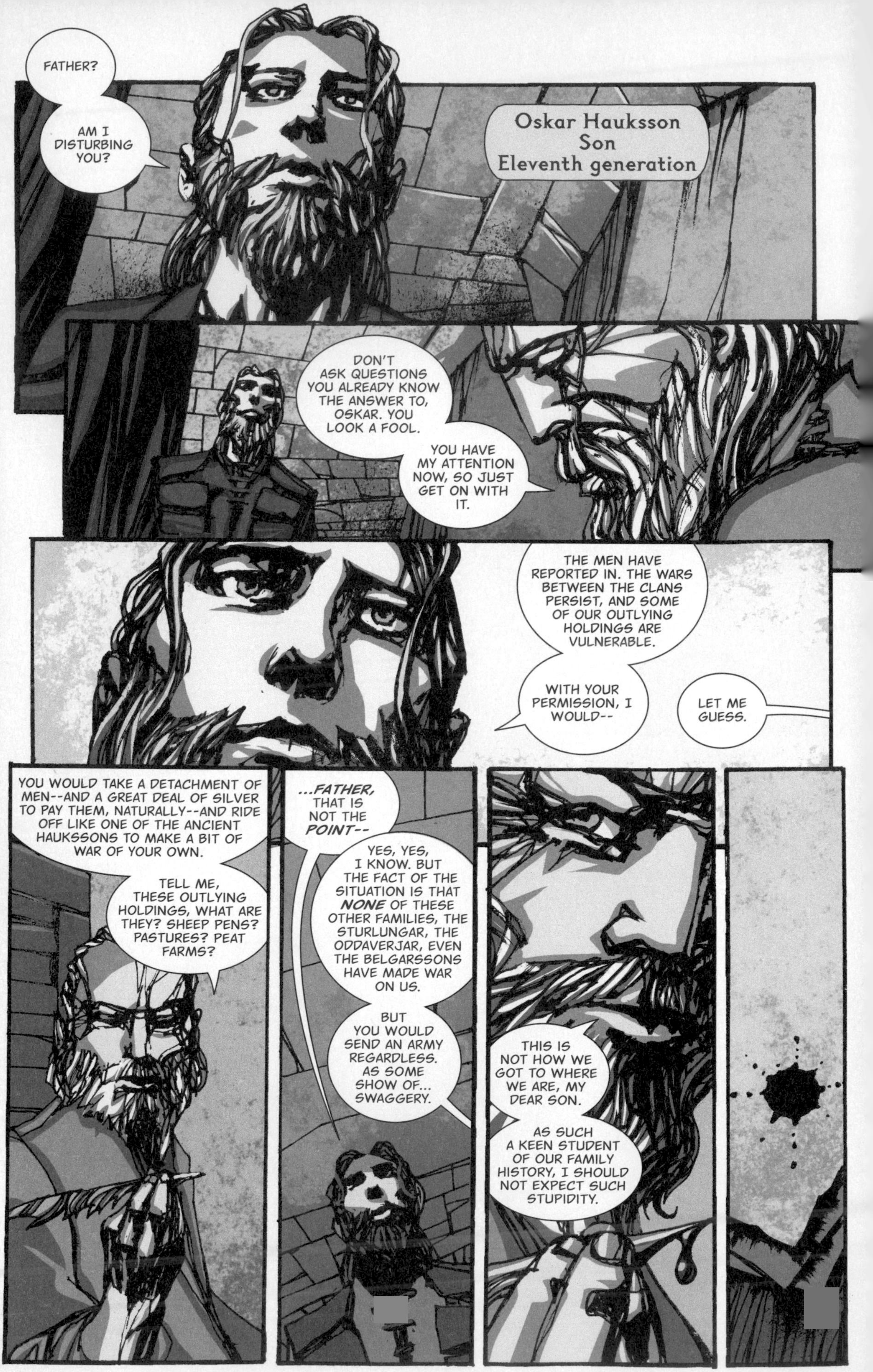
FATHER?
AM I DISTURBING YOU?
Oskar Hauksson Son Eleventh generation
DON'T ASK QUESTIONS YOU ALREADY KNOW THE ANSWER TO, OSKAR. YOU LOOK A FOOL.
YOU HAVE MY ATTENTION NOW, SO JUST GET ON WITH IT.
THE MEN HAVE REPORTED IN. THE WARS BETWEEN THE CLANS PERSIST, AND SOME OF OUR OUTLYING HOLDINGS ARE VULNERABLE.
WITH YOUR PERMISSION, I WOULD--
LET ME GUESS.
YOU WOULD TAKE A DETACHMENT OF MEN--AND A GREAT DEAL OF SILVER TO PAY THEM, NATURALLY--AND RIDE OFF LIKE ONE OF THE ANCIENT HAUKSSONS TO MAKE A BIT OF WAR OF YOUR OWN.
TELL ME, THESE OUTLYING HOLDINGS, WHAT ARE THEY? SHEEP PENS? PASTURES? PEAT FARMS?
...FATHER, THAT IS NOT THE POINT--
YES, YES, I KNOW. BUT THE FACT OF THE SITUATION IS THAT NONE OF THESE OTHER FAMILIES, THE STURLUNGAR, THE ODDAVERJAR, EVEN THE BELGARSSONS HAVE MADE WAR ON US.
BUT YOU WOULD SEND AN ARMY REGARDLESS. AS SOME SHOW OF... SWAGGERY.
THIS IS NOT HOW WE GOT TO WHERE WE ARE, MY DEAR SON.
AS SUCH A KEEN STUDENT OF OUR FAMILY HISTORY, I SHOULD NOT EXPECT SUCH STUPIDITY.

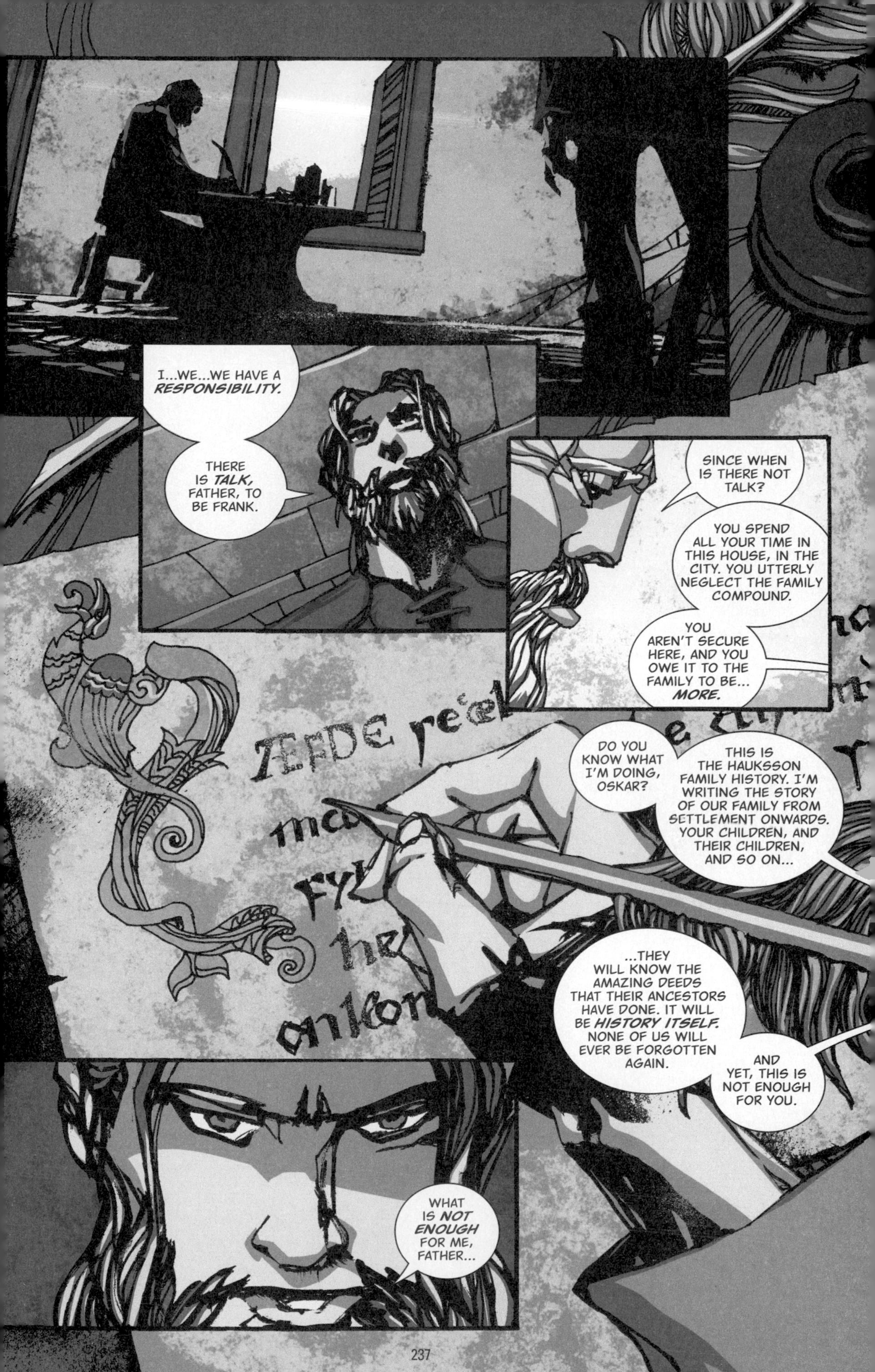

I...WE...WE HAVE A *RESPONSIBILITY.*
THERE IS *TALK,* FATHER, TO BE FRANK.
SINCE WHEN IS THERE NOT TALK?
YOU SPEND ALL YOUR TIME IN THIS HOUSE, IN THE CITY. YOU UTTERLY NEGLECT THE FAMILY COMPOUND.
YOU AREN'T SECURE HERE, AND YOU OWE IT TO THE FAMILY TO BE... *MORE.*
DO YOU KNOW WHAT I'M DOING, OSKAR?
THIS IS THE HAUKSSON FAMILY HISTORY. I'M WRITING THE STORY OF OUR FAMILY FROM SETTLEMENT ONWARDS. YOUR CHILDREN, AND THEIR CHILDREN, AND SO ON...
...THEY WILL KNOW THE AMAZING DEEDS THAT THEIR ANCESTORS HAVE DONE. IT WILL BE *HISTORY ITSELF.* NONE OF US WILL EVER BE FORGOTTEN AGAIN.
AND YET, THIS IS NOT ENOUGH FOR YOU.
WHAT IS *NOT ENOUGH* FOR ME, FATHER...

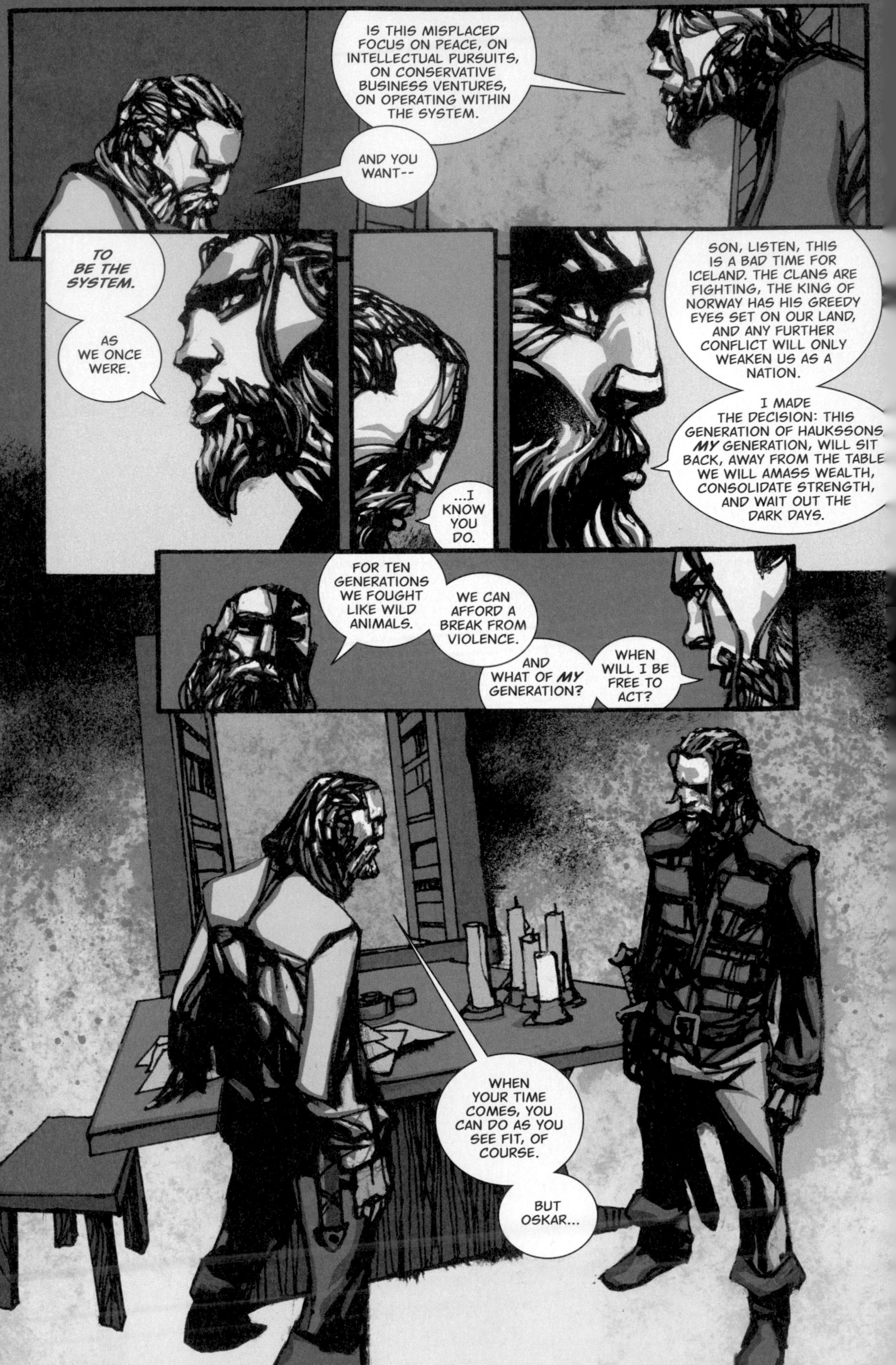
IS THIS MISPLACED FOCUS ON PEACE, ON INTELLECTUAL PURSUITS, ON CONSERVATIVE BUSINESS VENTURES, ON OPERATING WITHIN THE SYSTEM.
AND YOU WANT--
TO BE THE SYSTEM.
AS WE ONCE WERE.
...I KNOW YOU DO.
SON, LISTEN, THIS IS A BAD TIME FOR ICELAND. THE CLANS ARE FIGHTING, THE KING OF NORWAY HAS HIS GREEDY EYES SET ON OUR LAND, AND ANY FURTHER CONFLICT WILL ONLY WEAKEN US AS A NATION.
I MADE THE DECISION: THIS GENERATION OF HAUKSSONS, MY GENERATION, WILL SIT BACK, AWAY FROM THE TABLE. WE WILL AMASS WEALTH, CONSOLIDATE STRENGTH, AND WAIT OUT THE DARK DAYS.
FOR TEN GENERATIONS WE FOUGHT LIKE WILD ANIMALS.
WE CAN AFFORD A BREAK FROM VIOLENCE.
AND WHAT OF MY GENERATION?
WHEN WILL I BE FREE TO ACT?
WHEN YOUR TIME COMES, YOU CAN DO AS YOU SEE FIT, OF COURSE.
BUT OSKAR...

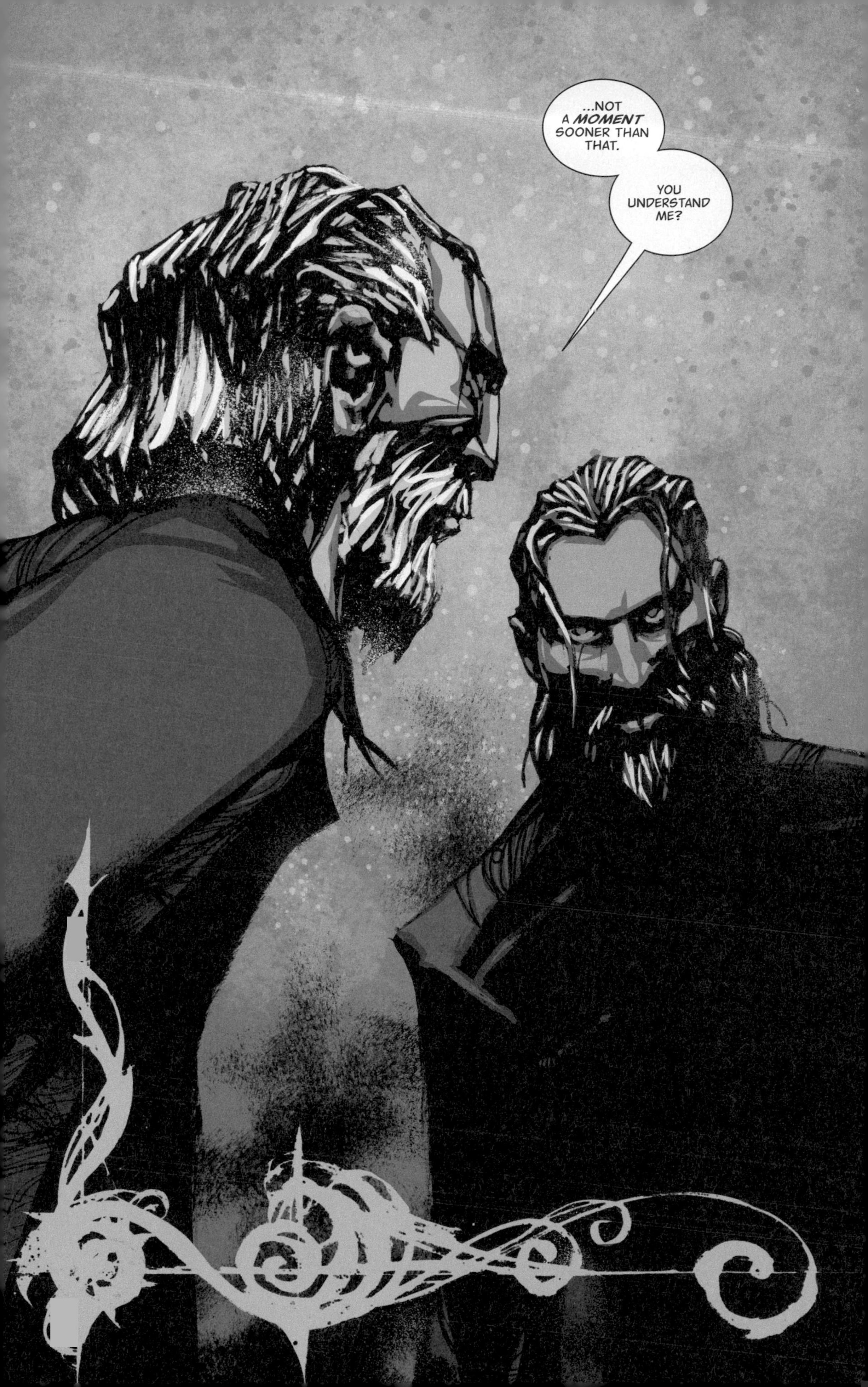
...NOT A *MOMENT* SOONER THAN THAT.
YOU UNDERSTAND ME?

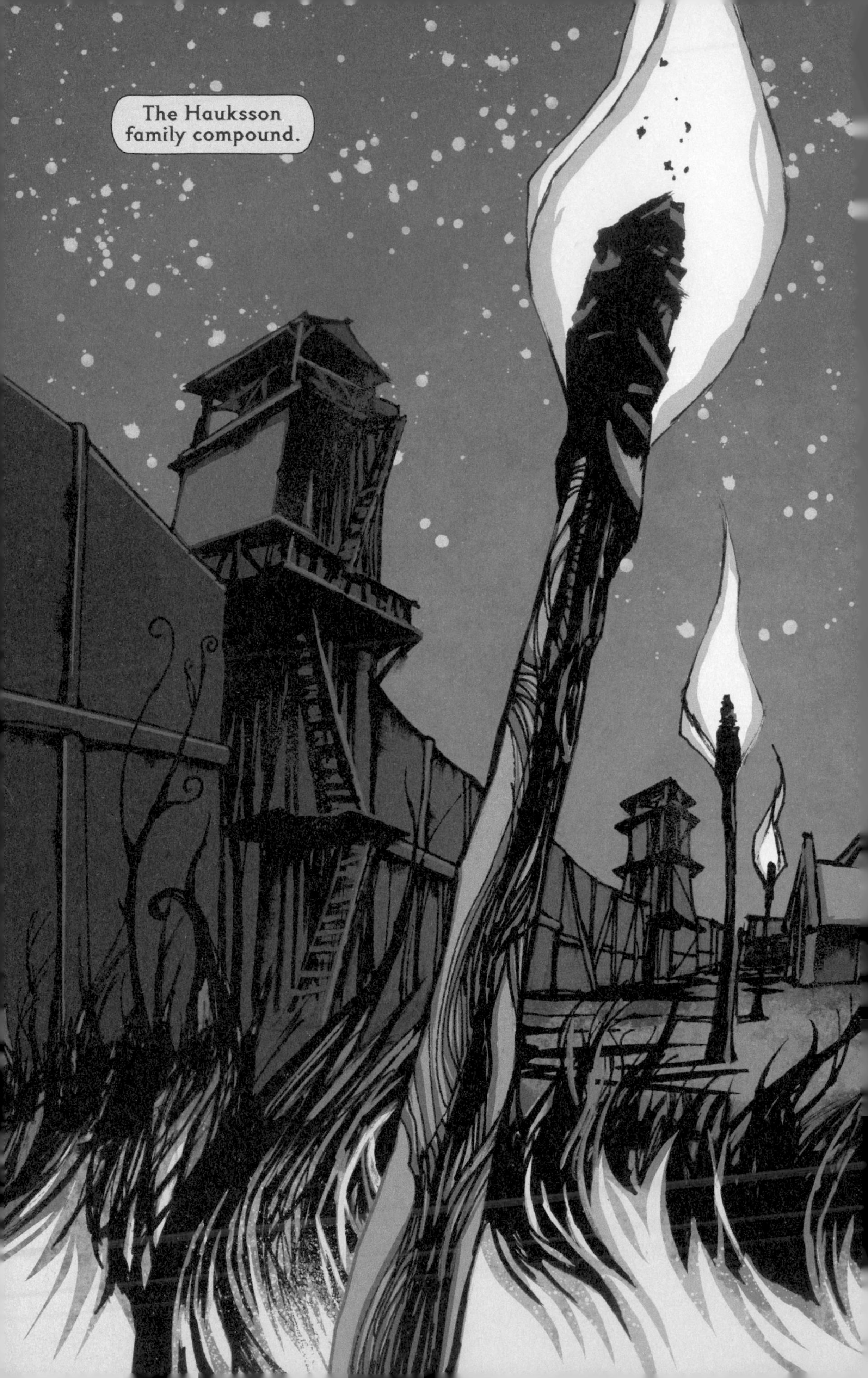
The Hauksson family compound.

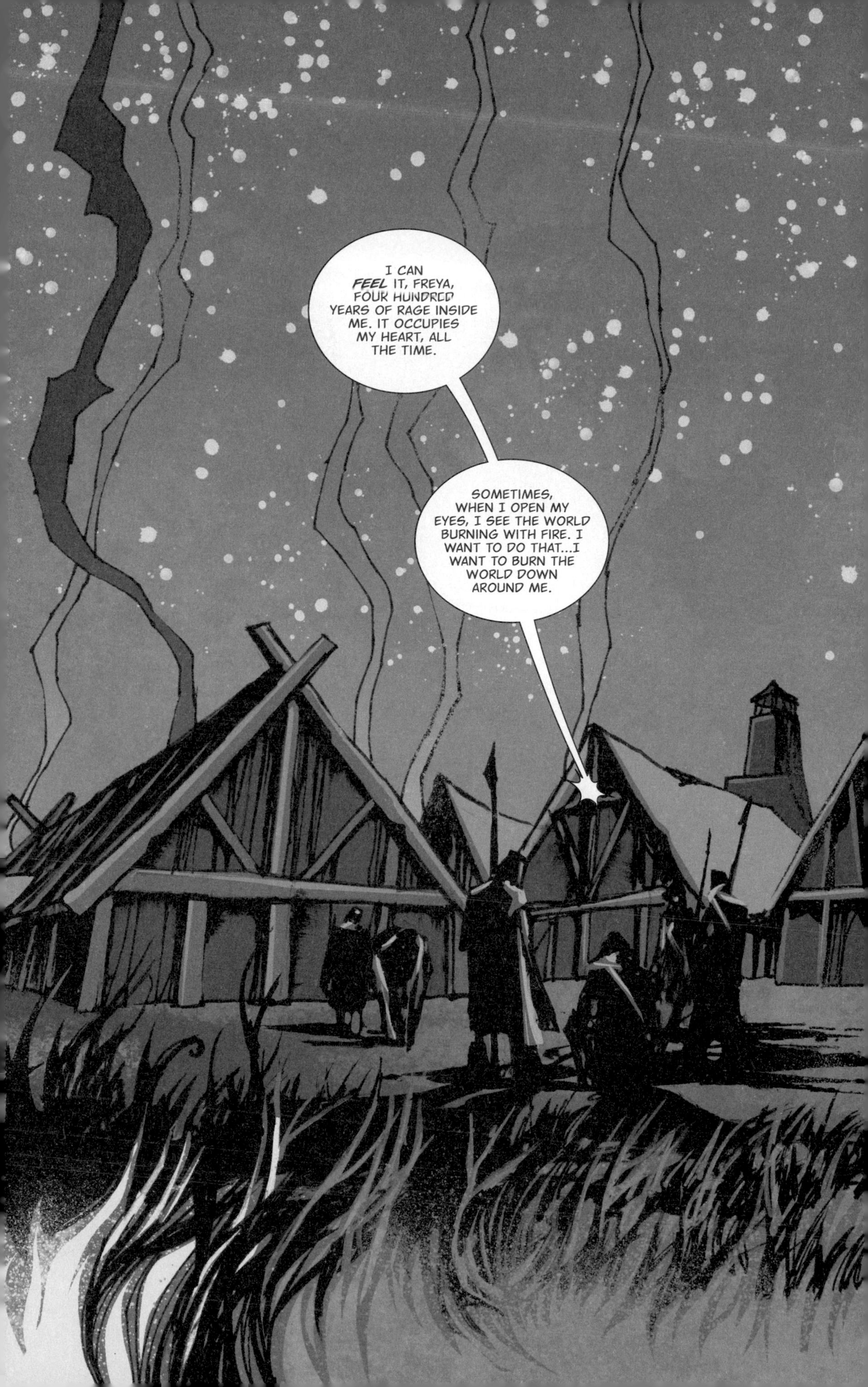
I CAN *FEEL* IT, FREYA, FOUR HUNDRED YEARS OF RAGE INSIDE ME. IT OCCUPIES MY HEART, ALL THE TIME.
SOMETIMES, WHEN I OPEN MY EYES, I SEE THE WORLD BURNING WITH FIRE. I WANT TO DO THAT...I WANT TO BURN THE WORLD DOWN AROUND ME.

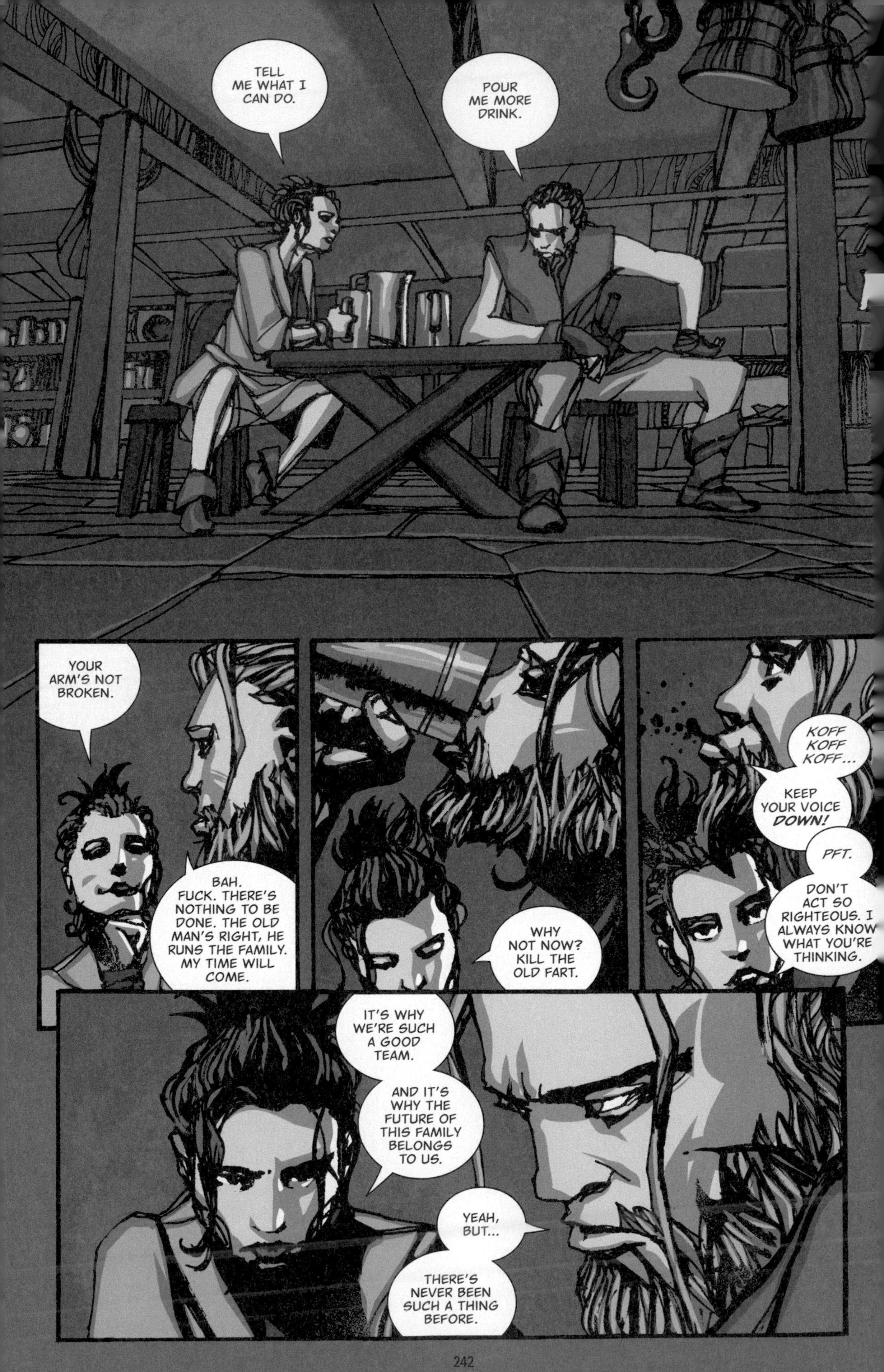
TELL ME WHAT I CAN DO.
POUR ME MORE DRINK.
YOUR ARM'S NOT BROKEN.
BAH. FUCK. THERE'S NOTHING TO BE DONE. THE OLD MAN'S RIGHT, HE RUNS THE FAMILY. MY TIME WILL COME.
WHY NOT NOW? KILL THE OLD FART.
KOFF KOFF KOFF...
KEEP YOUR VOICE *DOWN!*
PFT.
DON'T ACT SO RIGHTEOUS. I ALWAYS KNOW WHAT YOU'RE THINKING.
IT'S WHY WE'RE SUCH A GOOD TEAM.
AND IT'S WHY THE FUTURE OF THIS FAMILY BELONGS TO US.
YEAH, BUT...
THERE'S NEVER BEEN SUCH A THING BEFORE.

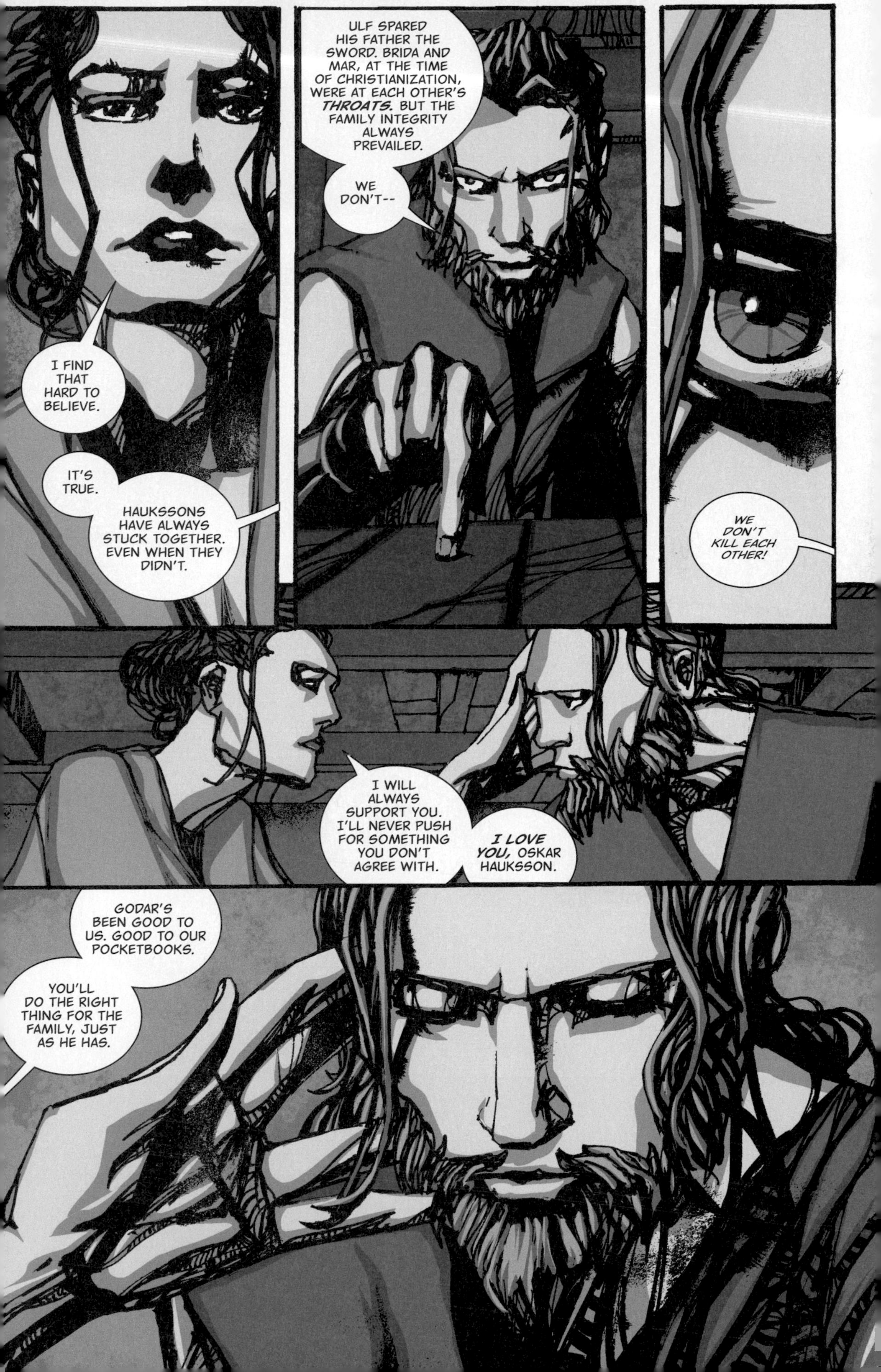
I FIND THAT HARD TO BELIEVE.
IT'S TRUE.
HAUKSSONS HAVE ALWAYS STUCK TOGETHER. EVEN WHEN THEY DIDN'T.
ULF SPARED HIS FATHER THE SWORD. BRIDA AND MAR, AT THE TIME OF CHRISTIANIZATION, WERE AT EACH OTHER'S *THROATS.* BUT THE FAMILY INTEGRITY ALWAYS PREVAILED.
WE DON'T--
WE DON'T KILL EACH OTHER!
I WILL ALWAYS SUPPORT YOU. I'LL NEVER PUSH FOR SOMETHING YOU DON'T AGREE WITH.
I LOVE YOU, OSKAR HAUKSSON.
GODAR'S BEEN GOOD TO US. GOOD TO OUR POCKETBOOKS.
YOU'LL DO THE RIGHT THING FOR THE FAMILY, JUST AS HE HAS.

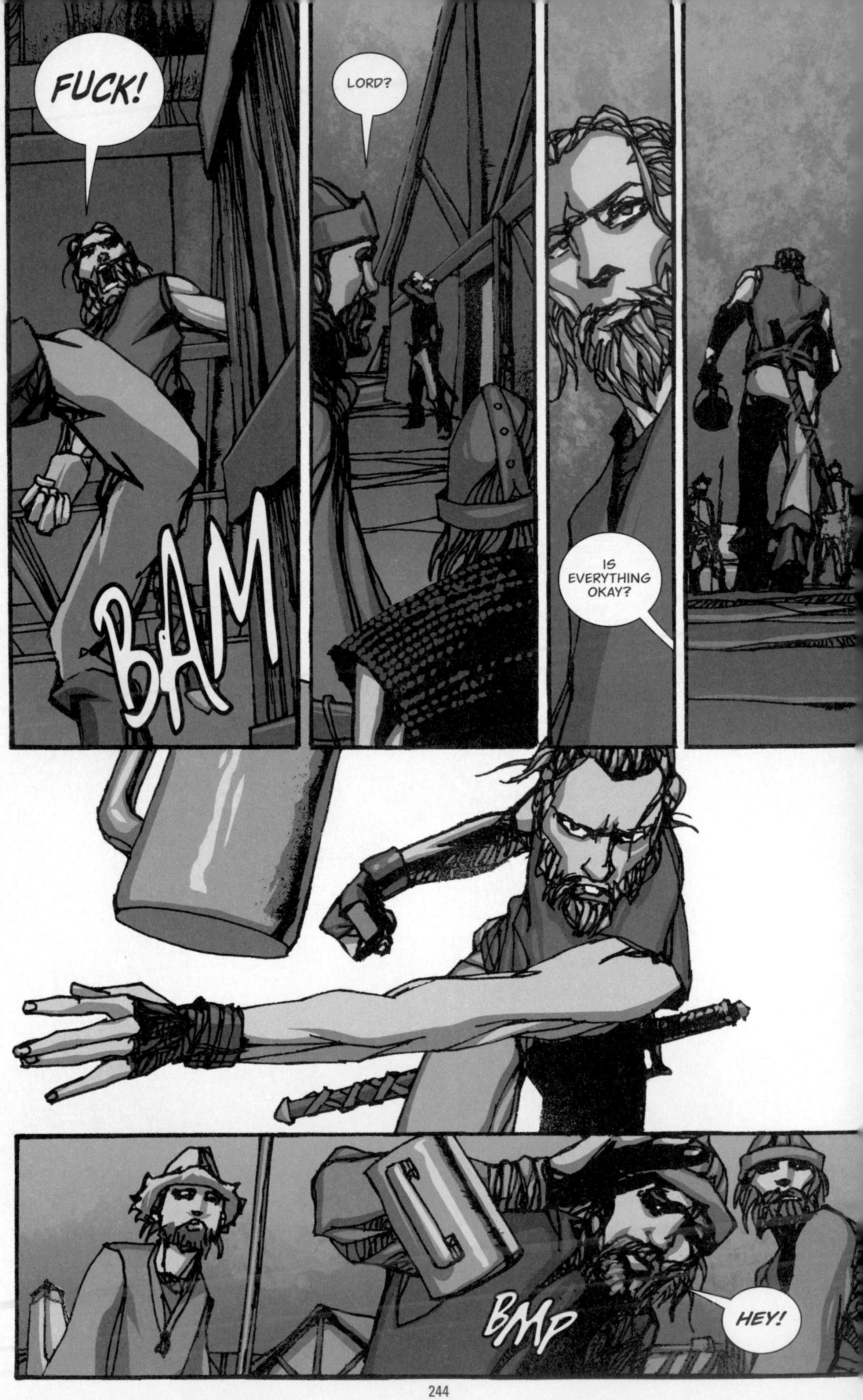
FUCK!
BAM
LORD?
IS EVERYTHING OKAY?
BMP
HEY!

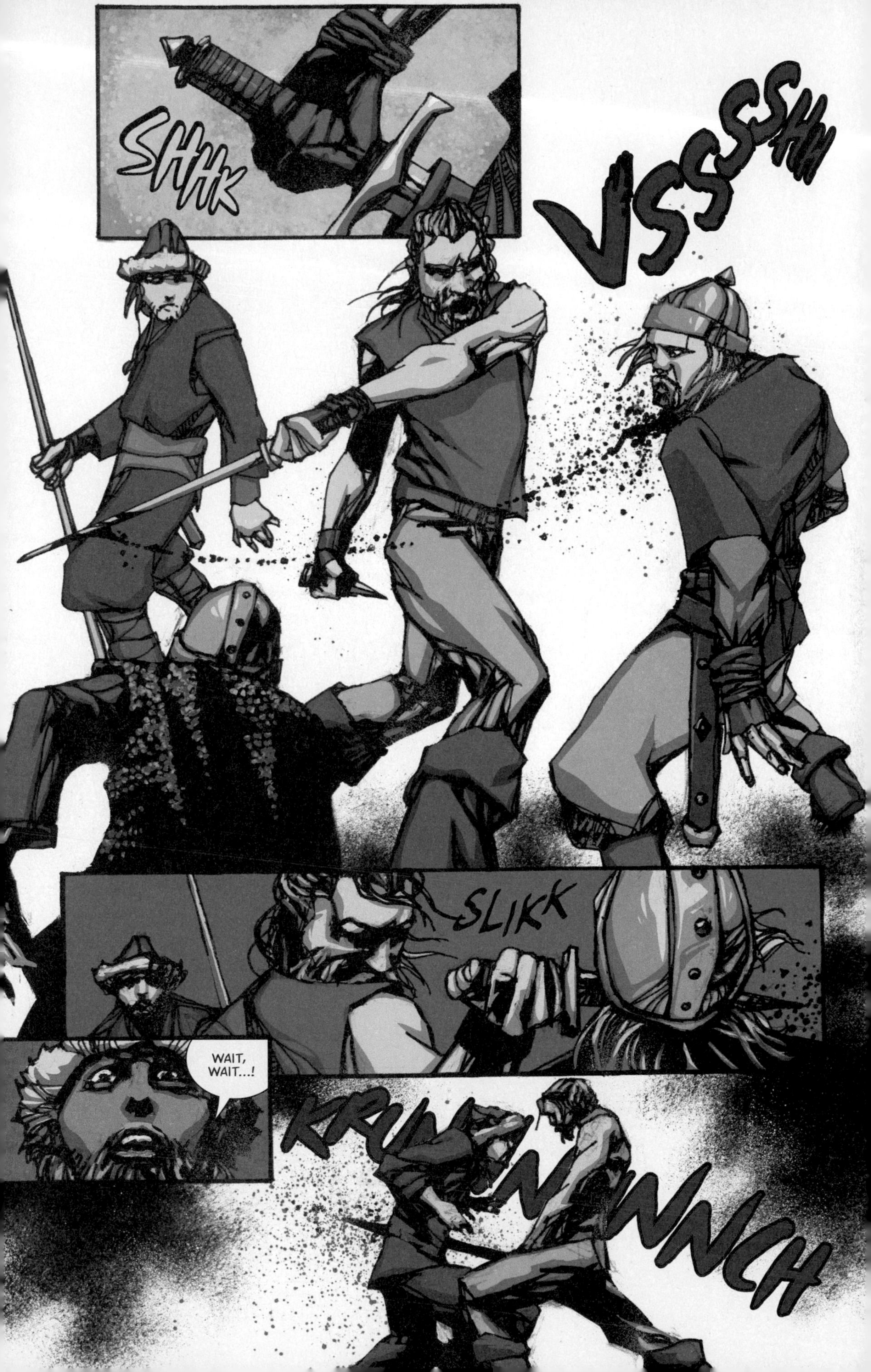
SHHK
VSSSSHH
SLIKK
WAIT, WAIT...!
KRUNNNNNCH

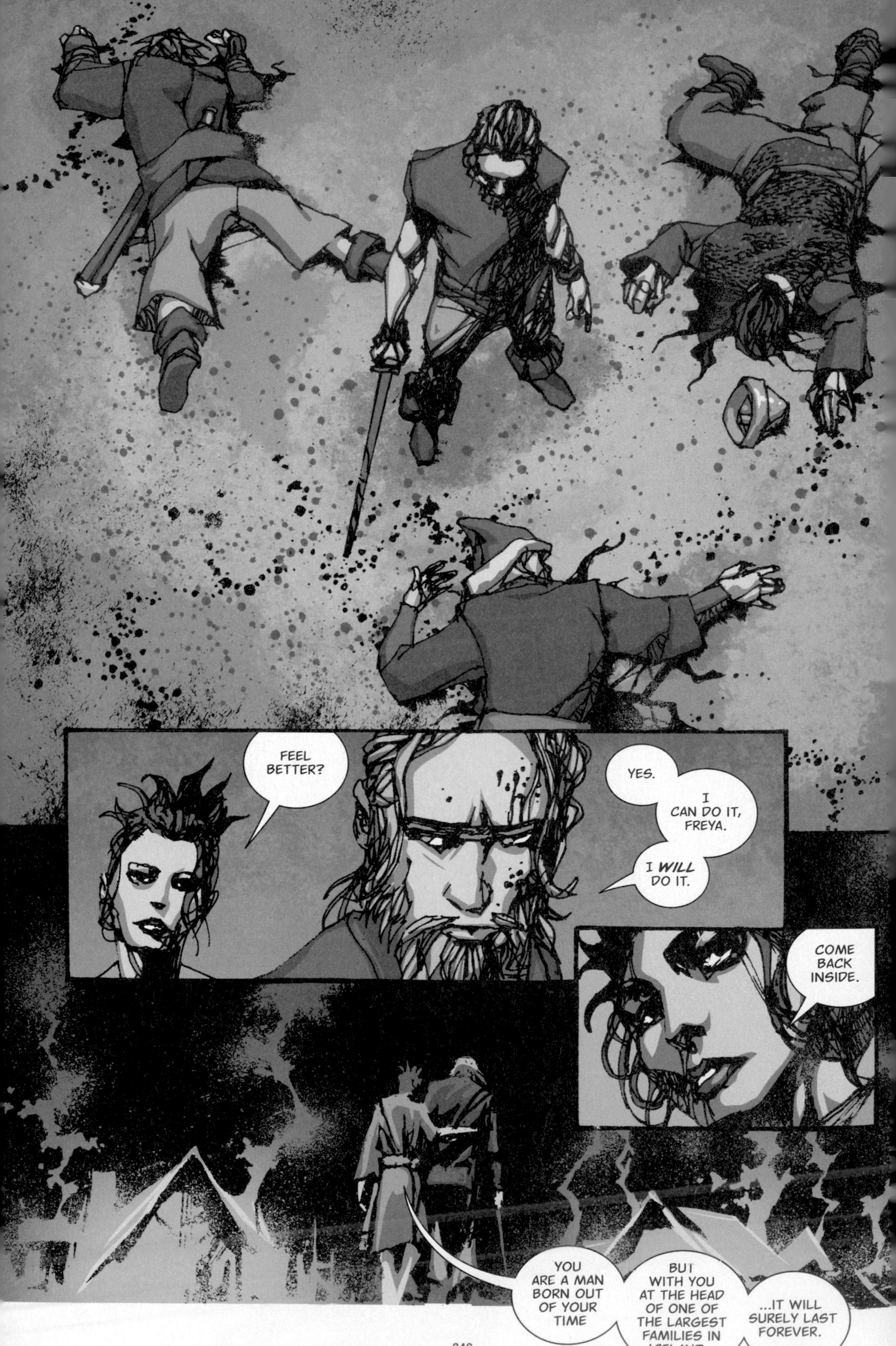
FEEL BETTER?
YES.
I CAN DO IT, FREYA.
I ***WILL*** DO IT.
COME BACK INSIDE.
YOU ARE A MAN BORN OUT OF YOUR TIME
BUT WITH YOU AT THE HEAD OF ONE OF THE LARGEST FAMILIES IN ICELAND...
...IT WILL SURELY LAST FOREVER.

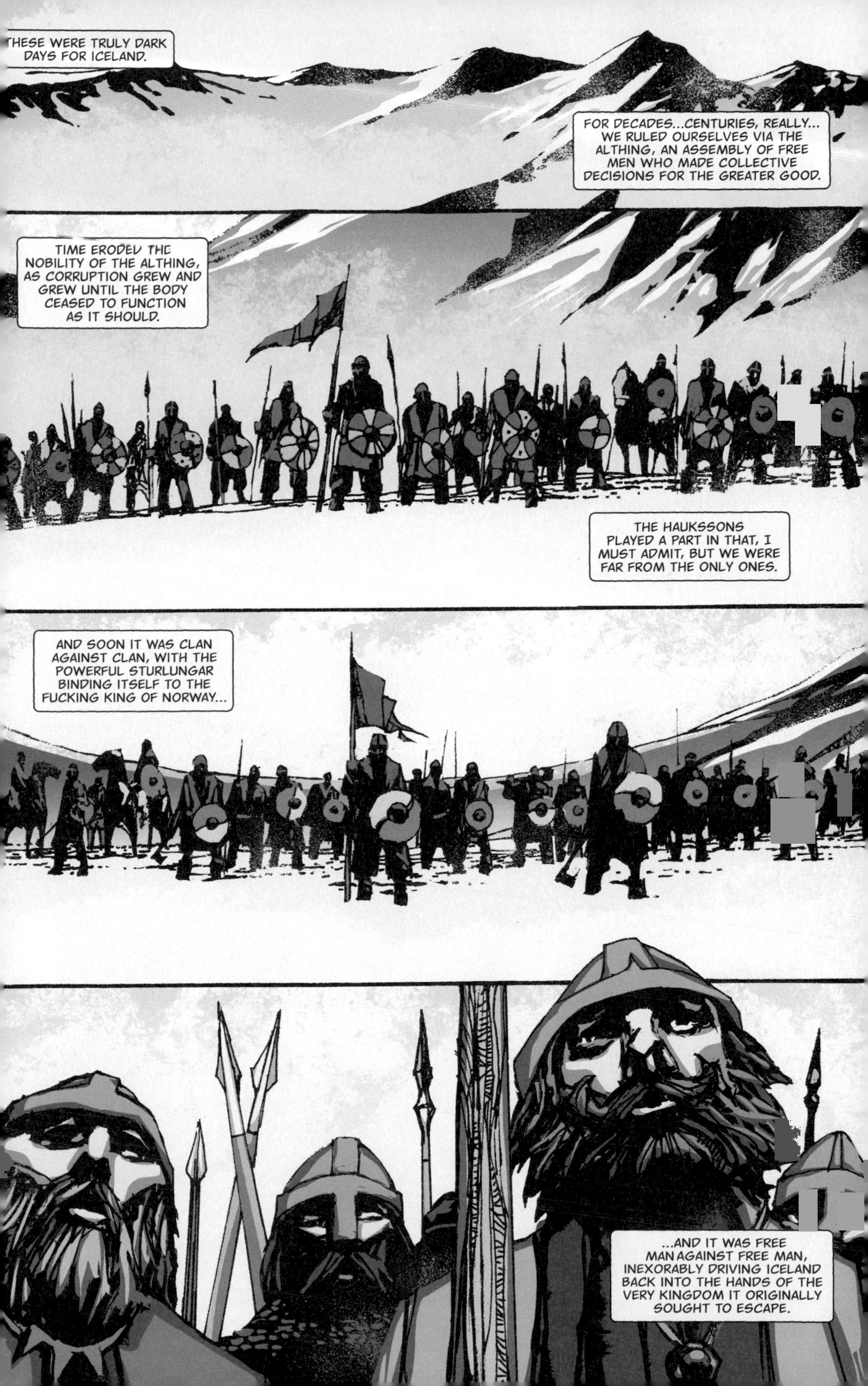
THESE WERE TRULY DARK DAYS FOR ICELAND.
FOR DECADES...CENTURIES, REALLY... WE RULED OURSELVES VIA THE ALTHING, AN ASSEMBLY OF FREE MEN WHO MADE COLLECTIVE DECISIONS FOR THE GREATER GOOD.
TIME ERODED THE NOBILITY OF THE ALTHING, AS CORRUPTION GREW AND GREW UNTIL THE BODY CEASED TO FUNCTION AS IT SHOULD.
THE HAUKSSONS PLAYED A PART IN THAT, I MUST ADMIT, BUT WE WERE FAR FROM THE ONLY ONES.
AND SOON IT WAS CLAN AGAINST CLAN, WITH THE POWERFUL STURLUNGAR BINDING ITSELF TO THE FUCKING KING OF NORWAY...
...AND IT WAS FREE MAN AGAINST FREE MAN, INEXORABLY DRIVING ICELAND BACK INTO THE HANDS OF THE VERY KINGDOM IT ORIGINALLY SOUGHT TO ESCAPE.

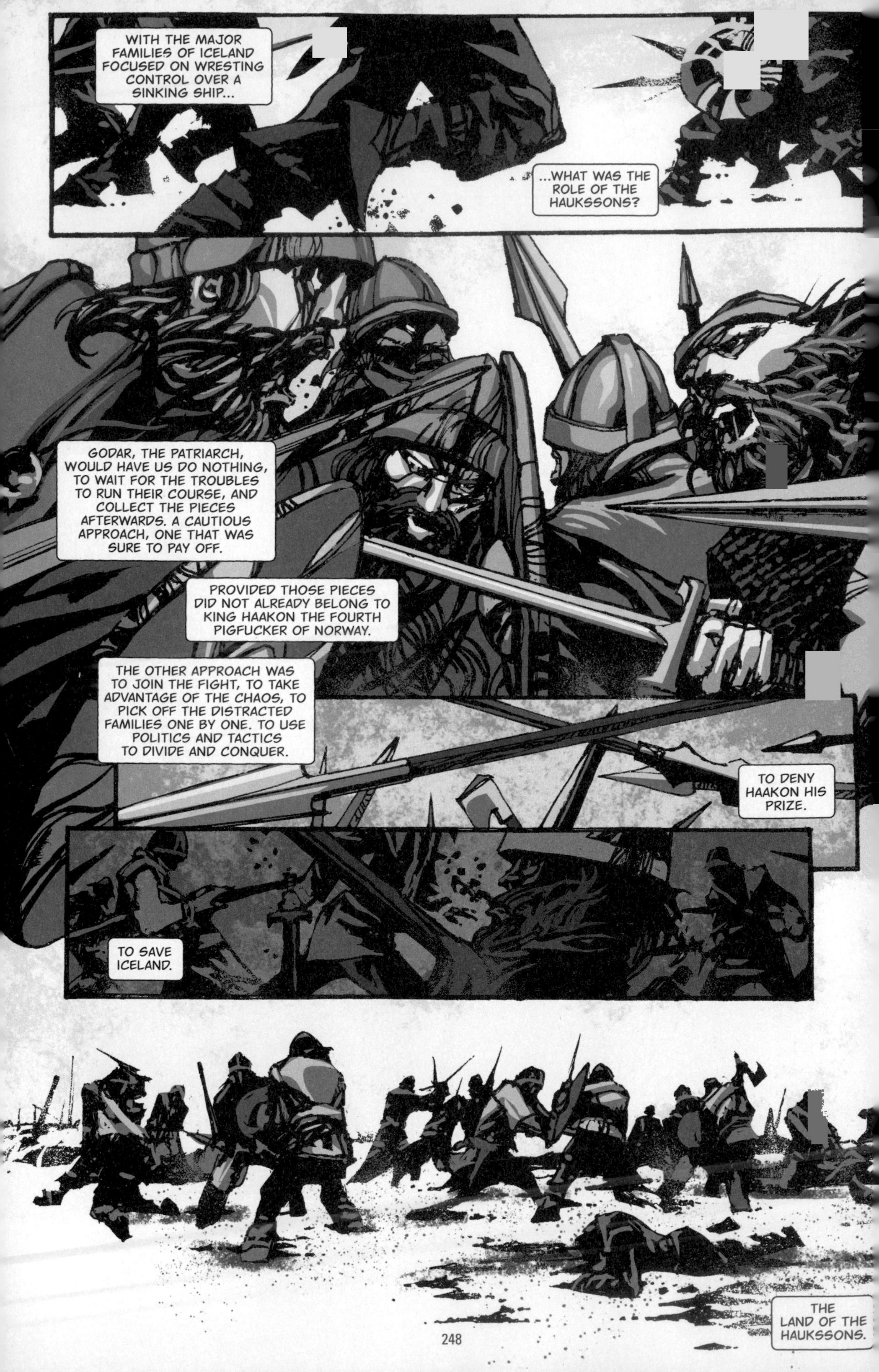
WITH THE MAJOR FAMILIES OF ICELAND FOCUSED ON WRESTING CONTROL OVER A SINKING SHIP...
...WHAT WAS THE ROLE OF THE HAUKSSONS?
GODAR, THE PATRIARCH, WOULD HAVE US DO NOTHING, TO WAIT FOR THE TROUBLES TO RUN THEIR COURSE, AND COLLECT THE PIECES AFTERWARDS. A CAUTIOUS APPROACH, ONE THAT WAS SURE TO PAY OFF.
PROVIDED THOSE PIECES DID NOT ALREADY BELONG TO KING HAAKON THE FOURTH PIGFUCKER OF NORWAY.
THE OTHER APPROACH WAS TO JOIN THE FIGHT, TO TAKE ADVANTAGE OF THE CHAOS, TO PICK OFF THE DISTRACTED FAMILIES ONE BY ONE. TO USE POLITICS AND TACTICS TO DIVIDE AND CONQUER.
TO DENY HAAKON HIS PRIZE.
TO SAVE ICELAND.
THE LAND OF THE HAUKSSONS.

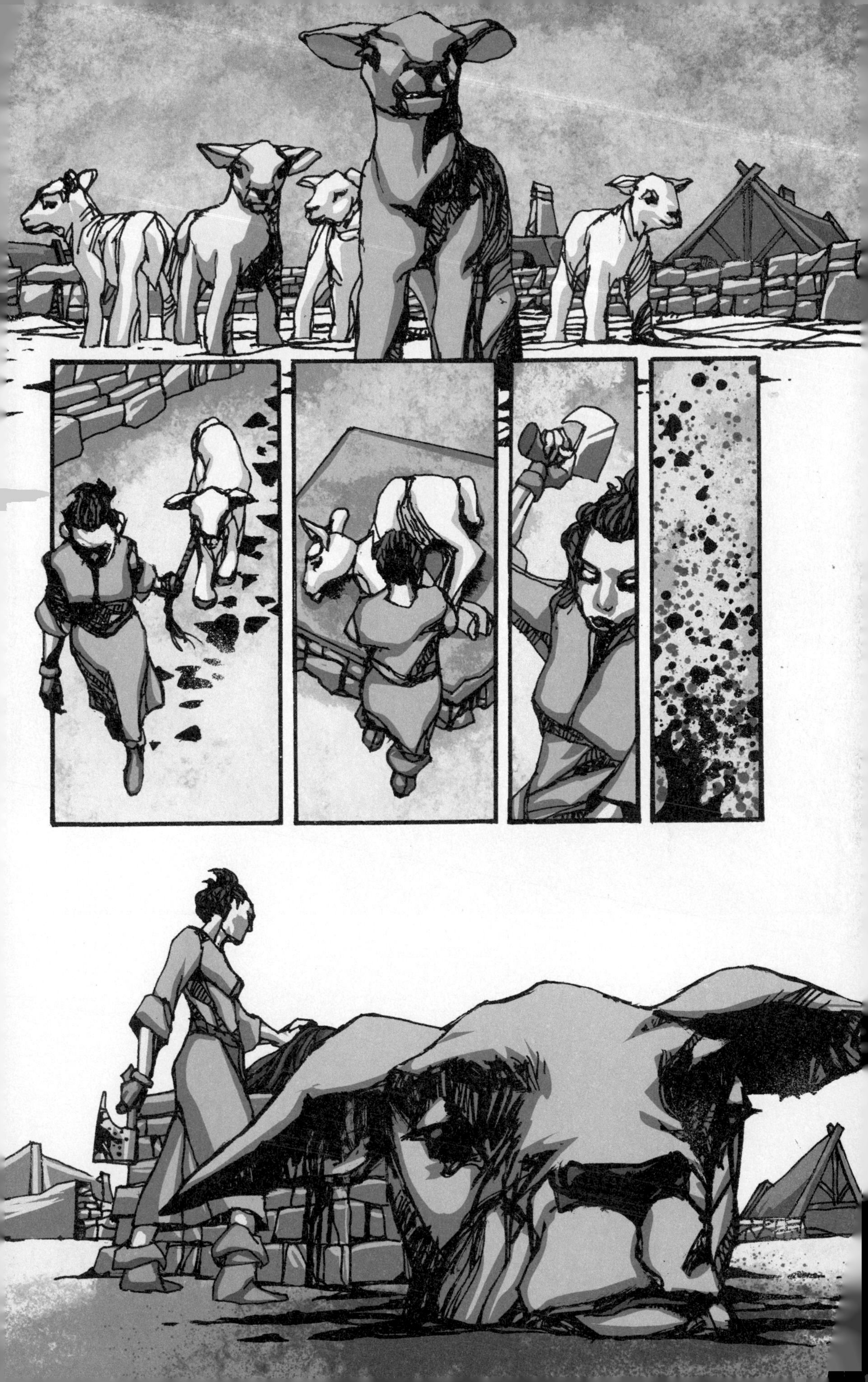

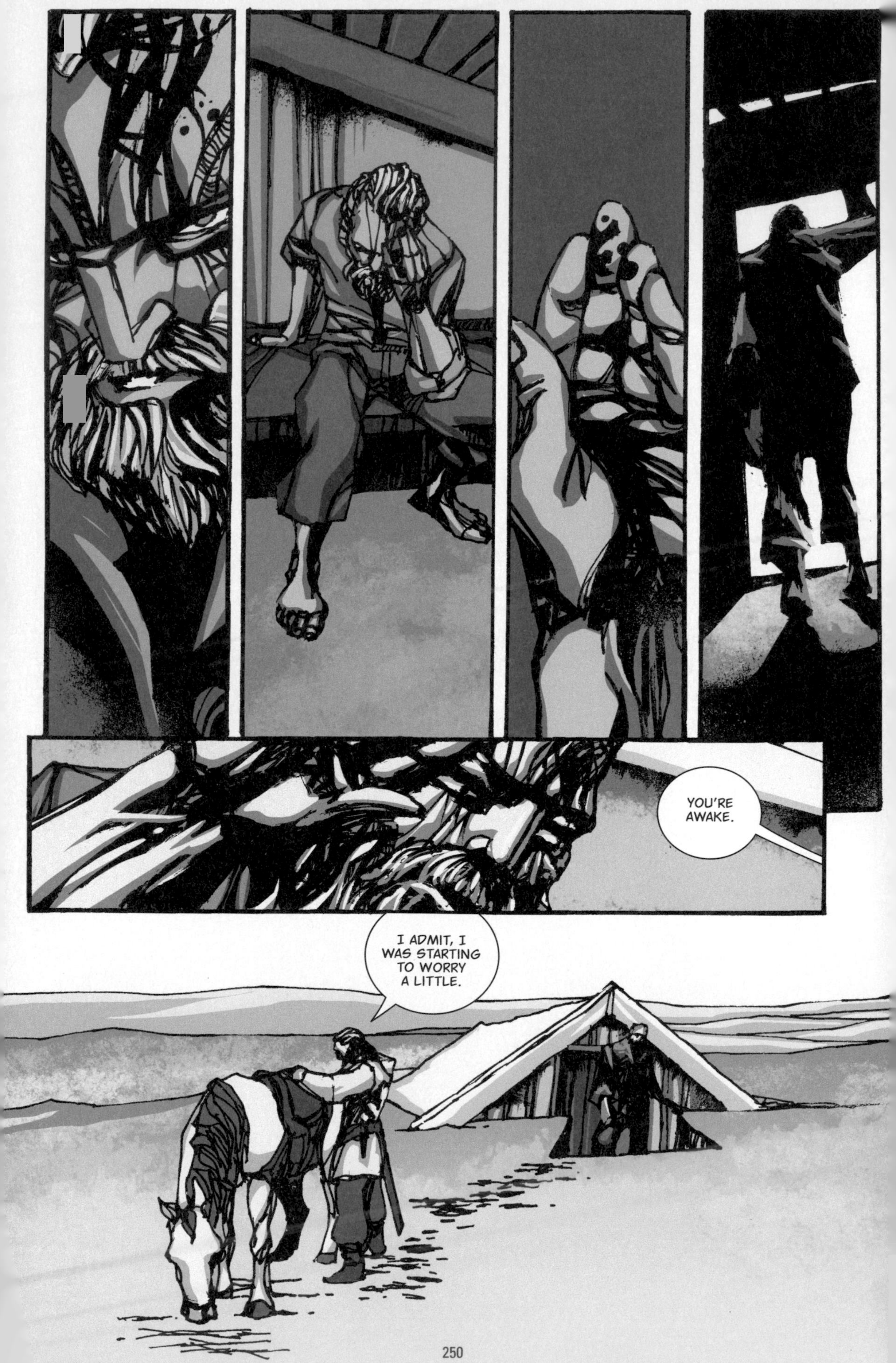
YOU'RE AWAKE.
I ADMIT, I WAS STARTING TO WORRY A LITTLE.

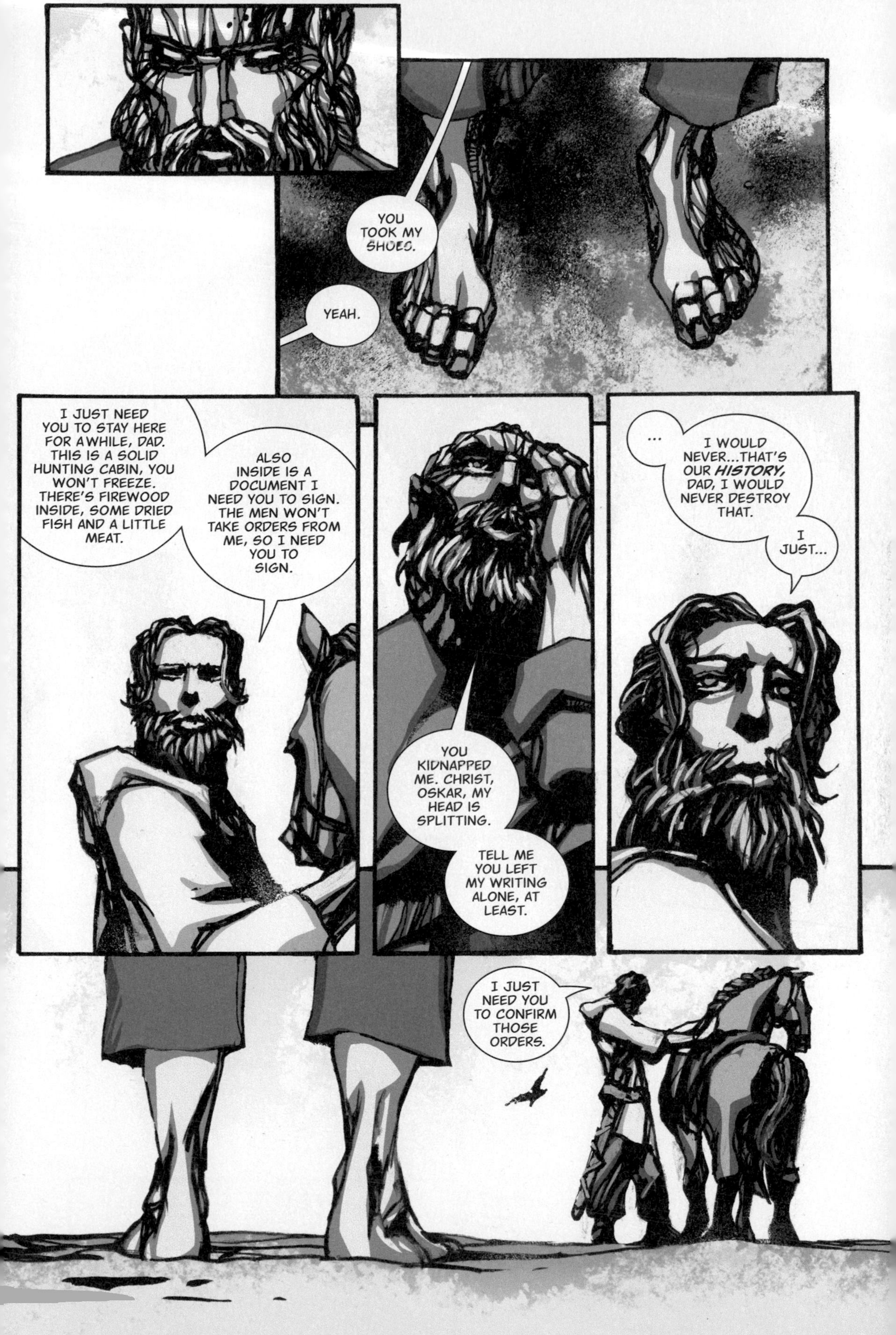

YOU TOOK MY SHOES.
YEAH.
I JUST NEED YOU TO STAY HERE FOR AWHILE, DAD. THIS IS A SOLID HUNTING CABIN, YOU WON'T FREEZE. THERE'S FIREWOOD INSIDE, SOME DRIED FISH AND A LITTLE MEAT.
ALSO INSIDE IS A DOCUMENT I NEED YOU TO SIGN. THE MEN WON'T TAKE ORDERS FROM ME, SO I NEED YOU TO SIGN.
YOU KIDNAPPED ME. CHRIST, OSKAR, MY HEAD IS SPLITTING.
TELL ME YOU LEFT MY WRITING ALONE, AT LEAST.
...
I WOULD NEVER...THAT'S OUR *HISTORY,* DAD, I WOULD NEVER DESTROY THAT.
I JUST...
I JUST NEED YOU TO CONFIRM THOSE ORDERS.

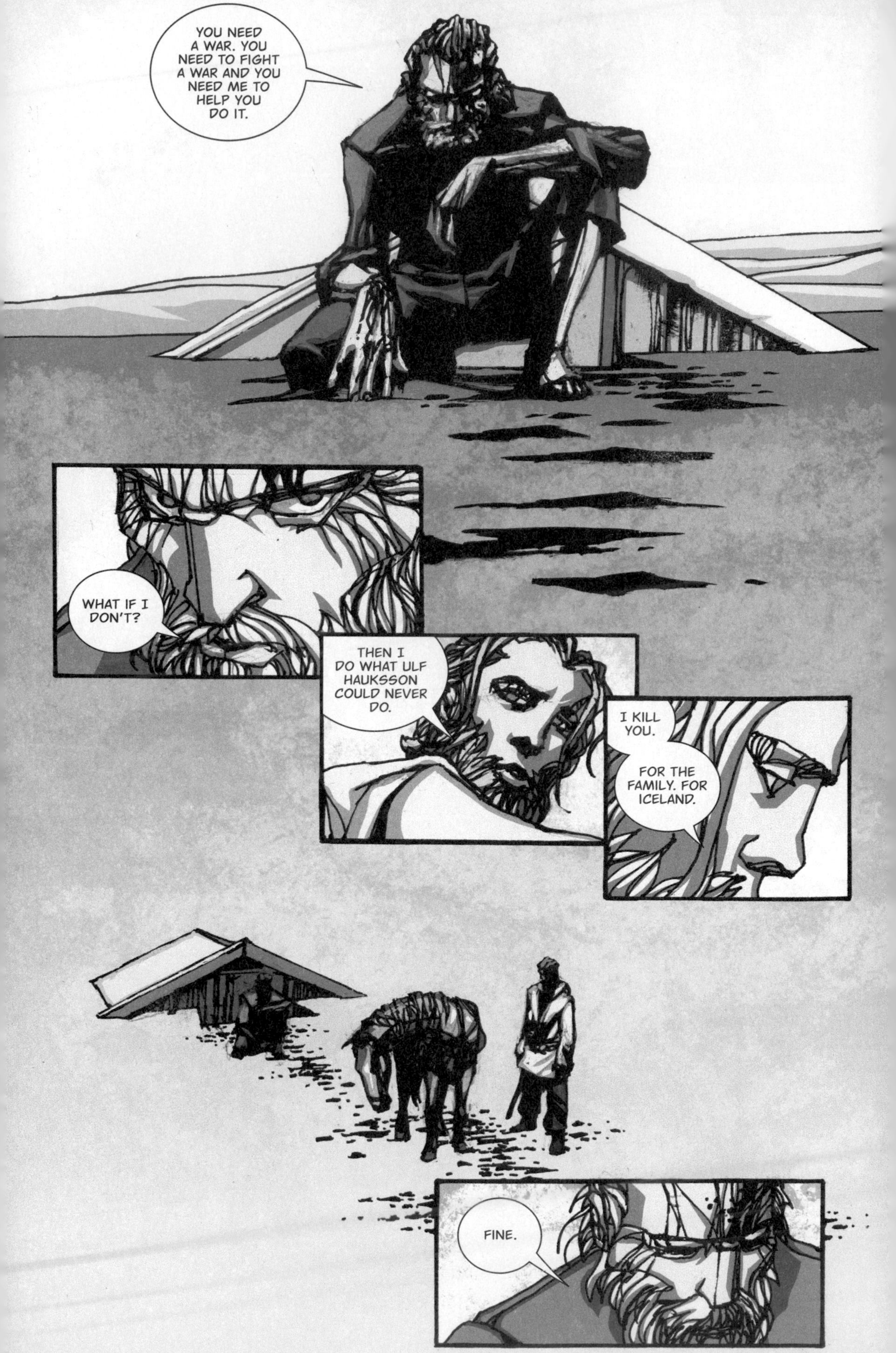
YOU NEED A WAR. YOU NEED TO FIGHT A WAR AND YOU NEED ME TO HELP YOU DO IT.
WHAT IF I DON'T?
THEN I DO WHAT ULF HAUKSSON COULD NEVER DO.
I KILL YOU.
FOR THE FAMILY. FOR ICELAND.
FINE.

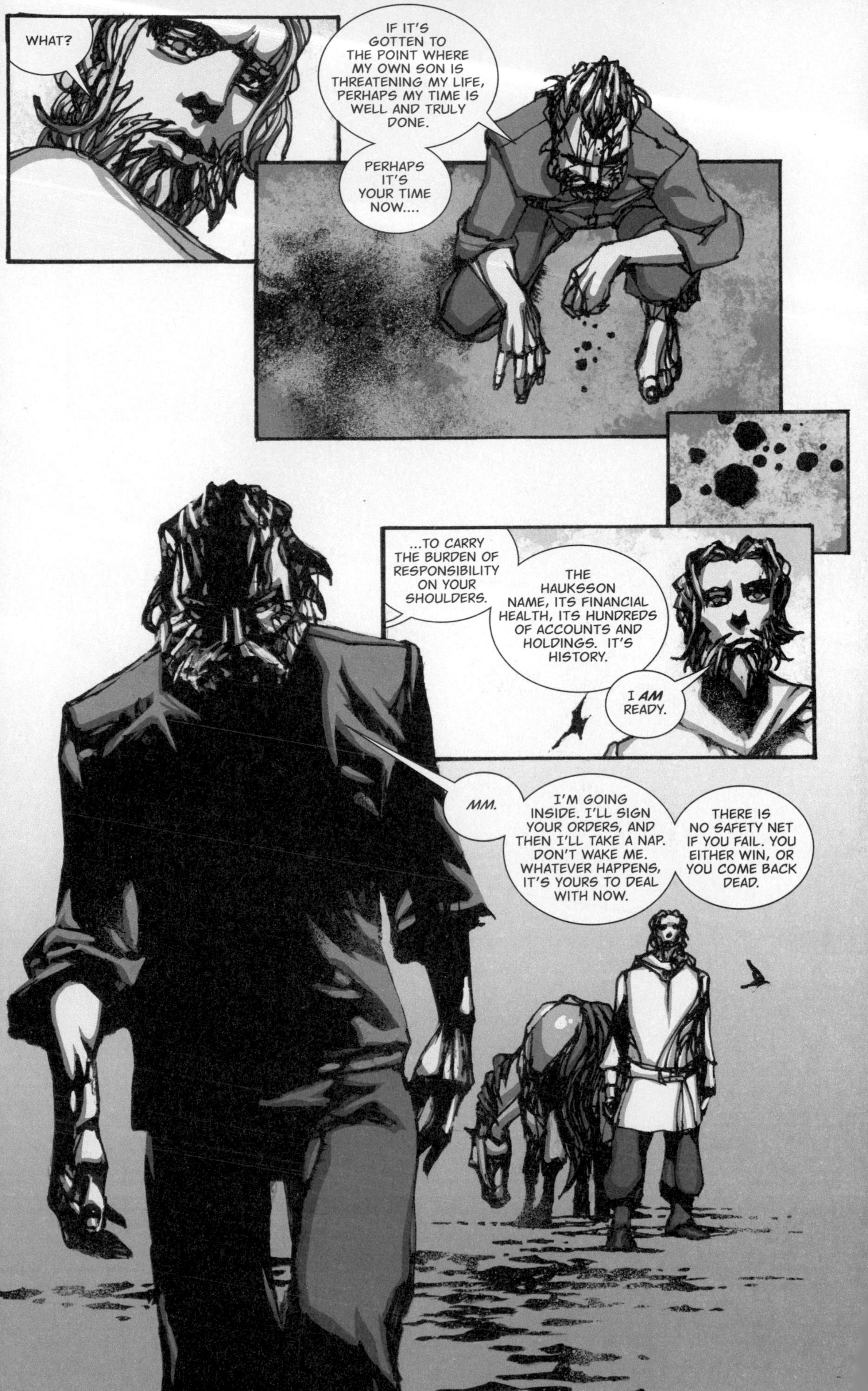
WHAT?
IF IT'S GOTTEN TO THE POINT WHERE MY OWN SON IS THREATENING MY LIFE, PERHAPS MY TIME IS WELL AND TRULY DONE.
PERHAPS IT'S YOUR TIME NOW....
...TO CARRY THE BURDEN OF RESPONSIBILITY ON YOUR SHOULDERS.
THE HAUKSSON NAME, ITS FINANCIAL HEALTH, ITS HUNDREDS OF ACCOUNTS AND HOLDINGS. IT'S HISTORY.
I *AM* READY.
MM.
I'M GOING INSIDE. I'LL SIGN YOUR ORDERS, AND THEN I'LL TAKE A NAP. DON'T WAKE ME. WHATEVER HAPPENS, IT'S YOURS TO DEAL WITH NOW.
THERE IS NO SAFETY NET IF YOU FAIL. YOU EITHER WIN, OR YOU COME BACK DEAD.

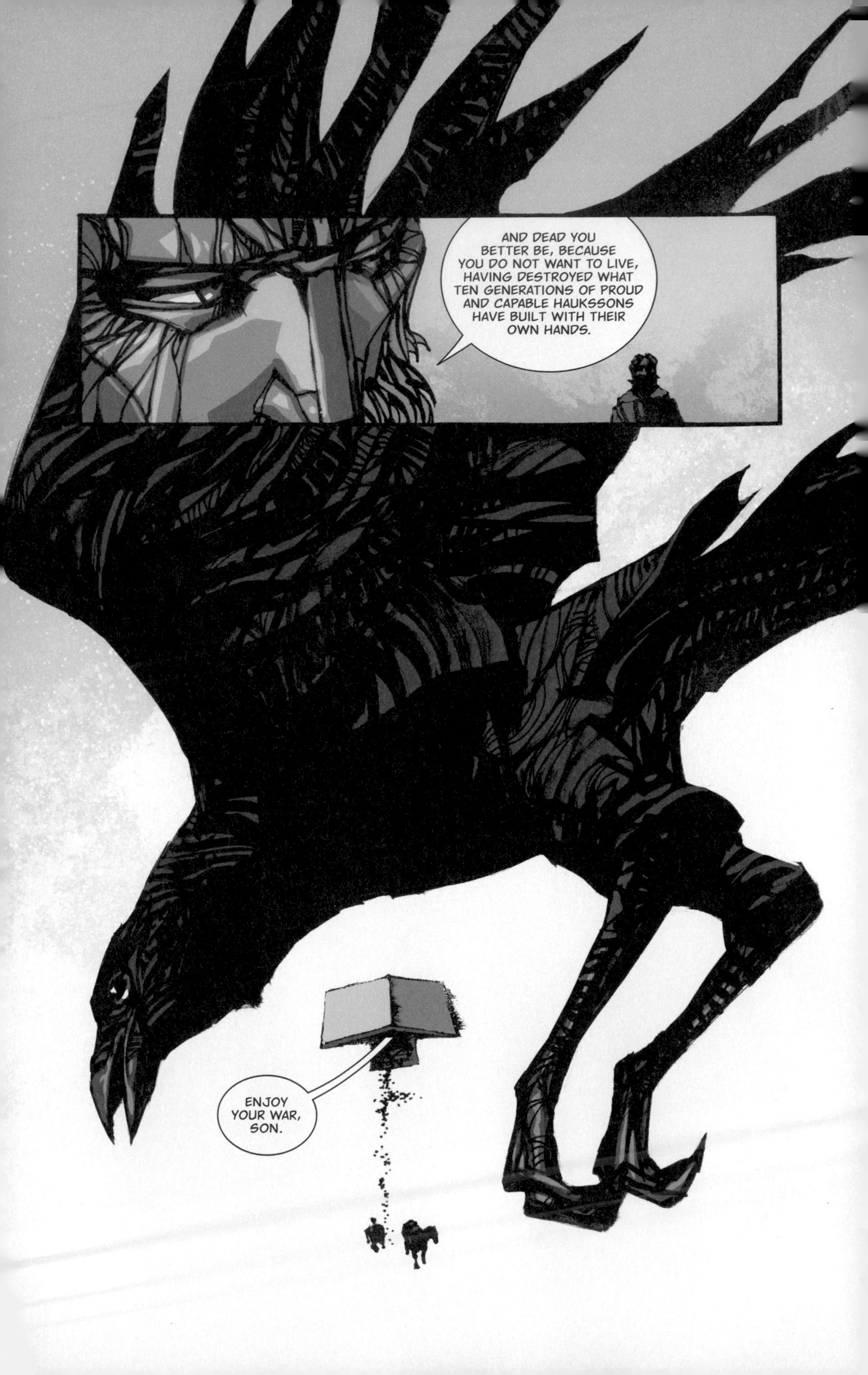
AND DEAD YOU BETTER BE, BECAUSE YOU DO NOT WANT TO LIVE, HAVING DESTROYED WHAT TEN GENERATIONS OF PROUD AND CAPABLE HAUKSSONS HAVE BUILT WITH THEIR OWN HANDS.
ENJOY YOUR WAR, SON.

Chapter VIII
Wealth
A.D. 1260

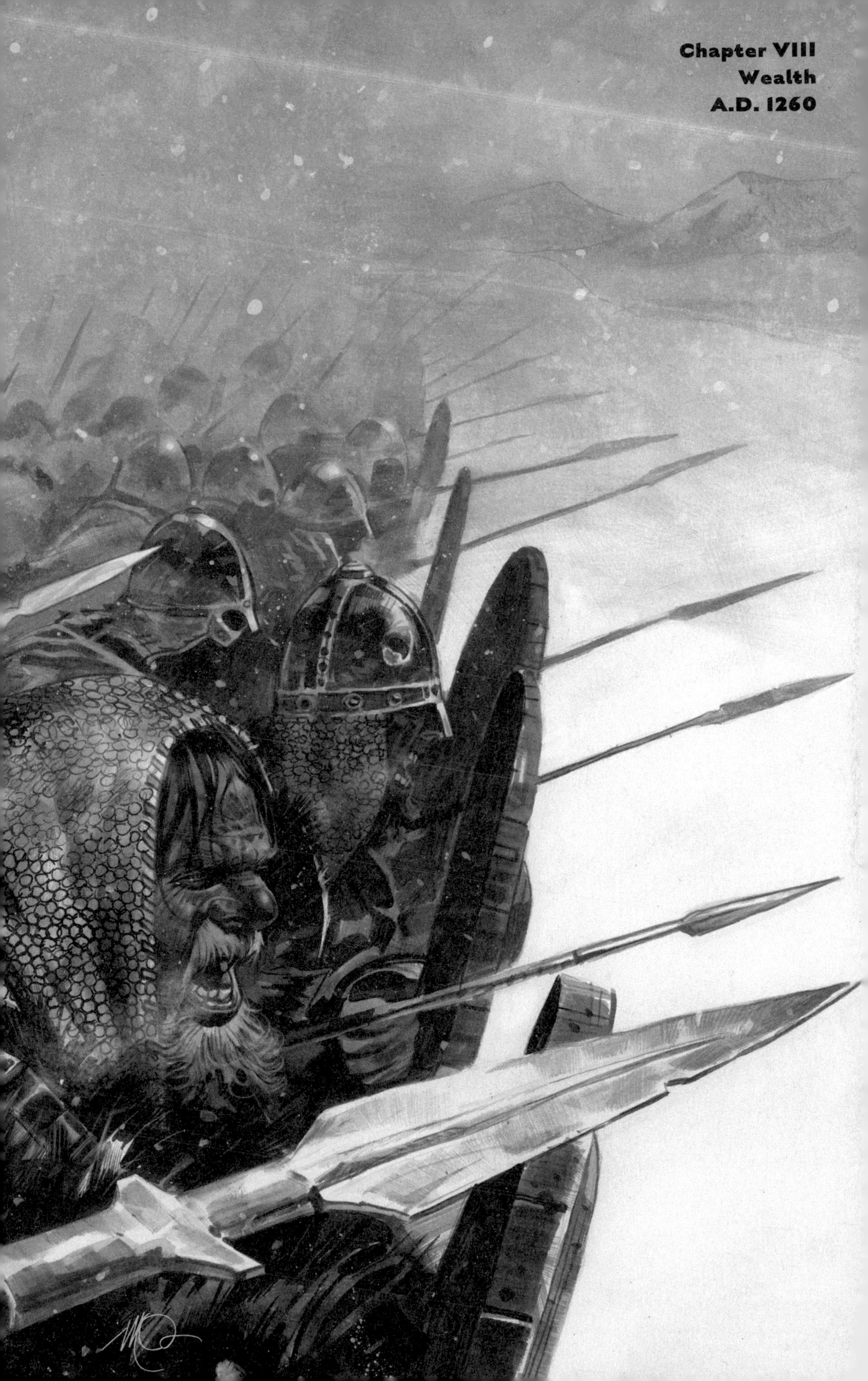

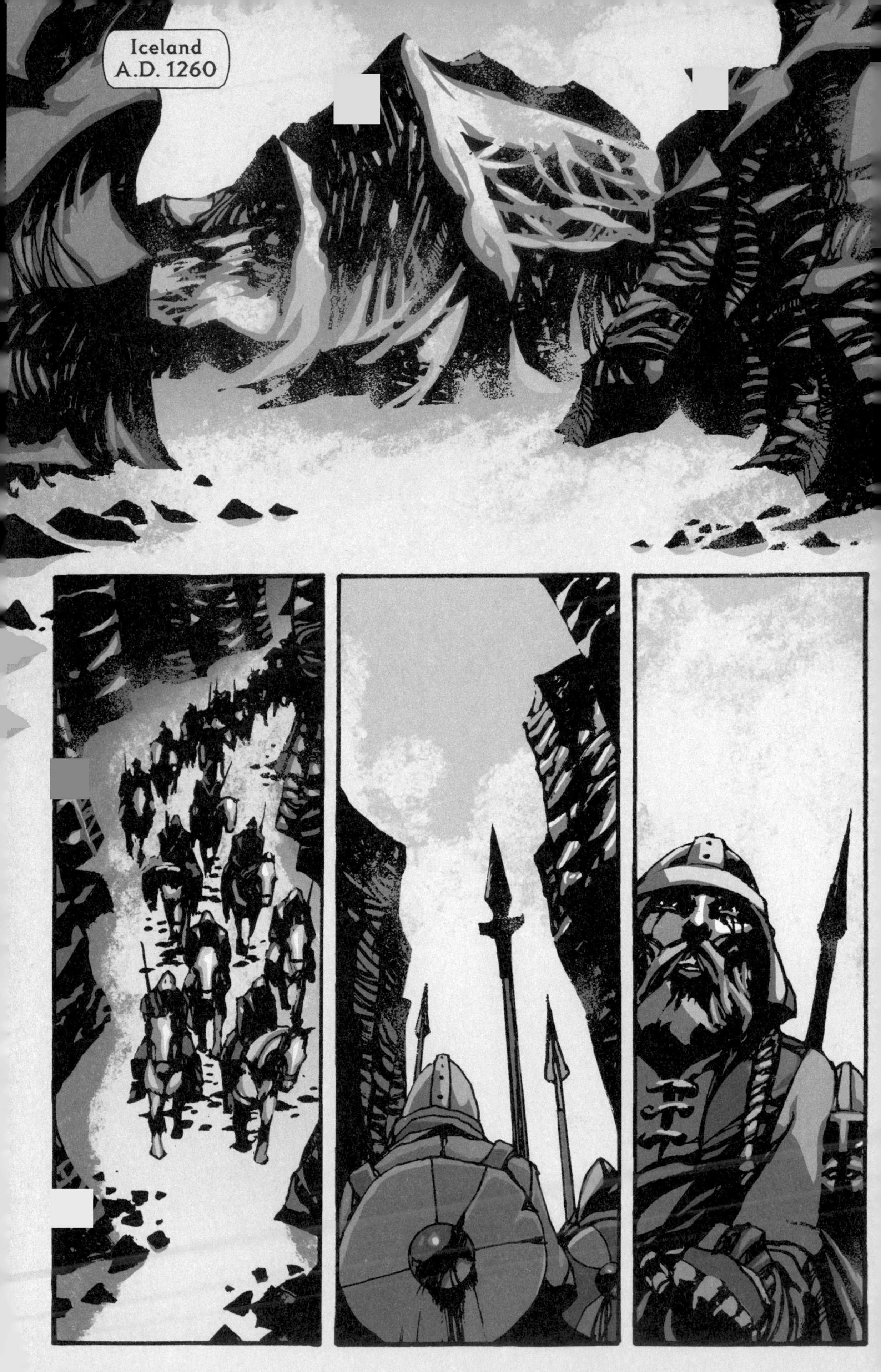
Iceland
A.D. 1260

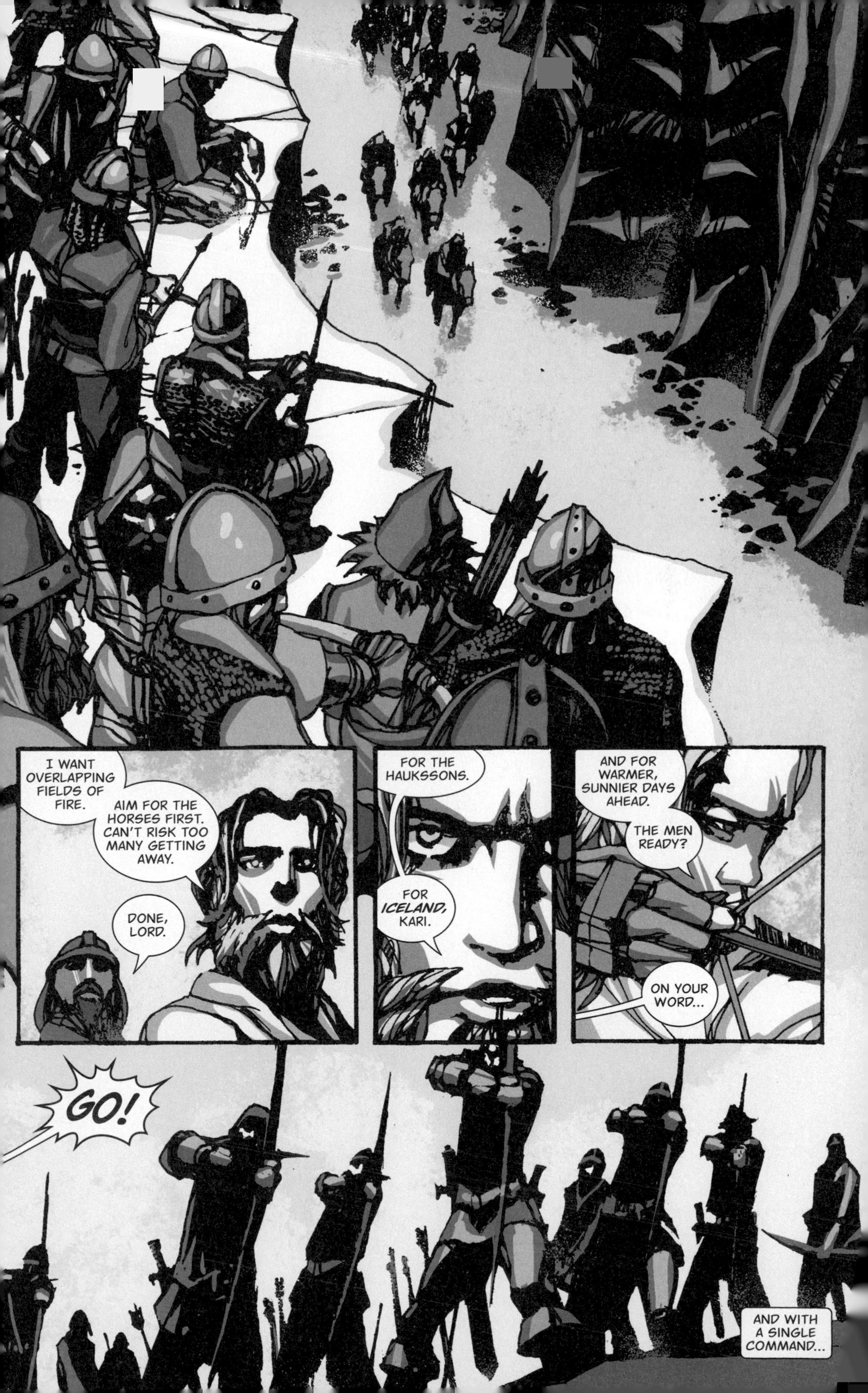
I WANT OVERLAPPING FIELDS OF FIRE.
AIM FOR THE HORSES FIRST. CAN'T RISK TOO MANY GETTING AWAY.
DONE, LORD.
FOR THE HAUKSSONS.
FOR ICELAND, KARI.
AND FOR WARMER, SUNNIER DAYS AHEAD.
THE MEN READY?
ON YOUR WORD...
GO!
AND WITH A SINGLE COMMAND...

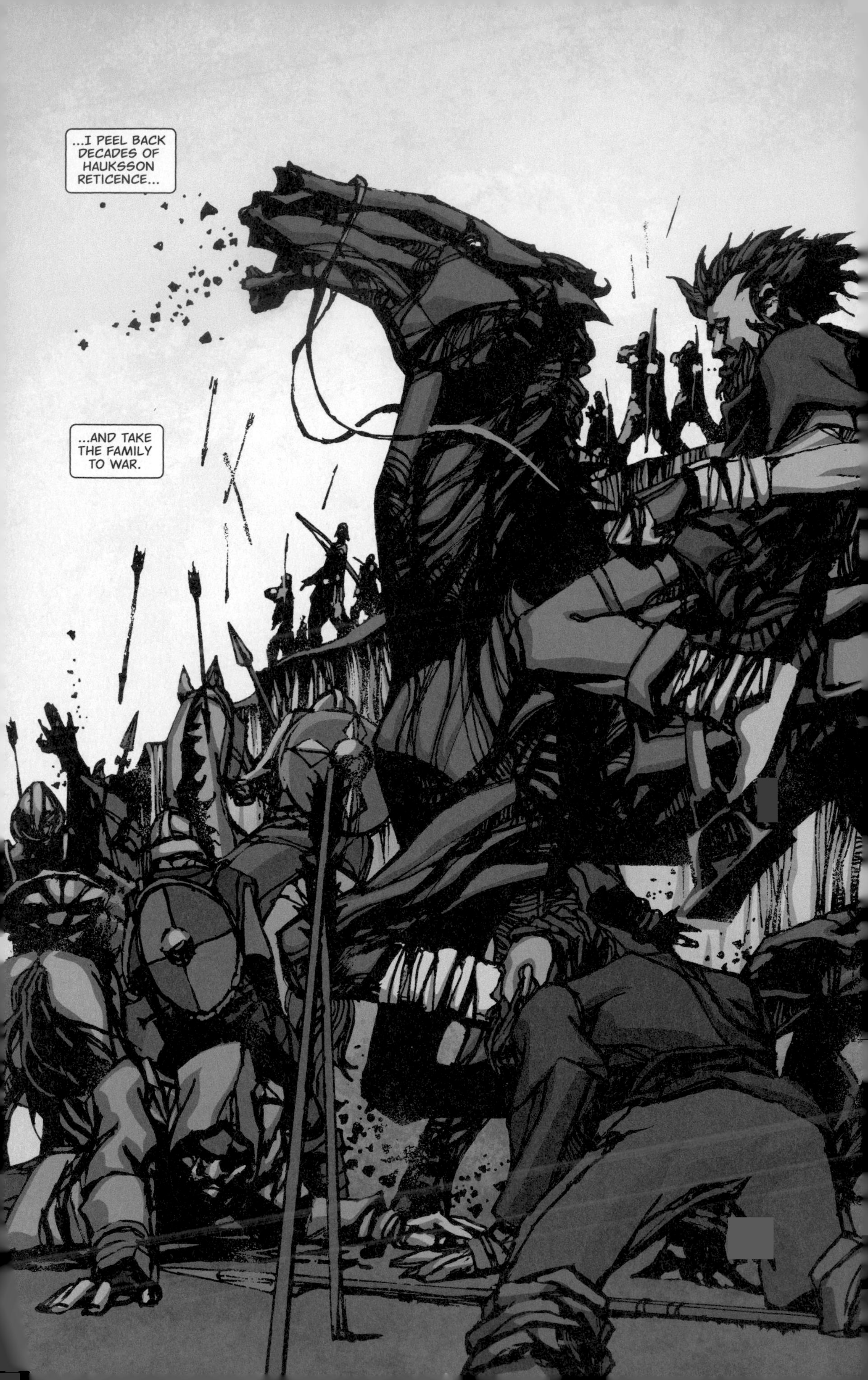
...I PEEL BACK DECADES OF HAUKSSON RETICENCE...
...AND TAKE THE FAMILY TO WAR.

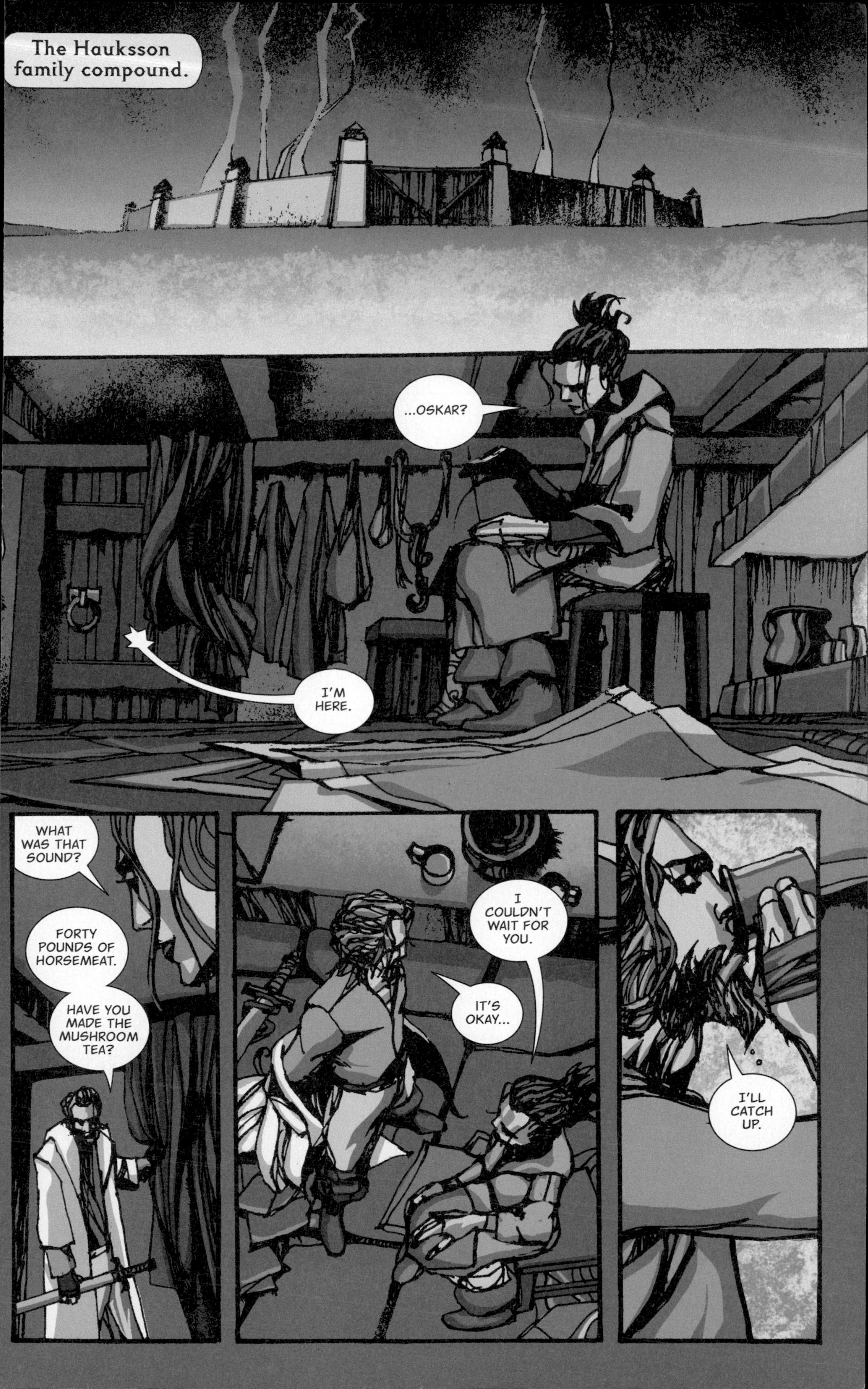
The Hauksson family compound.
...OSKAR?
I'M HERE.
WHAT WAS THAT SOUND?
FORTY POUNDS OF HORSEMEAT.
HAVE YOU MADE THE MUSHROOM TEA?
I COULDN'T WAIT FOR YOU.
IT'S OKAY...
I'LL CATCH UP.

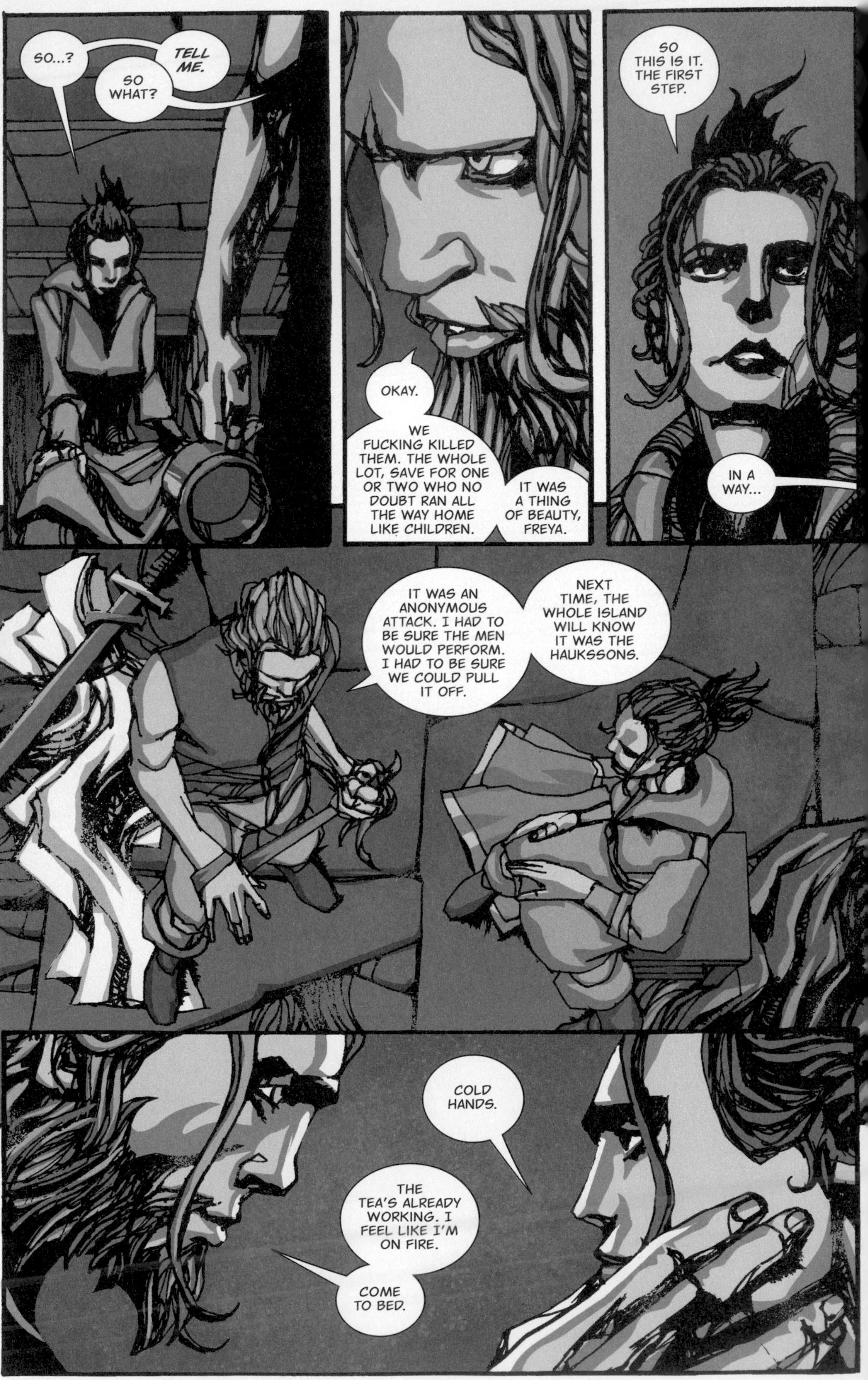
SO...?
TELL ME.
SO WHAT?
OKAY.
WE FUCKING KILLED THEM. THE WHOLE LOT, SAVE FOR ONE OR TWO WHO NO DOUBT RAN ALL THE WAY HOME LIKE CHILDREN.
IT WAS A THING OF BEAUTY, FREYA.
SO THIS IS IT. THE FIRST STEP.
IN A WAY...
IT WAS AN ANONYMOUS ATTACK. I HAD TO BE SURE THE MEN WOULD PERFORM. I HAD TO BE SURE WE COULD PULL IT OFF.
NEXT TIME, THE WHOLE ISLAND WILL KNOW IT WAS THE HAUKSSONS.
COLD HANDS.
THE TEA'S ALREADY WORKING. I FEEL LIKE I'M ON FIRE.
COME TO BED.

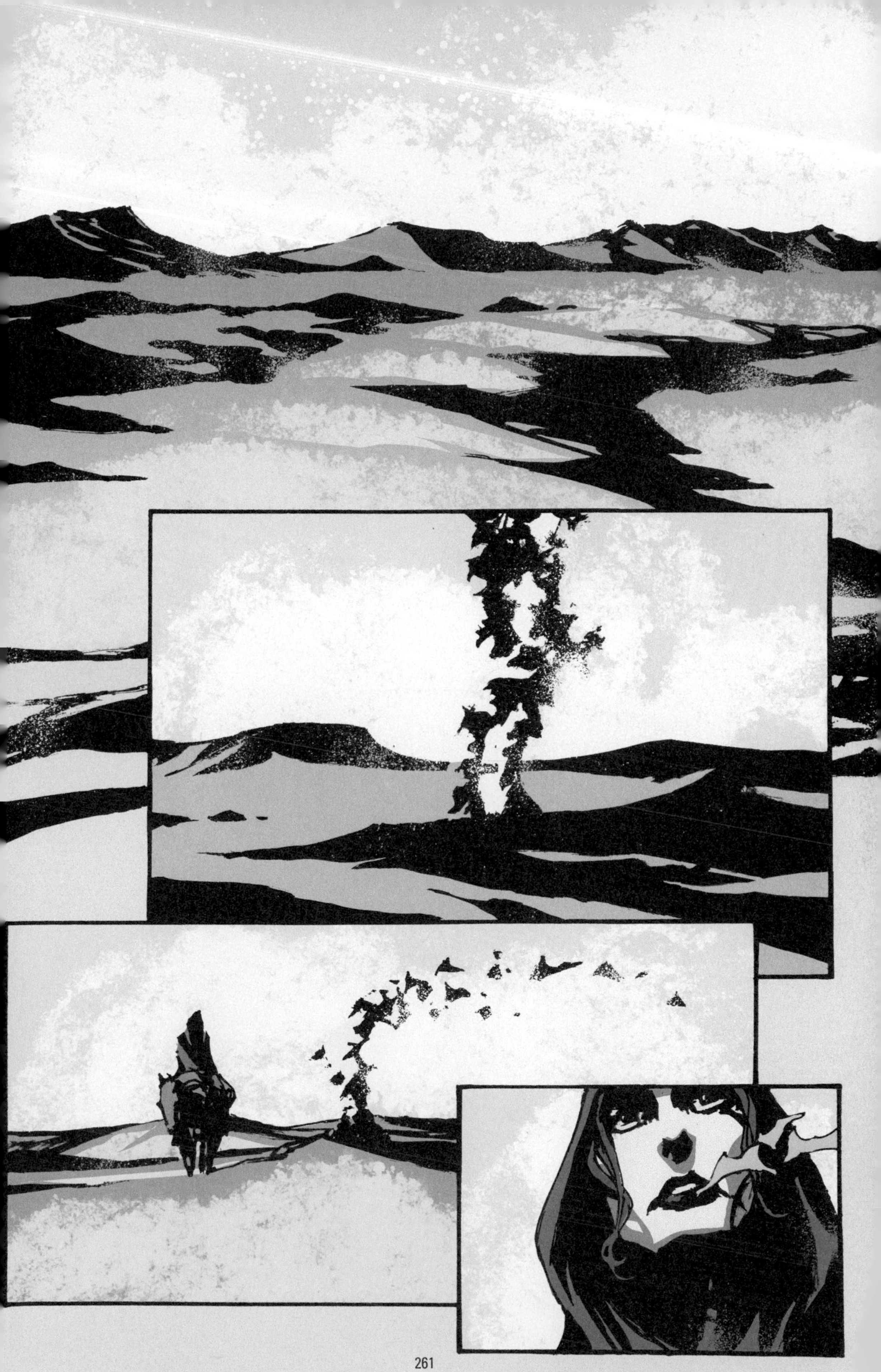

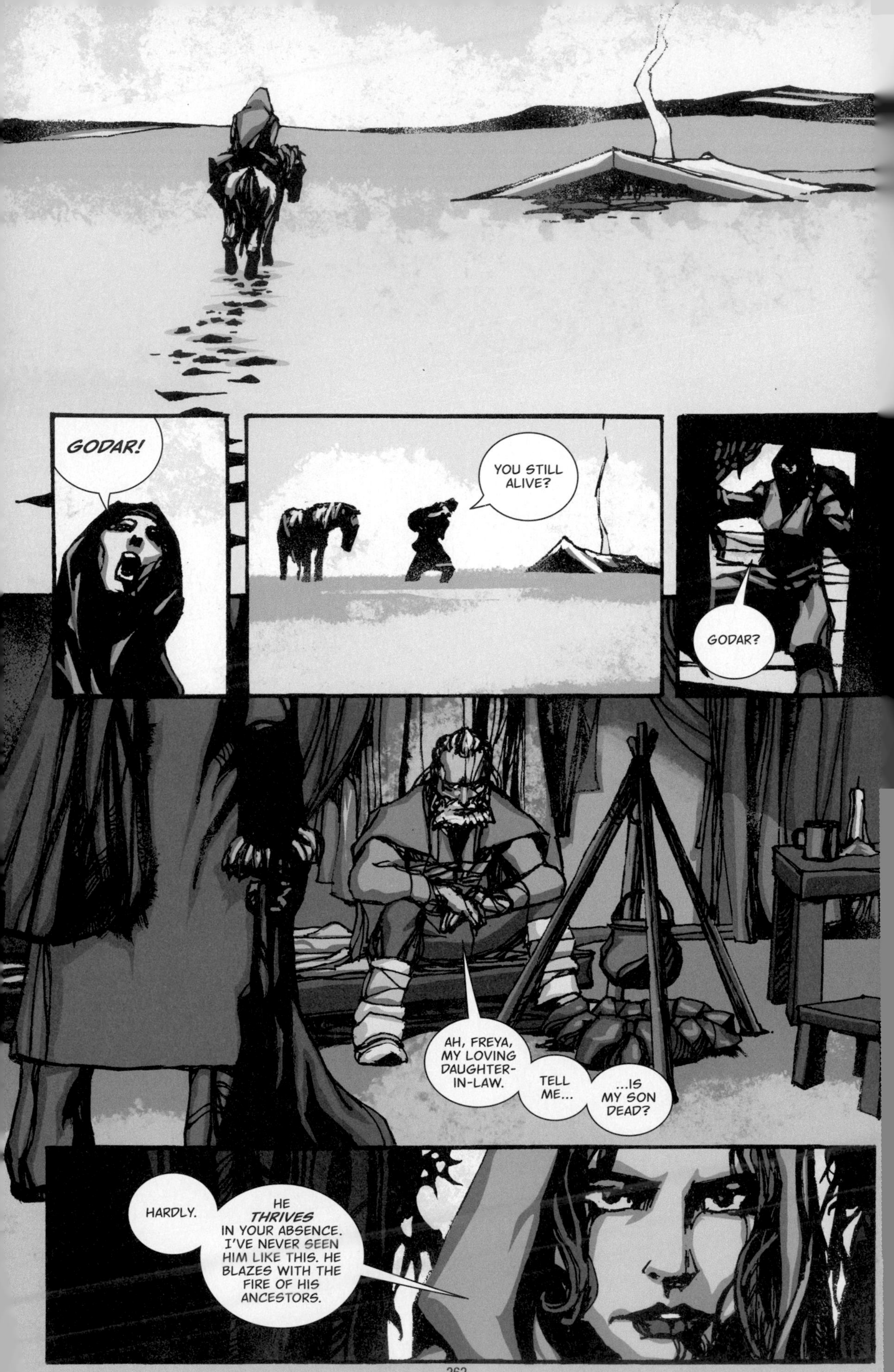
GODAR!
YOU STILL ALIVE?
GODAR?
AH, FREYA, MY LOVING DAUGHTER-IN-LAW.
TELL ME...
...IS MY SON DEAD?
HARDLY.
HE *THRIVES* IN YOUR ABSENCE. I'VE NEVER SEEN HIM LIKE THIS. HE BLAZES WITH THE FIRE OF HIS ANCESTORS.

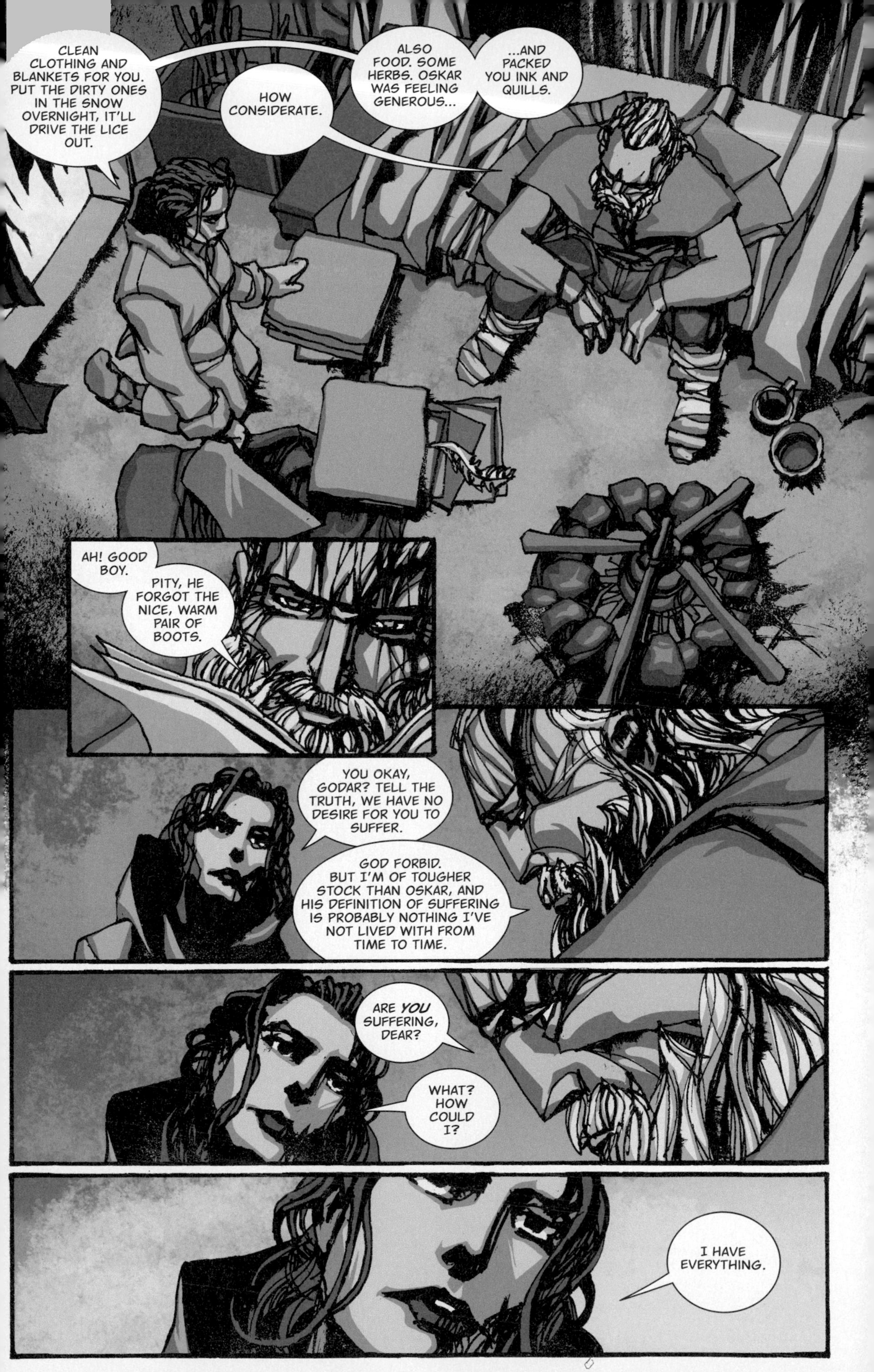
CLEAN CLOTHING AND BLANKETS FOR YOU. PUT THE DIRTY ONES IN THE SNOW OVERNIGHT, IT'LL DRIVE THE LICE OUT.
HOW CONSIDERATE.
ALSO FOOD. SOME HERBS. OSKAR WAS FEELING GENEROUS...
...AND PACKED YOU INK AND QUILLS.
AH! GOOD BOY.
PITY, HE FORGOT THE NICE, WARM PAIR OF BOOTS.
YOU OKAY, GODAR? TELL THE TRUTH, WE HAVE NO DESIRE FOR YOU TO SUFFER.
GOD FORBID. BUT I'M OF TOUGHER STOCK THAN OSKAR, AND HIS DEFINITION OF SUFFERING IS PROBABLY NOTHING I'VE NOT LIVED WITH FROM TIME TO TIME.
ARE *YOU* SUFFERING, DEAR?
WHAT? HOW COULD I?
I HAVE EVERYTHING.

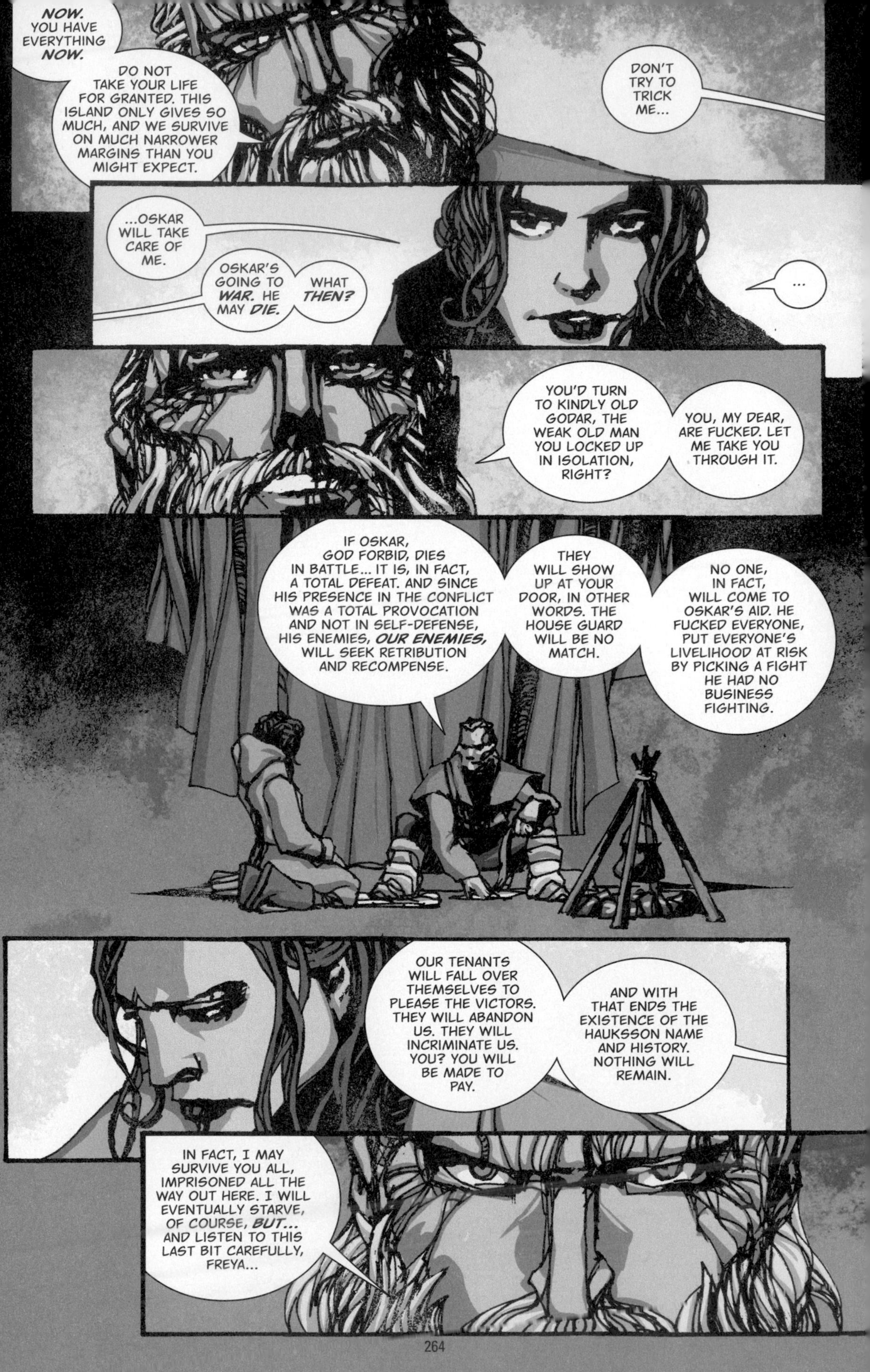
NOW. YOU HAVE EVERYTHING NOW.
DO NOT TAKE YOUR LIFE FOR GRANTED. THIS ISLAND ONLY GIVES SO MUCH, AND WE SURVIVE ON MUCH NARROWER MARGINS THAN YOU MIGHT EXPECT.
DON'T TRY TO TRICK ME...
...OSKAR WILL TAKE CARE OF ME.
OSKAR'S GOING TO WAR. HE MAY DIE.
WHAT THEN?
...
YOU'D TURN TO KINDLY OLD GODAR, THE WEAK OLD MAN YOU LOCKED UP IN ISOLATION, RIGHT?
YOU, MY DEAR, ARE FUCKED. LET ME TAKE YOU THROUGH IT.
IF OSKAR, GOD FORBID, DIES IN BATTLE... IT IS, IN FACT, A TOTAL DEFEAT. AND SINCE HIS PRESENCE IN THE CONFLICT WAS A TOTAL PROVOCATION AND NOT IN SELF-DEFENSE, HIS ENEMIES, OUR ENEMIES, WILL SEEK RETRIBUTION AND RECOMPENSE.
THEY WILL SHOW UP AT YOUR DOOR, IN OTHER WORDS. THE HOUSE GUARD WILL BE NO MATCH.
NO ONE, IN FACT, WILL COME TO OSKAR'S AID. HE FUCKED EVERYONE, PUT EVERYONE'S LIVELIHOOD AT RISK BY PICKING A FIGHT HE HAD NO BUSINESS FIGHTING.
OUR TENANTS WILL FALL OVER THEMSELVES TO PLEASE THE VICTORS. THEY WILL ABANDON US. THEY WILL INCRIMINATE US. YOU? YOU WILL BE MADE TO PAY.
AND WITH THAT ENDS THE EXISTENCE OF THE HAUKSSON NAME AND HISTORY. NOTHING WILL REMAIN.
IN FACT, I MAY SURVIVE YOU ALL, IMPRISONED ALL THE WAY OUT HERE. I WILL EVENTUALLY STARVE, OF COURSE, BUT... AND LISTEN TO THIS LAST BIT CAREFULLY, FREYA...

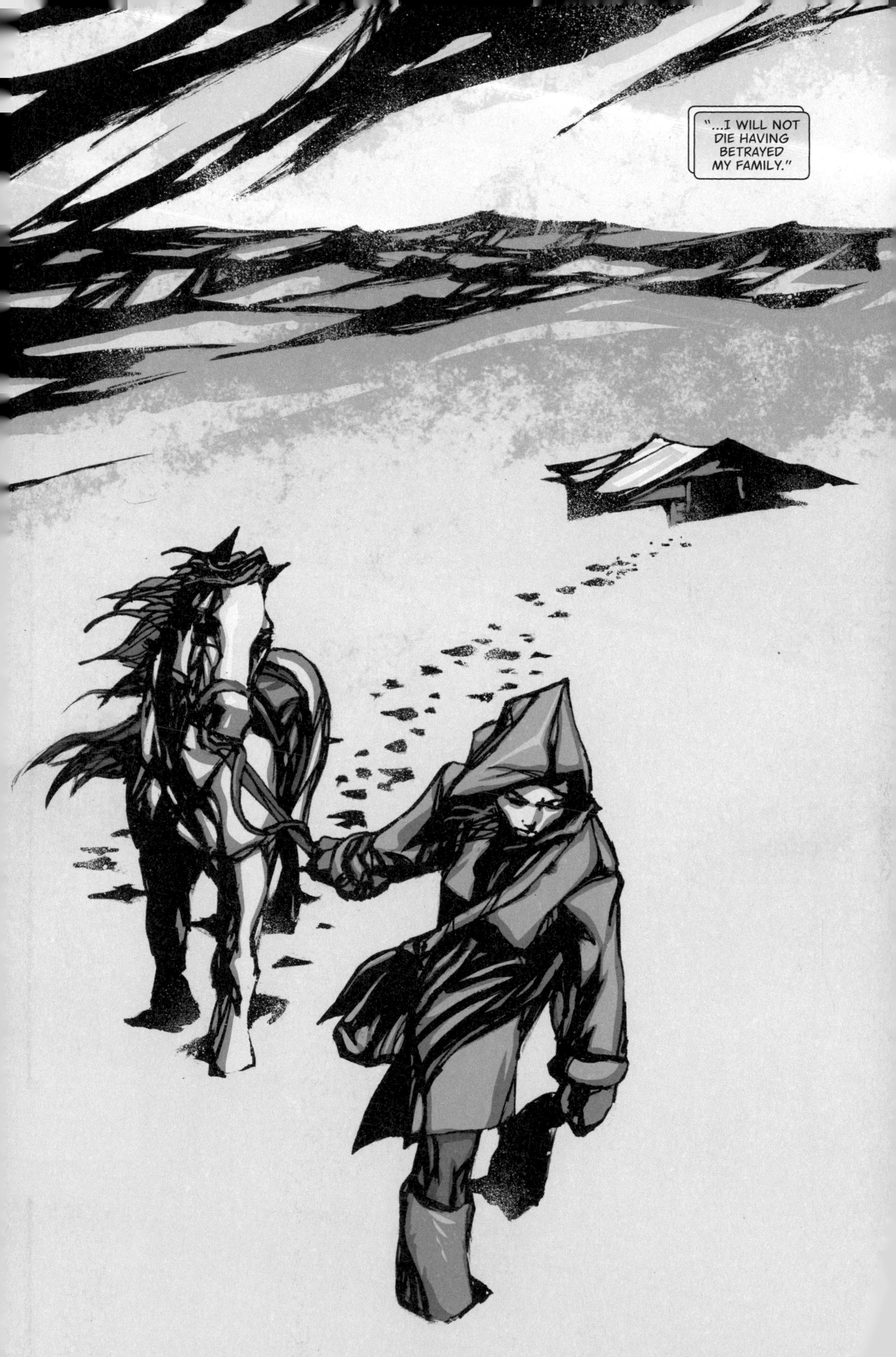
"...I WILL NOT DIE HAVING BETRAYED MY FAMILY."

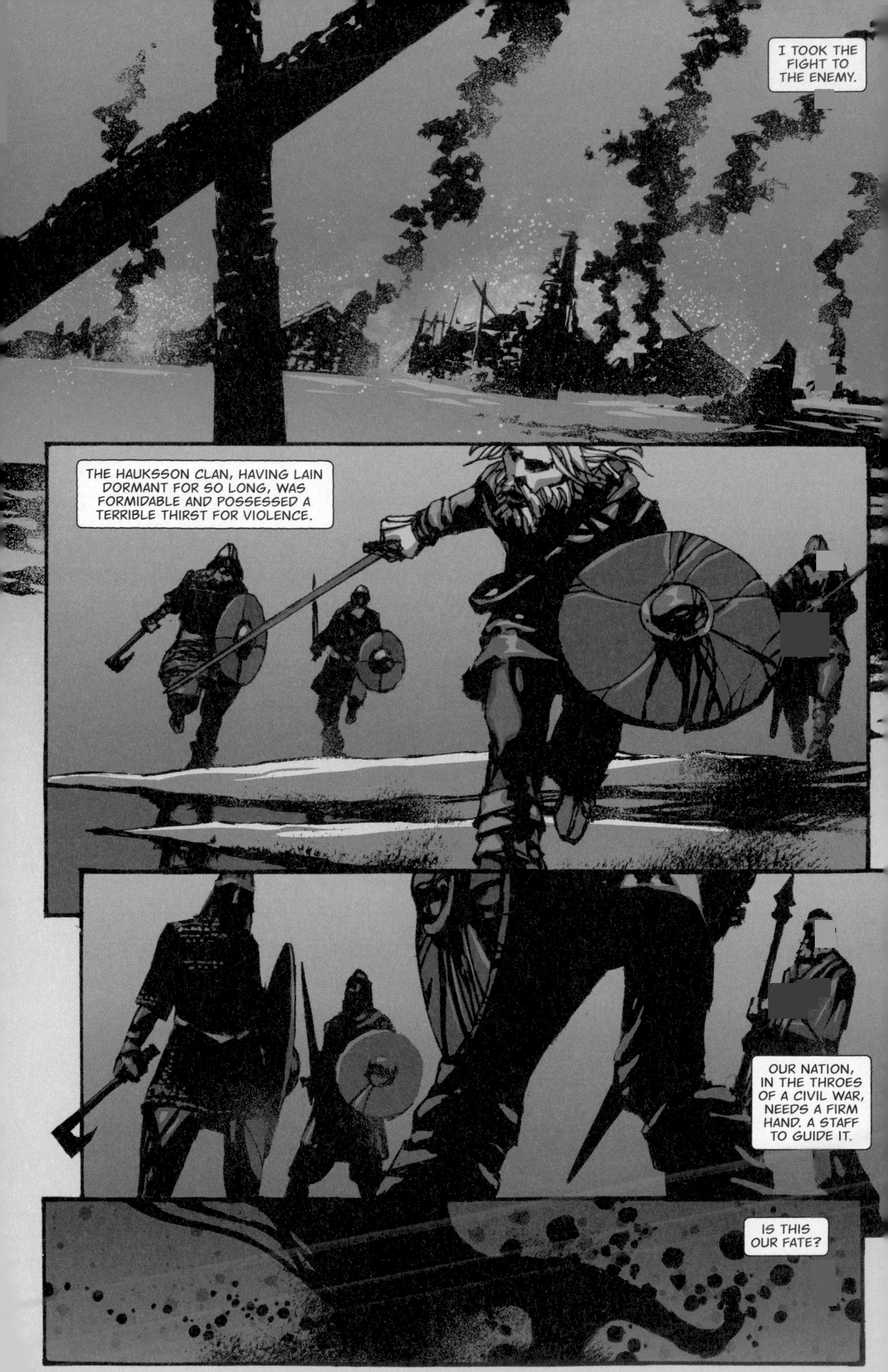

I TOOK THE FIGHT TO THE ENEMY.
THE HAUKSSON CLAN, HAVING LAIN DORMANT FOR SO LONG, WAS FORMIDABLE AND POSSESSED A TERRIBLE THIRST FOR VIOLENCE.
OUR NATION, IN THE THROES OF A CIVIL WAR, NEEDS A FIRM HAND. A STAFF TO GUIDE IT.
IS THIS OUR FATE?

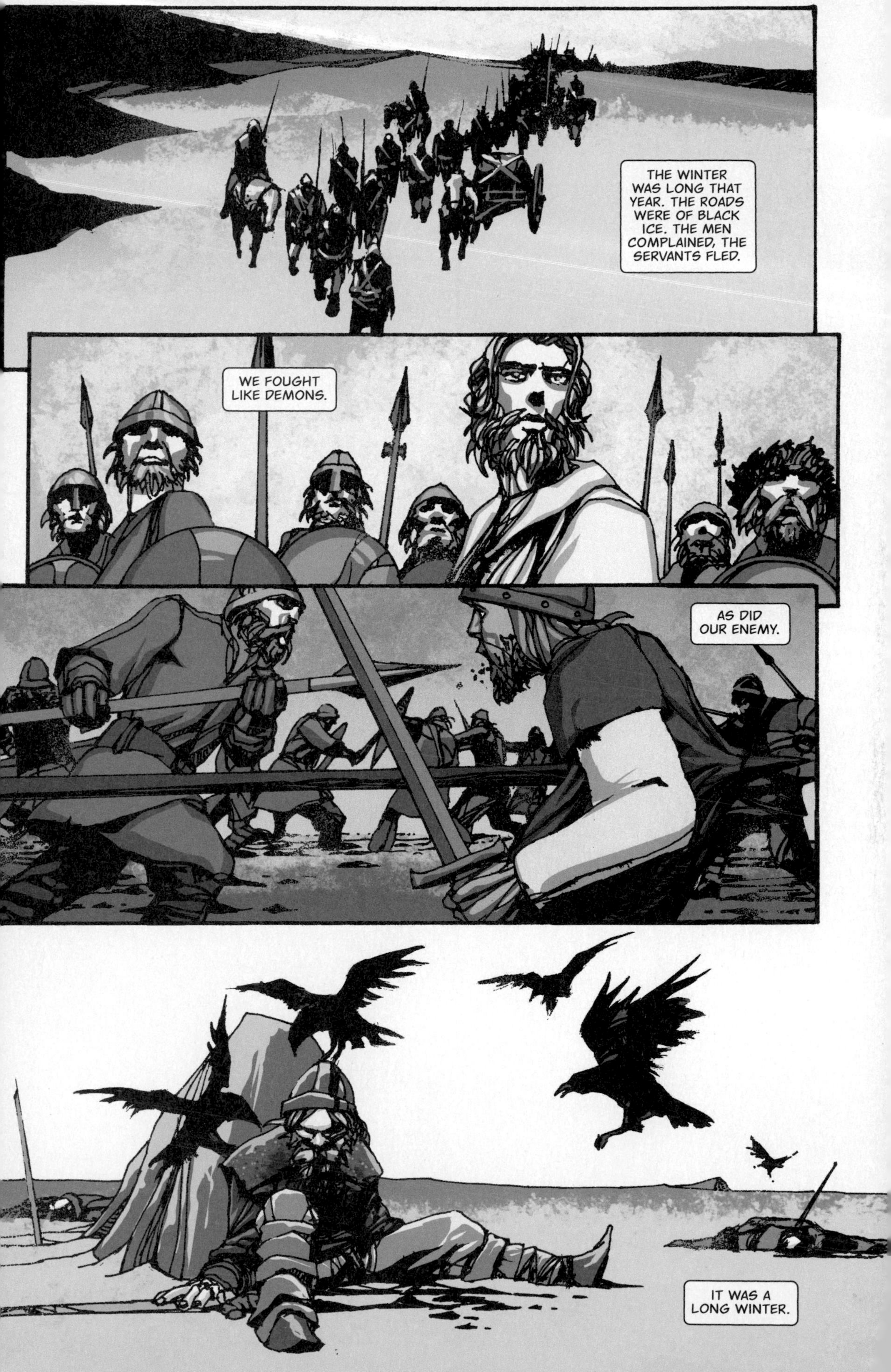
THE WINTER WAS LONG THAT YEAR. THE ROADS WERE OF BLACK ICE. THE MEN COMPLAINED, THE SERVANTS FLED.
WE FOUGHT LIKE DEMONS.
AS DID OUR ENEMY.
IT WAS A LONG WINTER.

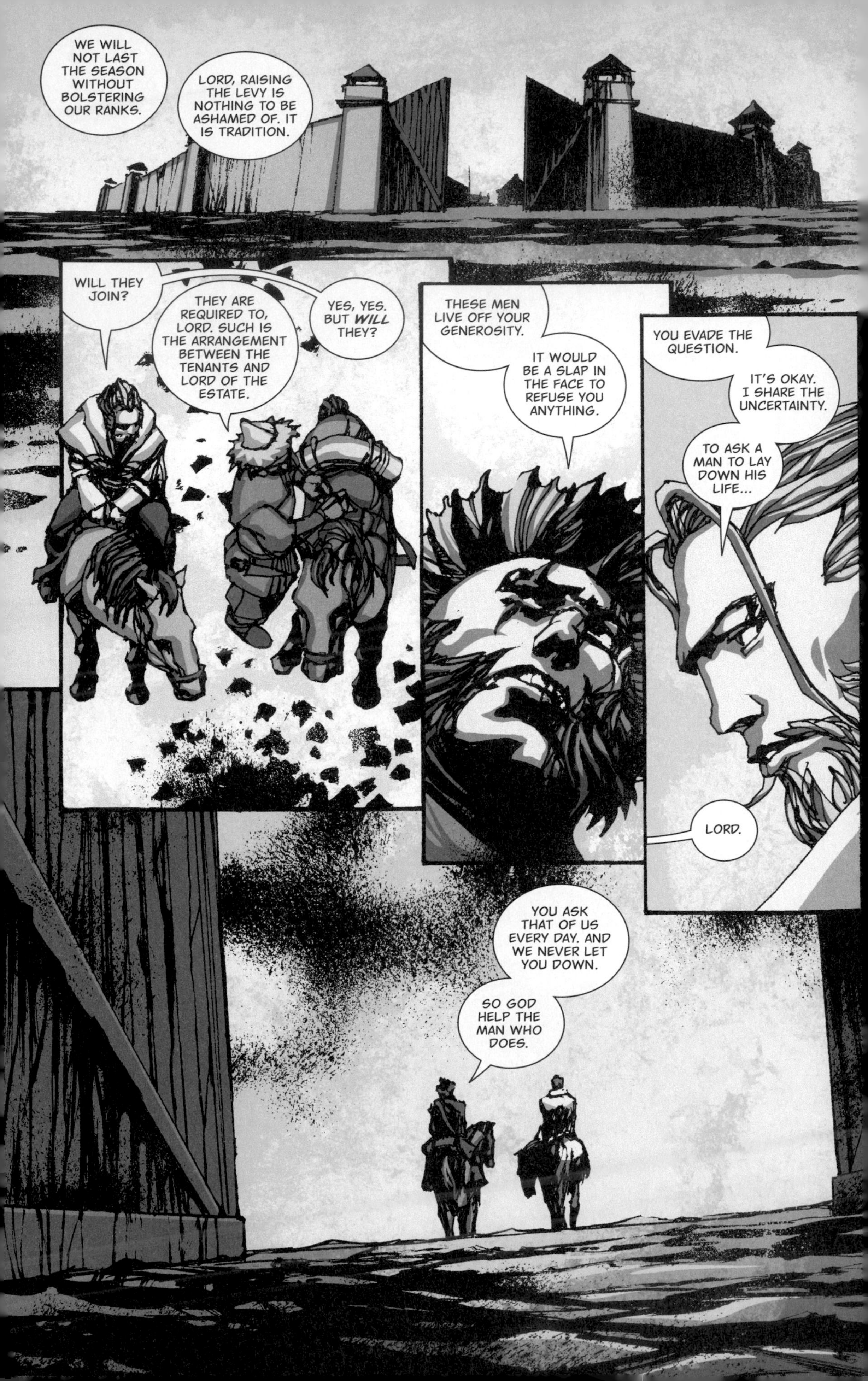
WE WILL NOT LAST THE SEASON WITHOUT BOLSTERING OUR RANKS.
LORD, RAISING THE LEVY IS NOTHING TO BE ASHAMED OF. IT IS TRADITION.
WILL THEY JOIN?
THEY ARE REQUIRED TO, LORD. SUCH IS THE ARRANGEMENT BETWEEN THE TENANTS AND LORD OF THE ESTATE.
YES, YES. BUT *WILL* THEY?
THESE MEN LIVE OFF YOUR GENEROSITY.
IT WOULD BE A SLAP IN THE FACE TO REFUSE YOU ANYTHING.
YOU EVADE THE QUESTION.
IT'S OKAY. I SHARE THE UNCERTAINTY.
TO ASK A MAN TO LAY DOWN HIS LIFE...
LORD.
YOU ASK THAT OF US EVERY DAY. AND WE NEVER LET YOU DOWN.
SO GOD HELP THE MAN WHO DOES.

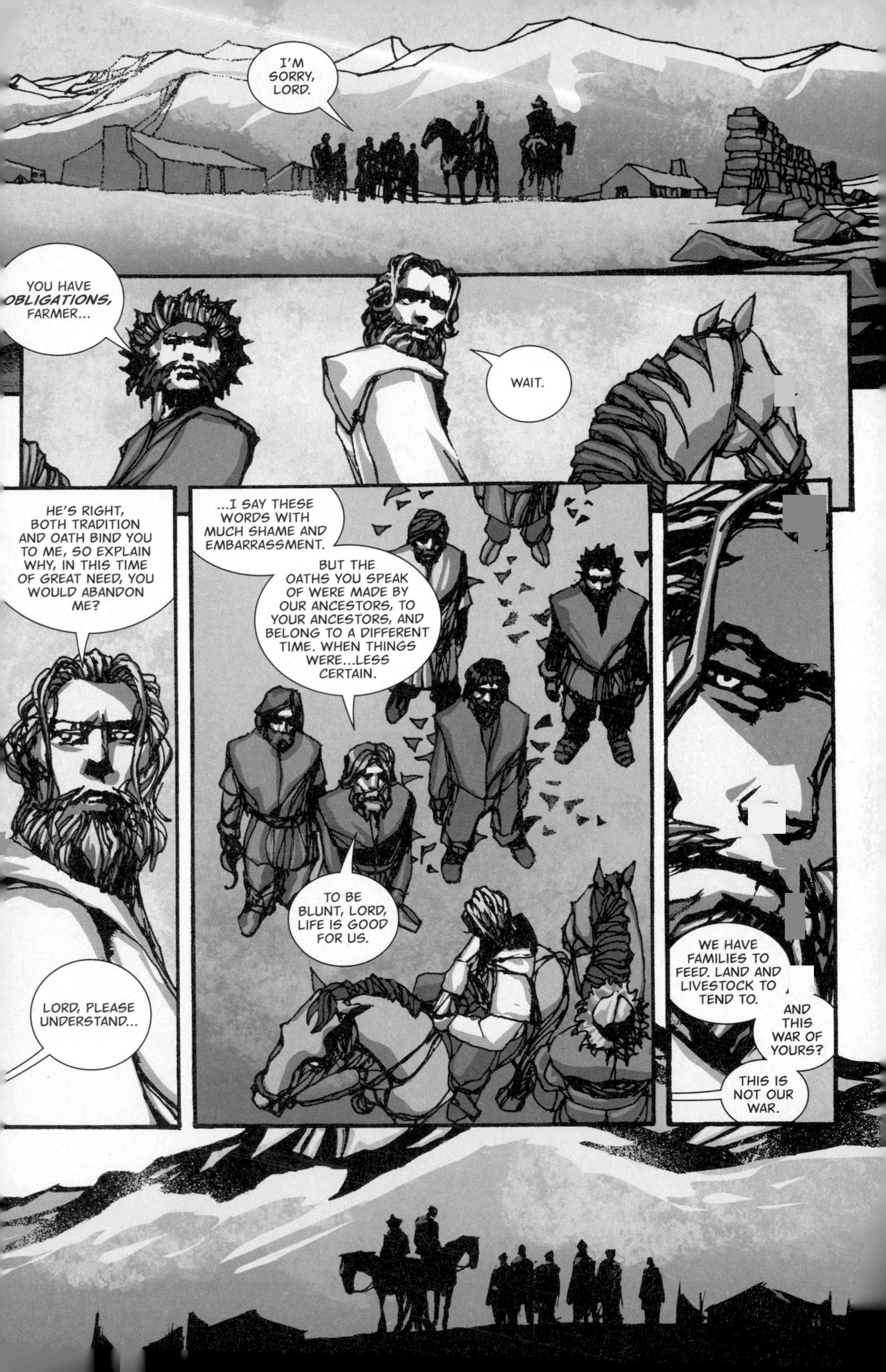
I'M SORRY, LORD.
YOU HAVE *OBLIGATIONS,* FARMER...
WAIT.
HE'S RIGHT, BOTH TRADITION AND OATH BIND YOU TO ME, SO EXPLAIN WHY, IN THIS TIME OF GREAT NEED, YOU WOULD ABANDON ME?
LORD, PLEASE UNDERSTAND...
...I SAY THESE WORDS WITH MUCH SHAME AND EMBARRASSMENT.
BUT THE OATHS YOU SPEAK OF WERE MADE BY OUR ANCESTORS, TO YOUR ANCESTORS, AND BELONG TO A DIFFERENT TIME. WHEN THINGS WERE...LESS CERTAIN.
TO BE BLUNT, LORD, LIFE IS GOOD FOR US.
WE HAVE FAMILIES TO FEED. LAND AND LIVESTOCK TO TEND TO.
AND THIS WAR OF YOURS?
THIS IS NOT OUR WAR.

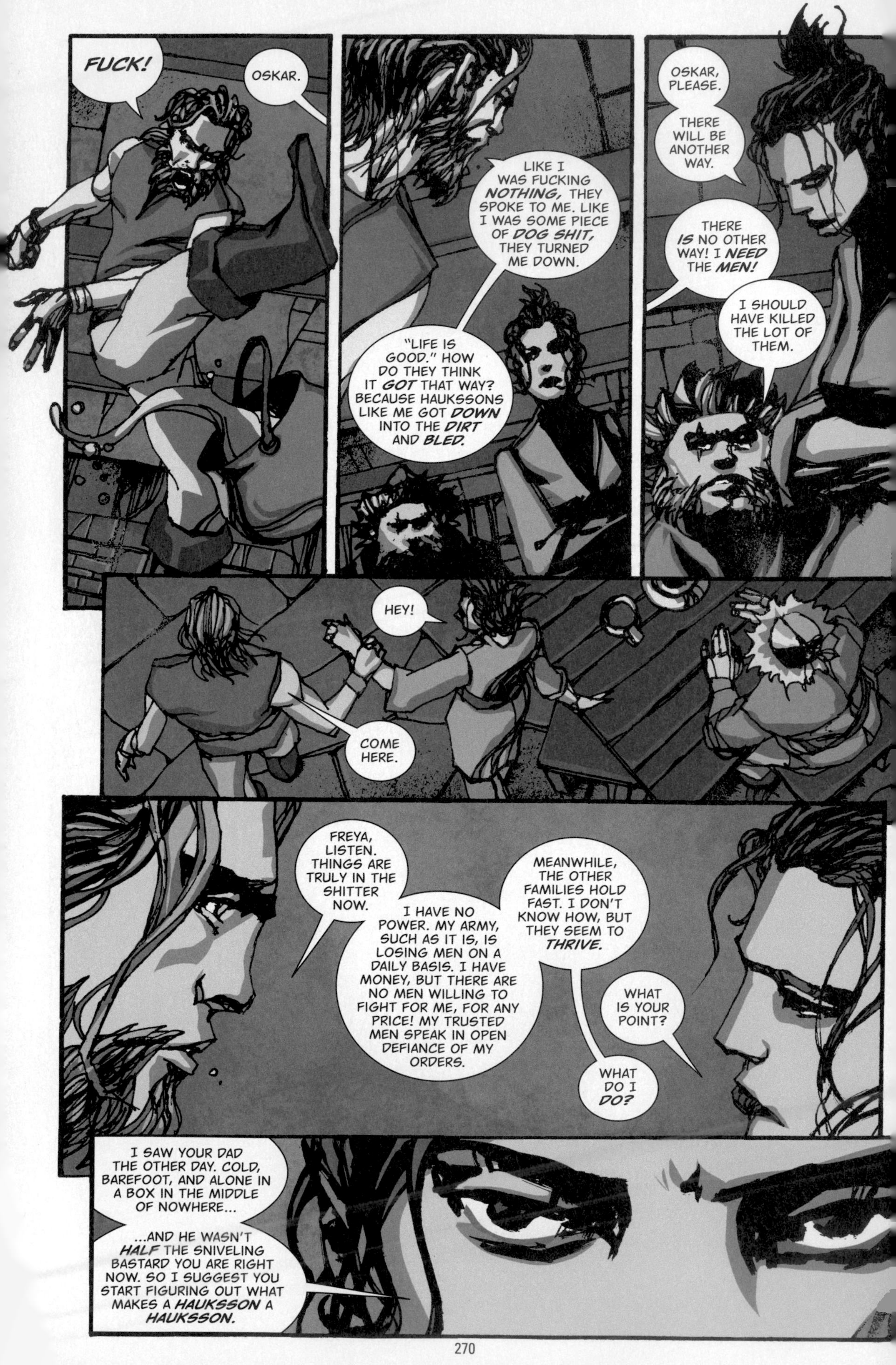
FUCK!
OSKAR.
LIKE I WAS FUCKING NOTHING, THEY SPOKE TO ME. LIKE I WAS SOME PIECE OF DOG SHIT, THEY TURNED ME DOWN.
"LIFE IS GOOD." HOW DO THEY THINK IT GOT THAT WAY? BECAUSE HAUKSSONS LIKE ME GOT DOWN INTO THE DIRT AND BLED.
OSKAR, PLEASE.
THERE WILL BE ANOTHER WAY.
THERE IS NO OTHER WAY! I NEED THE MEN!
I SHOULD HAVE KILLED THE LOT OF THEM.
HEY!
COME HERE.
FREYA, LISTEN. THINGS ARE TRULY IN THE SHITTER NOW.
I HAVE NO POWER. MY ARMY, SUCH AS IT IS, IS LOSING MEN ON A DAILY BASIS. I HAVE MONEY, BUT THERE ARE NO MEN WILLING TO FIGHT FOR ME, FOR ANY PRICE! MY TRUSTED MEN SPEAK IN OPEN DEFIANCE OF MY ORDERS.
MEANWHILE, THE OTHER FAMILIES HOLD FAST. I DON'T KNOW HOW, BUT THEY SEEM TO THRIVE.
WHAT DO I DO?
WHAT IS YOUR POINT?
I SAW YOUR DAD THE OTHER DAY. COLD, BAREFOOT, AND ALONE IN A BOX IN THE MIDDLE OF NOWHERE...
...AND HE WASN'T HALF THE SNIVELING BASTARD YOU ARE RIGHT NOW. SO I SUGGEST YOU START FIGURING OUT WHAT MAKES A HAUKSSON A HAUKSSON.

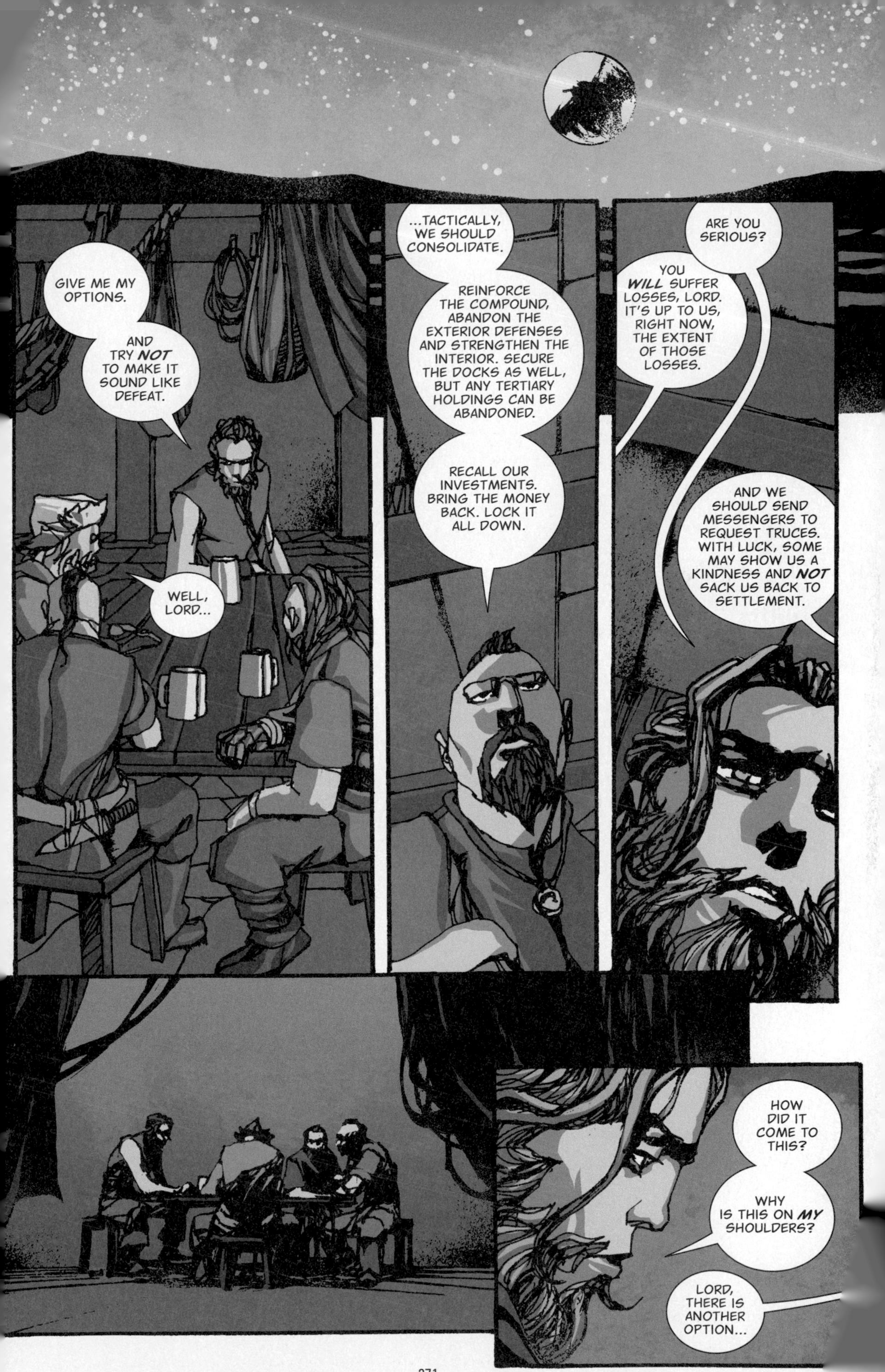
GIVE ME MY OPTIONS.
AND TRY NOT TO MAKE IT SOUND LIKE DEFEAT.
WELL, LORD...
...TACTICALLY, WE SHOULD CONSOLIDATE.
REINFORCE THE COMPOUND, ABANDON THE EXTERIOR DEFENSES AND STRENGTHEN THE INTERIOR. SECURE THE DOCKS AS WELL, BUT ANY TERTIARY HOLDINGS CAN BE ABANDONED.
RECALL OUR INVESTMENTS. BRING THE MONEY BACK. LOCK IT ALL DOWN.
ARE YOU SERIOUS?
YOU WILL SUFFER LOSSES, LORD. IT'S UP TO US, RIGHT NOW, THE EXTENT OF THOSE LOSSES.
AND WE SHOULD SEND MESSENGERS TO REQUEST TRUCES. WITH LUCK, SOME MAY SHOW US A KINDNESS AND NOT SACK US BACK TO SETTLEMENT.
HOW DID IT COME TO THIS?
WHY IS THIS ON MY SHOULDERS?
LORD, THERE IS ANOTHER OPTION...

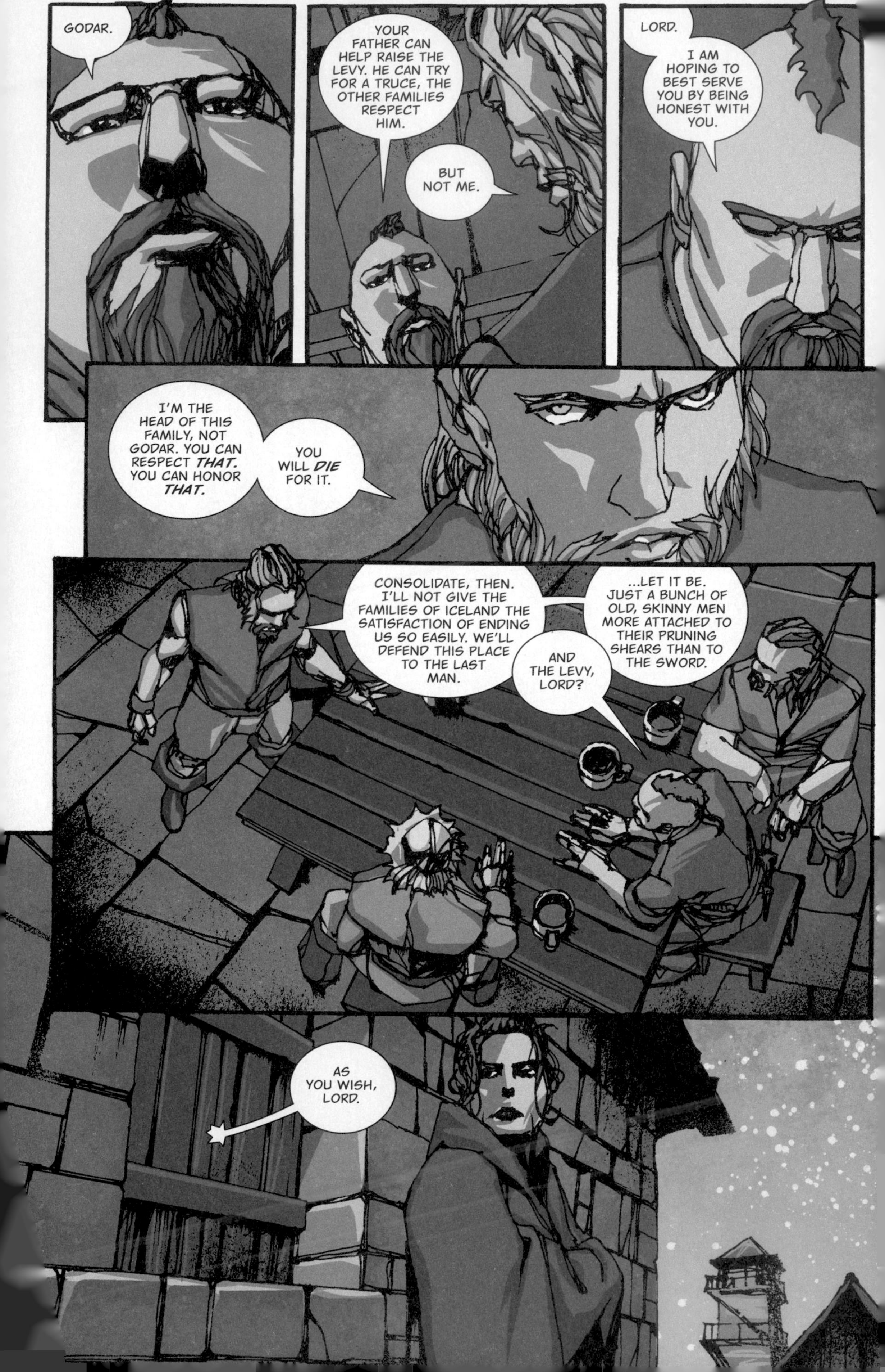
GODAR.
YOUR FATHER CAN HELP RAISE THE LEVY. HE CAN TRY FOR A TRUCE, THE OTHER FAMILIES RESPECT HIM.
BUT NOT ME.
LORD.
I AM HOPING TO BEST SERVE YOU BY BEING HONEST WITH YOU.
I'M THE HEAD OF THIS FAMILY, NOT GODAR. YOU CAN RESPECT *THAT.* YOU CAN HONOR *THAT.*
YOU WILL *DIE* FOR IT.
AND THE LEVY, LORD?
...LET IT BE. JUST A BUNCH OF OLD, SKINNY MEN MORE ATTACHED TO THEIR PRUNING SHEARS THAN TO THE SWORD.
CONSOLIDATE, THEN. I'LL NOT GIVE THE FAMILIES OF ICELAND THE SATISFACTION OF ENDING US SO EASILY. WE'LL DEFEND THIS PLACE TO THE LAST MAN.
AS YOU WISH, LORD.

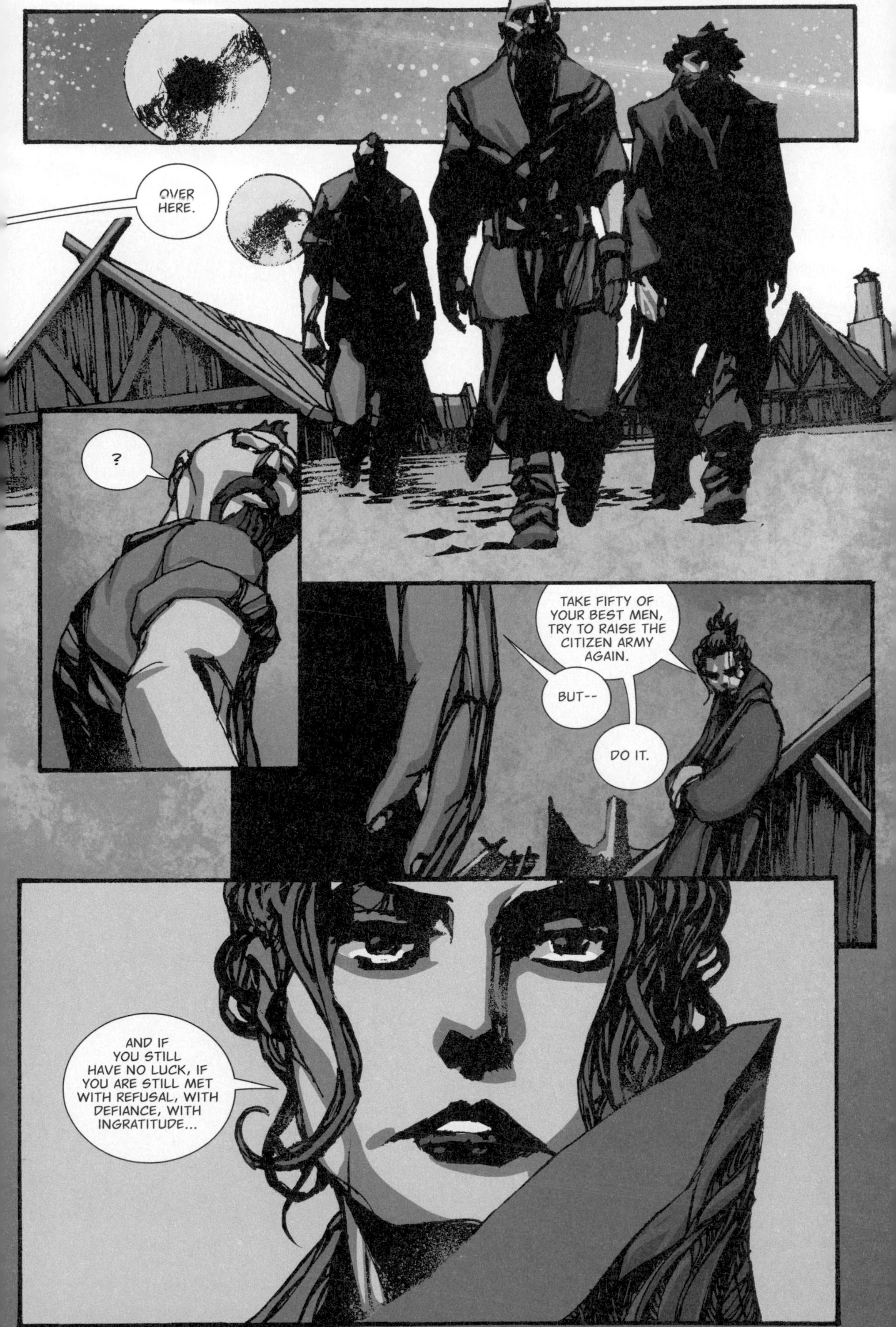
OVER HERE.
?
TAKE FIFTY OF YOUR BEST MEN, TRY TO RAISE THE CITIZEN ARMY AGAIN.
BUT--
DO IT.
AND IF YOU STILL HAVE NO LUCK, IF YOU ARE STILL MET WITH REFUSAL, WITH DEFIANCE, WITH INGRATITUDE...

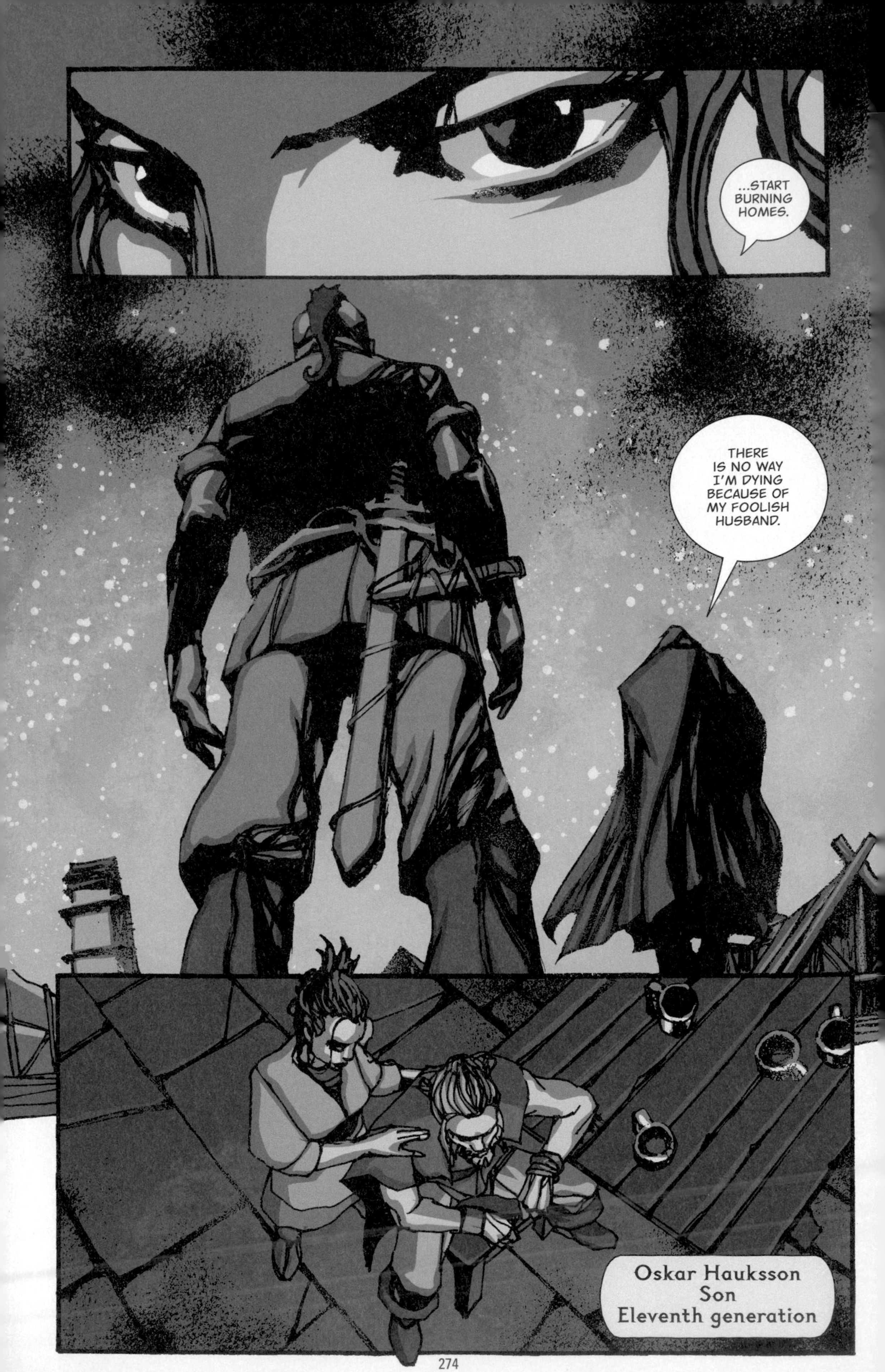
...START BURNING HOMES.
THERE IS NO WAY I'M DYING BECAUSE OF MY FOOLISH HUSBAND.
Oskar Hauksson
Son
Eleventh generation

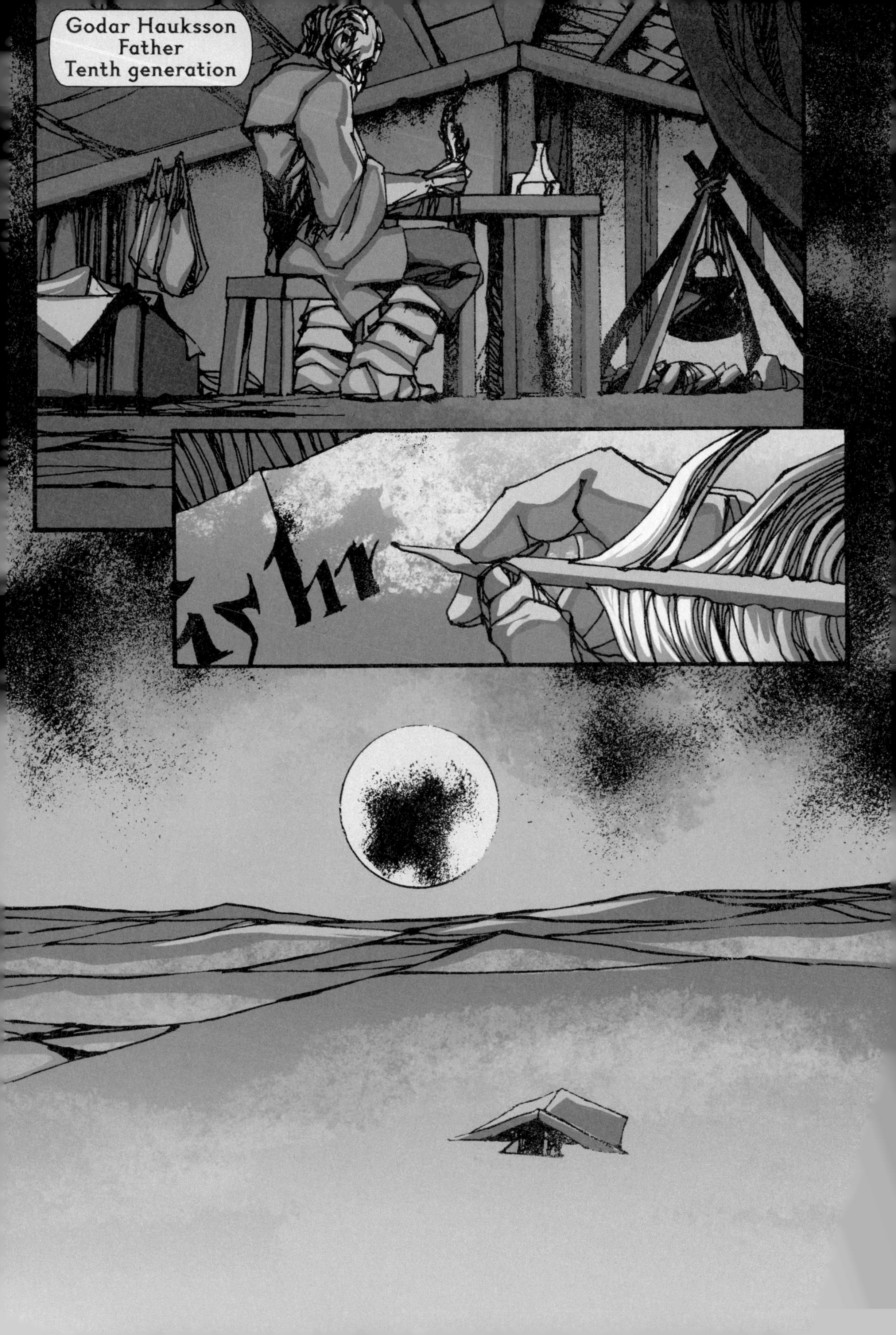
Godar Hauksson
Father
Tenth generation

Chapter IX
Waygone
A.D. 1260

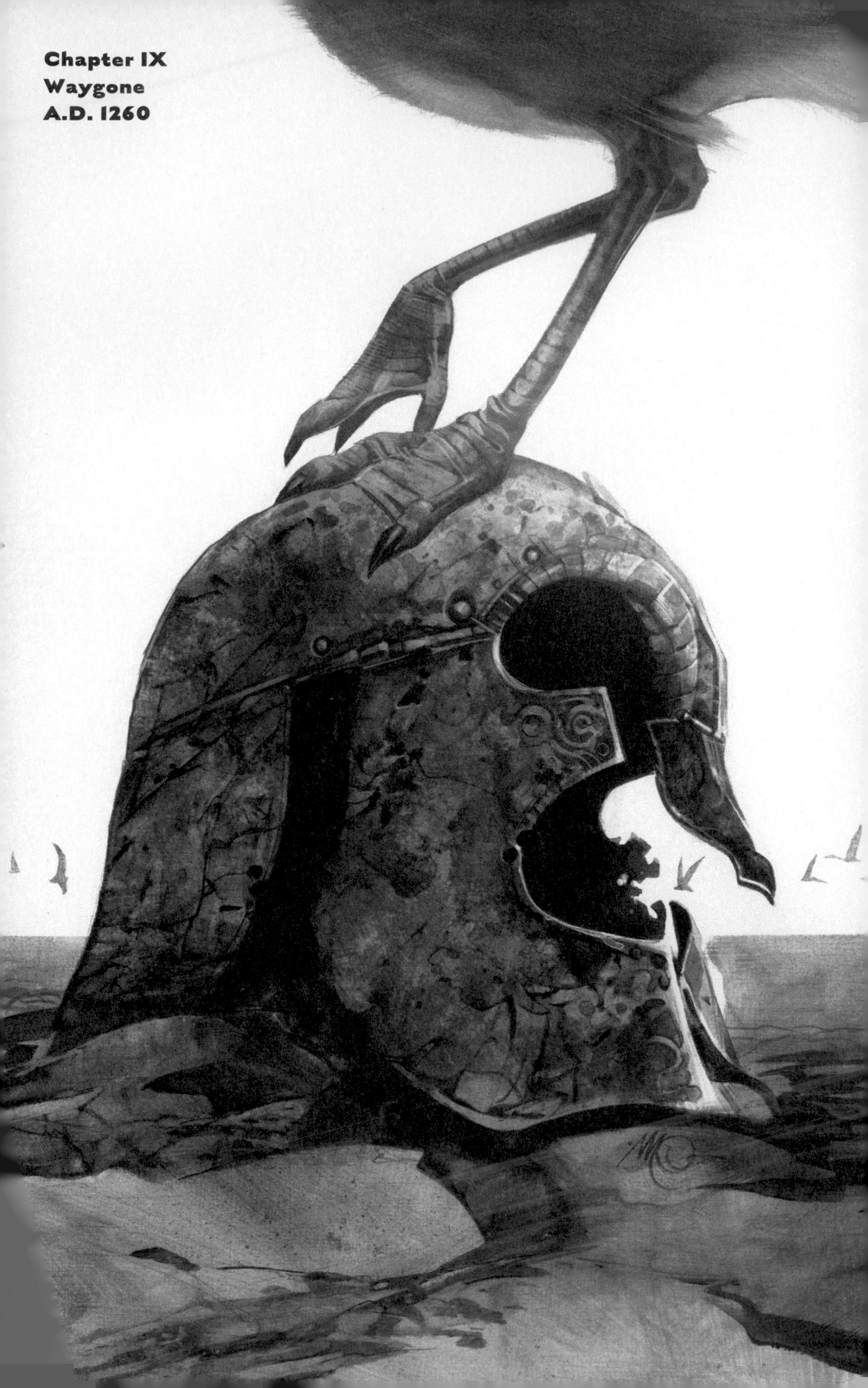

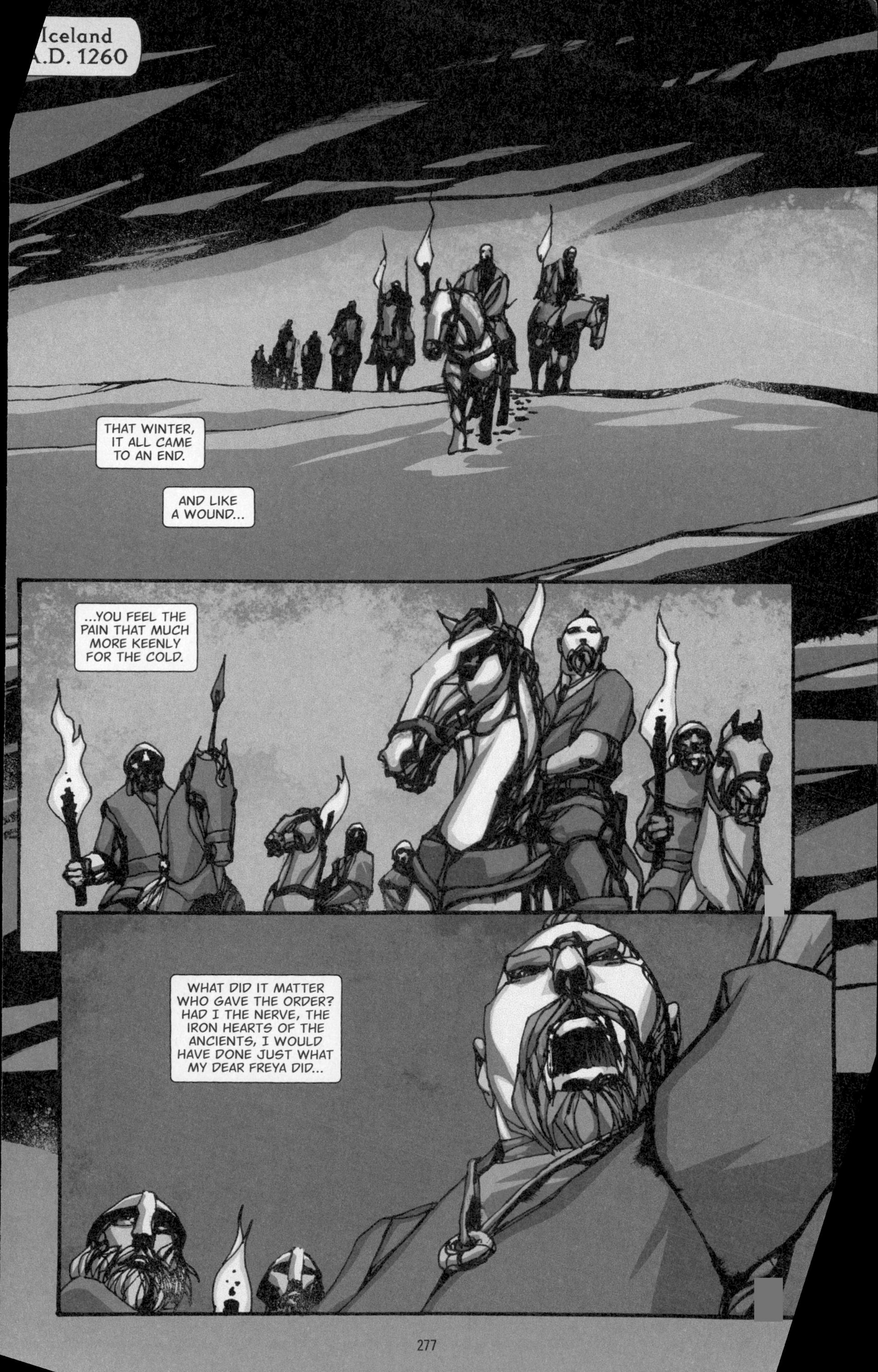
Iceland
A.D. 1260
THAT WINTER, IT ALL CAME TO AN END.
AND LIKE A WOUND...
...YOU FEEL THE PAIN THAT MUCH MORE KEENLY FOR THE COLD.
WHAT DID IT MATTER WHO GAVE THE ORDER? HAD I THE NERVE, THE IRON HEARTS OF THE ANCIENTS, I WOULD HAVE DONE JUST WHAT MY DEAR FREYA DID...

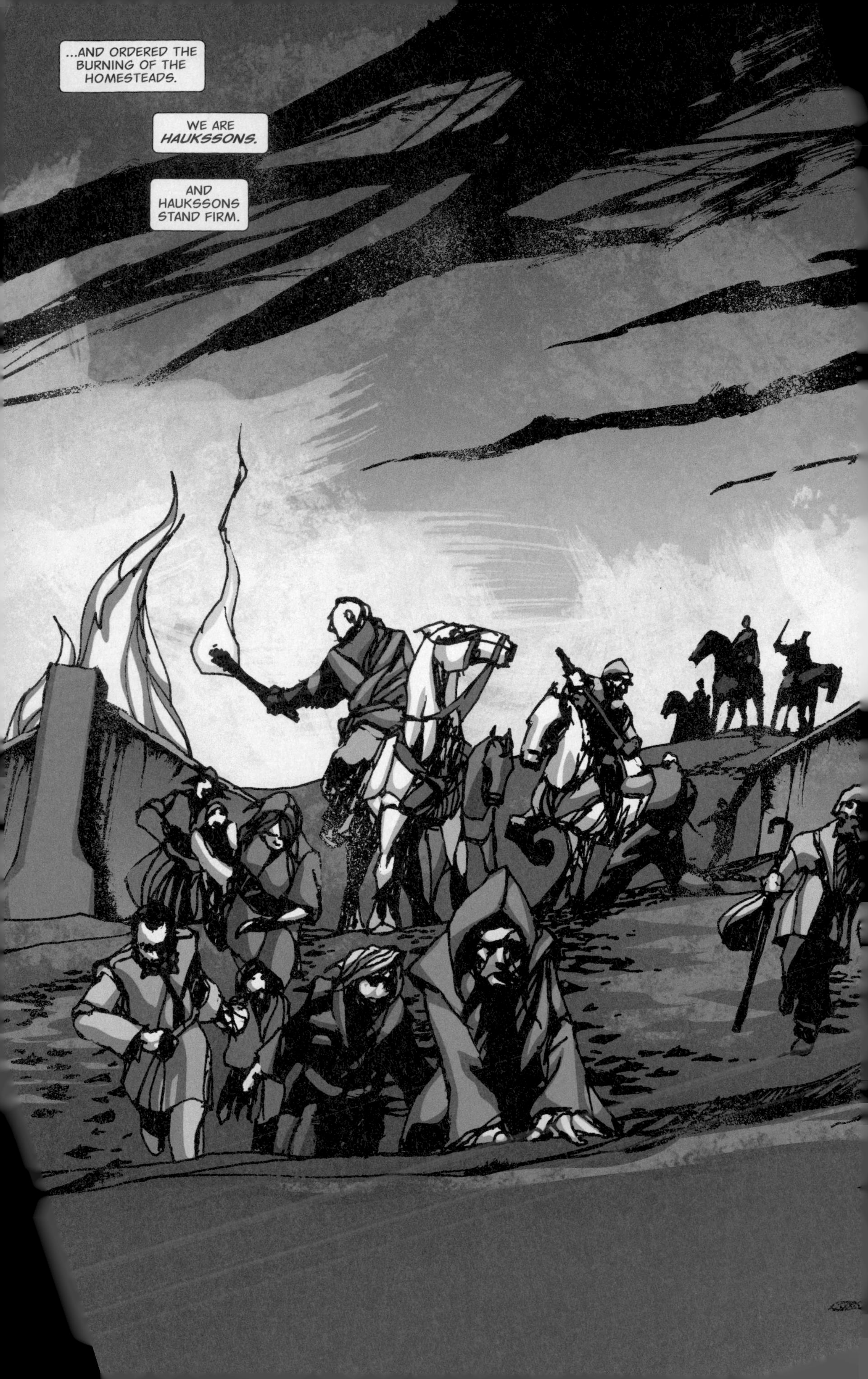
...AND ORDERED THE BURNING OF THE HOMESTEADS.
WE ARE *HAUKSSONS.*
AND HAUKSSONS STAND FIRM.

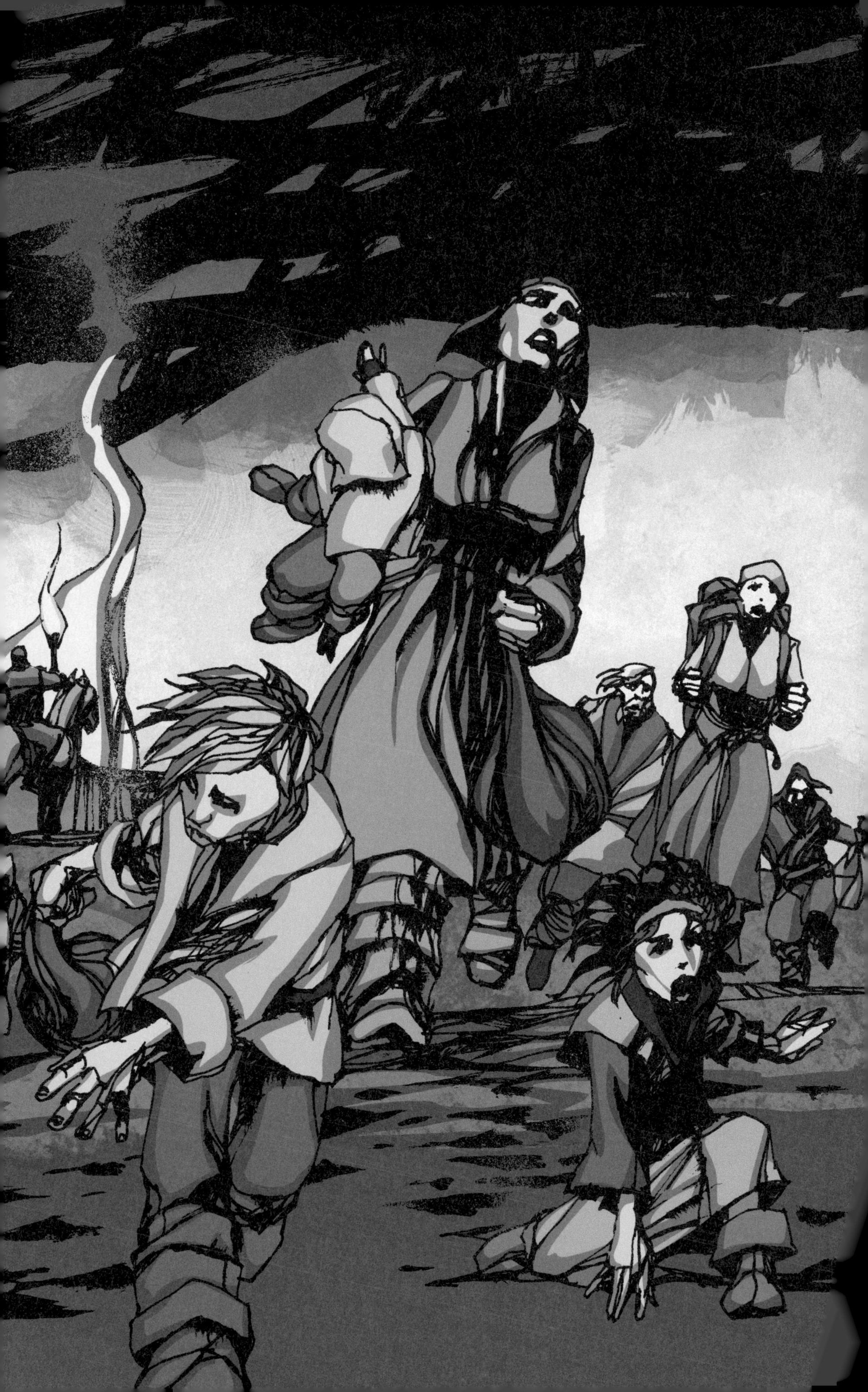

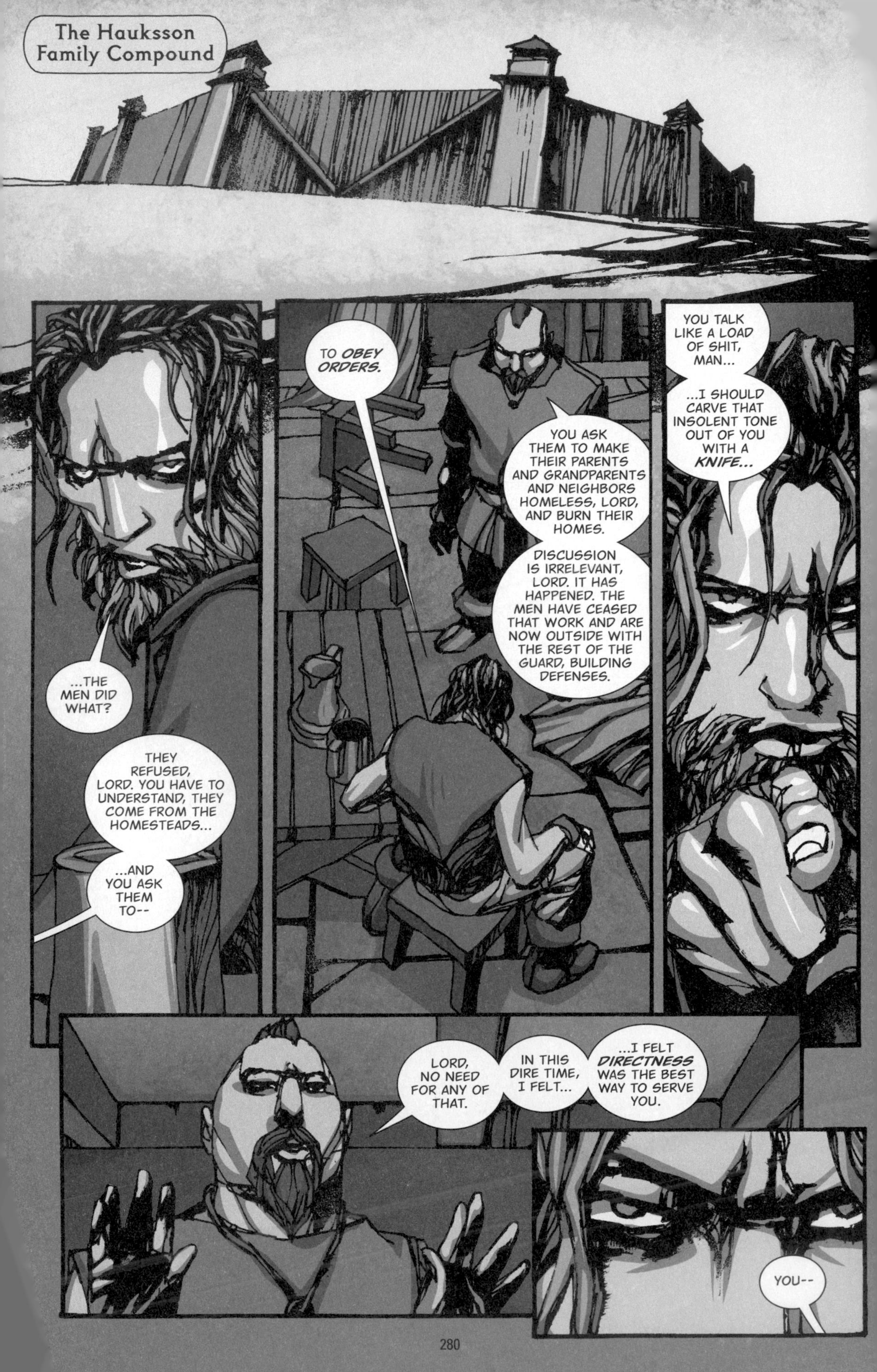
The Hauksson Family Compound
...THE MEN DID WHAT?
THEY REFUSED, LORD. YOU HAVE TO UNDERSTAND, THEY COME FROM THE HOMESTEADS...
...AND YOU ASK THEM TO--
TO OBEY ORDERS.
YOU ASK THEM TO MAKE THEIR PARENTS AND GRANDPARENTS AND NEIGHBORS HOMELESS, LORD, AND BURN THEIR HOMES.
DISCUSSION IS IRRELEVANT, LORD. IT HAS HAPPENED. THE MEN HAVE CEASED THAT WORK AND ARE NOW OUTSIDE WITH THE REST OF THE GUARD, BUILDING DEFENSES.
YOU TALK LIKE A LOAD OF SHIT, MAN...
...I SHOULD CARVE THAT INSOLENT TONE OUT OF YOU WITH A KNIFE...
LORD, NO NEED FOR ANY OF THAT.
IN THIS DIRE TIME, I FELT...
...I FELT DIRECTNESS WAS THE BEST WAY TO SERVE YOU.
YOU--

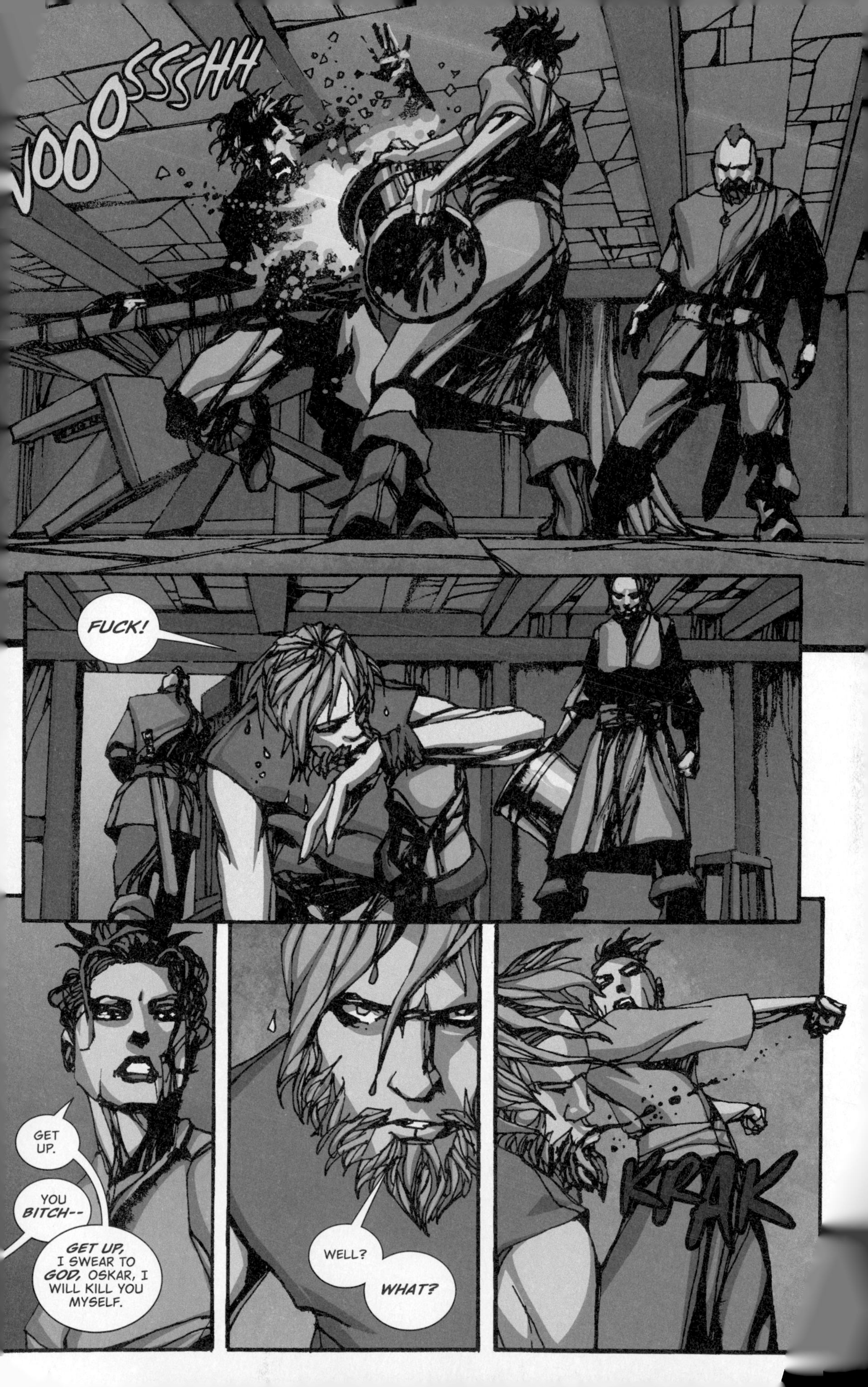
VOOOSSSHH
FUCK!
GET UP.
YOU BITCH--
GET UP, I SWEAR TO GOD, OSKAR, I WILL KILL YOU MYSELF.
WELL?
WHAT?
KRAK

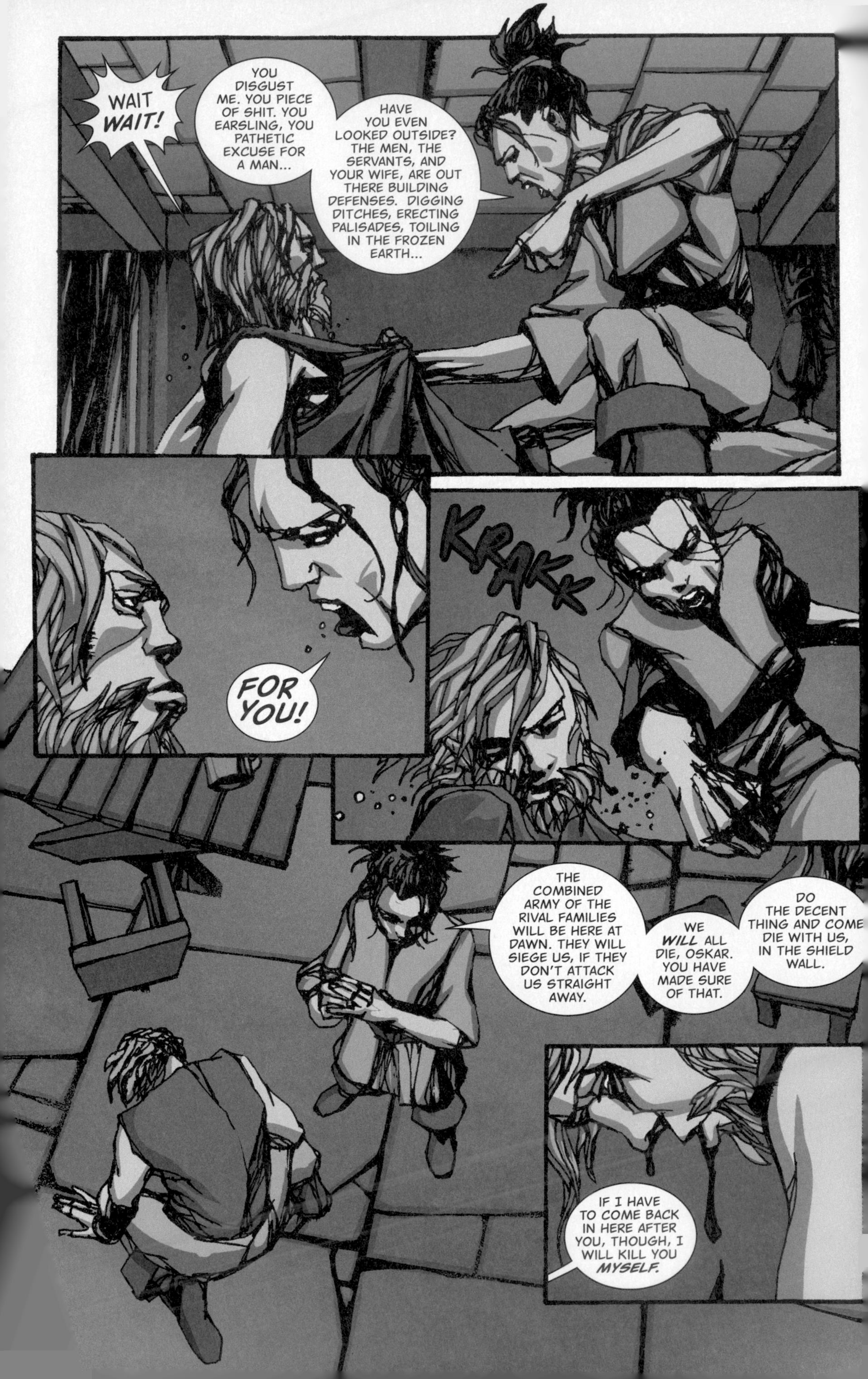
WAIT WAIT!
YOU DISGUST ME. YOU PIECE OF SHIT. YOU EARSLING, YOU PATHETIC EXCUSE FOR A MAN...
HAVE YOU EVEN LOOKED OUTSIDE? THE MEN, THE SERVANTS, AND YOUR WIFE, ARE OUT THERE BUILDING DEFENSES. DIGGING DITCHES, ERECTING PALISADES, TOILING IN THE FROZEN EARTH...
FOR YOU!
KRAKK
THE COMBINED ARMY OF THE RIVAL FAMILIES WILL BE HERE AT DAWN. THEY WILL SIEGE US, IF THEY DON'T ATTACK US STRAIGHT AWAY.
WE WILL ALL DIE, OSKAR. YOU HAVE MADE SURE OF THAT.
DO THE DECENT THING AND COME DIE WITH US, IN THE SHIELD WALL.
IF I HAVE TO COME BACK IN HERE AFTER YOU, THOUGH, I WILL KILL YOU MYSELF.

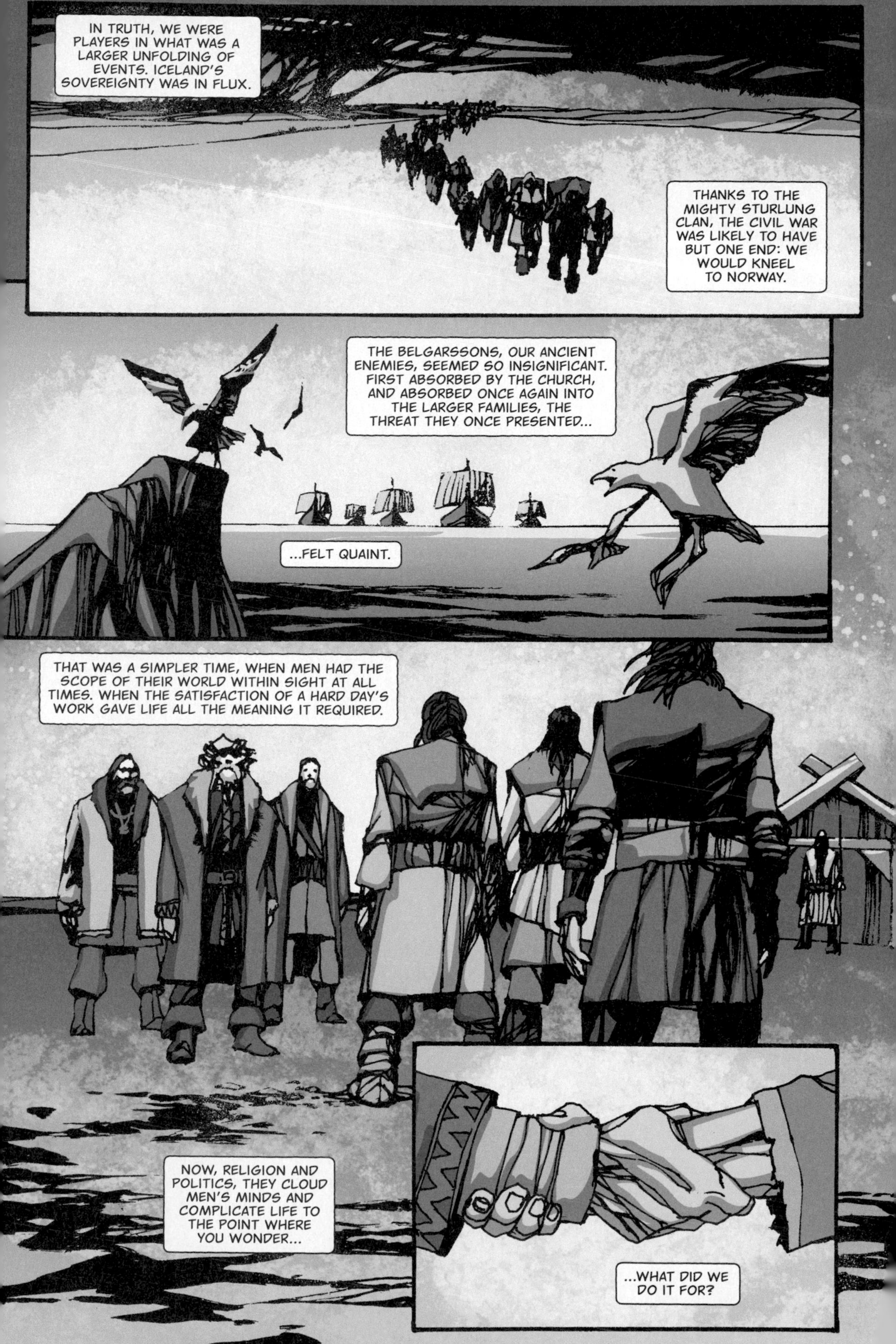
IN TRUTH, WE WERE PLAYERS IN WHAT WAS A LARGER UNFOLDING OF EVENTS. ICELAND'S SOVEREIGNTY WAS IN FLUX.
THANKS TO THE MIGHTY STURLUNG CLAN, THE CIVIL WAR WAS LIKELY TO HAVE BUT ONE END: WE WOULD KNEEL TO NORWAY.
THE BELGARSSONS, OUR ANCIENT ENEMIES, SEEMED SO INSIGNIFICANT. FIRST ABSORBED BY THE CHURCH, AND ABSORBED ONCE AGAIN INTO THE LARGER FAMILIES, THE THREAT THEY ONCE PRESENTED...
...FELT QUAINT.
THAT WAS A SIMPLER TIME, WHEN MEN HAD THE SCOPE OF THEIR WORLD WITHIN SIGHT AT ALL TIMES. WHEN THE SATISFACTION OF A HARD DAY'S WORK GAVE LIFE ALL THE MEANING IT REQUIRED.
NOW, RELIGION AND POLITICS, THEY CLOUD MEN'S MINDS AND COMPLICATE LIFE TO THE POINT WHERE YOU WONDER...
...WHAT DID WE DO IT FOR?

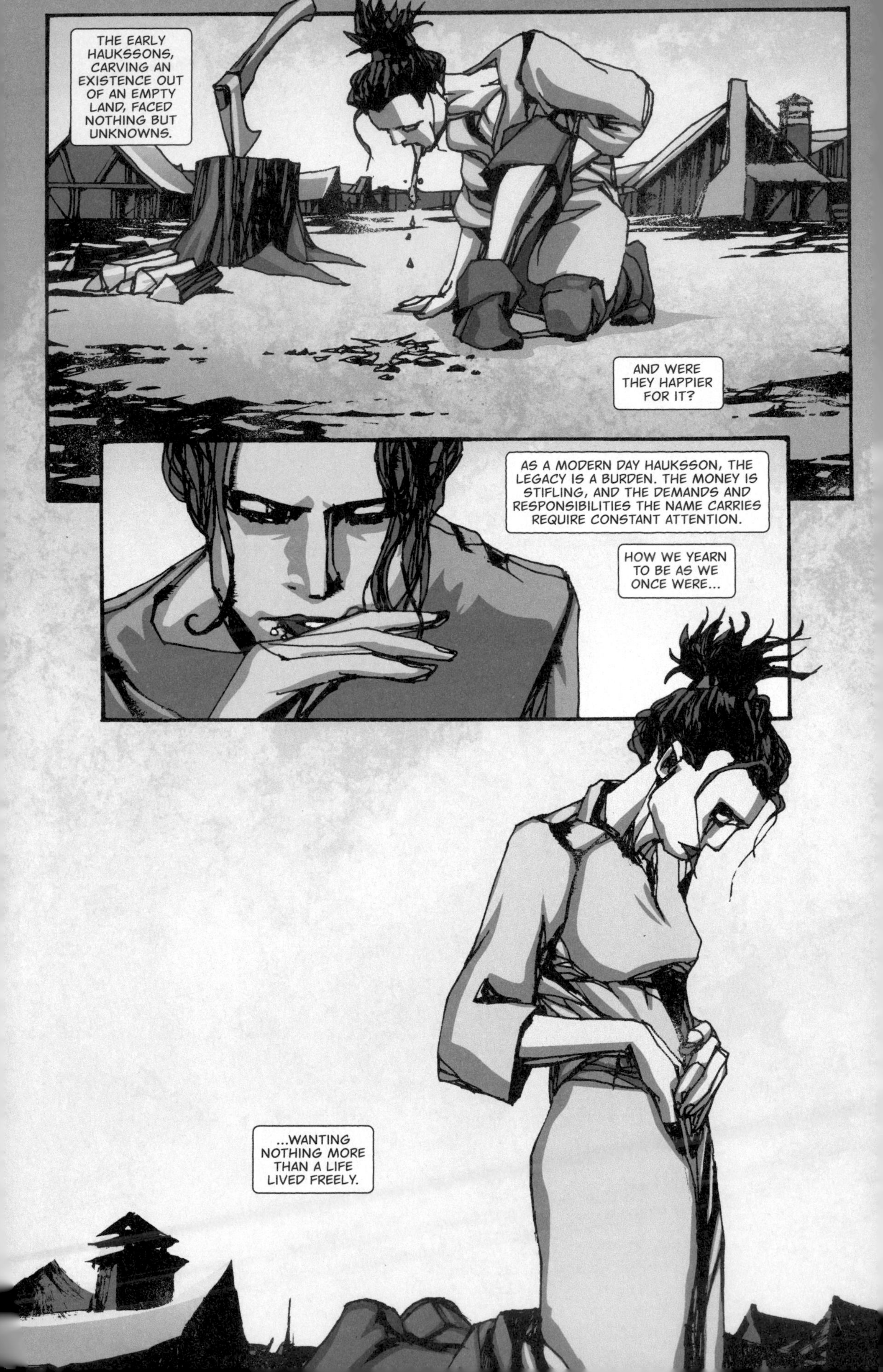
THE EARLY HAUKSSONS, CARVING AN EXISTENCE OUT OF AN EMPTY LAND, FACED NOTHING BUT UNKNOWNS.
AND WERE THEY HAPPIER FOR IT?
AS A MODERN DAY HAUKSSON, THE LEGACY IS A BURDEN. THE MONEY IS STIFLING, AND THE DEMANDS AND RESPONSIBILITIES THE NAME CARRIES REQUIRE CONSTANT ATTENTION.
HOW WE YEARN TO BE AS WE ONCE WERE...
...WANTING NOTHING MORE THAN A LIFE LIVED FREELY.

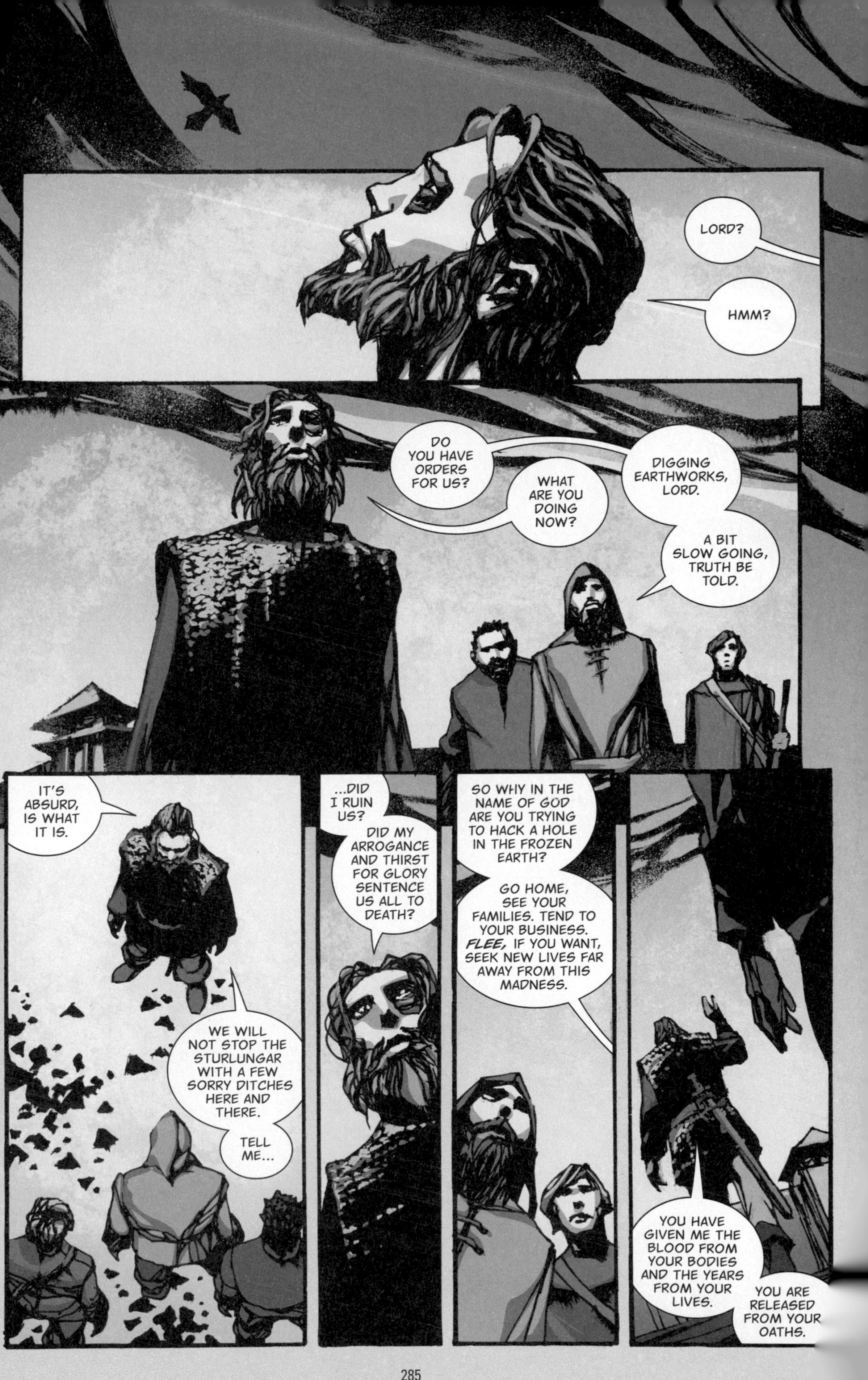
LORD?
HMM?
DO YOU HAVE ORDERS FOR US?
WHAT ARE YOU DOING NOW?
DIGGING EARTHWORKS, LORD.
A BIT SLOW GOING, TRUTH BE TOLD.
IT'S ABSURD, IS WHAT IT IS.
WE WILL NOT STOP THE STURLUNGAR WITH A FEW SORRY DITCHES HERE AND THERE.
TELL ME...
...DID I RUIN US?
DID MY ARROGANCE AND THIRST FOR GLORY SENTENCE US ALL TO DEATH?
SO WHY IN THE NAME OF GOD ARE YOU TRYING TO HACK A HOLE IN THE FROZEN EARTH?
GO HOME, SEE YOUR FAMILIES. TEND TO YOUR BUSINESS. FLEE, IF YOU WANT, SEEK NEW LIVES FAR AWAY FROM THIS MADNESS.
YOU HAVE GIVEN ME THE BLOOD FROM YOUR BODIES AND THE YEARS FROM YOUR LIVES.
YOU ARE RELEASED FROM YOUR OATHS.

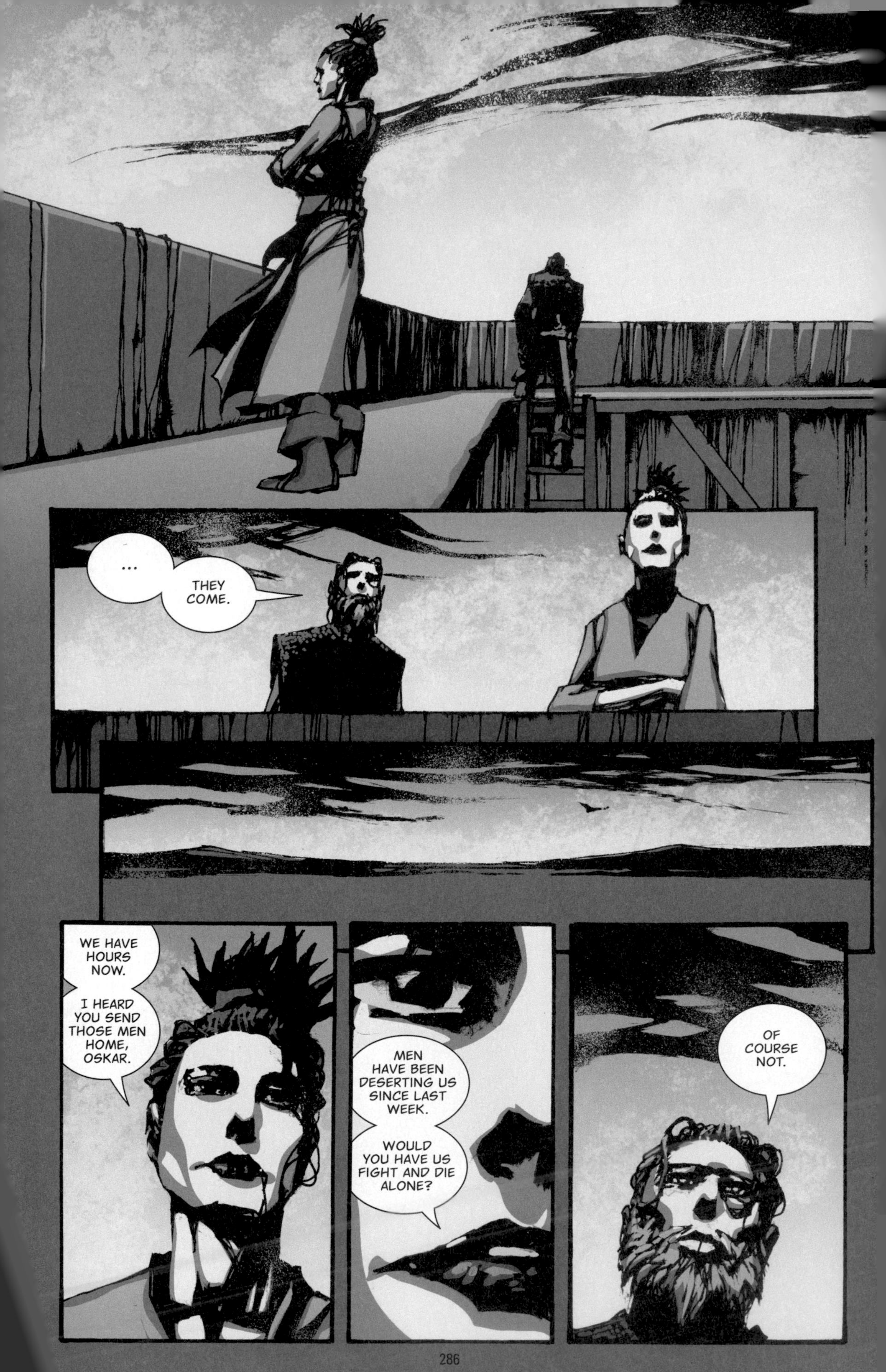
...
THEY COME.
WE HAVE HOURS NOW.
I HEARD YOU SEND THOSE MEN HOME, OSKAR.
MEN HAVE BEEN DESERTING US SINCE LAST WEEK.
WOULD YOU HAVE US FIGHT AND DIE ALONE?
OF COURSE NOT.

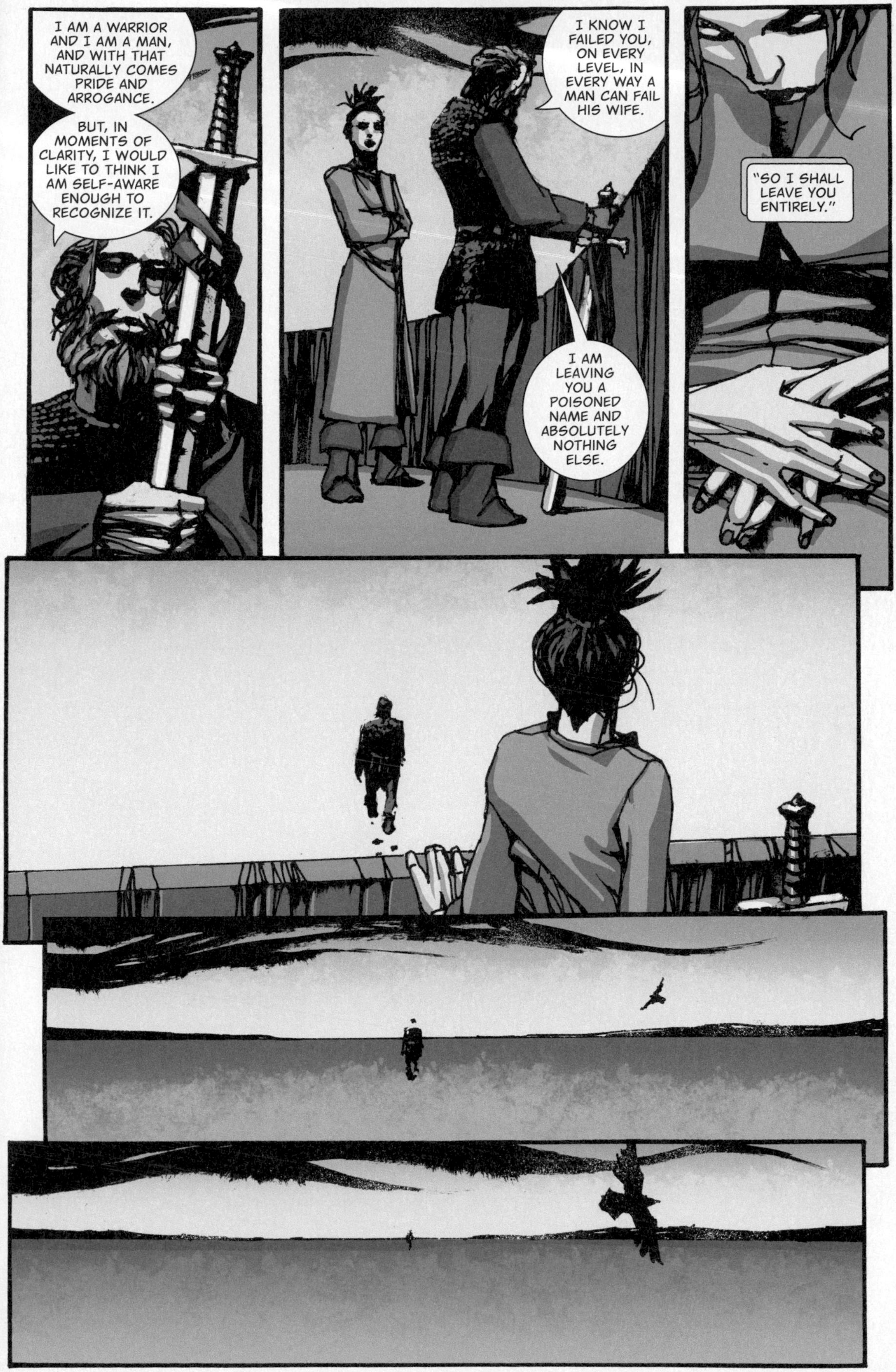
I AM A WARRIOR AND I AM A MAN, AND WITH THAT NATURALLY COMES PRIDE AND ARROGANCE.
BUT, IN MOMENTS OF CLARITY, I WOULD LIKE TO THINK I AM SELF-AWARE ENOUGH TO RECOGNIZE IT.
I KNOW I FAILED YOU, ON EVERY LEVEL, IN EVERY WAY A MAN CAN FAIL HIS WIFE.
I AM LEAVING YOU A POISONED NAME AND ABSOLUTELY NOTHING ELSE.
"SO I SHALL LEAVE YOU ENTIRELY."

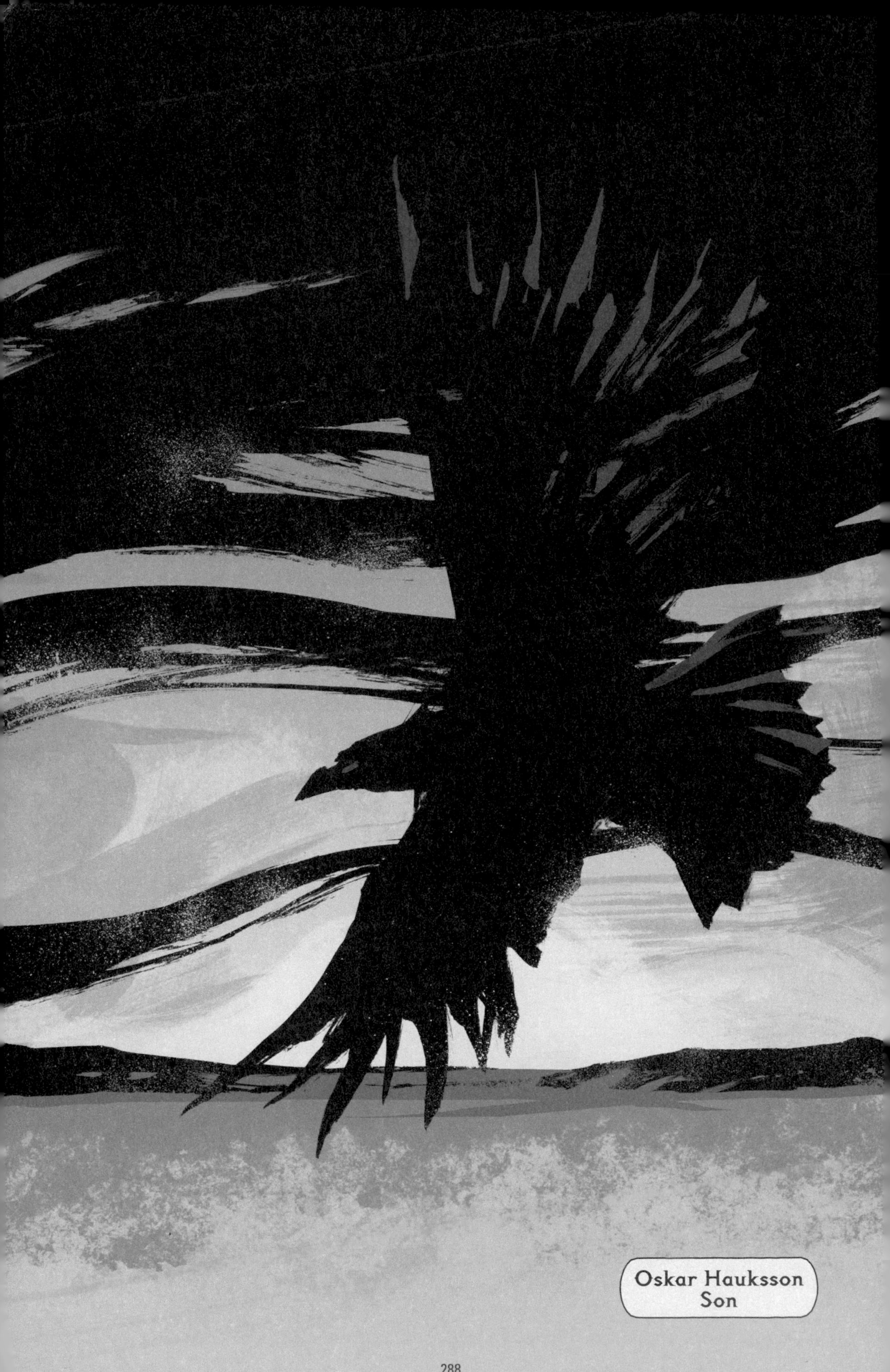
Oskar Hauksson
Son

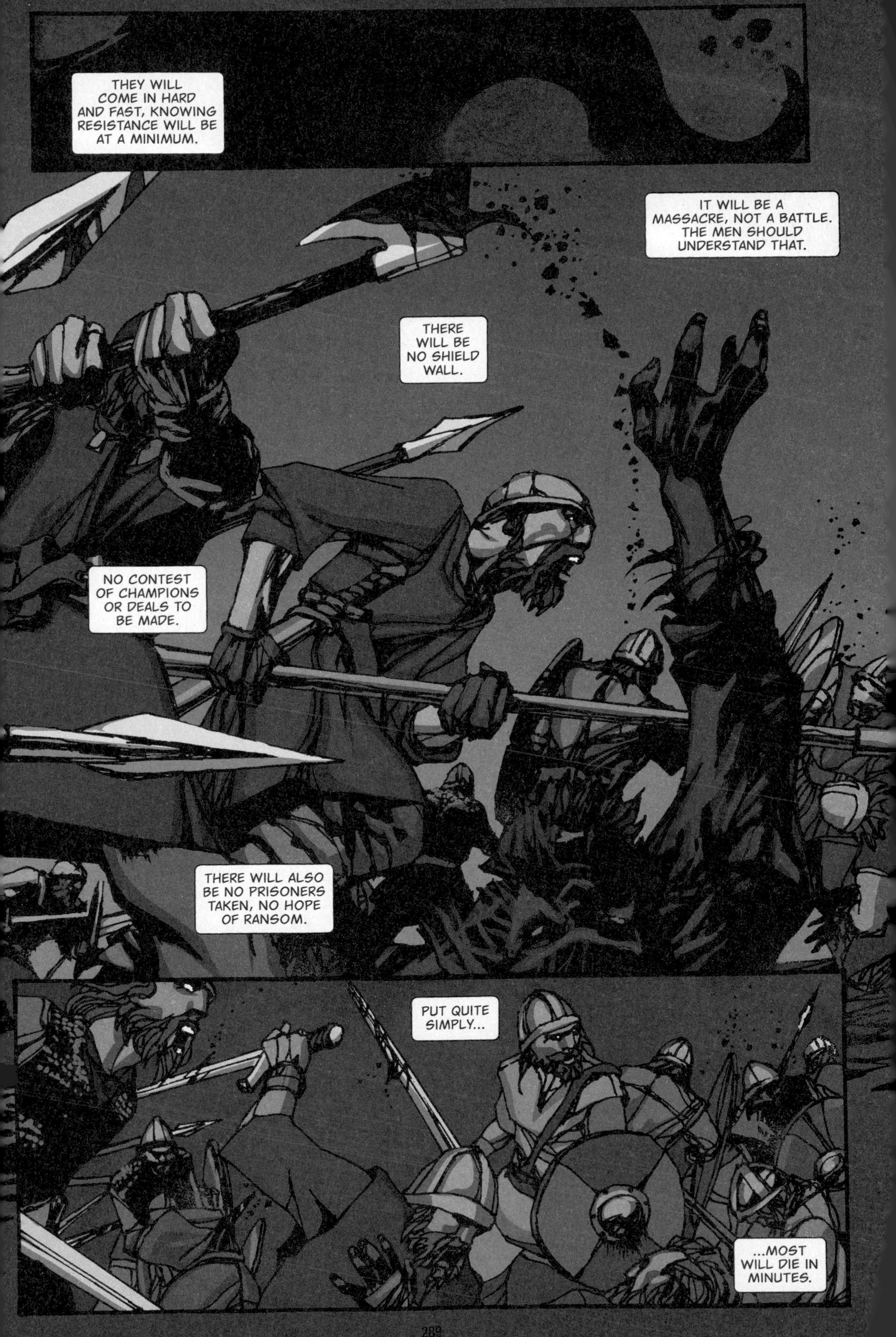
THEY WILL COME IN HARD AND FAST, KNOWING RESISTANCE WILL BE AT A MINIMUM.
IT WILL BE A MASSACRE, NOT A BATTLE. THE MEN SHOULD UNDERSTAND THAT.
THERE WILL BE NO SHIELD WALL.
NO CONTEST OF CHAMPIONS OR DEALS TO BE MADE.
THERE WILL ALSO BE NO PRISONERS TAKEN, NO HOPE OF RANSOM.
PUT QUITE SIMPLY...
...MOST WILL DIE IN MINUTES.

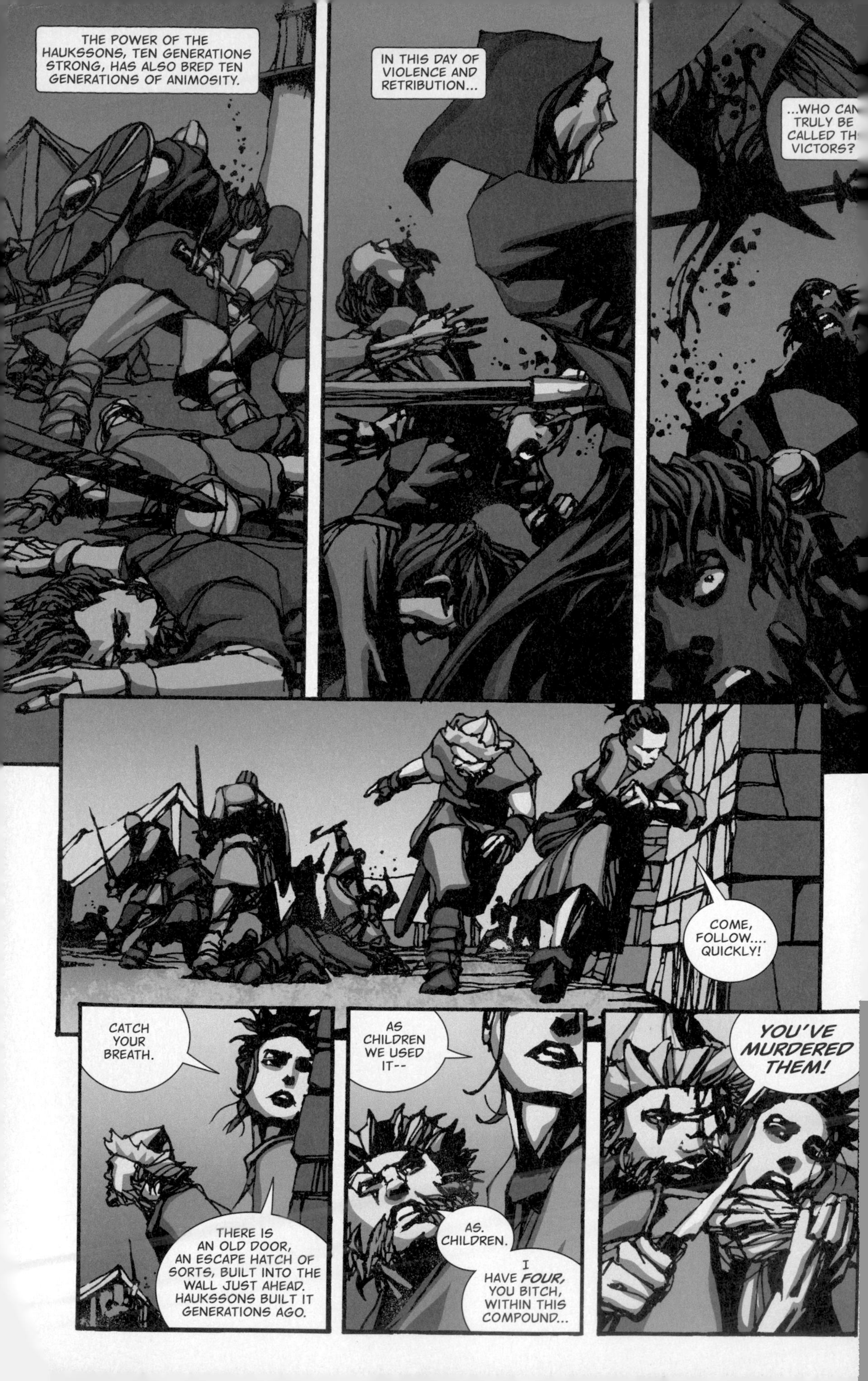
THE POWER OF THE HAUKSSONS, TEN GENERATIONS STRONG, HAS ALSO BRED TEN GENERATIONS OF ANIMOSITY.
IN THIS DAY OF VIOLENCE AND RETRIBUTION...
...WHO CAN TRULY BE CALLED THE VICTORS?
COME, FOLLOW.... QUICKLY!
CATCH YOUR BREATH.
THERE IS AN OLD DOOR, AN ESCAPE HATCH OF SORTS, BUILT INTO THE WALL JUST AHEAD. HAUKSSONS BUILT IT GENERATIONS AGO.
AS CHILDREN WE USED IT--
AS. CHILDREN.
I HAVE *FOUR,* YOU BITCH, WITHIN THIS COMPOUND...
YOU'VE MURDERED THEM!

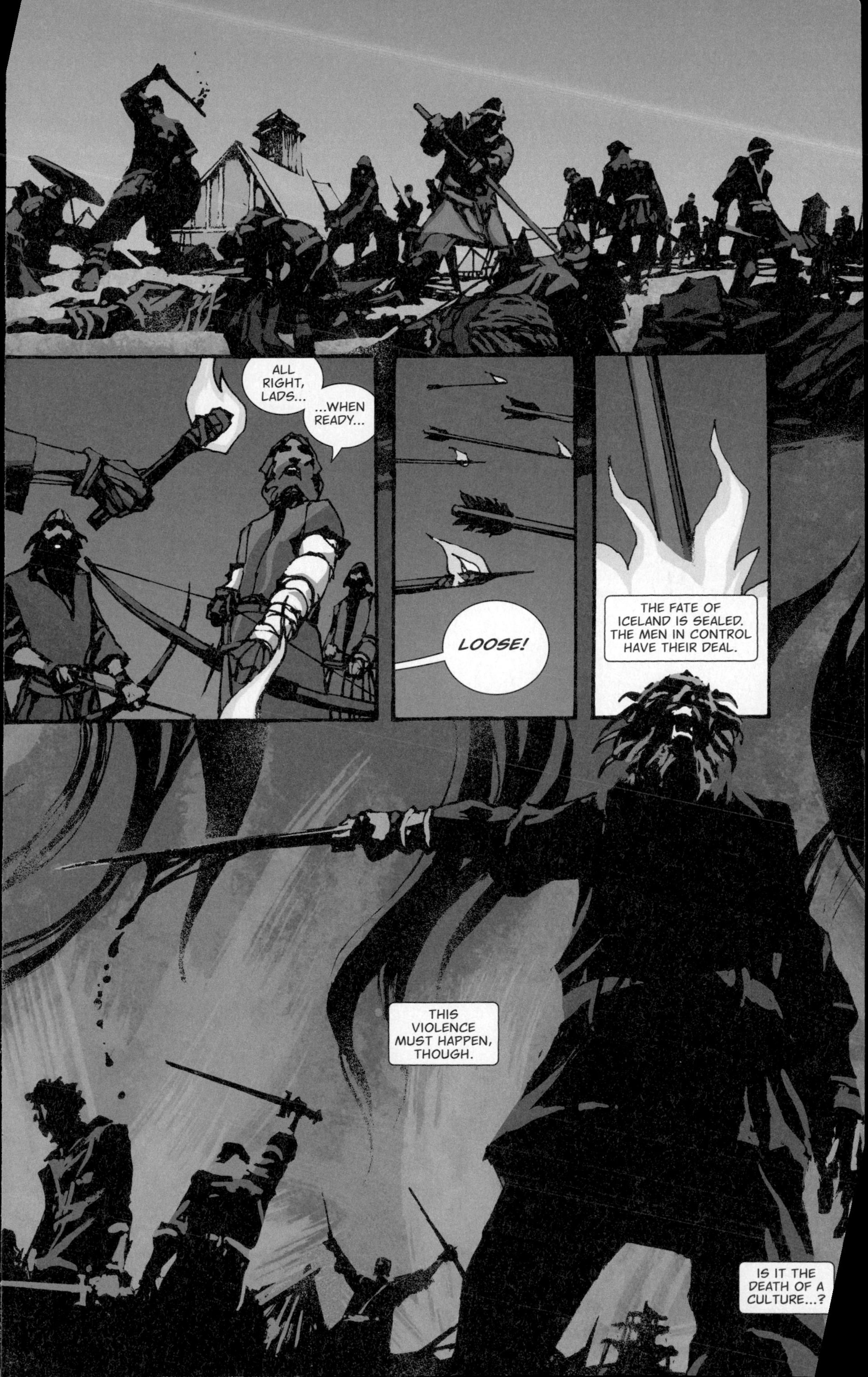
ALL RIGHT, LADS...
...WHEN READY...
LOOSE!
THE FATE OF ICELAND IS SEALED. THE MEN IN CONTROL HAVE THEIR DEAL.
THIS VIOLENCE MUST HAPPEN, THOUGH.
IS IT THE DEATH OF A CULTURE...?

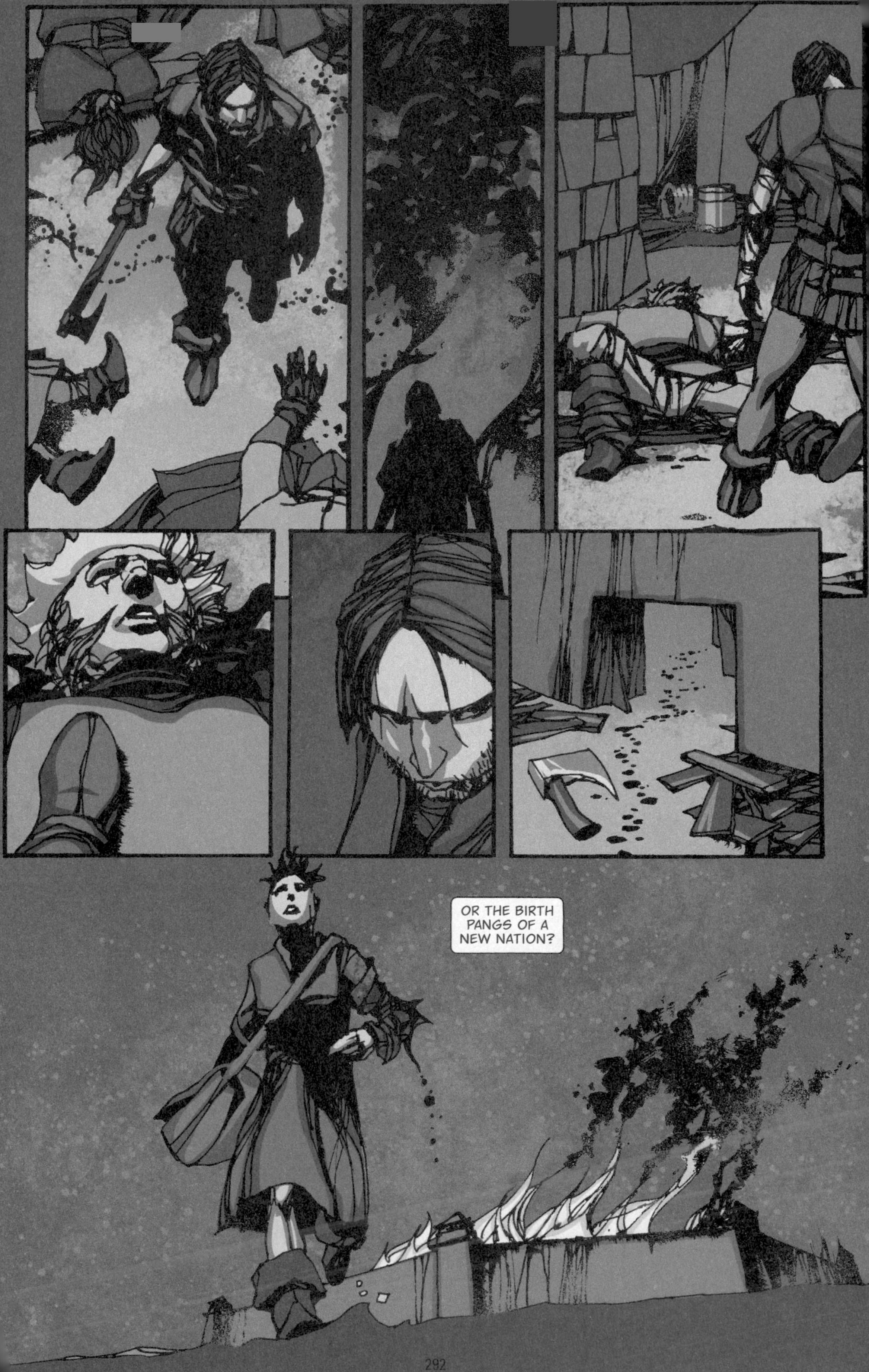
OR THE BIRTH PANGS OF A NEW NATION?

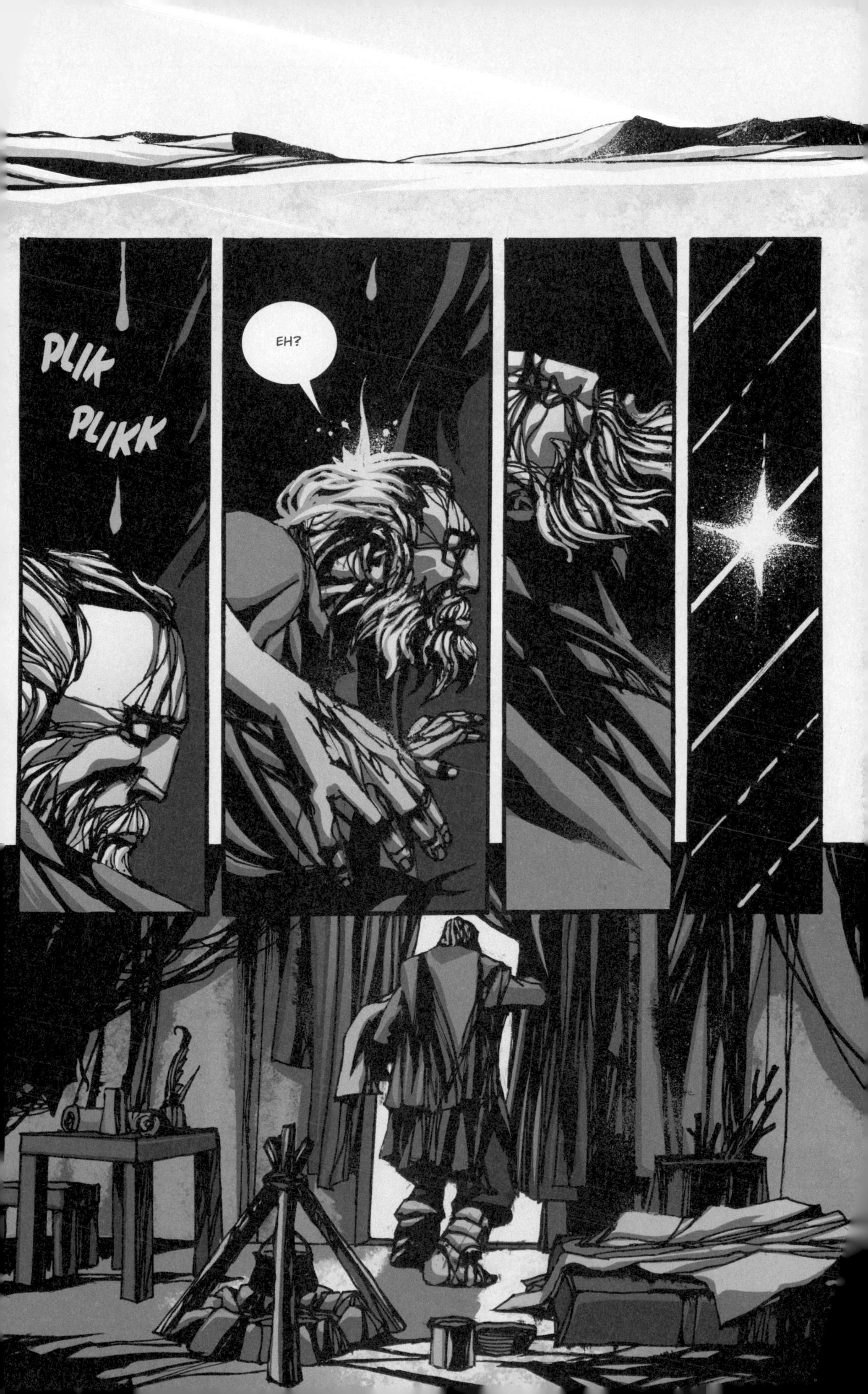
PLIK
PLIKK
EH?

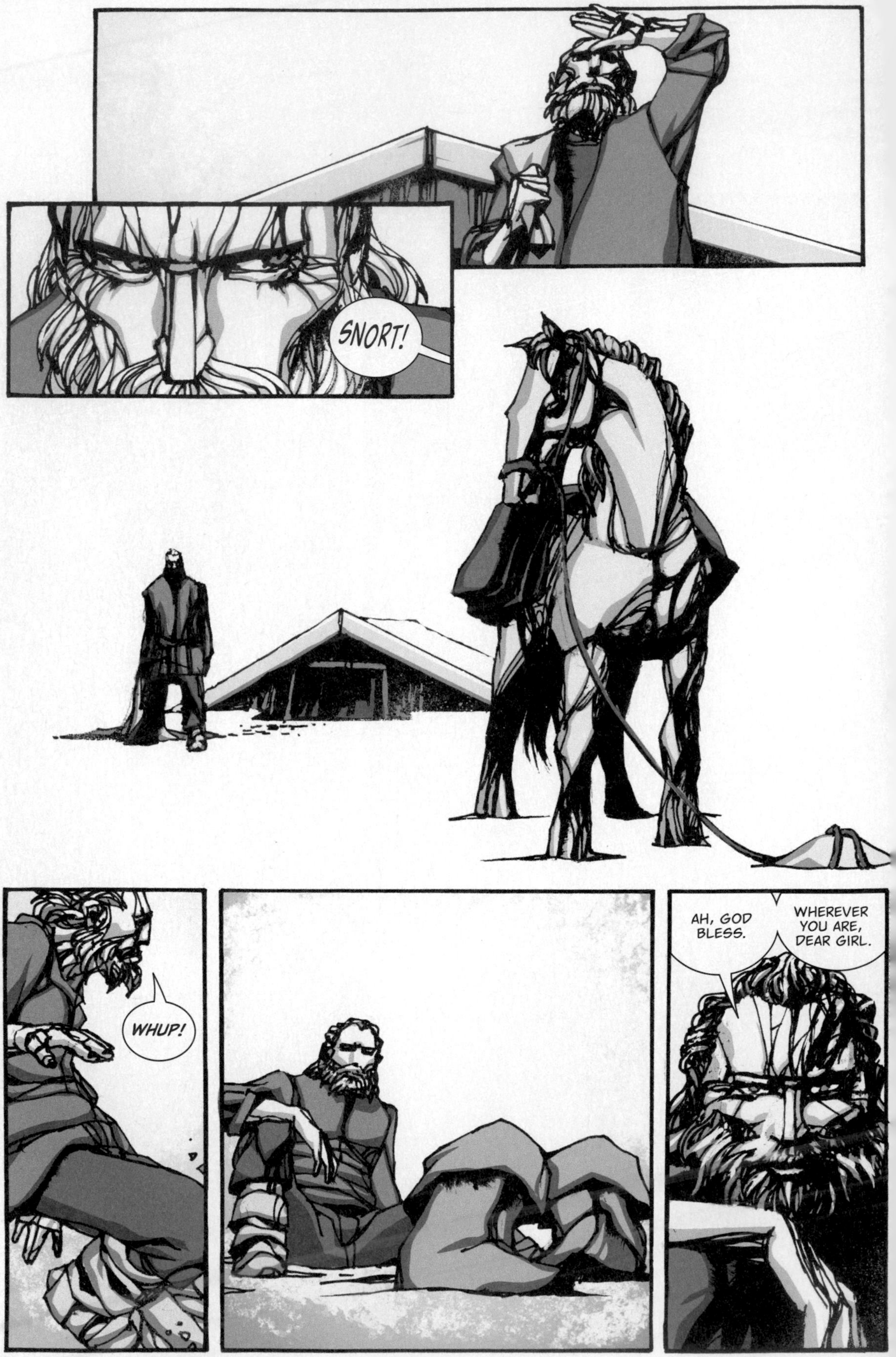
SNORT!
WHUP!
AH, GOD BLESS.
WHEREVER YOU ARE, DEAR GIRL.

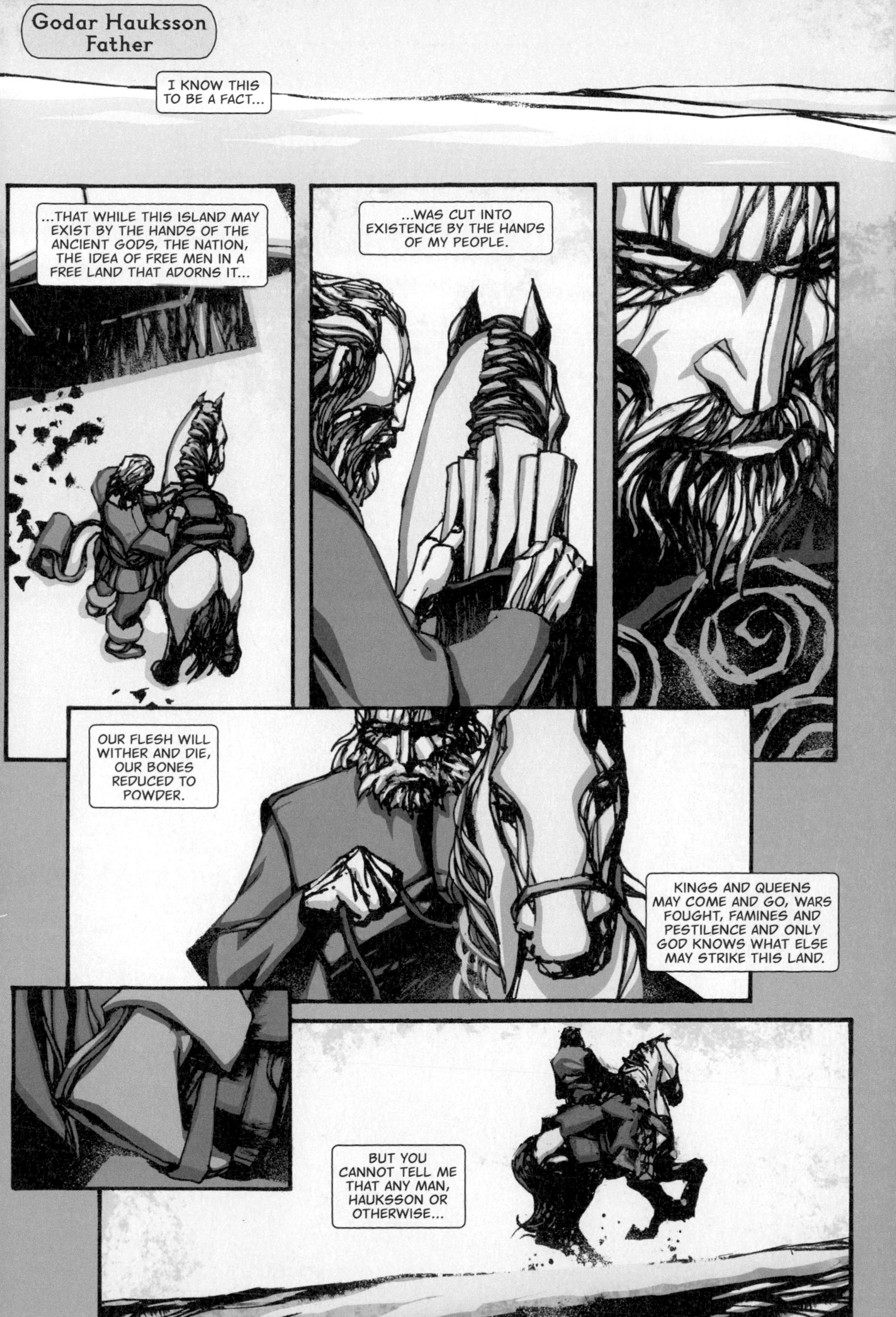
Godar Hauksson
Father
I KNOW THIS TO BE A FACT...
...THAT WHILE THIS ISLAND MAY EXIST BY THE HANDS OF THE ANCIENT GODS, THE NATION, THE IDEA OF FREE MEN IN A FREE LAND THAT ADORNS IT...
...WAS CUT INTO EXISTENCE BY THE HANDS OF MY PEOPLE.
OUR FLESH WILL WITHER AND DIE, OUR BONES REDUCED TO POWDER.
KINGS AND QUEENS MAY COME AND GO, WARS FOUGHT, FAMINES AND PESTILENCE AND ONLY GOD KNOWS WHAT ELSE MAY STRIKE THIS LAND.
BUT YOU CANNOT TELL ME THAT ANY MAN, HAUKSSON OR OTHERWISE...

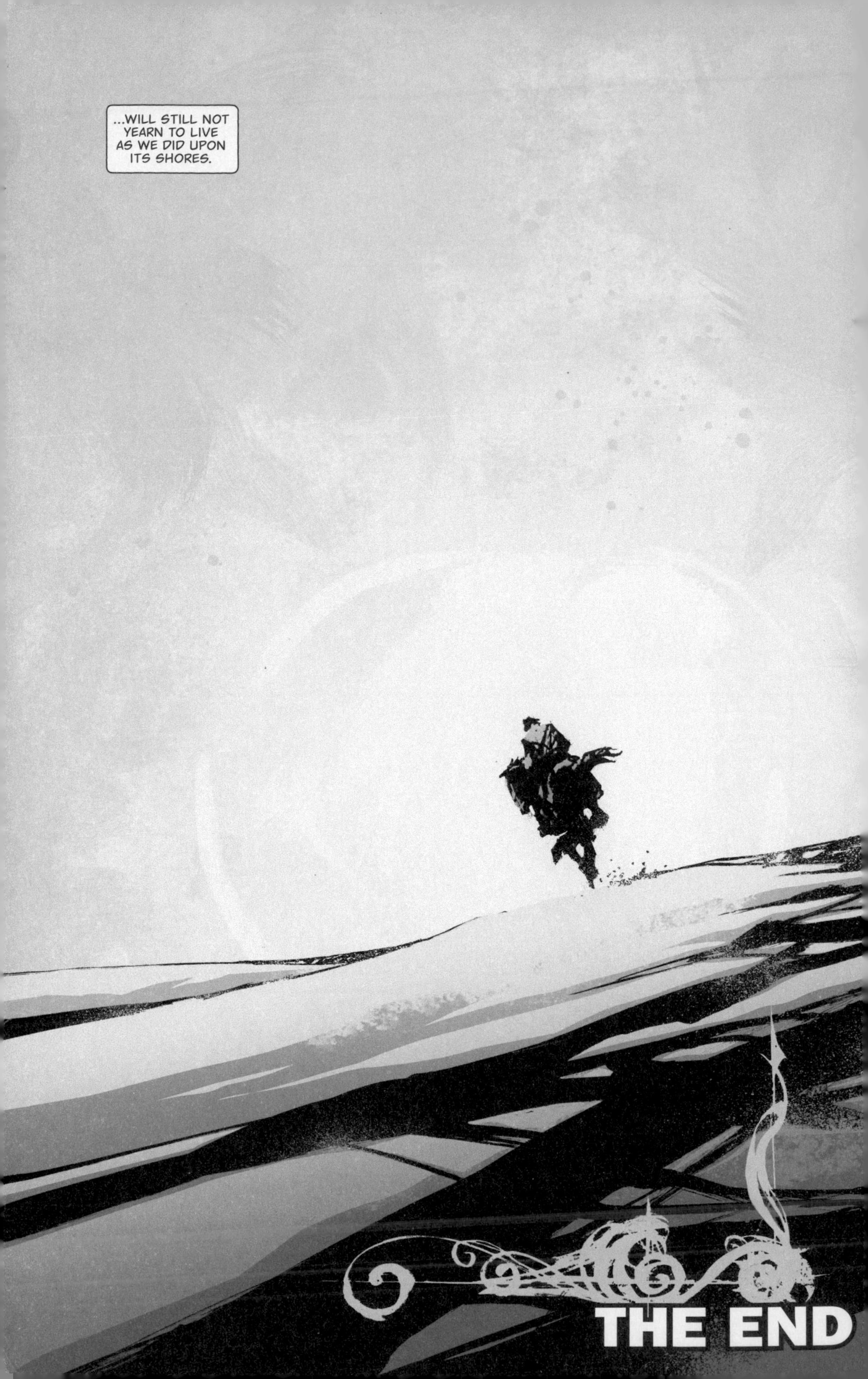
...WILL STILL NOT YEARN TO LIVE AS WE DID UPON ITS SHORES.
THE END